BLACKSTONE'S GUIDE TO

The Investigatory Powers Act 2016

BLACKSTONE'S GUIDE TO

The Investigatory Powers Act 2016

Simon McKay

Barrister

UNIVERSITY PRESS

Great Clarendon Street, Oxford, OX2 6DP,
United Kingdom

Oxford University Press is a department of the University of Oxford.
It furthers the University's objective of excellence in research, scholarship,
and education by publishing worldwide. Oxford is a registered trade mark of
Oxford University Press in the UK and in certain other countries

© Simon McKay 2017

The moral rights of the author have been asserted

First Edition published in 2017

Impression: 1

All rights reserved. No part of this publication may be reproduced, stored in
a retrieval system, or transmitted, in any form or by any means, without the
prior permission in writing of Oxford University Press, or as expressly permitted
by law, by licence or under terms agreed with the appropriate reprographics
rights organization. Enquiries concerning reproduction outside the scope of the
above should be sent to the Rights Department, Oxford University Press, at the
address above

You must not circulate this work in any other form
and you must impose this same condition on any acquirer

Crown copyright material is reproduced under Class Licence
Number C01P0000148 with the permission of OPSI
and the Queen's Printer for Scotland

Published in the United States of America by Oxford University Press
198 Madison Avenue, New York, NY 10016, United States of America

British Library Cataloguing in Publication Data
Data available

Library of Congress Control Number: 2017955854

ISBN 978–0–19–880175–7

Printed and bound by
CPI Group (UK) Ltd, Croydon, CR0 4YY

Links to third party websites are provided by Oxford in good faith and
for information only. Oxford disclaims any responsibility for the materials
contained in any third party website referenced in this work.

Foreword

In contrast to its ill-fated predecessor, the Communications Data Bill 2012, the Investigatory Powers Act 2016 achieves revolutionary change. It details intrusive capabilities—equipment interference, bulk collection of communications data, usage of bulk personal datasets—whose very existence was secret until 2015 and it provides for stronger control and oversight of these capabilities, notably by requiring judicial approval of warrants and notices that had previously been reserved to ministers. As a result, the Act significantly enhances the democratic control of electronic surveillance in the UK.

Transparency and stronger oversight were the core recommendations of my report, 'A Question of Trust' (2015), but to claim credit for their implementation in the Act would be naive. Larger forces were at work: the pressure for avowal that flowed from the Snowden disclosures and their use before the Investigatory Powers Tribunal; the realization that equivalent safeguards were going to be required if US service providers were to comply with requests for assistance; and legal pressure from the privacy-minded culture of the European institutions, influenced in turn by nations for whom intelligence-gathering has sinister historical resonances.

The degree of parliamentary scrutiny afforded to the Act fell short of what some (including the author) would have preferred. One might certainly wish that more MPs were at home on the digital front line. But parliamentary debates on the draft Bill and then the Bill occupied some twelve months and were informed by the reports of seven parliamentary committees, one of them privy to highly classified information. The Joint Bill Committee alone took some 2,400 pages of evidence, much of it from technical experts and NGOs, and made almost 200 recommendations, the vast majority of which were adopted.

With the strong powers confirmed or conferred by the Act now in place, attention will shift to the work of the Investigatory Powers Commission (as it should surely have been called), and to the courts. Legal challenges to the operation of the bulk powers—whose utility I examined in my Bulk Powers Review of 2016—are pending. Other likely areas of legal or regulatory controversy are the scope of targeted thematic powers, the safeguards on access to communications data, the conditions to be placed on data transfer, and the manner in which technical capability notices may in the future be used to require the removal of encryption. Brexit will impose its own complications, as the European Court of Justice sharpens its scrutiny of third countries which handle the personal data of EU citizens.

Foreword

This well-referenced handbook is a useful aid to understanding the Act. But as the threat picture, the law, and the technology continue their rapid evolution, the Act and its interpretation cannot be expected to stand still. We must hope that the author has the appetite for a second edition: it may be needed sooner rather than later.

David Anderson QC
Brick Court Chambers, London

Acknowledgements

The human rights lawyer, John Wadham, approached me in early 2016 with an invitation to consider jointly writing with him the Blackstones' Guide to the Investigatory Powers Act 2016. I was delighted to accept, not just because of the opportunity to work collaboratively with such a respected civil liberties practitioner, but also it was clear, even by then, that the legislation would be complex and John's experience and intelligence would make the task of trying to make sense of it considerably easier. However, by May 2016, John was called to undertake his essential work as the Chair of the National Preventative Mechanism and unable to participate in writing the text. It remains that without his original contact, it is unlikely I would have undertaken the project.

It was thereafter destined to be a largely a solitary work. The sheer complexity and vastness of the Bill required uninterrupted concentration—at least within my own intellectual limitations. That is not to say experts in their fields did not assist me; they were of considerable help, but in the main they had dedicated time, effort, and valuable resources to formulating submissions to and in some cases giving evidence before the various Committees reviewing the Bill and it is from this material I derived the greatest support. One of the Bill's architects, David Anderson QC, has been quick to point out in response to criticisms that the Act was ill thought out that it benefited from unparalleled expertise ranging from the compilation of the reports that previsioned reform to the high quality of the written and oral evidence provided to the Committees. I know some of those who contributed to this process but by no means all. However each deserves acknowledgment for their preparedness to grapple with the Bill's clauses—they are the pioneers discovering and mapping out a legal wilderness—and their contribution to this text has been invaluable. I am enormously grateful to David, who has contributed a vast amount to law reform in recent years and took the time to write the foreword to this work.

Above all, acknowledgment must be given to the whistle-blowers (leaving aside issues of culpability or justification) and those civil liberties organisations (Liberty, Privacy International, and Big Brother Watch, to name a few) and their advocates that held the state to account on the domestic and international stage. The widespread unlawfulness of aspects of state surveillance—for that it what it unquestionably was—is easily forgotten following the seismic avowals and reformation of recent times. It is important that those who catalysed change are recognised.

I would like to thank Professor Clive Walker QC, Emeritus Professor of Law at University of Leeds, for his friendship and support, not just for reading the draft chapters but in general, particularly over the last two or three years and Professor

Acknowledgements

David Ormerod QC, Law Commissioner and Professor of Law at Queen Mary's University.

Undertaking a project like this as a practitioner is only possible because professional clients continue to loyally instruct me. I am grateful to Séamus McIlroy and his colleagues for the thought-provoking instructions in this arena that take me back to my birthplace, Belfast, regularly. I wish him well as he makes the transition from solicitor to member of that august institution, the Northern Ireland Bar.

Finally, I would like to thank Fiona Sinclair and Peter Daniell at OUP and those working behind the scenes for their work on getting the book to completion, in particular Dipak at Newgen.

There is a post-script. Following the enactment of the Investigatory Powers Act 2016, the reports and events that carved out its course may easily be forgotten. One should not be: David Anderson's, A Question of Trust. Quite apart from the report being a reflection of David's success at making the difficult subject of state surveillance accessible to non-lawyers, its title should be etched on the minds of government, state actors, and agencies engaging in covert surveillance of whatever kind: in a free society, you are empowered to do so only in the service of the public interest and only whilst you hold the confidence of the people. Exceed the powers you are given, upset this delicate balance and as the events leading to the 2016 Act demonstrated, there will be reckoning. In this sense, it is as, Shakespeare's Antonio foresaw, that the past is prologue.

Any and all errors in the text are mine alone.

Table of Contents

TABLE OF CASES	xiii
TABLE OF LEGISLATION	xv
LIST OF ABBREVIATIONS	xli

1. AN INTRODUCTION TO THE INVESTIGATORY POWERS ACT 2016

A. Introduction	1.01
B. Evolution of the Investigatory Powers Act 2016	1.05
C. Provisions of General Application	1.59
D. Commencement	1.91
E. Preliminary Assessment of the Investigatory Powers Act 2016	1.94

2. GENERAL PRIVACY PROTECTIONS

A. Introduction	2.01
B. Section 1 IPA: The 'Overview' Provisions	2.06
C. Unlawful Interception	2.11
D. The Interception of Communications	2.19
E. Lawful Authority	2.39
F. Monetary Penalties for Certain Unlawful Interceptions	2.43
G. Civil Liability for Certain Unlawful Interceptions	2.54
H. Restriction on Requesting Interception by Overseas Authorities	2.55
I. Offence of Unlawfully Obtaining Communications Data	2.59
J. Abolition of Powers to Obtain Communications Data	2.62
K. Restriction on Use of Section 93 of the Police Act 1997	2.73

3. LAWFUL INTERCEPTION OF COMMUNICATIONS

A. Introduction	3.01
B. Warrants	3.06
C. Issuing Warrants	3.26
D. Approval of Warrants by Judicial Commissioners	3.45
E. Additional Safeguards	3.57
F. Warrants: Formalities	3.67
G. Other Forms of Lawful Interception	3.121

H. Restrictions on Handling and Disclosure of Intercept Material Obtained under Warrants	3.143
I. The Offence of Making Unauthorized Disclosures	3.163

4. AUTHORIZATIONS FOR OBTAINING COMMUNICATIONS DATA

A. Introduction	4.01
B. Authorization	4.06
C. Filtering	4.38
D. Relevant Public Authorities Other than Local Authorities	4.53
E. Local Authorities	4.63
F. Additional Protections	4.77
G. Unlawful Disclosure	4.98
H. Miscellaneous Provisions	4.102

5. RETENTION OF COMMUNICATIONS DATA

A. Introduction	5.01
B. Scope of Retention Powers	5.05
C. Pre-issue	5.12
D. Post-issue	5.17
E. Safeguards	5.24
F. Variation or Revocation of Notices	5.34
G. Enforcement	5.40

6. EQUIPMENT INTERFERENCE

A. Introduction	6.01
B. Warrants	6.05
C. Safeguards	6.52
D. Warrants: Post-issue Matters	6.66
E. Disclosure	6.104

7. BULK WARRANTS

A. Introduction	7.01
B. Bulk Interception Warrants	7.04
C. Bulk Acquisition Warrants	7.65
D. Bulk Equipment Interference Warrants	7.120

8. BULK PERSONAL DATASET WARRANTS

A. Introduction	8.01
B. Warrants	8.10

Table of Contents

C. Warrants: Post-issue Matters	8.54
D. Safeguards	8.79
E. Application of Part 7 to Other Parts of the IPA	8.95
9. OVERSIGHT ARRANGEMENTS	
A. Introduction	9.01
B. Judicial Commissioners	9.10
C. Reporting	9.49
D. The Investigatory Powers Tribunal	9.57
E. Advisory Bodies	9.85
10. ADDITIONAL POWERS, COMBINING WARRANTS, AND MISCELLANEOUS PROVISIONS	
A. Introduction	10.01
B. Additional Powers	10.03
C. Amendments to Other Enactments Relating to Investigatory Powers	10.52
D. Combined Warrants or Authorizations	10.59
E. Miscellaneous	10.125
APPENDIX: Investigatory Powers Act 2016	249
INDEX	503

Table of Cases

A v Director of Establishments [2009] UKSC 12 .... 6.01
Attorney General's Reference (No 5 of 2000) [2004] UKHL 40 .... 1.08
Big Brother Watch and Others v United Kingdom, Application No 58170/13
    (communicated on 9 January 2014) [2014] ECHR 93 . . .1.21, 1.25, 1.30, 1.34, 1.37, 4.02
British-Irish Rights Watch, The and Others v Security Service, GCHQ and the SIS IPT/
    01/77 (23 January 2003) 1.31
C v Police and Secretary of State, IPT/03/32/H 1.15
Chatwani and Others v National Crime Agency [2015] UKIPTrib 15_84_88-CH ... 3.45, 9.04
Digital Rights Ireland Limited v Minister for Communications (C-293/12)
    (8 April 2014) 1.21, 4.02, 5.02
Esbester v United Kingdom 1.07
Govell v United Kingdom 1.07
Gray and Others v News Group Newspapers Limited and Others [2011]
    EWHC 734 (Ch) 1.20
Harman and Hewitt v United Kingdom 1.07
Liberty and Others v United Kingdom, Application No 58243/00 (1 July 2008) 1.23
Malone v Commissioner of Police of the Metropolis [1979] Ch 344 .... 1.05
Malone v United Kingdom (1985) 7 EHRR 245 .... 1.05, 1.06, 3.01
Moran and Others v Police Scotland [2016] UKIPTrib 15/602/CH 4.83
Morgans v DPP[2000] 2 WLR, 386 .... 2.25
News Group Newspapers Limited and Others v The Commissioner of Police of the
    Metropolis [2015] UKIPTrib 14/176/H 4.83
Privacy International and Greennet and Others v (1) The Secretary of State for Foreign
    and Commonwealth Affairs (2) The Government Communications Headquarters,
    IPT 14/85/CH 14/120-126/CH 6.01
Privacy International and Others v Secretary of State for Foreign and Commonwealth
    Affairs and Others, IPT/13/92/CH 1.21, 3.07
Privacy International v Secretary of State for Foreign and Commonwealth Affairs and
    Others [2016] UKIPTrib 15/110/CH 4.02, 4.03, 7.02, 8.03, 8.04, 8.07
R v Allsopp and Others [2005] EWCA Crim 703 .... 1.23, 2.28
R v Coulson and Kuttner [2013] WLR (D) 262 .... 1.20, 1.25, 2.29, 2.30, 2.31
R v E [2004] Cr App R 29, [2004] EWCA Crim 1243 .... 2.28
R v Hammond, McIntosh and Gray [2002] EWCA Crim 1243 .... 2.26
R v McDonald, Rafferty and O'Farrell, Woolwich Crown Court (23 April 2002).... 2.27, 3.122
R v Moore and Burrows [2013] EWCA Crim 85 .... 1.18
R v Preston [1993] 4 All ER 651 .... 1.06, 3.01
R v Shayler [2001] 1 WLR 2206 .... 2.36
R v Smart and Beard (2002) Crim LR 684 .... 2.25
R v Walters, Newcastle Crown Court (unreported, 6 April 2017) 1.18
R (on the application of A) v B [2010] 1 WLR 1 .... 9.56

Table of Cases

R (on the application of NTL Group Limited) v Ipswich Crown Court [2002] EWHC 1585 (Admin), [2002] 3 WLR 1173 .... 1.17, 2.42

S and Marper v United Kingdom, Application Nos 30562/04 and 30566/04 (4 December 2008) ECtHR 1.33

Secretary of State for the Home Department v Rehman [2001] UKHL 47, [2003] 1 AC 153 .... 10.05

Secretary of State of the Home Department v Watson and Others (Case C-698/15) (21 December 2016) 1.38, 1.94, 4.02, 5.02, 8.05, 8.07

Table of Legislation

Statutes

Civil Contingencies Act 2004
   Pt 1 . . . . .10.06
Communications Act 2003
   Pt 1 . . . . .10.35
   Pt 2, Chap 1 .10.35
Computer Misuse Act 1990
   ss 1–3A. .2.68, 2.73
Constitutional Reform Act 2005
   Pt 3 . . . . .9.13
Counter-Terrorism Act 2008
   s 19 . . . . .8.03
Counter Terrorism and Security Act 2015
   Pt 3 . . . . .1.57
   s 21 . . . . .1.92
   s 52(3)(a) 1.92
Court of Session Act 1988 . . . . .4.37
   s 45 . . . . . .3.120, 5.42, 6.103, 7.108, 10.33
Criminal Justice Act 1991
   Pt 4 . . . . .3.136
Criminal Justice Act 2003
   s 154(1) 2.60, 3.118,
                 3.163, 4.100, 6.120, 7.60,
                 7.114, 7.118, 7.188, 8.91
Criminal Justice and Public Order Act 1994
   s 106(4) 3.136
Customs and Excise Management Act 1979
   s 1(1) 6.38, 10.69
   s 159 . . . . .3.130
Data Protection Act 1998. . . . . .8.09, 9.47
   s 2(a)–(f) 8.19
   s 69 . . . . .8.18
Data Retention and Investigatory Powers
   Act 2014 (DRIPA) 1.21, 1.38,
        1.39, 1.41, 1.57, 4.02, 4.05, 5.02
   s 2(3) 1.39
   s 7 . . . . .1.21, 1.41, 1.51
   s 7(2) 1.41
European Communities Act 1972
   s 2(2) 3.32, 6.25

Human Rights Act 1998. . . . . 1.07, 2.03,
                            2.10, 9.34
   s 6 . . . . .1.15
Immigration and Asylum Act 1999
   s 147 . . . . .3.141
   s 153 . . . . .3.141
   s 157 . . . . .3.141
   s 157A 3.141
Insolvency Act 1986
   s 429(2) 9.16
Intelligence Services Act 1994 (ISA) 1.04,
        6.02, 9.01, 10.09, 10.59, 10.60
   s 1(1) 10.63
   s 1(1)(a)–(b). .10.63
   s 1(2) 10.62
   s 1(2)(c) 10.54
   s 1(4) 10.62
   s 2(a)–(c) 10.63
   s 2(2)(a) 8.03
   s 3 .1.60, 2.07, 10.52
   s 3(1) 10.63
   s 3(1)(a)–(b)(ii) 10.63
   s 3(1)(b)(ii) 10.53
   s 3(2)(a)–(c) 10.63
   s 3(2)(c) 10.54
   s 4(2)(a) 8.03
   s 5 . . . . . . .1.60, 2.07, 4.97, 6.02, 9.27, 10.54,
        10.60, 10.96, 10.98, 10.103, 10.115
   ss 5–7 . . . . .9.27
   s 5(1) 10.61
   s 5(2)(a)(i)–(iii) 10.61
   s 5(3) 10.54
   s 5(3A) 10.54
   s 6(3) 9.27
   s 6(4) 9.27
   s 7 . . . . .6.02
Interception of Communications Act
   1985 (IOCA) . . . 1.01, 1.06–1.07, 1.08,
        2.11, 2.25, 3.01, 3.143, 3.155
   s 1 . . . . .3.155

Table of Legislation

s 1(1) 2.11
s 1(2) 3.155
s 1(3) 3.155
s 2............................1.06
s 6............................3.152
s 8............................1.06
s 9............................1.06
Investigatory Powers Act
2016 (IPA)........... 1.01–1.05, 1.07,
1.08, 1.14, 1.61, 1.62, 1.63, 1.72, 1.74,
1.91, 1.92, 1.94–1.99, 2.01, 2.04, 2.08,
2.15, 2.21, 2.24, 2.35, 2.66, 2.67, 3.06,
3.139. 3.143, 3.145, 3.153, 3.155, 4.02,
4.04, 4.77, 4.97, 5.02, 5.03, 6.02, 6.03,
6.95, 7.120, 7.171, 8.08, 8.12, 8.18,
8.75, 8.94, 8.95, 9.01, 9.09, 9.24, 9.25,
9.27, 9.32, 9.33, 9.34, 9.42, 9.45, 9.49,
9.53, 9.66, 9.67, 9.71, 9.85, 9.86, 10.02,
10.06, 10.09, 10.25, 10.59, 10.64,
10.124, 10.125, 10.128–10.133,
Appendix
Pt 1, General Privacy Protections 2.01,
2.03, 2.04, 2.05, 2.14, 2.68
Pts 2–7 ....2.06
Pt 2............ 1.59, 2.06, 2.21, 3.21,
8.95, 9.57, 10.18, 10.121, 10.123
Pt 2, Chap 1 ...... 1.58, 2.40, 2.44, 2.57,
3.05, 3.06, 3.10, 3.23, 3.46, 3.48,
3.59, 3.67, 3.75, 3.83, 3.99, 3.100,
3.106, 3.156, 3.160, 3.161, 3.162,
6.05, 7.49, 9.24, 10.34, 10.122
Pt 3............. 1.59, 2.06, 4.04, 4.05,
4.06, 4.16, 4.54, 4.64, 4.66, 4.67,
4.70, 4.75, 4.84, 4.89, 4.91, 4.92,
4.96, 4.98, 4.110–4.111, 5.24,
5.27, 9.58, 9.61, 9.63, 9.74,
9.75, 10.18, 10.34
Pt 4......... 1.59, 1.92, 2.06, 4.04, 5.01,
5.05, 5.30, 5.31, 9.07, 9.60,
9.61, 9.63, 9.70, 9.74
Pt 5......... 1.59, 2.06, 2.21, 2.41, 4.04,
6.04, 6.05, 6.11, 6.17, 6.19,
6.42, 6.55, 6.64, 6.66, 6.71,
6.93, 6.117, 6.118, 7.177, 10.18,
10.120, 10.121, 10.123, 10.131
Pt 6..........2.06, 4.04, 7.03, 9.49, 10.18
Pt 6, Chap 1 ...... 1.59, 2.06, 2.40, 2.44,
3.19, 7.03, 7.04, 9.24, 9.57

Pt 6, Chap 2 .... 1.59, 2.06, 7.03,
8.94, 9.58, 9.75
Pt 6, Chap 3 ...1.59, 2.06, 2.41, 2.69, 6.07,
7.03, 7.120, 7.125, 7.127, 7.149
Pt 6, Chap 5 ....2.69
Pt 7.... 1.59, 2.06, 4.04, 8.03, 8.08, 8.09,
8.10, 8.14, 8.16, 8.80, 8.89, 8.95, 9.47
Pt 8............. 1.60, 2.06, 2.07, 9.08,
9.11, 9.18, 9.38–9.40
Pt 9.......1.60, 2.07, 10.01, 10.10, 10.45
Pt 9, Chap 2 ....1.91
s 1.........................2.06, 2.07
s 1(3)(a)–(b)....................2.05
s 1(4) 2.05
s 1(4)(a) 1.59
s 1(5)(a)–(b)....................2.03
s 1(6)(a) 2.06
s 1(6)(a)–(c)....................1.59
s 1(6)(b)–(c)....................2.06
s 1(6)(d)–(e)................1.59, 2.06
s 1(7)(a)–(b)................1.60, 2.07
s 2............. 1.92, 2.19, 3.46, 5.25,
5.28, 6.43, 7.133, 8.36, 9.04,
9.34, 10.28, 10.50, 10.111
s 2(1) 3.154
s 2(1)(a)–(k)....................2.08
s 2(2) 2.08, 2.13, 2.14
s 2(5) 2.09
s 2(5)(a)–(c)....................2.09
s 3..............2.12, 2.15, 2.44, 3.22
s 3(1) 2.12, 6.10, 7.125, 10.57
s 3(1)(a)–(c)....................2.12
s 3(3)(a) 2.15
s 3(3)(b) 2.15
s 3(5) 2.15
s 3(6)(a) 2.12
s 3(6)(b) 2.12
s 3(6)(c) 2.12
s 3(7) 2.12, 3.21
s 4................2.15, 2.19, 2.20, 2.30
s 4(1) 2.20
s 4(1)(a) 2.22
s 4(1)(b) 2.22
s 4(2)(a) 2.22
s 4(2)(b) 2.22
s 4(2)(c) 2.22
s 4(4) 2.31
s 4(4)(a) 2.22

s 4(4)(b)	2.22	s 12(6)	2.66, 2.67
s 4(4)(a)–(b)	2.23	s 13	2.68
s 4(8)	2.36	s 13(1)	2.68, 2.71
s 4(8)(a)	2.36	s 13(1)(a)	2.68, 2.70
s 4(8)(b)(i)	2.36	s 13(1)(b)	2.68
s 4(8)(b)(ii)	2.36	s 13(2)(a)	2.71
s 5	2.20	s 13(2)(b)	2.71
s 5(1)	2.37	s 13(2)(c)(i)–(ii)	2.72
s 5(2)(a)–(b)	2.37	s 13(2)(c)(iii)	2.72
s 6	2.18, 2.51	s 13(3)	2.68
s 6(1)–(3)	2.18, 2.39	s 13(4)	2.69
s 6(1)(a)(i)	2.40	s 13(4)(a)	3.39
s 6(1)(a)(ii)	2.40	s 13(4)(b)	3.40
s 6(1)(b)	2.40	s 13(4)(c)	3.39, 3.40
s 6(1)(c)(i)	2.41	s 13(8)	2.69
s 6(1)(c)(ii)	2.42	s 14(1)	2.73
s 6(1)(c)(iii)	2.42	ss 15–43	3.06
s 6(7)	2.44	s 15	3.11
s 7	3.154	s 15(1)(a)–(c)	3.11
s 7(1)	2.44	s 15(2)	3.12
s 7(2)	2.43	s 15(2)(a)–(c)	3.13
s 7(3)(a)–(c)	2.44	s 15(3)	3.18, 3.19
s 7(4)	2.44	s 15(4)(a)	3.15
s 7(5)	2.45	s 15(4)(b)	3.15
s 7(5)(e)	3.155	s 15(4)(c)	3.15
s 7(6)	2.46	s 15(5)	3.11
s 8	3.154, 3.155	s 15(5)(a)	3.16
s 9	2.55	s 15(5)(a)(i)–(ii)	3.16
s 9(1)	2.56	s 15(5)(b)	3.17
s 9(2)(a)	2.56	s 15(5)(c)	3.17
s 9(2)(b)	2.56	s 15(6)	3.17
s 9(4)(a)(i)	2.60	s 15(7)	3.21
s 10	2.55, 2.63	s 16	3.14, 3.21, 9.68
s 10(1)	2.62	s 16(1)	3.21
s 10(1)(a)–(b)	2.57	s 16(3)(a)–(b)	3.22
s 10(2)	2.57	s 16(6)(a)–(c)	3.22
s 10(3)	1.69, 2.58	s 16(5)	3.21
s 11	2.73	s 17	3.106, 9.56
s 11(1)	2.59	s 17(1)	3.70, 3.84
s 11(2)	2.59	s 17(1)(a)–(b)	3.23
s 11(3)	2.59	s 17(2)	3.71
s 11(4)(a)–(b)	2.60	s 17(2)(a)–(c)	3.24
s 11(4)(c)(i)–(ii)	2.60	s 17(2)(c)	3.23
s 11(4)(d)	2.61	s 17(3)	3.72
s 12(2)	2.64	s 17(3)(a)(i)–(ii)	3.25
s 12(3)	2.65	s 17(3)(b)(i)–(ii)	3.25
s 12(4)	1.67, 1.68	s 17(4)	3.43
s 12(5)	2.63	s 18	3.145

s 18(1)(a)–(g)	3.26	s 23(4)	3.46
s 18(1)(h)	3.27	s 23(5)	3.47
s 18(3)	3.28	s 24(1)–(2)	3.48
s 19	3.32	s 24(3)	3.49, 10.119
s 19(1)	3.29, 3.43	s 24(4)(a)–(b)	3.50
s 19(1)(a)–(c)	3.29	s 25	10.119
s 19(1)(b)–(d)	3.36	s 25(2)	3.51
s 19(1)(d)	3.30	s 25(3)	10.119
s 19(2)	3.31, 3.43	s 25(3)(a)–(c)	3.52
s 19(2)(a)–(b)	3.31	s 25(5)(a)–(b)	3.53
s 19(2)(b)–(d)	3.41	s 25(4)(a)	3.53
s 19(2)(c)	3.31	s 25(4)(b)	3.54
s 19(2)(d)	3.31	s 25(6)	3.55
s 19(3)	3.29, 3.43	s 25(7)(a)–(b)	3.55
s 19(3)(a)–(c)	3.29	s 25(8)(a)–(b)	3.56
s 19(3)(b)–(d)	3.36, 3.42	ss 26–29	3.88
s 19(3)(d)	3.30	s 26(1)–(2)	3.57
s 19(5)	3.32	s 26(3)(a)–(e)	3.58
s 20	3.29, 3.33, 3.78, 3.100	s 27	3.60, 3.62
s 20(2)(a)	3.33	s 27(2)	3.61
s 20(2)(b)	3.33	s 27(3)–(4)(a)	3.60
s 20(2)(c)	3.33	s 27(4)(b)	3.59
s 20(3)(a)	3.34	s 27(5)	3.61
s 20(3)(b)	3.34	s 27(6)	3.60
s 20(4)	3.33	s 27(7)	3.62
s 20(5)	3.35, 3.44	s 27(8)(a)–(b)	3.62
s 20(6)	3.33	s 27(9)	3.59
s 21	3.45	s 27(10)(a)–(b)	3.62
s 21(1)(a)	3.36	s 27(11)–(12)	3.63
s 21(1)(b)	3.36	s 27(13)	3.63
s 21(1)(c)–(e)	3.42	s 28	3.65
s 21(1)(a)–(b)	3.42	s 28(2)	3.65
s 21(4)	3.78, 3.100	s 28(3)	3.66
s 21(4)(b)(i)	3.42	s 28(4)	3.66
s 21(4)(b)(ii)	3.42	s 29	3.65
s 21(5)	3.44	s 29(2)	3.65
s 21(6)	3.36	s 29(3)	3.66
s 22	3.37	s 30(1)	3.67
s 22(1)	3.37	s 30(2)–(4)	3.67
s 22(1)(c)–(e)	3.36	s 30(3)(b)	3.67
s 22(3)(a)(i)–(ii)	3.39	s 30(5)(a)	3.67
s 22(2)(a)–(b)(i)–(ii)	3.38	s 30(5)(b)	3.67
s 22(3)(b)(i)–(ii)	3.39	s 30(6)	3.68
s 22(4)(a)(i)–(ii)	3.40	s 30(6)(a)	3.104
s 22(4)(b)(i)–(ii)	3.40	s 31(1)–(2)	3.69
s 23	3.45, 3.88	s 31(3)	3.70
s 23(1)(a)–(b)	3.46	s 31(4)	3.71
s 23(2)(a)–(b)	3.46	s 31(5)	3.70

s 31(8) 3.83	s 37(2)(a)–(b) 3.93
s 31(9) 3.74	s 37(3) 3.94
s 31(9)(a) 3.90	s 38................................3.95
s 31(9)(b)..........................3.90	s 38(3) 3.96
s 31(10) 3.70	s 38(4) 3.95
s 31(6)–(7).........................3.72	s 38(4)(a)–(b) 3.95
s 32(1)(a) 3.75	s 38(5) 3.97
s 32(2)(a) 3.76	s 38(6)(a)(i)–(ii) 3.97
s 32(2)(b)(i).......................3.75	s 38(6)(b)..........................3.97
s 32(2)(b)(ii) 3.75	s 38(7)(a)–(b) 3.98
s 32(3) 3.76	s 38(8)(a) 3.98
s 33................................3.104	s 38(8)(b)..........................3.98
s 33(1) 3.77	s 39.....................3.101, 3.105
s 33(2)(a) 3.78	s 39(1) 3.99
s 33(2)(b)..........................3.78	s 39(2)(a) 3.100
s 33(2)(c)–(d) 3.78	s 39(2)(b)..........................3.100
s 33(5)(a)–(b) 3.77	s 39(5) 3.101
s 33(6) 3.79	s 39(6) 3.101
s 33(7) 3.80	s 39(8) 3.106
s 33(8) 3.81	s 40................................3.106
s 33(10) 3.82	s 40(1)(a)–(b) 3.102
s 34(1) 3.83	s 40(2) 3.103
s 34(2)(a)–(b) 3.83	s 40(3) 3.103
s 34(2)(b).........................3.83	s 40(4) 3.103, 3.104
s 34(3) 3.84	s 40(5) 3.103
s 34(4) 3.85	s 40(7) 3.05
s 34(5)(a) 3.83	s 40(8) 3.104
s 34(5)(b).........................3.83	s 41................3.107, 9.45, 9.72
s 34(6) 3.83	s 41(2) 3.108
s 35................................3.95	s 41(3) 3.108
s 35(1)(a)–(c).....................3.86	s 41(4) 3.108
s 35(2) 3.90	s 41(5) 3.109, 3.159
s 35(2)(a)–(e).....................3.87	s 41(6)(a)–(b) 3.110
s 35(3) 3.87, 3.95	s 42.......................3.111, 7.41
s 35(4) 3.88	s 42(2) 3.112
s 35(6)(a)(i)–(ii) 3.91	s 42(3)–(5).......................3.108
s 35(6)(b).........................3.88	s 42(3)(a) 3.113
s 35(6)(b)–(e) 3.92	s 42(3)(b)..........................3.113
s 36(5)(a) 3.88	s 42(3)(c) 3.114
s 36(5)(b).........................3.88	s 42(4) 3.114
s 36(6)(a)(i) 3.88	s 42(5) 3.114
s 36(6)(a)(ii).......................3.88	s 43................................7.41, 9.45
s 36(7)(a)–(c).....................3.88	s 43(1) 3.115
s 36(8) 3.89	s 43(2) 3.116
s 36(9) 3.89	s 43(4) 3.115
s 36(10) 3.90	s 43(5)(a) 3.116
s 37................................3.121	s 43(5)(b).........................3.116
s 37(1) 3.93	s 43(6) 3.117

s 43(7)(a)	3.118	s 53(7)(a)–(b)	3.146
s 43(7)(b)	3.118	s 53(8)	3.143
s 43(7)(c)	3.118	s 53(10)	3.143, 3.147
s 43(7)(d)	3.119	s 54	3.29, 3.143
s 43(8)	3.120	s 54(1)	3.150
ss 44–52	2.40	s 54(2)	3.151
s 44	2.26	s 54(5)	3.151
s 44(1)	3.121	s 55(1)–(2)	3.148
s 44(2)	3.122	s 55(3)	3.149
ss 45–48	3.123	s 55(5)(a)–(b)	3.149
s 45	9.30	s 55(6)(a)	3.149
s 45(1)(a)	3.124	s 55(6)(b)	3.149
s 45(2)	3.124	s 55(7)	3.149
s 45(2)(a)	3.124	s 56	3.152, 3.158, 7.63, 8.95, 9.56, 10.122
s 45(2)(b)	3.125	s 56(1)	3.151, 3.153, 7.46
s 45(2)(c)	3.125	s 56(2)	3.154
s 45(3)	3.124	s 56(3)	3.154, 3.157
s 46(1)	3.126	s 56(3)(a)	3.154
s 46(2)	1.67, 3.126	s 56(3)(b)–(c)	3.154
s 46(2)(a)	3.127	s 56(3)(d)	3.154
s 46(2)(b)	3.127	s 56(4)(a)	3.155
s 46(3)	3.128	s 56(4)(b)	3.155
s 46(4)	3.129	s 56(4)(c)	3.155
s 47	3.130, 9.30	s 56(4)(d)	3.155
s 48(1)	3.132	s 56(4)(e)	3.155
s 48(3)	3.131	ss 57–59	7.64, 8.95
s 48(3)(e)	3.154	s 57	3.156, 3.157
s 50	9.30	s 57(1)	3.163
s 50(1)–(2)	3.137	s 57(2)	3.156
s 51(1)	3.140	s 57(3)	3.157
s 52(1)	3.142	s 57(4)	3.157
s 52(2)	3.141, 3.142	ss 58–60	4.102
s 52(3)	1.67, 3.142	s 58	3.156, 3.158
s 52(4)	3.142	s 58(1)(a)	4.47
s 52(5)	1.67, 3.142	s 58(2)(a)–(c)	3.159
s 53	3.29, 3.59, 3.66	s 58(2)(c)	7.64
s 53(2)(a)	3.144	s 58(3)	3.159
s 53(2)(b)	3.144	s 58(4)	9.23
s 53(2)(c)	3.144	s 58(4)(a)	3.160
s 53(2)(d)	3.144	s 58(4)(b)	3.160
s 53(3)(a)	3.145	s 58(4)(c)	3.160
s 53(3)(b)	3.145	s 58(5)(a)	3.161
s 53(3)(c)	3.145	s 58(5)(b)	3.161
s 53(3)(d)	3.145	s 58(6)	3.161
s 53(3)(e)	3.145	s 58(7)	3.161, 10.123
s 53(4)	3.144	s 58(7)(a)	8.95
s 53(5)	3.144, 3.145	s 58(8)	3.162
s 53(7)	3.146, 4.56		

s 58(8)(a)	1.69	s 65(3)	4.33
s 58(9)	3.158	s 65(4)	4.34
s 59	3.156	s 65(5)	1.68
s 59(1)	3.166, 4.43	s 65(5)–(6)	4.34
s 59(2)(a)(i)–(ii)	3.163	s 66(1)	4.35
s 59(2)(b)(i)–(ii)	3.164	s 66(2)	4.35
s 59(2)(c)(i)–(ii)	3.164	s 66(3)	4.36
s 59(2)(d)	3.165	s 66(4)	4.36
s 59(3)	3.166	s 66(5)	4.37
s 60(1)(c)	4.48	s 67	4.15
s 61	4.06, 4.07, 4.13, 4.92, 5.37	s 67(1)(a)	4.39, 4.41, 4.49, 4.50
s 61(1)	4.10, 4.11, 4.34, 4.39, 4.43, 4.57	s 67(1)(b)	4.39
s 61(1)(a)	4.13, 4.56, 4.65	s 67(2)(a)	4.40
s 61(1)(b)	4.14	s 67(2)(b)	4.40
s 61(1)(c)	4.14	s 67(3)(a)	4.41
s 61(2)	4.12, 4.67, 4.68, 4.93	s 67(3)(b)	4.41
s 61(3)	4.15	s 67(4)	4.42, 4.49
s 61(4)	4.16	s 67(5)	4.42, 4.49
s 61(4)(a)–(b)	4.16	s 67(6)	1.70
s 61(4)(c)(i)–(ii)	4.17	s 68(2)(a)–(b)	4.43
s 61(5)	4.18	s 68(3)	4.44
s 61(6)	4.18	s 68(3)(a)–(c)	4.44
s 61(6)(a)	4.19	s 68(4)	4.43
s 61(6)(b)	4.20	s 68(5)	4.43
s 61(6)(b)(ii)	4.67	s 68(7)	4.86
s 61(6)(ii)	4.92, 4.93	s 69	4.45, 4.52
s 61(7)	4.08, 4.10, 4.11, 4.13, 4.30, 4.53, 4.56, 4.57, 5.37	s 69(1)(a)	4.46
s 61(7)(a)–(j)	1.92, 5.05, 5.24, 5.27	s 69(1)(b)(i)–(ii)	4.47
s 61(7)(b)	4.65	s 69(2)	4.49
s 61(7)(j)	4.13	s 69(3)(a)	4.50
s 61(8)	4.14	s 69(3)(b)	4.50
s 62	4.15	s 69(4)	4.50
s 62(1)	4.23	s 69(5)	4.51
s 62(3)(a)–(b)	4.25	s 69(6)(a)	4.52
s 62(4)(b)(i)–(iii)	4.26	s 69(6)(b)	4.52
s 62(5)(a)–(c)	4.27	s 69(7)	4.52
s 62(6)(a)–(b)	4.27	s 69(8)	4.52
s 62(7)(a)–(b)	4.21	s 69(9)	4.46
s 63(1)–(2)	4.28	s 70	4.06, 4.15, 4.53, 4.58
s 63(3)	4.28	s 70(1)	4.53, 4.58
s 63(3)(a)–(d)	4.28	s 70(3)	4.07, 4.55
s 63(3)(d)	4.67, 4.92, 4.94	s 70(3)(a)	4.09
s 64(1)(a)–(e)	4.30	s 70(3)(b)	4.09
s 64(2)(a)–(b)	4.31	s 70(4)(a)–(b)	4.09, 4.55
s 64(3)(a)–(b)	4.32	s 70(5)(a)–(b)	4.09
s 64(4)	4.29	s 70(6)(a)	4.10
s 65(1)–(2)	4.33	s 70(6)(a)–(b)	4.56
		s 70(6)(b)	4.10

s 70(7) 4.11	s 78(2) 4.66
s 71 .... 1.69, 4.59	s 78(3)(a)–(d) 4.67
s 71(1) 4.58	s 78(4) 4.68
s 71(2) 4.58	s 78(5) 4.69
s 71(3) 4.58	s 79(1) 4.87
s 72 .... 1.69	s 79(2)–(3) 4.87
s 72(1)–(2) 4.59	s 79(2)(b)–(c) 4.87
s 72(2) 4.60	s 79(4) 4.88
s 72(3) 1.66, 4.59	s 79(5) 4.89
s 73 .... 4.15, 4.98	s 79(6) 4.66
ss 73–75 .... 4.63	s 79(7) 4.66, 4.89
s 73(1) 4.64	s 80 .... 4.90
s 73(2) 4.07	s 80(1)(a)–(b) 4.90
s 73(2)(a)–(b) 4.64	s 80(2) 4.91
s 73(3) 4.65	s 80(3)(a)–(b) 4.92
s 73(4) 1.66, 1.69, 4.64	s 80(3)(b) 4.94
s 73(5) 1.66, 1.69, 4.64	s 80(3)(c) 4.92
s 73(6) 1.66, 4.64	s 80(4) 4.93
s 74 .... 4.06, 4.66	s 80(4)(b) 4.94
s 74(1)(a) 4.66	s 80(6) 4.90
s 74(1)(b) 4.66	s 81(1)(a)–(b) 4.96
s 74(2) 4.70	s 81(2) 4.97
s 74(3) 4.70, 4.71	s 81(3) 4.97
s 75 .... 4.15, 4.72, 4.76, 4.85	s 82(1) 4.98
s 75(1) 4.67, 4.72	s 82(1)(a)–(b) 4.98
s 75(2) 4.72	s 82(2) 4.99
s 75(4)(a)–(b) 4.74	s 82(3)(a)–(c) 4.100
s 75(5)(a) 4.75	s 82(3)(d) 4.101
s 75(5)(b) 4.75	s 83 .... 1.67, 4.103
s 75(6) 4.76	s 83(1) 4.103, 4.104
s 75(7) 4.72	s 83(1)(a) 4.102
s 76 .... 4.15	s 83(1)(b) 4.102
s 76(2) 4.78	s 83(2) 4.102
s 76(3) 4.78	s 83(3) 4.102
s 76(4)(b) 4.69, 4.95	s 83(4) 4.102
s 76(5)(a)–(d) 4.80	s 84(1)(2)(a)–(c) 4.16
s 76(6)(a)–(d) 4.81	s 85(1)–(2) 4.110
s 76(7)(a)–(c) 4.82	s 85(3)(a)–(c) 4.111
s 76(8) 4.77	s 85(4) 4.36
s 77 .... 4.15	s 85(4)(a)–(b) 4.36
s 77(1) 4.84	s 85(5) 4.35
s 77(2) 4.84	s 86(1)(a)–(b) 4.07
s 77(3) 4.84	s 87 .... 1.92
s 77(6)(a)–(b) 4.85	s 87(1)(a) 5.05
ss 78–79 .... 4.66	s 87(1)(b) 5.05
s 78(1) 4.66	s 87(2) 5.38
s 78(1)(a) 4.66	s 87(2)(a)–(c) 5.07
s 78(1)(b)(i)–(iii) 4.66	s 87(2)(d)–(f) 5.07

s 87(3)	5.38	s 94(1)–(3)	1.92
s 87(3)(a)	5.09	s 94(2)	5.35
s 87(3)(b)–(c)	5.10	s 94(3)	5.36
s 87(4)(a)–(d)	5.11	s 94(4)	5.37, 5.39
s 87(5)	5.12, 5.38	s 94(4)(a)	1.92
s 87(6)	5.13	s 94(4)(b)	1.92
s 87(7)	5.14, 5.38	s 94(5)	1.92, 5.37
s 87(8)	5.16	s 94(6)	5.39
s 87(8)(a)–(e)	5.15	s 94(7)	1.92, 5.38
s 87(9)(a)–(b)	5.06, 5.16	s 94(8)	1.92, 5.38
s 87(9)(c)–(d)	5.06	s 94(9)	1.92, 5.38
s 87(9)(e)	5.06	s 94(10)	5.35
s 87(10)	5.05	s 94(11)	1.92, 5.37
s 87(11)	5.06	s 94(12)	5.37
s 88	1.92, 5.08, 5.38	s 94(13)	5.34, 5.39
s 88(1)(a)–(e)	5.08	s 94(15)	5.36
s 88(2)	5.08	s 94(16)	5.34, 5.39
s 89(2)(a)	5.25, 5.28	s 95	1.92, 5.39
s 88(2)(a)–(g)	4.07	s 95(1)	5.40
s 89(2)(b)	5.25	s 95(1)–(3)	5.44
s 89(3)	5.26	s 95(2)	5.41
s 89(4)	5.26	s 95(3)	5.43
s 90	5.37	s 95(4)	5.41, 5.43
s 90(1)	1.67	s 95(5)	5.42
s 90(1)–(2)	5.17	s 96	6.35
s 90(3)	5.18	s 96(1)(e)–(f)	5.05
s 90(4)	5.19	s 96(1)–(2)(a)–(b)	5.05
s 90(5)	5.19	s 96(2)(c)	5.05
s 90(6)	5.20	s 96(2)(d)	5.10
s 90(7)	5.21	s 97	1.92, 5.39
s 90(8)	5.21	s 97(1)	5.44
s 90(9)(a)	5.22	s 97(2)	5.44
s 90(9)(b)	5.22	s 98	1.92
s 90(10)	5.23, 5.37	s 98(1)	5.06, 5.14
s 90(11)	5.23	s 99	7.149, 8.16
s 90(12)	5.22	s 99(1)(a)–(b)	6.05
s 90(13)	1.92, 5.20	s 99(2)(a)–(c)	6.06
s 90(13)–(16)	1.92	s 99(3)(a)–(b)	6.10
s 91(1)	5.27, 5.37	s 99(4)(a)	6.06
s 91(2)(a)–(b)	5.28	s 99(4)(b)	6.06
s 91(3)	5.29	s 99(5)(a)	6.11
s 92	1.92, 5.44	s 99(5)(b)	6.11
s 92(1)(a)–(c)	5.30	s 99(6)	6.10
s 92(2)	5.31	s 99(7)	6.11
s 92(3)	5.32	s 99(8)	6.10, 7.125
s 93	1.92, 5.33, 5.44	s 99(9)	6.07, 6.09
s 94	1.92, 5.23	s 99(11)	6.05
s 94(1)	5.34, 5.39	s 100	7.127

s 100(2)(a) 6.08	s 106. . . . . .6.32, 6.34, 6.39, 6.54
s 100(2)(c) 6.08	s 106(1)(a) 6.42
s 100(3) 6.08	s 106(1)(a)–(b) .6.20
s 100(5)(a)–(b) .6.58	s 106(1)(c) 6.22
s 101. . . . . .6.65	s 106(1)(d) 6.23
s 101(1) 6.12	s 106(1)–(2) 6.67
s 101(1)(a) 6.13	s 106(2) 6.36
s 101(1)(b) 6.13	s 106(2)(b) 6.42
s 101(1)(c) 6.13	s 106(3)(a) 6.36
s 101(1)(d) 6.14	s 106(5) 6.17
s 101(1)(e) 6.14	s 106(5)(a)–(c) .6.35
s 101(2)(a) 6.16	s 106(7)–(12) 6.38
s 101(2)(b) 6.16	s 106(8) 6.38
s 101(2)(c) 6.16	s 106(11) 6.21
s 101(2)(d)–(e) .6.16	s 106(13)(a)–(b) 6.38
s 102. . . . . .6.67	s 106(14) 6.33
s 102(1)(a) 6.29	s 107(1) 6.39
s 102(1)(a)–(b) .6.20	s 107(2) 6.39
s 102(1)(c) 6.22	s 107(3) 6.40
s 102(1)(d) 6.23	s 107(4)(a)–(b) .6.41
s 102(2)(a) 6.25, 6.29	s 107(4)(c)(i)–(iii) 6.41
s 102(2)(b) 6.25	s 107(5) 6.39
s 102(2)(c) 6.30	s 108. . . . . .6.66, 6.76, 6.87
s 102(2)(d)–(e) .6.30	s 108(1)(a)–(b) .6.42
s 102(3)(a)–(b) .6.26	s 108(2) 6.43
s 102(3)(c)–(d) .6.27	s 108(3) 6.43
s 102(4) 6.25	s 108(4) 6.44
s 102(5) 6.17, 6.42	s 108(5) 6.44
s 102(6) 6.28	s 109(2) 6.46
s 102(7) 6.21	s 109(3) 6.46
s 102(8) 6.24	s 109(4) 6.47
s 102(9) 6.25	s 110(2) 6.48
s 103. . . . . .6.42, 6.67	s 110(3)(a)–(c) .6.49
s 103(1)(b) 6.29	s 110(4) 6.49
s 103(1)(b)–(c) .6.20	s 110(5)(a) 6.50
s 103(1)(d) 6.22	s 110(5)(b) 6.50
s 103(1)(e) 6.23	s 110(6) 6.50
s 103(2)(b) 629	s 110(7) 6.51
s 103(3) 6.21	s 110(8) 6.51
s 104. . . . . .6.42, 6.67	s 110(9) 6.48
s 104(1)(a)–(b) .6.20	ss 111–114 . . . . .6.76, 6.87
s 104(1)(c) 6.22	s 111(1)–(2) 6.53
s 104(1)(d) 6.23	s 111(3) 6.53
s 104(2) 6.21	s 111(4)–(9) 6.54
s 104(3) 6.31	s 111(5) 6.87
s 105(1)–(2) 6.18	s 111(8) 6.53
s 105(3)–(4) 6.18	s 112. . . . . .6.56, 6.58
s 105(5)(a)–(b) .6.18	s 112(2) 6.57

s 112(3)	6.56	s 119(1)(a)	6.74
s 112(4)(a)	6.56	s 119(2)(b)	6.75
s 112(4)(b)	6.56	s 119(4)	7.75
s 112(5)	6.57	s 119(4)(b)	6.74
s 112(6)	6.56	s 120(3)	6.76
s 112(7)	6.58	s 120(4)(a)	6.76
s 112(9)	6.55	s 120(4)(b)	6.76
s 112(10)(a)–(b)	6.58	s 120(5)(a)(i)	6.76
s 112(11)–(12)	6.59	s 120(5)(b)	6.76
s 112(13)	6.59	s 120(6)	6.76
s 113	6.61	s 120(7)	6.76
s 113(2)	6.61	s 120(8)	6.76
s 113(3)	6.62	s 121(1)	6.77
s 113(4)	6.62	s 121(2)(a)–(c)	6.77
s 114	6.61	s 121(3)	6.78
s 114(2)	6.61	s 122	6.77
s 114(3)	6.62	s 122(1)–(3)	6.79
s 115	6.71	s 122(4)(a)	6.79
s 115(1)	6.64	s 122(4)(b)	6.79
s 115(2)	6.64	s 122(5)(a)–(b)	6.80
s 115(3)	6.72	s 122(6)(a)(i)–(ii)	6.80
s 115(3)–(5)	6.77	s 122(6)(b)	6.80
s 115(4)(a)–(b)	6.64	s 122(7)	6.81
s 115(5)	6.72	s 122(7)(a)–(b)	681
s 116(1)(a)–(b)	6.66	s 122(8)	682
s 116(2)(b)(i)	6.66	s 122(9)	6.82
s 116(2)(b)(ii)	6.66	s 122(10)(a)–(b)	6.83
s 116(3)(a)–(b)	6.45	s 123(1)(a)–(b)	6.85
s 117(1)	6.68	s 123(2)(a)	6.85
s 117(2)(a)	6.67	s 123(2)(b)	6.85
s 117(2)(b)	6.67	s 123(2)(c)–(d)	6.85
s 117(2)(c)	6.67	s 123(2)(e)–(f)	6.85
s 117(2)(d)	6.67	s 123(3)	6.85
s 117(3)	6.68	s 123(3)(a)(i)	6.86
s 117(4)	6.67	s 123(3)(a)(ii)	6.86
s 117(5)	6.68	s 123(3)(b)	6.86
s 117(6)	6.69	s 123(4)	6.86
s 117(7)	6.69	s 123(6)	6.85
s 117(8)	6.69	s 123(7)(a)–(b)	6.87
s 117(9)	6.70	s 123(8)	6.87
s 117(10)	6.70	s 123(9)	6.87
s 118(1)	6.71	s 123(10)	6.86
s 118(2)(a)–(b)	6.71	s 124(1)–(2)	6.88
s 118(2)(c)–(d)	6.71	s 124(3)	6.89
s 118(2)(e)–(f)	6.71	s 124(4)(a)–(c)	6.90
s 118(3)(a)–(b)	6.72	s 124(5)	6.91
s 118(4)	6.72	s 124(6)	6.91
s 118(5)	6.71	s 124(7)(a)–(b)	6.92

s 125 . . . . 6.93, 6.95	s 132(2) 6.111
s 125(1) 6.93	s 132(2)(b) 6.113
s 125(2)(a)–(b) 6.94	s 132(3)(a)–(f) 6.112
s 125(4) 6.93	s 132(4) 6.111
s 125(5) 6.95	s 133(1)(a)–(d) 6.114
s 125(6) 6.94	s 133(2)(a)–(c) 6.115
s 126 . . . . 9.45, 9.72	s 133(2)(c) 7.191
s 126(1) 6.96	s 133(3) 9.23
s 126(2) 6.97	s 133(3)(a) 6.116
s 126(3) 6.97	s 133(3)(b) 6.116
s 126(4) 6.96, 7.191	s 133(4) 10.123
s 126(5) 6.97	s 133(4)(a)–(b) 6.117
s 127 . . . . 7.169	s 133(5) 6.117
s 127(2) 6.98	s 133(6)(a) 1.69
s 127(3)(a) 6.99	s 133(6)(a)(i)–(ii) 6.118
s 127(3)(b) 6.99	s 133(6)(b) 6.118
s 127(3)(c) 6.100	s 134(2)(a) 6.120
s 127(4)(a)–(b) 6.100	s 134(2)(b) 6.120
s 127(5) 6.99	s 134(2)(c) 6.120
s 128 . . . . 7.169, 9.45	s 134(2)(d) 6.121
s 128(1) 6.101	s 134(3) 6.119
s 128(2)(a)–(b) 6.101	s 135(1)(a) 6.74, 7.51, 7.179
s 128(3) 6.102	s 136(1) 7.04
s 128(4)(a)–(b) 6.101	s 136(2) 7.05, 7.28
s 128(5) 6.101	s 136(3)(a)–(b) 7.05
s 128(6) 6.101	s 136(4)(a)–(d) 7.06
s 128(7) 6.103	s 136(5)(a)–(b) 7.07
s 129 . . . . 6.22, 6.55, 6.62	s 136(6) 7.07
s 129(1)–(2) 6.104	s 137(2)(a)–(b) 7.05
s 129(3)(a) 6.105	s 137(4) 7.05
s 129(3)(b)–(c) 6.105	s 137(5)(a)–(c) 7.05
s 129(3)(d)–(e) 6.105	s 138 . . . . 7.08
s 129(4)–(5) 6.104	s 138(1)(a) 7.09
s 129(7) 6.105	s 138(1)(b) 7.19, 7.27
s 129(8) 6.106	s 138(1)(b)(i) 7.09
s 129(9) 6.104	s 138(1)(b)–(d) 7.13
s 129(10) 6.104	s 138(1)(c) 7.09
s 129(11) 6.104, 6.107	s 138(1)(d)(i)–(ii) 7.09
s 130 . . . . 6.22	s 138(1)(e) 7.09
s 130(1)–(2) 6.108	s 138(1)(f) 7.09
s 131(1)–(2) 6.109	s 138(1)(g) 7.10, 7.13
s 131(3) 6.110	s 138(2) 7.19, 7.27
s 131(5)(a)–(b) 6.110	s 138(2)(a)–(b) 7.09
s 131(6)(a) 6.110	s 138(3) 7.09
s 131(6)(b) 6.110	s 138(4) 7.11, 7.131
s 131(7) 6.110	s 139 . . . . 7.09, 7.26
ss 132–134 . . . . 7.191	s 139(1)–(2) 7.12
s 132(1) 6.111	s 139(3)(a)–(e) 7.12

s 140(1)(a)–(c)	7.13	s 146(3)–(4)	7.33
s 140(1)(d)	7.13	s 147(1)(a)–(b)	7.34
s 140(2)(a)	7.14	s 147(2)	7.34
s 140(2)(b)	7.14	s 147(3)(a)–(b)	7.34
s 140(3)	7.15	s 147(4)(a)–(b)	7.35
s 140(4)	7.15	s 147(5)(a)–(b)	7.36
s 141(1)	7.08	s 148(1)	7.37
s 141(2)	7.08	s 148(2)	7.37
s 142	7.18, 7.20, 7.37, 7.48, 9.77, 9.78	s 148(3)(a)	7.37
s 142(3)	7.21	s 148(3)(b)	7.37
s 142(4)	7.18	s 148(3)(c)	7.37
s 142(5)	7.22	s 148(4)	7.37
s 142(6)	7.19	s 148(5)	7.38
s 142(7)	7.19	s 148(6)	7.38
s 142(8)	7.20	s 149	9.45, 9.72
s 142(9)(a)–(b)	7.20	s 149(1)	7.39
s 142(10)	7.20	s 149(2)	7.40
s 142(11)	7.18	s 149(3)	7.40
s 143(1)(a)	7.23	s 149(4)	7.39
s 143(1)(b)	7.23	s 149(5)	7.41
s 144	7.27	s 149(6)	7.40
s 144(1)	7.24	s 150	3.59, 3.66, 7.47, 7.53
s 144(2)	7.27	s 150(1)–(2)	7.42
s 144(2)(a)–(b)	7.25	s 150(2)	7.45
s 144(2)(c)–(d)	7.25	s 150(3)(a)	7.43
s 144(3)	7.24	s 150(3)(b)–(c)	7.43
s 144(4)	7.24	s 150(3)(d)	7.43
s 144(5)	7.26	s 150(3)(e)	7.43
s 144(6)(a)	7.27	s 150(4)–(5)	7.42
s 144(6)(b)	7.27	s 150(5)	7.45
s 144(6)(c)(i)–(ii)	7.27	s 150(6)	7.42
s 145(1)	7.28	s 150(7)	7.42
s 145(2)(a)	7.28	s 150(8)	7.42
s 145(2)(b)	7.28	s 150(9)	7.42, 7.44
s 145(3)(a)	7.28	s 151	7.42
s 145(3)(b)	7.28	s 151(1)–(2)	7.45
s 145(4)(a)–(b)	7.29	s 151(2)	7.46
s 145(5)	7.29	s 151(3)	7.46
s 145(6)(a)–(b)	7.30	s 152	7.42, 7.45, 7.47, 7.51, 7.59
s 145(7)	7.30	s 152(1)(a)–(c)	7.47
s 145(8)	7.30	s 152(2)	7.47, 7.48
s 145(9)	7.31	s 152(3)	7.47
s 145(10)	7.31	s 152(3)(a)–(b)	7.49, 7.52, 7.55
s 145(11)	7.31	s 152(3)(c)	7.52, 7.55
s 145(12)	7.28	s 152(3)(c)–(d)	7.49
s 145(13)	7.28	s 152(4)	3.18, 3.31, 3.78, 7.49
s 146(1)	7.32	s 152(5)	7.49, 7.50, 7.52
s 146(2)(a)–(b)	7.32	s 152(5)(a)	7.50

s 152(5)(b)	7.50
s 152(5)(c)	9.61
s 152(5)(c)–(d)	7.50
s 152(6)	7.50
s 152(7)	7.50
s 152(8)	7.50
s 153	7.59
s 153(1)	7.52
s 153(2)	7.52
s 153(3)	7.53
s 153(4)(a)–(b)	7.53
s 153(6)(b)–(c)	7.55
s 153(7)	7.55
s 153(9)	7.56
s 153(10)(a)–(b)	7.57
s 153(12)(a)–(b)	7.57
s 153(13)(a)	7.57
s 153(13)(b)	7.57
s 153(14)	7.57
s 154	7.58
s 155	7.62
s 155(1)(a)–(c)	7.59
s 155(2)(a)	7.60
s 155(2)(b)	7.60
s 155(2)(c)	7.60
s 155(2)(d)	7.61
s 155(3)	7.62
s 156(1)	7.63
s 156(2)	7.64
s 158	7.69
s 158(1)	7.69
s 158(1)(a)	7.80
s 158(1)(a)(i)	7.70
s 158(1)(a)–(d)	7.74
s 158(1)(b)	7.70, 7.88
s 158(1)(c)(i)–(ii)	7.71
s 158(1)(d)	7.71
s 158(1)(e)	7.72, 7.74
s 158(2)	7.73, 7.80, 7.88
s 158(2)(a)–(b)	7.70
s 158(3)	7.70
s 158(5)	7.65
s 158(6)	7.65, 7.66
s 158(6)(a)	7.98
s 158(6)(a)(i)–(iii)	7.67
s 158(6)(b)–(c)	7.67
s 158(7)	7.65, 7.66
s 158(7)(a)–(b)	7.68
s 158(8)	7.65
s 158(9)	7.69
s 159	7.88
s 159(1)(a)–(c)	7.74
s 159(2)(a)	7.75
s 159(2)(b)	7.75
s 159(3)	7.76
s 159(4)	7.76
s 160	1.61
s 160(1)	7.69
s 160(2)	7.69
s 161	7.79, 7.81, 7.98, 7.112
s 161(1)–(2)	7.78
s 161(3)	7.82
s 161(4)	7.79
s 161(5)	7.83
s 161(6)	7.80
s 161(7)	7.80
s 161(8)	7.81
s 161(9)(a)–(b)	7.81
s 161(10)	7.81
s 161(11)	7.79
s 162(1)(a)	7.84
s 162(1)(b)	7.84
s 163(1)	7.85
s 163(2)	7.88
s 163(2)(a)–(b)	7.86
s 163(2)(c)–(d)	7.86
s 163(3)	7.85
s 163(4)	7.85
s 163(6)(a)	7.88
s 163(6)(b)	7.88
s 163(6)(c)(i)–(ii)	7.88
s 164(1)	7.89
s 164(2)(a)	7.89
s 164(2)(b)	7.89
s 164(3)(a)	7.89
s 164(3)(b)	7.89
s 164(4)(a)–(b)	7.90
s 164(5)	7.90
s 164(6)(a)–(b)	7.91
s 164(7)	7.91
s 164(8)	7.91
s 164(9)	7.92
s 164(10)	7.92
s 164(11)	7.92
s 164(12)	7.89
s 165(1)	7.93

s 165(2)(a)–(b)	7.93
s 165(3)–(4)	7.94
s 166(1)(a)–(b)	7.95
s 166(2)	7.95
s 166(3)(a)–(b)	7.95
s 166(4)(a)–(b)	7.96
s 166(5)(a)–(b)	7.97
s 167(1)	7.98
s 167(2)	7/98
s 167(3)(a)	7.98
s 167(3)(b)	7.98
s 167(3)(c)	7.98
s 167(4)	7.98
s 167(5)	7.99
s 167(6)	7.99
s 168	9.45, 9.72
s 168(1)	7.100
s 168(2)	7.101
s 168(3)	7.101
s 168(4)	7.100
s 168(5)	7.101
s 169(2)	7.102
s 169(3)(a)	7.104
s 169(3)(b)	7.104
s 169(3)(c)	7.105
s 169(4)	7.105
s 169(5)	7.105
s 170	9.45
s 170(1)	7.106
s 170(2)	7.106
s 170(3)	7.106
s 170(4)	7.107
s 170(5)	7.108
s 171	7.112
s 171(1)–(2)	7.109
s 171(3)(a)	7.110
s 171(3)(b)–(c)	7.110
s 171(3)(d)	7.110
s 171(3)(e)	7.110
s 171(3)(f)	7.110
s 171(4)–(5)	7.109
s 171(6)–(7)	7.109
s 171(9)	7.109
s 171(10)	7.111
s 172	7.109
s 172(1)(a)–(b)	7.112
s 172(2)	7.112
s 172(3)	7.112
s 173	7.116, 7.190, 8.93
s 173(1)(a)–(c)	7.113
s 173(2)(a)	7.114, 7.118
s 173(2)(b)	7.114, 7.118
s 173(2)(c)	7.114, 7.118
s 173(2)(d)	7.115, 7.119
s 173(3)	7.116
s 176	7.121
s 176(1)(b)	7.154
s 176(1)(b)(i)	7.120
s 176(1)(b)(ii)–(iii)	7.120
s 176(1)(c)	7.121
s 176(2)(a)–(b)	7.121
s 176(4)(a)	7.123, 7.154
s 176(4)(b)(i)–(ii)	7.123
s 176(5)(a)–(b)	7.124
s 176(6)–(7)	7.125
s 176(9)	7.126
s 177(2)(a)	7.127
s 177(2)(c)	7.127
s 177(3)	7.127
s 178	7.128
s 178(1)	7.128
s 178(1)(a)	7.129
s 178(1)(a)–(e)	7.132
s 178(1)(b)	7.145
s 178(1)(b)(i)	7.129
s 178(1)(c)	7.129
s 178(1)(d)(i)–(ii)	7.129
s 178(1)(e)	7.129
s 178(1)(f)	7.130, 7.132
s 178(2)	7.145, 7.153
s 178(2)(a)–(b)	7.129
s 178(3)	7.129
s 178(4)	7.128
s 179	7.153
s 179(1)(a)–(c)	7.132
s 179(2)(a)	7.133
s 179(2)(b)	7.133
s 179(3)	7.134
s 179(4)	7.134
s 180(2)	7.136
s 180(3)	7.136
s 180(4)	7.137
s 181(2)	7.138
s 181(3)(a)–(c)	7.139
s 181(4)(a)	7.140
s 181(4)(b)	7.140

s 181(5)	7.140
s 181(6)	7.141
s 181(7)	7.141
s 181(8)	7.138
s 182(1)	7.128
s 182(2)	7.128
s 182(3)	7.128
s 182(4)	7.128
s 183	7.144, 7.146, 7.165, 7.176
s 183(1)–(2)	7.143
s 183(4)	7.144, 7.147
s 183(5)	7.144
s 183(6)	7.148
s 183(7)	7.145
s 183(8)	7.145
s 183(9)	7.146
s 183(10)(a)–(b)	7.146
s 183(11)	7.146
s 183(12)	7.144
s 184(1)(a)–(b)	7.149
s 184(2)(b)(i)	7.149
s 184(2)(b)(ii)	7.149
s 184(2)(a)	7.149
s 184(3)(a)–(b)	7.135
s 185(1)	7.150
s 185(2)	7.153
s 185(2)(a)–(b)	7.151
s 185(2)(c)–(d)	7.151
s 185(3)	7.150
s 185(4)	7.150
s 185(5)	7.152
s 185(6)(a)	7.153
s 185(6)(b)	7.153
s 185(6)(c)(i)–(ii)	7.153
s 186(1)	7.154
s 186(2)(a)–(b)	7.154
s 186(3)(a)	7.154
s 186(3)(b)	7.154
s 186(4)(a)–(b)	7.155
s 186(5)(a)–(b)	7.155
s 186(6)	7.155
s 186(7)(a)–(b)	7.156
s 186(8)	7.156
s 186(9)	7.156
s 186(10)	7.157
s 186(11)	7.158
s 186(12)	7.158
s 186(13)	7.154
s 186(14)	7.154
s 187(1)(a)–(b)	7.159
s 187(2)(a)–(b)	7.159
s 187(3)–(4)	7.160
s 188(1)(a)–(b)	7.161
s 188(2)	7.161
s 188(3)(a)–(b)	7.161
s 188(4)(a)–(b)	7.162
s 188(5)	7.163
s 188(6)(a)–(b)	7.164
s 189(1)	7.165
s 189(2)	7.165
s 189(3)(a)	7.165
s 189(3)(b)	7.165
s 189(3)(c)	7.165
s 189(4)	7.165
s 189(5)	7.166
s 189(6)	7.166
s 190	9.45, 9.72
s 190(1)	7.167
s 190(2)	7.168
s 190(3)	7.168
s 190(4)	7.167, 7.191
s 190(5)	7.169
s 190(6)	7.168
s 191	6.55, 6.62, 7.175, 7.181
s 191(1)–(2)	7.170
s 191(2)	7.174
s 191(3)(a)	7.71
s 191(3)(b)–(c)	7.171
s 191(3)(d)–(e)	7.171
s 191(4)–(5)	7.170
s 191(5)	7.174
s 191(7)	7.170, 7.171
s 191(8)	7.170
s 191(9)	7.170, 7.172
s 192(1)(a)–(b)	7.173
s 192(2)	7.174
s 193	7.174, 7.175, 7.179
s 193(1)(a)–(c)	7.175
s 193(2)	7.175, 7.176
s 193(3)	7.175
s 193(3)(a)–(b)	7.177, 7.180, 7.183
s 193(3)(c)	7.180, 7.183
s 193(3)(c)–(d)	7.177
s 193(4)	6.07, 6.27, 6.30, 6.67, 7.177
s 193(5)	7.177, 7.178, 7.180
s 193(5)(a)	7.178

s 193(5)(b)	7.178
s 193(5)(c)	9.61
s 193(5)(c)–(d)	7.178
s 193(6)	7.178
s 193(7)	7.178
s 193(8)	7178
s 194(1)	7.180
s 194(2)	7.180
s 194(3)	7.181
s 194(4)(a)–(b)	7.181
s 194(5)	7.182
s 194(6)(b)–(c)	7.183
s 194(7)	7.183
s 194(8)	7.183
s 194(9)	7.184
s 194(10)(a)–(b)	7.185
s 194(12)(a)–(b)	7.185
s 194(13)(a)	7.185
s 194(13)(b)	7.185
s 194(14)	7.185
s 195	7.186
s 196(1)(a)–(c)	7.187
s 196(2)(a)	7.188
s 196(2)(b)	7.188
s 196(2)(c)	7.188
s 196(2)(d)	7.189
s 196(3)	7.190
s 197	7.191
s 198	7.120
s 199	8.76
s 199(1)(a)	8.09
s 199(1)(b)	8.09
s 199(1)(c)–(d)	8.09
s 200(1)	8.42, 8.74, 8.77
s 200(1)–(2)	8.10
s 200(2)	8.42, 8.74
s 200(3)(a)–(b)	8.11
s 201	8.10
s 201(1)	8.12, 8.95
s 201(2)	8.13
s 201(3)	8.14
s 202(1)	8.26
s 202(1)–(2)(a)–(b)	8.15
s 202(2)	8.26
s 202(3)	8.14, 8.26
s 202(4)	8.19
s 203	8.16
s 203(1)(a)	8.16
s 203(1)(c)	8.16
s 203(2)(a)–(c)	8.16
s 204	8.22
s 204(1)	8.22
s 204(1)(e)	8.35
s 204(2)(a)–(b)	8.22
s 204(3)(a)	8.48
s 204(3)(a)(i)–(iii)	8.23
s 204(3)(b)	8.23
s 204(3)(c)(i)–(ii)	8.23
s 204(3)(d)	8.23
s 204(3)(e)	8.24
s 204(4)	8.25
s 204(5)	8.22
s 205	8.26
s 205(1)	8.26
s 205(1)(e)	8.35
s 205(2)(a)–(b)	8.26
s 205(3)(a)–(b)	8.26
s 205(4)(a)–(b)	827
s 205(5)	8.26
s 205(6)(a)	8.48
s 205(6)(a)(i)–(iii)	828
s 205(6)(b)	8.28
s 205(6)(c)(i)–(ii)	8.28
s 205(6)(d)	8.28, 8.83
s 205(6)(e)	8.29
s 205(7)	8.30
s 205(8)	8.31
s 205(9)	8.26
s 206	8.18
s 206(1)–(2)	8.32
s 206(3)	8.32
s 206(4)–(5)	8.33
s 206(6)(a)–(c)	8.18
s 206(7)	8.18
s 207	8.34, 8.51, 8.79
s 208(1)(a)–(c)	8.35
s 208(2)(a)	8.36
s 208(2)(b)	8.36
s 208(3)	8.37
s 208(4)	8.37
s 209(2)	8.39
s 209(3)	8.39
s 209(4)	8.40
s 210(2)	8.41
s 210(3)(a)–(b)	8.42
s 210(4)(a)	8.43

Table of Legislation

s 210(4)(b)	8.43	s 217	6.101
s 210(5)	8.43	s 217(1)(a)–(b)	8.64
s 210(6)	8.44	s 217(2)	8.64
s 210(7)	8.44	s 217(3)(a)–(b)	8.64
s 210(8)	8.14, 8.42	s 217(4)(a)–(b)	8.65
s 210(9)	8.41	s 217(5)(a)–(b)	8.66
s 211(1)	8.22, 8.27	s 218(1)	8.67
s 211(2)	8.22, 8.27	s 218(2)	8.67
s 211(4)	8.27	s 218(3)(a)	8.67
s 211(5)	8.27	s 218(3)(b)	8.67
s 212	8.47, 8.49, 8.67, 8.78, 8.90	s 218(3)(c)	8.67
s 212(1)–(2)	8.46	s 218(4)	8.67
s 212(3)(a)–(b)	8.50	s 219	8.68
s 212(4)(a)–(d)	8.51	s 219(1)–(2)	8.68
s 212(5)	8.47	s 219(2)(a)(i)	8.69
s 212(6)	8.52	s 219(2)(a)(ii)	8.69
s 212(7)	8.48	s 219(2)(b)	8.70
s 212(8)	8.48	s 219(3)	8.70
s 212(9)	8.49	s 219(3)(b)	9.61
s 212(10)(a)–(b)	8.49	s 219(4)(a)–(b)	8.72
s 212(11)	8.49	s 219(5)–(6)	8.73
s 212(12)	8.47	s 219(7)	8.71
s 213(1)(a)–(b)	8.53	s 219(8)	8.14, 8.74
s 213(2)(b)	8.53	s 220(1)(a)–(b)	8.75
s 213(3)(a)–(b)	8.38	s 220(2)	8.76
s 214(1)	8.54	s 220(3)	8.75
s 214(2)(a)–(b)	8.55	s 220(4)	8.75
s 214(2)(c)–(d)	8.55	s 220(5)	8.14
s 214(3)(b)	8.54	s 220(5)(a)–(b)	8.77
s 214(4)	8.54	s 221(1)(a)–(b)	8.78
s 214(5)	8.57	s 221(2)	8.78
s 214(6)	8.56	s 221(3)	8.79
s 215(1)	8.58	s 221(4)	8.78
s 215(2)(a)	8.58	s 222(1)	8.81
s 215(2)(b)	8.58	s 222(2)	8.81
s 215(3)(a)	8.58	s 222(3)	8.81
s 215(3)(b)	8.58	s 222(4)	8.81
s 215(4)(a)–(b)	8.59	s 222(5)(a)–(b)	8.83
s 215(5)	8.59	s 222(6)	8.83
s 215(6)(a)–(b)	8.60	s 222(7)(a)–(c)	8.84
s 215(7)	8.60	s 222(8)(a)–(b)	8.82
s 215(8)	8.60	s 222(9)–(10)	8.85
s 215(9)	8.61	s 222(11)	8.85
s 215(10)	8.61	s 222(12)	8.85
s 215(11)	8.61	s 222(13)	8.86
s 216(1)	8.62	s 223(1)	8.87
s 216(2)(a)–(b)	8.62	s 223(2)(a)–(b)	8.88
s 216(3)–(4)	8.63	s 223(3)–(5)	9.43

s 223(4)(a)–(b)	8.88
s 223(5)(a)	8.88
s 223(5)(b)	8.88
s 223(6)(a)–(b)	8.88
s 223(6)(a)–(e)	9.43
s 223(9)	2.16
s 223(14)	2.16
s 224(1)	9.48
s 224(1)(a)–(c)	8.89
s 224(2)(a)–(c)	8.90
s 224(2)(a)–(e)	9.49
s 224(2)(f)	9.50
s 224(2)(g)–(i)	9.51
s 224(3)	4.10, 8.90, 9.48
s 224(4)	9.52
s 224(4)(a)	8.91
s 224(4)(b)	8.91
s 224(4)(c)	8.91
s 224(4)(d)	8.92
s 224(5)	8.93, 9.48, 9.52
s 224(6)	9.54
s 224(7)	2.17, 9.53
s 224(8)	2.17, 9.54
s 224(9)	9.52
s 225	9.61, 9.63, 9.67, 9.70, 9.74
s 225(1)–(2)	8.94
s 225(3)(a)–(c)	8.95
s 225(4)	8.96
s 225(5)	8.95
s 225(6)(a)–(b)	8.95
s 225(7)	8.98
s 225(8)	8.99
s 225(9)–(10)	8.100
s 225(11)(a)–(b)	8.97
s 225(12)	8.98
s 225(13)	8.96
s 225(14)	8.95
s 227	1.93
s 227(1)(a)–(b)	9.11
s 227(2)–(4)	9.13
s 227(4)(e)	9.13
s 227(5)–(6)	9.14
s 227(7)	9.11
s 227(8)–(9)	9.21
s 227(10)	9.21
s 227(11)–(12)	9.22
s 227(13)(a)–(b)	9.11
s 228	1.93
s 228(1)–(3)	9.15
s 228(4)	9.16
s 228(5)(a)–(d)	9.16
s 229(1)	4.42
s 229(1)–(2)	9.24
s 229(3)(a)–(b)	9.25
s 229(3)(c)–(d)	9.27
s 229(3)(e)–(g)	9.27
s 229(3)(h)–(j)	9.27
s 229(4)(a)	9.28, 9.29
s 229(4)(c)	9.28
s 229(4)(d)(i)–(ii)	9.28
s 229(4)(e)	9.30
s 229(5)	9.24
s 229(6)(a)–(c)	9.18
s 229(7)(a)–(c)	9.18
s 229(8)	9.19, 9.23
s 230(1)–(2)	9.31
s 230(3)	9.32
s 230(4)(a)–(d)	9.32
s 231	2.03
s 231(1)	9.33
s 231(2)	9.34
s 231(4)(a)–(b)	9.35
s 231(6)(a)	9.37
s 231(6)(b)	9.37
s 231(7)	9.33
s 231(8)	9.50
s 231(9)	9.33
s 231(9)(a)–(b)	9.33
s 232	9.38
s 232(1)(a)–(b)	9.38
s 232(3)(a)–(d)	9.40
s 232(4)(a)–(b)	9.40
s 232(6)	9.39
s 233(1)	9.43
s 233(2)(a)–(h)	9.43
s 234(5)(e)–(f)	9.76
s 234(6)	9.76
s 234(10)	9.55
s 234(11)(a)–(b)	9.55
s 235(1)	9.45
s 235(2)–(3)	9.46
s 235(4)	9.46
s 235(5)	9.42
s 235(6)	9.36
s 236	1.97, 9.32
s 236(1)	9.41

Table of Legislation

s 236(2)	9.41	s 249(2)	10.129
s 237	9.47	s 249(3)–(5)	10.130
s 237(1)	9.47	s 249(6)	10.130
s 237(1)–(2)	9.47	s 249(7)	5.15, 10.131
s 238(1)–(2)	9.17	s 249(8)	10.128
s 238(3)	9.17	s 250(1)(a)–(b)	10.132
s 238(5)	9.23	s 250(2)–(4)	10.133
s 238(6)(a)	9.23	s 251	10.52
s 238(6)(b)–(c)	9.23	s 251(2)	10.03
s 238(7)	9.23	s 251(2)(a)	10.52
s 239	1.67	s 251(2)(b)	10.53
s 239(1)–(2)	9.44	s 251(3)(a)–(c)	10.54
s 239(3)	9.44	s 252	9.25, 9.61, 9.70, 9.73, 9.74, 10.43, 10.131
s 240(1)(a)–(f)	9.09		
s 240(2)(a)–(d)	9.09	s 252(1)	10.27
s 240(3)	1.67	s 252(1)(a)	10.49
s 240(3)–(5)	9.10	s 252(1)(a)–(b)	10.08
s 241	9.08, 9.20	s 252(1)(c)	10.08
s 242	9.81	s 252(3)(a)–(b)	10.06
s 242(1)	9.81	s 252(4)(a)–(b)	10.09
s 242(4)(a)–(b)	9.79, 9.83	s 252(5)	10.09
s 243(1)	9.63	s 252(7)	10.06
s 243(1)(a)	9.56	s 252(8)	10.12
s 243(1)(b)	9.57	s 253	1.67, 3.117, 4.36, 7.107, 9.60, 9.61, 9.70, 9.73, 9.74, 10.13, 10.43
s 243(1)(c)	9.58		
s 243(1)(d)	9.64	s 253(1)	10.27
s 243(1)(e)	9.65	s 253(1)(a)	10.49
s 243(1)(g)	9.66	s 253(1)(a)–(b)	10.15
s 243(1)(h)	9.66	s 253(1)(c)	10.15
s 243(1)(i)	9.67	s 253(2)(a)–(b)	10.14
s 243(1)(j)	9.68	s 253(3)	10.14, 10.18
s 243(2)(a)–(c)	9.69	s 253(4)(a)–(b)	10.18
s 243(3)	9.70	s 253(5)(a)–(e)	10.19
s 243(5)(a)(i)–(ii)	9.72	s 253(6)(a)–(d)	10.20
s 243(5)(b)	9.73	s 253(7)	10.17
s 243(5)(c)	9.74	s 253(8)	10.17
s 243(5)(d)(i)–(ii)	9.75	s 254	9.60
s 244	1.92, 9.07	s 254(1)	10.26
s 245	1.67, 9.84	s 254(2)(a)–(b)	10.27, 10.41
s 245(2)(a)–(b)	9.85	s 254(3)(a)–(b)	10.28
s 245(2)(c)–(d)	9.85	s 254(4)	10.29
s 245(3)	9.85	s 254(5)	10.29
s 246(1)–(3)	9.86	s 255(2)	10.30
s 246(5)	9.87	s 255(2)–(4)	10.42
s 246(6)	9.88	s 255(3)(a)–(e)	10.30
s 248	10.59	s 255(4)	10.36
s 249	1.92, 10.128	s 255(5)	10.32
s 249(1)	10.129	s 255(5)–(8)	10.47

s 255(6)(a)–(b)	10.37	s 261(6)	2.32
s 255(7)	1.69, 10.38, 10.42	s 261(6)(a)–(b)	1.80
s 255(8)	10.32	s 261(8)	1.81
s 255(8)–(12)	10.43	s 261(9)(a)–(b)	1.81
s 255(9)	10.33	s 261(10)(a)–(b)	1.76
s 255(10)	10.33	s 261(11)	1.76
s 255(10)(b)	10.34	s 261(12)	1.76
s 255(11)	10.33	s 261(13)	1.76
s 255(12)	10.35	s 261(14)(a)–(b)	1.82
s 256	10.43, 10.47	s 261(14)(c)	1.82
s 256(2)	10.39	s 262	1.83, 1.84, 1.87, 2.15
s 256(3)(a)–(b)	10.40	s 262(1)	1.83
s 256(4)(a)–(b)	10.40	s 262(2)	1.84
s 256(4)(c)	10.40	s 262(3)(a)–(b)	1.86
s 256(5)(a)–(b)	10.40	s 262(4)	2.38
s 256(5)(c)	10.40	s 262(4)(a)–(d)	1.85
s 256(6)	10.40	s 262(5)	1.83
s 256(7)	10.44	s 262(6)	1.83
s 256(8)(a)–(b)	10.41	s 262(7)	1.83
s 256(9)–(10)	10.42	s 262(8)	1.87
s 256(11)	10.44	s 263	1.76, 3.22, 7.05, 7.11
s 256(12)	10.43	s 263(1)	1.76, 1.77, 3.64, 6.60
s 257(1)	1.67, 10.40	s 263(2)(a)–(c)	1.88
s 257(1)–(2)	10.45	s 263(3)(a)–(c)	1.89
s 257(3)	10.48	s 263(4)	2.33
s 257(5)(a)–(b)	10.46	s 263(4)(a)–(e)	1.90
s 257(6)–(7)	10.46	s 263(5)	1.90
s 257(8)(a)–(b)	10.46	s 264	3.64, 6.60
s 257(9)	10.40, 10.47	s 265	2.21
s 257(10)	10.40, 10.47	s 266(1)	10.125
s 258(2)(a)–(b)	10.49	s 266(2)(a)–(b)	10.126
s 258(4)	10.51	s 266(3)(a)–(b)	10.127
s 259	10.55	s 267(1)	1.73
s 259(3)	10.56	s 267(1)(c)	9.44
s 259(6)	10.58	s 267(2)	1.66
ss 260–269	1.91	s 267(3)(a)–(k)	1.67
s 260(1)	1.61	s 267(4)(a)–(c)	1.68
s 260(2)	1.61	s 267(5)(a)–(g)	1.69
s 260(3)	1.62	s 267(7)	1.71
s 260(4)	1.62	s 267(8)	1.72
s 261	1.74, 2.15	s 267(9)	1.72
s 261(1)	1.74, 10.74	s 268	4.60
s 261(2)(a)–(b)	1.75	s 268(2)(a)–(c)	4.60
s 261(3)(a)(i)–(iii)	1.77	s 268(3)	4.61
s 261(3)(b)–(c)	1.77	s 268(4)	4.61
s 261(4)	1.78	s 268(5)–(6)	461
s 261(5)	5.10	s 268(8)–(10)	4.62
s 261(5)(a)–(c)	1.79	s 268(11)	4.60

Table of Legislation

s 270(2) 1.91	Sch 5, para 3(2)(a)–(b) 4.105
s 271(1) 1.92	Sch 5, para 3(3) 4.106
s 271(2) 1.67, 1.68	Sch 5, para 3(3)(a)–(e) 4.106
s 271(2)–(4) 1.91	Sch 5, para 3(3)(f) 4.107
s 272(2) 1.91, 1.92	Sch 5, para 3(5) 4.104
s 272(3) 1.93	Sch 5, para 3(6) 4.104
s 258(3)(a)–(b) 10.50	Sch 5, para 3(7) 4.107
Sch 1 . . . . .2.46–2.53	Sch 5, para 4 . . . . .1.70
Sch 1, Pt 1 . . . . 2.46, 2.47, 2.53, 2.59	Sch 5, para 4(2)–(3) 4.109
Sch 1, Pt 2 . . . . .2.46, 2.52, 2.53	Sch 5, para 5(a)–(b) 4.102
Sch 1, Pt 3 . . . . .2.59	Sch 5, para 8 .4.107
Sch 1, para 2(a)–(h) 2.47	Sch 5, para 69(a) 4.104
Sch 1, para 3(a) .2.48	Sch 6 . . . . .6.32, 6.35
Sch 1, paras 4–6 . . . . .2.48	Sch 6, Pt 1, Table 1 . . . . .6.32, 6.39
Sch 1, para 4 . . . . .2.48	Sch 6, Pt 2, Table 2 . . . . .6.33
Sch 1, para 4(g) .2.48	Sch 6, Pt 3 . . . . .6.34
Sch 1, para 5 . . . . .2.48, 2.50	Sch 6, Pt 3, para 2 . . . . .6.40
Sch 1, para 7 . . . . .2.48	Sch 7 . . . . .2.09, 9.08, 9.20, 9.26
Sch 1, para 8(1) .2.49	Sch 7, para 1(2) 9.19
Sch 1, para 8(4)(a) 2.49	Sch 7, para 1(2)(b) 9.26
Sch 1, para 8(4)(b) 2.49	Sch 7, para 2 .10.10
Sch 1, para 8(5) .2.49	Sch 7, para 2(3) 9.26
Sch 1, para 8(6) .2.49	Sch 7, para 4 . . . . .2.09
Sch 1, para 8(10) 2.49	Sch 7, para 4(2) 9.26
Sch 1, para 11(1) 2.51	Sch 7, para 4(4) 1.71
Sch 1, para 11(2) 2.51	Sch 7, para 5(3) 9.26
Sch 1, para 11(5) 2.51	Sch 7, para 5(5) 1.71
Sch 1, para 13(1) 2.53	Sch 8 . . . . .3.20, 10.59, 10.93–10.124,
Sch 2 . . . . .2.62	10.123, 10.124
Sch 3 . . . . .3.152, 7.63, 8.95	Sch 8, Pt 1 . . . . 10.93, 10.119
Sch 3, para 7 . . . . .3.152	Sch 8, Pt 2 . . . . 10.93, 10.120
Sch 3, para 14 .3.152	Sch 8, Pt 3 . . . . 10.93, 10.119
Sch 3, para 21 .3.152	Sch 8, Pt 4 . . . . .10.93
Sch 3, para 22 .3.152	Sch 8, para 1(b) 10.95
Sch 4 . . . . 4.07, 4.08, 4.10, 4.15,	Sch 8, para 1(e)–(f) 10.95
4.53, 4.58, 4.64, 4.65	Sch 8, para 2(a)–(c) 10.95
Sch 4, column 1 . . . . 4.08, 4.54, 4.58, 4.59	Sch 8, para 3(a) 10.95
Sch 4, column 2 . . . . 4.08, 4.09, 4.10,	Sch 8, para 3(c)–(d) 10.95
4.11, 4.55, 4.57, 4.58, 4.59	Sch 8, para 1(a) 10.96
Sch 4, column 3 . . . . .4.08, 4.10, 4.56	Sch 8, para 1(c)–(d) 10.96
Sch 4, column 4 . . . . .4.08, 4.13, 4.56	Sch 8, para 3(1)(b) 10.97
Sch 5 . . . . .4.103	Sch 8, para 4(a)–(d) 10.98
Sch 5, para 2(1) 4.103	Sch 8, para 5(a)–(d) 10.99
Sch 5, para 2(1)(b) 1.68	Sch 8, para 6(a)–(d) 10.99
Sch 5, para 2(2) 4.103	Sch 8, para 7(a)–(b) 10.100
Sch 5, para 2(3) 4.103	Sch 8, para 8(d)–(e) 10.102
Sch 5, para 3 . . . . .4.52	Sch 8, para 8(a)–(c) 10.103
Sch 5, para 3(1) 4.104	Sch 8, para 9(a)–(b) 10.102

Table of Legislation

Sch 8, para 10(a)–(c) 10.104
Sch 8, para 11(1)(a)–(c) 10.105
Sch 8, para 12(1)(a)–(c) 10.105
Sch 8, para 13(a)–(b) 10.106
Sch 8, para 14(a)–(b) 10.107
Sch 8, para 16(1) 10.108
Sch 8, para 16(2) 10.108
Sch 8, paras 17–18 ....10.109
Sch 8, para 19 ....10.110
Sch 8, para 20(1)(a)–(i) 10.111
Sch 8, para 20(2)(a)–(d) 10.112
Sch 8, para 20(3) 10.112
Sch 8, para 21(1) 10.114
Sch 8, para 21(2)(a)–(d) 10.115
Sch 8, para 21(3) 10.115
Sch 8, para 22(2) 10.115
Sch 8, para 22(1) 10.114
Sch 8, para 22(3) 10.115
Sch 8, para 23(1) 10.114
Sch 8, para 23(2) 10.115
Sch 8, para 24 ....10.116
Sch 8, para 24(2) 10.117
Sch 8, para 27(1)–(3) 10.118
Sch 8, para 28(1)–(2) 10.119
Sch 8, para 28(3)(a)–(c) 10.120
Sch 8, para 29(a)–(c) 10.120
Sch 8, para 30(1)–(3) 10.121
Sch 8, para 31(a)–(b) 10.122
Sch 8, para 32(1)–(2) 10.123
Sch 8, para 33 ....1.67
Sch 8, para 33(1)–(2) 10.124
Sch 9 ....1.13
Sch 9, para 3 ....1.92
Sch 9, paras 35 ....1.92
Sch 9, para 8 ....1.92
Sch 9, para 9 ....1.92
Sch 9, para 10. ....1.18, 1.19
Sch 10 ....1.13
Sch 10, Pt 1 ....10.72
Sch 10, Pt 8 ....1.92
Sch 10, paras 3–6 ....10.72
Justice and Security Act 2013
   s 2 ....9.55
Local Government etc (Scotland) Act 1994
   s 2 ....4.07
Mental Health (Care and Treatment)
   (Scotland) Act 2003
   s 281 ....3.139

s 284 ....3.139
National Health Service Act 2006
   s 4 ....3.137
   s 4(3A)(a) 3.137
National Health Service (Scotland) Act
   1978 ....3.138
   s 2(5) 3.138
National Health Service (Wales) Act 2006
   s 19 ....3.137
   s 23 ....3.137
Office of Communications Act 2002
   s 1 ....3.131
Official Secrets Act 1989 ....2.36
Patriot Act 2001
   s 215 ....1.22
Police Act 1996
   s 22A 4.90, 6.34
Police Act 1997 .... 1.07, 9.01, 9.09,
                              9.19, 10.64
   Pt III 1.04, 4.97, 9.27, 9.43, 9.53,
              9.75, 10.59, 10.64–10.70, 10.97,
                   10.99, 10.100, 10.105
   s 92 ....10.65
   s 93 .... 2.73, 10.70, 10.116, 10.117
   s 93(1)(a) 10.67
   s 93(1)(ab) 10.67
   s 93(1)(b) 10.67
   s 93(1A) 10.67
   s 93(2) 10.67
   s 93(2A) 10.68
   s 93(4) 10.69
   s 93(5) 10.66
   s 96 ....9.43, 10.116
   s 97 ....9.43, 10.116
   s 103 ....9.43
   s 103(1)–(2) 10.116
   s 103(4) 10.116
   s 103(6) 10.117
   s 104 ....9.43, 10.116
   s 105 ....9.43
Police and Criminal Evidence Act 1984 ...6.63
   s 9 ....4.83
   s 10 ....6.117
   s 11 ....2.09
Police Reform Act 2002
   s 9 ....9.02
Postal Services Act 2000
   s 105 ....3.130

Table of Legislation

s 125(3)	2.35
Prison Act 1952	3.135
s 47	3.134
Prison Act (Northern Ireland) 1953	3.135
s 13	3.134
Prisons (Interference with Wireless Telegraphy) Act 2012	
ss 1–4	9.27
Prisons (Scotland) Act 1989	3.135
s 14	3.136
s 39	3.134
Protection of Freedoms Act 2012	1.38, 4.05, 4.73, 9.05
Public Records Act 1958	3.145, 7.43, 7.110
Public Records Act (Northern Ireland) 1923	3.145, 7.43, 7.110
Regulation of Investigatory Powers Act 2000 (RIPA)	1.01, 1.02, 1.07, 1.08–1.17, 1.21, 1.24, 1.38, 1.45, 2.01, 2.11, 2.22, 2.26, 2.54, 2.63, 2.66, 2.67, 3.01, 3.06, 3.08, 3.23, 3.45, 3.75, 3.143, 3.152, 3.155, 4.04, 4.73, 4.97, 8.04, 9.01, 9.05, 9.09, 9.10, 9.13, 9.19, 9.21, 9.27, 9.28, 9.39, 9.56, 9.67, 9.79, 9.84, 10.09, 10.22, 10.59, 10.71–10.92, 10.99, 10.105
Pt I	1.01, 1.10, 1.11, 1.21, 1.57, 2.23, 3.126
Pt I, Chap I	1.10, 1.11, 1.25, 2.01, 3.01, 3.155, 3.156, 3.160, 3.161
Pt I, Chap II	1.10, 1.11, 2.01, 4.03, 4.04, 4.05, 4.83, 9.58, 9.74
Pt II	1.04, 1.12, 3.122, 9.05, 9.43, 9.65, 9.75, 10.67, 10.71, 10.72
Pt III	1.12, 9.28, 9.43, 10.71
Pt IV	1.12, 9.08, 10.71
s 1	2.14
s 1(1)	2.11, 3.155
s 1(2)	3.155
s 1(3)	2.04
s 1(4)	3.155
s 1(5)	3.155
s 1(6)	2.13
s 2	2.15
s 2(2)	2.22
s 2(2)(a)–(c)	2.22
s 2(7)	2.23, 2.30
s 2(8)	2.31
s 3(2)(a)	2.26
s 3(2)(b)	2.26
s 3(5)	2.23
s 5	1.27, 3.06
s 5(3)	1.31
s 5(3)(a)	1.29
s 5(3)(b)	1.29
s 5(3)(c)	1.29
s 5(6)	1.29
s 8	1.26, 1.27–1.37, 3.06
s 8(1)	1.28, 1.36, 3.06
s 8(1)(a)–(b)	1.28
s 8(2)	1.28, 1.31
s 8(3)	1.28
s 8(3)(a)–(b)	1.28
s 8(4)	1.25, 1.31, 1.32, 1.34, 1.36, 3.06, 3.09
s 8(4)(a)	1.29
s 8(4)(b)(i)	1.29
s 8(4)(b)(ii)	1.29
s 8(6)	1.29
s 11	9.72
s 11(9)	3.159
s 12	9.73, 10.13, 10.14
s 12(1)	10.18
s 14	10.128
s 15	1.34
s 16	1.34
s 16(3)	1.32, 1.36
s 16(3)–(4)	3.09
s 16(5)	1.32, 1.36
s 18	3.152
s 19	3.156
s 20	1.35
s 22	4.83, 9.75
s 23A	9.66
ss 25–38	10.116
s 26	10.80
s 26(2)(a)–(c)	10.80
s 26(2)(b)	10.79
s 26(3)(a)–(b)	10.81
s 26(8)(a)–(c)	10.82
s 26(9)	10.77
s 26(9)(a)	10.78
s 26(10)	10.79
s 28(2)(b)	10.89
s 28(3)(a)–(g)	10.88

s 28(5)	10.88	s 67A(7)(a)–(b)	9.80
s 29(2)(b)	10.89	s 67A(8) (a)–(b)	9.77
s 29(2)(c)(i)–(iii)	10.89	s 67A(8)(c)	9.77
s 29(3)(a)–(g)	10.88	s 68	9.76
s 29(6)	10.88	s 68(4)	9.82, 9.83
s 32	10.116	s 68(4A)	9.82
s 32(3)(a)–(c)	10.90	s 68(4B)	9.82
ss 32A–32B	10.89	s 68(4C)	9.83
ss 33–40	10.89	s 68(4D)	9.83
ss 35–39	9.43	s 68(4E)	9.83
s 36	10.91	s 68(4E)(a)–(b)	9.83
ss 41–42	10.89	s 68(5)(b)	9.70
s 41	10.91	s 68(6)(b)	9.71
s 42	10.91	s 68(7)	9.72
s 48(2)(a)	10.74	s 68(7)(f)	9.73
s 48(2)(b)–(c)	10.74	s 68(7)(k)	9.75
s 48(3)(a)–(b)	10.76	s 71	1.10
s 48(3)(c)(i)–(ii)	10.76	s 80	1.14, 1.15, 1.16, 1.18, 1.19
s 48(4)(a)–(b)	10.75	s 84(b)	1.29
s 49	9.28, 9.45	s 86(4)	9.78
s 51	9.43	s 86(4C)	9.78
s 54	9.43	s 110	10.120
s 55	9.43	Regulation of Investigatory Powers Act (Scotland) 2000 (RIP(S)A)	3.122, 9.09, 9.19, 9.27, 10.09, 10.59, 10.71, 10.99, 10.105
s 55	9.27		
s 59A	8.04		
s 64(1)	9.21		
s 65	9.56, 9.68	s 10	10.116
s 65(2)(c)	9.56	ss 13–16	10.116
s 65(5)(b)	9.57	ss 13–17	9.43
s 65(5)	9.63, 9.68	Scotland Act 1998	9.17
s 65(5)(c)	9.58, 9.59, 9.60	Security Service Act 1989	1.07, 1.46, 8.08
s 65(5)(czd)	9.65	s 1(2)–(4)	10.62
s 65(5)(d)	9.65	s 2(2)(a)	8.03
s 65(5)(f)	9.65	Serious Crime Act 2015	
s 65(6)	9.65	s 80	9.27
s 65(6A)	9.65	Telecommunications Act 1984	10.03
s 65(7)	9.66, 9.67	s 94	4.03, 8.03, 10.03
s 65(7ZB)	9.66	Terrorism Act 2000	
s 65(8)	9.67	Sch 7, para 9	3.130
s 65(9A)	9.68	Wireless Telegraphy Act 2006	3.131, 10.55–10.58
s 67(8)–(12)	9.81		
s 67A	9.77, 9.79, 9.80	Pt 2	3.131
s 67A(1)	9.78	ss 27–31	3.131
s 67A(2)	9.79	s 48	10.55
s 67A(3)(a) – (b)	9.79	s 48(1)	10.56
s 67A(4)	9.79	s 48(3A)	10.57
s 67A(5)	9.79	s 49	10.58
s 67A(6)(a)–(b)	9.80	s 115(3)	3.133

Table of Legislation

s 116 . . . . 2.34, 3.133
s 117 . . . . 2.34

Statutory Instruments

Data Retention (EC Directive)
   Regulations 2009 (SI 2009/859) . . . 1.39
Draft Investigatory Powers (Technical
   Capability) Regulations 2017,
   unpublished. 10.20
   Sch 1, para 8 . . . . 10.23
   Sch 1, para 10 . . . . 10.21
Investigatory Powers Act 2016
   (Commencement No 1 and
   Transitional Provisions) Regulations
   2016 (SI 2016/1233) 1.92
Police and Criminal Evidence (Northern
   Ireland) Order 1989 (SI 1989/1341)
   Art 13 . . . . 2.09
Regulation of Investigatory Powers
   (Covert Human Intelligence
   Sources: Relevant Sources) Order
   2013 (SI 2013/2788) 9.43, 10.84,
                                         10.85, 10.92
   art 2 . . . . 10.84
   art 3(2)(a)–(b) 10.85
   art 3(5) 10.87
Regulation of Investigatory Powers
   (Directed Surveillance and Covert
   Human Intelligence Sources)
   (Amendment) Order 2012 (SI
   2012/1500) 10.89
Regulation of Investigatory Powers
   (Directed Surveillance and Covert
   Human Intelligence Sources) Order
   2010 (SI 2010/521) 10.89
Regulation of Investigatory Powers
   (Maintenance of Interception
   Capability) Order 2002 (SI 2002/
   1931) 10.14, 10.20
Regulation of Investigatory Powers
   (Monetary Penalty Notices
   and Consents for
   Interceptions) Regulations 2011
   (SI 2011/1340) 2.43
State Hospitals Board for Scotland Order
   1995 (SI 1995/574)
   Art 5(1) 3.138
Transfer of Undertaking (Protection of
   Employment) Regulations (TUPE)
   2006 (SI 2006/246) 4.107

International Instruments

European Convention on Human Rights
   . . . . 2.03, 9.34
   Art 8 . . . . 1.05, 1.15, 1.35, 1.98, 4.03, 8.03
   Art 8(2) 1.31

European Directives

2002/58/EC Directive on Privacy and
   Electronic Communications 2.11
   Art 5(1) 2.11
   Art 15(1) 2.11

List of Abbreviations

BPD	Bulk Personal Dataset
CNE	computer network exploitation
DRIPA	Data Retention and Investigatory Powers Act 2014
DSO	Designated Senior Officer
ECtHR	European Court of Human Rights
ICR	internet connection record
IOCA	Interception of Communications Act 1985
IOCCO	Interception of Communications Commissioner's Office
IPA	Investigatory Powers Act
IPT	Investigatory Powers Tribunal
ISA	Intelligence Services Act 1994
ISC	Intelligence and Security Committee of Parliament
ISR	Independent Surveillance Review
NSA	National Security Agency
RIPA	Regulation of Investigatory Powers Act 2000
RUSI	Royal United Services Institute
SPOC	single point of contact
UK	United Kingdom

1
AN INTRODUCTION TO THE INVESTIGATORY POWERS ACT 2016

A.	Introduction	1.01
B.	Evolution of the Investigatory Powers Act 2016	1.05
	1. Overview of Legislation Governing the Interception of Communications	1.05
	2. Events Leading to Reform	1.20
	3. Section 8 RIPA	1.27
	4. Other Developments	1.38
	5. The Reviews	1.40
C.	Provisions of General Application	1.59
	1. Overview	1.59
	2. Review of Operation of Act	1.61
	3. The Making of Regulations	1.63
	4. Telecommunications Definitions	1.74
	5. Postal Definitions	1.83
	6. Data	1.88
D.	Commencement	1.91
E.	Preliminary Assessment of the Investigatory Powers Act 2016	1.94

A. INTRODUCTION

The Investigatory Powers Act 2016 (IPA) has changed the covert policing landscape beyond recognition. There were twelve sections in the Interception of Communications Act 1985 (IOCA) and the statute ran to fifteen pages. Part 1 of the Regulation of Investigatory Powers Act 2000 (RIPA), which repealed it, consisted of twenty-five sections. In the same time period, the IPA has multiplied in excess of tenfold, coming in at an eye-watering 272 provisions, ten schedules, and 305 pages. It has been described variously as a 'snooper's charter' 1.01

1. An Introduction to the Investigatory Powers Act 2016

permitting the 'tracking of everybody's web browsing history and hacking computers, phones, and tablets on an industrial scale'[1] and introducing 'world-leading transparency'.[2]

1.02 However, unpalatable to some, the impetus for the introduction of the IPA followed the revelations of former National Security Agency (NSA) contractor, Edward Snowden. That is not to say that reform of RIPA was not badly needed but the tipping point was the proliferation of litigation against the state that followed in the wake of allegations of mass collection of communications and the tenuous legal basis that existed for such activity to take place.

1.03 This work attempts to explain the IPA. Repeatedly, concerns were expressed at the haste with which the legislation was being passed and the lack of obvious structure to some of the provisions is evidence that these concerns were, at least in part, justified. The term 'future-proofing' was also coined with a frequency such that it became part of the lexicon of those with an interest—from whatever side of the divide—in this enormous statute. This undercurrent of attempting to ensure the IPA withstood the pace of technological developments is at odds with outstanding legal challenges about some of its provisions that, it is accepted by respected commentators, have implications for its future legality. If ever there was a Bill where it was sensible to pause or, at the very least, slow down the process of getting it on the statute book, the IPA was it.

1.04 Whatever the merit of these observations, the IPA is now the law. There remain serious questions that have been asked and will in due course be answered by the domestic and international courts but the one unarguable fact is that the United Kingdom (UK) now has the most comprehensive legislative framework for the conduct of technological surveillance in the world. That brings with it increased transparency and it may yet result in greater accountability. But since it is unassailable that it has arrived, those working in the industries affected by it, and investigators utilizing it, their advisers, lawyers, and judges must begin to grapple with the task of understanding it. With this in mind, the structure of this work (ie after this introductory chapter, which attempts to provide important historical context to the genesis of the legislation and introduce key and recurring definitions) follows each Part of the IPA in chronological order. The last chapter, Chapter 10, in addition to providing commentary on important and significant additional powers, looks at the scheme for the combination of warrants and provides an overview of some of the covert policing law to be found elsewhere in the Intelligence Services Act 1994 (ISA), Part III of the Police Act 1997, and the skeletal but surviving remains of Part II of the RIPA.

---

[1] 'Liberty launches legal challenge to "state spying" in snooper's charter' *Guardian* (10 January 2017) https://www.theguardian.com/world/2017/jan/10/liberty-launches-legal-challenge-to-state-spying-in-snoopers-charter.

[2] https://terrorismlegislationreviewer.independent.gov.uk/the-investigatory-powers-act-2016-an-exercise-in-democracy/.

B. EVOLUTION OF THE INVESTIGATORY POWERS ACT 2016

1. Overview of Legislation Governing the Interception of Communications

The use of covert investigatory powers has had a troubled history in the UK. Governments have, since the earliest times, had the power to intercept letters and this had some piecemeal and fragmentary statutory basis. Indeed, the interception of mail formed part of Shakespeare's plot in Henry VIII, where Norfolk says to Surrey: 'The cardinal's letters to the pope miscarried, And came to the eye o' the king: wherein was read, …'. It was not, however, until 1985 that there was any contemporary and specific legislation governing state surveillance[3] and, even then, the case that prompted it, *Malone v United Kingdom*,[4] which concerned the interception of communications, had its origins in a domestic decision some six years earlier[5] in 1979, when Megarry VC observed that it was an area 'crying out for legislation'. A government white paper followed[6] but concluded that no purpose would be served by embodying the then regime for the interception of communications in legislation.[7] However, the European Court of Human Rights (ECtHR) took a different view. It held that the existing law was 'somewhat obscure and open to different interpretations' and was 'lacking'. The existing legislative scheme did not have the necessary legal certainty, was not in accordance with the law, and, as a consequence, was a violation of Article 8 of the European Convention on Human Rights, the right to respect for family and private life.[8]

1.05

(a) *Interception of Communications Act 1985*
The government's response to the adverse decision in *Malone* was to introduce IOCA. This was later described by the House of Lords in *R v Preston*[9] as a 'short and difficult statute',[10] and which reflected the non-statutory practice prior to its enactment. IOCA provided for the lawful interception of communications in the course of their transmission by post or a private telecommunications system.[11] It created some oversight in the form of the Interception of Communications Commissioner[12] and a prohibition on the use of intercept product in legal proceedings.[13] Its legislative

1.06

---

[3] Interception of Communications Act 1985.
[4] (1985) 7 EHRR 245.
[5] *Malone v Commissioner of Police of the Metropolis* [1979] Ch 344.
[6] The Interception of Communications in Great Britain (1980) Cmnd 7873.
[7] *Hansard* (1 April 1981) HC cols 334–8 (Home Secretary).
[8] *Malone v United Kingdom* (1985) 7 EHRR 245, para 80.
[9] [1993] 4 All ER.
[10] *R v Preston* [1993] 4 All ER (Lord Mustill) 651.
[11] IOCA, s 2.
[12] ibid s 8.
[13] ibid s 9.

DNA can still be found in the IPA: those core provisions representing the canvas upon which the new statute has been painted.

1.07 What followed in the wake of IOCA was a raft of legislation dealing with other state surveillance-related issues, all of which was in response to either an adverse decision or expected adverse decision before the ECtHR: The Security Service Act 1989 in response to *Harman and Hewitt v United Kingdom*;[14] the ISA, following *Esbester v United Kingdom*;[15] and the Police Act 1997, which has its genesis in the decision in *Govell v United Kingdom*.[16] This led to respected commentators describing the law in this area as 'reactive'.[17] The one exception was RIPA, introduced in anticipation of the commencement of the Human Rights Act 1998 on 2 October 2000 (the two Acts came into force simultaneously). Interestingly, the key provisions of each of these statutes also remain; indeed, the IPA amends both the ISA and Police Act 1997: see Chapter 10, paragraphs 10.52–10.54 and 10.64–10.70.

(b) *Regulation of Investigatory Powers Act 2000*

1.08 RIPA built upon IOCA's foundations and created a more comprehensive regulatory scheme covering the interception of communications (it repealed IOCA in its entirety); acquisition and retention of communications data; surveillance activities, including the use of informers and undercover officers; accessing information protected by encryption and increased oversight, through the creation of the Investigatory Powers Tribunal. From its inception it has been roundly criticized for its complexity, even Lord Steyn in *Attorney General's Reference (No 5 of 2000)*[18] describing it as 'not easy to understand'.[19] It is unlikely that the IPA will be any easier on those judicial minds that will have to attempt to interpret its provisions in future legal proceedings.

1.09 RIPA was a landmark piece of legislation. For the first time in UK law, surveillance activities, other than the interception of communications and property interference, were comprehensively regulated. There was provision for the interception of communications on a private telecommunications system, the acquisition and retention of communications data and provisions in respect of encryption. It struck what Ferguson and Wadham described as 'fragile balance between the competing demands of privacy and surveillance' but failed to do so in 'a logical or structured way'.[20] Both observations were fair and well founded as history has made clear.

1.10 RIPA was in five parts. Part I contained two chapters. Chapter I was concerned with the interception of communications and Chapter II the acquisition and

---

[14] (1989) 67 DR 88.
[15] (1994) 18 EHRR CD 72.
[16] [1999] EHRLR 101 ECtHR.
[17] Y Akadeniz, N Taylor, and C Walker, 'Regulation of Investigatory Powers Act 2000 (1); BigBrother.gov.uk: State surveillance in the age of information and rights' [2001] Crim LR 73 and P Mirfield, 'Regulation of Investigatory Powers Act 2000 (2) Evidential Aspects' [2001] Crim LR 91; B Emmerson QC and A Ashworth QC, *Human Rights and Criminal Justice* (1st edn, Sweet & Maxwell 2001).
[18] [2004] UKHL 40.
[19] *Attorney General's Reference (No 5 of 2000)* [2004] UKHL 40, para 29.
[20] G Ferguson and J Wadham, 'Privacy and Surveillance: A Review of the Regulation of Investigatory Powers Act 2000' [2003] European Human Rights Law Review, Special Issue, 101.

B. Evolution of the Investigatory Powers Act 2016

disclosure of communications data. There were accompanying Codes of Practice issued under the provisions of section 71 of RIPA. The Code of Practice in relation to the Interception of Communications and Communications Data seemed to be in a perpetual state of revision.

1.11 The IPA repeals Part 1, Chapters 1 and 2 RIPA in their entirety. New draft Codes of Practice now exists.

1.12 Part II RIPA relates to the regulation of surveillance activities and the use and conduct of covert human intelligence sources. It creates a two-tier authorization process to reflect the nature of the intrusiveness that is likely to be engaged in, although the legitimacy of this has been questioned.[21] Part III is concerned with the investigation of data protected by encryption. These provisions remain in force. Part IV relates to oversight and, subject to the matters set out in Chapter 9 of this work, the provisions remain in force.

1.13 The full extent of the amendments to RIPA are set out in Schedules 9 and 10 IPA.

(c) *General Saving for Lawful Conduct*

1.14 Key provisions in RIPA, largely replicated in the IPA, were misunderstood. Perhaps surprisingly, this authorization and warrant scheme was and in relation to the provisions that remain is not mandatory: the surveillance and other covert activities investigators engaged in prior to RIPA coming into force were not and have not been made unlawful as a result of the legislation. This is expressly stated in section 80 RIPA, the 'general saving for lawful conduct', which provides that conduct that could or may be 'authorised by any warrant, authorisation or notice' under the statute should not be construed 'as making it unlawful to engage in any conduct' other than that which would constitute an unlawful act under it or as a result of some other provision. Nor did it require the issue, grant or giving of such a warrant, authorization or notice, or the taking of any step for or towards doing so 'before any such conduct of that description is engaged in [or] as prejudicing any power to obtain information by any means not involving conduct that may be authorised under [RIPA]'.

1.15 The effect of section 80 is not to obviate a public authority's requirement to act compatibly with a person's rights under section 6 of the Human Rights Act 1998 but a failure to do so does not make the conduct unlawful. Rather, it may not comply with the provisions of the RIPA. The Investigatory Powers Tribunal (IPT), the specialist tribunal set up to deal with complaints of non-compliance, considered the effect of section 80 in one of its earliest judgments: *C v Police and Secretary of State*, IPT/03/32/H. It held that surveillance by public authorities is not of itself unlawful at common law, nor does it necessarily engage Article 8 of the Convention. It was no more than a voluntary scheme of self-authorization.

1.16 The then Code of Practice on use and conduct of Covert Human Intelligence Sources reinforced this, at paragraph 2.10, 'public authorities are not required by the 2000 Act to seek or obtain an authorisation just because one is available' and referred expressly to section 80 RIPA.

---

[21] K Starmer, M Strange, and Q Whittaker and others, *Criminal Justice, Police Powers and Human Rights* (Blackstone Press 2001).

1. An Introduction to the Investigatory Powers Act 2016

1.17 It is also important to bear in mind that RIPA was not and is not a preferential legislative regime. That is to say that, where an alternative statutory basis exists for the conduct, a public authority may use this as the basis for its covert conduct: see *R (on the application of NTL Group Limited) v Crown Court at Ipswich*.[22]

1.18 The effect of section 80 RIPA, which is for all intents and purposes set out in like form in Schedule 9, paragraph 10 IPA is not to make authorization unnecessary but rather its effect is not to render unlawful conduct as a result of a failure to authorize, unless it would be an offence to do so. There remains the issue of compliance with the legislation in oversight terms and non-compliance may give rise to questions of abuse of process or admissibility where there is an allegation of entrapment, for example as in *R v Moore and Burrows*,[23] where the Court of Appeal held that 'authorisation and supervision of the operation' was one of the factors the court should consider when determining applications to stay proceedings or exclude evidence. Equally, for the corollary of this, see *R v Walters*.[24]

1.19 The effect of section 80 and now paragraph 10 of Schedule 9 remains controversial and amenable to further legal challenge.

2. Events Leading to Reform

1.20 There was a confluence of events that led to reform of this area of law. Domestically, revelations of widespread 'phone hacking' and the failure by the Metropolitan Police Service properly to consider the allegations forced a renewed investigation, which in fact resulted in a series of prosecutions, a related interlocutory appeal,[25] and convictions.[26] Multiple civil actions followed,[27] as well as a public inquiry chaired by Lord Justice Leveson and which became known pejoratively as the 'phone hacking inquiry'.[28]

1.21 The government also faced (and continues to face) challenges domestically before the IPT[29] and in Europe as a result of allegations that the Regulation of Investigatory Powers Act 2000 (RIPA) and other legislation, which regulates the interception of communications and other surveillance activities in the UK, lacks sufficient legal certainty and safeguards in relation to its use.[30] In a further unprecedented step, the government lifted the veil of secrecy around the practice of interception, in a statement prepared by the Director General of the Office for Security and Counter

---

[22] [2002] EWHC 1585 (Admin), [2002] 3 WLR 1173.
[23] [2013] EWCA Crim 85.
[24] Newcastle Crown Court (unreported, 6 April 2017) (Langstaff J).
[25] *R v Coulson and Kuttner* [2013] WLR (D) 262.
[26] ibid: sentencing remarks of Saunders J http://www.judiciary.gov.uk/wp-content/uploads/2014/07/sentencing-remarks-mr-j-saunders-r-v-coulson-others.pdf.
[27] See eg *Gray and Others v News Group Newspapers Limited and Others* [2011] EWHC 734 (Ch).
[28] 'An inquiry into the culture, practices and ethics of the press' (29 November 2012) HC 780–1.
[29] *Privacy International and Others v Secretary of State for Foreign and Commonwealth Affairs and Others*, IPT/13/92/CH.
[30] *Big Brother Watch and Others v United Kingdom*, Application No 58170/13 (communicated on 9 January 2014).

B. Evolution of the Investigatory Powers Act 2016

Terrorism, Charles Farr[31] (the Farr statement) in connection with proceedings before the IPT. Emergency legislation was introduced under the guise of a European Court of Justice decision affecting the Data Retention Directive[32] but which also amended aspects of the provisions in RIPA relating to interceptions.[33] It included provision for a review of aspects of Part 1 of RIPA by the Independent Reviewer of Terrorism Legislation, then Professor David Anderson QC.[34]

In the aftermath of NSA whistle-blower Edward Snowden's leaks concerning allegations of mass surveillance, the heads of the British intelligence services gave evidence in public before the Intelligence Services Committee of Parliament (ISC) for the first time in their combined history, the Chairman, Sir Malcolm Rifkind describing it as a 'very significant step forward in the transparency of our intelligence agencies'.[35] That said, the technical nature of the subject, which coins terms such as 'metadata' as frequently as opaque operational references such as 'PRISM', 'TEMPORA', and 'UPSTREAM', without any attempt to explain what they mean or refer to.[36] Internationally, in January 2014, President Obama announced reform of section 215 of the Patriot Act 2001 in the United States (US), which enabled bulk harvesting of telecommunications data[37] and in April 2017 section 702 of the Foreign Intelligence Surveillance Act 2008 was re-interpreted so as to minimise the collection of certain communications that merely mention a foreign intelligence target.

1.22

(a) *Early Legal Challenges*

The question of legal certainty was not new. There was an attempt to challenge oversight provisions and the protection against abuse of surveillance powers in *Liberty and Others v United Kingdom*.[38] The case concerned the previous regime under IOCA and resulted in an adverse finding against the UK.[39] It was not clear that RIPA, which was by the time the judgment was published on the statute book, met the standard the Court identified as being required:

1.23

[t]he Court does not consider that the domestic law at the relevant time indicated with sufficient clarity, so as to provide adequate protection against abuse of power, the scope or manner of the very wide discretion conferred on the State to intercept and examine external communications ... in particular ... the procedure to be followed for selecting for examination, sharing, storing and destroying intercepted material.

---

[31] https://www.privacyinternational.org/sites/privacyinternational.org/files/downloads/press-releases/witness_st_of_charles_blandford_farr.pdf.
[32] *Digital Rights Ireland Ltd and Others v Minister for Communications, Marine and Natural Resources and Others*, Case No 293/12 (8 April 2014).
[33] Data Retention and Investigatory Powers Act 2014 (DRIPA).
[34] ibid s 7.
[35] http://isc.independent.gov.uk/news-archive/7november2013-1.
[36] A guide to the terms can be found at http://www.theguardian.com/world/the-nsa-files.
[37] http://www.washingtonpost.com/world/national-security/obama-confronts-challenges-of-reforming-collection-of-americans-phone-records/2014/01/18/7d6de72c-806e-11e3-95c6-0a7aa80874bc_story.html.
[38] Application No 58243/00 (1 July 2008).
[39] For an excellent analysis of the decision see B Goold, '*Liberty v United Kingdom*: a new chance for another missed opportunity' [2009] PL.

1. An Introduction to the Investigatory Powers Act 2016

1.24 This short extract almost previsioned the terms of some of the later decisions before the domestic IPT. Judgment is awaited in Strasbourg in respect of a number of RIPA-related challenges.

1.25 In *Coulson and Kuttner*,[40] the Court of Appeal Criminal Division summarily dismissed the defence submission that the provisions of Part 1, Chapter 1 RIPA, lacked legal certainty. The issue of legal certainty is at the heart of the *Big Brother Watch and Others* application,[41] which at the time of writing has been communicated to the government and Privacy International's complaint to the IPT. The applications, in so far as they relate to Part I, Chapter I of RIPA, are principally concerned with external communications as defined in section 8(4) and depending on how it is received may influence the development of the law in relation to the question of what amounts to an interception more generally.

1.26 However, it was revelations of, to use a neutral term, mass collection of data on what appeared to be epidemic scale that gave an unstoppable momentum to reform. At its centre was section 8 RIPA.

3. Section 8 RIPA

1.27 The ISC accepted in 'Privacy and Security: a modern and transparent legal framework' that it was the 'current legal framework of external and internal communications has led to much confusion'. The provisions relating to external and internal communications, erroneously but understandably referred to as s 8(1) and 8(4) warrants were found in section 8 RIPA. The issue of an interception warrant was under section 5 RIPA: the nature of what was intercepted was governed by section 8 RIPA.

(a) Internal Communications

1.28 A warrant in respect of internal communications had to, under section 8(1) RIPA name or describe either one single person as the interception subject or a single set of premises where the interception is to take place.[42] It needed to be accompanied by one or more schedules setting out the addresses, numbers, apparatus or other factors, or a combination of factors that were then used for identifying the communications that may be or were to be intercepted.[43] These provisions, relating to the formulation of one or more schedules, correlated to section 8(3) RIPA, which extrapolated the effect of any 'factor' that had to identify communications that were likely to be or to include, communications from, or intended for, the person named or described or communications originating on, or intended for transmission to the premises named or described.[44] The Code of Practice set out a number of other requirements of a warrant, including the operational background, the person or

---

[40] [2013] WLR (D) 262, paras 44 and 45.
[41] Application No 58170/13 (4 September 2013).
[42] RIPA, s 8(1)(a)–(b).
[43] ibid s 8(2).
[44] ibid s 8(3)(a)–(b).

B. Evolution of the Investigatory Powers Act 2016

premises to which the application relates, a description of the communications, and conduct.[45]

(b) *External Communications*

1.29 Under section 8(4)(a) RIPA, the requirement to name a single person or premises did not apply to a warrant if the conduct authorized consisted in the interception of 'external communications' or conduct authorized in relation to any interception by section 5(6) RIPA. Section 8(4)(b) RIPA also had the same effect if at the time of the issue of the warrant a ministerial certificate was also issued certifying the descriptions of the intercepted material the examination of which he considered necessary and considered this necessary for the purposes of section 5(3)(a), (b), or (c) RIPA.[46] The Secretary of State was the only official who could issue the certificate in such circumstances.[47] In every other respect, the nature of the warrant was the same.

(c) *Competing Interpretations of Section 8 RIPA*

1.30 The effect of these provisions remains the battleground for the application to the ECtHR following Edward Snowden's revelations of systematic mass surveillance and data collection regimes in the US operating with the complicity of the UK, in the communicated case *Big Brother Watch and Others v United Kingdom*.[48]

1.31 One of the key issues in the case will be the question of legal certainty and quality of the provisions governing the acquisition of mass foreign intercept and communications data (the programmes that were known as PRISM and UPSTREAM) and the indiscriminate nature of the acquisition, use, storage, and destruction of material (said to be known as TEMPORA). This is likely to remain problematic for the government, notwithstanding a decision of the Investigatory Powers Tribunal in *The British-Irish Rights Watch and Others v Security Service, GCHQ and the SIS*[49] dismissing an application that the 'filtering process' was unlawful and holding:

> The provisions, in this case the right to intercept and access material covered by a s 8(4) warrant, and the criteria by reference to which it is exercised, are in our judgment sufficiently accessible and foreseeable to be in accordance with the law. The parameters in which te discretion to conduct interception is carried on, by reference to s 5(3) and subject to the safeguards referred to, a plain from the face of the statute. In this difficult and perilous area of national security, taking into account both the necessary narrow approach to Article 8(2) and the fact that the burden is placed on the Respondent, we are satisfied that the balance is properly struck.[50]

1.32 The former Interception Commissioner, Sir Anthony May, considered section 8(4) extensively in his 2013 Annual Report in light of the reporting of the Snowden

---

[45] Code of Practice, para 4.2.
[46] RIPA, sub-s 8(4)(b)(i) and (ii).
[47] ibid s 8(6).
[48] Application No 58170/13.
[49] IPT/01/77 (23 January 2003).
[50] *The British-Irish Rights Watch and Others v Security Service, GCHQ and the SIS*, para 39.

revelations.[51] Having reviewed the position, Sir Anthony concluded that 'what [his review] all boils down to' is that:

[A] section 8(4) warrant permits the interception of generally described (but not indiscriminate) external communications; this may only be lawfully *examined* if it is within a description certified by the Secretary of State as necessary for a statutory purpose; the selection for examination may not be referable to the communications of an individual who is known to be for the time being in the British Islands unless he or she is the subject of an individual authorisation under s 16(3) or (5); [and] the section 8(4) structure does not permit random trawling of communications. This would be unlawful. It only permits a search of communications referable to individuals the examination of whose communications are certified as necessary for a statutory purpose.[52]

1.33 These conclusions do not address the primary issue that is now before Strasbourg. This is encapsulated by the third question to the parties: is the UK's interception, search, analysis, dissemination, storage, and destruction of data relating to external communications in accordance with law and necessary in a democratic society?[53] The government's position appears to be that it intercepts but does not trawl unless the communication is, after filtering, identified as one that it wishes to examine. The difficulty with this was the absence of any statutory distinction between these processes, something the IPA attempts to address. It is reminiscent of the position in relation to the acquisition, use, and retention of DNA profiles and fingerprints that the ECtHR considered in *S and Marper v United Kingdom*.[54]

1.34 The provisions in section 8(4) RIPA need to be read in conjunction with section 16 headed 'extra safeguards in the case of certified warrants'. This implies such safeguards as exist are in addition to those that are set out in section 15. If the factual allegations set out in the *Big Brother Watch* application provide the framework for the Court's determination of the issues, then 'extra safeguards' are not what have been applied in practice since the acquisition of the intelligence through the TEMPORA programme is, on the face of it, arbitrary and disproportionate.

1.35 External communications was defined in section 20 RIPA as 'a communication sent or received outside the British Islands'. During the evolution of the Bill the minister, Mr Clarke, confirmed that where the communication 'was communicated via an internet service provider outside of the British Islands' this would 'not come within the definition of an external communication'.[55] This is also reflected in the Code of Practice[56] and confirmed in the Farr statement.[57] It follows that if the intercepted material derived from mass interception includes anything falling within this category, it is not only unlawful but a finding that there has been a violation of Article 8 seems inherently likely.

---

[51] Annual Report of the Interception of Communications Commissioner's Office (2013) paras 6.5.27 to 6.5.57 (IOCCO Report 2013).
[52] IOCCO 2013 Report, at para 6.5.38.
[53] *Big Brother Watch and Others v United Kingdom*, questions to the parties, question (3), 10.
[54] Application Nos 30562/04 and 30566/04 (4 December 2008) ECtHR.
[55] Standing Committee F (23 March 2000) col 160.
[56] Code of Practice, para 5.1.
[57] Farr statement, para 127.

B. Evolution of the Investigatory Powers Act 2016

1.36 The Interception Commissioner in his 2013 Annual Report dealt with how section 8(4) RIPA was in fact operated by intercepting agencies. Sir Anthony May noted that: 'any significant volume of digital data is literally useless unless its volume is first by filtering'.[58] Thereafter, the material was examined through the application of search material. The Commissioner concluded that in his judgment there was no undue invasion of privacy. This was for the following reasons:

> [It] cannot operate lawfully other than for a statutory purpose; it cannot operate lawfully other than pursuant to a warrant and one or more certificates issued by the Secretary of State; the Secretaries of State who sign warrants and give certificates are well familiar with the process; well able to judge by means of the written applications whether to grant or refuse the necessary permissions; and well supported by experienced senior officials who are independent from the interception agencies making the applications; if the warrant is up for renewal, the Secretary of State is informed in writing of the intelligence use the interception warrant has produced in the preceding period. Certificates are regularly reviewed and subject to modification by the Secretary of State; examination of interception material has to be in accordance with the certificate such that indiscriminate trawling is unlawful; with the exception of individuals under section 16(3) (or for very short periods under section 16(5)), examination of intercepted materials may not be referable to an individual who is in the British Islands; examination of material under section 16(3) referable to the communications of an individual who is within the British Islands is limited by a process equivalent to that for a section 8(1) warrant; the examination of the intercepted material is effected by search criteria constructed to comply with the s 8(4) process; the process is subject to Retention, Storage and Destruction policies and procedures which I have examined in detail ...[59]

1.37 These concerns have arguably been made good in the aftermath of Edward Snowden's revelations that communications data and intercept and related communications data have been acquired by GCHQ under the TEMPORA programme.[60] To be clear, there appears to be no dispute that mass interception is taking place; the government's position is that only limited amounts are in fact monitored. This issue forms the basis for one of the questions communication to the parties in *Big Brother Watch and Others v United Kingdom*.[61]

4. Other Developments

1.38 There were other significant developments in this area that inexorably led to the need to repeal at least parts of RIPA, including but not limited to the ill-fated Data Communications Bill that withered on the vine following a public outcry and divided government, the Protection of Freedoms Act 2012 that made provision for judicial approval of authorizations granted by local authorities. Snowden-related litigation generated a plethora of material on the subject of communications data and, following *Digital Rights Ireland Limited v Minister for Communications*,[62] the

---

[58] IOCCO Report 2013, para 6.5.40.
[59] ibid para 6.5.43.
[60] The acquisition of electronic traffic passing between the UK and the US via fibre-optic cables.
[61] [2014] ECHR 93.
[62] Case C-293/12, 8 April 2014.

1. An Introduction to the Investigatory Powers Act 2016

Data Retention and Investigatory Powers Act 2014 (DRIPA) was rushed through Parliament. The blurring of the line between what amounts to data and what is content was also gathering momentum (and continues to do so). Each has added to the understanding of the acquisition and use of data communications but the statutory framework under RIPA had not significantly changed.

(a) *Data Retention and Investigatory Powers Act 2014*

1.39 The lack of detail in DRIPA was of immediate and legitimate concern. Although 'relevant communications data' is defined in the 2009 Data Retention Regulations, these are probably ultra vires since the Directive under which they have been formulated has been declared invalid. Where the Regulations issued under DRIPA specify that the communications data, of the kind mentioned in the 2009 Regulations, it is to be read as a reference to that definition.[63] The absence of any meaningful parliamentary scrutiny and the provisions' close resemblance to those in the Communications Bill is also of concern. There is an argument that DRIPA was the former Bill in all but name and that it lacks legitimacy.

5. The Reviews

(a) *Overview*

1.40 Following what it described as the 'leak by Edward Snowden of stolen intelligence material in June 2013', the ISC undertook a review of technical surveillance capabilities in its report 'Privacy and Security: A modern and transparent legal framework'.[64] It looked at targeted and bulk interceptions, communications data, Bulk Personal Datasets, authorization and accountability, the legislative framework, and transparency. In many ways, what was most interesting about the report was its open use of such terms such as 'targeted' and 'bulk' interceptions—now common parlance in this area—but up until then the exclusive preserve of the intelligence services and an inner sanctum of government officials with whom members of the intelligence services engaged.

1.41 The DRIPA contained provision in section 7 requiring the home secretary to 'appoint the independent reviewer of terrorism legislation to review the operation and regulation of investigatory powers'. The terms of reference included in section 7(2) a requirement to consider six specific areas: (i) the current and future threats to the UK; (ii) the capabilities needed to combat those threats; (iii) safeguards to protect privacy; (iv) the challenge of changing technologies; (v) issues relating to transparency and oversight; and (vi) the effectiveness of existing legislation (including its proportionality) and the case for new or amending legislation.

1.42 The Royal United Services Institute (RUSI) was commissioned by the then deputy prime minister to convene an expert panel to undertake a review of surveillance 'in response to [Edward Snowden's] very serious allegation [of mass surveillance]'.

---

[63] DRIPA 2014, s 2(3).
[64] HC 1075 (12 March 2015).

B. Evolution of the Investigatory Powers Act 2016

The Independent Surveillance Review (as it became known) had terms of reference to 'look at the legality of UK surveillance programmes and the effectiveness of the regimes that govern them, and to suggest reforms we felt might be necessary'.

Each review began with a common acceptance that the intelligence services have a crucial role protecting UK citizens from threats to their safety but that, in order to do so, public confidence in their activities was critical.

1.43

(b) *Privacy and Security*

The ISC's report reached three main conclusions. First, the intelligence services do not seek to circumvent the law. Indeed, the report found they 'do not have the legal authority, the resources, the technical capability, or the desire to intercept every communication of British citizens, or of the internet as a whole: GCHQ are not reading the emails of everyone in the UK'. Secondly, the legal framework had 'developed piecemeal, and is unnecessarily complicated'. The ISC expressed 'serious concerns about the resulting lack of transparency, which is not in the public interest'. It recommended a new, single framework governing the activities of the intelligence services. Thirdly, in respect of the intelligence service's intrusive powers, a large number of recommendations were made, in particular in relation to bulk powers. These said the ISC 'are essential to improve transparency, strengthen privacy protections and increase oversight'.[65]

1.44

Although calls for reform from what was generally considered a conservative Committee were generally welcomed, there were problems with the ISC's analysis. It had published an earlier statement concluding that the allegations by Snowden of mass interception were unfounded.[66] This was later proved demonstrably incorrect, although the ISC may have blurred the concepts of interception and examination. In addition, it called for the scrapping of RIPA and the creation of a new framework for the intelligence services to operate within, distinct from law enforcement, without it seemed appreciating that RIPA also covered the activities of other public authorities.

1.45

However, some of the recommendations made by the ISC were built upon and traces of them can be seen in the IPA. The ISC recognized the weaknesses in the bulk acquisition and examination scheme, called for reform of the provisions in relation to the modification of warrants, suggested the introduction of new criminal offences for misuse of intelligence by the intelligence services, and highlighted the qualitatively differences in types of data, coining the phrase that was *not* later adopted: 'communications data plus'. In addition, it conceded that the use of the Security Service Act 1989 and ISA as a basis for the acquisition of Bulk Personal Datasets was tenuous and it called for increased retrospective review by commissioners (though expressly did not recommend judicial approval) and the right of appeal against a decision of the IPT.[67]

1.46

---

[65] ISC, Privacy and Security, 2.
[66] ISC, Statement on GCHQ's alleged interception of communications under the US PRISM programme (July 2013).
[67] ISC, Privacy and Security, 110–20.

(c) A Question of Trust

1.47 David Anderson QC was until recently the independent reviewer of terrorism and his critically acclaimed report 'A Question of Trust'[68] was published in June 2015. Although 'investigatory powers' was not defined, his terms of reference narrowed the scope of his review to 'communications data and interception' and the 'statutory oversight arrangements'.[69] His objectives were two-fold: 'to inform public and parliamentary debate' and to advance 'proposals for change'.[70]

1.48 The report examined comprehensively the concept of privacy. This was not confined to the law's approach to its meaning, scope, and application. Anderson sought to: '[l]ook under the surface of what we call privacy, in order better to understand the reasons why investigatory powers need to be limited and to inform the debate on the form that such limitations should take'.[71]

1.49 Privacy was at the heart of the Anderson review; if society accepts the use of intrusive techniques by the state, the only way it can avoid 'sleepwalking into a world which—although possibly safer—would be indefinably but appreciably poorer' was, wrote Anderson, through the existence of robust safeguards on their use.[72] As Anderson opined (and in doing so conceived the title of his report), '[the] question of trust is thus at the core of the issues to be considered in this Review'.[73]

1.50 Recent changes in privacy norms were not without relevance: they may not for example have a bearing on whether there is a reasonable expectation of privacy in a particular type of data at a particular time, said Anderson. They do not, however, amount to any sort of argument for dispensing with the constraints on the government's collection or use of data. Indeed, he reported, as more of our lives are lived online, and as more and more personal information can be deduced from our electronic footprint, the arguments for strict legal controls on the power of the state become if, anything, more compelling.[74]

1.51 In terms of threats, which under section 7 of DRIPA 2014 Anderson was specifically required to consider, his conclusion was that the UK faced 'a diverse range from a wide array of perpetrators'[75] but calibrating these was not 'an exact science', in part because of the inherent subjectivity of the fear a perceived threat provokes. When seeking to introduce intrusive powers, perspective was essential; 'claims of exceptional or unprecedented threat levels—particularly if relied upon for the purposes of curbing well-established liberties—should be approached with scepticism'.[76]

---

[68] David Anderson QC, 'A Question of Trust' https://terrorismlegislationreviewer.independent.gov.uk/wp-content/uploads/2015/06/IPR-Report-Print-Version.pdf.
[69] https://www.gov.uk/government/uploads/system/uploads/attachment_data/file/330749/Review_of_Communications_Data_and_Interception_Powers_Terms_of_Reference.pdf.
[70] See Anderson (n 68) para 1.12.
[71] ibid para 2.2.
[72] ibid paras 2.14–2.16.
[73] ibid para 2.17.
[74] ibid para 2.44.
[75] ibid para 3.1.
[76] ibid para 3.6.

B. Evolution of the Investigatory Powers Act 2016

Balanced against this, credible threats should be guarded against and, in doing so, privacy rights can be overridden where it is necessary and proportionate to do so.

1.52 National security threats take the form predominantly of the risk of terrorist or cyber-attack. The response to these threats is likely to involve the state use of covert investigatory powers, in particular the monitoring of electronic communications. Anderson concluded that 'the internet has complicated and magnified the threat in a number of ways' and that 'no-go areas' must be kept to a minimum[77] and any new legislation 'must be couched in technology-neutral language'.[78]

1.53 Anderson's report and recommendations were widely applauded and many formed the blueprint for the IPA. His report was readable, accessible, and reformative. At the heart of his recommendations was the introduction of a new oversight commission and judicial authorization of intrusive surveillance activities. His other key recommendations included the introduction of what he called 'a comprehensive and comprehensible new law', drafted 'from scratch', which should include a revision of the definitions of content and of communications data; the retention of communications should be in line with the requirements of EU law; a detailed operational case needs to be made out for the retention of Internet Connection Records, and a rigorous assessment conducted of the lawfulness, likely effectiveness, intrusiveness, and cost of requiring such data to be retained; bulk collection of intercepted material and associated data should be retained (subject to rulings of the courts) but used only subject to strict additional safeguard; reform of the scheme governing interception warrants and authorization for the acquisition of communications data; and additional protections for sensitive professions. He also recommended that the IPT should have an expanded jurisdiction and the capacity to make declarations of incompatibility; and its rulings should be subject to appeal on points of law.

(d) *Independent Surveillance Review*

1.54 The Independent Surveillance Review (ISR) was undertaken at the request of the then deputy prime minister, partly in response to allegations of mass surveillance following the disclosures made by Edward Snowden.

1.55 The existing legal framework authorizing the interception of communications was unclear, had not kept pace with developments in communications technology, and did not serve either the government or members of the public satisfactorily. The ISR recommended that a new, comprehensive, and clearer legal framework was required. Whatever this was, the activities it authorized needed to be demonstrably lawful, necessary, and proportionate. These conditions were essential if there was to be public confidence in the use of these powerful capabilities.

1.56 The ISR reported that, whilst warrants are an established and important legal mechanism authorizing the use of the state's most intrusive powers, the framework was complex, incomplete, and lacked legal clarity, particularly in light of outdated

---

[77] ibid paras 3.36–3.39.
[78] ibid para 4.1.

assumptions such as internal and external communications. It required radical overhaul, which the ISR reported, must include an enhanced role for the judiciary. The existing oversight regime operated in a series of layers, from ministerial oversight, parliamentary oversight, to the work of a number of judicial commissioners and the IPT:

> This system has grown in ad hoc ways and the public has limited knowledge and understanding of how it works. In the past few years a number of improvements have been made to the oversight regime, but further reform is required. Reorganisation and better resourcing of the existing setup could create a more streamlined, robust and systematic oversight regime that would be genuinely visible to the public and have a positive effect on the police and [intelligence services].

1.57 The ISR supported the views of the ISC and reported that the current surveillance powers were needed but that they required a new legislative framework and oversight regime. Specifically, it adopted David Anderson's suggestion that a comprehensive new law should replace RIPA 2000 Part I, DRIPA 2014, and Part 3 of the Counter Terrorism and Security Act 2015.

1.58 The ISR also agreed that there should be three different types of warrant for the interception and acquisition of communications and related data. This recommendation is largely reflected in the scheme set out in Part 2, Chapter 1 IPA. It also recommendedthe introduction of a National Intelligence and Surveillance Office and that judicial commissioners should authorize warrants in cases involving serious and organized crime and review ministerial decisions to authorize warrants in national security cases. Again, the ISR agreed with both the ISC and Anderson that a domestic right of appeal should be introduced in future legislation.

C. PROVISIONS OF GENERAL APPLICATION

1. Overview

1.59 The provisions in respect of the interception of communications are set out in Part 2 and Chapter 1, Part 6.[79] Acquisition and retention of communications data are found in Part 3 and Chapter 2, Part 6, and Part 4 respectively.[80] Equipment interference warrants are dealt with in Part 5 and Chapter 3, Part 6 and bulk personal dataset warrants in Part 7.[81]

1.60 Part 8 deals with oversight arrangements for the regimes in the IPA and under other Acts and Part 9 contains miscellaneous and general provisions including amendments to sections 3 and 5 of the Intelligence Services Act 1994 and provisions about national security and technical capability notices and combined warrants and authorizations.[82]

---

[79] IPA, s 1(4)(a).
[80] ibid s 1(6)(a)–(c).
[81] ibid s 1(6)(d)–(e).
[82] ibid s 1(7)(a)–(b).

C. Provisions of General Application

2. Review of Operation of Act

1.61 Section 160 IPA provides that the Secretary of State must, within the period of six months beginning with the end of the initial period, prepare a report (the report) on the operation of this Act.[83] The term 'initial period' means the period of five years and six months beginning with the day on which the Act was passed.[84]

1.62 The report must, in particular, take account of any report on the operation of the IPA made by a Select Committee of either or both Houses of Parliament.[85] The Secretary of State must publish the report and lay a copy of it before Parliament.[86]

3. The Making of Regulations

1.63 The power of the Secretary of State or the Treasury to make regulations under the IPA is vast. It is exercisable by statutory instrument, may be exercised so as to make different provision for different purposes or different areas, and includes power to make supplementary, incidental, consequential, transitional, transitory, or saving provision.

1.64 The exercise of what are known as Henry VIII clauses, those in statutes authorizing the executive to make secondary legislation that amends or repeals provisions in primary legislation is prolific and causing increasing concern to constitutional judges, lawyers and some parliamentarians. In a speech to King's College London on 12 April 2016, entitled, 'Ceding Power to the Executive; the Resurrection of Henry VIII', the former Lord Chief Justice and Chief Surveillance Commissioner, Lord Judge asked, 'are we ceding power to the executive which should be retained by Parliament?' And answered, 'we have done so, and we have become habituated to it'. His view was that:

> Unless strictly incidental to primary legislation, every Henry VIII clause, every vague skeleton bill, is a blow to the sovereignty of Parliament. And each one is a self-inflicted blow, each one boosting the power of the executive.
>
> ...
>
> I believe that our Parliament should give the same answer that the 1539 Commons gave to Thomas Cromwell and Henry VIII. Not the one it is thought to have given but the one they actually gave. Save in a national emergency, only statute can repeal, suspend, amend or dispense with statute.[87]

1.65 The Select Committee on the Constitution report on the Investigatory Powers Bill also expressed concern, although in more measured terms:

> In previous reports, we have criticised the framing of Henry VIII clauses in Bills presented to the House. We note that there are several Henry VIII powers in this Bill; however, while some are

---

[83] ibid s 260(1).
[84] ibid s 260(2).
[85] ibid s 260(3).
[86] ibid s 260(4).
[87] https://www.kcl.ac.uk/law/newsevents/newsrecords/2015-16/Ceding-Power-to-the-Executive---Lord-Judge---130416.pdf (last accessed 2 June 2017).

1. An Introduction to the Investigatory Powers Act 2016

significant—for instance those in clauses 67 and 69 which have the capacity to expand the operational scope of the regime for the collection of communications data under Part 3 of the Bill—we feel that the majority of uses of Henry VIII powers in this Bill raise no constitutional concerns.[88]

1.66 Sections 72(3) and 73(6) IPA set out the procedure for a statutory instrument containing regulations under section 71 to which section 72 applies, or under section 73(4) to which section 73(5) applies. These provisions relate to relevant public and local authorities capable of obtaining communications data and subject to an enhanced affirmative procedure: see Chapter 4, paragraphs 4.60–4.62.[89]

1.67 Regulations relating to certain provisions may not be made unless a draft of the statutory instrument has been laid before, and approved by a resolution of, each House of Parliament. Those provisions are: section 12(4) (abolition of powers relating to obtaining communications data) or 271(2)–(4) (power to make regulations in consequence of the IPA which amend or repeal any provision of primary legislation by then on the statute book); section 46(2) (interception by businesses for business purposes); section 52(5) (interception in accordance with overseas request); section 83 (variation or revocation of retention notices); section 90(1) (review of retention notices); section 239 (modification of Investigatory Powers or Judicial Commissioners' functions); section 240(3) (Investigatory Powers Commissioner for Northern Ireland); section 245 (Technical Advisory Board); 253 (technical capability notices); section 257(1) (review of technical capability notices); or paragraph 33 of Schedule 8 (combined warrants).[90]

1.68 Regulations relating to certain provisions may not be made unless a draft of the statutory instrument has been laid before, and approved by a resolution of either House of Parliament. Those provisions are: 12(4) (abolition of powers relating to obtaining communications data) or 271(2)–(4) (power to make regulations in consequence of the IPA which amend or repeal any provision of primary legislation) to which the requirement to place the regulations before both Houses does not apply; 65(5) (designated senior officers capable of cancelling authorizations for the obtaining of communications data); or paragraph 2(1)(b) of Schedule 5 (annual report by public authority to Secretary of State on filtering arrangements).[91]

1.69 A statutory instrument containing regulations relating to certain provisions is subject to annulment in pursuance of a resolution by either House of Parliament. Those provisions are: 10(3) (EU mutual assistance instrument or international mutual assistance agreement); section 52(3) (relevant international agreement); 58(8)(a) (disclosure by postal or telecommunications operator); section 71 (relevant public authorities and designated senior officers) but where section 72 (requirement to consult) does not apply; 73(4) (designated senior officers) but where section 73(5) (duty to consult) does not apply; 133(6)(a) (excepted disclosure by

---

[88] HL Paper 24 (11 July 2016).
[89] IPA, s 267(2).
[90] ibid s 267(3)(a)–(k).
[91] ibid s 267(4)(a)–(c).

C. Provisions of General Application

telecommunications operator); or 255(7) (the giving of national security or technical capability notices).[92]

1.70 A statutory instrument containing regulations under paragraph 4 of Schedule 5 (transfer scheme) is subject to annulment in pursuance of a resolution of the House of Commons.[93]

1.71 In the case of regulations relating to the coming into force of a Code of Practice, these require a draft to be laid before and approved by a resolution of both Houses of Parliament. In the case of a revised Code of Practice, the regulations must be laid before Parliament if the regulations have been made without a draft having been laid before and approved by a resolution of each House of Parliament.[94]

1.72 A statutory instrument containing regulations, which are subject to a particular parliamentary procedure under the IPA, may also include regulations subject to a different or no parliamentary procedure other than those referred to in paragraphs 1.66–1.68 above.[95] Where the regulations are subject to different parliamentary procedures, or one or more parliamentary procedure and no parliamentary procedure the statutory instrument is subject to a hierarchy of procedure. This is in descending order, the affirmative procedure (laid before, and approved by a resolution of, each House of Parliament), the negative procedure (annulment in pursuance of a resolution by either House of Parliament) or no procedure.[96]

1.73 Notwithstanding this comprehensive framework, there is a general saving that provision is not prevented from being included in regulations made under the IPA merely because the provision could have been included in other regulations that would have been subject to a different or no parliamentary procedure.[97]

4. Telecommunications Definitions

1.74 Telecommunications definitions, set out in section 261, apply to whole of the IPA.[98]

1.75 A 'communication' in relation to a telecommunications operator, telecommunications service or telecommunication system, includes, so is not limited to anything comprising speech, music, sounds, visual images. or data of any description, and signals serving either for the impartation of anything between persons, between a person and a thing or between things. or for the actuation or control of any apparatus.[99] The definition is concomitant on the meaning of telecommunications operator, service. or system.

1.76 A 'telecommunications operator' is a person who offers or provides a telecommunications service to persons in the UK, or controls or provides a telecommunication

---

[92] ibid s 267(5)(a)–(g).
[93] ibid s 67(6).
[94] ibid s 267(7) and paras 4(4) and 5(5) of Schedule 7.
[95] ibid s 267(8).
[96] ibid s 267(9).
[97] ibid s 267(1)).
[98] ibid s 261(1).
[99] ibid s 261(2)(a)–(b).

system that is either wholly or in part in or controlled from the UK.[100] A 'telecommunications service' is any service that consists in the provision of access to, and of facilities for making use of, any telecommunication system. The service and the system do not have to be provided by the same person.[101] Cases where the service is to be taken to consist in the provision of access to, and of facilities for making use of, a telecommunication system include any case where a service consists in or includes facilitating the creation, management, or storage of communications transmitted, or that may be transmitted, by means of such a system.[102] A 'telecommunication system' means a system, which includes the apparatus comprised in it that exists either wholly or partly in the UK or elsewhere for the purpose of facilitating the transmission of communications by any means involving the use of electrical or electromagnetic energy.[103] The term 'apparatus' is defined in section 263 (general definitions) and includes within its meaning any equipment, machinery, or physical or logical device and any wire or cable.[104]

(a) *Data: general*

1.77 The precursor to the meaning of entity data is the definition of 'data'. Data includes, so is not limited to, data that is not electronic data and any information, whether electronic or not.[105] Entity data means any data that is about an entity (a person or thing) or an association between an entity and a telecommunications service or system.[106] In addition it consists of, or includes, data that identifies or describes the entity including but not limited to by reference to its location and is not events data.[107]

1.78 Events data means any data that identifies or describes an event, including but not limited to by reference to its location on, in, or by means of a telecommunication system. The event consists of one or more entities engaging in a specific activity at a specific time.[108]

(b) *Communications Data*

1.79 Communications data, in relation to a telecommunications operator, service, or system, means three categories of entity or events data. The first is that which is, to be, or capable of being, held, or obtained by, or on behalf of, a telecommunications operator. This is subject to three qualifications: it is about an entity to which a telecommunications service is provided and relates to the provision of the service; is comprised in, included as part of, attached to, or logically associated with a communication, regardless of where it originates from or is going to, for the purposes of

---

[100] ibid s 261(10)(a)–(b).
[101] ibid s 261(11).
[102] ibid s 261(12).
[103] ibid s 261(13).
[104] ibid s 263(1).
[105] ibid s 263(1).
[106] ibid s 261(3)(a)(i)–(iii).
[107] ibid s 261(3)(b)–(c).
[108] ibid s 261(4).

C. Provisions of General Application

a telecommunication system by means of which the communication is being or may be transmitted; or does not fall within either of the first two qualifications but does relate to the use of a telecommunications service or system. The second is that which is available directly from a telecommunication system and falls within the parameters of the second qualification. The third is that which is or would be or capable of being held or obtained by, or on behalf of, a telecommunications operator, is about the architecture of a telecommunication system, and is not about a specific person.[109]

1.80 In no circumstances can communications data include any content of a communication or would-be content of a communication, other than systems data. Content for this purpose means any element of the communication, or any data attached to or logically associated with it, that reveals anything of what might reasonably be considered to be the meaning, if any, of the communication. This is subject to two exceptions: any meaning arising from the fact of the communication or from any data relating to the transmission of the communication is to be disregarded; and systems data.[110]

(c) Other Definitions

1.81 A public telecommunications service means any telecommunications service offered or provided to the public, or a substantial section of it, in any one or more parts of the UK.[111] A public telecommunication system means a telecommunication system located in the UK by means of which any public telecommunications service is provided, or that consists of parts of any other telecommunication system by means of which any such service is provided.[112]

1.82 A private telecommunication system means any telecommunication system that is not a public telecommunication system and is attached, directly or indirectly, to a public telecommunication system. It does not matter whether this is for the purposes of the communication in question.[113] It also includes apparatus that is both located in the UK and used, with or without other apparatus, for making the attachment to that public telecommunication system.[114]

5. Postal Definitions

1.83 Postal definitions, set out in section 262, apply to whole of the IPA.[115] They are interplay with a 'postal operator' (a person providing a postal service to persons in the UK) and 'postal service'.[116] This means a service that consists in one or more of the following: the collection, sorting, conveyance, distribution, and delivery, inside or outside the UK of

---

[109] ibid s 261(5)(a)–(c).
[110] ibid s 261(6)(a)–(b).
[111] ibid s 261(8).
[112] ibid s 261(9)(a)–(b).
[113] ibid s 261(14)(a)–(b).
[114] ibid s 261(14)(c).
[115] ibid s 262(1).
[116] ibid s 262(6).

postal items, and its main or one of its main purposes is to make available, or to facilitate, a means of transmission from place to place of postal items containing communications.[117] A postal item is any letter, postcard, or other such thing in writing as may be used by the sender for imparting information to the recipient, or any packet or parcel.[118]

1.84 The term 'communication' means in relation to a postal operator or postal service but not 'postal service' for the purposes of section 262; this includes anything transmitted by a postal service.[119]

(a) *Communications Data*

1.85 Communications data, in relation to a postal operator or postal service is determined by postal data. Postal data is data that identifies, purports to identify, or selects four derivatives of communications: any person, apparatus, or location to or from which a communication is or may be transmitted, apparatus through which, or by means of which, a communication is or may be transmitted, the time at which an event relating to a communication occurs, or the data or other data as data comprised in, included as part of, attached to or logically associated with a particular communication.[120] It includes, for the purposes of the present definition 'anything written on the outside of the item'.

1.86 Communications data is postal data comprised in, included as part of, attached to, or logically associated with a communication for the purposes of a postal service by means of which it is being or may be transmitted. It is irrelevant whether this relates to the sender, recipient, or other person. It also includes two types of related information, that about the use made by any person of a postal service but excluding any content of a communication falling outside what constitutes the postal data and information that is neither postal data or the first type of information but is, or is to be, or is capable of being held or obtained by or on behalf of a person providing a postal service, is about those to whom the service is provided, and relates to that service.[121]

(b) *Other Definitions*

1.87 A 'public postal service' as opposed to a postal service for the purposes of section 262, is a postal service that is offered or provided to the public, or a substantial section of the public, in any part or parts of the UK.[122]

6. Data

(a) *Identifying Data*

1.88 The term identifying data means three different types of data: that which may be used to identify, or assist in identifying, any person, apparatus, system, or service;

---

[117] ibid s 262(7).
[118] ibid s 262(5).
[119] ibid s 262(2).
[120] ibid s 262(4)(a)–(d).
[121] ibid s 262(3)(a)–(b).
[122] ibid s 262(8).

D. Commencement

that which may be used to identify, or assist in identifying, any event, or data which may be used to identify, or assist in identifying, the location of any person, event, or thing.[123]

1.89 Data that may be used to identify, or assist in identifying, any event includes, so is not limited to data relating to the fact, time, or duration of the event or type, method, or pattern of event.[124]

(b) *Systems Data*

1.90 Systems data means any data that enables or facilitates, or identifies, or describes anything connected with enabling or facilitating, the functioning of a postal service; telecommunication system (including any apparatus forming part of the system); any telecommunications service provided by means of a telecommunication system; a relevant system (including any apparatus forming part of the system); or any service provided by means of a relevant system.[125] For this purpose, a system is a relevant system if any communications or other information are held on or by means of it.[126]

D. COMMENCEMENT

1.91 The IPA received royal assent on 29 November 2016. On that date, sections Chapter 2 of Part 9, sections 260 to 269 came into force (review of operation of the IPA, definitions etc), and 270(2) and 271(2) to (4) (transitional and minor and consequential provision).[127]

1.92 Following the Investigatory Powers Act 2016 (Commencement No 1 and Transitional Provisions) Regulations 2016, the following provisions of the IPA came into force on 30 December 2016: section 2 (general duties in relation to privacy), so far as it applies to Part 4; paragraphs (a) to (j) of section 61(7) (purposes for which communications data may be obtained), for the purpose of the operation of sections 87 and 94; section 87 (powers to require retention of certain data), except subsection (1)(b); section 88 (matters to be taken into account before giving retention notices); section 90(13) (duty to keep a retention notice under review); section 92 (data integrity and security); section 93 (disclosure of retained data); section 94(1) to (3), (4)(a), (5), and (7) (variation or revocation of notices); section 94(8) except in so far as it applies to section 94(4)(b); section 94(9), (11) so far as it applies to section 90(13), and (13) to (16); section 95 (enforcement of notices and certain other requirements and restrictions); section 97 (extra-territorial application of Part 4); section 98 (Part 4: interpretation); section 244 (oversight by Information Commissioner in relation to Part 4); section 249 (payments towards certain compliance costs), for the

---

[123] ibid s 263(2)(a)–(c).
[124] ibid s 263(3)(a)–(c).
[125] ibid s 263(4)(a)–(e).
[126] ibid s 263(5).
[127] ibid s 272(2).

1. An Introduction to the Investigatory Powers Act 2016

purposes of the payment of a contribution in respect of costs incurred, or likely to be incurred, in complying with Part 4 and the purposes of paragraph 3 of Schedule 9 (transitional, transitory, and saving provision) only; paragraphs 3 to 5, 8, and 9 of Schedule 9, and section 270(1) so far as it relates to those paragraphs; paragraph 63 of Schedule 10 (minor and consequential provisions), and section 271(1) so far as it relates to that paragraph; and in Part 8 of Schedule 10, the repeals relating to sections 21 and 52(3)(a) of the Counter-terrorism and Security Act 2015, and section 271(1) so far as it relates to those repeals.[128]

1.93 Sections 227 and 228 (Investigatory Powers Commissioner and other Judicial Commissioners and their terms and conditions of appointment came into force at the end of January 2017.[129]

E. PRELIMINARY ASSESSMENT OF THE INVESTIGATORY POWERS ACT 2016

1.94 The level of expertise that was consulted in advance of the IP's enactment was unrivalled. Legislators had the benefit of three reviews and written and oral evidence from practitioners, regulators, and senior members of the judiciary. That said, the speed at which the Bill passed through the different stages of its evolution when challenges both here and in Strasbourg were pending was probably a mistake. This is particularly so in light of *Secretary of State of the Home Department v Watson and Others*.[130] Substantial amendment to the IPA, which is at least a significant risk to such a new and comprehensive regime, will inexorably impact on the public's confidence in the legislation. This is regrettable when this was a common feature of the reviews: the Anderson report was entitled 'A Question of Trust' for a reason and its *raison d'être* may be impugned if the decision in *Watson* is adverse to the government's position and those who drafted the IPA have to go back to the drawing board.

1.95 The opportunity to simplify as far as possible the complex has been missed. Although some procedural patterns emerge that enhance understanding (such as applications for and the requirements of warrants and the process for obtaining judicial approval) in many respects, the IPA remains as opaque as its predecessors and many of the provisions are unnecessarily unwieldy, fail to follow a logical order, and involve a confusing matrix of cross-referencing.

1.96 Notwithstanding this, the IPA is accompanied by a dizzying array of draft Codes of Practice, some of which have already undergone significant revision. Their detail is to be welcomed but it is troubling at a constitutional level that so much material is delegated to draft Codes and is not embodied in statutory form. On the subject of constitutional concerns, the vast scope for the use of regulations in this already pervasive and highly intrusive legislation is deeply troubling. The words of Lord

---

[128] ibid s 272(2) and art 2.
[129] ibid s 272(3).
[130] Case C-698/15 (21 December 2016).

E. Preliminary Assessment of the Investigatory Powers Act 2016

Judge quoted in paragraph 1.64 above are a sombre warning that the crucial boundary demarking the separation of powers is in danger of become perilously blurred.

1.97 Much will depend on not just the outcomes of the numerous challenges on the powers set out in the IPA but also on the detail of the provisions and how these will be interpreted in due course. There are some obvious areas of high risk: the scope for the erosion of end-to-end encryption; the operation of judicial approval in practice and how the Investigatory Powers Commissioner and Judicial Commissioners will apply judicial review principles; the protections afforded, in much weakened form, to sensitive professions and their practical implications for disclosure in criminal proceedings and how, the new super-regulator, the Office of the Investigatory Powers Commissioner, will cope with the vast expansion of its functions. At the time of writing there have been four major terrorist attacks in as many months in the UK and questions about the efficacy of the intelligence services are gathering momentum. A report by David Anderson QC on the intelligence services' own review of their handling of intelligence prior to the attacks has been ordered but, in future, this is precisely the sort of issue that could and should be referred to the Investigatory Powers Commissioner under section 236 IPA by the ISC. Managing such a commitment alongside the other pressures of its office will be extremely demanding.

1.98 As the many and complex provisions of the IPA begin to be confronted by those working with them, it will occur to many that few of the powers that are set out in 300 or so pages are in fact new but rather consolidate existing powers under a raft of provisions, sometimes found in the most unlikely corners of the driest legislation. Their consolidation is a positive thing but there is a cogent argument to say that the IPA represents a significant missed opportunity to create a single legislative regime for surveillance powers and achieve some consistency. For example it is a remarkable feature of the statutory scheme that legal challenges to its provisions can take place in the civil courts and the first-tier tribunal, as well as the IPT yet in the criminal courts there remains a prohibition on any disclosure that reveal even the evidence of an interception warrant. There is also significant incongruity in creating specific provision for privacy protection based around human rights protections, in particular Article 8, the right to respect for family and private life, yet error reporting does not arise merely where evidence of such a breach exists: see Chapter 2, paragraphs 2.08–2.10 and Chapter 9, paragraphs 9.33–9.37.

1.99 David Anderson QC wrote in 'A Question of Trust' that: 'an opportunity now exists to take a system characterized by confusion, suspicion and incessant legal challenge, and transform it into a world-class framework for the regulation of strong and vital powers'. The former independent reviewer of terrorism legislation added ruefully that he hoped 'that opportunity will be taken'. Had the government built to his plans, it might have been, but too many of the foundations of the old structure may have irreversibly undermined the stability of the new.

2
GENERAL PRIVACY PROTECTIONS

A.	Introduction	2.01
B.	Section 1 IPA: The 'Overview' Provisions	2.06
C.	Unlawful Interception	2.11
D.	The Interception of Communications	2.19
	1. Conduct Amounting to Interception of Communications	2.19
	2. Conduct that is not Interception	2.37
E.	Lawful Authority	2.39
F.	Monetary Penalties for Certain Unlawful Interceptions	2.43
	1. Schedule 1 IPA	2.46
G.	Civil Liability for Certain Unlawful Interceptions	2.54
H.	Restriction on Requesting Interception by Overseas Authorities	2.55
I.	Offence of Unlawfully Obtaining Communications Data	2.59
J.	Abolition of Powers to Obtain Communications Data	2.62
K.	Restriction on Use of Section 93 of the Police Act 1997	2.73

A. INTRODUCTION

2.01 The Investigatory Powers Act 2016 (IPA), unlike its predecessor, the Regulation of Investigatory Powers Act 2000 (RIPA), prefaces the main parts of the new legislation with Part 1, 'General Privacy Protections', which includes an 'overview of the Act'. In fact, it is a confluence of structure and substance. The former is an attempt to provide a 'bird's eye view' of the constituent parts of what is unquestionably extensive and complex legislation but the latter, it might be said, has little to do with the subject of privacy protections and, in reality, subsumes elements of the former Part 1, Chapters 1 and 2 of RIPA, which dealt with the interception of communications and acquisition, retention, and use of communications data not previously associated with privacy protections of a general nature.

2.02 On 9 February 2016, the Intelligence and Security Committee of Parliament (ISC) published its report on the draft Investigatory Powers Bill. It was of

2. General Privacy Protections

the view that privacy protections were a cause for concern. Specifically, the ISC said:

> Overall, the privacy protections are inconsistent and in our view need strengthening. We recommend that an additional Part be included in the new legislation to provide universal privacy protections, not just those that apply to sensitive professions.[1]

2.03 The initial response from government was to insert in the Bill, under the heading 'Part 1', the sub-heading referred to above. Although the BBC reported that privacy protections had been added[2] this was roundly condemned by legal[3] and other commentators, including former National Security Agency (NSA) whistle-blower Edward Snowden, who took to social media to note that: 'Headline: revised bill adds privacy safeguards. Reality: government changes one header'.[4] In fact, the only changes to the Bill were to navigate the reader to those clauses in it that purported to provide privacy protections in respect of the particular resource being considered for authority to use or to the Human Rights Act 1998 and other legislation.[5] By the time the Bill approached royal assent, some additional but limited work had been done on what could fairly qualify as privacy protections. These are now embodied in Part 1 of the Act. Such privacy protections as exist may be undermined by section 231 IPA (non-compliance with the IPA constituting breach of a European Convention on Human Rights (ECHR) right not of itself a serious error): see Chapter 9, paragraphs 9.34–9.38.

2.04 Arguably, there was in fact a reduction in privacy protections in Part 1 of the IPA since, in the Bill, the tort of unlawful interception of communications that was previously provided for in section 1(3) RIPA was originally omitted. During the parliamentary evolution of RIPA, section 1(3) was explained because of the need for interception to 'be within the legal framework and for a lawful purpose'.[6] It may have been considered that the existence of other remedies made the need for a specific tort redundant but this was far from clear and it was a curious omission. There were a number of calls for its reintroduction in the IPA during the Committee stages and a variation of the former provision found its way into Part 1: see paragraph 2.54, below.[7]

2.05 Part 1 of the IPA contains fourteen sections and deals primarily with the offences and penalties in relation to the existing offence of unlawful interception of communications and the new offence of unlawfully obtaining of communications data.[8] It also deals with restrictions for the taking place of the acquisition of communications

---

[1] Intelligence and Security Committee of Parliament, Report on the Investigatory Powers Bill, HC 795, para 5.
[2] http://www.bbc.co.uk/news/uk-politics-35689432 (last accessed 11 March 2016).
[3] Jack of Kent, 'Privacy is Surveillance': Part 1 of the Investigatory Powers Bill (2 March 2016) http://jackofkent.com/2016/03/privacy-is-surveillance-part-1-of-the-investigatory-powers-bill/ (last accessed 11 March 2016).
[4] https://twitter.com/Snowden/status/705132001431560192 (last accessed 11 March 2016).
[5] IPA, s 1(5)(a)–(b).
[6] *Hansard*, HL vol 613, col 1416 (Lord Bassam).
[7] See eg the written evidence of Scottish PEN to the House of Commons Bill Committee, para 10 http://www.publications.parliament.uk/pa/cm201516/cmpublic/investigatorypowers/Memo/IPB19.htm (last accessed 25 January 2017).
[8] IPA, s 1(3)(a)–(b).

data, equipment interference, and 'certain requests about' the interception of communications.[9] There provisions have little to do with privacy protections, either general or specific. It does direct the reader to where the various powers can be found in the various Parts of the Act but this adds little to that found in the index.

B. SECTION 1 IPA: THE 'OVERVIEW' PROVISIONS

2.06 Section 1 provides an overview of where the regimes provided for by Parts 2 to 7 can be found in the main body of the statute. The provisions in respect of the interception of communications are set out in Part 2 and Chapter 1, Part 6 (bulk interception).[10] The provisions in respect of acquisition and retention of communications data are set out in Part 3 and Chapter 2, Part 6 and Part 4, respectively.[11] Equipment interference warrants are dealt with in Part 5 and Chapter 3, Part 6, and bulk personal dataset warrants in Part 7.[12]

2.07 Section 1 also provides that Part 8 deals with oversight arrangements for the regimes in the Act (and elsewhere) and that Part 9 contains miscellaneous and general provisions, including amendments to sections 3 and 5 of the Intelligence Services Act 1994 (ISA) and provisions about national security and technical capability notices and combined warrants and authorizations.[13]

2.08 The general duties in relation to privacy were significantly overhauled after the Committee stages of the Bill's evolution but remain limited in their effect. Such provisions as were later introduced were largely a repetition of protections already built into the application process for the use of the resources available under the IPA. Any public authority deciding whether to use any of the powers available to it is subject to four mandatory duties prior to doing so.[14] These are: whether what is sought to be achieved through the use of the particular resource could reasonably be achieved by other less intrusive means; whether a higher level of protection should be applied in relation to the information obtained as a result of its use because of its particular sensitivity; the public interest in the integrity and security of telecommunication systems and postal services, and any other aspects of the public interest in the protection of privacy.[15]

2.09 A non-exhaustive list of examples of information of particular sensitivity is provided in section 2(5). It includes items subject to legal privilege, information identifying or confirming a journalistic source, and relevant confidential information for the purposes of Schedule 7.[16] Paragraph (4) of Schedule 7 defines this as information

---

[9] ibid s 1(4).
[10] ibid s 1(6)(a).
[11] ibid s 1(6)(b)–(c).
[12] ibid s 1(6)(d)–(e).
[13] ibid s 1(7)(a)–(b).
[14] ibid s 2(1)(a)–(k).
[15] ibid s 2(2).
[16] ibid s 2(75)(a)–(c).

held in confidence by a member of a profession and consists of personal records or journalistic material which are (or would be if held in England and Wales) excluded material as defined by section 11 of the Police and Criminal Evidence Act 1984. Presumably, section 13 of the Police and Criminal Evidence (Northern Ireland) Order 1989, which is in the same terms as section 11 of PACE, should also be caught by the definition although is not mentioned. Communications between Members of Parliament and their constituents are also included.

2.10   The duties apply 'contextually' and are subject to the need to have regard to other considerations relevant to the operational context. Again, a non-exhaustive list of what may amount to other considerations is provided, including the interests of national security or of the economic well-being of the United Kingdom (UK), the public interest in preventing or detecting serious crime, other considerations relevant to the necessity and proportionality of the conduct that will be engaged in, the requirements of the Human Rights Act 1998, and other requirements of public law.

C. UNLAWFUL INTERCEPTION

2.11   The offence of unlawful interception has existed since the IOCA[17] and has remained largely unchanged, at least in substance, in both the RIPA[18] and now the IPA. It is a requirement under Article 5(1) of the Directive on Privacy and Electronic Communications that:

> [Member] States shall ensure the confidentiality of communications and the related traffic data by means of a public communications network and publicly available electronic communications services, through national legislation. In particular, they shall prohibit listening, tapping, storage or other kinds of interception or surveillance of communications and the related traffic data by persons other than users, without the consent of the users concerned, except when legally authorised to do so in accordance with Article 15(1). This paragraph shall not prevent technical storage that is necessary for the conveyance of a communication without prejudice to the principle of confidentiality.[19]

2.12   Whilst the offence is to the same effect in section 3 IPA, it has been substantially restructured in section 3(1) but it is still the case that the offence is committed if a person intentionally and without lawful authority intercepts a communication in the UK in the course of its transmission by means of either a public postal service or a public or private telecommunications system.[20] A person found guilty of the offence may on summary conviction in England and Wales be fined[21] or in Scotland or Northern Ireland be subject to a fine not exceeding the statutory maximum[22] or, on conviction on indictment in the UK, to imprisonment for a term not exceeding

---

[17] IOCA, s 1(1).
[18] RIPA, s 1(1).
[19] Directive 2002/58/EC.
[20] IPA, s 3(1)(a)–(c).
[21] ibid s 3(6)(a).
[22] ibid s 3(6)(b).

C. Unlawful Interception

two years or to a fine, or to both.[23] The prosecution of either of the offences requires the consent of the Director of Public Prosecutions of England and Wales for offences committed within that jurisdiction and in Northern Ireland, the Director of Public of Prosecutions for Northern Ireland.[24]

The previous provision found in section 1(6) RIPA relating to the exclusion from criminal liability for a person intercepting a communication in the course of its transmission by means of a private telecommunications system who has the right to control the operation of the system or who carries out the interception with the express or implied consent of someone who does is now found in section 2(2) IPA. 2.13

The 'right to control the operation or use of the system' should be interpreted following consideration of the equivalent provision in section 1(6) RIPA by the Court of Appeal in *R v Stanford*,[25] which held it was wider than 'the right to operate or use the system' and meant 'authorise or forbid'. One of the objectives of the former section 1, now section 2(2) IPA, was to protect the privacy of private telecommunications systems, which would be undermined if the effect of the old section 1(6) gave unfettered access to persons with the ability to operate and use a telecommunications system.[26] This decision is unlikely to be affected by the new legislative scheme in Part 1 IPA. 2.14

Whereas section 2 RIPA set out the definitions relevant to the meaning and location of interception these are now found in different parts of the IPA that are not easy to follow. Although sections 3 and 4 provide for the meaning of interception[27] and interception within the UK,[28] the meaning of public and private telecommunications systems and public postal service are now found in sections 261 and 262.[29] These are dealt with in Chapter 1 of this work: paragraphs 1.86–1.96. 2.15

A public telecommunications system is one located in the UK by means of which any public communications service is provided or which consists of any other parts of any telecommunications system by means of which any such service is provided.[30] Its private counterpart has three elements: that it is not a public telecommunications system, that it is attached, directly or indirectly, to a public system, and that it includes apparatus for making the attachment that is located in the UK.[31] 2.16

A public postal service is a postal service[32] offered or provided to the public or a substantial section of the public within the UK.[33] 2.17

---

[23] ibid s 3(6)(c).
[24] ibid s 3(7).
[25] [2006] EWCA Crim 258.
[26] See also C Walker, 'Email interception and RIPA: the Court of Appeal rules on "the Rights to Control" defence' (2006) Communications Law, 2006 WL 1652477 (UK).
[27] IPA, s 3(3)(a).
[28] ibid s 3(3)(b).
[29] ibid s 3(5).
[30] ibid s 223(9).
[31] ibid s 223(14).
[32] Defined in ibid s 224(7).
[33] ibid s 224(8).

D. THE INTERCEPTION OF COMMUNICATIONS

1. Conduct Amounting to Interception of Communications

2.18   Section 6 provides the definition of 'lawful authority': see paragraphs 2.39–2.42 below.[34]

2.19   Section 4 IPA, formerly provided for in section 2 RIPA, breaks down into three discrete elements: interception in relation to telecommunication systems; interception in relation to postal services; and what is meant by interception of communications carried out in the UK. It belies the straightforward statements in the Home Office fact sheet that '[interception of communications in] practice means listening to a phone call or reading an email'[35] or in the draft Code of Practice issued concurrently with the Bill that:

> Section 4 of the Act provides that a person intercepts a communication in the course of its transmission by means of a telecommunication system if they perform a 'relevant act' in relation to the system and the effect of that act is to make any content of the communication available at a 'relevant time' to a person who is not the sender or intended recipient of the communication.[36]

2.20   Section 4 IPA has to be read alongside the following provision, section 5, which identifies conduct that is not interception. For the purposes of the new legislation:

> [A] person intercepts a communication in the course of its transmission by means of a telecommunication system if, and only if—(a) the person does a relevant act in relation to the system, and (b) the effect of the relevant act is to make any content of the communication available, at a relevant time, to a person who is not the sender or intended recipient of the communication.[37]

2.21   The term 'person' was defined in clause 225(1) of the Bill, as limited to 'the purposes of the IPA, except Parts 2 and 5'. It included, so was not therefore limited to, 'an organisation and any association or combination of persons'. Solicitor and respected commentator Graham Smith raised legitimate concerns about the lack of precision in the definition and whether 'person' extends to circumstances where the process is entirely automated.[38] However, whilst unsatisfactory, it was likely that, even if entirely computerized, the process is conceived by a person at some point in its evolution or operation and makes available to a person, in principle, content. In the event, it became academic, since the term does not appear in the index of defined expressions in section 265 IPA.

---

[34] ibid s 6(1)–(3).
[35] https://www.gov.uk/government/uploads/system/uploads/attachment_data/file/473739/Factsheet-Targeted_Interception.pdf.
[36] Interception of Communications, draft Code of Practice.
[37] IPA, s 4(1).
[38] Graham Smith, Evidence to Investigatory Powers Review (3 October 2014) paras 70–3 https://terrorismlegislationreviewer.independent.gov.uk/wp-content/uploads/2015/06/Submissions-H-Z.pdf.

D. The Interception of Communications

(a) Relevant Act
This simplifies to a limited extent the old section 2(2) RIPA, which was the subject to a number of exceptions. The IPA creates the new terms of 'relevant act'[39] and 'relevant time'.[40] The definition of the former in fact mirrors the former section 2(2)(a)–(c) RIPA, so, modifying or interfering with the system or its operation,[41] monitoring transmissions made by means of the system,[42] or made by wireless telegraphy to or from apparatus that is part of the system.[43] Modifying for the purpose of this provision remains as it was under RIPA and includes 'attaching any apparatus to or otherwise modifying or interfering with any part of the system'.[44] This includes any wireless apparatus that is part of the system.[45]

2.22

(b) Relevant Time
The term 'relevant time' is limited to transmissions by means of a telecommunications system and relates to 'any time while the communication is being transmitted and any time when the communication is stored in or by the system (whether before or after its transmission)'.[46] This is elaborated upon in section 3(5) and includes circumstances where 'the communication is diverted or recorded at the relevant time' so that the content is available to a person (so not limited to the intended recipient) subsequent to the interception. This incorporates the former section 2(7) RIPA, which dealt with the issue compositely, but Part 1 IPA now fragments the definitions.

2.23

(c) In the Course of Transmission
The term 'in the course of transmission' has been the subject of a number of reported decisions that are unlikely to be affected by the restructuring of the definitions under the IPA.

2.24

In *R v Smart and Beard*,[47] a decision under the IOCA (which made no provision for interception of communications on private communications systems), the Court of Appeal considered whether calls recorded by a covert listening device installed in the second defendant's car constituted an interception of communications. The court held, applying the decision of the House of Lords in *Morgans v DPP*,[48] that there was no interception of an electrical impulse or signal passing through a public telecommunications system.

2.25

---

[39] IPA, s 4(1)(a).
[40] ibid s 4(1)(b).
[41] ibid s 4(2)(a).
[42] ibid s 4(2)(b).
[43] ibid s 4(2)(c).
[44] ibid s 4(4)(a).
[45] ibid s 4(4)(b).
[46] ibid s 4(4)(a)–(b).
[47] (2002) Crim LR 684.
[48] [2000] 2 WLR, 386.

2.26 Following the enactment of RIPA, the Court of Appeal considered in *R v Hammond, McIntosh and Gray*[49] whether a telephone conversation between an undercover police officer and a defendant that was recorded was an interception. The court held there was no third party involved and the other party, the undercover police officer, had consented to the recording. There was no interception in fact, since the recording that took place did not happen during the course of transmission. Even if there had been, in the circumstances, the role of the officer was that of a consenting party so as to create an exception for an interception without a warrant in any event under section 3(2)(a) or (b) RIPA. This contingent ruling would remain unchanged in light of the effect of section 44 IPA (interception with consent).

2.27 A similar issue arose in the first instance decision of *R v McDonald, Rafferty and O'Farrell*.[50] An undercover officer used a recording device attached to the earpiece of a telephone to record conversations. The officer was not at the time authorized under Part II in relation to his conduct, although it was open to the relevant public authority to have done so. It was not disputed, unsurprisingly, that if the recordings were intercepts, authorization under Part I RIPA would have been required. Astill J held that:

> [T]he system begins at point A with the start of the transmission of electrical or electromagnetic energy or pulses into which the sound waves of the speaker have been converted and the systems ends at point B when these electrical or electromagnetic energy or pulses cease on being converted into sound waves by the receiver in the hand of the recipient ... an interception is an interference of one sort or another between a starting point A and a finishing point B. It is not concerned with events before or after.[51]

2.28 The Court of Appeal considered the question again in *R v E*[52] and *R v Allsopp and Others*.[53] In both cases, listening devices in motor vehicles had picked up telephone conversations that the defence had argued amounted to interceptions. The court held that since the recordings took place after transmission they did not amount to interceptions of communications and were therefore admissible.

2.29 In *R v Coulson and Kuttner*,[54] the Court of Appeal reviewed these authorities and did not depart from them.

2.30 The court in *Coulson* was concerned with whether, once a voicemail (a stored communication) had been accessed, it ceased to be in the course of its transmission. RIPA section 2(7), replaced by section 4 IPA, was 'at the heart of the appeal'. The Court of Appeal held that there was no good reason why 'the first receipt of the communication should be considered as bringing the transmission to an end'.[55] The storage of the message during transmission is not transient and it is not relevant that

---

[49] [2002] EWCA Crim 1243.
[50] Woolwich Crown Court (23 April 2002).
[51] *R v McDonald*, at p 24 of the judgment.
[52] [2004] Cr App R 29, [2004] EWCA Crim 1243.
[53] [2005] EWCA Crim 703.
[54] [2013] WLR (D) 262.
[55] *R v Coulson and Kuttner* [2013] WLR (D) 262, para 27.

D. The Interception of Communications

it may already have been listened to at the time of interception. Judge CJ held, at paragraph 26:

> The scope of the provision is put beyond doubt, in our view, by the reference in section 2(7) to the system by means of which 'the communication is being, or has been, transmitted'. The words 'has been transmitted' are totally inconsistent with the appellants' suggestion that the extension is limited to transient storage prior to first access. These words make entirely clear that the course of transmission may continue notwithstanding that the voicemail message has already been received and read by the intended recipient.

2.31 The ruling in *Coulson*[56] did not, perhaps surprisingly, consider the question of content. Under RIPA section 2(8), content, unlike storage, was subject to the restriction of during, not after transmission. Section 4(4) IPA now emphatically extends the definition to, somewhat counter-intuitively, the period after transmission.

2.32 The meaning of 'content' in relation to a communication is found in section 261(6), and extends to a telecommunications operator, service, or system, each of which are given their own meanings: see Chapter 1, paragraphs 1.74–1.87. It is any element of the communication, or any data attached to or logically associated with it, which 'reveals anything of what might reasonably be considered to be the meaning (if any) of the communication'. It creates two exceptions. First, content is not any meaning arising from the fact of the communication or from data relating to its transmission and, secondly, it excludes systems data.

2.33 Systems data is defined in section 263(4) and means any data that enables or facilitates or identifies or describes any data connected with enabling or facilitating the functioning of either a postal service, a telecommunications system, or service a 'relevant system' (a system holding any communications or other information on or by means of it), or any service provided by such a system.

2.34 The meanings of 'wireless telegraphy' and 'wireless telegraphy apparatus' have the same meaning as in sections 116 and 117 of the Wireless Telegraphy Act 2006, respectively.

2.35 In the IPA, determining whether a postal item is in the course of its transmission by means of a postal service requires consideration of section 125(3) of the Postal Services Act 2000. A postal packet should be read so as to apply to a postal item.

2.36 Interception of a communication is carried out in the UK if, and only if—so must be strictly interpreted[57]—in two circumstances.[58] First, the relevant act or, in the case of a postal item, interception is carried out by conduct within the UK.[59] Secondly, the communication, whether by means of a public postal or public or private telecommunications system, is intercepted in the course of its transmission.[60] In

---

[56] [2013] WLR (D) 262.
[57] *R v Shayler* [2001] 1 WLR 2206, para 43 (in the context of the Official Secrets Act 1989, in which the same words appear).
[58] IPA, s 4(8).
[59] ibid s 4(8)(a).
[60] ibid s 4(8)(b)(i).

the case of private communications systems, there is an added requirement that the sender or intended recipient of the communication is in the UK.[61]

2. Conduct that is not Interception

2.37 There are two express forms of conduct that fall outside the definition of interception. It does not include references to the interception of any communication broadcast for general reception.[62] The other form of conduct is limited to interception by means of a postal service and excludes any conduct connected with related postal data or necessary for identifying postal data 'comprised in, included as part of, attached to, or logically associated with a communication'.[63]

2.38 The term 'postal data' is defined in section 262(4) and is that which identifies or purports to identify any person, apparatus, or location to or from which a communication is or may be transmitted or time at which an event relating to the communication occurs. It also identifies or selects (or purports to identify or select) apparatus through which or by means of which a communication is or may be transmitted or identifies the data or other data comprised in, included as part of, attached, or logically associated with the communication. Data for this purpose includes anything written on the outside of the item: see Chapter 1, paragraphs 1.85–1.90.

E. LAWFUL AUTHORITY

2.39 The new Act defines 'lawful authority' for the first time. Generally, where there is a form of warrant or authorization in place, some other statutory power or a court order this will constitute lawful authority. Where it is in accordance with a warrant or authority under the Act, it is lawful 'for all other purposes'.[64]

2.40 The following warrants will constitute lawful authority: a targeted interception warrant or mutual assistance warrant under Chapter 1 of Part 2;[65] a bulk interception warrant under Chapter 1 of Part 6;[66] and an authorization under sections 44 to 52 IPA (interception authorized by circumstances, eg consent, interception in prisons etc).[67]

2.41 Where the communications are stored in or by a telecommunication system, lawful authority extends to the interception if it is carried out in accordance with a targeted equipment interference warrant under Part 5 or a bulk equipment interference warrant under Chapter 3 of Part 6, IPA.[68]

---

[61] ibid s 4(8)(b)(ii).
[62] ibid s 5(1).
[63] ibid s 5(2)(a)–(b).
[64] ibid s 6(1)–(3).
[65] ibid s 6(1)(a)(i).
[66] ibid s 6(1)(a)(ii).
[67] ibid s 6(1)(b).
[68] ibid s 6(1)(c)(i).

2.42 Two new circumstances constituting lawful authority have been added to reflect the decision in *R (on the application of NTL) v Ipswich Crown Court*.[69] Where the interception is in the exercise of any statutory power that is exercised for the purpose of obtaining information or taking possession of any document or other property,[70] or is carried out in accordance with a court order made for that purpose, this will constitute lawful authority.[71]

F. MONETARY PENALTIES FOR CERTAIN UNLAWFUL INTERCEPTIONS

2.43 Monetary penalties were first introduced by statutory instrument[72] on 16 June 2011 for the purposes of complying with the Council Directives 95/46/EC and 2002/58/EC (processing and free movement of personal data and privacy and electronic communications respectively) by amending section 1(1) of RIPA and providing a new Schedule A1. These requirements are now set out in section 6 of the new Act but unsurprisingly are to the same effect. A monetary penalty notice may be served where there has been interception without lawful authority but no offence is committed. It requires the person served with it to pay the sum of money specified in it.[73]

2.44 The Investigatory Powers Commissioner may serve a monetary penalty notice on a person if two conditions referred to as 'A' and 'B' are met.[74] Condition A is that the Commissioner considers that an interception[75] has taken place in the UK, in the course of its transmission by means of a public telecommunication system without lawful authority and at the time of the interception, it was not an attempt to act in accordance with an interception warrant[76] which might, in the opinion of the Investigatory Powers Commissioner, explain the interception.[77] Condition B is that the Investigatory Powers Commissioner does not consider that the person has committed an offence under section 2.[78]

2.45 The amount of a monetary penalty determined by the Investigatory Powers Commissioner under this section cannot exceed £50,000.[79]

---

[69] [2002] EWHC 1585 (Admin), [2002] 3 WLR 1173.
[70] IPA, s 6(1)(c)(ii).
[71] ibid s 6(1)(c)(iii).
[72] Regulation of Investigatory Powers (Monetary Penalty Notices and Consents for Interceptions) Regulations 2011 (SI 2011/1340).
[73] IPA, s 7(2).
[74] ibid s 7(1).
[75] This has the meaning set out in ibid s 3.
[76] This means a targeted interception warrant or mutual assistance warrant under Chapter 1 of Part 2 or bulk interception warrant under Chapter 1 of Part 6: IPA, s 6(7).
[77] IPA, s 7(3)(a)–(c).
[78] ibid s 7(4).
[79] ibid s 7(5).

1. Schedule 1 IPA

2.46 Schedule 1 (which makes further provision about monetary penalty notices) has effect.[80] This is in two parts, monetary penalty notices (Part 1) and information provisions (Part 2).

2.47 Part 1 of Schedule 1 specifies the payment period for the penalty but not less than twenty-eight days after service.[81] The formalities of the content of notices are set out in paragraph 2(a)–(h) of Schedule 1 and includes the requirement to specify the grounds on which it is served and the basis for the determination of the monetary penalty, as well as the right of appeal.

2.48 There are two enforcement obligations set out Schedule 1. These are a requirement on the part of the person on whom the notice is served to cease interception activities[82] and such other specified steps set out in the notice. There are detailed provisions in paragraphs 4 to 6 of Schedule 1 relating to consultation prior to service of a notice, including the service of a notice of intent (and the formalities of their content).[83] There is the right to an oral hearing[84] before the Investigatory Powers Commissioner who is empowered to, amongst other things, vary or cancel a notice of intent.[85] The provisions on the exercise of the Investigatory Powers Commissioner's powers to vary or cancel are set out in Schedule 1, paragraph 7.

2.49 Interestingly, the right of appeal against the notice or refusal to vary or cancel it is made to the First-tier Tribunal, not the Investigatory Powers Tribunal.[86] The tribunal must allow an appeal against a notice where it was 'not in accordance with the law'[87] or where the notice involved the exercise of discretion by the Investigatory Powers Commissioner, that this ought to have been exercised differently.[88] In any other case, any appeal must be dismissed.[89] Appeals against a refusal to vary or cancel a notice may be allowed where the tribunal considers it is appropriate but must otherwise dismiss the appeal. In carrying out is appellate function in respect of either form of appeal, the tribunal may review the factual basis upon which any notice was based.[90]

2.50 Paragraph 5 of Schedule 1 makes provision for enforcement of monetary penalty notices in the county court and High Court in England, Wales, and Northern Ireland and the Sheriff's Court in Scotland.

2.51 The Investigatory Powers Commissioner is mandated to prepare and issue any guidance on how the functions under section 6 IPA and Schedule 1 will be

---

[80] ibid s 7(6).
[81] IPA, Schedule 1, para 1(1).
[82] ibid para 3(a).
[83] ibid para 4.
[84] ibid para 4(g).
[85] ibid para 5.
[86] ibid para 8(1).
[87] ibid para 8(4)(a).
[88] ibid para 8(4)(b).
[89] ibid para 8(5).
[90] ibid para 8(6) and 8(10).

exercised.[91] This must deal with the manner in which the Investigatory Powers Commissioner will deal with circumstances giving rise to the service of a monetary penalty notice, the amount of the penalty, and its enforcement.[92] The guidance must be published but the form and manner of this is a matter for the Investigatory Powers Commissioner.[93]

2.52 Part 2 of Schedule 1 relates to information notices. It is open to the Investigatory Powers Commissioner to request a person on whom either a notice of intent or substantive notice may be served to 'provide such information as the Investigatory Powers Commissioner reasonably requires for the purpose of deciding whether to serve it'.[94] Part 2 specifies the requirements of information notices, appeals, and enforcement and the requirement on the Office of Communications to provide technical assistance in connection with the Investigatory Powers Commissioner's functions.

2.53 Perhaps surprisingly, appeals under either Part 1 or Part 2 are not to the Investigatory Powers Tribunal but to the First-tier Tribunal.

G. CIVIL LIABILITY FOR CERTAIN UNLAWFUL INTERCEPTIONS

2.54 Civil liability arises if four conditions are met. Condition A is that the interception is carried out in the UK. Condition B is that interception takes place whilst the communication is in the course of its transmission by means of a private telecommunication system, or in the course of its transmission, by means of a public telecommunication system, to or from apparatus that is part of a private telecommunication system. Condition C is that the interception is carried out by, or with the express or implied consent of, a person who has the right to control the operation or use of the private telecommunication system and Condition D is that the interception is carried out without lawful authority. A claimant can be either the sender or recipient or intended recipient of the communication. This replaces the previous provision in RIPA: see paragraph 2.04 above.

H. RESTRICTION ON REQUESTING INTERCEPTION BY OVERSEAS AUTHORITIES

2.55 Sections 9 and 10 IPA deal with requests from outside the UK, the former providing for requests that are not made under a European Union mutual assistance agreement and the latter, those that are.

---

[91] ibid para 11(1).
[92] ibid para 11(2).
[93] ibid para 11(5).
[94] ibid Part 2, para 13(1).

2.56 Where a person representing any authorities of a country or territory outside the UK believes an individual will be in the British Isles and a request is made to carry out the interception of that individual's communications (either sent or intended for) at that time, then the request to intercept may not be made by or on behalf of a person in the UK unless two criteria are met.[95] These are either the existence of a targeted interception warrant authorizing the interception of the individual's communications[96] or a targeted examination warrant in respect of a selection of the individual's communications.[97]

2.57 Requests for assistance under a EU mutual assistance instrument, and for assistance in accordance with an international mutual assistance agreement[98] are also subject to qualifying criteria namely that a mutual assistance warrant must have been issued under Chapter 1 of Part 2 authorizing the making of the request.[99]

2.58 The two instruments referred to, an EU mutual assistance instrument and an international mutual assistance agreement are defined as an EU instrument and an international agreement respectively, which: (a) relates to the provision of mutual assistance in connection with, or in the form of, the interception of communications; (b) requires the issue of a warrant, order, or equivalent instrument in cases in which assistance is given, and is designated as an EU mutual assistance instrument or mutual assistance agreement by regulations made by the Secretary of State.[100]

I. OFFENCE OF UNLAWFULLY OBTAINING COMMUNICATIONS DATA

2.59 A new offence of unlawfully obtaining communications data is created in Part 1. Its scope is limited to a 'relevant person', that is, a person holding an office rank or position with a relevant public authority (relevant public authority is defined in Part 3).[101] The person must be acting without lawful authority and knowingly or recklessly obtain communications data from either a telecommunications operator or postal operator.[102] The offence is not committed if the relevant person acted in the reasonable belief that he or she had lawful authority to obtain the communications data.[103] As to when the offence is committed by a body corporate or Scottish partnership, see Chapter 10, paragraphs 10.125–10.127.

---

[95] IPA, s 9(1).
[96] ibid s 9(2)(a).
[97] ibid s 9(2)(b).
[98] ibid s 10(1)(a)–(b).
[99] ibid s 10(2).
[100] ibid s 10(3).
[101] ibid s 11(2).
[102] ibid s 11(1).
[103] ibid s 11(3).

2.60 On summary conviction in England, Wales, and Scotland, the offence attracts a maximum term of imprisonment not exceeding twelve months,[104] or a fine (in Scotland, not exceeding the statutory maximum), or both.[105] In Northern Ireland, the maximum term may not exceed six months, a fine not exceeding the statutory maximum, or both.[106]

2.61 On conviction on indictment, the person found guilty is liable to be sentenced to a term of imprisonment not exceeding two years or to a fine, or to both.[107]

J. ABOLITION OF POWERS TO OBTAIN COMMUNICATIONS DATA

2.62 Schedule 2 IPA, repeals certain information powers so far as they enable public authorities to secure the disclosure by a telecommunications operator or postal operator of communications data without the consent of the operator and is given has effect by section 10(1) IPA.

2.63 Section 10 IPA provides for limits on the power to obtain communications data. It creates a 'general information power', which is defined as any power to obtain information or documents conferred by statute other than the Act or RIPA 2000 and does not deal with either telecommunications operators or class of postal operators or any class of either.[108] Telcommunications operators and postal operators are defined in Chapter 1, paragraphs 1.76 and 1.83.

2.64 Any general information power, which would enable a public authority to secure the disclosure by a telecommunications operator or postal operator of communications data without the consent of the operator, and does not involve a court order or other judicial authorization or warrant and is not a regulatory power or a relevant postal power, is to be read as not enabling the public authority to secure such a disclosure.[109] However, the Secretary of State may by regulations modify any enactment affected by this provision.[110]

2.65 Where a regulatory power or relevant postal power which enables a public authority to secure the disclosure by a telecommunications operator or postal operator of communications data without the consent of the operator may only be exercised by the public authority for that purpose if it is not possible for the authority to use a power under this Act to secure the disclosure of the data.[111]

---

[104] Or, in England and Wales, 6 months, if the offence was committed before the commencement of s 154(1) of the Criminal Justice Act 2003: IPA, s 9(4)(a)(i).
[105] IPA, s (11)(4)(a)–(b).
[106] ibid s 11(4)(c)(i)–(ii).
[107] ibid s 11(4)(d).
[108] ibid s 12(5).
[109] ibid s 12(2).
[110] ibid s 12(4).
[111] ibid s 12(3).

2.66   There are a series of definitions provided in section 12(6), IPA. The word power, in addition to 'general information power', is subject to no fewer than four additional sub-definitions: 'power', which includes, so presumably is not limited to, 'part of a power' and 'regulatory power', which means any power to obtain information or documents conferred by statute other than the IPA and the RIPA 2000 and exercisable for the purpose of regulatory functions. 'Regulatory functions' is not defined.

2.67   A 'relevant postal power' is defined as any power to obtain information or documents that is conferred by statute other than the IPA and RIPA and 'is exercisable in connection with the conveyance or expected conveyance of any postal item into or out of the UK'. Finally, references to powers include duties and references to enabling and exercising are to be read as including references to requiring and performing.[112]

2.68   The penultimate provision in Part 1, section 13 IPA relates to restrictions on interference with equipment. It creates a prohibition on the part of any of the intelligence services to obtain communications, private information or equipment data or engage in any other conduct which could be authorized by an equipment interference warrant except under the authority of such a warrant.[113] It is subject to two conditions. First, the intelligence service considers that, in the absence of a warrant, the conduct would constitute one or more offences under sections 1 to 3A of the Computer Misuse Act 1990 (computer misuse offences)[114] and, secondly, there is a British Islands connection.[115] However, it does not restrict the ability on the part of an intelligence service to apply for a warrant where these criteria are not met.[116] The no doubt intended corollary of this is that there is no legal requirement to do so. Indeed, the general saving provisions would prevent allegations of unlawfulness, if made, succeeding: see Chapter 1, paragraphs 1.14–1.19.

2.69   The definitions of communications, private information, and equipment data are found elsewhere in the Act[117] and equipment interference warrant means either a targeted or bulk warrant under Chapter 5 or Chapter 3 of Part 6 IPA, respectively.[118]

2.70   The determinative criterion for the operation of the prohibition in section 13(1)(a) IPA is highly subjective, depending on the intelligence service's own assessment of whether the conduct would amount to an offence.

2.71   There is an attempt to define the purposes of the interference set out in section 13(1) IPA (obtaining communications data etc). There is some commonality in the definitions but each is parasitic on the term 'a British Islands connection'. 'British Islands connection' means that any of the conduct would take place in the British

---

[112] ibid s 12(6).
[113] ibid s 13(1).
[114] ibid s 13(1)(a).
[115] ibid s 13(1)(b).
[116] ibid s 13(3).
[117] ibid s 138.
[118] ibid s 13(4).

Islands, whether or not the location of the equipment that it is proposed is interfered with is within the British Islands. The geographical reach of this provision appears, therefore, to be greater than its jurisdictional scope, since the ambit of the protection afforded by a requirement to authorize extends to the Channel Islands and the Isle of Man.[119] It is subject to the intelligence service believing that any of the equipment affected would be in the British Islands while the interference is taking place.[120]

Each of the purposes of the interference is predicated on some actual or perceived belief that a person affected (either because he or she is a person to whom a communication has been sent by or private information relating to that person is or may be obtained) is 'for the time being' in the British Islands.[121] Equipment data is that which forms part of, or is connected with, communications or private information falling within either the communications or private information affected.[122]

2.72

K. RESTRICTION ON USE OF SECTION 93 OF THE POLICE ACT 1997

There is a similar prohibition on the use of section 93 of the Police Act 1997 for the purpose of obtaining communications, private information, or equipment data (these terms have the same definitions as those used in section 11). Where authorization to engage in conduct could be authorized by a targeted equipment interference warrant if the applicant considers that the conduct would (unless done under lawful authority) constitute one or more offences under sections 1 to 3A of the Computer Misuse Act 1990 (computer misuse offences), such an application should be made under this Act.[123]

2.73

---

[119] ibid s 13(2)(a).
[120] ibid s 13(2)(b).
[121] ibid s 13(2)(c)(i)–(ii).
[122] ibid s 13(2)(c)(iii).
[123] ibid s 14(1).

3
LAWFUL INTERCEPTION OF COMMUNICATIONS

A.	Introduction	3.01
B.	Warrants	3.06
	1. Types of Warrants	3.06
C.	Issuing Warrants	3.26
	1. Secretary of State's Power to Issue Warrants	3.29
	2. Grounds on Which Warrants May Be Issued	3.33
D.	Approval of Warrants by Judicial Commissioners	3.45
	1. Introduction	3.45
	2. Non-urgent Cases	3.46
	3. Urgent Cases	3.48
E.	Additional Safeguards	3.57
	1. Members of Parliament	3.57
	2. Items Subject to Legal Privilege	3.59
	3. Journalistic Material and Sources	3.64
F.	Warrants: Formalities	3.67
	1. Requirements that Must Be Met by Warrants	3.69
	2. Duration of Warrants	3.75
	3. Renewal of Warrants	3.77
	4. Modification of Warrants	3.83
	5. Cancellation of Warrants	3.99
	6. Special Rules for Certain Mutual Assistance Warrants	3.102
	7. Implementation of Warrants	3.107
	8. Service of Warrants outside the United Kingdom	3.111
	9. Duty of Postal and Telecommunications Operators	3.115
G.	Other Forms of Lawful Interception	3.121
	1. Consent	3.121
	2. Interception for Administrative, Enforcement, or Regulatory Purposes	3.123
	3. Interception in Prisons and Other Institutions	3.134
H.	Restrictions on Handling and Disclosure of Intercept Material Obtained under Warrants	3.143
	1. Handling Intercept Material	3.143
	2. Privileged Items	3.148
	3. Disclosure of Intercept Material	3.150
I.	The Offence of Making Unauthorized Disclosures	3.163

3. Lawful Interception of Communications

A. INTRODUCTION

3.01 The Birkett Report, a Privy Council review into the interception of communications in 1957, noted that the power to do so had existed from 'the earliest times' and had been recognized in successive Acts of Parliament. More recently, Nick Herbert MP, in a speech to Parliament in 2013 in response to Edward Snowden's disclosures, said that 'the Spanish Armada was said to have been averted as much by the pen of Queen Elizabeth's spymaster, Sir Francis Walsingham, as by the Royal Navy'.[1] In modern times, the regulation of the interception of communications was cemented by the Interception of Communications Act 1985 (IOCA). This 'short but difficult'[2] statute was introduced following the adverse decision in *Malone v United Kingdom*[3] in the European Court of Human Rights, which was concerned exclusively with public communications systems. The IOCA was later repealed and replaced with Part 1, Chapter 1 of the Regulation of Investigatory Powers Act 2000 (RIPA), which introduced a framework for interception on both public and private communications systems and attempted to bring the former provisions in the IOCA up to date with technological advances.

3.02 The case for the interception of communications by the state is in principle compelling. The Intelligence and Security Committee of Parliament (ISC) in its report 'Privacy and Security' said that:

> The targeted interception of communications (primarily in the UK) is an essential investigative capability, which the [intelligence] Agencies require in order to learn more about individuals who are plotting against the UK.[4]

3.03 The Independent Reviewer of Terrorism Legislation, David Anderson QC, in his seminal report 'A Question of Trust', opined that interception 'can be of vital importance for intelligence, for disruption and for the detection and investigation of crime'.[5] In a briefing paper for the House of Commons on the Investigatory Powers Bill,[6] as it then was, the corollary of the case for interception was equally clear:

> The Bill, and the powers for which it would provide, raise questions of profound importance. These include the balance to be struck between privacy and security; the extent to which Parliament, and the public, should be aware of conduct exercised on their behalf; and the trust that should be placed in the agencies and Government not to abuse powers that have the potential to be deeply intrusive.

---

[1] http://www.wscountytimes.co.uk/news/opinion/arundel-south-downs-mp-nick-herbert-striving-to-balance-liberty-and-security-1-5188075 (accessed 27 January 2017).
[2] *R v Preston* [1993] 4 All ER 651 (Lord Mustill).
[3] (1985) 7 EHRR 14.
[4] Privacy and Security, HC 1075 (12 March 2015) page 23.
[5] David Anderson QC, 'A Question of Trust' (June 2015).
[6] J Dawson, Investigatory Powers Bill Briefing Paper, House of Commons Library, Number 7518 (11 March 2016).

The concept of 'targeted' interception, which now features expressly in the IPA, was admitted for the first time in March 2015, see Chapter 3, paragraphs 3.12 to 3.14.[7]   3.04

Part 2, Chapter 1 IPA contains twenty-nine sections, dealing with pre-issue matters, the issuing of warrants, and post-issue implementation issues. There is a draft Code of Practice running to 101 pages. This is not considered detail in this chapter but should be read alongside the provisions in Part 2, Chapter 1.   3.05

B. WARRANTS

1. Types of Warrants

(a) Background

The lawful interception of communications by warrant was previously provided for in six sections of RIPA. This number has more than quadrupled in the IPA and the provisions are found in Part 2, Chapter 1, sections 15 to 43. Under the former regime, a warrant was issued under section 5 RIPA, and section 8, provided for its content; section 8(1) related to what became known as 'internal communications' and section 8(4) 'external communications'. This in turn led to the terms section 8(1) and 8(4) warrants being used to define the nature of the warrant, although, strictly speaking, all warrants were issued under section 5 and section 8 governed content only. Only external communications were defined in RIPA. The use of the term 'internal' evolved for the purpose of distinguishing between external communications and those that were not. This already confusing position was exacerbated, as the interception of 'internal' communications did not necessarily mean that the interception did not take place outside the United Kingdom (UK).   3.06

The distinction was dealt with in the government's evidence to the Investigatory Powers Tribunal in *Privacy International and Others v Secretary of State for Foreign and Commonwealth Affairs and Others*:[8]   3.07

[An] email from a person in London to a person in Birmingham will be an internal, not external, communication for the purposes of RIPA and the Code, whether or not it is routed via IP addresses outside the British Islands, because the intended recipient is not any of the servers that handle the communication whilst en route (whether that server be located inside, or outside, the British Islands). Indeed, the sender of the email cannot possibly know at the time of sending (and is highly unlikely to have any interest in) how that email is routed, or what servers will handle it on its way to the intended recipient.[9]

The government during the passage of what became RIPA recognized that internal communications will from time to time inexorably be caught up as part of a warrant intercepting external communications: 3.08

It is just not possible to ensure that only external communications are intercepted. That is because modern communications are often routed in ways that are not all intuitively obvious ... An

---

[7] Privacy and Security (n 4) paras 42–45.
[8] IPT/13/92/CH.
[9] Statement of Charles Farr (Farr Statement), para 129 https://www.privacyinternational.org/sites/default/files/Witness%20st%20of%20Charles%20Blandford%20Farr_0.pdf (accessed 31 May 2016).

internal communication—say, a message from London to Birmingham—may be handled on its journey by Internet service providers in, perhaps, two different countries outside the United Kingdom. We understand that. The communication might therefore be found on a link between those two foreign countries. Such a link should clearly be treated as external, yet it would contain at least this one internal communication. There is no way of filtering that out without intercepting the whole link including the internal communication.[10]

3.09 Where this occurred, the government stated:

In practice, this means (for example) that if the content of a Google search made by an individual known to be in the British Islands had been intercepted pursuant to an interception warrant under section 8(4) of RIPA, it could not be selected to be read, or even looked at, on the basis of any factor referable to that individual (save in the limited circumstances set out in sections 16(3)–(4)).[11]

3.10 These ambiguous and complex arrangements are at least in part responsible for the new Part 2, Chapter 1 IPA.

3.11 Section 15 IPA replaces the previous single interception warrant scheme and creates three types of warrants: targeted interception, targeted examination, and mutual assistance warrants.[12] Since section 15(5) provides matters common to both targeted and mutual assistance warrants these are considered first.

(b) *Targeted Warrants*

3.12 A targeted interception warrant authorizes or requires the person to whom it is addressed to secure, by any conduct described in it, to intercept communications and/or obtain secondary data. It can also authorize or require disclosure of the product obtained through the use of the warrant.[13]

3.13 The interception of communications is in the course of transmission by means of a postal or telecommunications system that must be described in the warrant and secondary data is obtained as a derivative of the interception. Disclosure is to the person to whom the warrant is addressed or someone acting on his or her behalf.[14]

3.14 A warrant to intercept communications and/or obtain secondary data only authorizes the person to whom it is addressed to secure it. Disclosure of the product obtained is limited to the warrant's addressee or someone acting on his or her behalf. It does not authorize disclosure to anyone else. Obtaining secondary data is provided for in section 16: see paragraphs 3.21 to 3.22 below.

(c) *Mutual Assistance Warrants*

3.15 Unlike a targeted interception warrant, a mutual assistance warrant is limited to the interception of communications (so not secondary data) and disclosure. It authorizes

---

[10] Lord Bassam, *Hansard*, col 323 (12 July 2000).
[11] Farr Statement (n 9) para 141.
[12] IPA, s 15(1)(a)–(c).
[13] ibid s 15(2).
[14] ibid s 15(2)(a)–(c).

or requires the person to whom it is addressed to secure, by any conduct described in the warrant, any one or more of three possible actions. The first is the making of a request, in accordance with an EU mutual assistance instrument or an international mutual assistance agreement, for the provision of any assistance of a kind described in the warrant.[15] The second is the provision to the competent authorities of a country or territory outside the UK, in accordance with such an instrument or agreement, of any assistance of a kind described in the warrant.[16] In both cases this is in connection with, or in the form of, an interception of communications. The third is the disclosure, in any manner described in the warrant, of anything obtained under the warrant to the person to whom the warrant is addressed or to any person acting on that person's behalf.[17]

(d) *Matters Common to Targeted Interception and Mutual Assistance Warrants*

3.16 In relation to either targeted interception or mutual assistance warrants the warrant, in addition to the conduct described in it, also authorizes a raft of other conduct including 'anything which it is necessary to undertake in order to do what is expressly authorised or required by the warrant'.[18] This encompasses the interception of communications not described in the warrant and obtaining secondary data from such communications.[19]

3.17 Two other forms of conduct are also authorized. First, any conduct by any person which is conduct in pursuance of a requirement imposed by or on behalf of the person to whom the warrant is addressed to be provided with assistance in giving effect to the warrant.[20] Secondly, any conduct for obtaining related systems data from any postal operator or telecommunications operator.[21] The terms 'related systems data' and 'relevant communication' in this second form of conduct are defined in section 15(6) IPA. The former means, in relation to a warrant, 'systems data relating to a relevant communication or to the sender or recipient, or intended recipient, of a relevant communication (whether or not a person)'. The latter is defined as any communication intercepted in accordance with the warrant in the course of its transmission by means of a postal service or telecommunication system, or, any communication from which secondary data is obtained.

(e) *Targeted Examination Warrants*

3.18 This warrant authorizes the person to whom it is addressed to carry out the selection of relevant content for examination, that would be otherwise a breach of the prohibition in section 152(4) (the prohibition on attempting to identify communications of individuals in the British Islands): see Chapter 7, paragraphs 7.47–7.51.[22]

---

[15] ibid s 15(4)(a).
[16] ibid s 15(4)(b).
[17] ibid s 15(4)(c).
[18] ibid s 15(5)(a).
[19] ibid s 15(5)(i)–(ii).
[20] ibid s 15(5)(b).
[21] ibid s 15(5)(c).
[22] ibid s 15(3).

3. Lawful Interception of Communications

3.19   The term 'relevant content', in relation to a targeted examination warrant, means any content of communications intercepted by an interception authorized or required by a bulk interception warrant under Chapter 1 of Part 6.[23]

3.20   Schedule 8 sets out the provisions enabling the combination of targeted interception warrants with certain other warrants or authorizations (including targeted examination warrants).[24] This is dealt with in Chapter 10, paragraphs 10.93–10.124.

(f) *Obtaining Secondary Data*

3.21   Section 16 applies only for the purposes of Part 2.[25] It makes provision in relation to communications transmitted by means of a postal service and by means of a telecommunication system. As to the former, references to obtaining secondary data from the communication are references to obtaining such data in the course of the transmission of the communication.[26] Secondary data in this connection means systems data which is comprised in, included as part of, attached to, or logically associated with the communication (whether by the sender or otherwise).[27]

3.22   In respect of the latter, references to obtaining secondary data from the communication are references to obtaining such data either while the communication is being transmitted, or at any time when the communication is stored in or by the system, whether before or after its transmission.[28] This reflects the changes in section 3 IPA: see Chapter 2, paragraphs 2.12–2.18. Secondary data includes that which relates to communications transmitted by means of a postal system but also identifying data which, is comprised in, included as part of, attached to, or logically associated with the communication (whether by the sender or otherwise), is capable of being logically separated from the remainder of the communication and, if it were so separated, would not reveal anything of what might reasonably be considered to be the meaning (if any) of the communication, disregarding any meaning arising from the fact of the communication or from any data relating to the transmission of the communication.[29] The terms 'systems data' and 'identifying data' are defined in section 263 IPA and dealt with in Chapter 1: see paragraphs 1.88–1.90.

(g) *Targets of Warrants*

3.23   A warrant issued under the provisions of Part 2, Chapter 1 may target a particular person, organization, or a single set of premises but the term also subsumes testing the apparatus and training activities.[30] This was not previously provided for under RIPA.

---

[23] ibid s 15(3).
[24] ibid s 15(7).
[25] ibid s 16(1).
[26] ibid s 3(7).
[27] ibid s 16(5).
[28] ibid s 16(3)(a)–(b).
[29] ibid s 16(6)(a)–(c).
[30] ibid s 17(1)(a)–(b) and (2)(c).

3.24 In addition, a targeted interception warrant or targeted examination warrant (so excluding mutual assistance warrants) may target a group of persons who share a common purpose or who carry on, or may carry on, a particular activity, more than one person or organization, or more than one set of premises, where the conduct authorized or required by the warrant is for the purposes of a single investigation or operation or testing or training activities.[31]

3.25 The meaning of the term 'testing or training activities' is determined by the nature of the warrant and in each case is pervasive. In the case of a targeted interception warrant it means the testing, maintenance, or development of apparatus, systems, or other capabilities relating to the interception of communications in the course of their transmission by means of a telecommunication system or to the obtaining of secondary data from communications transmitted by means of such a system, or the training of persons who carry out, or are likely to carry out such interception, or the obtaining of such data.[32] Where the warrant is a targeted examination warrant it means the testing, maintenance, or development of apparatus, systems, or other capabilities relating to the selection of relevant content for examination, or the training of persons who carry out, or are likely to carry out, the selection of relevant content for examination.[33]

C. ISSUING WARRANTS

3.26 There are nine domestic intercepting authorities: the heads of the intelligence services (MI5, MI6, and GCHQ), the National Crime Agency, the Police of the Metropolis, the Police Service of Northern Ireland, the Police Service of Scotland, Her Majesty's Revenue and Customs, and Defence Intelligence.[34]

3.27 In addition, it includes a person who is the competent authority of a country or territory outside the UK for the purposes of an EU mutual assistance instrument or an international mutual assistance agreement.[35]

3.28 An application for the issue of a warrant in this chapter may only be made on behalf of an intercepting authority by a person holding office under the Crown.[36]

1. Secretary of State's Power to Issue Warrants

(a) *Requirements*

3.29 On the application by or on behalf of an intercepting authority a targeted interception or mutual assistance warrant may be issued if four requirements are met.[37]

---

[31] ibid s 17(2)(a)–(c).
[32] ibid s 17(3)(a)(i)–(ii).
[33] ibid s 17(3)(b)(i)–(ii).
[34] ibid s 18(1)(a)–(g).
[35] ibid s 18(1)(h).
[36] ibid s 18(3).
[37] ibid s 19(1) and (3).

The first three are that Secretary of State must consider that the warrant is necessary on any of the grounds falling within section 20, that the conduct authorized by the warrant is proportionate to what is sought to be achieved by that conduct, and that satisfactory arrangements made for the purposes of sections 53 and 54 IPA (safeguards relating to disclosure and other matters) are in force in relation to the warrant.[38]

3.30 The fourth requirement is that, other than where the Secretary of State considers that there is an urgent need to issue the warrant, the decision to issue the warrant has been approved by a judicial commissioner.[39]

3.31 Applications for targeted examination warrants are limited to the intelligence agencies.[40] Again, the Secretary of State must be satisfied that the issue of the warrant is necessary or that one of the statutory grounds is met and that the conduct authorized is proportionate to the operational objective.[41] Two further requirements must then be met. The Secretary of State must consider that the warrant is or may be necessary to authorize the selection of relevant content for examination in breach of the prohibition in section 152(4) (prohibition on attempting to identify communications of individuals in the British Islands)[42] and except in urgent cases a judicial commissioner has approved the warrant.[43]

3.32 The scheme under section 19 IPA is subject to two prohibitions on the power of the Secretary of State to issue warrants. The first, in respect of all three warrant types, is that the application is a 'relevant Scottish application' and in respect of targeted interception warrants and targeted examination warrants that the warrant is necessary only for the purpose of preventing or detecting serious crime.[44] In neither type of case can warrants be issued. However, this provision does not prevent the Secretary of State from doing anything under this section for the purposes specified in section 2(2) of the European Communities Act 1972.[45]

2. Grounds on Which Warrants May Be Issued

3.33 Applications for targeted interception or targeted examination warrants can only be issued if it is necessary on grounds falling within section 20 IPA. It must be necessary on any one of three grounds: in the interests of national security;[46] for the purpose of preventing or detecting serious crime;[47] or in the interests of the economic well-being of the UK so far as those interests are also relevant to the interests

---

[38] ibid s 19(1)(a)–(c) and (3)(a)–(c).
[39] ibid s 19(1)(d) and (3)(d).
[40] ibid s 19(2).
[41] ibid s 19(2)(a)–(b).
[42] ibid s 19(2)(c).
[43] ibid s 19(2)(d).
[44] ibid s 19(4)(a)–(b).
[45] ibid s 19(5).
[46] ibid s 20(2)(a).
[47] ibid s 20(2)(b).

C. Issuing Warrants

of national security.[48] In relation to the third ground, a warrant may be considered necessary on this ground only if the information which it is considered necessary to obtain is information relating to the acts or intentions of persons outside the British Islands.[49] Necessary for the purposes of any of the grounds upon which a warrant made be obtained does not include the activities of a trade union in the British Islands 'of itself'.[50]

The position in respect of mutual assistance warrants is narrower. It must be necessary for the purpose of giving effect to the provisions of an EU mutual assistance instrument or an international mutual assistance agreement,[51] and the circumstances appear to the Secretary of State to be equivalent to those in which the Secretary of State would issue a warrant for the purposes of preventing or detecting serious crime.[52] 3.34

There is a prohibition on the issuing of a warrant if it is considered necessary for one of the statutory grounds only for the purpose of gathering evidence for use in any legal proceedings.[53] 3.35

(a) Warrants: Scotland (Prevention or Detection of Crime)

The Scottish Ministers may, on an application made by or on behalf of any of the intercepting authorities, issue a targeted interception warrant if the application is a 'relevant Scottish application'[54] and the Scottish Ministers consider that the warrant is necessary for the purposes of preventing or detecting serious crime.[55] Necessary for this purpose does not include the activities of a trade union in the British Islands 'of itself'.[56] In addition, there are mirror provisions to those applying to the Secretary of State set out in section 19(1)(b)–(d) and (3)(b)–(d), namely proportionality, arrangements (safeguards relating to disclosure) and, other than in urgent cases, a requirement for judicial approval by a commissioner.[57] 3.36

(b) Relevant Scottish Application

The term 'relevant Scottish application' is defined in section 22 IPA. It is not straightforward. It is subject to three conditions one of which must be met before a warrant can be issued. Condition A relates to targeted interception of examination warrants. Conditions B and C relate to mutual assistance warrants.[58] 3.37

Condition A is that the application is for the issue of a targeted interception warrant or a targeted examination warrant, and the warrant, if issued, would relate to 3.38

---

[48] ibid s 20(2)(c).
[49] ibid s 20(4).
[50] ibid s 20(6).
[51] ibid s 20(3)(a).
[52] ibid s 20(3)(b).
[53] ibid s 20(5).
[54] ibid s 21(1)(a).
[55] ibid s 21(1)(b).
[56] ibid s 21(6).
[57] ibid s 22(1)(c)–(e).
[58] ibid s 22(1).

3. Lawful Interception of Communications

either a person or who is or premises which are in Scotland (or is reasonably believed by the applicant to be in Scotland), at the time of the issue of the warrant.[59]

3.39 For Condition B to be satisfied the application must meet two requirements. The first is compliance with section 13(4)(a) and (c) IPA (ie that the application if granted would constitute a mutual assistance warrant for the purposes of that section) so the making of a request or the making of such a request and disclosure.[60] The second requirement is geographical: the application must be made by, or on behalf of, the chief constable of the Police Service of Scotland, or by, or on behalf of, the Commissioners for Her Majesty's Revenue and Customs or the Director General of the National Crime Agency for the purpose of preventing or detecting serious crime in Scotland.[61]

3.40 Condition C requires that the application is for the issue of a mutual assistance warrant that would comply with section 13(4)(b) and (c) so the provision of assistance or the provision of such assistance and disclosure.[62] The geographical requirement is that the warrant, if issued, would relate to a person who is or premises, which are in Scotland, or is reasonably believed by the applicant to be in Scotland, at the time of the issue of the warrant.[63]

(c) *Warrants: Scotland (Other Grounds)*

3.41 The provisions in respect of an application to issue a targeted examination warrant made by or on behalf of the head of an intelligence service to Scottish Ministers broadly mirror those applicable to the Secretary of State in section 19(2)(b)–(d) IPA. However, the application must be a relevant Scottish application and the Scottish Ministers consider that the warrant is necessary on the ground that it is necessary for the prevention and detection of serious crime.

3.42 Similarly, the provisions in relation to an application to Scottish Ministers to issue a mutual assistance warrant by or on behalf of an intercepting authority reflect the scheme under section 19(3)(b)–(d)[64] subject to the same requirements (i.e. it is a relevant Scottish application and for the prevention and detection of serious crime).[65] However, two further criteria must also be met. The first is that it is necessary for the purpose of giving effect to the provisions of an EU mutual assistance instrument or an international mutual assistance agreement[66] and the second is that the circumstances must appear to the Scottish Ministers to be equivalent to those in which the Scottish Ministers would issue a warrant on the ground that it is necessary for the purposes of the prevention and detection of serious crime.[67]

---

[59] ibid s 22(2)(a)–(b)(i)–(ii).
[60] ibid s 22(3)(a)(i)–(ii).
[61] ibid s 22(3)(b)(i)–(ii).
[62] ibid s 22(4)(a)(i)–(ii).
[63] ibid s 22(4)(b)(i)–(ii).
[64] ibid s 21(1)(c)–(e).
[65] ibid s 21(1)(a)–(b).
[66] ibid s 21(4)(b)(i).
[67] ibid s 21(4)(b)(ii)

D. Approval of Warrants by Judicial Commissioners

3.43 In being satisfied that it is necessary and proportionate for the purposes of section 19(1) and (3) the same test applies as in section 17(4), namely, whether the information which it is considered necessary to obtain under the warrant could reasonably be obtained by other means.

3.44 The prohibition in section 20(5) IPA that a warrant may not be considered necessary if it is considered necessary on any ground only for the purpose of gathering evidence for use in any legal proceedings is repeated in section 21(5), the only distinction being that applications to Scottish Ministers are limited to the single ground of prevention and detection of serious crime.

D. APPROVAL OF WARRANTS BY JUDICIAL COMMISSIONERS

1. Introduction

3.45 The oversight arrangements are set out in Chapter 9. One of the Independent Reviewers of Terrorism Legislation, David Anderson QC's recommendations in 'A Question of Trust' was the introduction of judicial authorization. A new framework for judicial approval is introduced in sections 21 to 23 IPA. It emulates the scheme under RIPA 2000 for the approval of intrusive surveillance, so it is not entirely novel. Approval is distinct from authorization: see eg *Chatwani and Others v National Crime Agency* [2015] UKIPTrib 15_84_88-CH, para 15.

2. Non-urgent Cases

3.46 A judicial commissioner, when determining whether to approve the decision by an interception authority to issue a warrant under Part 2, Chapter 1, must review two aspects of the decision. The first is whether the warrant is necessary on any of the relevant grounds (in the case of an application for a warrant made to Scottish Ministers, the only ground available is prevention and detection of serious crime). The second is that the conduct that would be authorized by the warrant is proportionate to what is sought to be achieved by that conduct.[68] The principles to be applied are the same principles that would be applied by a court on an application for judicial review and the judicial commissioner should 'consider the [necessity and proportionality of the application] with a sufficient degree of care' so as to ensure compliance with section 2 of the IPA (general duties in relation to privacy): see Chapter 2, paragraphs 2.08–2.10.[69]

3.47 Where a judicial commissioner refuses to approve a decision to issue a warrant written reasons for the refusal must be provided to the person who decided to issue it.[70] In such an event and assuming the judicial commissioner was not an

---

[68] ibid s 23(1)(a)–(b).
[69] ibid s 23(2)(a)–(b).
[70] ibid s 23(4).

Investigatory Powers Commissioner, the application for approval may be put before an Investigatory Powers Commissioner for a decision whether or not to approve the decision to issue the warrant.[71]

3. Urgent Cases

3.48 Where a warrant under Part 2, Chapter 1 has been issued without the approval of a judicial commissioner, and the person who decided to issue the warrant considered that there was an urgent need to issue it, the person who decided to issue the warrant must inform a judicial commissioner that it has been issued.[72]

3.49 The judicial commissioner must then, before the end of the relevant period (the period ending with the third working day after the day of issue) decide whether to approve the decision to issue the warrant, and provide notification of the decision to the person who issued it.[73]

3.50 Where a judicial commissioner refuses to approve the decision to issue a warrant, the warrant ceases to have effect (unless already cancelled), and it may not be renewed. There is no right in such circumstances to then ask the Investigatory Powers Commissioner to review the decision.[74]

(a) Failure to Approve Warrants Issued in Urgent Cases

3.51 Where a judicial commissioner refuses to approve the decision to issue a warrant in an urgent case, the person to whom the warrant was addressed must, so far as is reasonably practicable, secure that anything in the process of being done under the warrant stops as soon as possible.[75]

3.52 The judicial commissioner (so presumably the judicial commissioner refusing to approve the decision to issue) also has powers to direct that any of the material obtained under the warrant is destroyed, impose conditions as to the use or retention of any of that material or in the case of a targeted examination warrant, impose conditions as to the use of any relevant content selected for examination under the warrant.[76]

3.53 The persons affected by the refusal 'an affected person'—either the person who decided to issue the warrant—or, the person to whom it was addressed have a freestanding right to make representations to the judicial commissioner who has refused to approve it as to what should happen to the material obtained as a result of the warrant having been issued.[77] The judicial commissioner can also formally require representations from an affected party.[78]

---

[71] ibid s 23(5).
[72] ibid s 24(1)–(2).
[73] ibid s 24(3).
[74] ibid s 24(4)(a)–(b).
[75] ibid s 25(2).
[76] ibid s 25(3)(a)–(c).
[77] ibid s 25(5)(a)–(b).
[78] ibid s 25(4)(a).

E. Additional Safeguards

3.54 Where representations are received, whether as a result of a formal requirement or not, the judicial commissioner must have regard to these when deciding what should happen to the material.[79]

3.55 There is a right of review limited to the person who decided to issue the warrant who may ask the Investigatory Powers Commissioner to review the decision.[80] On such a review under the Investigatory Powers Commissioner may confirm the original decision, or make a fresh determination.[81]

3.56 No unlawfulness arises from anything done or in the process of being done before it could be stopped or which it is not reasonably practicable to stop under the warrant before it ceases to have effect.[82]

E. ADDITIONAL SAFEGUARDS

1. Members of Parliament

3.57 Where an interception authority makes an application to the Secretary of State for the issue of either a targeted interception warrant (where the purpose is to authorize or require the interception of communications sent by, or intended for, a person who is a member of a relevant legislature) or a targeted examination warrant (where the purpose is to authorize the selection for examination of the content of such communications), the Secretary of State must before deciding whether to issue the warrant, consult the prime minister.[83]

3.58 The term 'member of a relevant legislature' means a member of either House of Parliament, a member of the Scottish Parliament, a member of either the National Assembly for Wales or the Northern Ireland Assembly, or a member of the European Parliament elected for the UK.[84]

2. Items Subject to Legal Privilege

3.59 Chapter 1, Part 2 IPA provides for two circumstances relating to legal privilege: deliberate acquisition and selection for examination following acquisition, whether deliberate or incidental. In each case, arrangements must be in place under sections 53 or 150 (safeguards relating to retention and disclosure of material), depending on the circumstances, prior to the warrant being issued.[85]

3.60 Where an application is made for a targeted interception or mutual assistance warrant to authorize or require the interception of items subject to legal privilege

---

[79] ibid s 25(4)(b).
[80] ibid s 25(6).
[81] ibid s 25(7)(a)–(b).
[82] ibid 2 25(8)(a)–(b).
[83] ibid s 26(1)–(2).
[84] ibid s 26(3)(a)–(e).
[85] ibid s 27(4)(b) and (9).

3. Lawful Interception of Communications

or the purpose of a targeted examination warrant is to select items subject to legal privilege for examination then section 27 IPA imposes a number of additional conditions. The person issuing the warrant must have regard to the public interest in the confidentiality of items subject to legal privilege and consider that there are exceptional and compelling circumstances that make it necessary to do so.[86] The threshold of 'exceptional and compelling' will not be met unless the public interest in obtaining the information outweighs the public interest in maintaining the confidentiality of the legal privilege; there are no other means by which the information could reasonably be obtained and, in cases where the substantive ground upon which the warrant is obtained in the prevention and detection of serious crime, obtaining the information is necessary for the preventing death or significant injury.[87]

3.61 The application must also contain a statement that the purpose is or includes the acquisition or selection for examination of items subject to legal privilege.[88] A warrant may not be issued if the only basis for it being necessary is on the ground of the economic well-being of the UK.[89]

3.62 The position is broadly similar in cases where there is a risk of items subject to legal privilege being included in 'relevant communications'.[90] For the purposes of section 27, this is either that acquired through targeted interception or mutual assistance warrant or the communications selected for examination.[91] In such cases, in addition to a statement that there is a likelihood of items of legal privilege being included, an assessment of how likely this is must be included on the warrant.[92]

3.63 There is detailed provision for cases where the material sought has been created or is held with the intention of furthering a criminal purpose (and which is therefore not or no longer privileged). In cases where a targeted interception or mutual assistance warrant seeks to obtain such material or a targeted examination warrant authorizes the selection of such material for examination, three conditions arise. First, the application must contain a statement that the material would, but for it being created or held for this purpose, be subject to legal privilege. The second, in the case of a targeted examination warrant, is that the application must specifically authorize the selection of such items. The third condition is that the application must set out the reasons for believing the material was created or held for such a purpose.[93] The person issuing the warrant may only then do so if it is considered that the material is likely to have been created or is held with the intention of furthering a criminal purpose.[94]

---

[86] ibid s 27(3)–(4)(a).
[87] ibid s 27(6).
[88] ibid s 27(2).
[89] ibid s 27(5).
[90] ibid s 27(7).
[91] ibid s 27(10)(a)–(b).
[92] ibid s 27(8)(a)–(b).
[93] ibid s 27(11)–(12).
[94] ibid s 27(13).

3. Journalistic Material and Sources

3.64 Journalistic material means, in summary, material created or acquired for the purposes of journalism but not material created or acquired with the intention of furthering a criminal purpose. Confidential journalistic material is either a communication consisting of journalistic material which either the sender, recipient, or intended recipient of the communication holds in confidence or other journalistic material which a person holds in confidence.[95] A journalistic source is 'an individual who provides material intending the recipient to use it for the purposes of journalism or knowing that it is likely to be so used'.[96]

3.65 The position in respect of confidential journalistic material and journalistic sources follows a similar procedure under sections 28 and 29 IPA, introduced at a late stage of the Bill's evolution, although the threshold is considerably lower than that for legal privilege. If the application for a targeted interception or mutual assistance warrant relates to communications which are or contain confidential journalistic material or is a targeted examination warrant authorizing the selection of journalistic material that is confidential journalistic material for examination, then in both cases it must contain a statement to this effect.[97]

3.66 The person to who the application is made may only issue the warrant if arrangements are in place under sections 53 or 150 (safeguards relating to retention and disclosure of material)[98] that include specific arrangements for the handling, retention, use, and destruction of any confidential journalistic material.[99]

F. WARRANTS: FORMALITIES

3.67 The decision to issue a warrant under Chapter 1 is the Secretary of State's alone, or in the case of a warrant to be issued by the Scottish Ministers, a member of the Scottish Government.[100] Whoever issues it, the person who has taken the decision to do so must, unless it is not reasonably practicable, sign it.[101] In such circumstances, the requirement to sign may be delegated to a designated senior official and the warrant must contain a statement to this effect.[102] This derogation does not obviate the requirement for the minister to have personally and expressly authorized the issue of the warrant and this too must be stated in it in such circumstances.[103] However, the position is different for mutual assistance warrants: see paragraph 3.34 above.[104]

---

[95] The full definition can be found in ibid s 264.
[96] ibid s 263(1).
[97] ibid s 28(2) and 29(2).
[98] ibid s 28(4).
[99] ibid s 28(3) and 29(3).
[100] ibid s 30(1).
[101] ibid s 30(2)–(4).
[102] ibid s 30(5)(a).
[103] ibid s 30(5)(b).
[104] ibid s 30(3)(b).

3. Lawful Interception of Communications

3.68 The post of 'senior official' for the purpose of a warrant to be issued by the Secretary of State means a member of the Senior Civil Service or a member of the Senior Management Structure of Her Majesty's Diplomatic Service. In the case of a warrant to be issued by the Scottish Ministers, it means a member of the staff of the Scottish Administration who is a member of the Senior Civil Service.[105]

1. Requirements that Must Be Met by Warrants

3.69 There are a number of additional formalities that a warrant must comply with. It must specify whether it is a targeted interception warrant, a targeted examination warrant, or a mutual assistance warrant and must be addressed to the person by whom, or on whose behalf, the application for the warrant was made.[106]

3.70 Where the warrant is applied for in reliance of section 17(1) IPA (particular person or organization, or to a single set of premises), it must name or describe that person or organization or those premises.[107] If it relates to more than one person or organization, or more than one set of premises but where the conduct authorized or required by the warrant is for the purposes of a single investigation or operation, the warrant must describe the investigation or operation, and name, or describe as many of those persons or organizations, or as many of those sets of premises, as it is reasonably practicable to name or describe.[108] References to communications from or intended to a person or organization, includes those owned, controlled, or operated by that person or organization.[109]

3.71 If the warrant is applied for under section 17(2) IPA (a group of persons who share a common purpose or who carry on, or may carry on, a particular activity), it must describe that purpose or activity, and name or describe as many of those persons as it is reasonably practicable to name or describe.[110]

3.72 If the warrant relates to any testing or training activities under section 17(3) IPA, it must first describe those activities. Secondly, it must name or describe insofar as it is reasonably practicable to do so, in the case of a targeted interception warrant communications or secondary data from or intended for the person who will or may be the subject of the interception. In the case of a targeted examination warrant, the content of communications from, or intended for that person that may be selected for examination.[111]

3.73 Where either a targeted interception warrant or mutual assistance warrant authorizes or requires the interception of communications described in the warrant, or a targeted examination warrant authorizes the selection of the content of communications for examination, the warrant must specify the addresses, numbers, apparatus,

---

[105] ibid s 30(6).
[106] ibid s 31(1)–(2).
[107] ibid s 31(3).
[108] ibid s 31(5).
[109] ibid 31(10).
[110] ibid s 31(4).
[111] ibid s 31(6)–(7).

or other factors, or combination of factors, that are to be used for identifying the communications.[112]

The terms factor and combination of factors, are subject to non-exhaustive definition in section 31(9) IPA. It must be one that identifies communications that are likely to be or to include communications from, or intended for, any person named or described in the warrant, or communications originating on, or intended for transmission to, any premises named or described in the warrant. 3.74

2. Duration of Warrants

In general terms a warrant issued under Part 2, Chapter 1 IPA ceases to have effect after a period of six months from the date of issue.[113] It may be renewed prior to expiration, in which case it will last for a further six months from the day after it would have otherwise expired.[114] As with RIPA, there is no limit to the number of times a warrant can be renewed. A warrant may also be cancelled, in which case it ceases to have effect from that date.[115] 3.75

If it is an urgent warrant, that is, a warrant issued without judicial approval from a judicial commissioner and where the person who issued it considered there was an urgent need to issue it,[116] it ceases to have effect on the fifth working day after the date of issue: see paragraphs 3.48–3.56 above.[117] 3.76

3. Renewal of Warrants

A warrant may be renewed at any time prior to expiration (the 'renewal period'), by 'an instrument' issued by the person who issued it or, presumably, his or her successor in office. Instrument is not defined but is likely to be some form to be used for the purpose of renewal.[118] The renewal period is in urgent cases the relevant period or in every other case the period of thirty days ending with the day the warrant would cease to have effect if it was not renewed.[119] 3.77

Four conditions must be met before renewal is possible. The first is that the warrant continues to be necessary on any of the grounds set out in sections 20 or 21(4), as appropriate.[120] The second is that the conduct that would be authorized by the renewed warrant continues to be proportionate to that which is sought to be achieved by that conduct.[121] The third is that, in the case of a targeted examination warrant, the appropriate person considers that the warrant continues to be necessary 3.78

---

[112] ibid s 31(8).
[113] ibid s 32(2)(b)(i).
[114] ibid s 32(2)(b)(ii).
[115] ibid s 32(1)(a).
[116] ibid s 32(3).
[117] ibid s 32(2)(a).
[118] ibid s 33(1).
[119] ibid s 33(5)(a)–(b).
[120] ibid s 33(2)(a).
[121] ibid s 33(2)(b).

to authorize the selection of relevant content for examination in breach of the prohibition in section 152(4). The final condition is that the decision to renew the warrant has been approved by a judicial commissioner.[122]

3.79 As with an original warrant, the decision to renew a warrant must be taken personally by the minister and the instrument renewing the warrant must be signed by that person.[123]

3.80 Any renewal of a warrant requires approval by a judicial commissioner as it applied in relation to a decision to issue a warrant.[124]

3.81 The provisions in respect of Members of Parliament and items subject to legal privilege apply in relation to a decision to renew a warrant as they applied in relation to a decision to issue a warrant.[125]

3.82 Certain mutual assistance warrants are subject to additional provisions: see paragraphs 3.102 to 3.106 below.[126]

4. Modification of Warrants

(a) Modification of Warrants Issued by the Secretary of State or Scottish Ministers

3.83 A warrant issued under Part 2, Chapter 1 may be modified at any time by an instrument issued by the person making the modification.[127] The scope of modification is limited to adding, varying, or removing a name or description of a person or set of premises to which the original warrant relates or any factor specified in it.[128] Insofar as the modification relates to adding or varying a name or description (so not including removing a name or description) it is categorized as a major modification.[129] A minor modification includes the removal of a name or description and adding, varying, or removing any factor specified in the warrant in accordance with section 31(8) IPA.[130] The provisions are only concerned with modifications that affect the conduct authorized or required by it.[131]

3.84 There is no power to modify the details required under section 17(1) IPA (particular person, organization or single set of premises), in a warrant where this is the only proposed modification.[132]

3.85 As with the issue of the warrant, the decision to modify must be taken personally by the person making the modification and that person must also sign the instrument making the modification.[133]

---

[122] ibid s 33(2)(c)–(d).
[123] ibid s 33(6).
[124] ibid s 33(7).
[125] ibid s 33(8).
[126] ibid s 33(10).
[127] ibid s 34(1).
[128] ibid s 34(2)(a)–(b).
[129] ibid s 34(5)(a).
[130] ibid s 34(2)(b) and (5)(b).
[131] ibid s 34(6).
[132] ibid s 34(3).
[133] ibid s 34(4).

F. Warrants: Formalities

(b) *Persons Entitled to Make Modifications*

3.86 A major modification may be made by the Secretary of State or, in appropriate cases, a member of the Scottish Government or a senior official acting on behalf of his or her behalf. Where the senior official performs this function, the minister or member of the Scottish Government must be notified personally of the modification and the reasons for it.[134]

3.87 A minor modification may be made by any of the persons identified in paragraph 3.86 and the person to whom the warrant is addressed or a person who holds a senior position in the same public authority (these are limited to intercepting authorities) as the person to whom the warrant is addressed.[135] However, such persons are also empowered to make a major modification where there is an urgent need to do so.[136]

3.88 The provisions about persons entitled to make modifications are subject to the special rules in cases involving Members of Parliament, lawyers, and journalists.[137] The scheme for issuing a warrant in these cases under sections 26 to 29 IPA applies to major modifications.[138] In the case of a member of Parliament, the Secretary of State must make any modification personally.[139] In cases involving legal privilege or confidential journalistic material, the Secretary of State or, in appropriate cases, a member of the Scottish Government, must make the modification.[140] However, a senior official may sign the instrument for the Secretary of State or Scottish Minister in urgent cases.[141] In each case, the modification does not take effect until a judicial commissioner has approved it.[142] The provisions in relation to judicial approval in such cases apply to modifications and section 23 IPA should be read accordingly.[143]

3.89 A senior official may sign the instrument for the Secretary of State or Scottish Minister where it is not reasonably practicable for them to do so but it must then contain a statement that this is the case and that the minister has personally and expressly authorized the modification.[144]

3.90 If at any time any of the persons considers that any factor specified in a warrant in accordance with section 35(2) IPA (addresses, numbers, apparatus), is no longer relevant for identifying communications which, in the case of that warrant, are likely to be, or to include, communications falling within section 31(9)(a) or (b) IPA (identification communications including from or intended for any person or premises), the person must modify the warrant by removing that factor.[145]

---

[134] ibid s 35(1)(a)–(c).
[135] ibid s 35(2) (a)–(e).
[136] ibid s 35(3).
[137] ibid s 35(4).
[138] ibid s 35(4).
[139] ibid s 36(5)(a).
[140] ibid s 36(6)(a)(i).
[141] ibid s 36(6)(a)(ii).
[142] ibid s 36(5)(b) and (6)(b).
[143] ibid s 36(7)(a)–(c).
[144] ibid s 36(8) and (9).
[145] ibid s 36(10).

3.91 The range of persons holding a senior position in a public or intercepting authority is broad. In the case of any of the intelligence services, the person is a member of the Senior Civil Service or a member of the Senior Management Structure of Her Majesty's Diplomatic Service, or the person holds a position in the intelligence service of equivalent seniority to such a person.[146]

3.92 In the National Crime Agency, this is a grade 2 officer or above. In the metropolitan police force, the Police Service of Northern Ireland or the Police Service of Scotland, a person is of or above the rank of superintendent. In Her Majesty's Revenue and Customs, the person is a member of the Senior Civil Service and, in the case of the Ministry of Defence, the person is a member of the Senior Civil Service, or the person is of or above the rank of brigadier, commodore, or air commodore.[147]

(c) *Modifications: Requirement to Notify*

3.93 Where a modification has been made a judicial commissioner must be notified as soon as reasonably practicable of this and the reasons for it.[148] Modifications in urgent cases and those involving safeguarded information concerning parliamentarians, lawyers, and journalists are not subject to this requirement.[149]

3.94 Where the senior official has made a modification in any case, the Secretary of State or, as the case may be, a member of the Scottish Government, must be notified personally of and the reasons for the modification.[150]

(d) *Approval of Major Modifications: Urgent Cases*

3.95 The requirements consequent on a major modification of a warrant under section 35(3) are set out in section 38 IPA. The key actors are the appropriate person, the senior official (see paragraph 3.68 above) and designated senior official. If it is a case involving a major modification of a warrant it is 'a designated senior official' but if it relates to cases involving Members of Parliament, lawyers, and journalists, it is a judicial commissioner.[151] The latter is defined as a senior official designated by the Secretary of State or, where appropriate, Scottish Ministers for the purposes of section 35 IPA.[152]

3.96 The first requirement is on the person who made the modification who must inform a designated senior official that it has been made.[153]

3.97 The second requirement is that the appropriate person must, before the end of the fifth working day following the modification (the relevant period), decide whether to approve the decision to make the modification, and notify the person

---

[146] ibid s 35(6)(a)(i)–(ii).
[147] ibid s 35(6)(b)–(e).
[148] ibid s 37(1).
[149] ibid s 37(2)(a)–(b).
[150] ibid s 37(3).
[151] ibid s 38(4)(a)–(b).
[152] ibid s 38(4).
[153] ibid s 38(3).

of the senior official's decision.[154] Where this is a designated senior official, a judicial commissioner must be notified as soon as reasonably practicable after the decision has been made of what the decision is and, if it is to approve, particulars of the modification.[155] The Secretary of State or, where appropriate, Scottish Ministers must also be notified personally of the matters notified to the judicial commissioner.[156]

3.98 In the event the appropriate person refuses to approve the decision to make the modification there are two practical consequences: the warrant has effect as if the modification had not been made and as far as reasonably practicable secure that anything in the process of being done under the warrant as a result of the modification ceases as soon as possible.[157] Where the appropriate person is a judicial commissioner, there is no right to have the decision reviewed by the Investigatory Powers Commissioner. However, this does not affect the lawfulness of anything done under the warrant as a result of the modification before it ceases to have effect (this must mean up to the time when it was reasonably practicable to secure anything in the process of being done is stopped).[158] Neither does anything done before it could be stopped or anything done that it was not reasonably practicable to stop.[159]

5. Cancellation of Warrants

3.99 Any of the appropriate persons have discretion to cancel a warrant issued under Chapter 1 at any time.[160]

3.100 There are two circumstances where it is mandatory for any of the appropriate persons to cancel a Chapter 1 warrant: where they consider a warrant issued is no longer necessary on any relevant grounds (those set out in section 20 and, where appropriate, section 21(4)),[161] or the conduct authorized by the warrant is no longer proportionate to what is sought to be achieved by that conduct.[162]

3.101 Where a warrant is cancelled under section 39 IPA, the person to whom the warrant was addressed must, so far as is reasonably practicable, secure that anything in the process of being done under the warrant stops as soon as possible.[163] There is no scope to renew a warrant cancelled under this section.[164]

---

[154] ibid s 38(5).
[155] ibid s 38(6)(a)(i)–(ii).
[156] ibid s 38(6)(b).
[157] ibid s 38(7)(a)–(b).
[158] ibid s 38(8)(a).
[159] ibid s 38(8)(b).
[160] ibid s 39(1).
[161] ibid s 39(2)(a).
[162] ibid s 39(2)(b).
[163] ibid s 39(5).
[164] ibid s 39(6).

6. Special Rules for Certain Mutual Assistance Warrants

3.102 Within the category of mutual assistance warrants special rules apply where the warrant is a 'relevant mutual assistance warrant'. This is a mutual assistance warrant (see paragraphs 3.15–3.17, above) issued for the purposes of a request for assistance made under an EU or international mutual assistance instrument or agreement by the competent authorities of a country or territory outside the UK and either the interception subject is or the targeted property is also outside the UK.[165]

3.103 The decision to issue and renew a relevant mutual assistance warrant may be taken by a senior official designated by the Secretary of State for that purpose.[166] In both cases, the warrant must contain a statement that the warrant is a relevant mutual warrant (i.e. that it is issued for the purposes of a request for assistance made under an EU or international mutual assistance instrument or agreement and specify whether it relates to the interception subject or premises).[167]

3.104 The references in section 33 IPA (renewal of warrants), to the 'appropriate person' include, in the case of a mutual assistance warrant, references to that senior official.[168] The designation of 'senior official' has the same meaning as that set out in section 30(6)(a) IPA: see paragraph 3.68, above.[169]

3.105 In cases where a relevant mutual assistance warrant was issued or the last renewal was by a senior official and the Secretary of State or senior official believes that the interception subject is in the UK, that person must cancel the warrant in accordance with the provisions in section 39 IPA.[170]

3.106 The reference to 'interception subject' only appears in section 40 IPA, notwithstanding section 17 IPA, which deals with 'subject-matter of warrants' contemplates the scope and reach of the warrants available under Part 2, Chapter 1. In relation to a relevant mutual assistance warrant, section 39(8) defines this as meaning 'the person, group of persons or organization about whose communications information is sought by the interception to which the warrant relates'.

7. Implementation of Warrants

3.107 Section 41 IPA relates to the implementation of targeted interception and mutual assistance warrants.

3.108 In giving effect to a warrant to which this section applies, the intercepting authority may if it needs to act through, or together with, such other persons as the intercepting authority may require to provide the authority with assistance.[171] Where it requires such assistance the intercepting authority may serve

---

[165] ibid s 40(1)(a)–(b).
[166] ibid s 40(2) and (4).
[167] ibid s 40(3) and (5).
[168] ibid s 40(4).
[169] ibid s 40(8).
[170] ibid s 40(7).
[171] ibid s 41(2).

or make arrangements to serve a copy of the warrant, including outside of the UK, on any person who it considers may be able to provide such assistance.[172] Service outside the UK is dealt with in section 42(3)–(5) IPA: see paragraphs 3.111–3.114 below.

The provision of assistance in giving effect to either type of warrant includes any disclosure to the intercepting authority, or to persons acting on behalf of the intercepting authority, of anything obtained under the warrant.[173]

3.109

Service of a copy of the warrant envisages service of it in its entirety but also includes service of one or more schedules contained in the warrant with the omission of the remainder of the warrant, and the service of a copy of the warrant with the omission of any schedule contained in the warrant.[174]

3.110

8. Service of Warrants outside the United Kingdom

Where service of a copy of a warrant on a person outside the UK is necessary, there are a number of ways that this can take place under section 42, although it is not exhaustive (and includes service by electronic or other means).

3.111

Service must take place in such a way so as to bring the contest of the warrant to the attention of the person who the intercepting authority considers may be able to provide assistance in relation to it.[175]

3.112

Methods of service include serving a copy of the warrant at the person's principal office within the UK[176] or, if the person has no such office in the UK, at any place in the UK where the person carries on business or conducts activities. If the person has specified an address in the UK as one at which the person, or someone on the person's behalf, will accept service of documents of the same description as a copy of a warrant, service can take place by serving it at that address.[177]

3.113

Service can also take effect by making a copy of the warrant available for inspection whether to the person or his or her agent at a place in the UK.[178] However, this is only permissible where it is not reasonably practicable for a copy to be served by any other means and the intercepting authority (the person to whom it is addressed) takes such steps, as the authority considers appropriate for the purpose of bringing the contents of the warrant, and the availability of a copy for inspection, to the attention of the person.[179] These steps must be taken as soon as reasonably practicable after the copy of the warrant is made available for inspection.[180]

3.114

---

[172] ibid s 41(3) and (4).
[173] ibid s 41(5).
[174] ibid s 41(6)(a)–(b).
[175] ibid s 42(2).
[176] ibid s 42(3)(a).
[177] ibid s 42(3)(b).
[178] ibid s 42(3)(c).
[179] ibid s 42(4).
[180] ibid s 42(5).

9. Duty of Postal and Telecommunications Operators

3.115 The consequence of service of a copy of a warrant is to impose a duty on 'a relevant operator' to take all steps for giving effect to the warrant that are notified to the relevant operator by or on behalf of the intercepting authority[181] and which would not otherwise be reasonably practicable for it to take.[182] Where they knowingly fail to do so, it is an offence.

3.116 The term 'relevant operator' means a postal operator or a telecommunications operator and it is irrelevant whether or not it is in the UK.[183] However, where it is outside the UK a determination whether it is reasonably practicable for a relevant operator outside the UK to take any steps in a country or territory outside the UK for giving effect to a warrant, must take into account at least two factors: first, any requirements or restrictions under the law of that country or territory that are relevant to the taking of those steps;[184] and, secondly, the extent to which it is reasonably practicable to give effect to the warrant in a way that does not breach any of those requirements or restrictions.[185]

3.117 Where obligations have been imposed on a relevant operator under section 253 IPA (maintenance of technical capability), the steps that it is reasonably practicable for it to take include every step that it would have been reasonably practicable for it to take if it had complied with all of those obligations.[186]

(a) *Offence of Failing to Comply with Duty*

3.118 A person who knowingly fails to comply with the duty is guilty of an either way offence. On summary conviction in England and Wales, he or she is liable to imprisonment for a term not exceeding twelve months (or six months if the offence was committed before the commencement of section 154(1) of the Criminal Justice Act 2003), or to a fine, or both.[187] On summary conviction in Scotland to imprisonment for a term not exceeding twelve months, or to a fine not exceeding the statutory maximum, or both.[188] In Northern Ireland, the maximum sentence on summary conviction is imprisonment for a term not exceeding six months, or to a fine not exceeding the statutory maximum, or both.[189]

3.119 On conviction on indictment, the maximum sentence is imprisonment for a term not exceeding two years or to a fine, or both.[190]

---

[181] ibid s 43(1).
[182] ibid s 43(4).
[183] ibid s 43(2).
[184] ibid s 43(5)(a).
[185] ibid s 43(5)(b).
[186] ibid s 43(6).
[187] ibid s 43(7)(a).
[188] ibid s 43(7)(b).
[189] ibid s 43(7)(c).
[190] ibid s 43(7)(d).

The duty imposed is enforceable by civil proceedings by the Secretary of State for an injunction, or for specific performance of a statutory duty under section 45 of the Court of Session Act 1988, or for any other appropriate relief.[191] 3.120

G. OTHER FORMS OF LAWFUL INTERCEPTION

1. Consent

Where the sender and the intended recipient of the communication to be intercepted both consent to its interception it may be authorized under section 37.[192] 3.121

If the communication is one sent by, or intended for a person who has consented to its interception then the interception may be authorized if surveillance of the interception has been authorized under Part II of RIPA or RIP(S)A:[193] as the application of this see *R v McDonald, Rafferty and O'Farrell*.[194] 3.122

2. Interception for Administrative, Enforcement, or Regulatory Purposes

Sections 45 to 48 IPA provide for interception 'for administrative or enforcement purposes'. 3.123

The first category is interception by providers of postal or telecommunications services. The interception of a communication may be authorized under section 45(1)(a) IPA if it is carried out by or on behalf of a person who provides a postal or telecommunications service. The interception must be for one of the three purposes set out in section 45(2) IPA, the first of which is the provision or operation of the service.[195] This is defined as including, so is not exhaustive, anything done for the purpose of identifying, combating, or preventing any thing that could affect any system providing the service or apparatus attached to the system.[196] 3.124

The second purpose relates to the enforcement in relation to the service of any statutory provision relating to the use of postal or telecommunications services or the content of communications transmitted by means of such services.[197] The third purpose relates to the provision of services or facilities aimed at preventing or restricting the viewing or publication of the content of communications transmitted by such services.[198] 3.125

The second category relates to interception by businesses etc for monitoring and record-keeping purposes.[199] These replace the provisions in RIPA, Part I relating 3.126

---

[191] ibid s 43(8).
[192] ibid s 44(1).
[193] ibid s 44(2).
[194] Woolwich Crown Court (unreported) 23 April 2002) (Astill J).
[195] IPA, s 45(2)(a).
[196] ibid s 45(3).
[197] ibid s 45(2)(b).
[198] ibid s 45(2)(c).
[199] ibid s 46(1).

3. Lawful Interception of Communications

to lawful business monitoring in the workplace. Like its predecessor, the new Act authorizes the interception of work place emails, providing such conduct is authorized by regulations made under section 46(2) IPA.

3.127 The conduct that may be authorized and specified in the regulations must appear to the Secretary of State to constitute a legitimate practice reasonably required for the purpose, in connection with the carrying on of any relevant activities of monitoring or keeping a record of either communications by means of which transactions are entered into in the course of the relevant activities,[200] or other communications relating to the relevant activities or taking place in the course of the carrying on of those activities.[201]

3.128 The regulations must not authorize the interception of any communication except in the course of its transmission using apparatus or services provided by or to the person carrying on the relevant activities for use (whether wholly or partly) in connection with those activities.[202]

3.129 The term 'relevant activities' is defined as any business, any activities of a government department, the Welsh Government, a Northern Ireland department or any part of the Scottish Administration, any activities of a public authority, and any activities of any person or office holder on whom functions are conferred by or under any enactment.[203]

3.130 Section 47 IPA authorizes the interception of a communication in the course of its transmission by means of a public postal service if it is carried out by an officer of Revenue and Customs under section 159 of the Customs and Excise Management Act 1979, as applied by virtue of section 105 of the Postal Services Act 2000 (power to open postal items etc), 'that section and another enactment'. It is also authorized if it is carried out under paragraph 9 of Schedule 7 to the Terrorism Act 2000 (port and border controls).

3.131 There are specific provisions relating to the regulatory functions of Office of Communications (OFCOM[204]) insofar as these relate to the interception of communications. These fall individually within the definition of a 'relevant matter' in section 48(3). There are three. The first is the grant of wireless telegraphy licences under the Wireless Telegraphy Act 2006; the second is the prevention or detection of anything that constitutes wireless telegraphy; and the third is the enforcement of Part 2 of the Wireless Telegraphy Act 2006 (other than sections 27 to 31) or any other enactment not covered by those provisions but which relates to wireless telegraphy.

3.132 Where a relevant matter arises, OFCOM is authorized by section 48(1) IPA to intercept a communication in the course of its transmission, obtain by or in connection with the interception information about the sender or recipient or intended

---

[200] ibid s 46(2)(a).
[201] ibid s 46(2)(b).
[202] ibid s 46(3).
[203] ibid s 46(4).
[204] Established by s 1 of the Office of Communications Act 2002.

G. Other Forms of Lawful Interception

recipient of the communication and, or, the disclosure of anything obtained as a consequence of this conduct.

3.133 The terms interference and wireless telegraphy emanate from the Wireless Telegraphy Act 2006, sections 115(3) and 116 respectively.

3. Interception in Prisons and Other Institutions

(a) *Prisons*

3.134 The interception of communications in a prison continues to be governed by prison rules. The provisions are found in section 47 of the Prison Act 1952, section 39 of the Prisons (Scotland) Act 1989, or section 13 of the Prison Act (Northern Ireland) 1953. As to the difficulties associated with their application see *R v Knaggs* [2015] EWCA Crim 1007.

3.135 The term 'prison' is broad and means any prison, young offender institution, young offenders' centre, secure training centre, secure college, or remand centre, which is under the general superintendence of, or is provided by, the Secretary of State under the Prison Act 1952, the Department of Justice in Northern Ireland under the Prison Act (Northern Ireland) 1953, or Scottish Ministers under the Prisons (Scotland) Act 1989.

3.136 It also includes any contracted-out prison, within the meaning of Part 4 of the Criminal Justice Act 1991 or section 106(4) of the Criminal Justice and Public Order Act 1994, and any legalized police cells within the meaning of section 14 of the Prisons (Scotland) Act 1989.

(b) *Psychiatric Hospitals*

3.137 The interception of communications in high-security psychiatric hospitals,[205] other than in Scotland, is authorized if it is in accordance with a relevant direction given to the premises under section 4(3A)(a) of the National Health Service Act 2006 or section 19 or section 23 of the National Health Service (Wales) Act 2006.[206]

3.138 In Scotland the interception of communications is authorized if it takes place in a state hospital,[207] and it is conduct in pursuance of, and in accordance with, any direction given to the State Hospitals Board for Scotland under section 2(5) of the National Health Service (Scotland) Act 1978 (regulations and directions as to the exercise of their functions by health boards) as applied by Article 5(1) of the State Hospitals Board for Scotland Order 1995.

3.139 Additionally, in Scotland there are powers to withhold correspondence of certain persons detained in hospital as well as their use of telephones under sections 281 and 284 of the Mental Health (Care and Treatment) (Scotland) Act 2003 respectively. Where such powers are used, the interception is authorized under the IPA.

---

[205] This has the same meaning as in s 4 of the National Health Service Act 2006.
[206] IPA, s 50(1)–(2).
[207] This has the same meaning as in the National Health Service (Scotland) Act 1978.

3. Lawful Interception of Communications

(c) Immigration Detention Facilities

3.140 The interception of communications taking place in immigration detention facilities is authorized under section 51(1) if it is conduct in exercise of any power conferred by or under relevant rules.

3.141 The term 'immigration detention facilities' is also broad and means any removal centre, short-term holding facility or pre-departure accommodation as defined by section 147 of the Immigration and Asylum Act 1999. The reference to 'relevant rules' means in respect of each category of facility, rules made under sections 153, 157 and 157A of the Immigration and Asylum Act 1999 respectively.[208]

(d) Interception in Accordance with Overseas Requests

3.142 Where the interception of a communication in the course of its transmission by means of a telecommunication system takes place in accordance with an overseas request it is authorized by section 52(1) if four conditions (A to D) are met. Condition A is that the interception is carried out by or on behalf of a telecommunications operator, and relates to the use of a telecommunications service provided by the telecommunications operator.[209] Condition B is that the interception is carried out in response to a request made in accordance with a relevant international agreement[210] by the competent authorities of a country or territory outside the UK.[211] Condition C is that the interception is carried out for the purpose of obtaining information about the communications of an individual who is outside the UK or the person making the request or carrying out the interception believes the person is outside the UK.[212] Condition D is that any further conditions specified in regulations made by the Secretary of State for the purposes of this section are met.[213]

H. RESTRICTIONS ON HANDLING AND DISCLOSURE OF INTERCEPT MATERIAL OBTAINED UNDER WARRANTS

1. Handling Intercept Material

3.143 As under RIPA and, indeed, the IOCA 1985 before it, the IPA imposes mandatory requirements on the 'issuing authority' (the relevant Secretary of State[214]) to ensure, in relation to every targeted interception or mutual assistance warrant issued by them, that arrangements are in force for securing that the material obtained under the warrant is properly handled. Material obtained under a warrant or a copy of such material and handed to any overseas authorities (an authority of a country or

---

[208] IPA, s 52(2).
[209] ibid s 52(2).
[210] This means an international agreement to which the UK is a party.
[211] IPA, s 52(3).
[212] ibid s 52(4).
[213] ibid s 52(5).
[214] ibid s 53(10).

H. Restrictions on Handling and Disclosure of Intercept Material

territory outside the UK) is excluded from this requirement but is governed by section 54.[215]

3.144 The requirements as to the handling of the material are met if the number of persons to whom any of the material is disclosed or otherwise made available,[216] the extent to which any of the material is disclosed or otherwise made available,[217] the extent to which any of the material is copied[218] and the number of copies that are made[219] is limited to the minimum that is necessary for the authorized purposes. In addition, the requirements must include arrangements for securing that every copy made of any of that material is stored, for so long as it is retained, in a secure manner[220] and that in relation to the material obtained under a warrant if every copy made of any of that material (if not destroyed earlier) is destroyed as soon as there are no longer any relevant grounds for retaining it.[221]

3.145 The term 'necessary for the authorised purposes' means 'if, and only if' (so therefore narrowly interpreted) any one or more of five criteria are met. First, it is, or is likely to become, necessary on any of the grounds falling within section 18 (i.e. it is or is likely to be necessary on any of the grounds upon which the warrant was originally issued).[222] Secondly, it is necessary for facilitating the carrying out of any functions under the IPA of the Secretary of State, the Scottish Ministers or the person to whom the warrant is or was addressed.[223] Thirdly, it is necessary for facilitating the carrying out of any functions of the judicial commissioners or the Investigatory Powers Tribunal under or in relation to the IPA.[224] Fourthly, it is necessary to ensure that a prosecutor conducting a criminal prosecution has the information needed to the fairness of any prosecution.[225] And fifthly, it is necessary for the performance of any duty imposed on any person by the Public Records Act 1958 or the Public Records Act (Northern Ireland) 1923.[226] If these criteria cease to exist, the material must be destroyed.[227]

3.146 There is a reporting obligation provided for by section 53(7) where a communication containing confidential journalistic material or reveals the identity of a source is intercepted through the use of a targeted interception warrant or mutual assistance warrant is retained (so not on being intercepted per se). In such circumstances, the person to whom the warrant is addressed must inform the Investigatory Powers Commissioner as soon as is reasonably practicable.[228]

---

[215] ibid s 53(8).
[216] ibid s 53(2)(a).
[217] ibid s 53(2)(b).
[218] ibid s 53(2)(c).
[219] ibid s 53(2)(d).
[220] ibid s 53(4).
[221] ibid s 53(5).
[222] ibid s 53(3)(a).
[223] ibid s 53(3)(b).
[224] ibid s 53(3)(c).
[225] ibid s 53(3)(d).
[226] ibid s 53(3)(e).
[227] ibid s 53(5).
[228] ibid s 53(7)(a)–(b).

3.147 The word 'copy' and copied in this context is broad and is to be read as 'any copy, extract or summary of the material which identifies the material as having been obtained under the warrant, and any record which refers to any interception or to the obtaining of any material is a record of the identities of the persons to or by whom the material was sent, or to whom the material relates'.[229]

2. Privileged Items

3.148 Where an item subject to legal privilege has been obtained under a targeted interception or mutual assistance warrant and is retained following its examination for purposes other than its destruction, the person to whom the warrant is addressed must inform the Investigatory Powers Commissioner of the retention of the item as soon as reasonably practicable.[230]

3.149 Other than in cases where the public interest in retention of the item outweighs the public interest in the confidentiality of items subject to items subject to legal privilege and retention is necessary in the interests of national security or for the purpose of preventing death or serious injury,[231] the Investigatory Powers Commissioner must either direct the item is destroyed or impose conditions as to the retention and use of the item.[232] In determining which of these alternatives is appropriate, the Commissioner may require representations to be made by affected persons.[233] These are either the person to whom the warrant was or is addressed or the issuing authority.[234] Where the Commissioner requires representations, these must be considered when determining whether the items should be destroyed or conditions imposed.[235]

3. Disclosure of Intercept Material

(a) *Disclosure Overseas*

3.150 In cases involving disclosure of intercept material or copies of intercept material the issuing authority, so relevant Minister, must ensure, in relation to every targeted interception or mutual assistance warrant, that arrangements are in force for securing that it is handled properly.[236]

3.151 The mandatory requirements set out in section 54(2) and (5) IPA apply 'to such extent (if any) as the issuing authority considers appropriate': see paragraphs 3.44 and 3.45 above. In addition, there is a requirement to ensure to such an extent as the minister considers appropriate, if any, that there would be not be the equivalent of a breach of section 56(1) IPA.

---

[229] ibid s 53(10).
[230] ibid s 55(1)–(2).
[231] ibid s 55(5)(a)–(b).
[232] ibid s 55(3).
[233] ibid s 55(6)(a).
[234] ibid s 55(7).
[235] ibid s 55(6)(b).
[236] ibid s 54(1).

H. Restrictions on Handling and Disclosure of Intercept Material

(b) *Exclusion of Matters from Legal Proceedings*

3.152 Section 56 replaces the former section 18 RIPA and section 6 IOCA, the prohibition from disclosure in legal proceedings. The prohibition is subject to a number of exceptions. These are set out in Schedule 3. They include the exceptions provided for in RIPA (so, lawful interception other than by warrant, proceedings before the Investigatory Powers Tribunal and other 'sensitive' proceedings,[237] for example). The exceptions previously set out in section 18 RIPA relating to disclosure in criminal proceedings are now set out in detail in Schedule 3, paragraph 21 and remained largely unchanged. There is now express provision in respect of employment proceedings,[238] inquiries, and inquests[239] and closed material proceedings cases.[240]

3.153 It remains the position under the IPA that no evidence may be adduced, question asked, assertion or disclosure made, or other thing done in, for the purposes of or in connection with any legal proceedings or Inquiries Act proceedings which in any manner either discloses, in circumstances from which its origin in interception-related conduct may be inferred any content of an intercepted communication, or any secondary data obtained from a communication, or tends to suggest that any interception-related conduct has or may have occurred or may be going to occur.[241] The extension to secondary data reflects the introduction of that concept in the new legislation.

3.154 The term 'interception-related conduct' is also new and defined in section 56(2) IPA. There are five categories. The first is conduct that is, or in the absence of any lawful authority would constitute, the offence of unlawful interception, as provided for in section 3(1).[242] This extends to a limited number of persons listed in section 56(3) but who are in effect intercepting authorities, ie Crown office-holders, proper officers of Revenue and Customs, the police, and relevant postal and telecommunications operators.[243] The second and third categories are breaches of the restrictions imposed under sections 9 and 10: see Chapter 2, paragraphs 2.55–2.58.[244] The fourth category is the making of an application by a person for a warrant or the issue of a warrant,[245] and the final category is the imposition on any person to provide assistance in giving effect to either a targeted or mutual assistance warrant.[246]

3.155 It also includes conduct under RIPA and IOCA (so as to ensure the effect of the IPA extends to operations involving the interception of communications that traverse the period relating to the different regimes). Conduct that was or would have been[247] an offence under either section 1(1) and (2) RIPA and section 1 IOCA

---

[237] For example, those before the Special Immigration Appeals Commission or Proscribed Organisations Appeal Commission.
[238] ibid Schedule 3, para 14.
[239] ibid Schedule 3, para 22.
[240] ibid Schedule 3, para 7.
[241] ibid s 56(1).
[242] ibid s 56(2)(a).
[243] ibid s 56(3).
[244] ibid s 56(2)(b)–(c).
[245] ibid s 56(2)(d).
[246] ibid s 56(2)(e).
[247] Sections 1(5) RIPA 2000 and 1(2) and (3) IOCA 1985.

falls within the meaning of interception-related conduct,[248] as does the making of an application for or the issue of a warrant under either statute.[249] Also subsumed within the definition is a breach by the Secretary of State of the provisions in section 1(4) RIPA relating to the restrictions on requesting assistance under mutual assistance agreements (now provided for by section 8 IPA).[250] Finally, so too is the equivalent provision in Chapter 1, Part 1 RIPA to section 43(1) IPA (duty to provide assistance).[251]

(c) *Duty Not to Make Unauthorized Disclosures*

3.156 Sections 57 and 58 relate to unauthorized disclosures in relation to interception warrants issued under Chapter 1 of Part 2 IPA or Chapter 1, Part 1 of RIPA.[252] The provisions unravel the former section 19 RIPA, which dealt with the offence of making unlawful disclosure, now found in section 59 IPA.

3.157 There are six categories of persons who are either an intercepting authority or person holding office or employed by organizations engaged in the interception of communications that are caught by section 57 IPA.[253] They are the same as those set out in section 56(3) IPA: see paragraph 3.154 above. A disclosure by a person within one of the categories will be unauthorized if it relates to a warrant and discloses the existence or contents of the warrant, details of its issue, renewal, or modification, the existence or contents of any requirement to provide assistance in giving effect to the warrant, steps taken in pursuance of a warrant, or the requirement to take steps or the material obtained.[254]

3.158 A disclosure will not be unauthorized if it is an excepted disclosure. Section 58 IPA provides for the meaning of this. It is complex and creates four 'heads' of excepted disclosure. The provision does not affect the operation of the prohibition in section 56.[255]

3.159 The first head relates to disclosures authorized under the terms of the warrant. There are three types of disclosure: a disclosure authorized by the warrant; a disclosure authorized by the person to whom the warrant is or was addressed or under any arrangements made by that person for the purposes of this section (unless it is a mutual assistance warrant addressed to a person who is the competent authority for the purposes of mutual assistance); or, a disclosure authorized by the terms of any requirement to provide assistance in giving effect to the warrant.[256] This last exception includes any requirement for disclosure imposed by virtue of section 41(5) IPA or, section 11(9) of RIPA, if applicable.

---

[248] IPA, s 56(4)(a) and (b).
[249] ibid s 56(4)(d).
[250] ibid s 56(4)(c).
[251] ibid s 56(4)(e).
[252] ibid s 57(2).
[253] ibid s 57(3).
[254] ibid s 57(4).
[255] ibid s 58(9).
[256] ibid s 58(2)(a)–(c) and (3).

The second head relates to oversight bodies. Disclosures in respect of Chapter 1, Part 2 IPA or Chapter 1, Part 1 RIPA 2000 to or authorized by a judicial commissioner or, if applicable, the Interception of Communications Commissioner will not fall within the meaning of unauthorized disclosures.[257] Nor will a disclosure to the Independent Police Complaints Commission for the purposes of facilitating the carrying out of any of its functions.[258]   3.160

The third head relates to disclosures by legal advisers. There are two categories. The first is a disclosure by a legal adviser in contemplation of, or in connection with, any legal proceedings and for the purposes of those proceedings will not be an unauthorized disclosure.[259] The second is a disclosure by a professional legal adviser to his or her client or a representative of the client or by the client or representative to the professional legal adviser in connection with the provision of advice to the client about the effect of the 'the relevant provisions' will be 'excepted'.[260] These are the provisions of Chapter 1, Part 2 IPA and Chapter 1, Part 1 of RIPA 2000.[261] If the disclosure is made for the purposes of the furtherance of a criminal purpose, then it falls outside the meaning of this head.[262]   3.161

The final head relates to disclosures of a more general nature. A disclosure by postal or telecommunications operator in accordance with a requirement imposed by regulations made by the Secretary of State and relates to the number of warrants issued under Chapter 1, Part 2 is included as is a disclosure of information about warrants in general.[263]   3.162

I. THE OFFENCE OF MAKING UNAUTHORIZED DISCLOSURES

A person who makes an unauthorized disclosure for the purposes of section 57(1) IPA commits an offence. A person who is guilty of the offence may be sentenced on summary conviction in England and Wales to imprisonment for a term not exceeding twelve months (or six months, if the offence was committed before the commencement of section 154(1) of the Criminal Justice Act 2003), or to a fine, or to both.[264]   3.163

In Scotland a person who is guilty of the offence may be sentenced to imprisonment for a term not exceeding twelve months, or to a fine not exceeding the statutory maximum, or to both.[265] In Northern Ireland, on summary conviction a   3.164

---

[257] ibid s 58(4)(a) and (b).
[258] ibid s 58(4)(c).
[259] ibid s 58(5)(a).
[260] ibid s 58(5)(b).
[261] ibid s 58(7).
[262] ibid s 58(6).
[263] ibid s 58(8).
[264] ibid s 59(2)(a)(i)–(ii).
[265] ibid s 59(2)(b)(i)–(ii).

person who is guilty of the offence may be sentenced to imprisonment for a term not exceeding six months, or to a fine not exceeding the statutory maximum, or to both.[266]

3.165 On conviction on indictment, a person who is guilty of the offence may be liable to imprisonment for a term not exceeding five years or to a fine, or to both.[267]

3.166 It is a defence for the person charged with an offence under section 59(1) IPA to show that they could not reasonably have been expected, after first becoming aware of the matter disclosed, to take steps to prevent the disclosure.[268] As to the when the offence is committed by a body corporate or Scottish partnership, see Chapter 10, paragraphs 10.125–10.127.

---

[266] ibid s 59(2)(c)(i)–(ii).
[267] ibid s 59(2)(d).
[268] ibid s 59(3).

4
AUTHORIZATIONS FOR OBTAINING COMMUNICATIONS DATA

A.	Introduction	4.01
B.	Authorization	4.06
	1. The Designated Senior Officer	4.07
	2. The Power to Authorize	4.12
	3. Internet Connection Records	4.21
	4. Authorizations and Authorized Notices	4.29
	5. Duration and Cancellation of Authorizations and Notices	4.33
	6. Duties of Telecommunications Operators in Relation to Authorizations	4.35
C.	Filtering	4.38
	1. Filtering	4.38
	2. Filtering Arrangements	4.40
	3. Use of Filtering Arrangements Following Authorization	4.43
	4. Filtering Arrangements: Secretary of State's Duties	4.45
D.	Relevant Public Authorities Other than Local Authorities	4.53
	1. Relevant Public Authorities and Designated Senior Officers	4.53
	2. Adding or Removing Relevant Public Authorities from the Table	4.58
E.	Local Authorities	4.63
	1. Local Authority Authorizations: Judicial Approval	4.72
F.	Additional Protections	4.77
	1. Use of a Single Point of Contact (SPOC)	4.77
	2. Authorizations to Identify or Confirm Journalistic Sources: Judicial Approval	4.83
	3. Collaboration Agreements	4.87
	4. Lawfulness of Conduct Authorized by Part 3, IPA	4.96
G.	Unlawful Disclosure	4.98
H.	Miscellaneous Provisions	4.102
	1. Transfer and Agency Arrangements with Public Authorities: Regulations	4.102
	2. Extra-territorial Application of Part 3	4.110

4. Authorizations for Obtaining Communications Data

A. INTRODUCTION

4.01 The acquisition, retention, and use of communications data, described in the former Code of Practice on the Acquisition and Disclosure of Communications Data as the 'who, when and where of a communication but not the content',[1] has been one of the consistently controversial aspects of covert policing law over the last two decades.

4.02 It has also been significantly litigated both domestically[2] and in Europe.[3] The United Kingdom (UK) had to pass emergency legislation in the form of the Data Retention and Investigatory Powers Act 2014 (DRIPA) in response to one adverse judgment. The legality of DRIPA was in turn challenged. The Grand Chamber of the European Court of Justice in *Secretary of State of the Home Department v Watson and Others*[4] delivering judgment on 21 December 2016 stated that DRIPA 'exceeds the limit of what is strictly necessary and cannot be considered to be justified, within a democratic society'[5]. At the time of writing, the matter has been referred back to the Court of Appeal. David Anderson QC, the former Independent Reviewer of Terrorism Legislation, acknowledged the judgment has 'significance' for the Investigatory Powers Act (IPA).[6] On 8 September 2017, the bulk communications data regime was referred to the Grand Chamber by the Investigatory Powers Tribunal in *Privacy International v Secretary of State for Foreign and Commonwealth Affairs*.[7]

4.03 Part 1, Chapter 2 of the Regulation of Investigatory Powers Act 2000 (RIPA) provided a statutory framework for the acquisition and disclosure of communications data. Following the disclosures by former National Security Agency contractor Edward Snowden in 2013, it emerged that the UK intelligence services (MI5, MI6, and GCHQ) used section 94 of the Telecommunications Communications Act 1984 to acquire and use of what is now known as 'bulk' data constituting communications data that included considerable volumes of data about biographical details, commercial and financial activities, communications, and travel. The use of the provisions and the directions were publicly 'avowed' by the intelligence services

---

[1] Code of Practice (the RIPA Code of Practice), para 2.13 https://www.gov.uk/government/uploads/system/uploads/attachment_data/file/426248/Acquisition_and_Disclosure_of_Communications_Data_Code_of_Practice_March_2015.pdf.

[2] *Privacy International v Secretary of State for Foreign and Commonwealth Affairs and Others* [2016] UKIPTrib 15_110-CH.

[3] For example, in the European Court of Human Rights: *Big Brother Watch and Others v United Kingdom* [2014] ECHR 93 and in the European Court of Justice: *Digital Rights Ireland Limited v Minister for Communications* C-293/12 (8 April 2014).

[4] Case C-698/15 (21 December 2016).

[5] ibid para 107.

[6] https://terrorismlegislationreviewer.independent.gov.uk/cjeu-judgment-in-watson/ (last accessed 19 January 2017).

[7] IPT/15/110/CH.

in March and November 2015, respectively, and the practice prior to this has been held to violate Article 8 of the European Convention on Human Rights by the Investigatory Powers Tribunal.[8]

4.04 An attempt to address these developments as well as technological advances has influenced the drafting of Part 3 of the IPA. The enormity of the undertaking is reflected in the twenty-four provisions in the IPA that replace the five in the now repealed Part 1, Chapter II RIPA. In addition, the retention of communications data has evolved to its own discrete Part (Part 5) and 'bulk collection' two substantial Parts, Parts 6 and 7 IPA. A Code of Practice running to seventy-eight pages supplemented the provisions in RIPA. The IPA has published a draft Code of Practice on Communications Data, which is 124 pages in its current form.[9] It is incongruous that a prior incarnation of Parts 3 and 4 of the IPA, the Communications Data Bill, was abandoned owing to public concern and the absence of any political consensus, although the IPA was passed without substantial amendment.[10]

4.05 Part 1, Chapter 2 RIPA provided for the lawful acquisition of communications data, obtaining and disclosing communications data, the formalities of authorization, and arrangements for payments to those complying with a notice served in accordance with its provisions. The Data Retention and Investigatory Powers Act (DRIPA) provided for, amongst other things, the making of regulations including those to deal with the requirements to be met before giving a retention notice and the maximum time for the retention of data (not longer than twelve months). The structure of Part 3 IPA is authorization, including the introduction of 'filtering' and the duties on those served with notices. It then makes provision for the position of public authorities that are not local authorities, local authorities, which following the Protection of Freedoms Act 2012, were required to obtain judicial approval following authorization, collaboration, and the new offences that may be committed following unlawful disclosure.

B. AUTHORIZATION

4.06 The power to grant authorizations is provided for in section 61 of Part 3 IPA. The scheme adopts the new terminology of 'targeted' authorizations, the corollary of the post-Snowden allusion and UK government 'avowal' to the authorization of 'bulk' acquisition of data. Central to the authorization process is the Designated Senior Officer (DSO). Unlike many of the various personalities identified in the RIPA Code of Practice, which remain in the new draft Code of Practice, the DSO is now a creation of the new statute and, although this role is defined in later sections of Part 3,

---

[8] *Privacy International v Secretary of State for Foreign and Commonwealth Affairs and Others* [2016] UKIPTrib 15_110-CH, para 13.
[9] https://www.gov.uk/government/uploads/system/uploads/attachment_data/file/557862/IP_Bill_-_Draft_CD_code_of_practice.pdf (last accessed 19 January 2017).
[10] 'Blunkett shelves access to data plans' *Guardian* (19 June 2002).

sections 70 (relevant public authorities) and 74 (local authorities) IPA, it makes sense to set out the meaning and functions of the DSO at the outset of this chapter.

1. The Designated Senior Officer

4.07 The power to grant authorizations under section 61 IPA lies with a DSO. This role is defined in section 70(3) and Schedule 4 IPA, in respect of a public authority that is not a local authority and section 73(2) IPA, in respect of a public authority that is a local authority.[11] The term 'local authority' is defined as a district, county, or county borough council in England, Wales, and Northern Ireland, a council constituted under section 2 of the Local Government etc (Scotland) Act 1994 and any London borough or Common Council of the City of London. The Council of the Isles of Scilly is also included in the definition.[12]

4.08 Schedule 4 IPA consists of four columns. Column 1 describes the 'relevant public authority' (the authority), column 2 the minimum office, rank, or position to be held by the DSO, column 3 the type of communications data that the DSO may obtain, and column 4 the paragraphs of section 61(7) that correlate to the exercise of the relevant power: see paras, 4.13–4.14, below.

4.09 The DSO means an individual who holds with the authority as a minimum the rank specified in column 2.[13] This is subject to the where an office, rank, or position is specified by reference to a particular branch, agency, or other part of the authority or responsibility for functions of a particular description.[14] In these circumstances, a person is a DSO if he holds the office, rank, or position (it must then be a higher rank than that specified in column 2[15]), or has responsibility for those functions.[16] The draft Code of Practice provides some detail of the requirements of the role.[17]

4.10 Columns two and three of Schedule 4 specify different ranks and different types of communications data capable of being acquired.[18] For example, in any police force in the UK, an inspector may authorize the acquisition of entity data,[19] and a superintendent, all forms of communications data: see paragraphs 4.53–4.57 below. This is subject to meeting the requirements of section 61(1) and (7): see paragraph 4.13 below.[20]

4.11 Where there is more than one entry in relation to an authority in column 2 (for example the Home Office, which specifies a number officers, ranks, or positions, the requirement to comply with section 61(1) and (7) applies in relation to each.[21]

---

[11] IPA, s 86(1)(a)–(b).
[12] ibid s 88(2)(a)–(g).
[13] ibid s 70(3)(a).
[14] ibid s 70(4)(a)–(b).
[15] ibid s 70(3)(b).
[16] ibid s 70(5)(a)–(b).
[17] Draft Code of Practice, paras 4.11–4.27.
[18] IPA, s 70(6)(a).
[19] Defined in IPA, s 224(3) and dealt with in Chapter 1.
[20] IPA, s 70(6)(b).
[21] ibid s 70(7).

B. Authorization

2. The Power to Authorize

Under section 61(2) IPA, a DSO may authorize any officer employed by their organization to engage in any conduct that is for the purpose of obtaining the data from any person, and relates to data derived from a telecommunication system. This is subject to three broad requirements being met.

4.12

(a) *Requirements under Section 61*

The first is that it is necessary to obtain communications data for one of the statutory purposes set out in section 61(7) IPA.[22] These are the interests of national security, preventing, or detecting crime or of preventing disorder, the interests of the economic well-being of the UK (so far as those interests are also relevant to the interests of national security), the interests of public safety, the purpose of protecting public health the purpose of assessing or collecting any tax, duty, levy, or other imposition, contribution, or charge payable to a government department, the purpose of preventing death or injury or any damage to a person's physical or mental health, or of mitigating any injury or damage to a person's physical or mental health or assisting investigations into alleged miscarriages of justice. In addition, where a person has died or is unable to identify him or herself because of a physical or mental condition to assist in identifying or obtaining information about the person, her next of kin, or other persons connected to the person or connected to the reasons for her death. Finally, it may also be for the purpose of exercising functions relating to the regulation of financial services or markets, or financial stability.[23] These correspond to the matters referred to it column 4.

4.13

The second requirement is that it is necessary to obtain the data either for the purposes of a specific investigation or operation or for the purposes of testing, maintaining, or developing equipment, systems, or other capabilities relating to the availability or obtaining of communications data.[24] Necessary for these purposes does not include the activities of a trade union in the British Islands 'of itself'.[25] Finally, the conduct authorized by the authorization must be proportionate to the objective sought by obtaining it.[26] Further guidance is provided for in the draft Code of Practice.[27]

4.14

(b) *Permissible Conduct*

Authorization is subject to the application of seven further provisions: sections 62, 63, 70, 73, 75, 67, 76, and 77 and Schedule 4 IPA, insofar as it relates to restrictions affecting certain authorities.[28]

4.15

---

[22] ibid s 61(1)(a).
[23] ibid s 61(7)(j).
[24] ibid s 61(1)(b).
[25] ibid s 61(8).
[26] ibid s 61(1)(c).
[27] Draft Code of Practice, 21–23.
[28] IPA, s 61(3).

4. Authorizations for Obtaining Communications Data

4.16 Section 61(4) IPA provides for particular permissible authorized conduct. It includes obtaining the communications data themselves from any person or telecommunication system and asking any person whom the authorized officer believes is, or may be, in possession of the communications data or capable of obtaining it to obtain it if not in possession of it and disclose it to a person identified by, or in accordance with, the authorization.[29] References in Part 3 IPA to telecommunications operators, telecommunications service, and telecommunications systems apply to postal operators, postal services, and postal systems.[30]

4.17 The permissible conduct also includes requiring by notice a telecommunications operator whom the authorized officer believes is, or may be, in possession of the communications data obtain it if not already in possession of it and disclose it to a person identified by, or in accordance with, the authorization.[31]

(c) *Limits on Authorization*

4.18 There is provision in section 61(5) and (6) IPA imposing limits on the scope of an authorization. An authorization may relate to data whether or not in existence at the time of the authorization, may authorize the obtaining or disclosure of data by a person who is not an authorized officer, or any other conduct by such a person, which enables or facilitates the obtaining of the communications data concerned, and may, in particular, require a telecommunications operator who controls or provides a telecommunication system to obtain or disclose data relating to the use of a telecommunications service provided by another telecommunications operator in relation to that system.

4.19 An authorization may not authorize any conduct consisting in the interception of communications in the course of their transmission by means of a telecommunication system.[32]

4.20 In addition, an authorization may not authorize an authorized officer to engage in the permissible conduct referred to in paragraphs 4.10 and 4.11 above unless it is to an authorized officer or an officer of the same authority as an authorized officer.[33]

3. Internet Connection Records

4.21 An internet connection record (ICR) is communications data which may be used to identify, or assist in identifying, a telecommunications service to which a communication is transmitted by means of a telecommunication system for the purpose of obtaining access to, or running, a computer file, or computer program, and comprises data generated or processed by a telecommunications operator in the process

---

[29] ibid s 61(4)(a)–(b).
[30] ibid s 84(1)(2)(a)–(c).
[31] ibid s 61(4)(c)(i)–(ii).
[32] ibid s 61(6)(a).
[33] ibid s 61(6)(b).

B. Authorization

of supplying the telecommunications service to the sender of the communication (whether or not a person).[34]

4.22 The provisions in relation to ICRs caused civil liberty groups particular concern, Big Brother Watch stating that, 'no evidence was presented to clearly outline how they will work, exactly how much they will cost and whether or not they are technically feasible or beneficial'.[35] Further guidance is provided for in the draft Code of Practice.[36] The Bill was amended at a late stage to provide for an entirely discrete section on restrictions in relation to ICRs.

4.23 A DSO of a local authority may not grant an authorization for the purpose of obtaining data which is, or can only be, obtained by processing an ICR.[37]

4.24 A DSO of a relevant public authority may not grant an authorization for the purpose of obtaining data that is, or can only be obtained by processing, an ICR record unless one of three conditions is met.

4.25 Condition A is that the DSO considers it is necessary for one of the statutory purposes to obtain the data to identify which person or apparatus is using the internet service, where the service and time of use are already known but the identity of the person or apparatus using the service is not known.[38]

4.26 Condition B is that the DSO considers it is necessary for one of the statutory purposes other than preventing or detecting crime to identify one of three things: which internet communications service is being used, and when and how it is being used, by a person or apparatus whose identity is already known; where or when a person or apparatus whose identity is already known is obtaining access to, or running, a computer file or computer program that wholly or mainly involves making available, or acquiring, material whose possession is a crime; or which internet service is being used, and when and how it is being used, by a person or apparatus whose identity is already known.[39]

4.27 Condition C applies in the same way as Condition B except that the purpose for which the data is to be obtained, in addition to identifying the three things referred to in Condition B, is the prevention or detection of crime where it is a serious or other relevant crime.[40] The meaning of 'other relevant crime' is a crime which is not a serious crime but would be an offence for which an individual who has reached the age of 18 or, in relation to Scotland or Northern Ireland, 21 is capable of being sentenced to imprisonment for a term of twelve months or more (disregarding any enactment prohibiting or restricting the imprisonment of individuals who have no previous convictions), or is an offence by a person who is not an individual, or

---

[34] ibid s 62(7)(a)–(b).
[35] https://www.bigbrotherwatch.org.uk/wp-content/uploads/2016/05/Big-Brother-Watch-Investigatory-Powers-Bill-Briefing.pdf (last accessed 17 January 2017).
[36] Draft Code of Practice, 15–17 and 53–55.
[37] IPA, s 62(1).
[38] ibid s 62(3)(a)–(b).
[39] ibid s 62(4)(b)(i)–(iii).
[40] ibid s 62(5)(a)–(c).

4. Authorizations for Obtaining Communications Data

which involves, as an integral part of it, the sending of a communication or a breach of a person's privacy.[41]

4.28 A DSO may not grant an authorization for the purposes of a specific investigation or a specific operation if the officer is working on that investigation or operation unless there are exceptional circumstances.[42] Four examples of these are provided in section 63(3) IPA, and include an imminent threat to life or another emergency, the investigation, or operation gives rise due to the interests of national security to a need to keep knowledge of it to a minimum, there is a 'rare' opportunity to obtain information in the interests of national security, and the time to act is short but the need to obtain the information significant or the size of the authority concerned makes it impracticable to have a DSO who is not also working on the investigation or operation concerned.[43]

4. Authorizations and Authorized Notices

4.29 An authorization must be applied for, and granted, in writing but if not, in a manner that produces a record of its having been applied for or granted.[44] The draft Code of Practice envisages '[the] applicant (the person involved in conducting an investigation) completes an application form, setting out for consideration by the designated senior officer, the necessity and proportionality of a specific requirement for acquiring communications data'.[45]

4.30 There are five mandatory requirements of an authorization. It must specify the office, rank, or position held by the DSO granting it, the ground or grounds in section 61(7) IPA, upon which it is based, the nature of the conduct authorized, the data or description of data to be obtained and the person or description of persons to whom the data is to be or may be disclosed, and how such persons will be identified.[46]

4.31 Where an authorization authorizes a person to impose requirements by notice on a telecommunications operator must in addition to the five requirements referred to above, specify the operator concerned and the nature of the requirements that are to be imposed. However, it need not then specify 'the other contents of the notice'.[47] The decision whether to also disclose the other contents of the notice is at the discretion of the public authority.

4.32 The requirements of the notice must specify the office, rank, or position held by the person giving it, the requirements that are being imposed, and the telecommunications operator on whom the requirements are being imposed. It must also be in

---

[41] ibid s 62(6)(a)–(b).
[42] ibid s 63(1)–(2).
[43] ibid s 63(3)(a)–(d).
[44] ibid s 64(4).
[45] Draft Code of Practice, para 4.7.
[46] IPA, s 64(1)(a)–(e).
[47] ibid s 64(2)(a)–(b).

writing or, if not, 'in a manner that produces a record of its having been given'.[48] The draft Code of Practice provides some elaboration of the mandatory requirements of the application form.[49]

5. Duration and Cancellation of Authorizations and Notices

4.33 An authorization lasts for one month beginning with the date on which it is granted but may be renewed at any time before its expiration.[50] This is by way of the grant of a further authorization and the period of renewal runs from the end of the last period of authorization.[51] However, a notice is not affected by the failure to renew; it only ceases to have effect if cancelled.

4.34 There is an obligation in section 65(4) on a DSO who has granted an authorization to cancel if they consider that the requirements in section 61(1) IPA are no longer met: see paragraphs 4.13 to 4.14 above.[52] If the DSO is no longer available to perform this function regulations will set out the person who will carry out the function in their place.[53]

6. Duties of Telecommunications Operators in Relation to Authorizations

4.35 A telecommunications operator is required to comply with a notice.[54] In obtaining or disclosing communications data, in response to 'a request or requirement for the data in pursuance of an authorization, (which ought to be the notice) to obtain or disclose the data, a telecommunications operator must do so in a way that minimizes the amount of data that needs to be processed for this purpose'.[55] The definition of telecommunications operator does not limit the type of communications data for these purposes.[56] For the definition of telecommunications operator, see Chapter 1, paragraph 1.76.

4.36 Neither duty requires the telecommunications operator to take any steps that it is not reasonably practicable to take.[57] Where these arise under section 253 (maintenance of technical capability), section 66(4) IPA provides that 'the steps which it is reasonably practicable for [the telecommunications operator] to take include every step which it would have been reasonably practicable for [him] to take if [he] had complied with all of those obligations'. Guidance on what is reasonably practicable

---

[48] ibid s 64(3)(a)–(b).
[49] Draft Code of Practice, paras 4.9–4.10.
[50] IPA, s 65(1)–(2).
[51] ibid s 65(3).
[52] ibid s 65(4).
[53] ibid s 65(5)–(6).
[54] ibid s 66(1).
[55] ibid s 66(2).
[56] ibid s 85(5).
[57] ibid s 66(3).

4. Authorizations for Obtaining Communications Data

is found in section 85(4) IPA, and includes any requirements or restrictions under the law of that country or territory as are relevant to the taking of any steps and the extent to which it is reasonably practicable to comply with the duty in a way any such requirements or restrictions as may exist.[58]

4.37 The duties imposed are enforceable by the Secretary of State by civil proceedings for an injunction, or for specific performance of a statutory duty under section of the Court of Session Act 1988, or for any other appropriate relief.[59]

C. FILTERING

1. Filtering

4.38 Filtering is an entirely new statutory provision. In summary, it limits the volume of communications data provided to the applicant public authority but only to the extent it specifies such filters at the time of authorization. The draft Code of Practice describes how it will assist public authorities by:

> Providing a mechanism for pulling fragmented communications data together and providing a more complete analysis. With the increasing use of a wider range of online communications services and communications networks, the communications data required to answer operational questions is becoming more fragmented ... Reducing analytic burden on public authorities and getting an operational answer in the shortest possible time to facilitate the timely recovery of forensic evidence, eliminate individuals without further more intrusive activity, and identify witnesses while events remain fresh in their memories; and ... Managing proportionality and collateral intrusion. A public authority will only be provided with the data that directly answers its question, as opposed to all the data originally required to conduct the analysis.[60]

4.39 The Secretary of State may establish, maintain, and operate arrangements for the purposes of assisting a DSO who is considering whether to grant an authorization, to determine whether the facts meet the three requirements of section 61(1): see paragraphs 4.13 and 4.14 above.[61] The arrangements may also deal with facilitating the lawful, efficient, and effective obtaining of communications data from any person by an authority in pursuance of an authorization.[62] This is known as 'filtering' and the arrangements 'filtering arrangements'.

2. Filtering Arrangements

4.40 The filtering arrangements may, in particular, involve the obtaining of communications data in pursuance of an authorization, known as 'the target data', by means of a

---

[58] ibid s 85(4)(a)–(b).
[59] ibid s 66(5).
[60] Draft Code of Practice, para 9.3.
[61] IPA, s 67(1)(a).
[62] ibid s 67(1)(b).

C. Filtering

request to the Secretary of State to obtain the target data on behalf of an authorized officer,[63] and the Secretary of State then obtaining, processing, and disclosing the target data or data from which the target data may be derived.[64]

Filtering arrangements may, in particular, involve the generation or use of information for the purpose mentioned in section 67(1)(a) IPA (assisting a DSO),[65] or for the purposes of supporting, maintaining, overseeing, or the operation or administration of the arrangements, the functions of the Investigatory Powers Commissioner.[66] 4.41

Insofar as the filtering arrangements relate to the functions of the Investigatory Powers Commissioner they must involve the generation and retention of such information or documents, as the Investigatory Powers Commissioner considers appropriate for the purposes of the functions of their office but only to the extent necessary for the purposes of keeping under review the exercise by authorities of functions under this Part under section 229(1) of this Act (main oversight functions of the Investigatory Powers Commission).[67] The Secretary of State must consult with the Investigatory Powers Commissioner about the arrangements.[68] 4.42

3. Use of Filtering Arrangements Following Authorization

Section 59(1) IPA provides for the use of the filtering arrangements in respect of an authorization. They may be used to obtain, disclose, and process (and temporarily retain) communications data in pursuance of an authorization but only if the authorization specifically authorizes their use for these purposes.[69] The requirements of section 61(1) must be met and the DSO must specifically consider whether the use of the filtering arrangements is proportionate to the objective to be achieved through their use.[70] Unless these criteria are satisfied, the DSO is prohibited from granting an authorization.[71] 4.43

Where a DSO uses the filtering arrangements the decision must be recorded.[72] It must expressly address three matters: first, whether the communications data may be obtained and disclosed through their use; secondly, the processing of data under them (and its temporary retention for that purpose) is authorized; and, thirdly, if the processing of data under them is authorized, the description of data that may be processed.[73] 4.44

---

[63] ibid s 67(2)(a).
[64] ibid s 67(2)(b).
[65] ibid s 67(3)(a).
[66] ibid s 67(3)(b).
[67] ibid s 67(4).
[68] ibid s 67(5).
[69] ibid s 68(2)(a)–(b).
[70] ibid s 68(4).
[71] ibid s 68(5).
[72] ibid s 68(3).
[73] ibid s 68(3)(a)–(c).

4. Filtering Arrangements: Secretary of State's Duties

4.45 Under section 69 IPA, the Secretary of State must secure a raft of duties that arise through the use of filtering arrangements. They fall into five categories: acquisition, retention, access, security, and functioning.

(a) *Acquisition*

4.46 As to the first, the Secretary of State must secure that no 'authorisation data' is obtained or processed under the filtering arrangements except for the purposes of an authorization.[74] Authorization data is defined in section 69(9) IPA. It is characteristically opaque and means data derived or that may be derived from an authorization 'or any data from that data is, or may be derived'. This may mean data that is or may be derived from the original data but which is not secondary data as that term is defined in the Act.

4.47 There is an additional duty in respect of data that has been obtained or processed under the filtering arrangements, and is to be disclosed in pursuance of an authorization or for the purpose of section 58(1)(a) (assisting a DSO determine whether the requirements for granting an authorization are made out: see paragraph 4.41 above) is disclosed only to the person to whom the data is to be disclosed in pursuance of the authorization or where appropriate to the DSO concerned.[75]

4.48 Finally, there is a duty to secure that any authorization data which is obtained under the filtering arrangements in pursuance of an authorization is immediately destroyed once the purposes of the authorization have been met or if, at any time, it ceases to be necessary to retain the data for the purpose or purposes concerned.[76]

(b) *Retention*

4.49 The duties on the Secretary of State extend to securing that data (other than authorization data) which is retained under the filtering arrangements is disclosed only in four prescribed circumstances, for the purpose mentioned in section 67(1)(a) IPA, for the purposes of support, maintenance, oversight, operation, or administration of the arrangements, to the Investigatory Powers Commissioner for the purposes of the functions of the Commissioner mentioned in section 67(4) or (5) IPA, or otherwise as authorized by law.[77]

(c) *Access*

4.50 Only the Secretary of State and designated individuals are permitted to read, obtain, or otherwise process data for the purposes of support, maintenance, oversight, operation, or administration of the filtering arrangements.[78] The term 'designated' in this connection means an individual designated by the Secretary of State for this

---

[74] ibid s 69(1)(a).
[75] ibid s 69(1)(b)(i)–(ii).
[76] ibid s 60(1)(c).
[77] ibid s 69(2).
[78] ibid s 69(3)(a).

purpose.[79] No other persons are permitted to access or use the filtering arrangements except in pursuance of an authorization or for the purpose mentioned in section 67(1)(a) IPA.[80]

(d) *Security*

Under section 69(5) IPA, the Secretary of State must put in place and maintain an adequate security system to govern access to, and use of, the filtering arrangements and to protect against any abuse of the power of access, and impose measures to protect against unauthorized or unlawful data retention, processing, access, or disclosure. 4.51

(e) *Functioning*

The final duty on the Secretary of State under section 69 relates to putting in place and maintaining procedures to ensure that the filtering arrangements are functioning properly.[81] This extends to the regular testing of relevant software and hardware) to ensure that the filtering arrangements are functioning properly. There is also a duty to report annually to the Investigatory Powers Commissioner about the functioning of the filtering arrangements during that year.[82] This report must, in particular, contain information about the destruction of authorization data during the reporting period.[83] Where the Secretary of State believes that significant processing errors relating to the filtering arrangements have occurred this must be immediately reported to the Investigatory Powers Commissioner.[84] Schedule 5, paragraph (3) IPA imposes a requirement that any report must also be made to the Secretary of State (by the public authority). 4.52

D. RELEVANT PUBLIC AUTHORITIES OTHER THAN LOCAL AUTHORITIES

1. Relevant Public Authorities and Designated Senior Officers

Section 70 IPA gives effect to Schedule 4, a table identifying within four columns, 'relevant public authorities', the relevant rank to be held by their DSOs and the type of communications data that they may obtain ('entity data' or 'all data') and the relevant paragraphs of section 61(7) IPA.[85] Entity data is dealt with in Chapter 1: see para 1.77. 4.53

---

[79] ibid s 69(4).
[80] ibid s 69(3)(b).
[81] ibid s 69(6)(a).
[82] ibid s 69(6)(b).
[83] ibid s 69(7).
[84] ibid s 69(8).
[85] ibid s 70(1).

4.54 A relevant public authority (the authority) for the purposes of Part 3 IPA is set out in column 1 of the table, and includes police forces, including the Ministry of Defence and armed forces police, National Crime Agency, HM Revenue and Customs, the intelligence services, some government departments, and other public authorities.

4.55 A DSO means an individual who holds with the authority an office, rank, or position, specified in column 2 of the table or higher or has responsibility for functions of that description.[86] The applicability of the DSO holding higher office, rank, or offices arises where it is specified by reference to a particular branch, agency, or other part of the authority or responsibility for functions of a particular description.[87]

4.56 A DSO may grant an authorization limited to obtaining communications data of the kind specified in the corresponding entry in column 3 of the table, in respect of that authority and only if the requirements of section 61(1)(a) and (7) IPA, specified in the corresponding entry in column 4 of the table are met.[88] By way of example, a DSO in a police force holding the rank of inspector or above may obtain entity data and a superintendent or above, all data, for any of the purposes in section 61(7) IPA, except tax collection, the investigation of miscarriages of justice, and the regulation of financial markets. A general duties or other level four officer or above in the Security Service can obtain entity communications data and a general duties or other level three officer or above can obtain all communications data but only in the interests of national security, for the purpose of preventing or detecting crime or of preventing disorder or in the interests of the economic well-being of the UK.

4.57 Where there is more than one entry in relation to the authority in column 2 of the table and a person is a DSO of the authority by virtue of subsection (3) as it applies to more than one of those entries, the requirements of section 61(1) and (7) must be met in relation to each entry.

2. Adding or Removing Relevant Public Authorities from the Table

4.58 Section 71(1) IPA provides that the Secretary of State may by regulations modify section 70 or Schedule 4. There is no limit to the power to do so but the Act envisages four areas in particular where modification may be required. These are by adding or removing a public authority from column 1 of the table, modifying an entry in respect of the DSO in column 2 of the table, the imposition or removal of restrictions on the authorizations that may be granted by a DSO with the authority and the imposition or removal of restrictions on the circumstances in which or purposes for which such authorizations may be granted by a DSO.[89] The power to make regulations under section 70(1) IPA includes power to make such modifications in

---

[86] ibid s 70(3).
[87] ibid s 70(4)(a)–(b).
[88] ibid s 70(6)(a)–(b).
[89] ibid s 71(2).

D. Relevant Public Authorities Other than Local Authorities

any enactment as appropriate in consequence of a person becoming, or ceasing to be, a relevant public authority because of regulations under that subsection.[90]

Where regulations under section 71 IPA, other than those that remove a public authority from the list in column 1 of the table and make consequential modifications and/or modify column 2 of the table in a way that does not involve replacing an office, rank, or position specified in that column in relation to the authority with a lower office, rank, or position in relation to that authority, there is a mandatory requirement that the Secretary of State consult both the Investigatory Powers Commissioner, and the public authority to which the modifications relate.[91] Any statutory instrument containing such regulations may not be made except in accordance with the enhanced affirmative procedure.[92] 4.59

(a) *Enhanced Affirmative Procedure*

The enhanced affirmative procedure is set out in section 268 IPA, and is engaged where the Secretary of State has consulted under section 72(2) IPA, in relation to making regulations and a period of at least twelve weeks has elapsed (beginning with the day on which the consultation commenced), and the Secretary of State considers it appropriate to proceed with making the regulations.[93] Various time limits are imposed, these begin with the day on which the draft regulations were laid before Parliament but no account is to be taken of any time during which Parliament is dissolved or prorogued or during which either House is adjourned for more than four days.[94] 4.60

In these circumstances, the Secretary of State must then place before Parliament draft regulations, and an explanatory document relating to the draft regulations.[95] If, after the end of a forty-day period, the draft regulations are approved by a resolution of each House of Parliament, the Secretary of State may make regulations in the terms of the draft.[96] However, if either House of Parliament resolves, or a committee of either House charged with reporting on the draft regulations recommends within a thirty-day period and the House to which the recommendation is made does not by resolution reject the recommendation within that period, the Secretary of State must have regard to any representations, resolution of either House of Parliament, and any recommendations of a committee of either House of Parliament charged with reporting on the draft regulations made during a sixty-day period. If then the draft regulations are approved by a resolution of each House of Parliament, the Secretary of State may make regulations in the terms of the draft regulations.[97] 4.61

Alternatively, if at the end of the sixty-day period the Secretary of State wishes to proceed with the draft regulations but with material changes, the Secretary of State 4.62

---

[90] ibid s 71(3).
[91] ibid s 72(1)–(2).
[92] ibid s 72(3).
[93] ibid s 268(2)(a)–(c).
[94] ibid s 268(11).
[95] ibid s 268(3).
[96] ibid s 268(4).
[97] ibid s 268(5)–(6).

may go through the same procedure in order to attempt to have the regulations approved.[98]

E. LOCAL AUTHORITIES

4.63　Sections 73 to 75 IPA, impose restrictions in relation to the grant of authorizations by local authorities.

4.64　A local authority is a relevant public authority for the purposes of Part 3 IPA.[99] However, a local authority's DSO means an individual who holds with the authority the position of director, head of service, or service manager (or equivalent), or a higher position.[100] As with Schedule 4, the Secretary of State may by regulations amend the provision in respect of DSOs[101] but must consult the Commissioner and the local authority concerned.[102] Again, any statutory instrument may not be made except in accordance with the enhanced affirmative procedure: see paragraphs 4.60–4.62 above.[103]

4.65　A DSO of a local authority has significantly less scope to authorize than those set out in Schedule 4 and may grant an authorization for obtaining communications data only if section 61(1)(a) is met in relation to a purpose within section 61(7)(b) IPA (prevention and detection or crime or disorder).[104]

4.66　The scope to authorize is further limited by section 74 IPA, which requires the authority to be party to a collaboration agreement. This can be either as a supplying authority or a subscribing authority or both.[105] The Secretary of State must certify the collaboration agreement having regard to such guidance as is published under section 79(6) and (7) IPA.[106] A 'collaboration agreement' for this purpose is not straightforward.[107] It is an agreement that recognizes the concept of the supplying authority and subscribing authority and where the former puts the disposal of the latter the services of its DSO or other officers.[108] It expands the number of persons who are otherwise capable of authorizing or who may be authorized under Part 3 IPA.[109] Any one of three conditions needs to be met. First, the DSO from the supplying authority must be authorized to grant authorizations to the subscribing authority. Second, the 'other officers' must be permitted to be subject of an authorization by the DSO of the subscribing authority. Thirdly, officers of

---

[98] ibid s 268(8)–(10).
[99] ibid s 73(1).
[100] ibid s 73(2)(a)–(b).
[101] ibid s 73(4).
[102] ibid s 73(5).
[103] ibid s 73(6).
[104] ibid s 73(3).
[105] ibid s 74(1)(a).
[106] ibid s 74(1)(b).
[107] But is not, perhaps self-evidently, a police collaboration agreement: ibid s 78(1).
[108] ibid s 78(1)(a).
[109] ibid s 78(2).

E. Local Authorities

the supplying authority act as single points of contact for officers of the subscribing authority.[110] The formalities of collaboration agreements that are not police collaboration agreements are set out in sections 78 to 79 IPA: see paragraphs 4.87–4.89 below.

4.67 In cases where the first condition is met there are four consequences. First, section 61 has effect as it the reference to 'any officer' in section 61(2) IPA is a reference to the subscribing authority and the reference in section 61(6)(b)(ii) the reference to 'an officer of the same relevant public authority' included a reference to an officer of the supplying officer. Second, section 63(3)(d) IPA (the size of the public authority does not make it practicable for the DSO not to work on the investigation), has effect as if the reference to the relevant public authority were a reference to both authorities. Third, Part 3 IPA has effect as if the DSO of the supplying authority had the power to grant an authorization to the subscribing authority and had other equivalent functions to their counterpart who would have dealt with the application and, fourthly, section 75(1) IPA (judicial authorization), applies as if it was granted by the DSO of the subscribing authority.[111]

4.68 Section 78(4) IPA has the same effect in cases where the second condition is met except that the reference to 'any officer' in section 61(2) is a reference to the supplying authority.

4.69 In cases where the third condition is met, section 76(4)(b) IPA (persons acting as a SPOC), has effect as if the references to the relevant public authority were references to the subscribing authority.[112]

4.70 Section 74(2) IPA prescribes that DSO of a local authority may only grant an authorization to an officer of a relevant public authority that is a supplying authority under a collaboration agreement to which the local authority is a party.[113] Where this is the DSO's local authority, that DSO may authorize under Part 3 IPA.

4.71 If a local authority is itself a supplying authority under a collaboration agreement, the persons within section 74(3) IPA include officers of the local authority.

1. Local Authority Authorizations: Judicial Approval

4.72 Section 75 IPA, provides for applications for judicial approval of local authority authorizations, other than those relating to authorizations to identify or confirm journalistic sources.[114] No authorization by a DSO has effect until a relevant judicial authority approves it.[115] This means in England and Wales a justice of the peace, in Scotland a sheriff, and in Northern Ireland a district judge in the magistrates' court.[116]

---

[110] ibid s 78(1)(b)(i)–(iii).
[111] ibid s 78(3)(a)–(d).
[112] ibid s 78(5).
[113] ibid s 74(3).
[114] ibid s 75(1).
[115] ibid s 75(2).
[116] ibid s 75(7).

4. Authorizations for Obtaining Communications Data

(a) *Procedure*

4.73 The procedure under this section is not new. Local authorities have had to seek judicial approval for the acquisition of communications data and directed surveillance under RIPA (as amended by the Protection of Freedoms Act 2012).

4.74 There is no requirement on the part of the local authority to give notice of the application to the person to whom the authorization relates or their legal representatives.[117]

4.75 The relevant judicial authority may approve the authorization if, and only if, two criteria are met. First, at the time of granting approval, there were reasonable grounds for considering that the requirements of Part 3 IPA, were satisfied in relation to the authorization.[118] Second, at the time when the approval is being considered, there are reasonable grounds for considering that the requirements of Part 3 would be satisfied if an equivalent new authorization were granted at that time.[119]

4.76 Where, on an application under section 75 IPA the relevant judicial authority refuses to approve the grant of the authorization, the relevant judicial authority may make an order quashing the authorization.[120]

F. ADDITIONAL PROTECTIONS

1. Use of a Single Point of Contact (SPOC)

4.77 The SPOC was a creation of the RIPA Code of Practice but the role is now recognized in the text of the IPA. A SPOC acts as such if he is an officer with the relevant public authority and is responsible for advising officers within that authority about applying for authorizations or DSOs about granting authorizations. A SPOC may also be an applicant for an authorization and may also be a DSO. Neither precludes the person being granted or granting an authorization.[121] The draft Code of Practice provides guidance on the role and responsibilities of the SPOC.[122]

4.78 Other than in exceptional circumstances the DSO must consult the person acting as the SPOC.[123] Exceptional circumstances may include an imminent threat to life or another emergency or the interests of national security.[124]

4.79 It is envisaged that the SPOC may provide advice in respect of the application, the granting of the authorization, and matters consequential on the granting of an authorization.

4.80 As to the application, the SPOC may, in particular, advise on the most appropriate methods for obtaining data where the data concerned is processed by more than

---

[117] ibid s 75(4)(a)–(b).
[118] ibid s 75(5)(a).
[119] ibid s 75(5)(b).
[120] ibid s 75(6).
[121] ibid s 76(8).
[122] Draft Code of Practice paras 4.28–4.41.
[123] IPA, s 76(2).
[124] ibid s 76(3).

F. Additional Protections

one telecommunications operator, the cost, and resource implications, for both the authority in obtaining and telecommunications operator in disclosing the data. In addition to any unintended consequences of the proposed authorization, and any issues as to the lawfulness of the proposed authorization.[125]

In respect of advice to the DSO on granting the authorization, the SPOC in addition to the matters referred to in paragraph 4.76, may consider whether it is reasonably practical to obtain the data sought in pursuance of the proposed authorization.[126] 4.81

Finally, in relation to post-authorization matters the SPOC may provide advice on whether requirements imposed by virtue of an authorization have been met, the use in support of operations or investigations of communications data obtained in pursuance of an authorization, and any other effects of an authorization.[127] 4.82

2. Authorizations to Identify or Confirm Journalistic Sources: Judicial Approval

The original RIPA Code of Practice did not make any provision for protecting communications data involving information relating to journalists. It was later revised in March 2015 and provided guidance that an application for communications data by a police force or law enforcement agency which is designed to identify a journalist's source should not be made under the former section 22 RIPA, but should be made under section 9 of the Police and Criminal Evidence Act 1984 (PACE), which requires judicial authorization and provides various procedural safeguards.[128] Adverse judgments of the Investigatory Powers Tribunal[129] and findings by the Interception of Communications Commissioner's Office[130] where police forces had used Part 1, Chapter 2 RIPA to obtain communications data where there was a risk that confidential journalistic information may be acquired led to these changes being introduced. 4.83

There is now provision to obtain approval from a judicial commissioner where the DSO has granted an authorization in relation to the obtaining of communications data for the purpose of identifying or confirming a journalistic source, or 'source of journalistic information' and where there is no imminent threat to life.[131] In such circumstances, the authorization will not take effect until approval is given.[132] However, as with other applications for approval in Part 3, a relevant public authority is not required to seek judicial approval but rather it is open to it to do so.[133] 4.84

---

[125] ibid s 76(5)(a)–(d).
[126] ibid s 76(6)(a)–(d).
[127] ibid s 76(7)(a)–(c).
[128] RIPA Code of Practice, paras 3.78–3.84.
[129] *News Group Newspapers Limited and Others v The Commissioner of Police of the Metropolis* [2015] UKIPTrib 14_176-H and *Moran and Others v Police Scotland* [2016] UKIPTrib 15_602-CH.
[130] http://www.iocco-uk.info/docs/Press%20statement%2025-11-2015.pdf (last accessed 19 January 2017).
[131] IPA, s 77(1).
[132] ibid s 77(2).
[133] ibid s 77(3).

4.85 Where application is made the provisions as to notice, the test applied, and power to quash the authorization are identical to an application for judicial approval under section 75 IPA, except that in addition, a judicial commissioner must also in particular have regard to the public interest in protecting a source of journalistic information and the need for there to be another overriding public interest before a relevant public authority seeks to identify or confirm a source of journalistic information.[134]

4.86 The term, 'source of journalistic information' is defined in section 163(1) IPA and means 'an individual who provides material intending the recipient to use it for the purposes of journalism or knowing that it is likely to be so used'. This broadens the scope of who may be caught by the provision; the DSO will need to consider the intention of the person providing the information to the journalist and not whether that person is in fact a source.

3. Collaboration Agreements

4.87 There are formalities that must be met when a collaboration agreement is entered into. It must be in writing and either published or the fact that the agreement has been made must be published.[135] It may provide for payments to be made between the parties to the agreement.[136] An agreement may be varied by way of a subsequent agreement and brought to an end by agreement between the parties to it.[137]

4.88 Section 79(4) IPA provides that it is open to a relevant public authority to enter into a collaboration agreement as supplying authority, subscribing authority, or both, even where it would not otherwise have the power to do so.

4.89 The Secretary of State may, but only after consultation, direct a relevant public to enter into a collaboration agreement. The threshold is that the Secretary of State considers that entering into the agreement would assist the effective exercise by either the authority or another relevant public authority of its functions under Part 3 IPA.[138] The Code of Practice must include guidance on the criteria the Secretary of State will use when considering whether to impose the requirement on a relevant public authority.[139]

4.90 There is further provision about police collaboration agreements in section 80 IPA. The section applies where the chief officer of a police force in England and Wales (including the National Crime Agency) has entered into a police collaboration agreement under section 22A of the Police Act 1996 and under its terms a DSO of 'force 1' is permitted to grant authorizations to officers of a collaborating police force, officers of this force are permitted to be granted authorizations by the collaborating police force and officers of 'force 1' act as SPOCs for a collaborating police force.[140]

---

[134] ibid s 77(6)(a)–(b).
[135] ibid s 79(2)–(3).
[136] ibid s 79(1).
[137] ibid s 79(2)(b)–(c).
[138] ibid s 79(5).
[139] ibid s 79(7).
[140] ibid s 80(1)(a)–(b).

F. Additional Protections

Collaborating police force is defined in section 80(6) IPA, as a force whose chief officer is part to a police collaboration agreement.

4.91 The DSOs, SPOCs, and those who may be granted authorization under a police collaboration agreement are additional to those who could otherwise act as such under Part 3 IPA.[141]

4.92 Where the DSO of 'force 1' is acting in that capacity for a collaborating force, section 61 (the power to grant authorization) and section 63(3)(d) IPA is to be read accordingly. So, the reference to 'an officer of the authority' in section 61(2) IPA should be read as an officer of the collaborating authority. Section 61(6)(ii) IPA should be read to include an officer of 'force 1'.[142] Part 3 IPA has effect as if the DSO of force 1 had the power to grant an authorization to the collaborating police force and had other equivalent functions to his or her counterpart, who would have dealt with the authorization.[143]

4.93 In cases where officers of 'force 1' can be granted authorization by a DSO of the collaborating police force, section 61(2) IPA should be read as if 'officer of the authority' were a reference to an officer in 'force 1' and in subsection 6(ii) the reference to an officer of the same relevant public authority, read as if it were a reference to 'force 1' and the collaborating police force.[144]

4.94 In both cases, section 63(3)(d) IPA should read as if the reference to relevant public authority were a reference to 'force 1' and the collaborating police force.[145]

4.95 Where officers of 'force 1' act as DSOs and SPOCs for officers of a collaborating police force section 76(4)(b) IPA should be read as if the reference to the relevant public authority was a reference to 'force 1' and the collaborating police force.

4. Lawfulness of Conduct Authorized by Part 3, IPA

4.96 Conduct engaged in under the provisions of Part 3 IPA is lawful for all purposes if it is authorized or is undertaken as a consequence of a notice given in pursuance of an authorization and the conduct is in accordance with that authorization or notice.[146]

4.97 Any person engaging in conduct that is incidental to, or is reasonably undertaken in connection with, conduct that is lawful for all purposes, whether or not the person who engages in it is authorized or is acting having been given a notice will not be subject to any civil liability. This exclusion extends conduct that is not itself conduct for which an authorization is capable of being granted under any of the enactments mentioned in section 81(3) IPA, and might reasonably have been expected to have been sought in the case in question.[147] The enactments are any provision in the IPA RIPA, Part III of the Police Act 1997, or section 5 of the Intelligence Services Act 1994.[148]

---

[141] ibid s 80(2).
[142] ibid s 80(3)(a)–(b).
[143] ibid s 80(3)(c).
[144] ibid s 80(4).
[145] ibid s 80(3)(b) and (4)(b).
[146] ibid s 81(1)(a)–(b).
[147] ibid s 81(2).
[148] ibid s 81(3).

G. UNLAWFUL DISCLOSURE

4.98 The scope of the offence of making an unauthorized disclosure under section 73 IPA is limited to telecommunications operators, or any person employed or engaged for the purposes of such a business.[149] The offence is committed in two circumstances. First, tipping off the person subject of the authorization, where the disclosure is to any person of any requirement imposed on the operator by Part 3 IPA to disclose communications relating to that person and second, the more general offence of disclosing any request made in pursuance of an authorization for the operator to disclose such data. In both cases, the disclosures must be made without reasonable excuse.[150]

4.99 What constitutes a reasonable excuse is not exhaustively defined but it will include where the disclosure is made with the permission of the relevant public authority seeking to obtain the data from the operator. Such permission does not need to be contained in any notice requiring the operator to disclose the data.[151] Where an operator makes a statement for the purposes of an investigation into an allegation an offence has been committed, this is also likely to constitute reasonable excuse.

4.100 On summary conviction in Scotland, England, and Wales, a person guilty of the offence is liable to a term of imprisonment not exceeding twelve months (in England and Wales, if the offence was committed before the commencement of section 154(1) of the Criminal Justice Act 2003, the maximum term is six months) or a fine or to both. In Scotland, the fine cannot exceed the statutory maximum. In Northern Ireland, the maximum term of imprisonment may not exceed six months, or a fine not exceeding the statutory maximum, or both.[152] As to when the offence is committed by a body corporate or Scottish partnership, see Chapter 10, paragraphs 10.125–10.127.

4.101 On conviction on indictment, a person guilty of the offence is liable to a term of imprisonment not exceeding two years or to a fine, or to both.[153]

H. MISCELLANEOUS PROVISIONS

1. Transfer and Agency Arrangements with Public Authorities: Regulations

4.102 The Secretary of State may by regulations provide for any function under sections 58 to 60 IPA (filtering arrangements) that is exercisable by the Secretary of State to be exercisable instead by another public authority.[154] This may include the modification

---

[149] ibid s 82(1).
[150] ibid s 82(1)(a)–(b).
[151] ibid s 82(2).
[152] ibid s 82(3)(a)–(c).
[153] ibid s 82(3)(d).
[154] ibid s 83(1)(a).

H. Miscellaneous Provisions

of any enactment about a public authority for this purpose and impose requirements or confer other functions on a public authority in connection with transferred functions.[155] Such regulations may also provide for the Secretary of State to transfer such functions back from the public authority.[156] In such circumstances, the Secretary of State may also by regulations 'modify' any enactment relating to a public authority for the purpose of enabling or otherwise facilitating this function.[157] Any such regulation permitting modification, do not affect the Secretary of State's responsibility for the exercise of the functions concerned.[158] However, it does not apply in relation to any function of the Secretary of State of making regulations.[159]

Section 83 IPA gives effect to Schedule 5. This imposes on a public authority exercising functions under any regulations as provided for under section 83(1) IPA a requirement to report at least once in each calendar year to the Secretary of State on the discharge of the functions and any such other things specified in the regulations.[160] The regulations may modify the requirement in relation to the calendar year insofar as it relates to the date the regulations come into force or are revoked.[161] The Secretary of State may also agree that any report by the public authority can be combined with any other requirement on it to make a report.[162] 4.103

Where there is a provision in any regulations for a transfer of functions, the Secretary of State is empowered to make a scheme for the transfer of property, rights, or liabilities.[163] This may be included in the regulations under section 83(1) IPA, but if not, must be laid before Parliament.[164] The scope of any such scheme is vast and may adversely impact on those affected by it (the scheme may provide for discretionary compensation awards in such circumstances[165]) and may include the power to modify any enactment.[166] It broadly encompasses transfer of property, rights and liabilities, and tax provisions where transfer takes place. 4.104

The things that may be transferred may include the transfer of property rights and liabilities that could not otherwise be transferred and those rights arising after the making of the scheme.[167] 4.105

Any transfer scheme may make 'consequential, supplementary, incidental, transitory or saving provision'. Paragraph 3(3) of Schedule 5 sets out six areas that may in particular be provided for. They include the ability to create rights or impose liabilities in respect of any property or rights transferred and in respect of anything 4.106

---

[155] ibid Schedule 5, para 5(a)–(b).
[156] ibid s 83(1)(b).
[157] ibid s 83(2).
[158] ibid s 83(3).
[159] ibid s 83(4).
[160] IPA, Schedule 5, para 2(1).
[161] ibid para 2(2).
[162] ibid para 2(3).
[163] ibid para 3(1).
[164] ibid para 3(6).
[165] ibid para 3(5).
[166] ibid para 69(a).
[167] ibid para 3(2)(a)–(b).

transferred, make provision about the continuing effect of things done by or behalf or in relation to the transferor. They may also make provision about the continuation of things on behalf of the transferor that may be on going at the time of transfer, including legal proceedings and to treat references to the transferee as the transferor in documents or instruments. In addition, they make provision for the shared use or ownership of property.[168]

4.107 Rights and liabilities include references to those relating to a contract of employment, including those relating to civil servants.[169] In respect of the latter, any scheme may provide for a person employment by the civil service to become an employee of the transferee, including the terms of their employment and vice versa.[170] If the Transfer of Undertaking (Protection of Employment) Regulations (TUPE) 2006[171] do not apply to the transfer, the scheme may make the same or similar provision.[172]

4.108 Any transfer scheme may provide for modification by agreement and to have effect from the date when the original scheme came into effect.

4.109 In respect of the tax consequences of transfers under any scheme, the Treasury may by regulations provide for varying the way a relevant tax has effect in relation to or done for the purposes of or in relation to anything transferred under any scheme. This includes provision for tax to apply, or apply with modifications, for anything transferred to be treated in a specified way and to require or empower the Secretary of State to permit or specify tax arrangements for anything transferred.[173]

2. Extra-territorial Application of Part 3

4.110 An authorization or notice under Part 3 may relate to conduct outside the UK and persons outside the UK.[174]

4.111 In the case of a notice to be given to a person outside the UK, there are a number of ways notice may be given to the person including by way of or electronic service (but other means of service are not excluded). It may be given by delivering it to the person's principal office within the UK or, if the person has no such office in the UK, to any place in the UK where the person carries on business or conducts activities. If the person has specified an address in the UK as one at which the person, or someone on the person's behalf, will accept documents of the same description as a notice, by delivering it to that address. Service may also be given by notifying the person by such other means as the authorized officer considers appropriate including notification to the person orally.[175]

---

[168] ibid para 3(3)(a)–(e).
[169] ibid para 3(7).
[170] ibid para 8.
[171] SI 2006/246.
[172] IPA, Schedule 5, para 3(3)(f).
[173] ibid para 4(2)–(3).
[174] IPA, s 85(1)–(2).
[175] ibid s 85(3)(a)–(c).

5
RETENTION OF COMMUNICATIONS DATA

A. Introduction	5.01
B. Scope of Retention Powers	5.05
C. Pre-issue	5.12
D. Post-issue	5.17
E. Safeguards	5.24
1. Judicial Approval	5.24
2. Other Safeguards	5.30
F. Variation or Revocation of Notices	5.34
1. Matters Common to Variation and Revocation	5.35
G. Enforcement	5.40
1. Extra-territoriality	5.44

A. INTRODUCTION

Part 4 of the Investigatory Powers Act 2016 (IPA), which makes provision for the retention of communications data, extends over only nine sections but they are among the most controversial. It broadly covers six areas, the scope of power to retain data by way of a retention notice, pre-issue, post-issue, safeguards, variation, and revocation of notices and enforcement. The draft Code on Communications Data, published concurrently with the original Investigatory Powers Bill, also covers retention. 5.01

The regulation of the acquisition, use, and retention of communications data has had an unhappy recent history. The EU Data Retention Directive was held to be invalid following *Digital Rights Ireland* in the European Court of Justice.[1] This led to the government introducing emergency legislation in the form of the Data Retention and Investigatory Powers Act 2014 (DRIPA), described by the Law Society as 'an affront to parliamentary sovereignty and the rule of law'.[2] DRIPA has 5.02

---

[1] Case C-293/12 *Digital Rights Ireland Limited v Minister for Communications*.
[2] https://www.lawsociety.org.uk/ … /acquisition-and-disclosure-of-communications-data/ (last accessed 29 January 2017).

5. Retention of Communications Data

now been subject to an adverse judgment by the European Court of Justice and is awaiting consideration by the Court of Appeal.[3] There are likely to be implications for the IPA but the extent of these is not known at the time of writing.

5.03 The IPA provides for the retention of communications data, including internet connection records (ICRs) for twelve months. The inclusion of ICRs has been particularly controversial, the operational case published by the government, being criticized roundly by civil liberties groups,[4] communications service providers,[5] and the former Independent Reviewer of Terrorism Legislation, David Anderson QC, the latter expressing the view that:

> I have no doubt that the retained records of user interaction with the internet (whether or not via web logs) would be useful ... that is not enough on its own to justify the introduction of a new obligation on CSPs, particularly one which could be portrayed as potentially very intrusive on their customers' activities.[6]

5.04 Despite the intensity of criticism, the Bill remained unchanged after the debate stage.

B. SCOPE OF RETENTION POWERS

5.05 Through the mechanism of the issue and service of a retention notice the Secretary of State may require a telecommunications operator to retain relevant communications data if it is considered that it is necessary and proportionate to do so for one or more of the purposes falling within paragraphs (a) to (j) of section 61(7) IPA (purposes for which communications data may be obtained): see Chapter 4, paragraphs 4.13 to 4.14.[7] Necessary for these purposes does not include the activities of a trade union in the British Islands 'of itself'.[8] A judicial commissioner must also have approved the decision.[9] The requirement of judicial approval was a late amendment to the original Bill. The provisions of Part 4 IPA also apply to postal operators and services and references to telecommunications operator and service have effect accordingly.[10] Any reference to a telecommunication system should be read where appropriate as if it was reference to a postal service.[11]

---

[3] Case C-698/15 *Secretary of State of the Home Department v Watson and Others* (21 December 2016).
[4] See eg Privacy International, 'The database of you: Internet Connection Records will allow the UK Government to document everything we do online' https://www.privacyinternational.org/node/1011.
[5] See eg the evidence of British Telecom to the Joint Committee on the Investigatory Powers Bill (the Joint Committee), 21 http://www.parliament.uk/documents/joint-committees/draft-investigatory-powers-bill/written-evidence-draft-investigatory-powers-committee.pdf.
[6] A Question of Trust (June 2015) para 14.33.
[7] IPA, s 87(1)(a).
[8] ibid s 87(10).
[9] ibid s 87(1)(b).
[10] ibid s 96(1)–(2)(a)–(b) and (e)–(f).
[11] ibid s 96(2)(c).

B. Scope of Retention Powers

Relevant communications data is defined in section 87(11).[12] Under the Code of Practice issued under RIPA, it was referred to as the 'who', 'when', and 'where' of the communication, not content. The new provisions include the 'who', the sender and recipient, the 'when', the time or duration of the communication, and the 'where', the location of the system.[13] It also includes the type, method, or pattern or fact of communication and the telecommunications system or part of that system which conveys or may convey the transmission.[14] It also includes ICRs.

The scope of a retention notice is vast. It may relate to a particular operator or any description of operators, require the retention of all data or any description of data, and identify the period or periods for which data is to be retained.[15] Whilst pervasive, these provisions are at least specific. However, it may also impose other requirements or restrictions in relation to the retention of data, make different provision for different purposes, and relate to data whether or not in existence at the time of the giving, or coming into force, of the notice.[16]

Under section 88 IPA, 'Safeguards', there are five matters that the Secretary of State must take into account. These are the likely benefits of the notice, the likely number of users (if known) of any telecommunications service to which the notice relates, the technical feasibility of complying with the notice, the likely cost of complying with the notice, and any other effect of the notice on the telecommunications operator (or description of operators) to whom it relates.[17] It is a non-exhaustive list. There is also a mandatory requirement that before giving such a notice, the Secretary of State must take reasonable steps to consult any operator to whom it relates.[18]

A retention notice must not require any data to be retained for more than twelve months. Determining the commencement of the period to which the notice relates is not straightforward and falls into three broad categories. It begins with in the case of communications data relating to a specific communication, the day of the communication concerned.[19]

In the case of entity data which does relate to a specific communication but does fall within the definition of 'communications data' in section 261(5) IPA, the day on which the entity concerned ceases to be associated with the telecommunications service concerned or (if earlier) the day on which the data is changed, and in any other case, the day on which the data is first held by the operator concerned.[20] Also see section 96(2)(d) as to how this provision should be read in relation to postal operators and services. Entity data is dealt with in Chapter 1: see paragraph 1.77.

---

[12] ibid s 98(1).
[13] ibid s 87(9)(a)–(b) and (e).
[14] ibid s 87(9)(c)–(d).
[15] ibid s 87(2)(a)–(c).
[16] ibid s 87(2)(d)–(f).
[17] ibid s 88(1)(a)–(e).
[18] ibid s 88(2).
[19] ibid s 87(3)(a).
[20] ibid s 87(3)(b)–(c).

5.11 A retention notice must also not require a systems operator (a person who controls or provides a telecommunication system) to retain data that relates to the use of a telecommunications service provided by another telecommunications operator in relation to that system, is or may be processed by the system operator as a result of being comprised in, included as part of, attached to, or logically associated with a communication transmitted by means of that system by another telecommunications operator, is not needed by the system operator for the functioning of the system in relation to that communication, and is not retained or used by the system operator for any other lawful purpose. These requirements are subject to it being reasonably practicable to separate from other data that is subject to the notice.[21]

C. PRE-ISSUE

5.12 A retention notice which relates to data already in existence when the notice comes into force imposes a requirement to retain the data for only so much of a period of retention as occurs on or after the coming into force of the notice.[22]

5.13 A retention notice comes into force when the notice is given to the operator or a description of operators concerned or, if later, at the time or times specified in the notice.[23]

5.14 Notice is given by giving or publishing it in such manner as the Secretary of State considers appropriate for bringing it to the attention of the operator or description of operators to whom it relates.[24] It must be in writing.[25]

5.15 There are five requirements a retention notice must specify: first, the operator, or description of operators, to whom it relates; secondly, the data which is to be retained; thirdly, the period or periods for which the data is to be retained; fourthly, any other requirements, or any restrictions, in relation to the retention of the data; and, fifthly, the information required by section 249(7) IPA (the level or levels of contribution in respect of costs incurred as a result of the notice).[26]

5.16 There is some elaboration of what 'requirements' or 'restrictions' means in respect of the fourth requirement in section 87(8) IPA. It may, in particular, include a requirement to retain the data in such a way that it can be transmitted efficiently and effectively in response to requests and requirements or restrictions in relation to the obtaining (whether by collection, generation, or otherwise), generation, or processing of two types of data: data for retention or retained data.[27]

---

[21] ibid s 87(4)(a)–(d).
[22] ibid s 87(5).
[23] ibid s 87(6).
[24] ibid s 87(7).
[25] ibid s 98(1).
[26] ibid s 87(8)(a)–(e).
[27] ibid s 87(9)(a)–(b).

D. POST-ISSUE

5.17 A telecommunications operator has the right to refer a retention notice or part of a notice given back to the Secretary of State for review.[28] The time period or circumstances will be provided for by regulations made by the Secretary of State.

5.18 Where a notice given relates to a description of operators, each operator may make a reference under section 90(1) but only in relation to the notice or part of the notice that applies to it.[29]

5.19 Where a referral has been made, there is no requirement for the operator who has referred the retention notice to comply with it, until the Secretary of State has reviewed the notice.[30] The Secretary of State must review any notice or part of any notice referred.[31]

5.20 There are a number of other mandatory requirements on the Secretary of State on a referral being made, including consulting the Technical Advisory Board (Board), and the Investigatory Powers Commissioner.[32] In addition, the Secretary of State must keep a retention notice under review, whether or not it is subject to a referral.[33]

5.21 The Board must consider the technical requirements and the financial consequences, for the operator who has made the reference, of the notice or part of the notice referred[34] and the Investigatory Powers Commissioner must consider whether the notice or part referred is proportionate.[35]

5.22 There are limited procedural requirements to be met on the referral being considered by the Board and the Investigatory Powers Commissioner in that both must give the operator concerned and the Secretary of State the opportunity to provide evidence, or make representations, to them before reaching their conclusions.[36] They must then report their conclusions to the operator and the Secretary of State.[37] A copy of the report must be provided to the operator or it may be published in such a manner as the Secretary of State determines is appropriate for the purposes of bringing it to the attention of the operator.[38]

5.23 The Secretary of State is not bound by the conclusions of the Board or the Investigatory Powers Commissioner and, upon receiving the report, may either vary or revoke the retention notice under section 94 IPA (variation or revocation of notices) or give a notice to the operator concerned confirming its effect.[39] However, this can

---

[28] ibid s 90(1)–(2).
[29] ibid s 90(3).
[30] ibid s 90(4).
[31] ibid s 90(5).
[32] ibid s 90(6).
[33] ibid s 90(13).
[34] ibid s 90(7).
[35] ibid s 90(8).
[36] ibid s 90(9)(a).
[37] ibid s 90(9)(b).
[38] ibid s 90(12).
[39] ibid s 90(10).

only be done if the Investigatory Powers Commissioner has approved the Secretary of State's decision.[40]

E. SAFEGUARDS

1. Judicial Approval

(a) *Notices*

5.24 A retention notice requires the approval of a judicial commissioner who must review the Secretary of State's conclusions as to whether the requirement to be imposed by the notice to retain relevant communications data is necessary and proportionate for one or more of the purposes set out in section 61(7)(a)–(j) of Part 3 IPA.

5.25 The principles applied by the judicial commissioner in doing are those as would be applied by a court on an application for judicial review.[41] The judicial commissioner is required to carry out this function 'with a sufficient degree of care as to ensure … [compliance] with the duties imposed by section 2 IPA (general duties in relation to privacy)': see Chapter 2, paragraphs 2.08–2.10.[42]

5.26 If a judicial commissioner refuses to approve the decision to give a retention notice written reasons for the refusal must be provided to the Secretary of State.[43] In these circumstances, the Secretary of State may ask the Investigatory Powers Commissioner to approve the decision to give the retention notice. This is not a review of the judicial commissioner's decision but rather a reconsideration of the original ministerial decision.[44]

(b) *Variations*

5.27 A variation of a retention notice requires the approval of the Investigatory Powers Commissioner who must review the Secretary of State's conclusions as to whether the requirement to be imposed by the notice as varied or confirmed to retain relevant communications data is necessary and proportionate for one or more of the purposes set out in section 61(7)(a)–(j) of Part 3 IPA.[45]

5.28 The principles applied by the Investigatory Powers Commissioner in doing are those as would be applied by a court on an application for judicial review.[46] The Investigatory Powers Commissioner is required to carry out this function 'with a sufficient degree of care as to ensure … [compliance] with the duties imposed by section 2 IPA (general duties in relation to privacy)'.[47]

---

[40] ibid s 90(11).
[41] ibid s 89(2)(a).
[42] ibid s 89(2)(b).
[43] ibid s 89(3).
[44] ibid s 89(4).
[45] ibid s 91(1).
[46] ibid s 89(2)(a).
[47] ibid s 91(2)(a)–(b).

Where the Investigatory Powers Commissioner refuses to approve a decision to vary a retention notice, or to give a notice confirming the effect of a retention notice, the Investigatory Powers Commissioner must give the Secretary of State written reasons for the refusal.[48]

5.29

2. Other Safeguards

There are a number of mandatory obligations on a telecommunications operator who retains relevant communications data under Part 4 IPA. There is a mirroring requirement in that it must secure that the data is of the same integrity, and subject to at least the same security and protection, as the data on any system from which it is derived. It must also secure, by appropriate technical and organizational measures, that the data can be accessed only by specially authorized personnel, and protect, by appropriate technical and organizational measures, the data against accidental or unlawful destruction, accidental loss or alteration, or unauthorized or unlawful retention, processing, access, or disclosure.[49]

5.30

There is an obligation on the part of a telecommunications operator to destroy any relevant communications data if the retention of it ceases to be authorized by way of retention notice under Part 4 IPA and is not otherwise authorized by law.[50]

5.31

The destruction of the data may take place not less than monthly intervals as appear to the operator to be practicable.[51]

5.32

A telecommunications operator must take steps to protect against unlawful disclosure of any retained relevant communications data by putting in place adequate security systems (including technical and organizational measures) governing those persons who may have access to it.[52]

5.33

F. VARIATION OR REVOCATION OF NOTICES

The Secretary of State has the power to vary or revoke in whole or part a retention notice.[53] Where it is revoked, this does not prevent the giving of a further retention notice in respect of the same data or operator or description of operators.[54]

5.34

1. Matters Common to Variation and Revocation

In the case of either a revocation or variation, the Secretary of State must give, or publish, notice of this in such manner as the Secretary of State considers appropriate

5.35

---

[48] ibid s 91(3).
[49] ibid s 92(1)(a)–(c).
[50] ibid s 92(2).
[51] ibid s 92(3).
[52] ibid s 93.
[53] ibid s 94(1) and (13).
[54] ibid s 94(16).

5. Retention of Communications Data

for bringing the variation or revocation to the attention of the telecommunications operator (or description of operators) to whom it relates.[55]

5.36 A variation or revocation comes into force when notice of it is given or published or if later than this, at the time or times specified in the notice.[56]

(a) *Variation*

5.37 No variation of retention notice is permitted without the necessary authorization requirements set out in section 61 IPA being considered and met (so, at least one of the statutory purposes must be met in section 61(7) IPA and the Secretary of State must consider it necessary and proportionate).[57] It requires judicial approval of a judicial commissioner unless it is a variation following a review by the Secretary of State under section 90, in relation to a retention notice but only so far as the variation is concerned and other than one varied following the referral.[58] Similarly, judicial approval is required in relation to a decision under section 90(10) to vary or confirm a variation as it is in relation to a decision to vary or confirm a retention notice, and section 91(1) IPA is to be read as a reference to the requirement to be imposed by the variation as varied or confirmed.[59]

5.38 Section 87(2) (scope of a retention notice) and (5) IPA (duty to retain where data already exists) apply in relation to a variation as they apply in relation to a retention notice, except the references to the variation coming into force are to read in place of those relating to the original notice.[60] Similarly, section 87(3) and (7) and section 88 IPA apply in relation to the variation as they apply to the original notice.[61]

5.39 Section 94(1), (4), (13), and (16) applies and section 95 (enforcement of notices) and section 97 IPA (extra-territoriality) apply in relation to a varied retention notice, as they apply to the original notice.[62]

G. ENFORCEMENT

5.40 A telecommunications operator given a retention notice and who retains relevant communications data and is therefore required to secure it and protect it against unlawful disclosure must comply with both the requirements and restrictions imposed.[63]

5.41 A telecommunications operator, or any person employed or engaged for the purposes of the business of a telecommunications operator, must not disclose the

---

[55] ibid s 94(2) and (10).
[56] ibid s 94(3) and (15).
[57] ibid s 94(4).
[58] ibid s 94(5) and (11).
[59] ibid 94(12).
[60] ibid s 94(7).
[61] ibid s 94(8) and (9).
[62] ibid s 94(6).
[63] ibid s 95(1).

G. Enforcement

existence or contents of a retention notice to any other person other than with the permission of the Secretary of State.[64]

These duties are enforceable by civil proceedings by the Secretary of State for an injunction, or for specific performance of a statutory duty under section 45 of the Court of Session Act 1988, or for any other appropriate relief.[65] 5.42

There is an identical prohibition on disclosure of the existence or contents of a retention notice on the Information Commissioner or her staff without the permission of the Secretary of State but this is not included in the duties enforceable by way of civil proceedings.[66] 5.43

1. Extra-territoriality

A retention notice and any requirement or restriction imposed by virtue of a retention notice or by section 92 (data security), 93 (unlawful disclosure), or 95(1) to (3) IPA (enforcement) may relate to conduct outside the United Kingdom (UK) and persons outside the UK[67] but proceedings to enforce the duty to comply with requirements or restrictions do not apply to a person outside the UK.[68] 5.44

---

[64] ibid s 95(2) and (4).
[65] ibid s 95(5).
[66] ibid s 95(3) and (4).
[67] ibid s 97(1).
[68] ibid s 97(2).

6
EQUIPMENT INTERFERENCE

A.	Introduction	6.01
B.	Warrants	6.05
	1. Types of Warrants	6.05
	2. Scope of Warrants	6.10
	3. Subject Matter of Warrants	6.12
	4. Issuing Warrants	6.17
	5. Approval of Warrants by Judicial Commissioners	6.42
C.	Safeguards	6.52
	1. Members of Parliament	6.52
	2. Items Subject to Legal Privilege	6.55
	3. Confidential Journalistic Material and Journalistic Sources	6.60
	4. Requirements that Must Be Met by Warrants	6.63
D.	Warrants: Post-issue Matters	6.66
	1. Duration of Warrants	6.66
	2. Renewal of Warrants	6.67
	3. Modification of Warrants	6.71
	4. Modification of Warrants Issued by Law Enforcement Chiefs	6.84
	5. Cancellation of Warrants	6.93
	6. Implementation of Warrants	6.96
	7. Service of Warrants	6.98
	8. Duty of Telecommunications Operators to Assist with Implementation	6.101
E.	Disclosure	6.104
	1. Safeguards	6.104
	2. Duty Not to Make Unauthorized Disclosures	6.111
	3. Excepted Disclosures	6.114
	4. Offence of Making Unauthorized Disclosure	6.119

A. INTRODUCTION

The state's engagement in equipment interference, also known as computer network exploitation (CNE), has only been publicly admitted since early 2015 when the government published a draft Code of Practice on the use of the technique. This avowal, 6.01

6. Equipment Interference

as it has become known, was in response to *Privacy International and Greennet and Others v (1) The Secretary of State for Foreign and Commonwealth Affairs (2) The Government Communications Headquarters*,[1] an application to the Investigatory Powers Tribunal (IPT) alleging, amongst other things, that the legislative scheme such as it was under which CNE was conducted was unlawful. Although the IPT found that the practice was lawful, it was not prepared to make a finding on whether acts outside the British Islands were unlawful. The tribunal did conclude that prior to the publication of the draft Code of Practice the conduct of the intelligence services had been unlawful insofar as it related to the handling of legal professional privilege. An application for judicial review of the decision failed on the ground that the High Court did not have jurisdiction to consider such a challenge following *A v Director of Establishments*.[2] A reflection of the government's *volte face* in terms of this previously highly secret technique can be seen on the Security Service (MI5) website, which now publishes details of the practice.[3]

6.02 Prior to the Investigatory Powers Act 2016 (IPA), equipment interference, or 'hacking' as it is less elegantly known, was said to be provided for by sections 5 and 7 of the Intelligence Services Act 1994, as amended. The former was a pervasive power exercisable by the relevant Secretary of State to issue a warrant in the most general terms providing it was necessary to the discharge of the intelligence services' functions and proportionate. The latter made lawful activities outside the British Islands that might otherwise be rendered unlawful in the United Kingdom (UK) providing a warrant was in place. These two sections have been replaced with thirty-seven new provisions in the IPA and a draft Code of Practice that runs to 134 pages.

6.03 The draft Code of Practice sets out a number of requirements of applications for warrants, including but not limited to, identification of targets (where known) and the equipment, the nature, and extent of the interference proposed, the operational objective, an assessment of collateral intrusion, and whether any legal privilege will be obtained.[4] Opinion on the draft Code was polarized. Privacy International described it was 'too little too late'[5] and the Home Office that 'there are limits on what can be said in public about this work. But it is imperative that the government is as open as it can be about these capabilities and how they are used'.[6] As to the provisions in the IPA, David Anderson QC, the Independent Reviewer of Terrorism Legislation, who conceived in 'A Question of Trust'[7] the need for a comprehensive

---

[1] IPT 14/85/CH 14/120-126/CH.
[2] [2009] UKSC 12.
[3] https://www.mi5.gov.uk/equipment-interference (last accessed 6 February 2017).
[4] Draft Code of Practice, para 4.6.
[5] https://www.openrightsgroup.org/ourwork/reports/equipment-interference-code-of-practice (last accessed 6 February 2017).
[6] https://www.theguardian.com/uk-news/2015/feb/06/uk-security-services-capable-bypassing-encryption-draft-code (last accessed 6 February 2017).
[7] Report of the Investigatory Powers Review (June 2015).

legislative structure to be in place, described them as introducing 'world-leading standards of transparency'.[8]

The regulation of Equipment Interference, other than bulk equipment interference, forms Part 5 of the IPA.   6.04

B. WARRANTS

1. Types of Warrants

As with interception warrants under Part 2, Chapter 1, there are two kinds of warrants which may be issued under Part 5, targeted equipment interference warrants and targeted examination warrants.[9] The scheme for obtaining warrants is also similar to that for the interception of communications. Any conduct carried out in accordance with a warrant under Part 5 is lawful for all purposes.[10]   6.05

A targeted equipment interference warrant authorizes or requires a person to whom it is addressed to obtain equipment data, communications, and any other information.[11] Obtaining communications is not subject to exhaustive definition but includes monitoring, observing, or listening to a person's communications 'or other activities' or the recording of such.[12]   6.06

A targeted examination warrant authorizes the person to whom it is addressed to carry out the selection of protected material acquired through the use of a bulk equipment interference warrant under Part 6, Chapter 3 for the purpose of examination in breach of the prohibition on seeking to identify the communications of or private information relating to individuals in the British Isles, contrary to section 193(4).[13]   6.07

(a) *Equipment Data*

Equipment data is systems data or identifying data (see Chapter 1, paragraphs 1.88–1.90) comprising three elements which: first, is for the purposes of a relevant system (any system on or by means of which the data is held),[14] comprised in, included as part of, attached to, or logically associated with a communication but not limited to just the sender, or any other item of information;[15] secondly, is capable of being logically separated from the remainder of the communication or the item of information; and, thirdly, if so separated would not reveal anything of what might reasonably be considered to be the meaning, if any, of the communication or the item   6.08

---

[8] https://terrorismlegislationreviewer.independent.gov.uk/the-investigatory-powers-act-2016-an-exercise-in-democracy/#more-2849 (last accessed 7 February 2917).
[9] ibid s 99(1)(a)–(b).
[10] ibid s 99(11).
[11] ibid s 99(2)(a)–(c).
[12] ibid s 99(4)(a)–(b).
[13] ibid s 99(9).
[14] ibid s 100(3).
[15] ibid s 100(2)(a).

6. Equipment Interference

of information. Where the meaning is clear or can be inferred from the fact of the communication or the existence of the item of information or from any data relating to either, this should disregarded for the purpose of the definition.[16]

(b) *Protected Material*

6.09 Protected material is any material obtained under a bulk equipment interference warrant, other than material which is equipment data and/or information except a communication or equipment data, which is not private information.[17]

2. Scope of Warrants

6.10 In addition to authorizing the acquisition of communications, equipment data, and any other information, a targeted equipment interference warrant must also authorize or require the person to whom it is addressed to secure this and may also authorize that person to secure the disclosure, in any manner described in the warrant, of anything obtained under it.[18] However, it does not authorize conduct that would amount to the unlawful interception of a communication contrary to section 3(1) IPA, other than in respect of a stored communication or with lawful authority.[19] In this connection, 'stored communication' means stored by the telecommunications system, whether before or after transmission.[20]

6.11 A warrant issued under Part 5 also authorizes consequential conduct that it is necessary to undertake to facilitate what is expressly authorized or required by the warrant, including conduct for securing the obtaining of communications, equipment data or other information[21] (but not conduct that would constitute an offence of unlawful interception as described in paragraph 6.10, above)[22] and any conduct by any person to whom the warrant is addressed or who is acting on their behalf to provide assistance in giving effect to the warrant.[23]

3. Subject Matter of Warrants

(a) *Targeted Equipment Interference Warrants*

6.12 A targeted equipment interference warrant may relate to any one or more of eight matters set out in section 101(1) IPA. Each relates to equipment and broadly falls into three categories: ownership, location, and use.

6.13 There are three ownership 'matters': equipment belonging to, used by or in the possession of: a particular person or organization;[24] a group of persons who share a

---

[16] ibid s 100(2)(c).
[17] ibid s 99(9).
[18] ibid s 99(3)(a)–(b).
[19] ibid s 99(6).
[20] ibid s 99(8).
[21] ibid s 99(5)(a).
[22] ibid s 99(7).
[23] ibid s 99(5)(b).
[24] ibid s 101(1)(a).

common purpose or who carry on, or may carry on, a particular activity;[25] and more than one person or organization (where the interference is for the purpose of a single investigation or operation).[26]

There are two location matters, either equipment in a particular location,[27] or in more than one location, where the interference is for the purpose of the same investigation or operation.[28]

6.14

The third category, use, is equipment that is being, or may be used for three purposes: a particular activity or activities of a particular description; to test, maintain, or develop capabilities relating to interference with equipment for the purpose of obtaining communications, equipment data, or other information; or for the training of persons who carry out, or are likely to carry out, such interference with equipment.

6.15

(b) *Targeted Examination Warrants*

A targeted examination warrant may relate to any one or more of narrower—since it involves the examination of the product of bulk equipment interference that has already taken place—but broadly similar matters. In addition to testing, maintenance, or development and/or training,[29] those matters are a particular person or organization,[30] a group of persons who share a common purpose or who carry on, or may carry on, a particular activity;[31] and/or more than one person or organization, where the conduct authorized by the warrant is for the purpose of a single investigation or operation.[32]

6.16

4. Issuing Warrants

There are three entities that may apply to the Secretary of State for the issue of a targeted equipment interference warrant under Part 5: the intelligence services (MI5, MI6, and GCHQ), Defence Intelligence (part of the Ministry of Defence), and law enforcement. The intelligence services may, subject to certain restrictions, seek a warrant on the grounds of national security, the economic well-being of the UK so far as relevant to national security and the prevention and detection of serious crime.[33] Defence Intelligence is limited to applying on national security grounds only and law enforcement, to preventing or detecting serious crime, or preventing death or injury, although in the case of Police Service Northern Ireland, this extends to protecting the interests of national

6.17

---

[25] ibid s 101(1)(b).
[26] ibid s 101(1)(c).
[27] ibid s 101(1)(d).
[28] ibid s 101(1)(e).
[29] ibid s 101(2)(d)–(e).
[30] ibid s 101(2)(a).
[31] ibid s 101(2)(b).
[32] ibid s 101(2)(c).
[33] ibid s 102(5).

6. Equipment Interference

security.[34] Only the intelligence services are entitled to apply for a targeted examination warrant under Part 5.

6.18 The decision to issue a warrant on behalf of the intelligence services and the Chief of Defence Intelligence must be taken personally by the Secretary of State or where the equipment or person is or believed to be in Scotland, Scottish Ministers.[35] The person who issues it must also sign it or, if it is not reasonably practicable for that person to do so, a senior official designated by the Secretary of State or, where necessary, Scottish Ministers.[36] In these circumstances, the warrant must contain a statement that it was not reasonably practicable for the warrant to be signed by the person who issued it but that person has personally and expressly authorized the issue of it.[37]

(a) *Matters Common to All Applications for Warrants under Part 5*

6.19 There are a number of matters that are common to applications for targeted equipment interference warrants or, in the case of the intelligence services, targeted examination warrants under Part 5 by any of the entities permitted to apply.

6.20 In each case, the Secretary of State considers that it is necessary to issue the warrant on the particular ground upon which the application is made and that it is proportionate to what is to be achieved.[38]

6.21 The matters to be taken into account when considering the necessity and proportionality of issuing a warrant includes of whether what is sought through the issue of the warrant could reasonably be achieved by other means.[39]

6.22 The Secretary of State must consider that satisfactory arrangements are in force for the purposes of sections 129 and 130 (safeguards in relation to retention and disclosure of material including disclosure overseas).[40]

6.23 Except where the Secretary of State considers that there is an urgent need to issue the warrant, in each case, the decision to issue a warrant must be approved by a judicial commissioner.[41]

(b) *The Intelligence Services*

6.24 An application for a targeted equipment interference or targeted examination warrant must be made by or on behalf of the head of an intelligence service. If it is on behalf of the head of the service, the person applying must hold office under the Crown.[42]

---

[34] ibid s 106(5).
[35] ibid s 105(1)–(2).
[36] ibid s 105(3)–(4).
[37] ibid s 105(5)(a)–(b).
[38] ibid s 102(1)(a)–(b) (intelligence services); s 103(1)(b)–(c) (intelligence services where equipment believed to be in Scotland); s 104(1)(a)–(b) (Chief of Defence Intelligence); and s 106(1)(a)–(b) (law enforcement).
[39] ibid s 102(7), 103(3), 104(2), and 106(11), respectively.
[40] ibid s 102(1)(c), 103(1)(d), 104(1)(c), and 106(1)(c), respectively.
[41] ibid s 102(1)(d), 103(1)(e), 104(1)(d), and 106(1)(d), respectively.
[42] ibid s 102(8).

The restriction on the Secretary of State to issue a targeted equipment interference warrant are where the only ground for considering the warrant to be necessary is for the purpose of preventing or detecting serious crime.[43] In addition, in the case of both a targeted equipment interference and examination warrant, the warrant, if issued, would authorize interference only with equipment or person which or who would be or the Secretary of State believes would be in Scotland at the time of the issue of the warrant.[44] However, the restrictions on issuing a warrant in relation to equipment or persons either in or believed to be in Scotland would not prevent the Secretary of State from implementing any treaties for the purposes of section 2(2) of the European Communities Act 1972.[45]

The Secretary of State may only issue a targeted examination warrant if it is considered necessary on one of the three grounds available to it (set out in paragraph 6.17, above) and it is proportionate to do so.[46]

There are two other requirements before the Secretary of State can issue a targeted examination warrant. First, it is considered that the warrant is or may be necessary to authorize the selection of protected material for examination in breach of the prohibition in section 193(4) (see paragraph 6.09, above), and the decision to issue the warrant has been approved by a judicial commissioner unless it is urgent.[47]

A targeted interference warrant may be considered necessary in the interests of the economic well-being of the UK only if the interference with equipment is considered necessary for the purpose of obtaining information relating to the acts or intentions of persons outside the British Islands.[48]

(c) *Intelligences Services: Scotland*

In addition to those matters common to all applications, Scottish Ministers may issue a targeted equipment interference or examination warrant where an application is made by or on behalf of the intelligence services where the warrant authorizes interference only with equipment which or person who is or Scottish Ministers believe is in Scotland at the time the warrant is issued.[49] Scottish Ministers may only issue warrants on the ground that it is necessary for the purposes of preventing or detecting serious crime.[50]

As in the case of targeted examination warrants issued by the Secretary of State, the Scottish Ministers will also need to be satisfied it is proportionate to issue the warrant,[51] that in the case of a targeted examination warrant it is considered that

6.25

6.26

6.27

6.28

6.29

6.30

---

[43] ibid s 102(2)(a).
[44] ibid s 102(2)(b) and (4).
[45] ibid s 102(9).
[46] ibid s 102(3)(a)–(b).
[47] ibid s 102(3)(c)–(d).
[48] ibid s 102(6).
[49] ibid s 102(1)(a) and (2)(a).
[50] ibid s 103(1)(b) and (2)(b).
[51] ibid s 102(2)(c).

6. Equipment Interference

the warrant is or may be necessary to authorize the selection of protected material for examination in breach of the prohibition in section 193(4) (see paragraph 6.09, above), and the decision to issue the warrant has been approved by a judicial commissioner unless it is urgent.[52]

(d) *Chief of Defence Intelligence*

6.31 In the case of an application made by or on behalf of the Chief of Defence Intelligence, the Secretary of State must consider that the matters common to all applications and set out in paragraphs 6.19 to 6.23 above are satisfied. Where it is made on behalf of the Chief of Defence Intelligence that person must hold office under the Crown.[53]

(e) *Law Enforcement Officers: Schedule 6 IPA*

6.32 Section 106 of the Act provides for law enforcement officers to apply to their chief for the issue of a targeted equipment warrant. The provision needs to be read alongside Schedule 6 of the Act, which identifies, in Part 1, Table 1 and in three columns the chiefs, their delegates where appropriate and those officers who may make an application for a warrant (police force law enforcement officials). Typically, any chief constable of a police force may issue a warrant and the function may be delegated to a designated assistant chief constable or, where not practicable, any assistant chief constable within that force. In the case of the metropolitan police, the function may be delegated to a commander. In Scotland, it may be delegated to the deputy or assistant chief constable. In the case of the National Crime Agency, the Director General is its 'chief' and any senior officer designated by the Director General may issue a warrant. A member of the relevant police force, collaborative force, or National Crime Agency officer included in a collaboration agreement may apply for a warrant.

6.33 Part 2, Table 2 of Schedule 6 sets out in the same schematic the position in relation to non-police force law enforcement officials,[54] including senior immigration officers, Revenue and Customs, the Competition and Markets Authority, and Police Investigations and Review Commissioner in Scotland.

6.34 Part 3 of Schedule 6 defines what is meant by collaborative police force. Collaborative agreements are provided for by section 22A of the Police Act 1996. A collaborative force is where two forces are parties to such an agreement and where one police force to the agreement is able to apply under section 106 to the chief officer of the other. There are similar arrangements for agreements with the National Crime Agency, which permits NCA officers to apply to the relevant chief officer and for the collaborating police force to apply to the NCA's Director General where appropriate.

---

[52] ibid s 102(20)(d)–(e).
[53] ibid s 104(3).
[54] The terms 'designated customs official' and 'immigration officer' are defined in ibid s 106(14).

B. Warrants

(f) *Police Law Enforcement Officials*
Section 96 gives effect to Schedule 6.[55] 6.35

In addition to the matters common to all applications and set out in paragraphs 6.19 to 6.23, above) a police force law enforcement chief may, on an application made by an appropriate law enforcement officer issue a targeted equipment interference warrant. Such applications are limited to the prevention or detection of serious crime or where it is necessary for the purpose of preventing death or any injury or damage to a person's physical or mental health or of mitigating any injury or damage to a person's physical or mental health.[56] Necessary for the prevention and detection of crime does not include the activities of a trade union in the British Islands 'of itself'.[57] 6.36

In an urgent case an appropriate delegate may exercise the power to issue the warrant if it is not reasonably practicable for a law enforcement chief to consider the application. 6.37

(g) *Other Law Enforcement Officials*
In addition to the matters common to all applications, non-police law enforcement officials may only apply for the issue of a warrant where the serious crime sought to be prevented or which is being investigated relates to their functions. So, a chief immigration official can only issue if the serious crime is an immigration or nationality offence[58] and Revenue and Customs in relation to an 'assigned matter' for the purposes of section 1(1) of the Customs and Excise Management Act 1979 (any matter in relation to which the Commissioners are for the time being required in pursuance of any enactment to perform any duties).[59] There are similar provisions in respect of other non-police law enforcement officials.[60] 6.38

(h) *Restriction on Issue of Warrants to Certain Law Enforcement Officers*
In the original Bill restrictions on certain law enforcement chiefs was found in clause 117 and was sensibly moved to follow consecutively what became section 106. Broadly speaking, the chief officer of any police force, as well as the Police Investigations and Review Commissioner in Scotland and the chairman or a deputy chairman of the Independent Police Complaints Commission may not issue a targeted equipment interference warrant unless they consider that there is a British Islands connection.[61] Other law enforcement chiefs identified in Schedule 6, Part 1, Table: Part 1 are not so restricted.[62] Note there is no equivalent provision in respect of the Police Ombudsman of Northern Ireland. 6.39

---

[55] ibid s 106(5)(a)–(c).
[56] ibid s 106(3)(a).
[57] ibid s 106(2).
[58] Defined further in ibid s 106(13)(a)–(b).
[59] ibid s 106(8).
[60] ibid s 106(7)–(12).
[61] ibid s 107(1) and (2).
[62] ibid s 107(5).

6. Equipment Interference

6.40 The Director General of the National Crime Agency may not issue a targeted equipment interference warrant on the application of a member of a collaborative police force[63] unless the Director General considers that there is a British Islands connection.[64]

6.41 What constitutes a British Islands connection is extremely broad and arises if any of the conduct authorized by the warrant would take place in the British Islands (regardless of the location of the equipment that would, or may, be interfered with), or any of the equipment which would, or may, be interfered with would, or may, be in the British Islands at some time while the interference is taking place.[65] In addition, a purpose of the interference is to obtain communications sent by, or to, a person who is, or whom the law enforcement officer believes to be, for the time being in the British Islands information relating to an individual who is, or whom the law enforcement officer believes to be, for the time being in the British Islands, or equipment data which forms part of, or is connected with, communications or information relating to either of these purposes.[66]

5. Approval of Warrants by Judicial Commissioners

(a) *Approval of Warrants: Non-urgent Cases*

6.42 Other than in urgent cases, a warrant under Part 5 can only be issued if the decision to issue it has been approved by a judicial commissioner. In deciding whether to approve the judicial commissioner must review conclusions reached by the person who has decided to issue the warrant as to two matters. The first is whether the warrant is necessary on any relevant grounds and, secondly, whether the conduct that would be authorized by the warrant is proportionate to the objective to be met through its use.[67] Relevant grounds means any ground open to the relevant applicant under sections 102(5), 103, 104, and 106(1)(a), and (2)(b).[68]

6.43 In determining whether to approve the same principles as would be applied by a court on an application for judicial review are applicable[69] and the judicial commissioner should 'consider the [necessity and proportionality of the application] with a sufficient degree of care' so as to ensure compliance with section 2 of the IPA (general duties in relation to privacy): see Chapter 2, paragraphs 2.08–2.10.

6.44 A judicial commissioner who refuses to approve a decision to issue a warrant must give the person written reasons for the refusal.[70] The applicant in such circumstances may then ask the Investigatory Powers Commissioner for approval, unless

---

[63] As defined in para 2 of Part 3 of ibid Schedule 6.
[64] ibid s 107(3).
[65] ibid s 107(4)(a)–(b).
[66] ibid s107(4)(c)(i)–(iii).
[67] ibid s 108(1)(a)–(b).
[68] ibid s 108(3).
[69] ibid s 108(2).
[70] ibid s 108(4).

the Investigatory Powers Commissioner was the judicial commissioner who refused it at first instance.[71]

(b) *Approval of Warrants: Urgent Cases*

An urgent warrant is a warrant issued without the approval of a judicial commissioner and where the person who issued it considered there was an urgent need to issue it without prior judicial approval.[72] 6.45

In cases where the warrant has been issued on an urgent basis and without prior approval the person who issued the warrant must inform a judicial commissioner that it has been issued.[73] There is no time limit specified within which the judicial commissioner should be informed. However, the judicial commissioner must decide whether to approve the decision to issue the warrant, and notify the applicant of the decision within the 'relevant period'. This is the period ending with the third working day after the day on which the warrant was issued.[74] 6.46

Where a judicial commissioner refuses to approve the decision to issue an urgent warrant, the warrant ceases to have effect (unless previously cancelled), and it may not be renewed.[75] Refusal has a number of effects. 6.47

(c) *Consequences where Judicial Commissioner Refuses to Approve in Urgent Cases*

Where a judicial commissioner refuses to approve the issue of a warrant in an urgent case, the person to whom the warrant was addressed must, so far as is reasonably practicable, secure that anything in the process of being done under the warrant stops as soon as possible.[76] The lawfulness of anything in the process of being done at the time the warrant ceases to have effect but which has already been done or cannot be stopped is not affected.[77] There are different provisions in respect of each warrant type. 6.48

Where the decision to refuse to approve relates to a targeted equipment interference warrant, the judicial commissioner has discretion to direct certain things take place on cessation. The first is to authorize further interference with equipment for the purpose of securing that anything in the process of being done under the warrant stops as soon as possible. The second is to direct that any of the material obtained under the warrant is destroyed; or the third is to impose conditions as to the use or retention of the material.[78] In the case of a targeted examination warrant, the judicial commissioner has discretion to impose any conditions as to the use of any protected material selected for examination under the warrant.[79] 6.49

---

[71] ibid s 108(5).
[72] ibid s 116(3)(a)–(b).
[73] ibid s 109(2).
[74] ibid s 109(3).
[75] ibid s 109(4).
[76] ibid s 110(2).
[77] ibid s 110(9).
[78] ibid s 110(3)(a)–(c).
[79] ibid s 110(4).

6. Equipment Interference

6.50 There are number of procedural mechanisms that may take effect on the judicial commissioner refusing to approve an urgent warrant. The first relate to an 'affected party'(the person who issued the warrant or the person to whom it is addressed).[80] The judicial commissioner may invite representations about how to exercise their discretion on cessation of either type of warrant.[81] Where an affected party makes representations (whether or not at the judicial commissioner's invitation), these must be considered when the judicial commissioner considers whether to exercise discretion on cessation of the warrant.[82]

6.51 The second is a right of person who authorized the issue of the urgent warrant to seek a review of the judicial commissioner's decision by the Investigatory Powers Commissioner.[83] Where such a right is exercised the Investigatory Powers Commissioner may either confirm the original decision not to approve or make a fresh determination.[84]

C. SAFEGUARDS

1. Members of Parliament

6.52 The provisions in relation to the position of Members of Parliament were originally located within the first few clauses of Part 5 of the Bill but later moved under the heading 'additional safeguards'. Amendments were later made to strengthen the position in relation to equipment interference and parliamentarians.

6.53 Where an application is made to the Secretary of State for a targeted equipment interference or examination warrant the purpose of which is to obtain or examine protected material consisting of communications sent by, or intended for, a person who is a member of 'a relevant legislature' (i.e. either House of Parliament or the Scottish Parliament, the National Assemblies of Wales or Northern Ireland, or the European Parliament)[85] or their private information[86] before deciding to issue the warrant, the Secretary of State must consult the Prime Minister.[87]

6.54 The amendments added following publication of the Bill related to applications by law enforcement chiefs or an appropriate delegate for targeted equipment interference warrants in such circumstances. Whereas, in any other case, a law enforcement chief may issue the warrant on an application being made by an officer under section 106, there is a prohibition from doing so in a case involving a parliamentarian's communications or private information without the approval of the Secretary of State

---

[80] ibid s 110(6).
[81] ibid s 110(5)(a).
[82] ibid s 110(5)(b).
[83] ibid s 110(7).
[84] ibid s 110(8).
[85] ibid s 111(8).
[86] ibid s 111(1)–(2).
[87] ibid s 111(3).

C. Safeguards

who may only give approval if the Prime Minister approves the issue of the warrant. The only exception to this requirement is where equipment is in Scotland or the law enforcement chief believes the equipment to be there at the time the warrant is issued.[88]

2. Items Subject to Legal Privilege

6.55 Part 5 provides for two circumstances relating to the acquisition of legal privilege: deliberate and incidental acquisition. In each case, arrangements must be in place under sections 129 or 191 (safeguards relating to retention and disclosure of material),[89] although the former provision is required to be met in the case of any warrant prior to issue.

6.56 Where an application is made for a warrant to authorize or require interference with equipment for the purpose of obtaining items subject to legal privilege or the purpose of a targeted examination warrant is to examine items subject to legal privilege then section 112 of the Act imposes a number of additional conditions. The person issuing the warrant must have regard to the public interest in the confidentiality of items subject to legal privilege[90] and consider that there are exceptional and compelling circumstances that make it necessary to do so.[91] The threshold of 'exceptional and compelling' will not be met unless the public interest in obtaining the information outweighs the public interest in maintaining the confidentiality of the legal privilege, there are no other means by which the information could reasonably be obtained and in cases where the substantive ground upon which the warrant is obtained in the prevention and detection of serious crime, obtaining the information is necessary for the preventing death or significant injury.[92]

6.57 The application must also contain a statement that the purpose is or includes the acquisition or examination of items subject to legal privilege.[93] A warrant may not be issued if the only basis for it being necessary is on the ground of the economic well-being of the UK.[94]

6.58 The position is broadly similar in cases where there is a risk of items subject to legal privilege being included in 'relevant material'.[95] For the purposes of section 112, this is either that acquired through targeted equipment interference or the protected material selected for examination.[96] In such cases, in addition to a statement that there is a likelihood of items of legal privilege being included, an assessment of how likely this is must be included on the warrant.[97]

---

[88] ibid s 111(4)–(9).
[89] ibid s 112(4)(b) and (9).
[90] ibid s 112(3).
[91] ibid s 112(4)(a).
[92] ibid s 112(6).
[93] ibid s 112(2).
[94] ibid s 112(5).
[95] ibid s 112(7).
[96] ibid s 112(10)(a)–(b).
[97] ibid s 100(5)(a)–(b).

6.59 There is detailed provision for cases where the material sought has been created or is held with the intention of furthering a criminal purpose (and which, therefore, is not or no longer privileged). In cases where a targeted equipment interference warrant seeks to obtain such material or a targeted examination warrant authorizes the selection of such material for examination, three conditions arise. The first condition is that the application must contain a statement that the material would, but for it being created or held for this purpose, be subject to legal privilege. The second condition, in the case of a targeted examination warrant, is that it must specifically authorize the selection of such items; the third condition is that it must set out the reasons for believing the material was created or held for such a purpose.[98] The person issuing the warrant may only then do so if it is considered that the material is likely to have been created or is held with the intention of furthering a criminal purpose.[99]

3. Confidential Journalistic Material and Journalistic Sources

6.60 Journalistic material means, in summary, material created or acquired for the purposes of journalism but not material created or acquired with the intention of furthering a criminal purpose. Confidential journalistic material is either a communication consisting of journalistic material which either the sender, recipient or intended recipient of the communication holds in confidence or other journalistic material which a person holds in confidence.[100] A journalistic source is 'an individual who provides material intending the recipient to use it for the purposes of journalism or knowing that it is likely to be so used'.[101]

6.61 The position in respect of confidential journalistic material and journalistic sources follows a similar procedure under sections 113 and 114 IPA, introduced at a late stage of the Bill's evolution, although the threshold is considerably lower than that for legal privilege. If the application for a targeted equipment interference warrant relates to communications which are or contain confidential journalistic material or is a targeted examination warrant authorizing the selection of journalistic material that is confidential journalistic material for examination then in both cases it must contain a statement to this effect.[102]

6.62 The person to who the application is made may only issue the warrant if arrangements are in place under section 129 or section 191 IPA (safeguards relating to retention and disclosure of material)[103] that include specific arrangements for the handling, retention, use, and destruction of any confidential journalistic material.[104]

---

[98] ibid s 112(11)–(12).
[99] ibid s 112(13).
[100] The full definition can be found in ibid s 264.
[101] ibid s 263(1).
[102] ibid s 113(2) and 114(2).
[103] ibid s 113(4).
[104] ibid s 113(3) and 114(3).

4. Requirements that Must Be Met by Warrants

There are a number of additional formalities that a warrant must include, although unlike warrants issued under the Police and Criminal Evidence Act 1984, there is no express provision making non-compliance unlawful.

6.63

A warrant under Part 5 must state whether it is a targeted equipment interference or a targeted examination warrant[105] and must be addressed to the applicant. So, for example, the appropriate head of the relevant intelligence service or law enforcement chief or their delegate if applicable.[106] In the case of a targeted examination warrant, the warrant must also describe the type of equipment that it is proposed will be interfered with and the extent of the conduct authorized.[107]

6.64

There are two tables set out in section 101, setting out the 'matter'(for example, who belongs to the equipment being interfered with) and the formalities that must be addressed in the warrant in respect of the matter (the name or description of the person or organization). The tables set out the requirements of section 101 (subject matter of warrants)[108] and how these need to be dealt with in the body of the warrant. The first table relates to targeted examination warrants and table two, targeted examination warrants.

6.65

D. WARRANTS: POST-ISSUE MATTERS

1. Duration of Warrants

A warrant issued under Part 5 is of six months duration, commencing on the day of issue.[109] Where it has been renewed this period recommences the day following what would have been day of the warrant's expiration.[110] An urgent warrant is of five working days duration, commencing the day after it was issued. This is known as the relevant period. A warrant will cease to have effect unless it is renewed or is cancelled or otherwise eases to have effect (for example it is an urgent warrant but not given later approval by a judicial commissioner under section 108) at the end of the relevant period.[111]

6.66

2. Renewal of Warrants

There are three common renewal conditions that closely mirror the original basis for the warrant being issued. It must necessary on any relevant grounds (those set out in sections 102, 103, 104, and 106(1)–(2) depending on the entity seeking

6.67

---

[105] ibid s 115(1).
[106] ibid s 115(2).
[107] ibid s 115(4)(a)–(b).
[108] See paras 6.12–6.16 above.
[109] ibid s 116(2)(b)(i).
[110] ibid s 116(2)(b)(ii).
[111] ibid s 116(1)(a)–(b).

authorization),[112] proportionate to the objective sought by engaging in the conduct[113] and a judicial commissioner has approved the renewal.[114] Renewing a targeted examination warrant in respect of the selection of protected material for examination in breach of the prohibition in section 193(4) must also be considered to be necessary.[115]

6.68 If each of the renewal conditions is met then a warrant may be renewed providing this is done before the expiration of the renewal period. The renewal period is in urgent cases the relevant period or in every other case the period of 30 days ending with the day the warrant would cease to have effect if it was not renewed).[116] It is done so by the 'appropriate person', who is in fact the person holding the office who issued the warrant originally (for example, the Secretary of State in the case of the intelligence service and Chief of Defence Intelligence) and by instrument.[117]

6.69 In cases of renewals of warrants for the intelligence services and Chief of Defence Intelligence, the Secretary of State must sign the instrument[118] or in the case of the intelligence services in Scotland, a member of the Scottish Government must personally decide to renew and sign the instrument.[119] In law enforcement renewals the person who renews it must sign the instrument.[120]

6.70 The provisions in relation to Members of Parliament, legal privilege and confidential journalistic material apply in relation to renewal as they applied in relation to the decision to issue the warrant.[121] So too do the provisions in relation to approval by judicial commissioners and references to the person who issued the warrant should be read for the purposes of renewal as the person who has decided to renew it.[122]

3. Modification of Warrants

(a) *Modification of Warrants Issued by the Secretary of State or Scottish Ministers*

6.71 A warrant issued at ministerial level under Part 5 (so those relating to the intelligence services and the Chief of Defence Intelligence) may be modified at any time by an instrument issued by the person making the modification.[123] The scope of modification is limited to adding or removing the subject matter,[124] adding, varying, or removing a name or names or description or descriptions included in the original

---

[112] ibid s 117(2)(a) and (4).
[113] ibid s 117(2)(b).
[114] ibid s 117(2)(d).
[115] ibid s 117(2)(c).
[116] ibid s 117(5).
[117] ibid s 117(1) and (3).
[118] ibid s 117(6).
[119] ibid s 117(7).
[120] ibid s 117(8).
[121] ibid s 117(10).
[122] ibid s 117(9).
[123] ibid s 118(1).
[124] ibid s 118(2)(a)–(b).

D. Warrants: Post-issue Matters

warrant[125] and adding, varying, or removing the description or descriptions of types of equipment included in the warrant under section 115.[126] The provisions are only concerned with modifications that affect the conduct authorized or required by it.[127]

6.72 There is no power to modify the details required under section 115(3) and (5) (details to be included in warrants) in cases of targeted equipment interference or examination warrants where the proposed modifications relate only to equipment belonging to or, used by or in the possession of a particular problem or organization and at a particular location.[128]

6.73 As with the issue of the warrant, the decision to modify must be taken personally by the person making the modification and that person must also sign the instrument making the modification.[129]

(b) Persons Entitled to Make Modifications

6.74 The persons who may make modifications depend on whether the warrant is urgent. In non-urgent cases, a warrant issued by the Secretary of State relating to the intelligence services or Chief of Defence Intelligence, may only be modified by the person holding that office or a senior official acting on their behalf.[130] In the case of a warrant issued by Scottish Minsters, modifications are limited to a member of the Scottish Government or a senior official on their behalf. The meaning of senior official in this context is not straightforward. In the case of a warrant on behalf of the intelligence services, it is a the person who is a member of the Senior Civil Service or Senior Management Structure of Her Majesty's Diplomatic Service, or person who holds a position in the intelligence service of equivalent seniority to such a person.[131] There is provision in relation to the Ministry of Defence, although it is not clear where the power for Scottish Minsters to issue warrants on its behalf derive from. In such cases, a senior official means a member of the Senior Civil Service, or the person is of or above the rank of brigadier, commodore, or air commodore.[132]

6.75 In urgent cases either the person to whom the warrant is addressed or a person who holds a senior position in the same public authority as the addressee may also make modifications.[133]

6.76 There is provision for modifications in cases involving Members of Parliament, lawyers and journalists. The scheme for issuing a warrant in these cases under sections 111 to 114 applies to modifications unless it relates to removing any matter, name, or description from the warrant.[134] In the case of a Member of Parliament, the

---

[125] ibid s 118(2)(c)–(d).
[126] ibid s 118(2)(e)–(f).
[127] ibid s 118(5).
[128] ibid s 118(3)(a)–(b).
[129] ibid s 118(4).
[130] ibid s 119(1)(a).
[131] ibid s 135(1)(a).
[132] ibid s 119(4)(b).
[133] ibid s 119(2)(b) and (4).
[134] ibid s 120(3).

Secretary of State must make any modification personally.[135] In cases involving legal privilege or confidential journalistic material, the Secretary of State, or in appropriate cases, a member of the Scottish Government must make the modification.[136] However, a senior official may sign the instrument if it is not reasonably practicable for the Secretary of State or Scottish Minister to do so but it must then contain a statement that this is the case and that the Minister has personally and expressly authorized the modification.[137] In each case, the modification does not take effect until a judicial commissioner has approved it.[138] The provisions in relation to judicial approval in such cases apply to modifications and section 108 should be read accordingly.[139]

(c) *Modifications: Requirement to Notify*

6.77 Where a modification has been made a judicial commissioner must be notified as soon as reasonably practicable of this and the reasons for it.[140] Modifications removing any matter, name or description in accordance with section 115(3) to (5), urgent cases and those involving safeguarded information concerning parliamentarians, lawyers, and journalists are not subject to this requirement.[141] There is further provision about judicial approval in these cases in section 122.

6.78 Where the senior official has made a modification in any case, the Secretary of State or, as the case may be, a member of the Scottish Government must be notified personally of and the reasons for the modification.[142]

(d) *Judicial Approval of Modifications in Urgent and Safeguarded Cases*

6.79 Where a modification has been made on the grounds of urgency or in a warrant concerned with information relating to parliamentarians, legal privilege or confidential journalistic material or sources has been modified without approval of a judicial commissioner on an urgent basis, the person who made the modification must inform the appropriate person that it has been made.[143] In urgent cases this is a designated senior official: see para 6.74, above.[144] In safeguarded cases, it is a judicial commissioner.[145]

6.80 The appropriate person must, within the period ending with the third working day after the modification (the relevant period), decide whether to approve the decision and notify the person who made the modification of this.[146] Where this is made

---

[135] ibid s 120(4)(a).
[136] ibid s 120(5)(a)(i).
[137] ibid s 120(7) and (8).
[138] ibid s 120(4)(b) and (5)(b).
[139] ibid s 120(6).
[140] ibid s 121(1).
[141] ibid s 121(2)(a)–(c).
[142] ibid s 121(3).
[143] ibid s 122(1)–(3).
[144] ibid s 122(4)(a).
[145] ibid s 122(4)(b).
[146] ibid s 122(5)(a)–(b).

D. Warrants: Post-issue Matters

by a designated senior official, notification of the decision must be given to a judicial commissioner as soon as reasonably practicable and if this is to approve the modification, provide particulars.[147] The Secretary of State or, where appropriate, Scottish Ministers must also be notified personally where this is the case.[148]

6.81 The consequence of a refusal to approve a modification are that Secretary of State or member of the Scottish Government in appropriate cases must be notified of the decision, the warrant has effect as if the modification had not been made (unless it has otherwise ceased to have effect) and as far as reasonably practicable secure that anything in the process of being done as a result of the modification ceases as soon as possible.[149] In safeguarded cases, there is no further right in such circumstances to ask the Investigatory Powers Commissioner to review the decision.[150]

6.82 In addition, and as with warrants case in the event of a refusal to approve a decision to modify a targeted equipment interference warrant, the designated senior official may authorize further interference with equipment for the purpose only of securing that anything in the process of being done under the warrant as a result of the modification stops as soon as possible.[151] In these circumstances, the designated senior official must personally notify the Secretary of State or, as the case may be, a member of the Scottish Government.[152]

6.83 Again, as with warrants, the lawfulness of anything done or being done before it could be stopped or which it is not reasonably practicable to stop under the warrant as a consequence of the modification before it ceases to have effect is not affected.[153]

4. Modification of Warrants Issued by Law Enforcement Chiefs

(a) *Non-urgent Cases*

6.84 The scheme for modification of warrants by law enforcement chiefs broadly reflects the position in respect of modification of other warrants.

6.85 A law enforcement chief or appropriate delegate (if they issued the warrant) may modify a warrant at any time.[154] Modifications made in such circumstances are limited to adding to the matters to which the warrant relates,[155] removing a matter to which the warrant relates,[156] adding, varying, or removing but only in relation to a matter to which the warrant relates a name or description to the names or descriptions included in the warrant,[157] adding to, varying, or removing the descriptions

---

[147] ibid s 122(6)(a)(i)–(ii).
[148] ibid s 122(6)(b).
[149] ibid s 122(7)(a)–(b).
[150] ibid s 122(7).
[151] ibid s 122(8).
[152] ibid s 122(9).
[153] ibid s 122(10)(a)–(b).
[154] ibid s 123(1)(a)–(b).
[155] ibid s 123(2)(a).
[156] ibid s 123(2)(b).
[157] ibid s 123(2)(c)–(d).

of types of equipment included in the warrant.[158] However, a modification to a targeted examination warrant, relating to only the equipment belonging to, used, or in the possession of a particular person or organization or varying or removing the description of this on the warrant is impermissible.[159] A decision to modify must be taken personally by the person making it and be by way of instrument signed by that person.[160]

6.86 As with the original warrant a modification, other than where this relates to removing any matter, name, or description, may be made only if the person making the modification considers that the warrant as modified continues to be necessary on any relevant grounds[161] (preventing or detecting crime or preventing death or injury etc) and the conduct authorized by the modification is proportionate to the operational objective,[162] and, other than in urgent cases (except those relating to Members of Parliament[163]) the modification has been approved by a judicial commissioner.[164]

6.87 Judicial approval is required following a decision to modify and section 108 IPA (the provisions relating to judicial approval) should be read accordingly: see paras 6.42–6.44.[165] Similarly, the provisions in relation to warrants and safeguarded information in sections 111 to 114 should be read across so as to apply to the decision to modify: see paras 6.52–6.62.[166] However, section 111(5), which relates to Members of Parliament, needs to be read by substituting references to the warrant being issued with references to modification as appropriate.[167]

(b) *Urgent Cases*

6.88 Again, the position in urgent modification cases reflects that relating to other warrants subject to modification in such circumstances. Where a modification has been made on an urgent basis, the person who made it must inform a judicial commissioner that it has been made.[168]

6.89 The judicial commissioner must then, within the period ending with the third working day after the modification (the relevant period), decide whether to approve the decision and notify the person who made the modification of this.[169]

6.90 The consequence of a refusal to approve a modification are that person who issued the warrant must be notified of the decision, the warrant has effect as if the modification had not been made (unless it has otherwise ceased to have effect) and as

---

[158] ibid s 123(2)(e)–(f).
[159] ibid s 123(3).
[160] ibid s 123(6).
[161] ibid s 123(3)(a)(i) and (4).
[162] ibid s 123(3)(a)(ii).
[163] ibid s 123(10).
[164] ibid s 123(3)(b).
[165] ibid s 123(7)(a)–(b).
[166] ibid s 123(8).
[167] ibid s 123(9).
[168] ibid s 124(1)–(2).
[169] ibid s 124(3).

D. Warrants: Post-issue Matters

far as reasonably practicable secure that anything in the process of being done as a result of the modification ceases as soon as possible.[170] There is no right to ask the Investigatory Powers Commissioner to review the decision.

In addition, and as with warrants in the event of a refusal to approve a decision to modify a targeted equipment interference warrant, the judicial commissioner may authorize further interference with equipment for the purpose only of securing that anything in the process of being done under the warrant as a result of the modification stops as soon as possible.[171] In these circumstances, the judicial commissioner must notify the person who issued it.[172] 6.91

Again, as with warrants, the lawfulness of anything done or being done before it could be stopped or which it is not reasonably practicable to stop under the warrant as a consequence of the modification before it ceases to have effect is not affected.[173] 6.92

5. Cancellation of Warrants

Any person who issues a warrant under Part 5 may, under section 125 IPA, cancel it at any time.[174] The section describes those who issue warrants as 'appropriate persons' for the purposes of cancellation.[175] 6.93

The basis upon which cancellation may arise reflects the basis upon which the warrant was issued. Where it is no longer considered necessary having regard to the grounds upon which it was issued or proportionate to the underlying objective for which it was issued then it may be cancelled.[176] The requirement to cancel is mandatory albeit the decision is based on the subjective view of the person who issued the warrant. Once cancelled the warrant cannot be renewed.[177] 6.94

Where a warrant is cancelled under section 125 IPA, the person to whom the warrant was addressed must, so far as is reasonably practicable, secure that anything in the process of being done under the warrant stops as soon as possible.[178] There is nothing in the Act about how cancellation is to be notified. 6.95

6. Implementation of Warrants

For the purposes of implementation of a targeted equipment interference warrant, the person to whom it is addressed, 'the implementing authority', may in addition to its own role in implementing the warrant act through, or together with other persons as the implementing authority may require to assist it to do so.[179] This 6.96

---

[170] ibid s 124(4)(a)–(c).
[171] ibid s 124(5).
[172] ibid s 124(6).
[173] ibid s 124(7)(a)–(b).
[174] ibid s 125(1).
[175] ibid s 125(4).
[176] ibid s 125(2)(a)–(b).
[177] ibid s 125(6).
[178] ibid s 125(5).
[179] ibid s 126(1).

6. Equipment Interference

includes disclosure to the implementing authority of any material obtained under the warrant.[180]

6.97 Where the implementing authority requires assistance with implementation, it may serve or make arrangements to serve a copy of the warrant—either with or without one or more of the schedules contained in it—on such persons it requires assistance from.[181] This includes service outside the UK.[182]

7. Service of Warrants

6.98 The requirement of service is to bring the contents of the warrant to the attention of the person who the implementing authority considers may be able to provide assistance in relation to it.[183]

6.99 Where service is to take place outside of the UK if may be done so by serving a copy of the warrant at the person's principal office within the UK or, if the person has no such office in the UK, at any place in the UK where the person carries on business or conducts activities.[184] If the person to be served has specified an address in the UK as one at which the person, or someone on the person's behalf, will accept service of documents serve may take place at that address but must be as soon as reasonably practicable after a copy of the warrant is made available for inspection.[185]

6.100 Service may also take place by making it available for inspection (whether to the person or to someone acting on the person's behalf) at a place in the UK.[186] However, this is only possible where it is not reasonably practicable for a copy to be served by any of the other two mechanisms and the implementing authority takes such steps as it considers appropriate for the purpose of bringing the contents of the warrant, and the availability of a copy for inspection, to the attention of the person.[187]

8. Duty of Telecommunications Operators to Assist with Implementation

6.101 Where a telecommunications operator has been served with a copy of a targeted equipment interference warrant issued by the Secretary of State or by the Scottish Ministers it must take all steps for giving effect to the warrant.[188] The same obligation on the part of the telecommunications operator arises where the warrant was addressed to a law enforcement officer, its terms approved by the Secretary of State

---

[180] ibid s 126(4).
[181] ibid s 126(2) and (5).
[182] ibid s 126(3).
[183] ibid s 127(2).
[184] ibid s 127(3)(a).
[185] ibid s 127(3)(b) and (5).
[186] ibid s 127(3)(c).
[187] ibid s 127(4)(a)–(b).
[188] ibid s 128(1).

of Scottish Minister as the case may be and these have been notified to it by or on behalf of the law enforcement officer.[189] Before the Secretary of State or Scottish Ministers give approval it must be considered necessary for the telecommunications operator to take the required steps and proportionate to the objective in taking them.[190] There is no requirement to take any steps that it is not reasonably practicable for the telecommunications operator to take.[191] The position is more onerous in respect of fulfilling a requirement under section 253 IPA (maintenance of technical capability).[192] This is dealt with in Chapter 10, paras 10.13–10.17.

6.102 The term 'law enforcement officer' is limited for this purpose to a constable of the Police Service of Scotland, a member of the Police Service of Northern Ireland or Metropolitan Police Service or officers in the National Crime Agency of Revenue and Customs.[193]

6.103 The duties on the telecommunications operator are enforceable but only against a person in the UK by way of civil proceedings for injunctive relief, in Scotland specific performance under section 45 of the Court of Session Act 1988 or any other appropriate relief.[194]

E. DISCLOSURE

1. Safeguards

(a) *Retention and Disclosure of Material*

6.104 There is a requirement on the part of any issuing authority to ensure, in relation to every targeted equipment interference warrant issued by that authority, that it has arrangements in force for securing that the number of persons to whom any of the material derived from the warrant is disclosed, the extent to which it is disclosed or otherwise made available and the extent to which the material is copied and the number of copies that are made is limited to minimum number necessary for the authorized purposes.[195] Every copy must be stored for as long as it is retained securely and must be destroyed as soon as there is no longer any relevant grounds—which in this context means authorized purposes—for retaining it unless it is destroyed sooner.[196] This does not apply to material, including any copy of the material, obtained under the warranted handed over to any overseas authorities (a country or territory outside the UK).[197]

---

[189] ibid s 128(2)(a)–(b).
[190] ibid s 128(4)(a)–(b).
[191] ibid s 128(5).
[192] ibid s 128(6).
[193] ibid s 128(3).
[194] ibid s 128(7).
[195] ibid s 129(1)–(2).
[196] ibid s 129(4)–(5).
[197] ibid s 129(9), (10), and (11).

6.105 Authorized purposes are limited to five purposes. The first purpose is that it is, or is likely to be, necessary on any of the relevant grounds (that is, the grounds upon or purpose for which the warrant was issued).[198] The second and third purposes are that it is necessary for facilitating the carrying out of functions under the Act by the Secretary of State, Scottish Ministers, or the person to whom the warrant is addressed or by the judicial commissioners or the Investigatory Powers Tribunal.[199] The fourth and fifth purposes are that it is necessary for the purpose of legal proceedings or the performance of the functions of any person under any enactment.[200]

6.106 If any item containing confidential journalistic material or identifies a journalist's source is retained following its examination the person retaining it must notify the Investigatory Powers Tribunal as soon as reasonably practicable.[201]

6.107 Copy has the same meaning as it does when used in the context of intercept warrants: see Chapter 3, paragraph 3.147.[202] Issuing authority means the Secretary of State, Scottish Ministers, or law enforcement chief that issued the warrant.[203]

(b) *Safeguards Relating to Disclosure of Material or Data Overseas*

6.108 Where the material or copies of the material obtained from a targeted equipment interference warrant is to be handed over to an overseas authority, the issuing authority must ensure that arrangements are in force for securing that the overseas authority has corresponding requirements to those imposed on it to such an extent if any the issuing authority considers appropriate.[204]

(c) *Safeguards Relating to Legal Privilege*

6.109 Where an item subject to legal privilege has been obtained under a targeted equipment interference warrant and is retained following its examination for purposes other than its destruction, the person to whom the warrant is addressed must inform the Investigatory Powers Commissioner of the retention of the item as soon as reasonably practicable.[205]

6.110 Other than in cases where the public interest in retention of the item outweighs the public interest in the confidentiality of items subject to items subject to legal privilege and retention is necessary in the interests of national security or for the purpose of preventing death or serious injury,[206] the Investigatory Powers Commissioner must either direct the item is destroyed or impose conditions as to the retention and use of the item.[207] In determining which of these alternatives is

---

[198] ibid s 129(3)(a) and (7).
[199] ibid s 129(3)(b)–(c).
[200] ibid s 129(3)(d)–(e).
[201] ibid s 129(8).
[202] ibid s 129(11).
[203] ibid s 129(11).
[204] ibid s 130(1)–(2).
[205] ibid s 131(1)–(2).
[206] ibid s 131(5)(a)–(b).
[207] ibid s 131(3).

E. Disclosure

appropriate the Commissioner may require representations to be made by affected persons.[208] These are either the person to who the warrant was or is addressed or the issuing authority: see paragraph 6.106 above.[209] Where the Commissioner requires representations, these must be considered when determining whether the items should be destroyed or conditions imposed.[210]

2. Duty Not to Make Unauthorized Disclosures

6.111 There is a duty imposed on those who may become aware of the existence or content of a warrant, details of its issue, renewal, or modification, details of any requirement to provide assistance, steps taken in pursuance of a warrant or any requirement to take such steps, and any material obtained under it in a form that identifies it as having been so obtained not to make an unauthorized disclosure of those matters.[211]

6.112 The categories of persons are any applicant for a warrant, person holding office under the Crown, person employed by or for the purposes of a police force, telecommunications operator, employee of, or person engaged for the purposes of any business of a telecommunications operator. It also includes any person to whom the matters, subject of the prohibition on disclosure, have been disclosed.[212]

6.113 A disclosure of the matters not be disclosed by a person caught by the duty not to will not make an unauthorized disclosure, if it is an excepted disclosure.[213]

3. Excepted Disclosures

6.114 An excepted disclosure may fall within four categories or 'heads': authorized disclosures, disclosures in connection with oversight bodies or legal proceedings and those of a general nature.[214]

6.115 The first head, authorized disclosures, means a disclosure authorized by the warrant, by the person to whom the warrant is or was addressed or under arrangements made by that person or by the terms of any requirement to provide assistance in giving effect to the warrant, including its implementation.[215]

6.116 The second head, disclosure in connection with oversight bodies, means a disclosure made to, or authorized by, a judicial commissioner[216] or the Independent Police Complaints Commission for the purposes of it carrying out any of its functions.[217]

---

[208] ibid s 131(6)(a).
[209] ibid s 131(7).
[210] ibid 131(6)(b).
[211] ibid s 132(1), (2), and (4).
[212] ibid s 132(3)(a)–(f).
[213] ibid s 132(2)(b).
[214] ibid s 133(1)(a)–(d).
[215] ibid s 133(2)(a)–(c).
[216] ibid s 133(3)(a).
[217] ibid s 133(3)(b).

6.117 The third head, legal proceedings, means a disclosure in contemplation of, or in connection with, any legal proceedings, and for the purposes of those proceedings a disclosure made by a professional legal adviser to their client or a representative of their client, or by their client, or by a representative of their client, to the legal adviser in connection with the giving of advice about the effect of the provisions of Part 5 IPA.[218] This does not include a disclosure with a view to furthering a criminal purpose.[219] This reflects the definition of legal privilege in section 10 of the Police and Criminal Evidence Act 1984.

6.118 The fourth head, disclosures of a general nature, means a disclosure made by a telecommunications operator in accordance with a requirement imposed by regulations made by the Secretary of State, which relates to the number of warrants under Part 5 to which the operator has given effect or has been involved in giving effect.[220] In addition, a disclosure of information that does not relate to any particular warrant under Part 5 IPA but relates to such warrants in general is also required.[221]

4. Offence of Making Unauthorized Disclosure

6.119 The offence of making an authorized disclosure is committed if a person makes a disclosure contrary to the duty not to knowing it was in breach of that duty. It is a defence to show that the accused could not reasonably have been expected, after first becoming aware of the matter disclosed, to take steps to prevent the disclosure.[222] As to when the offence is committed by a body corporate or Scottish partnership, see Chapter 10, paragraphs 10.125–10.127.

6.120 A person guilty of the offence of making an unauthorized disclosure is liable on summary conviction in England and Wales to imprisonment for a term not exceeding twelve months (or six months, if the offence was committed before the commencement of section 154(1) of the Criminal Justice Act 2003), or to a fine, or both.[223] On summary conviction in Scotland to imprisonment for a term not exceeding twelve months, or to a fine not exceeding the statutory maximum, or both.[224] In Northern Ireland the maximum sentence on summary conviction is imprisonment for a term not exceeding six months, or to a fine not exceeding the statutory maximum, or both.[225]

6.121 On conviction on indictment, the maximum sentence is imprisonment for a term not exceeding five years or to a fine, or both.[226]

---

[218] ibid s 133(4)(a)–(b).
[219] ibid s 133(5).
[220] ibid s 133(6)(a)(i)–(ii).
[221] ibid s 133(6)(b).
[222] ibid s 134(3).
[223] ibid s 134(2)(a).
[224] ibid s 134(2)(b).
[225] ibid s 134(2)(c).
[226] ibid s 134(2)(d).

7
BULK WARRANTS

A.	Introduction	7.01
B.	Bulk Interception Warrants	7.04
	1. Bulk Interception Warrants	7.04
	2. Power to Issue Bulk Interception Warrants	7.08
	3. Approval of Warrants by Judicial Commissioners	7.13
	4. Requirements that Must Be Met by Warrants	7.16
	5. Duration of Warrants	7.23
	6. Renewal of Warrants	7.24
	7. Modification of Warrants	7.28
	8. Cancellation of Warrants	7.37
	9. Implementation of Warrants	7.39
	10. Safeguards	7.42
	11. Safeguards Relating to Examination of Material	7.47
	12. Additional Safeguards	7.52
	13. Offence of Breaching Safeguards Relating to Examination of Material	7.59
	14. Application of Other Restrictions in Relation to Warrants	7.63
C.	Bulk Acquisition Warrants	7.65
	1. Bulk Acquisition Warrants	7.65
	2. Approval of Warrants by Judicial Commissioners	7.74
	3. Requirements that Must Be Met by Warrants	7.77
	4. Duration of Warrants	7.84
	5. Renewal	7.85
	6. Modification of Warrants	7.89
	7. Cancellation of Warrants	7.98
	8. Implementation of Warrants	7.100
	9. Service of Warrants	7.102
	10. Duty of Operators to Assist with Implementation	7.106
	11. Safeguards	7.109
	12. Offence of Breaching Safeguards Relating to Examination of Data	7.113
	13. Offence of Making Unauthorized Disclosure	7.117

7. Bulk Warrants

D. Bulk Equipment Interference Warrants	7.120
1. Bulk Equipment Interference Warrants	7.120
2. Power to Issue Bulk Equipment Interference Warrants	7.128
3. Approval of Warrants	7.132
4. Failure to Approve Warrant Issued in Urgent Case	7.138
5. Requirements that Must Be Met by Warrants	7.142
6. Duration of Warrants	7.149
7. Renewal of Warrants	7.150
8. Modification of Warrants	7.154
9. Cancellation of Warrants	7.165
10. Implementation of Warrants	7.167
11. Safeguards	7.170
12. Additional Safeguards	7.180
13. Offence of Breaching Safeguards Relating to Examination of Material	7.187
14. Application of Other Restrictions in Relation to Warrants	7.191

A. INTRODUCTION

7.01 The use of bulk powers, in particular in relation to external communications, has been one of the most controversial aspects of state surveillance in recent years, equal only to the undercover police scandal.[1] Liberty and other respected commentators described the scope of the power as 'breath-taking'.[2]

7.02 A legal challenge has, at the time of writing, been launched.[3] On 8 September 2017, the Investigatory Powers Tribunal in *Privacy International v Secretary of State for Foreign and Commonwealth Affairs*[4] referred the question of the bulk collection of communications data to the Grand Chamber.

7.03 Part 6 of the IP Act has three chapters each concerned with the use of discrete covert resources set out in the preceding parts but in bulk. Chapter 1 relates to interception, Chapter 2, acquisition communications data, and Chapter 3, equipment interference. There is a draft Code of Practice in respect of the bulk acquisition of communications data; the other draft Codes incorporate bulk acquisition as part of their narrative. The draft Codes are not considered as part of this chapter but must be read alongside the text of the statute.

---

[1] See https://www.ucpi.org.uk.

[2] Liberty's briefing on Part 6 of the Investigatory Powers Bill for Committee Stage in the House of Commons (April 2016) https://www.liberty-human-rights.org.uk/sites/default/files/Liberty%27s%20Briefing%20on%20Part%206%20of%20the%20Investigatory%20Powers%20Bill%20for%20Committee%20Stage%20in%20the%20House%20of%20Commons.pdf (last accessed 2 June 2017).

[3] 'Liberty launches legal challenge to state spying in snooper's charter' *Guardian* (10 January 2017) https://www.theguardian.com/world/2017/jan/10/liberty-launches-legal-challenge-to-state-spying-in-snoopers-charter (last accessed 3 June 2017).

[4] IPT/15/110/CH.

B. BULK INTERCEPTION WARRANTS

1. Bulk Interception Warrants

A bulk interception warrant is a warrant issued under Part 6, Chapter 1, which meets two conditions, referred to as A and B.[5]

7.04

Condition A is that the main purpose of the warrant is one or more of either the interception of overseas-related communications or the obtaining of secondary data from such communications.[6] Overseas-related communications means communications sent or received by individuals who are outside the British Islands.[7] Secondary data for the purposes of Chapter 1 is less straightforward; they are sub-species of systems and identifying data, defined much later in the statute in section 263 and dealt with in chapter 1 of this work: see paragraphs 1.88–1.90. It includes systems data comprised in, included as part of, attached to, or logically associated with the communication and is not confined to the sender.[8] It is also identifying data of the same type but in addition capable of being logically separated from the remainder of the communication, and if it were so separated, would not reveal anything of what might reasonably be considered to be the meaning—assuming it had any—of the communication, 'disregarding any meaning arising from the fact of the communication or from any data relating to the transmission of the communication'.[9] References to obtaining secondary data in this connection are where doing so it would constitute an interception (ie whilst the communication is being transmitted, or at any time when the communication is stored in or by the system, whether before or after its transmission).[10]

7.05

Condition B is that the warrant authorizes or requires the person to whom it is addressed to secure, by any conduct described in the warrant, any one or more of four types of conduct. The first is the interception of communications as described in the warrant. The second is the obtaining of secondary data from those communications as described in the warrant. The third is the selection for examination of intercepted content or secondary data obtained under the warrant and the fourth is the disclosure, in any manner described in the warrant, of anything obtained under the warrant to the person to whom the warrant is addressed or to any person acting on that person's behalf.[11]

7.06

In addition, a bulk interception warrant also authorizes incidental conduct, including anything necessary to undertake in order to do what is expressly authorized or required by the warrant, including the interception of communications not

7.07

---

[5] ibid s 136(1).
[6] ibid s 136(2).
[7] ibid s 136(3)(a)–(b).
[8] ibid s 137(4).
[9] ibid s 137(5)(a)–(c).
[10] ibid s 137(2)(a)–(b).
[11] ibid s 136(4)(a)–(d).

described in the warrant, and conduct for obtaining secondary data from such communications and assistance by any person in giving effect to the warrant.[12] Finally, it also authorizes any conduct for obtaining related systems data from any telecommunications operator. The term 'related systems data' in this connection means systems data relating to a relevant communication or to the sender or recipient, or intended recipient, of a relevant communication. This does not need to be a person. A 'relevant communication' means any communication intercepted in accordance with the warrant in the course of its transmission by means of a telecommunication system, or any communication from which secondary data is obtained under the warrant.[13]

2. Power to Issue Bulk Interception Warrants

7.08 An application for the issue of a bulk interception warrant may only be made by or on behalf of the head of the intelligence services. Where it is the latter, the person applying must hold office under the Crown. Applications are made to the Secretary of State under section 138 of the IPA. The decision to issue a warrant must be taken personally by the Secretary of State.[14] Before it is issued, the Secretary of State must also sign the warrant.[15]

7.09 Before a bulk interception warrant can be issued the Secretary of State must consider six conditions have been met: the main purpose of the warrant is either or both the interception of overseas-related communications, and the obtaining of secondary data from such communications;[16] it is in the interests of national security,[17] preventing or detecting serious crime or in the interests of the economic well-being of the United Kingdom (UK) so far as those interests are also relevant to the interests of national security[18] (but only where this relates to the acts or intentions of persons outside the British Islands);[19] the conduct authorized is proportionate to the operational objective to which the conduct relates;[20] each of the specified operational purposes is a purpose for which the examination of intercepted content or secondary data obtained under the warrant is or may be necessary, and the examination of intercepted content or secondary data for each such purpose is necessary on any of the grounds on which the Secretary of State considers the warrant to be necessary;[21] satisfactory arrangements made for the purposes of safeguards relating to disclosure are in force in relation to the warrant;[22] and where a telecommunications operator

---

[12] ibid s 136(5)(a)–(b).
[13] ibid s 136(6).
[14] ibid s 141(1).
[15] ibid s 141(2).
[16] ibid s 138(1)(a).
[17] ibid s 138(1)(b)(i).
[18] ibid s 138(2)(a)–(b).
[19] ibid s 138(3).
[20] ibid s 138(1)(c).
[21] ibid s 138(1)(d)(i)–(ii).
[22] ibid s 138(1)(e).

outside the UK is likely to be required to provide assistance in giving effect to the warrant if it is issued, the Secretary of State has complied with the requirements of section 139:[23] see paragraph 7.12 below.

7.10 The decision to issue a bulk warrant must be approved by a judicial commissioner.[24]

7.11 A bulk warrant may not be issued if it is considered necessary only for the purpose of gathering evidence for use in any legal proceedings.[25] Legal proceedings are defined in section 263 IPA as civil or criminal proceedings in or before a court or tribunal or proceedings before a service officer in respect of military disciplinary proceedings.

(a) *Additional Requirements: Warrants Affecting Overseas Operators*

7.12 Where an application for a bulk interception warrant has been made, and the Secretary of State considers that a telecommunications operator outside the UK is likely to be required to provide assistance in giving effect to the warrant if it is issued it is a mandatory requirement that there is consultation with the operator before any warrant is issued.[26] The Secretary of State must take into account a number of matters (although it is not clear whether this is as part of the consultation or independent of it) including but not limited to the likely benefits of the warrant if issued; the likely number of users (if known) of any telecommunications service which is provided by the operator and to which the warrant relates; the technical feasibility of complying with any requirement that may be imposed on the operator to provide assistance in giving effect to the warrant; the likely cost of complying with any such requirement; and any other effect of the warrant on the operator.[27]

3. Approval of Warrants by Judicial Commissioners

7.13 Under section 138(1)(g) a decision to issue a bulk interception warrant, in common with other forms of warrant, requires the approval of a judicial commissioner. In doing so, the judicial commissioner is required to review the Secretary of State's conclusions under section 138(1)(b)–(d): see paragraph 7.09 above.[28] In addition, the review must include any of the additional matters taken into account by the Secretary of State: see paragraph 7.12 above.[29]

7.14 The principles applied by the judicial commissioner in doing are those as would be applied by a court on an application for judicial review.[30] The judicial commissioner is required to carry out this function 'with a sufficient degree of care as to ensure ... [compliance] with the duties imposed by section 2 (general duties in relation to privacy)': see Chapter 2, paragraphs 2.08–2.10.[31]

---

[23] ibid s 138(f).
[24] ibid s 138(1)(g).
[25] ibid s 138(4).
[26] ibid s 139(1)–(2).
[27] ibid s 139(3)(a)–(e).
[28] ibid s 140(1)(a)–(c).
[29] ibid s 140(1)(d).
[30] ibid s 140(2)(a).
[31] ibid s 140(2)(b).

7.15 If a judicial commissioner refuses to approve the decision to issue a warrant written reasons for the refusal must be provided to the Secretary of State.[32] In these circumstances, the Secretary of State may ask the Investigatory Powers Commissioner to approve the decision to issue the warrant. This is not a review of the judicial commissioner's decision but rather a reconsideration of the original Ministerial decision. If the Investigatory Powers Commissioner made the decision to refuse, there is no scope to have the decision reconsidered further.[33]

4. Requirements that Must Be Met by Warrants

7.16 There are a number of requirements that must be met by warrants. The majority of these fall within the category of 'operational purposes'.

(a) Non-operational Purpose Requirements

7.17 There are two non-operational purpose requirements. First, the warrant must contain a provision stating that it is a bulk interception warrant and, secondly, it must be addressed to the head of the intelligence service by whom, or on whose behalf, the application for the warrant was made.

(b) Operational Purposes: Procedural Matters

7.18 The term 'specified operational purposes' means the operational purposes specified in the warrant in accordance with section 142.[34] These are set out on a list maintained by the heads of the intelligence services and known as 'the list of operational purposes'. They are the purposes that the intelligence services consider are operational purposes for which intercepted content or secondary data obtained under bulk interception warrants may be selected for examination.[35]

7.19 An operational purpose may be specified in the list of operational purposes only with the approval of the Secretary of State.[36] Approval may only be given if the Secretary of State is satisfied that the operational purpose is specified in a greater level of detail than the descriptions contained in section 138(1)(b) or (2), national security, preventing or detecting serious crime and economic well-being of the UK respectively.[37]

7.20 The Secretary of State must provide the list of operational purposes to the Intelligence and Security Committee (ISC) at the end of each relevant three-month period.[38] This means the period of three months beginning with the day on which section 142 comes into force, and each successive period of three months

---

[32] ibid s 140(3).
[33] ibid s 140(4).
[34] ibid s 142(11).
[35] ibid s 142(4).
[36] ibid s 142(6).
[37] ibid s 142(7).
[38] ibid s 142(8).

thereafter.[39] The Prime Minister must review the list of operational purposes at least once a year.[40]

(c) *Operational Purposes: Requirements*
A bulk interception warrant must specify the operational purposes for which any intercepted content or secondary data obtained under the warrant may be selected for examination.[41]

7.21

The warrant may, in particular, specify all of the operational purposes, which at the time the warrant is issued, are specified in the list of operational purposes.[42]

7.22

5. Duration of Warrants

A bulk interception warrant that has not earlier been cancelled ceases to have effect at the end of the period of six months beginning with the day on which the warrant was issued.[43] If it has been renewed it ceases to have effect the day after the day at the end of which the warrant would ceased to have effect if it had not been renewed.[44]

7.23

6. Renewal of Warrants

(a) *General*
A bulk interception warrant may be renewed at any time during the renewal period—the thirty-day period ending with the day at the end of which the warrant would otherwise cease to have effect—by an instrument issued by the Secretary of State.[45] This is subject to the renewal conditions being met and a number of complicated exceptions. The decision to renew must be taken personally by the Secretary of State. The Secretary of State must also sign the renewal instrument.[46]

7.24

The renewal conditions reflect the original basis upon which the warrant was issued. It must be necessary on one or more of the available grounds (national security, preventing and detecting serious crime, economic well-being of the UK), and the conduct authorized proportionate to the operational objective.[47] The requirements as to the necessity of the operational purposes and examination of intercepted content or secondary data must also be met and the decision to issue requires the approval of a judicial commissioner.[48]

7.25

---

[39] ibid s 142(9)(a)–(b).
[40] ibid s 142(10).
[41] ibid s 142(3).
[42] ibid s 142(5).
[43] ibid s 143(1)(a).
[44] ibid s 143(1)(b).
[45] ibid s 144(1) and (3).
[46] ibid s 144(4).
[47] ibid s 144(2)(a)–(b).
[48] ibid s 144(2)(c)–(d).

7.26   When considering whether to approve the decision to renew, the judicial commissioner must carry out the review in the same way as the original decision to issue the warrant except that there is no requirement to consider the additional requirements set out in section 139: see paragraph 7.12 above.[49] This is subject to the same exceptions as apply to renewal generally.

(b) *Exceptions*

7.27   The renewal provisions are subject to exceptions but only in the case of the renewal of a bulk interception warrant that has been modified so that it no longer authorizes or requires the interception of communications or the obtaining of secondary data. In such circumstances there is no requirement that the Secretary of State considers the warrant is necessary on one or more of the available grounds.[50] Instead, the requirement that the Secretary of State considers the examination of intercepted content or secondary data continues to be necessary should be read as a reference to those grounds (but as set out in section 138(1)(b) or (2) and not as repeated in sub-section (2) of section 144).[51] The judicial commissioner must also consider this variation of the authorization scheme when determining whether to approve the renewal in the case of a modified warrant and section 140 is to be given effect accordingly: see paras 7.13–7.15 above.[52]

7. Modification of Warrants

7.28   A bulk interception warrant may be modified at any time by an instrument issued by the person making the modification.[53] There are two types of modification, major and minor. The former is a modification adding or varying any operational purpose as a purpose for which any intercepted content or secondary data obtained under the warrant may be selected for examination.[54] The latter is a modification providing that the warrant no longer authorizes or requires (to the extent that it did so previously) the interception of any communications in the course of their transmission or the obtaining of any secondary data from communications by means of a telecommunications system.[55] Although this appears to subvert Condition A set out in section 136(2), such a modification does not prevent the warrant from being a bulk interception warrant.[56] Any modification is limited only to conduct authorized or required by the warrant.[57]

7.29   A major modification must be made by the Secretary of State, and is limited to circumstances where it is considered necessary on any of the available grounds upon

---

[49] ibid s 144(5).
[50] ibid s 144(6)(a).
[51] ibid s 144(6)(b).
[52] ibid s 144(6)(c)(i)–(ii).
[53] ibid s 145(1).
[54] ibid s 145(2)(a) and (3)(a).
[55] ibid s 145(2)(b) and (3)(b).
[56] ibid s 145(12).
[57] ibid s 145(13).

B. Bulk Interception Warrants

which the warrant could be issued.[58] Unless it is an urgent modification, it does not take effect until a judicial commissioner has approved it.[59]

7.30 The Secretary of State or senior official acting on their behalf may make a minor modification.[60] However, where a senior official makes it the Secretary of State must be notified personally of the modification and the reasons for making it.[61] There is a mandatory requirement on both the Secretary of State and a senior official to modify where either considers that any operational purpose specified in a warrant is no longer a purpose for which the examination of intercepted content or secondary data obtained under the warrant is or may be necessary. In such circumstances that operational purpose should be removed.[62]

7.31 The decision to modify in either case must be taken personally by the person making it and that person must sign the instrument.[63] In the case of a major modification made by the Secretary of State but where it is not reasonably practicable for that person to sign the instrument, it may be signed by a senior official designated by the Secretary of State for that purpose.[64] The instrument making the modification must in such circumstances contain a statement to this effect and that the Secretary of State has personally and expressly authorized the making of the modification.[65]

(a) Approval of Major Modifications: Non-urgent Cases

7.32 When determining whether to approve a decision to make a major modification of a bulk interception warrant, a judicial commissioner must review the Secretary of State's conclusions as to whether the modification is necessary on any of the available grounds upon which it could be issued.[66] The same principles apply to the approval of major modifications as apply to the approval of warrants: see paragraphs 7.13–7.15 above.[67]

7.33 As with the approval of warrants there is a duty to provide reasons to the Secretary of State where approval is refused and in cases where the refusal is by a judicial commissioner other than the Investigatory Powers Commissioner there is a right to ask for the decision to modify to be reconsidered by the senior Commissioner.[68]

(b) Approval of Major Modifications: Urgent Cases

7.34 Where the Secretary of State makes a major modification without and considered that there was an urgent need to make the modification a judicial commissioner must be informed that the modification has been made.[69] The judicial commissioner

---

[58] ibid s 145(4)(a)–(b).
[59] ibid s 145(5).
[60] ibid s 145(6)(a)–(b).
[61] ibid s 145(7).
[62] ibid s 145(8).
[63] ibid s 145(9).
[64] ibid s 145(10).
[65] ibid s 145(11).
[66] ibid s 146(1).
[67] ibid s 146(2)(a)–(b).
[68] ibid s 146(3)–(4).
[69] ibid s 147(1)(a)–(b) and (2).

must then, before the end of the relevant period (the period ending with the third working day after the day on which the modification was made) decide whether to approve the decision to make the modification and notify the Secretary of State of the judicial commissioner's decision.[70]

7.35 If the judicial commissioner refuses to approve the decision the warrant—unless it no longer has effect for some other reason, such as, for example, cancellation—it has effect as if the modification had not been made, and the person to whom the warrant is addressed must, so far as is reasonably practicable, secure that anything in the process of being done under the warrant by virtue of that modification stops as soon as possible. There is no right to have the decision reconsidered by the Investigatory Powers Commissioner in such circumstances.[71]

7.36 The refusal to approve an urgent modification does not affect the lawfulness of anything done under the warrant by virtue of the modification prior to the modification ceasing to have effect. If anything is in the process of being done under the warrant by virtue of the modification when it ceases to have effect anything done before that thing could be stopped, or anything done which it is not reasonably practicable to stop is not unlawful.[72]

8. Cancellation of Warrants

7.37 The Secretary of State or a senior official acting on his or her behalf may cancel a bulk interception warrant at any time.[73] However, where any of the 'cancellation conditions' apply, cancellation is mandatory.[74] There are three cancellation conditions. The first is that the warrant is no longer necessary in the interests of national security, except where the warrant has been modified so that it no longer authorizes or requires the interception of communications or the obtaining of secondary data.[75] The second is that the conduct authorized by the warrant is no longer proportionate to what it seeks to achieve.[76] The third is that the examination of intercepted content or secondary data obtained under the warrant is no longer necessary for any of the specified operational purposes provided for by section 142: see paragraphs 7.18 to 7.22 above.[77]

7.38 There are two consequences of cancellation: the person to whom the warrant was addressed must, so far as is reasonably practicable, secure that anything in the process of being done under the warrant stops as soon as possible,[78] and a warrant that has been cancelled may not be renewed.[79]

---

[70] ibid s 147(3)(a)–(b).
[71] ibid s 147(4)(a)–(b).
[72] ibid s 147(5)(a)–(b).
[73] ibid s 148(1).
[74] ibid s 148(2).
[75] ibid s 148(3)(a) and (4).
[76] ibid s 148(3)(b).
[77] ibid s 148(3)(c).
[78] ibid s 148(5).
[79] ibid s 148(6).

B. Bulk Interception Warrants

9. Implementation of Warrants

7.39 For the purposes of implementation of a bulk interception warrant, the person to whom it is addressed, 'the implementing authority', may in addition to its own role in implementing the warrant act through, or together with other persons as the implementing authority may require to assist it to do so.[80] This includes disclosure to the implementing authority of any material obtained under the warrant.[81]

7.40 Where the implementing authority requires assistance with implementation, it may serve or make arrangements to serve a copy of the warrant—either with or without one or more of the schedules contained in it—on such persons it requires assistance from.[82] This includes service outside the UK.[83]

7.41 The provisions in sections 42 (service of warrants) and 43 (duty of operators to assist with implementation) apply in relation to a bulk interception warrant as they apply in relation to a targeted interception warrant: see Chapter 3, paragraphs 3.111–3.117.[84]

10. Safeguards

(a) Retention and Disclosure of Material

7.42 There is a requirement on the part of the Secretary of State to ensure, in relation to every bulk interception warrant issued that arrangements in force for securing that the requirements of section 152 are met (examination of material: see paragraphs [insert] below) and that the number of persons to whom any of the material derived from the warrant is disclosed, the extent to which it is disclosed or otherwise made available and the extent to which the material is copied and the number of copies that are made is limited to minimum number necessary for the authorized purposes.[85] Every copy must be stored for as long as it is retained securely and must be destroyed as soon as there is no longer any relevant grounds—which in this context means authorized purposes—for retaining it unless it is destroyed sooner.[86] This does not apply to material, including any copy of the material, obtained under the warranted handed over to any overseas authorities (a country or territory outside the UK).[87] This is provided for in section 151: see paragraphs 7.47–7.51 below.[88]

7.43 Authorized purposes are limited to five purposes. The first is that it is, or is likely to be, necessary on any of the relevant grounds (that is, the grounds upon or purpose

---

[80] ibid s 149(1).
[81] ibid s 149(4).
[82] ibid s 149(2) and (6).
[83] ibid s 149(3).
[84] ibid s 149(5).
[85] ibid s 150(1)–(2).
[86] ibid s 150(4)–(5).
[87] ibid s 150(6), (7), and (9).
[88] ibid s 150(8).

7. Bulk Warrants

for which the warrant was issued).[89] The second and thirdly are that it is necessary for facilitating the carrying out of functions under the Act by the Secretary of State, Scottish Ministers, or the person to whom the warrant is addressed or by the judicial commissioners or the Investigatory Powers Tribunal.[90] The fourth is that it is necessary for a prosecutor conducting a criminal prosecution to have the information so as to determine what may be required to ensure the fairness of the proceedings.[91] The fifth is that it is necessary for the performance of any duty imposed on any person by the Public Records Act 1958 or the Public Records Act (Northern Ireland) 1923.[92]

7.44   Copy has the same meaning as it does when used in the context of intercept warrants: see Chapter 3, paragraph 3.147.[93]

(b) *Disclosure of Material Overseas*

7.45   Where the material or copies of the material obtained from a bulk interception warrant is to be handed over to an overseas authority, the Secretary of State must ensure that arrangements are in force for securing that the overseas authority has corresponding requirements to those imposed on the Secretary of State to such an extent if any the issuing authority considers appropriate.[94] The requirements are provided for in sections 150(2) and (5) and 152: see paragraphs 7.42 to 7.44 above and paragraphs 7.147–7.151 below.

7.46   The arrangements must also ensure that restrictions are in force which would prevent, to such extent (if any) as the Secretary of State considers appropriate, the doing of anything in, for the purposes of or in connection with any proceedings outside the UK which would result in a prohibited disclosure (a disclosure which, if made in the UK, would breach the prohibition in section 56(1): see Chapter 3, paragraphs 3.152–3.155.[95]

11. Safeguards Relating to Examination of Material

7.47   The section 152 requirements will be met in relation to the intercepted content and secondary data obtained under a warrant for the purposes of section 150 if the selection of any of the intercepted content or secondary data for examination is carried out only for the specified purposes, is necessary and proportionate in all the circumstances, and meets any of the selection conditions.[96] The term 'specified purposes' is defined in sub-section (2) and the 'selection conditions' are set in sub-section (3).

---

[89] ibid s 150(3)(a).
[90] ibid s 150(3)(b)–(c).
[91] ibid s 150(3)(d).
[92] ibid s 150(3)(e).
[93] ibid s 150(9).
[94] ibid s 151(1)–(2).
[95] ibid s 151(2) and (3).
[96] ibid s 152(1)(a)–(c).

B. Bulk Interception Warrants

The specified purposes means only so far as is necessary for the operational purposes specified in the warrant—that in existence at the time of the selection—in accordance with section 142: see paragraphs 7.18 to 7.22 above.[97]

7.48

There are four selection conditions each of which relates to the prohibition on the intercepted content not at any time being selected for examination if any criteria used for the selection are referable to an individual known to be in the British Islands at that time, and the purpose of using those criteria is to identify the content of communications sent by, or intended for, that individual (whether or not that person's identity is known).[98] The first two conditions are that the selection of the intercepted content for examination does not breach the prohibition and that the person to whom the warrant is addressed considers that the selection of the intercepted content for examination would not breach the prohibition.[99] The second two are that the selection of the intercepted content for examination in breach of that prohibition is authorized by either sub-section (5) or by a targeted examination warrant issued under Chapter 1 of Part 2.[100]

7.49

Authorization by virtue of sub-section (5) occurs where four circumstances exist. The first is that the criteria referable to an individual have been, or are being, used for the selection of intercepted content for examination in circumstances falling within the first two selection conditions: see paragraph 7.49 above.[101] The second is where at any time it appears to the person to whom the warrant is addressed that there has been a relevant change of circumstances in relation to the individual that would mean that the selection of the relevant content for examination would breach the prohibition.[102] Change circumstances for this purpose means either the individual has entered the British Islands, or a belief by the person to whom the warrant is addressed that the individual was outside the British Islands was in fact mistaken.[103] The third and fourth are that since a change of circumstances became known a written authorization to examine the relevant content using those criteria has been given by a senior officer, and the selection is made before the end of the permitted period.[104] This is the fifth working day following the day after the person to whom the warrant is addressed knows of the change of circumstances.[105] Where authorization is given under section 152(5), the person to whom the warrant is addressed must notify the Secretary of State that the selection is being carried out.[106]

7.50

A senior officer for the purposes of section 152 has the same meaning as senior official in section 135(1)(a): see Chapter 6, paragraph 6.74.

7.51

---

[97] ibid s 152(2).
[98] ibid s 152(4).
[99] ibid s 152(3)(a)–(b).
[100] ibid s 152(3)(c)–(d).
[101] ibid s 152(5)(a).
[102] ibid s 152(5)(b).
[103] ibid s 152(6).
[104] ibid s 152(5)(c)–(d).
[105] ibid s 152(7).
[106] ibid s 152(8).

12. Additional Safeguards

(a) *Items Subject to Legal Privilege*

7.52 Where the selection of the intercepted content for examination does not breach the prohibition is section 152(3)(a)–(b) or is authorized under section 152(3)(c) and at least a purpose of using the criteria to be used for the selection of the intercepted content for examination is to identify any items subject to legal privilege, or the use of the criteria is likely to identify such items, the intercepted content may be selected for examination.[107] The 'criteria' is a reference back to section 152(5) but in this context is referred to as 'the relevant criteria'. Its use is subject to the approval of a senior official acting on behalf of the Secretary of State who has approved the use of those criteria.[108]

7.53 The senior official in deciding whether to give an approval must have regard to the public interest in the confidentiality of items subject to legal privilege[109] and may only do so if two conditions are met. First, that the arrangements made for safeguarding retention and disclosure of the material under section 150 include specific arrangements for the handling, retention, use, and destruction of items subject to legal privilege, and where a purpose is to identify any items subject to legal privilege, the senior official considers that there are exceptional and compelling circumstances that make the use of the relevant criteria necessary.[110]

7.54 The threshold of 'exceptional and compelling' will not be met unless the public interest in obtaining the information outweighs the public interest in maintaining the confidentiality of the legal privilege, there are no other means by which the information could reasonably be obtained and obtaining the information is necessary in the interests of national security or for the preventing death or significant injury.[111]

7.55 Where the selection of the intercepted content for examination does not breach the prohibition is section 152(3)(a)–(b) or is authorized under section 152(3)(c) and at least a purpose of using the criteria to be used for the selection of the intercepted content for examination is to identify communications that, if they were not made with the intention of furthering a criminal purpose, would be items subject to legal privilege, and the person to whom the warrant is addressed considers that the communications are likely to be communications made with the intention of furthering a criminal purpose, the intercepted content may be selected for examination. This again is referred to as 'the relevant criteria' for this purpose and the communications are referred to as 'the targeted communications' for this purpose. Its use is subject to the approval of a senior official acting on behalf of the Secretary of State who has approved the use of those criteria.[112] Approval can only be given if the

---

[107] ibid s 153(1).
[108] ibid s 153(2).
[109] ibid s 153(3).
[110] ibid 153(4)(a)–(b).
[111] IPA, s 153(5)(a)–(c).
[112] ibid s 153(6)(b)–(c).

B. Bulk Interception Warrants

official considers that the targeted communications are likely to be communications made with the intention of furthering a criminal purpose.[113]

7.56 Where an item subject to legal privilege has been intercepted in accordance with a bulk interception warrant and is retained following its examination for purposes other than its destruction, the person to whom the warrant is addressed must inform the Investigatory Powers Commissioner of the retention of the item as soon as reasonably practicable.[114]

7.57 Other than in cases where the public interest in retention of the item outweighs the public interest in the confidentiality of items subject to items subject to legal privilege and retention is necessary in the interests of national security or for the purpose of preventing death or serious injury,[115] the Investigatory Powers Commissioner must either direct the item is destroyed or impose conditions as to the retention and use of the item.[116] In determining which of these alternatives is appropriate the Commissioner may require representations to be made by affected persons.[117] These are either the person to who the warrant was or is addressed or the Secretary of State.[118] Where the Commissioner requires representations, these must be considered when determining whether the items should be destroyed or conditions imposed.[119]

(b) *Confidential Journalistic Material*

7.58 In cases where a communication which has been intercepted in accordance with a bulk interception warrant is retained, following its examination, for purposes other than the destruction of the communication, and it is a communication containing confidential journalistic material, the person to whom the warrant is addressed must inform the Investigatory Powers Commissioner as soon as is reasonably practicable.[120]

13. Offence of Breaching Safeguards Relating to Examination of Material

7.59 The offence of breaching safeguards relating to examination of material is committed if a person selects for examination any intercepted content or secondary data (the material) obtained under a bulk interception warrant knowing or believing that the selection of that material does not comply with a requirement imposed by section 152 or 153 and the person deliberately selects the material for examination in breach of that requirement. As to the requirements of sections 152 and 153, see

---

[113] ibid s 153(7).
[114] ibid s 153(9).
[115] ibid s 153(12)(a)–(b).
[116] ibid s 153(10)(a)–(b).
[117] ibid s 153(13)(a).
[118] ibid s 153(14).
[119] ibid s 153(13)(b).
[120] ibid s 154.

paragraphs 7.47–7.57 above.[121] As to when the offence is committed by a body corporate or Scottish partnership, see Chapter 10, paragraphs 10.125–10.127.

7.60 A person guilty of the offence of making an unauthorized disclosure is liable on summary conviction in England and Wales to imprisonment for a term not exceeding twelve months (or six months, if the offence was committed before the commencement of section 154(1) of the Criminal Justice Act 2003), or to a fine, or both.[122] On summary conviction in Scotland to imprisonment for a term not exceeding twelve months, or to a fine not exceeding the statutory maximum, or both.[123] In Northern Ireland the maximum sentence on summary conviction is imprisonment for a term not exceeding six months, or to a fine not exceeding the statutory maximum, or both.[124]

7.61 On conviction on indictment, the maximum sentence is imprisonment for a term not exceeding five years or to a fine, or both.[125]

7.62 The consent of the relevant Director of Public Prosecutions is required before criminal proceedings for an offence under section 155 may be instituted against a person in England, Wales, or Northern Ireland.[126]

14. Application of Other Restrictions in Relation to Warrants

7.63 The provisions in relation to the exclusion of matters from legal proceedings etc that apply in relation to bulk interception warrants set out in section 56 and Schedule 3 also apply in relation to targeted interception warrants: see Chapter 3, paras 3.152–3.155.[127]

7.64 Similarly the provisions relating to the duty not to make unauthorized disclosures apply in relation to bulk interception warrants as they apply in relation to targeted interception warrants, so sections 57 to 59 and section 58(2)(c) should be read accordingly: see Chapter 3, paras 3.156–3.166.[128]

C. BULK ACQUISITION WARRANTS

1. Bulk Acquisition Warrants

7.65 A bulk acquisition warrant is a warrant which authorizes or requires the person to whom it is addressed to secure, by any conduct described in the warrant, any one or more of a series of specified activities set out in section 158(6) and (7).[129]

---

[121] ibid s 155(1)(a)–(c).
[122] ibid s 155(2)(a).
[123] ibid s 155(2)(b).
[124] ibid s 155(2)(c).
[125] ibid s 155(2)(d).
[126] ibid s 155(3).
[127] ibid s 156(1).
[128] ibid s 156(2).
[129] ibid s 158(5).

C. Bulk Acquisition Warrants

It may relate to data whether or not in existence at the time of the issuing of the warrant.[130]

7.66 The specified activities fall into two substantive categories; those set out in sub-section (6); and incidental thereto, those set out in sub-section (7).

7.67 The former are, first of all, those requiring a telecommunications operator to disclose to a person any communications data in the possession of the operator, to obtain any communications data which is not in the possession of the operator but which the operator is capable of obtaining, or to disclose to a person any such data. The person and communications data must be specified in the warrant.[131] The second are those requiring the selection for examination of communications data obtained under the warrant, and the third are those requiring the disclosure of communications data obtained under the warrant to the person to whom the warrant is addressed or to any person acting on that person's behalf.[132] The selection for examination and disclosure of communications must be described in the warrant.

7.68 The latter is any conduct which it is necessary to undertake in order to do what is expressly authorized or required by the warrant, and conduct by any person which is in pursuance of a requirement, imposed by or on behalf of the person to whom the warrant is addressed, to be provided with assistance in giving effect to the warrant.[133]

7.69 An application for the issue of a bulk acquisition warrant may only be made by or on behalf of the head of the intelligence services.[134] Where it is the latter, the person applying must hold office under the Crown.[135] Applications are made to the Secretary of State under section 158 of the IPA. The decision to issue a warrant must be taken personally by the Secretary of State.[136] Before it is issued, the Secretary of State must also sign the warrant.[137]

7.70 Before a bulk acquisition warrant can be issued, the Secretary of State must consider that it is in the interests of national security,[138] preventing or detecting serious crime or in the interests of the economic well-being of the UK so far as those interests are also relevant to the interests of national security[139] (but only where this relates to the acts or intentions of persons outside the British Islands)[140] and that the conduct authorized is proportionate to the operational objective to which the conduct relates.[141]

7.71 In addition, the Secretary of State must consider that each of the specified operational purposes is a purpose for which the examination of communications data

---

[130] ibid s 158(8).
[131] ibid s 158(6)(a)(i)–(iii).
[132] ibid s 158(6)(b)–(c).
[133] ibid s 158(7)(a)–(b).
[134] ibid s 158(1).
[135] ibid s 158(9).
[136] ibid s 160(1).
[137] ibid s 160(2).
[138] ibid s 158(1)(a)(i).
[139] ibid s 158(2)(a)–(b).
[140] ibid s 158(3).
[141] ibid s 158(1)(b).

obtained under the warrant is or may be necessary, and the examination of that data for each such purpose is necessary on any of the grounds on which the Secretary of State considers the warrant to be necessary[142] and that satisfactory arrangements made for the purposes of safeguards relating to disclosure are in force in relation to the warrant.[143]

7.72 The decision to issue a bulk warrant must be approved by a judicial commissioner.[144]

7.73 The fact that the communications data which would be obtained under a warrant relates to the activities in the British Islands of a trade union is not, of itself, sufficient to establish that the warrant is necessary in the interests of national security or on that ground and a ground falling within sub-section (2): see para 7.70 above.

2. Approval of Warrants by Judicial Commissioners

7.74 Under section 158(1)(e) a decision to issue a bulk acquisition warrant, in common with other forms of warrant, requires the approval of a judicial commissioner. In doing so the judicial commissioner is required to review the Secretary of State's conclusions under section 158(1)(a)–(d): see paragraphs 7.70–7.71 above.[145]

7.75 The principles applied by the judicial commissioner in doing are those as would be applied by a court on an application for judicial review.[146] The judicial commissioner is required to carry out this function 'with a sufficient degree of care as to ensure ... [compliance] with the duties imposed by section 2 (general duties in relation to privacy)': see Chapter 2, paragraphs 2.08–2.10.[147]

7.76 If a judicial commissioner refuses to approve the decision to issue a warrant written reasons for the refusal must be provided to the Secretary of State.[148] In these circumstances, the Secretary of State may ask the Investigatory Powers Commissioner to approve the decision to issue the warrant. This is not a review of the judicial commissioner's decision but rather a reconsideration of the original Ministerial decision. If the Investigatory Powers Commissioner made the decision to refuse, there is no scope to have the decision reconsidered further.[149]

3. Requirements that Must Be Met by Warrants

7.77 As with bulk interception warrants, there are a number of requirements that must be met by warrants. The majority of these fall within the category of 'operational purposes'.

---

[142] ibid s 158(1)(c)(i)–(ii).
[143] ibid s 158(1)(d).
[144] ibid s 158(1)(e).
[145] ibid s 159(1)(a)–(c).
[146] ibid s 159(2)(a).
[147] ibid s 159(2)(b).
[148] ibid s 159(3).
[149] ibid s 159(4).

C. Bulk Acquisition Warrants

(a) *Non-operational Purpose Requirements*

7.78 There are two non-operational purpose requirements. First, the warrant must contain a provision stating that it is a bulk acquisition warrant and, secondly, it must be addressed to the head of the intelligence service by whom, or on whose behalf, the application for the warrant was made.[150]

(b) *Operational Purposes: Procedural Matters*

7.79 The term 'specified operational purposes' means the operational purposes specified in the warrant in accordance with section 161.[151] These are set out on a list maintained by the heads of the intelligence services and known as 'the list of operational purposes'. They are the purposes that the intelligence services consider are operational purposes for which communications data obtained under bulk acquisition warrants may be selected for examination.[152]

7.80 An operational purpose may be specified in the list of operational purposes only with the approval of the Secretary of State.[153] Approval may only be given if the Secretary of State is satisfied that the operational purpose is specified in a greater level of detail than the descriptions contained in section 158(1)(a) or (2), national security, preventing or detecting serious crime and economic well-being of the UK respectively.[154]

7.81 The Secretary of State must provide the list of operational purposes to the Intelligence and Security Committee of Parliament (ISC) at the end of each relevant three-month period.[155] This means the period of three months beginning with the day on which section 161 comes into force, and each successive period of three months thereafter.[156] The prime minister must review the list of operational purposes at least once a year.[157]

(c) *Operational Purposes: Requirements*

7.82 A bulk acquisition warrant must specify the operational purposes for which any communications data obtained under the warrant may be selected for examination.[158]

7.83 The warrant may, in particular, specify all of the operational purposes, which at the time the warrant is issued, are specified in the list of operational purposes.[159]

4. Duration of Warrants

7.84 A bulk acquisition warrant that has not earlier been cancelled ceases to have effect at the end of the period of six months beginning with the day on which the warrant

---

[150] ibid s 161(1)–(2).
[151] ibid s 161(11).
[152] ibid s 161(4).
[153] ibid s 161(6).
[154] ibid s 161(7).
[155] ibid s 161(8).
[156] ibid s 161(9)(a)–(b).
[157] ibid s 161(10).
[158] ibid s 161(3).
[159] ibid s 161(5).

was issued.[160] If it has been renewed it ceases to have effect the day after the day at the end of which the warrant would ceased to have effect if it had not been renewed.[161]

5. Renewal

7.85 A bulk acquisition warrant may be renewed at any time during the renewal period—the thirty-day period ending with the day at the end of which the warrant would otherwise cease to have effect—by an instrument issued by the Secretary of State.[162] This is subject to the renewal conditions being met and a number of complicated exceptions. The decision to renew must be taken personally by the Secretary of State. The Secretary of State must also sign the renewal instrument.[163]

7.86 The renewal conditions reflect the original basis upon which the warrant was issued. It must be necessary on one or more of the available grounds (national security, preventing and detecting serious crime, economic well-being of the UK) and the conduct authorized proportionate to the operational objective.[164] The requirements as to the necessity of the operational purposes for the examination of the communications data must also be met and the decision to issue requires the approval of a judicial commissioner.[165]

7.87 When considering whether to approve the decision to renew, the judicial commissioner must carry out the review in the same way as the original decision to issue the warrant.

(a) Exceptions

7.88 The renewal provisions are subject to exceptions but only in the case of the renewal of a bulk acquisition warrant that has been modified so that it no longer authorizes or requires the examination of the communications data. In such circumstances there is no requirement that the Secretary of State considers the warrant is necessary on one or more of the available grounds.[166] Instead, the requirement that the Secretary of State considers the examination of the communications data continues to be necessary should be read as a reference to those grounds (but as set out in section 158(1)(b) or (2) and not as repeated in sub-section (2) of section 163).[167] The judicial commissioner must also consider this variation of the authorization scheme when determining whether to approve the renewal in the case of a modified warrant and section 159 is to be given effect accordingly: see paras 7.74–7.76 above.[168]

---

[160] ibid s 162(1)(a).
[161] ibid s 162(1)(b).
[162] ibid s 163(1) and (3).
[163] ibid s 163(4).
[164] ibid s 163(2)(a)–(b).
[165] ibid s 163(2)(c)–(d).
[166] ibid s 163(6)(a).
[167] ibid s 163(6)(b).
[168] ibid s 163(6)(c)(i)–(ii).

C. Bulk Acquisition Warrants

6. Modification of Warrants

7.89 A bulk acquisition warrant may be modified at any time by an instrument issued by the person making the modification.[169] There are two types of modification, major and minor. The former is a modification adding or varying any operational purpose as a purpose for which any communications data obtained under the warrant may be selected for examination.[170] The latter is a modification providing that the warrant no longer authorizes or requires (to the extent that it did so previously) the acquisition or disclosure of communications data that forms the first of the substantive specified activities: see paragraph 7.67 above.[171] Any modification is limited only to conduct authorized or required by the warrant.[172]

7.90 A major modification must be made by the Secretary of State, and is limited to circumstances where it is considered necessary on any of the available grounds upon which the warrant could be issued.[173] Unless it is an urgent modification, it does not take effect until a judicial commissioner has approved it.[174]

7.91 The Secretary of State or senior official acting on his or her behalf may make a minor modification.[175] However, where a senior official makes it the Secretary of State must be notified personally of the modification and the reasons for making it.[176] There is a mandatory requirement on both the Secretary of State and a senior official to modify where either considers that any operational purpose specified in a warrant is no longer a purpose for which the examination of intercepted content or secondary data obtained under the warrant is or may be necessary. In such circumstances, that operational purpose should be removed.[177]

7.92 The decision to modify in either case must be taken personally by the person making it and that person must sign the instrument.[178] In the case of a major modification made by the Secretary of State but where it is not reasonably practicable for that person to sign the instrument, it may be signed by a senior official designated by the Secretary of State for that purpose.[179] The instrument making the modification must in such circumstances contain a statement to this effect and that the Secretary of State has personally and expressly authorized the making of the modification.[180]

(a) *Approval of Major Modifications by Judicial Commissioners*

7.93 When determining whether to approve a decision to make a major modification of a bulk acquisition warrant, a judicial commissioner must review the Secretary of

---

[169] ibid s 164(1).
[170] ibid s 164(2)(a) and (3)(a).
[171] ibid s 164(2)(b) and (3)(b).
[172] ibid s 164(12).
[173] ibid s 164(4)(a)–(b).
[174] ibid s 164(5).
[175] ibid s 164(6)(a)–(b).
[176] ibid s 164(7).
[177] ibid s 164(8).
[178] ibid s 164(9).
[179] ibid s 164(10).
[180] ibid s 164(11).

7. Bulk Warrants

State's conclusions as to whether the modification is necessary on any of the available grounds upon which it could be issued.[181] The same principles apply to the approval of major modifications as apply to the approval of warrants: see paragraph 7.74–7.76 above.[182]

7.94 As with the approval of warrants there is a duty to provide reasons to the Secretary of State where approval is refused and in cases where the refusal is by a judicial commissioner other than the Investigatory Powers Commissioner there is a right to ask for the decision to modify to be reconsidered by the senior Commissioner.[183]

(b) *Approval of Major Modifications Made in Urgent Cases*

7.95 Where the Secretary of State makes a major modification without and considered that there was an urgent need to make the modification a judicial commissioner must be informed that the modification has been made.[184] The judicial commissioner must then, before the end of the relevant period (the period ending with the third working day after the day on which the modification was made) decide whether to approve the decision to make the modification and notify the Secretary of State of the judicial commissioner's decision.[185]

7.96 If the judicial commissioner refuses to approve the decision the warrant—unless it no longer has effect for some other reason, such as, for example, cancellation—has effect as if the modification had not been made, and the person to whom the warrant is addressed must, so far as is reasonably practicable, secure that anything in the process of being done under the warrant by virtue of that modification stops as soon as possible. There is no right to have the decision reconsidered by the Investigatory Powers Commissioner in such circumstances.[186]

7.97 The refusal to approve an urgent modification does not affect the lawfulness of anything done under the warrant by virtue of the modification prior to the modification ceasing to have effect. If anything is in the process of being done under the warrant by virtue of the modification when it ceases to have effect anything done before that thing could be stopped, or anything done which it is not reasonably practicable to stop is not unlawful.[187]

7. Cancellation of Warrants

7.98 The Secretary of State or a senior official acting on his or her behalf may cancel a bulk interception warrant at any time.[188] However, where any of the 'cancellation

---

[181] ibid s 165(1).
[182] ibid s 165(2)(a)–(b).
[183] ibid s 165(3)–(4).
[184] ibid s 166(1)(a)–(b) and (2).
[185] ibid s 166(3)(a)–(b).
[186] ibid s 166(4)(a)–(b).
[187] ibid s 166(5)(a)–(b).
[188] ibid s 167(1).

conditions' apply, cancellation is mandatory.[189] There are three cancellation conditions. The first is that the warrant is no longer necessary in the interests of national security, except where the warrant has been modified so that it no longer authorizes or requires the carrying out of the first of the substantive specified activities in section 158(6)(a): see paragraph 7.67.[190] The second is that the conduct authorized by the warrant is no longer proportionate to what it seeks to achieve.[191] The third is that the examination of communications data obtained under the warrant is no longer necessary for any of the specified operational purposes provided for by section 161: see paragraphs 7.79–7.83 above.[192]

7.99 There are two consequences of cancellation: the person to whom the warrant was addressed must, so far as is reasonably practicable, secure that anything in the process of being done under the warrant stops as soon as possible;[193] and a warrant that has been cancelled may not be renewed.[194]

8. Implementation of Warrants

7.100 For the purposes of implementation of a bulk acquisition warrant, the person to whom it is addressed, 'the implementing authority', may in addition to its own role in implementing the warrant act through, or together with other persons as the implementing authority may require to assist it to do so.[195] This includes disclosure to the implementing authority of any material obtained under the warrant.[196]

7.101 Where the implementing authority requires assistance with implementation, it may serve or make arrangements to serve a copy of the warrant—either with or without one or more of the schedules contained in it—on such persons it requires assistance from.[197] This includes service outside the UK.[198]

9. Service of Warrants

7.102 Service of a bulk acquisition warrant must take effect in such a way as to bring the contents of the warrant to the attention of the person whom the implementing authority considers may be able to provide assistance in relation to it.[199]

7.103 There are a number of ways service can take place though it is not exhaustive (and includes service by electronic or other means).

---

[189] ibid s 167(2).
[190] ibid s 167(3)(a) and (4).
[191] ibid s 167(3)(b).
[192] ibid s 167(3)(c).
[193] ibid s 167(5).
[194] ibid s 167(6).
[195] ibid s 168(1).
[196] ibid s 168(4).
[197] ibid s 168(2) and (5).
[198] ibid s 168(3).
[199] ibid s 169(2).

7.104　Methods of service include serving a copy of the warrant at the person's principal office within the UK or, if the person has no such office in the UK, at any place in the UK where the person carries on business or conducts activities.[200] If the person has specified an address in the UK as one at which the person, or someone on the person's behalf, will accept service of documents of the same description as a copy of a warrant, service can take place by serving it at that address.[201]

7.105　Service can also take effect by making a copy of the warrant available for inspection whether to the person or their agent at a place in the UK.[202] However this is only permissible where a person is outside the UK and it is not reasonably practicable for a copy to be served by any other means and the implementing authority (the person to whom it is addressed) takes such steps, as the authority considers appropriate for the purpose of bringing the contents of the warrant, and the availability of a copy for inspection, to the attention of the person.[203] These steps must be taken as soon as reasonably practicable after the copy of the warrant is made available for inspection.[204]

10. Duty of Operators to Assist with Implementation

7.106　The consequence of service of a copy of a warrant is to impose a duty on a telecommunications operator to take all steps for giving effect to the warrant that are notified to the operator by or on behalf of the implementing authority[205] and which would not otherwise be reasonably practicable for it to take.[206] It is irrelevant whether or not it is in the UK.[207]

7.107　Where obligations have been imposed on a telecommunications operator under section 253 (technical capability notices), the steps that it is reasonably practicable for it to take include every step that it would have been reasonably practicable for it to take if it had complied with all of those obligations.[208]

7.108　The duty imposed is enforceable by civil proceedings by the Secretary of State for an injunction, or for specific performance of a statutory duty under section 45 of the Court of Session Act 1988, or for any other appropriate relief.[209]

11. Safeguards

(a) *Retention and Disclosure of Data*

7.109　There is a requirement on the part of the Secretary of State to ensure, in relation to every bulk acquisition warrant issued that arrangements in force for securing that the

---

[200] ibid s 169(3)(a).
[201] ibid s 169(3)(b).
[202] ibid s 169(3)(c).
[203] ibid s 169(4).
[204] ibid s 169(5).
[205] ibid s 170(1).
[206] ibid s 170(3).
[207] ibid s 170(2).
[208] ibid s 170(4).
[209] ibid s 170(5).

C. Bulk Acquisition Warrants

requirements of section 172 are met (examination of material: see paragraph 7.112 below) and that the number of persons to whom any of the material derived from the warrant is disclosed, the extent to which it is disclosed or otherwise made available and the extent to which the material is copied and the number of copies that are made is limited to minimum number necessary for the authorized purposes.[210] Every copy must be stored for as long as it is retained securely and must be destroyed as soon as there is no longer any relevant grounds—which in this context means authorized purposes—for retaining it unless it is destroyed sooner.[211] This does not apply to material, including any copy of the material, obtained under the warrant handed over to any overseas authorities (a country or territory outside the UK).[212] In such circumstances, the Secretary of State must ensure arrangements as considered appropriate are in force for securing that communications data obtained under the warrant or any copy of such data is handed over or given only if such corresponding requirements will apply.[213]

7.110 Authorized purposes are limited to six purposes. The first is that it is, or is likely to be, necessary on any of the relevant grounds (that is, the grounds upon or purpose for which the warrant was issued).[214] The second and third purposes are that it is necessary for facilitating the carrying out of functions under the Act by the Secretary of State, Scottish Ministers, or the person to whom the warrant is addressed or by the judicial commissioners or the Investigatory Powers Tribunal.[215] The fourth purpose is that it is necessary for a prosecutor conducting a criminal prosecution to have the information so as to determine what may be required to ensure the fairness of the proceedings.[216] The fifth purpose is that it is necessary for use as evidence in legal proceedings[217] and, finally, the sixth purpose is that it is necessary for the performance of any duty imposed on any person by the Public Records Act 1958 or the Public Records Act (Northern Ireland) 1923.[218]

7.111 Copy has the same meaning as it does when used in the context of intercept warrants: see Chapter 3, paragraph 3.147.[219]

(a) *Examination of Data*

7.112 The requirements for the purposes of section 171 are met in relation to the communications data obtained under a warrant if any selection of the data for examination is carried out only for the specified purposes and are necessary and proportionate in all the circumstances.[220] The term 'only for the specified purposes' relates to those

---

[210] ibid s 171(1)–(2).
[211] ibid s 171(4)–(5).
[212] ibid s 171(6)–(7).
[213] ibid s 171(9).
[214] ibid s 171(3)(a).
[215] ibid s 171(3)(b)–(c).
[216] ibid s 171(3)(d).
[217] ibid s 171(3)(e)
[218] ibid s 171(3)(f).
[219] ibid s 171(10).
[220] ibid s 172(1)(a)–(b).

specified in the warrant (at the time of the selection) and is a reference back to the operational purposes provided for in section 161: see paragraphs 7.79–7.83.[221]

12. Offence of Breaching Safeguards Relating to Examination of Data

7.113   There are three ingredients to the offence of breaching safeguards relating to the examination of data. The person must select for examination any communications data obtained under a bulk acquisition warrant, know or believe that the selection of that data for examination does not comply with a requirement relating to examination of data safeguards, and deliberately selects that data for examination in breach of that requirement.[222] As to the when the offence is committed by a body corporate or Scottish partnership, see Chapter 10, paragraphs 10.125–10.127.

7.114   A person guilty of the offence is liable on summary conviction in England and Wales to imprisonment for a term not exceeding twelve months (or six months, if the offence was committed before the commencement of section 154(1) of the Criminal Justice Act 2003), or to a fine, or both.[223] On summary conviction in Scotland to imprisonment for a term not exceeding twelve months, or to a fine not exceeding the statutory maximum, or both.[224] In Northern Ireland the maximum sentence on summary conviction is imprisonment for a term not exceeding six months, or to a fine not exceeding the statutory maximum, or both.[225]

7.115   On conviction on indictment, the maximum sentence is imprisonment for a term not exceeding two years or to a fine, or both.[226]

7.116   The consent of the relevant Director of Public Prosecutions is required before criminal proceedings for an offence under section 173 may be instituted against a person in England, Wales, or Northern Ireland.[227]

13. Offence of Making Unauthorized Disclosure

7.117   It is an offence for a telecommunications operator caught by the provisions of section 170 (duty of operators to assist with implementation) to assist in giving effect to a bulk acquisition warrant, or any person employed or engaged for the purposes of the business of such an operator, to disclose to any person, without reasonable excuse, the existence or contents of the warrant.

7.118   A person guilty of the offence is liable on summary conviction in England and Wales to imprisonment for a term not exceeding twelve months (or six months, if the offence was committed before the commencement of section 154(1) of the Criminal Justice Act 2003), or to a fine, or both.[228] On summary conviction in

---

[221] ibid s 172(2) and (3).
[222] ibid s 173(10(a)–(c).
[223] ibid s 173(2)(a).
[224] ibid s 173(2)(b).
[225] ibid s 173(2)(c).
[226] ibid s 173(2)(d).
[227] ibid s 173(3).
[228] ibid s 173(2)(a).

Scotland to imprisonment for a term not exceeding twelve months, or to a fine not exceeding the statutory maximum, or both.[229] In Northern Ireland the maximum sentence on summary conviction is imprisonment for a term not exceeding six months, or to a fine not exceeding the statutory maximum, or both.[230]

On conviction on indictment, the maximum sentence is imprisonment for a term not exceeding two years or to a fine, or both.[231] As to when the offence are committed by a body corporate or Scottish partnership, see Chapter 10, paragraphs 10.125–10.127. 7.119

D. BULK EQUIPMENT INTERFERENCE WARRANTS

1. Bulk Equipment Interference Warrants

A bulk equipment interference warrant is a warrant issued under Part 6, Chapter 3. It authorizes or requires the person to whom it is addressed to secure interference with any equipment for the purpose of obtaining communications.[232] This means anything comprising speech, music, sounds, visual images, or data of any description and 'signals serving either for the impartation of anything between persons, between a person and a thing or between things or for the actuation or control of any apparatus'.[233] Signals in this context mean non-physical forms of transmission and reception such as electrical impulse or radio wave but it is not further defined in the IPA. In addition, it extends to equipment data and any other information.[234] 7.120

The main purpose of a bulk equipment interference warrant is to obtain one or more of overseas-related communications, information, or equipment data.[235] These terms are defined in section 176. Overseas-related communications means communications sent or received by individuals who are outside the British Islands and overseas-related information is information of individuals who are outside the British Islands.[236] 7.121

Overseas-related equipment data means equipment data forming part of, or connected with, overseas-related communications or overseas-related information. It also means equipment data that would or may assist in establishing the existence of overseas-related communications or overseas-related information or in obtaining such communications or information or it would or may assist in developing capabilities in relation to obtaining overseas-related communications or overseas-related information. 7.122

---

[229] ibid s 173(2)(b).
[230] ibid s 173(2)(c).
[231] ibid s 173(2)(d).
[232] ibid s 176(1)(b)(i).
[233] ibid s 198.
[234] ibid s176(1)(b)(ii)–(iii).
[235] ibid s 176(1)(c).
[236] ibid s 176(2)(a)–(b).

7.123 The warrant has mandatory and discretionary elements. It must authorize or require the person to whom it is addressed to secure the obtaining of the communications, equipment data, or other information to which the warrant relates.[237] It may also authorize or require the person to whom it is addressed to secure the selection for examination, in any manner described in the warrant, of any material obtained under the warrant, and the disclosure, in any manner described in the warrant, of any such material to the person to whom the warrant is addressed or to any person acting on that person's behalf.[238]

7.124 The warrant also authorizes incidental conduct, including that which it is necessary to undertake in order to do what is expressly authorized or required by the warrant, including conduct for securing the obtaining of communications, equipment data, or other information and that, in pursuance of a requirement imposed by or on behalf of the person to whom the warrant is addressed, to be provided with assistance in giving effect to the warrant.[239]

7.125 A warrant under Part 6, Chapter 3 may not authorize a person to engage in conduct, in relation to a communication other than a stored communication which would (unless done with lawful authority) constitute an offence of unlawful interception under section 3(1) and does not authorize a person to engage in conduct which could not be expressly authorized under the warrant because of this restriction.[240] Stored communication has the same meaning as set out in section 99(8): see Chapter 6, paragraph 6.10.

7.126 Any conduct that is carried out in accordance with a bulk equipment interference warrant is lawful for all purposes.[241]

(a) *Meaning of Equipment Data*

7.127 Equipment data for the purposes of Part 6, Chapter 3 has the same meaning as that provided for in section 100. It is systems data or identifying data comprising three elements which, first, is for the purposes of a relevant system (any system on or by means of which the data is held),[242] comprised in, included as part of, attached to, or logically associated with a communication but not limited to just the sender, or any other item of information.[243] Secondly, it is data that is capable of being logically separated from the remainder of the communication or the item of information and, thirdly, if so separated, would not reveal anything of what might reasonably be considered to be the meaning, if any, of the communication or the item of information. Where the meaning is clear or can be inferred from the fact of the communication or the existence of the item

---

[237] ibid s 176(4)(a).
[238] ibid s 176(4)(b)(i)–(ii).
[239] ibid s 176(5)(a)–(b).
[240] ibid s 176(6)–(7).
[241] ibid s 176(9).
[242] ibid s 177(3).
[243] ibid s 177(2)(a).

D. Bulk Equipment Interference Warrants

of information or from any data relating to either, this should disregarded for the purpose of the definition.[244]

2. Power to Issue Bulk Equipment Interference Warrants

7.128 An application for the issue of a bulk interception warrant may only be made by or on behalf of the head of the intelligence services.[245] Where it is the latter, the person applying must hold office under the Crown.[246] Applications are made to the Secretary of State under section 178 of the IPA. The decision to issue a warrant must be taken personally by the Secretary of State.[247] Before it is issued, the Secretary of State must also sign the warrant.[248] If it is not reasonably practicable for a warrant to be signed by the Secretary of State the warrant may be signed by a senior official providing it is personally and expressly authorized by the Secretary of State and the warrant in such circumstances must contain a statement to this effect.[249]

7.129 Before a bulk interception warrant can be issued, the Secretary of State must consider whether five conditions have been met: the main purpose of the warrant is either or both the interception of overseas-related communications, information, or equipment data;[250] it is in the interests of national security,[251] preventing or detecting serious crime or in the interests of the economic well-being of the UK so far as those interests are also relevant to the interests of national security[252] (but only where this relates to the acts or intentions of persons outside the British Islands);[253] the conduct authorized is proportionate to the operational objective to which the conduct relates;[254] each of the specified operational purposes is a purpose for which the examination of material obtained under the warrant is or may be necessary, and the examination of material for each such purpose is necessary on any of the grounds on which the Secretary of State considers the warrant to be necessary;[255] and satisfactory arrangements made for the purposes of safeguards relating to disclosure are in force in relation to the warrant.[256]

7.130 The decision to issue a bulk warrant must be approved by a judicial commissioner, unless there is an urgent need to issue it without prior approval.[257]

---

[244] ibid s 177(2)(c).
[245] ibid s 178(1).
[246] ibid s 178(4).
[247] ibid s 182(1).
[248] ibid s 182(2).
[249] ibid s 182(3) and (4).
[250] ibid s 178(1)(a).
[251] ibid s 178(1)(b)(i).
[252] ibid s 178(2)(a)–(b).
[253] ibid s 178(3).
[254] ibid s 178(1)(c).
[255] ibid s 178(1)(d)(i)–(ii).
[256] ibid s 178(1)(e).
[257] ibid s 178(1)(f).

7.131 A warrant may be considered necessary on the available grounds only if the interference with equipment which would be authorized by the warrant is considered necessary for the purpose of obtaining information relating to the acts or intentions of persons outside the British Islands.[258]

3. Approval of Warrants

(a) *Non-urgent Cases*

7.132 Under section 178(1)(f) a decision to issue a bulk equipment interference warrant, in common with other forms of warrant, requires the approval of a judicial commissioner unless it is an urgent case. In doing so the judicial commissioner is required to review the Secretary of State's conclusions under section 178(1)(a)–(e).[259]

7.133 The principles applied by the judicial commissioner in doing are those as would be applied by a court on an application for judicial review.[260] The judicial commissioner is required to carry out this function 'with a sufficient degree of care as to ensure ... [compliance] with the duties imposed by section 2 (general duties in relation to privacy)': see Chapter 2, paragraphs 2.08–2.10.[261]

7.134 If a judicial commissioner refuses to approve the decision to issue a warrant written reasons for the refusal must be provided to the Secretary of State.[262] In these circumstances, the Secretary of State may ask the Investigatory Powers Commissioner to approve the decision to issue the warrant. This is not a review of the judicial commissioner's decision but rather a reconsideration of the original Ministerial decision. If the Investigatory Powers Commissioner made the decision to refuse, there is no scope to have the decision reconsidered further.[263]

(b) *Urgent Cases*

7.135 An urgent warrant is a warrant issued without the approval of a judicial commissioner and where the person who issued it considered there was an urgent need to issue it without prior judicial approval.[264]

7.136 In cases where the warrant has been issued on an urgent basis and without prior approval, the Secretary of State must inform a judicial commissioner that it has been issued.[265] There is no time limit specified within which the judicial commissioner should be informed. However, the judicial commissioner must decide whether to approve the decision to issue the warrant, and notify the applicant of the decision within the 'relevant period'. This is the period ending with the third working day after the day on which the warrant was issued.[266]

---

[258] ibid s 138(4).
[259] ibid s 179(1)(a)–(c).
[260] ibid s 179(2)(a).
[261] ibid s 179(2)(b).
[262] ibid s 179(3).
[263] ibid s 179(4).
[264] ibid s 184(3)(a)–(b).
[265] ibid s 180(2).
[266] ibid s 180(3).

D. Bulk Equipment Interference Warrants

Where a judicial commissioner refuses to approve the decision to issue an urgent warrant, the warrant ceases to have effect (unless previously cancelled), and it may not be renewed.[267] Refusal has a number of effects. 7.137

4. Failure to Approve Warrant Issued in Urgent Case

Where a judicial commissioner refuses to approve the issue of a warrant in an urgent case, the person to whom the warrant was addressed must, so far as is reasonably practicable, secure that anything in the process of being done under the warrant stops as soon as possible.[268] The lawfulness of anything in the process of being done at the time the warrant ceases to have effect but which has already been done or cannot be stopped is not affected.[269] 7.138

Where the decision to refuse to approve is taken, the judicial commissioner has discretion to direct certain things take place on cessation. First, the judicial commissioner may authorize further interference with equipment for the purpose of securing that anything in the process of being done under the warrant stops as soon as possible. Secondly, the judicial commissioner may direct that any of the material obtained under the warrant is destroyed; or, thirdly, the judicial commissioner may impose conditions as to the use or retention of the material.[270] 7.139

There are number of procedural mechanisms that may take effect on the judicial commissioner refusing to approve an urgent warrant. The first relate to an 'affected party' (the Secretary of State or the person to whom it is addressed).[271] The judicial commissioner may invite representations about how to exercise their discretion on cessation of either type of warrant.[272] Where an affected party makes representations (whether or not at the judicial commissioner's invitation), these must be considered when the judicial commissioner considers whether to exercise discretion on cessation of the warrant.[273] 7.140

The second is a right of the Secretary of State to seek a review of the judicial commissioner's decision by the Investigatory Powers Commissioner.[274] Where such a right is exercised the Investigatory Powers Commissioner may either confirm the original decision not to approve or make a fresh determination.[275] 7.141

5. Requirements that Must Be Met by Warrants

As with all bulk warrants, there are a number of requirements that must be met by bulk equipment interference warrants. The majority of these fall within the category of 'operational purposes'. 7.142

---

[267] ibid s 180(4).
[268] ibid s 181(2).
[269] ibid s 181(8).
[270] ibid s 181(3)(a)–(c).
[271] ibid s 181(5).
[272] ibid s 181(4)(a).
[273] ibid s 181(4)(b).
[274] ibid s 181(6).
[275] ibid s 181(7).

7. Bulk Warrants

(a) *Non-operational Purpose Requirements*

7.143 There are two non-operational purpose requirements. First, the warrant must contain a provision stating that it is a bulk acquisition warrant and, secondly, it must be addressed to the head of the intelligence service by whom, or on whose behalf, the application for the warrant was made.[276]

(b) *Operational Purposes: Procedural Matters*

7.144 The term 'specified operational purposes' means the operational purposes specified in the warrant in accordance with section 183.[277] These are set out on a list maintained by the heads of the intelligence services and known as 'the list of operational purposes'.[278] They are the purposes that the intelligence services consider are the operational purposes for which material obtained under bulk equipment interference warrants may be selected for examination.[279]

7.145 An operational purpose may be specified in the list of operational purposes only with the approval of the Secretary of State.[280] Approval may only be given if the Secretary of State is satisfied that the operational purpose is specified in a greater level of detail than the descriptions contained in section 178(1)(b) or (2), national security, preventing or detecting serious crime, and economic well-being of the UK, respectively.[281]

7.146 The Secretary of State must provide the list of operational purposes to the Intelligence and Security Committee (ISC) at the end of each relevant three-month period.[282] This means the period of three months beginning with the day on which section 183 comes into force, and each successive period of three months thereafter.[283] The Prime Minister must review the list of operational purposes at least once a year.[284]

(c) *Operational Purposes: Requirements*

7.147 A bulk equipment interference warrant must specify the operational purposes for which any material obtained under the warrant may be selected for examination.[285]

7.148 The warrant may, in particular, specify all of the operational purposes, which at the time the warrant is issued, are specified in the list of operational purposes.[286]

6. Duration of Warrants

7.149 A warrant issued under Part 6, Chapter 3 is of six months duration, commencing on the day of issue.[287] Where it has been renewed this period recommences the day

---

[276] ibid s 183(1)–(2).
[277] ibid s 183(12).
[278] ibid s 183(5).
[279] ibid s 183(4).
[280] ibid s 183(7).
[281] ibid s 183(8).
[282] ibid s 183(9).
[283] ibid s 183(10)(a)–(b).
[284] ibid s 183(11).
[285] ibid s 183(4).
[286] ibid s 183(6).
[287] ibid s 184(2)(b)(i).

D. Bulk Equipment Interference Warrants

following what would have been day of the warrant's expiration.[288] An urgent warrant is of five working days duration, commencing the day after it was issued.[289] In both cases, this is known as the relevant period. A warrant will cease to have effect unless it is renewed or is cancelled or otherwise eases to have effect (for example it is an urgent warrant but not given later approval by a judicial commissioner under section 99) at the end of the relevant period.[290]

7. Renewal of Warrants

A bulk equipment interference warrant may be renewed at any time during the renewal period—the thirty-day period ending with the day at the end of which the warrant would otherwise cease to have effect—by an instrument issued by the Secretary of State.[291] In the case of an urgent warrant that has not been renewed, the relevant period: see paragraphs 7.135–7.137. This is subject to the renewal conditions being met and a number of complicated exceptions. The decision to renew must be taken personally by the Secretary of State. The Secretary of State must also sign the renewal instrument.[292] 7.150

The renewal conditions reflect the original basis upon which the warrant was issued. It must be necessary on one or more of the available grounds (national security, preventing and detecting serious crime, or economic well-being of the UK) and the conduct authorized proportionate to the operational objective.[293] The requirements as to the necessity of the operational purposes and examination of the material must also be met and the decision to issue requires the approval of a judicial commissioner.[294] 7.151

When considering whether to approve the decision to renew, the judicial commissioner must carry out the review in the same way as the original decision to issue the warrant.[295] This is subject to the same exceptions as apply to renewal generally. 7.152

(a) Exceptions

The renewal provisions are subject to exceptions but only in the case of the renewal of a bulk interception warrant that has been modified so that it no longer authorizes or requires the securing of interference with any equipment or the obtaining of any communications, equipment data, or other information. In such circumstances there is no requirement that the Secretary of State considers the warrant is necessary on one or more of the available grounds.[296] Instead, the requirement that the 7.153

---

[288] ibid s 184(2)(b)(ii).
[289] ibid s 184(2)(a).
[290] ibid s 184(1)(a)–(b).
[291] ibid s 185(1) and (3).
[292] ibid s 185(4).
[293] ibid s 185(2)(a)–(b).
[294] ibid s 185(2)(c)–(d).
[295] ibid s 185(5).
[296] ibid s 185(6)(a).

Secretary of State considers the examination of the material continues to be necessary should be read as a reference to those grounds (but as set out in section 178(2) and not as repeated in sub-section (2) of section 185).[297] The judicial commissioner must also consider this variation of the authorization scheme when determining whether to approve the renewal in the case of a modified warrant and section 179 is to be given effect accordingly: see paras 7.132–7.134 above.[298]

8. Modification of Warrants

7.154 A bulk equipment interference warrant may be modified at any time by an instrument issued by the person making the modification.[299] There are two types of modification: major and minor. The former is a modification adding or varying any operational purpose as a purpose for which any material obtained under the warrant may be selected for examination or a modification adding or varying any description of conduct authorized by the warrant.[300] The latter is the removal, as opposed to adding or varying, the operational purpose or description of conduct: see paragraphs 7.144–7.148 above.[301] Where the modification no longer authorizes or requires the securing of interference with equipment or the obtaining of any communications, equipment data or other information such a modification does not prevent the warrant from being a bulk interception warrant, notwithstanding that it may no longer meet the requirements of section 176(1)(b) and (4)(a): see paragraphs 7.120 and 7.126 above.[302] Any modification is limited only to conduct authorized or required by the warrant.[303]

7.155 A major modification relating to the operational purpose must be made by the Secretary of State, and is limited to circumstances where it is considered necessary on any of the available grounds upon which the warrant could be issued.[304] The same requirements apply in relation to the description of the conduct except that, in addition, the conduct authorized by the modification must be proportionate to the operational objective.[305] Unless it is an urgent modification, it does not take effect until a judicial commissioner has approved it.[306]

7.156 The Secretary of State or senior official acting on his or her behalf may make a minor modification.[307] However, where a senior official makes it the Secretary of State must be notified personally of the modification and the reasons for making

---

[297] ibid s 185(6)(b).
[298] ibid s 185(6)(c)(i)–(ii).
[299] ibid s 186(1).
[300] ibid s 186(2)(a)–(b) and (3)(a).
[301] ibid s 186(3)(b).
[302] ibid s 186(13).
[303] ibid s 186(14).
[304] ibid s 186(4)(a)–(b).
[305] ibid s 186(5)(a)–(b).
[306] ibid s 186(6).
[307] ibid s 186(7)(a)–(b).

D. Bulk Equipment Interference Warrants

it.[308] There is a mandatory requirement on both the Secretary of State and a senior official to modify where either considers that any operational purpose specified in a warrant is no longer a purpose for which the examination of the material obtained under the warrant is or may be necessary. In such circumstances that operational purpose should be removed.[309]

7.157 The decision to modify in either case must be taken personally by the person making it and that person must sign the instrument.[310]

7.158 In the case of a major modification made by the Secretary of State but where it is not reasonably practicable for that person to sign the instrument, it may be signed by a senior official designated by the Secretary of State for that purpose.[311] The instrument making the modification must in such circumstances contain a statement to this effect and that the Secretary of State has personally and expressly authorized the making of the modification.[312]

(a) Approval of Major Modifications Made in Non-urgent Cases

7.159 When determining whether to approve a decision to make a major modification of a bulk equipment interference warrant, a judicial commissioner must review the Secretary of State's conclusions as to whether the modification is necessary on any of the available grounds upon which it could be issued or, in the case of a major modification, adding or varying any description of conduct whether it is proportionate to what is sought to be achieved by that conduct.[313] The same principles apply to the approval of major modifications as apply to the approval of warrants: see paragraphs 7.132–7.137 above.[314]

7.160 As with the approval of warrants there is a duty to provide reasons to the Secretary of State where approval is refused and in cases where the refusal is by a judicial commissioner other than the Investigatory Powers Commissioner there is a right to ask for the decision to modify to be reconsidered by the senior Commissioner.[315]

(b) Approval of Major Modifications Made in Urgent Cases

7.161 Where the Secretary of State makes a major modification because it was considered that there was an urgent need to make the modification a judicial commissioner must be informed that the modification has been made.[316] The judicial commissioner must then, before the end of the relevant period (the period ending with the third working day after the day on which the modification was made) decide

---

[308] ibid s 186(8).
[309] ibid s 186(9).
[310] ibid s 186(10).
[311] ibid s 186(11).
[312] ibid s 186(12).
[313] ibid s 187(1)(a)–(b).
[314] ibid s 187(2)(a)–(b).
[315] ibid s 187(3)–(4).
[316] ibid s 188(1)(a)–(b) and (2).

whether to approve the decision to make the modification and notify the Secretary of State of the judicial commissioner's decision.[317]

7.162 If the judicial commissioner refuses to approve the decision the warrant—unless it no longer has effect for some other reason, such as, for example, cancellation—has effect as if the modification had not been made, and the person to whom the warrant is addressed must, so far as is reasonably practicable, secure that anything in the process of being done under the warrant by virtue of that modification stops as soon as possible. There is no right to have the decision reconsidered by the Investigatory Powers Commissioner in such circumstances.[318]

7.163 Where the decision is to refuse to approve the warrant, the judicial commissioner may authorize further interference with equipment for the purpose of enabling the person to whom the warrant is addressed to secure that anything in the process of being done under the warrant by virtue of the modification stops as soon as possible.[319]

7.164 The refusal to approve an urgent modification does not affect the lawfulness of anything done under the warrant by virtue of the modification prior to the modification ceasing to have effect. If anything is in the process of being done under the warrant by virtue of the modification when it ceases to have effect anything done before that thing could be stopped, or anything done which it is not reasonably practicable to stop is not unlawful.[320]

9. Cancellation of Warrants

7.165 The Secretary of State or a senior official acting on his or her behalf may cancel a bulk equipment interference warrant at any time.[321] However, where any of the 'cancellation conditions' apply, cancellation is mandatory.[322] There are three cancellation conditions. The first is that the warrant is no longer necessary in the interests of national security, except where the warrant has been modified so that it no longer authorizes or requires the securing of interference with any equipment or the obtaining of any communications, equipment data, or other information.[323] The second is that the conduct authorized by the warrant is no longer proportionate to what it seeks to achieve.[324] The third is that the examination of material obtained under the warrant is no longer necessary for any of the specified operational purposes provided for by section 183: see paragraphs 7.144–7.148 above.[325]

7.166 There are two consequences of cancellation: the person to whom the warrant was addressed must, so far as is reasonably practicable, secure that anything in the process of

---

[317] ibid s 188(3)(a)–(b).
[318] ibid s 188(4)(a)–(b).
[319] ibid s 188(5).
[320] ibid s 188(6)(a)–(b).
[321] ibid s 189(1).
[322] ibid s 189(2).
[323] ibid s 189(3)(a) and (4).
[324] ibid s 189(3)(b).
[325] ibid s 189(3)(c).

being done under the warrant stops as soon as possible;[326] and a warrant that has been cancelled may not be renewed.[327]

10. Implementation of Warrants

For the purposes of implementation of a bulk equipment interference warrant, the person to whom it is addressed, 'the implementing authority', may in addition to its own role in implementing the warrant act through, or together with other persons as the implementing authority may require to assist it to do so.[328] This includes disclosure to the implementing authority of any material obtained under the warrant.[329]

Where the implementing authority requires assistance with implementation, it may serve or make arrangements to serve a copy of the warrant—either with or without one or more of the schedules contained in it—on such persons it requires assistance from.[330] This includes service outside the UK.[331]

The provisions in sections 127 (service of warrants) and 128 (duty of operators to assist with implementation) apply in relation to a bulk equipment interference warrant as they apply in relation to a targeted interception warrant: see Chapter 3, paragraphs 3.111–3.117.[332]

7.167

7.168

7.169

11. Safeguards

(a) *Retention and Disclosure of Material*

There is a requirement on the part of the Secretary of State to ensure, in relation to every bulk equipment interference warrant issued, that it has arrangements in force for securing that the number of persons to whom any of the material derived from the warrant is disclosed, the extent to which it is disclosed or otherwise made available and the extent to which the material is copied and the number of copies that are made is limited to minimum number necessary for the authorized purposes.[333] Every copy must be stored for as long as it is retained securely and must be destroyed as soon as there is no longer any relevant grounds—which in this context means authorized purposes—for retaining it unless it is destroyed sooner.[334] This does not apply to material, including any copy of the material, obtained under the warranted handed over to any overseas authorities (a country or territory outside the UK).[335]

7.170

---

[326] ibid s 189(5).
[327] ibid s 189(6).
[328] ibid s 190(1).
[329] ibid s 190(4).
[330] ibid s 190(2) and (6).
[331] ibid s 190(3).
[332] ibid s 190(5).
[333] ibid s 191(1)–(2).
[334] ibid s 191(4)–(5).
[335] ibid s 191(7), (8), and (9).

7. Bulk Warrants

7.171　Authorized purposes are limited to five purposes. The first is that it is, or is likely to be, necessary on any of the relevant grounds (that is, the grounds upon or purpose for which the warrant was issued).[336] The second and third are that it is necessary for facilitating the carrying out of functions under the Act by the Secretary of State, Scottish Ministers, or the person to whom the warrant is addressed or by the judicial commissioners or the Investigatory Powers Tribunal.[337] The fourth and fifth are that it is necessary for the purpose of legal proceedings or the performance of the functions of any person under any enactment.[338]

7.172　Copy has the same meaning as it does when used in the context of intercept warrants: see Chapter 3, paragraph 3.147.[339]

(b) Disclosure of Material Overseas

7.173　In cases involving disclosure of material or copies of material obtained under a bulk equipment interference warrant the Secretary of State must ensure, in relation to every such warrant, that arrangements are in force for securing that it is handled in accordance with the applicable requirements.[340]

7.174　The requirements are those corresponding to the provisions in section 191(2) and (5) and 193 and apply 'to such extent (if any) as the Secretary of State considers appropriate'.[341]

(c) Examination of Material

7.175　The section 193 requirements will be met in relation to the material obtained under a warrant for the purposes of section 191 if the selection of any of the material for examination is carried out only for the specified purposes, is necessary and proportionate in all the circumstances, and meets any of the selection conditions.[342] The term 'specified purposes' is defined in sub-section (2) and the 'selection conditions' are set in sub-section (3).

7.176　The specified purposes mean only so far as is necessary for the operational purposes specified in the warrant—in existence at the time of the selection—in accordance with section 183: see paragraphs 7.144–7.148 above.[343]

7.177　There are four selection conditions each of which relates to the prohibition on the protected material not at any time being selected for examination if any criteria used for the selection are referable to an individual known to be in the British Islands at that time, and the purpose of using those criteria is to identify the protected material consisting of communications sent by, or intended for, that individual (whether

---

[336] ibid s 191(3)(a) and (7).
[337] ibid s 191(3)(b)–(c).
[338] ibid s 191(3)(d)–(e).
[339] ibid s 191(9).
[340] ibid s 192(1)(a)–(b).
[341] ibid s 192(2).
[342] ibid s 193(1)(a)–(c).
[343] ibid s 193(2).

or not their identity is known).[344] The first two conditions are that the selection of the protected material for examination does not breach the prohibition and that the person to whom the warrant is addressed considers that the selection of the protected material for examination would not breach the prohibition.[345] The second two are that the selection of the protected material for examination in breach of that prohibition is authorized by either sub-section (5) or by a targeted examination warrant issued under Part 5.[346]

7.178 Authorization by virtue of sub-section (5) occurs where four circumstances exist. The first is that the criteria referable to an individual have been, or are being, used for the selection of protected material (redefined as 'the relevant material' for this purpose) for examination in circumstances falling within the first two selection conditions.[347] The second is where at any time it appears to the person to whom the warrant is addressed that there has been a relevant change of circumstances in relation to the individual that would mean that the selection of the relevant material for examination would breach the prohibition.[348] A change of circumstances for this purpose means either that the individual has entered the British Islands or a belief by the person to whom the warrant is addressed that the individual was outside the British Islands was in fact mistaken.[349] The third and fourth are that since a change of circumstances became known a written authorization to examine the relevant material using those criteria has been given by a senior officer, and the selection is made before the end of the permitted period.[350] This is the fifth working day following the day after the person to whom the warrant is addressed knows of the change of circumstances.[351] Where authorization is given under section 193(5), the person to whom the warrant is addressed must notify the Secretary of State that the selection is being carried out.[352]

7.179 A senior officer for the purposes of section 193 has the same meaning as senior official in section 135(1)(a): see Chapter 6, paragraph 6.74.

12. Additional Safeguards

(a) *Items Subject to Legal Privilege*

7.180 Where the selection of the protected material for examination does not breach the prohibition in section 193(3)(a)–(b) or is authorized under section 193(3)(c) and at least a purpose of using the criteria to be used for the selection of the intercepted content for examination is to identify any items subject to legal privilege, or the

---

[344] ibid s 193(4).
[345] ibid s 193(3)(a)–(b).
[346] ibid s 193(3)(c)–(d).
[347] ibid s 193(5)(a).
[348] ibid s 193(5)(b).
[349] ibid s 193(6).
[350] ibid s 193(5)(c)–(d).
[351] ibid s 193(7).
[352] ibid s 193(8).

use of the criteria is likely to identify such items, the material may be selected for examination.[353] The 'criteria' is a reference back to section 193(5) but, in this context, is referred to as 'the relevant criteria'. It use is subject to the approval of a senior official acting on behalf of the Secretary of State, who has approved the use of those criteria.[354]

7.181 The senior official in deciding whether to give an approval must have regard to the public interest in the confidentiality of items subject to legal privilege[355] and may only do so if two conditions are met. First, that the arrangements made for safeguarding retention and disclosure of the material under section 191 include specific arrangements for the handling, retention, use and destruction of items subject to legal privilege, and where a purpose is to identify any items subject to legal privilege, the senior official considers that there are exceptional and compelling circumstances that make the use of the relevant criteria necessary.[356]

7.182 The threshold of 'exceptional and compelling' will not be met unless the public interest in obtaining the information outweighs the public interest in maintaining the confidentiality of the legal privilege, there are no other means by which the information could reasonably be obtained and in cases where the substantive ground upon which the warrant is obtained in the prevention and detection of serious crime, obtaining the information is necessary for the preventing death or significant injury.[357]

7.183 Where the selection of the material for examination does not breach the prohibition is section 193(3)(a)–(b) or is authorized under section 193(3)(c) and at least a purpose of using the criteria to be used for the selection of the material for examination is to identify communications or other information that, if they were not made with the intention of furthering a criminal purpose, would be items subject to legal privilege, and the person to whom the warrant is addressed considers that the communications are likely to be communications made with the intention of furthering a criminal purpose, the material may be selected for examination. This again is referred to as 'the relevant criteria' for this purpose and the communications are referred to as the targeted communications' for this purpose. Its use is subject to the approval of a senior official acting on behalf of the Secretary of State who has approved the use of those criteria.[358] Approval can only be given if the official considers that the targeted communications or other information are likely to be communications made with the intention of furthering a criminal purpose.[359]

7.184 Where an item subject to legal privilege has been obtained in accordance with a bulk equipment interference warrant and is retained following its examination for purposes other than its destruction, the person to whom the warrant is addressed

---

[353] ibid s 194(1).
[354] ibid s 194(2).
[355] ibid s 194(3).
[356] ibid 194(4)(a)–(b).
[357] ibid s 194(5).
[358] ibid s 194(6)(b)–(c).
[359] ibid s 194(7) and (8).

D. Bulk Equipment Interference Warrants

must inform the Investigatory Powers Commissioner of the retention of the item as soon as reasonably practicable.[360]

Other than in cases where the public interest in retention of the item outweighs the public interest in the confidentiality of items subject to items subject to legal privilege and retention is necessary in the interests of national security or for the purpose of preventing death or serious injury,[361] the Investigatory Powers Commissioner must either direct the item is destroyed or impose conditions as to the retention and use of the item.[362] In determining which of these alternatives is appropriate the Commissioner may require representations to be made by affected persons.[363] These are either the person to who the warrant was or is addressed or the Secretary of State.[364] Where the Commissioner requires representations, these must be considered when determining whether the items should be destroyed or conditions imposed.[365] 7.185

(b) *Confidential Journalistic Material*

In cases where material which has been obtained in accordance with a bulk equipment interference warrant is retained, following its examination, for purposes other than the destruction of the communication, and it is a communication containing confidential journalistic material, the person to whom the warrant is addressed must inform the Investigatory Powers Commissioner as soon as is reasonably practicable.[366] 7.186

13. Offence of Breaching Safeguards Relating to Examination of Material

There are three ingredients to the offence of breaching safeguards relating to the examination of data. The person must select for examination any material obtained under a bulk equipment interference warrant, know or believe that the selection of that data for examination does not comply with a requirement relating to the safeguards for the examination of material or items subject to legal privilege and deliberately selects that data for examination in breach of that requirement.[367] As to when the offence is committed by a body corporate or Scottish partnership, see Chapter 10, paragraphs 10.125–10.127. 7.187

A person guilty of the offence is liable on summary conviction in England and Wales to imprisonment for a term not exceeding twelve months (or six months, if the offence was committed before the commencement of section 154(1) of the Criminal Justice Act 2003), or to a fine, or both.[368] On summary conviction in Scotland to imprisonment for a term not exceeding twelve months, or to a fine 7.188

---

[360] ibid s 194(9).
[361] ibid s 194(12)(a)–(b).
[362] ibid s 194(10)(a)–(b).
[363] ibid s 194(13)(a).
[364] ibid s 194(14).
[365] ibid s 194(13)(b).
[366] ibid s 195.
[367] ibid s 196(1)(a)–(c).
[368] ibid s 196(2)(a).

7. Bulk Warrants

not exceeding the statutory maximum, or both.[369] In Northern Ireland the maximum sentence on summary conviction is imprisonment for a term not exceeding six months, or to a fine not exceeding the statutory maximum, or both.[370]

7.189 On conviction on indictment, the maximum sentence is imprisonment for a term not exceeding two years or to a fine, or both.[371]

7.190 The consent of the relevant Director of Public Prosecutions is required before criminal proceedings for an offence under section 173 may be instituted against a person in England, Wales, or Northern Ireland.[372]

14. Application of Other Restrictions in Relation to Warrants

7.191 The provisions in relation to the duty not to make unauthorized disclosures, set out in sections 132 to 134, apply in relation to bulk equipment interference warrants as they apply in relation to targeted equipment interference warrants, but as if the reference in section 133(2)(c) to a requirement for disclosure imposed by virtue of section 126(4) were a reference to such a requirement imposed by virtue of section 190(4).[373]

---

[369] ibid s 196(2)(b).
[370] ibid s 196(2)(c).
[371] ibid s 196(2)(d).
[372] ibid s 196(3).
[373] ibid s 197.

8
BULK PERSONAL DATASET WARRANTS

A.	Introduction	8.01
B.	Warrants	8.10
	1. When Part 7 Is Engaged	8.10
	2. Types of Warrants	8.12
	3. Class BPD Warrants	8.23
	4. Specific BPD Warrants	8.27
	5. Specific BPD: Additional Requirements	8.33
	6. Approval of Warrants by Judicial Commissioners	8.36
	7. Consequences Where Judicial Commissioner Refuses to Approve in Urgent Cases	8.42
	8. Requirements that Must Be Met by Warrants	8.46
C.	Warrants: Post-issue Matters	8.54
	1. Duration of Warrants	8.54
	2. Renewal of Warrants	8.55
	3. Modification of Warrants	8.59
	4. Judicial Approval	8.63
	5. Cancellation of Warrants	8.68
	6. 'Lazarus' or Non-renewal or Cancellation of BPD Warrants	8.69
	7. Acquisition of Bulk Personal Datasets outside Statutory Scheme	8.76
D.	Safeguards	8.79
	1. General	8.79
	2. Items Subject to Legal Privilege	8.82
	3. Items Subject to Legal Privilege	8.87
	4. Criminal Offence: Breaching Safeguards	8.90
E.	Application of Part 7 to Other Parts of the IPA	8.95
	1. Application for a 'Direction'	8.95
	2. Judicial Approval for Directions and Variations to Directions	8.99

A. INTRODUCTION

Bulk personal datasets are described by the Security Service (MI5) on its website **8.01** self-effacingly as 'sets of personal information about a large number of individuals, the majority of whom will not be of any interest to MI5'.[1] Big Brother Watch describes them as holding 'personal information on everyone'.[2] There is at least a consensus that they include the electoral roll, telephone directories, or travel-related data but the full extent is not known. The draft Code of Practice on the Security and Intelligence Agencies' retention and use of bulk personal datasets (the draft Code of Practice) describes them in the following terms:

> For the purposes of the Act and this code, a set of data that has been obtained by a Security and Intelligence Agency comprises a BPD where it includes personal data relating to a number of individuals, and the nature of that set is such that the majority of individuals contained within it are not, and are unlikely to become, of interest to the Security and Intelligence Agencies in the exercise of their statutory functions. Typically these datasets are very large, and of a size, which means they cannot be processed manually.[3]

8.02 According to MI5's website, 'the datasets are held on electronic systems for the purposes of analysis, although analysts will only actually look at the data relating to the minority who are of intelligence interest'. The apparent openness about their existence belies the fact that they have been used for decades but the Intelligence and Security Committee only avowed this use as recently as 12 March 2015.[4]

8.03 Part 7 of the IPA provides a relatively comprehensive scheme for the authorization, acquisition, retention, use, and destruction of bulk personal datasets. It consists of twenty-eight sections and at the time of writing a draft Code of Practice consisting of 72 pages. Prior to the IPA's enactment this area was regulated by four provisions in different statutes: section 94 of the Telecommunications Act 1984, section 2(2)(a) of the Security Service Act 1989 (the 1989 Act), sections 2(2)(a) and 4(2)(a) of the Intelligence Services Act 1994 (ISA) and section 19 of the Counter-Terrorism Act 2008. Each relates to the acquisition of information in the discharge of the functions of the intelligence services. The adequacy of the framework under section 94 of the Telecommunications Act 1994 for acquiring, retaining and using bulk personal datasets and bulk communications data was the subject of legal challenge in *Privacy International v (1) Secretary of State for Foreign and Commonwealth Affairs and Others*.[5] The Investigatory Powers Tribunal held that the respective regimes for their use did not comply with Article 8 of the European Convention on Human Rights until March and November 2015.

8.04 The key holdings in the *Privacy International* judgment were time-limited largely as a result of the avowal referred to in paragraph 8.02 above, and the publication of 'Handling Arrangements' on 4 November 2015. The Regulation of Investigatory Powers Act 2000 had also been amended in March 2015 to extend the Intelligence Commissioner's reach to oversight of the intelligence services use, including misuse of bulk personal datasets.[6]

---

[1] https://www.mi5.gov.uk/bulk-data.
[2] https://www.bigbrotherwatch.org.uk/wp-content/uploads/2016/03/Bulk-Personal-Datasets.pdf.
[3] Draft Code of Practice, para 2.2.
[4] ISC Report, Privacy and Security: A Modern and Transparent Legal Framework (12 March 2015) HC 1075.
[5] [2016] UKIPTrib 15_110-CH.
[6] Regulation of Investigatory Powers Act 2000, s 59A.

A. Introduction

The acquisition, use, and retention of bulk personal datasets remain controversial. The effect of the decision in *Secretary of State of the Home Department v Watson and Others*[7] has inextricable implications for their use. The ISC initially questioned their necessity, a position unsurprisingly adopted by civil liberties groups. In response, David Anderson QC, the then independent reviewer of terrorism legislation, was commissioned to carry out a Bulk Powers Review. Anderson reported in August 2016. He noted: 8.05

> They [bulk personal databases] play an important part in identifying, understanding and averting threats in Great Britain, Northern Ireland and further afield. After close examination of numerous case studies, the Review concluded that other techniques could sometimes (though not always) be used to achieve these objectives: but that they would often be less effective, more dangerous, more resource-intensive, more intrusive or slower.[8]

His final reported concluded: 8.06

> This Report has declared the powers under review to have a clear operational purpose. But like an old-fashioned snapshot, it will fade in time. The world is changing with great speed, and new questions will arise about the exercise, utility and intrusiveness of these strong capabilities. If adopted, my recommendation will enable those questions to be answered by a strong oversight body on a properly informed basis.[9]

The IPT considered further issues in the *Privacy International* litigation, at a hearing in June 2017. The issues before the IPT were whether sharing or granting access to bulk communications data and bulk personal datasets with foreign intelligence agencies and UK law enforcement agencies was lawful and whether the collection, retention and use of these datasets is lawful under EU law. Privacy International's lawyers argued that the 'strong oversight' Anderson recommended does not exist. On the question of the effect of the decision in *Watson*, they submitted it is 8.07

> binding authority that the safeguards presently in place are inadequate. In particular, there is general and indiscriminate retention, no prior independent authorisation for access, no requirement for data to be retained in the EU and no notification provision.[10]

On 8 September 2017, the bulk communications data regime was referred to the Grand Chamber by the IPT.[11] 8.08

It should be emphasized that the IPA does not create *new* powers in respect of bulk personal datasets but rather provides an authorization matrix for their acquisition and use. Nor is their acquisition limited to Part 7: see paras 8.95–8.98 below. This is also recognized in the draft Code of Practice that refers to acquisition via the 1989 Act and ISA as 'information gateways'.[12] Even the ISC had to concede the 8.09

---

[7] Case C-698/15 (21 December 2016).
[8] https://terrorismlegislationreviewer.independent.gov.uk/bulk-powers-review-report/#more-2790
[9] https://terrorismlegislationreviewer.independent.gov.uk/wp-content/uploads/2016/08/Bulk-Powers-Review-final-report.pdf.
[10] https://privacyinternational.org/sites/default/files/1.%20Claimant%27s%20Skeleton%20for%20June%20hearing.pdf (last accessed 3 June 2017).
[11] IPT/15/110/CH.
[12] Draft Code of Practice, para 2.11 (last updated 23 February 2017).

8. Bulk Personal Dataset Warrants

use of this legislation as a basis for collecting the data was 'implicit'.[13] However, for the first time the powers are placed on a tangible statutory basis that enables some degree of foreseeability, in Strasbourg jurisprudential terms, of the activities of the intelligence services in this area.[14]

B. WARRANTS

1. When Part 7 Is Engaged

8.10 Bulk Personal Dataset (BPD) warrants are only available to the intelligence services. An intelligence service retains a bulk personal dataset if four circumstances are met. First, it obtains a set of information that includes personal data relating to a number of individuals.[15] Personal data for the purposes of Part 7 of the IPA has the same meaning as in the Data Protection Act 1998, except that it also includes data relating to a deceased individual where the data would be personal data within the meaning of that Act if it related to a living individual. Secondly, the nature of the set is such that the majority of those on it are of no interest to the intelligence service or are unlikely to become of interest to it in the exercise of its functions.[16] Thirdly, after any initial examination of the contents, the intelligence service retains the set for the purpose of the exercise of its functions; and, fourthly, the set is held, or is to be held, electronically for analysis in the exercise of those functions.[17] The draft Code of Practice states that the intelligence service 'should complete this initial examination as soon as reasonably practicable'. This, it says, 'will depend on many different factors', including taking possession of the dataset and, in some cases, getting it translated.[18]

8.11 In order to exercise the power to retain and/or examine a bulk personal dataset warrant, authorization under Part 7 is required unless one of a number of exemptions applies.[19]

2. Types of Warrants

8.12 There are two types of warrant. These are, first, a class bulk personal dataset warrant (a class BPD warrant), which authorizes an intelligence service to retain, or to retain and examine, any bulk personal dataset of a class described in the warrant and, secondly, a specific bulk personal dataset warrant (a specific BPD warrant) authorizing the retention and/or examination of any bulk personal dataset described in the warrant.[20]

---

[13] ISC, Privacy and Security, 6.
[14] See also the draft Code of Practice, paras 2.11–2.13.
[15] IPA, s 199(1)(a).
[16] ibid s 199(1)(b).
[17] ibid s 199(1)(c)–(d).
[18] Draft Code of Practice, para 2.6.
[19] IPA, s 200(1)–(2) and s 201.
[20] ibid s 200(3)(a)–(b).

B. Warrants

(a) *Scope*

There is no requirement to obtain a warrant where an intelligence service exercises the power to retain or examine a bulk personal dataset if it obtained the bulk personal dataset under a warrant or other authorization issued or given under some other provision of the IPA.[21]

There is no requirement to obtain a warrant if at any time a bulk personal dataset is being retained or examined for the purpose of enabling any of the information contained in it to be destroyed.[22]

Reference is made in section 202(3) to three other provisions in different parts of Part 7, in sections 210(8), 219(8), and 220(5). Each of these provisions relates to circumstances when exceptions apply in cases where a judicial commissioner refuses to approve a specific BPD warrant, the non-renewal or cancellation of BPD warrants, and initial examinations.[23]

(b) *Class BPD Warrants: Restrictions on Use*

There are some limited restrictions on the use of class BPD warrants where the head of the intelligence service considers that the bulk personal dataset consists of, or includes, protected data or health records or a substantial proportion of the bulk personal dataset consists of sensitive personal data.[24] In such circumstances, there is a general prohibition on the retention and/or examination of the material.

(c) *Protected Data*

Protected data is defined for the purposes of Part 7 in section 203 and is a broader concept than 'protected material', which is provided for in section 99 (equipment interference): see Chapter 6, paragraph 6.09 above. It means data contained in a bulk personal dataset that is not systems data or data that is not private information (including information relating to a person's private and family life, so presumably as this understood in human rights' jurisprudence).[25] In addition, it includes 'identifying data' included in the bulk personal dataset capable of being logically separated from it and if it was,

would not reveal anything of what might reasonably be considered to be the meaning (if any) of any of the data which would remain in the bulk personal dataset or of the bulk personal dataset itself, disregarding any meaning arising from the existence of that data or (as the case may be) the existence of the bulk personal dataset or from any data relating to that fact.[26]

This less than straightforward provision is an attempt to circumscribe the scope of the bulk data that can be accessed by way of a class BPD warrant by excluding content (other than that capable of being inferred from the nature of the data itself).

8.13

8.14

8.15

8.16

8.17

8.18

---

[21] ibid s 201(1).
[22] ibid s 201(2).
[23] ibid s 201(3).
[24] ibid s 202(1)–(2)(a)–(b).
[25] ibid s 203(10(a) and (c).
[26] ibid s 203(2)(a)–(c).

8.19 Health records, which are subject to additional protections in section 206, means records consisting of information relating to the physical or mental health or condition of an individual that was made by or on behalf of a health professional in connection with the care of that individual and was obtained by the intelligence service from a health professional or a health service body or from a person acting on behalf of a health professional or a health service body in relation to the record or the copy: see paragraphs 8.33–8.34 below.[27] The terms 'health professional' and 'health service body' are found in section 69 of the Data Protection Act 1998 and have the same meaning for the purposes of the IPA.[28]

8.20 Similarly, 'sensitive personal data' means personal data consisting of information about an individual (whether living or deceased) which is of a kind mentioned in section 2(a) to (f) of the Data Protection Act 1998.[29]

8.21 A similar prohibition applies where the head of the intelligence service considers that the nature of the bulk personal dataset, or the circumstances in which it was created, is or are such that its retention, or retention and examination, by the intelligence service raises novel or contentious issues which ought to be considered by the Secretary of State and a judicial commissioner on an application for a specific BPD warrant.

8.22 The draft Code of Practice makes extensive provision at paragraphs 4.31–4.58 (and Chapter 7) in respect of protected data, setting out:

> [A] scheme that enables the Secretary of State to impose additional controls in relation to the selection for examination of any protected data in the dataset relating to an individual who is known to be in the British Islands at the time of the selection. The scheme applies on a dataset by dataset basis having regard to the range of factors set out below, including the nature and intrusiveness of the protected data in the dataset.[30]

3. Class BPD Warrants

8.23 An application for the issue of a class BPD warrant may only be made by or on behalf of the head of the intelligence services.[31] Where it is the latter, the person applying must hold office under the Crown.[32] Applications are made to the Secretary of State under section 204 of the IPA. There are a number of formalities. The application must include a description of the class of bulk personal datasets to which the application relates, and in a case where authorization is sought for the examination of bulk personal datasets of that class, the operational purposes that it is proposing should be specified in the warrant.[33] The decision to issue a warrant must be taken

---

[27] ibid s 206(6)(a)–(c).
[28] ibid s 206(7).
[29] ibid s 202(4).
[30] Draft Code of Practice, para 4.36.
[31] IPA, s 204(1).
[32] ibid s 204(5).
[33] ibid s 2014(2)(a)–(b).

B. Warrants

personally by the Secretary of State.[34] Before it is issued, the Secretary of State must also sign the warrant.[35] When completing a warrant application the intelligence service 'must ensure that the case for the warrant is presented in the application in a fair and balanced way. In particular all reasonable efforts should be made to take account of information, which supports or weakens the case for the warrant'.[36]

(a) *Conditions to Be Met Prior to Issue*

8.24 Before a class BPD warrant can be issued the Secretary of State must consider whether the conditions for doing so have been met. These are: whether it is in the interests of national security, preventing or detecting serious crime, or in the interests of the economic well-being of the United Kingdom (UK) so far as those interests are also relevant to the interests of national security,[37] that the conduct authorized is proportionate to the operational objective to which the conduct relates;[38] each of the specified operational purposes is a purpose for which the examination of material obtained under the warrant is or may be necessary, and the examination of material for each such purpose is necessary on any of the grounds on which the Secretary of State considers the warrant to be necessary;[39] and satisfactory arrangements made for the purposes of safeguards relating to disclosure are in force in relation to the warrant.[40]

8.25 The decision to issue a class BPD warrant must be approved by a judicial commissioner.[41]

8.26 The fact that the retention and examination of bulk personal datasets that would be obtained under a warrant relates to the activities in the British Islands of a trade union is not, of itself, sufficient to establish that the warrant is necessary in the interests of national security or on any of the other available grounds.[42]

4. Specific BPD Warrants

8.27 An application for the issue of a specific BPD warrant may only be made by or on behalf of the head of the intelligence services.[43] Where it is the latter, the person applying must hold office under the Crown.[44] Applications are made to the Secretary of State under section 205 of the IPA. Applications are limited to two categories of cases. Case 1 is where authorization is sought to retain, or to retain

---

[34] ibid s 211(1).
[35] ibid s 211(2).
[36] Draft Code of Practice, para 4.5.
[37] IPA, s 204(3)(a)(i)–(iii).
[38] ibid s 204(3)(b).
[39] ibid s 204(3)(c)(i)–(ii).
[40] ibid s 204(3)(d).
[41] ibid s 204(3)(e).
[42] ibid s 204(4).
[43] ibid s 205(1).
[44] ibid s 205(9).

8. Bulk Personal Dataset Warrants

and examine, a bulk personal dataset, and this does not fall within a class described in a class BPD warrant.[45] Case 2 is where the circumstances are the same as Case 1 but where either section 202(1), (2), or (3) prevents retention, or retention and examination, of the bulk personal dataset in reliance on the class BPD warrant, or the intelligence service at any time considers that it would be appropriate to seek a specific BPD warrant.[46] If it is the former, an explanation for this must be provided in the application.[47]

8.28 As with class BPD warrants, there are a number of formalities. The application must include a description of the class of bulk personal datasets to which the application relates, and in a case where authorization is sought for the examination of bulk personal datasets of that class, the operational purposes that it is proposing should be specified in the warrant.[48] The decision to issue a warrant must be taken personally by the Secretary of State.[49] Before it is issued, the Secretary of State must also sign the warrant.[50] If it is not reasonably practicable for a warrant to be signed by the Secretary of State, the warrant may be signed by a senior official providing it is personally and expressly authorized by the Secretary of State and the warrant in such circumstances must contain a statement to this effect.[51]

(a) *Conditions to Be Met Prior to Issue*

8.29 Before a specific BPD warrant can be issued, the Secretary of State must consider whether the conditions for doing so have been met. These are: whether it is in the interests of national security, preventing or detecting serious crime, or in the interests of the economic well-being of the UK so far as those interests are also relevant to the interests of national security;[52] that the conduct authorized is proportionate to the operational objective to which the conduct relates;[53] each of the specified operational purposes is a purpose for which the examination of material obtained under the warrant is or may be necessary, and the examination of material for each such purpose is necessary on any of the grounds on which the Secretary of State considers the warrant to be necessary;[54] and satisfactory arrangements made for the purposes of safeguards relating to disclosure are in force in relation to the warrant.[55]

8.30 The decision to issue a specific BPD warrant must be approved by a judicial commissioner unless it is considered that there is an urgent need to issue the warrant.[56]

---

[45] ibid s 205(2)(a)–(b).
[46] ibid s 205(3)(a)–(b).
[47] ibid s 205(5).
[48] ibid s 205(4)(a)–(b).
[49] ibid s 211(1).
[50] ibid s 211(2).
[51] ibid s 211(4) and (5).
[52] ibid s 205(6)(a)(i)–(iii).
[53] ibid s 205(6)(b).
[54] ibid s 205(6)(c)(i)–(ii).
[55] ibid s 205(6)(d).
[56] ibid s 205(6)(e).

8.31 The fact that the retention and examination of bulk personal datasets that would be obtained under a warrant relates to the activities in the British Islands of a trade union is not, of itself, sufficient to establish that the warrant is necessary in the interests of national security or on any of the other available grounds.[57]

8.32 A specific BPD warrant relating to a bulk personal dataset, referred to as 'dataset A' may also authorize the retention or examination of other bulk personal datasets, referred to as the 'replacement datasets' that do not exist at the time of the issue of the warrant but may subsequently reasonably be regarded as replacements for dataset A.[58]

5. Specific BPD: Additional Requirements

(a) *Health Records*

8.33 The Secretary of State may only issue a specific BPD warrant if there are exceptional and compelling circumstances that make it necessary to authorize the retention and/or the examination of health records.[59] Where such an application is made and the purpose, or one of the purposes, of the warrant is to authorize the retention and/or the examination of health records, it must contain a statement to that effect.[60]

8.34 Where it is not the purpose or one of the purposes to retain and/or examine health records but the head of the intelligence service considers that the bulk personal dataset includes, or is likely to include, health records, the application must contain a statement that the bulk personal dataset includes health records or it is likely to do so and an assessment of how likely this is.[61]

(b) *Protected Data*

8.35 If the decision is to issue a specific BPD warrant in circumstances where protected data will be retained, the Secretary of State may impose conditions that must be satisfied before protected data retained in reliance on the warrant may be selected for examination. This is 'on the basis of criteria which are referable to an individual known to be in the British Islands at the time of selection'.[62]

6. Approval of Warrants by Judicial Commissioners

(a) *Approval of Warrants: Non-urgent Cases*

8.36 Under sections 204(3)(e) and 205(6)(e) a decision to issue a Class or Specific BPD warrant, in common with other forms of warrant, requires the approval of a judicial commissioner. In doing so, the judicial commissioner is required to review the

---

[57] ibid s 205(7).
[58] ibid s 205(8).
[59] ibid s 206(3).
[60] ibid s 206(1)–(2).
[61] ibid s 206(4)–(5).
[62] ibid s 207.

Secretary of State's conclusions as to whether the conditions for issue have been met: see paragraphs 8.24 and 8.29 above.[63]

8.37 The principles applied by the judicial commissioner in doing so are those as would be applied by a court on an application for judicial review.[64] The judicial commissioner is required to carry out this function 'with a sufficient degree of care as to ensure ... [compliance] with the duties imposed by section 2 (general duties in relation to privacy)': see Chapter 2, paragraphs 2.08–2.10.[65]

8.38 If a judicial commissioner refuses to approve the decision to issue a warrant, written reasons for the refusal must be provided to the Secretary of State.[66] In these circumstances, the Secretary of State may ask the Investigatory Powers Commissioner to approve the decision to issue the warrant. This is not a review of the judicial commissioner's decision but rather a reconsideration of the original ministerial decision. If the Investigatory Powers Commissioner made the decision to refuse, there is no scope to have the decision reconsidered further.[67]

(b) *Approval of Specific BPD Warrants: Urgent Cases*

8.39 An urgent warrant is a warrant issued without the approval of a judicial commissioner and where the person who issued it considered there was an urgent need to issue it without prior judicial approval.[68] It is limited to specific BPD warrants.

8.40 In cases where the warrant has been issued on an urgent basis and without prior approval, the Secretary of State must inform a judicial commissioner that it has been issued.[69] There is no time limit specified within which the judicial commissioner should be informed. However, the judicial commissioner must decide whether to approve the decision to issue the warrant, and notify the applicant of the decision within the 'relevant period'. This is the period ending with the third working day after the day on which the warrant was issued.[70]

8.41 Where a judicial commissioner refuses to approve the decision to issue an urgent warrant, the warrant ceases to have effect (unless previously cancelled), and it may not be renewed.[71] Refusal has a number of effects.

7. Consequences Where Judicial Commissioner Refuses to Approve in Urgent Cases

8.42 Where a judicial commissioner refuses to approve the issue of a warrant in an urgent case, the head of the intelligence service to whom the warrant was addressed must,

---

[63] ibid s 208(1)(a)–(c).
[64] ibid s 208(2)(a).
[65] ibid s 208(2)(b).
[66] ibid s 208(3).
[67] ibid s 208(4).
[68] ibid s 213(3)(a)–(b).
[69] ibid s 209(2).
[70] ibid s 209(3).
[71] ibid s 209(4).

so far as is reasonably practicable, secure that anything in the process of being done under the warrant stops as soon as possible.[72] The lawfulness of anything in the process of being done at the time the warrant ceases to have effect but which has already been done or cannot be stopped is not affected.[73]

Where the decision to refuse to approve is taken, the judicial commissioner has discretion to direct certain things take place on cessation: he or she may either direct that the whole or part of a bulk personal dataset retained in reliance of the warrant is destroyed or impose conditions as to the use or retention of part or all of the personal dataset.[74] Where conditions are imposed, an intelligence service is not to be regarded as being in breach of section 200(1) or (2) where it then retains or examines a bulk personal dataset.[75] 8.43

There are number of procedural mechanisms that may take effect on the judicial commissioner refusing to approve an urgent warrant. The first relates to an 'affected party' (the Secretary of State or the head of the intelligence service to whom it is addressed).[76] The judicial commissioner may invite representations about how to exercise their discretion on cessation of the warrant.[77] Where an affected party makes representations (whether or not at the judicial commissioner's invitation), these must be considered when the judicial commissioner considers whether to exercise discretion on cessation of the warrant.[78] 8.44

The second is a right of the Secretary of State to seek a review of the judicial commissioner's decision by the Investigatory Powers Commissioner.[79] Where such a right is exercised, the Investigatory Powers Commissioner may either confirm the original decision not to approve or make a fresh determination.[80] 8.45

8. Requirements that Must Be Met by Warrants

There are a number of requirements that must be met by warrants. The majority of these fall within the category of 'operational purposes'. 8.46

(a) *Non-operational Purpose Requirements*

There are two non-operational purpose requirements. First, the warrant must contain a provision stating that it is a either a class or specific BPD warrant and, secondly, it must be addressed to the head of the intelligence service by whom, or on whose behalf, the application for the warrant was made.[81] 8.47

---

[72] ibid s 210(2).
[73] ibid s 210(9).
[74] ibid s 210(3)(a)–(b).
[75] ibid s 210(8).
[76] ibid s 210(5).
[77] ibid s 210(4)(a).
[78] ibid s 210(4)(b).
[79] ibid s 210(6).
[80] ibid s 210(7).
[81] ibid s 212(1)–(2).

(b) *Operational Purposes: Procedural Matters*

8.48 The term 'specified operational purposes' means the operational purposes specified in the warrant in accordance with section 212.[82] These are set out on a list maintained by the heads of the intelligence services and known as 'the list of operational purposes'. They are the purposes that the intelligence services consider are the operational purposes for which data contained in bulk personal datasets obtained under specific or class BPD warrants may be selected for examination.[83]

8.49 An operational purpose may be specified in the list of operational purposes only with the approval of the Secretary of State.[84] Approval may only be given if the Secretary of State is satisfied that the operational purpose is specified in a greater level of detail than the descriptions contained in section 204(3)(a) or 205(6)(a) (depending on the type of warrant)), national security, preventing or detecting serious crime, and economic well-being of the UK, respectively.[85]

8.50 The Secretary of State must provide the list of operational purposes to the Intelligence and Security Committee (ISC) at the end of each relevant three-month period.[86] This means the period of three months beginning with the day on which section 212 comes into force, and each successive period of three months thereafter.[87] The prime minister must review the list of operational purposes at least once a year.[88]

(c) *Operational Purposes: Requirements*

8.51 A class BPD warrant must include a description of the class of bulk personal datasets to which the warrant relates and specify the operational purposes for which any data contained in the bulk personal datasets of that class may be selected for examination.[89]

8.52 A specific BPD warrant must include a description of the bulk personal datasets to which the warrant relates, where the warrant authorizes the retention or examination of replacement datasets, include a description that will enable those datasets to be identified, and specify the operational purposes for which any data contained in the bulk personal datasets of that class may be selected for examination. In addition, where the Secretary of State has imposed conditions under section 207 because protected data is included, it must specify those conditions: see paragraph 8.35 above.[90]

8.53 Either class of warrant may, in particular, specify all of the operational purposes, which at the time the warrant is issued are specified in the list of operational purposes.[91]

---

[82] ibid s 212(12).
[83] ibid s 212(5).
[84] ibid s 212(7).
[85] ibid s 212(8).
[86] ibid s 212(9).
[87] ibid s 212(10)(a)–(b).
[88] ibid s 212(11).
[89] ibid s 212(3)(a)–(b).
[90] ibid s 212(4)(a)–(d).
[91] ibid s 212(6).

C. WARRANTS: POST-ISSUE MATTERS

1. Duration of Warrants

A class or specific BPD warrant that has not earlier been cancelled or renewed ceases to have effect at the end of the period of six months beginning with the day on which the warrant was issued.[92] This is referred to as the 'relevant period'. If it has been renewed, the relevant period has effect from the day after the day at the end of which the warrant would have ceased to have effect if it had not been renewed.[93] 8.54

2. Renewal of Warrants

A class or specific BPD warrant may be renewed at any time during the renewal period—the thirty-day period ending with the day at the end of which the warrant would otherwise cease to have effect—by an instrument issued by the Secretary of State.[94] This is subject to the renewal conditions being met and a number of complicated exceptions. The decision to renew must be taken personally by the Secretary of State. The Secretary of State must also sign the renewal instrument.[95] 8.55

The renewal conditions reflect the original basis upon which the warrant was issued. It must be necessary on one or more of the available grounds (national security, preventing and detecting serious crime, economic well-being of the UK) and the conduct authorized proportionate to the operational objective.[96] The requirements as to the necessity of the operational purposes and examination of the bulk personal datasets or class of personal datasets must also be met and the decision to issue requires the approval of a judicial commissioner.[97] 8.56

When considering whether to approve the decision to renew, the judicial commissioner must carry out the review in the same way as the original decision to issue the warrant: see paragraphs 8.36–8.38 above.[98] 8.57

The provisions in relation to protected data apply in relation to the renewal of a specific BPD warrant as they applied in relation to its issue. It does not matter whether any conditions were imposed on the issue of the warrant.[99] 8.58

3. Modification of Warrants

A class or specific BPD warrant may be modified at any time by an instrument issued by the person making the modification.[100] There are two types of modification: major 8.59

---

[92] ibid s 213(1)(a)–(b).
[93] ibid s 213(2)(b).
[94] ibid s 214(1) and (3)(b).
[95] ibid s 214(4).
[96] ibid s 214(2)(a)–(b).
[97] ibid s 214(2)(c)–(d).
[98] ibid s 214(6).
[99] ibid s 214(5).
[100] ibid s 215(1).

and minor. The former is a modification adding, varying, or removing any operational purpose as a purpose for which bulk personal datasets of a class described in the warrant may be selected for examination.[101] The latter relates only to a specific DPD warrant and is a modification adding, varying, or removing any operational purpose as a purpose for which the bulk personal dataset described in the warrant may be selected for examination.[102]

8.60　A major modification must be made by the Secretary of State, and is limited to circumstances where it is considered necessary on any of the available grounds upon which the warrant could be issued.[103] Unless it is an urgent modification, it does not take effect until a judicial commissioner has approved it.[104]

8.61　The Secretary of State or senior official acting on his or her behalf may make a minor modification.[105] However, where a senior official makes it, the Secretary of State must be notified personally of the modification and the reasons for making it.[106] There is a mandatory requirement on both the Secretary of State and a senior official to modify where either considers that any operational purpose specified in a warrant is no longer a purpose for which the examination of any bulk personal datasets obtained under the warrant is or may be necessary. In such circumstances, that operational purpose should be removed.[107]

8.62　The decision to modify in either case must be taken personally by the person making it and that person must sign the instrument.[108] In the case of a major modification made by the Secretary of State but where it is not reasonably practicable for that person to sign the instrument, it may be signed by a senior official designated by the Secretary of State for that purpose.[109] The instrument making the modification must in such circumstances contain a statement to this effect and that the Secretary of State has personally and expressly authorized the making of the modification.[110]

4. Judicial Approval

(a) *Non-urgent Cases*

8.63　When determining whether to approve a decision to make a major modification of a class or specific BPD warrant, a judicial commissioner must review the Secretary of State's conclusions as to whether the modification is necessary on any of the available grounds upon which it could be issued.[111] The same principles apply to the

---

[101] ibid s 215(2)(a) and (3)(a).
[102] ibid s 215(2)(b) and (3)(b).
[103] ibid s 215(4)(a)–(b).
[104] ibid s 215(5).
[105] ibid s 215(6)(a)–(b).
[106] ibid s 215(7).
[107] ibid s 215(8).
[108] ibid s 215(9).
[109] ibid s 215(10).
[110] ibid s 215(11).
[111] ibid s 216(1).

C. Warrants: Post-issue Matters

approval of major modifications as apply to the approval of warrants: see paragraphs 8.36–8.38 above.[112]

As with the approval of warrants, there is a duty to provide reasons to the Secretary of State where approval is refused and, in cases where the refusal is by a judicial commissioner other than the Investigatory Powers Commissioner, there is a right to ask for the decision to modify to be reconsidered by the senior Commissioner.[113]   **8.64**

(b) *Urgent Cases*

Where the Secretary of State makes a major modification to a warrant without approval and considered that there was an urgent need to make the modification, a judicial commissioner must be informed that the modification has been made.[114] The judicial commissioner must then, before the end of the relevant period (the period ending with the third working day after the day on which the modification was made) decide whether to approve the decision to make the modification and notify the Secretary of State of the judicial commissioner's decision.[115]   **8.65**

If the judicial commissioner refuses to approve the decision, the warrant—unless it no longer has effect for some other reason, such as, for example, cancellation—has effect as if the modification had not been made, and the person to whom the warrant is addressed must, so far as is reasonably practicable, secure that anything in the process of being done under the warrant by virtue of that modification stops as soon as possible. There is no right to have the decision reconsidered by the Investigatory Powers Commissioner in such circumstances.[116]   **8.66**

The refusal to approve an urgent modification does not affect the lawfulness of anything done under the warrant by virtue of the modification prior to the modification ceasing to have effect. If anything is in the process of being done under the warrant by virtue of the modification, when it ceases to have effect anything done before that thing could be stopped, or anything done which it is not reasonably practicable to stop is not unlawful.[117]   **8.67**

5. Cancellation of Warrants

The Secretary of State or a senior official acting on his or her behalf may cancel a class or specific BPD warrant at any time.[118] However, where any of the 'cancellation conditions' apply, cancellation is mandatory.[119] There are three cancellation conditions. The first is that the warrant is no longer necessary on any of the available   **8.68**

---

[112] ibid s 216(2)(a)–(b).
[113] ibid s 216(3)–(4).
[114] ibid s 217(1)(a)–(b) and (2).
[115] ibid s 217(3)(a)–(b).
[116] ibid s 217(4)(a)–(b).
[117] ibid s 217(5)(a)–(b).
[118] ibid s 218(1).
[119] ibid s 218(2).

grounds upon which it was issued.[120] The second is that the conduct authorized by the warrant is no longer proportionate to what it seeks to achieve.[121] The third is that the examination of bulk personal datasets of a class described in the warrant (in the case of a class warrant) or a bulk personal dataset (in the case of a specific warrant) obtained under the warrants is no longer necessary for any of the specified operational purposes provided for by section 212: see paragraphs 8.48–8.50 above.[122]

6. 'Lazarus' or Non-renewal or Cancellation of BPD Warrants

(a) *Applications*

8.69 In circumstances where a class BPD warrant or a specific BPD warrant ceases to have effect because it expires without having been renewed or because it is cancelled, provision is made in section 219 for the intelligence service to whom the warrant was addressed to apply to the Secretary of State for a further warrant, a non-renewable or cancellation warrant, to retain and, or examine that material retained during the currency of the warrant. The author has referred to these as 'Lazarus' warrants, reflecting the highly unusual nature of a scheme of resurrecting warrants after the expiration of the original instrument. Any such application must be made before the end of the period of five working days beginning with the day on which the warrant ceases to have effect.[123]

8.70 Such an application, in the case of a specific BPD warrant, is for authorization to retain and/or examine the whole or any part of the material retained by the intelligence service in reliance on the warrant which has ceased to have effect.[124] In the case of an application for a class BPD warrant, it is for authorization to retain and/or examine bulk personal datasets of a class that is described in a way that would otherwise have authorized the retention and/or the examination of the whole or any part of such material.[125]

8.71 In addition, there is provision to allow for the material to be retained and/or examined pending the intelligence service making a decision as to whether to apply for either warrant.[126] Where this is the case, the application is also made to the Secretary of State, within the same time-frame. The Secretary of State then has two options He or she may either direct that any of the material to which the application relates be destroyed or authorize the retention and/or examination of any of the material, subject to the imposition of any such conditions as the Secretary of State considers appropriate. The period for which the Secretary of State may authorize retention may not exceed three months and it requires the approval of a judicial commissioner.[127]

---

[120] ibid s 218(3)(a) and (4).
[121] ibid s 218(3)(b).
[122] ibid s 218(3)(c).
[123] ibid s 219(1)–(2).
[124] ibid s 219(2)(a)(i).
[125] ibid s 219(2)(a)(ii).
[126] ibid s 219(2)(b).
[127] ibid s 219(3).

Where, during any period when retention has been authorized pending a decision on whether application for a warrant and the head of the intelligence to whom the original warrant was issued then decides to make such an application, it must be made as soon as reasonably practicable and before the period of retention authorized has expired.[128]   8.72

(b) *Approval of Warrants*
When determining whether to approve a decision of the Secretary of State, the judicial commissioner must apply the same principles as would be applied by a court on an application for judicial review and consider the matter with a sufficient degree of care as to ensure compliance with the duties imposed by section 2 (general duties in relation to privacy): see Chapter 2, paragraphs 2.08–2.10.[129]   8.73

As with the approval of warrants, there is a duty to provide reasons to the Secretary of State where approval is refused and, in cases where the refusal is by a judicial commissioner other than the Investigatory Powers Commissioner, there is a right to ask for the decision to modify to be reconsidered by the senior Commissioner.[130]   8.74

Where either type of BPD warrant ceases to have effect because it expires without having been renewed or it is cancelled, an intelligence service is not to be regarded as in breach of section 200(1) or (2) as a consequence of its retention or examination of any material to which the warrant related during any of four specified periods of time. These are: the 'first period', consisting of five working days beginning with the day on which the warrant ceases to have effect; the 'second period' beginning with the day on which the head of the intelligence service makes an application for a warrant in relation to the material and ending with the determination of the application; the 'third period', being any period during which the retention or examination of the material is authorized pending a decision on whether to seek a warrant; and the 'fourth period', where a decision is taken during the third period to apply for a warrant and consisting of the period, if applicable, beginning with the expiry of the authorization pending a decision on whether to make an application for a warrant and ending with the determination of that application.[131]   8.75

7. Acquisition of Bulk Personal Datasets outside Statutory Scheme

(a) *Initial Examinations: Time Limits*
There are limited procedural safeguards where an intelligence service obtains a set of information otherwise than as a result of the operation of a warrant or other authorization issued or given under the IPA and the head of that intelligence service believes that it includes, or may include, personal data relating to a number of individuals, and its nature is, or may be, such that the majority of the individuals are   8.76

---

[128] ibid s 219(7).
[129] ibid s 219(4)(a)–(b).
[130] ibid s 219(5)–(6).
[131] ibid s 219(8).

not, and are unlikely to become, of interest to the intelligence service in the exercise of its functions.[132] In such circumstances, the head of the intelligence service must take three steps between the dates commencing with the day the belief that the requirement to take the steps is formed[133] and not later than the date ending—in the case of a set of information created in the UK—three months later or, if created outside the UK, six months.[134] This is known as the permitted period.

8.77 The first step is a requirement to carry out an initial examination of the set for the purpose of deciding whether, if it were thereafter retained and held electronically for analysis for the purposes of the exercise of its functions, the intelligence service would in fact be retaining a bulk personal dataset for the purposes of section 199: see paragraph 8.10 above. Steps two and three are consequential on step one being satisfied. If the intelligence service would be retaining a bulk personal dataset and decides to retain the set and hold it electronically for analysis (step two), an application for a specific BPD warrant must then be made as soon as reasonably practicable after making that decision (step three). Step three does not apply if the retention of the dataset is authorized by a class BPD warrant.[135]

8.78 If an application for a specific BPD warrant is made in accordance with step three, no breach of section 200(1) arises as a result of retaining or examination of the bulk personal dataset (if this is necessary for the purposes of determining whether an application is necessary) during the period between steps two and three.[136]

D. SAFEGUARDS

1. General

8.79 The Secretary of State must ensure arrangements are in place in respect of each type of warrant which authorizes examination of bulk personal datasets of a class described in the warrant or of a bulk personal dataset for securing the selection of data contained in the dataset or datasets for examination is carried out only for the specified purposes and is necessary and proportionate.[137] The term 'specified purposes' means it is selected for examination for the operational purposes specified in the warrant and set out in section 212: see paragraphs 8.48–8.50.[138] The term 'specified in the warrant' means specified in the warrant at the time of the selection.[139]

8.80 In addition, there is a mandatory requirement on the Secretary of State to ensure in relation to every specific BPD warrant which specifies conditions imposed under

---

[132] ibid s 220(1)(a)–(b).
[133] ibid s 220(3).
[134] ibid s 220(4).
[135] ibid s 220(2).
[136] ibid s 220(5)(a)–(b).
[137] ibid s 221(1)(a)–(b).
[138] ibid s 221(2).
[139] ibid s 221(4).

D. Safeguards

section 207 that arrangements are in force for securing that any selection for examination of protected data on the basis of criteria which are referable to an individual known to be in the British Islands at the time of the selection is in accordance with the conditions specified in the warrant.[140]

8.81 There is no express provision in respect of confidential journalistic material or material that may identify journalistic sources in Part 7. This is provided for in the draft Code of Practice.[141]

2. Items Subject to Legal Privilege

(a) *Examination*

8.82 Where the selection of protected data retained in reliance on a specific BPD warrant for examination is made and at least a purpose, of using the criteria to be used for the selection of the data for examination is to identify any items subject to legal privilege, or the use of the criteria is likely to identify such items, the data may be selected for examination.[142] If the 'relevant criteria' is referable to an individual known to be in the British Islands at the time of the selection, the Secretary of State and subsequently a judicial commissioner must approve the use of the criteria.[143] In any other case, its use is subject to the approval of a senior official acting on behalf of the Secretary of State who has approved the use of those criteria.[144]

8.83 When determining whether to approve the relevant criteria identified by the Secretary of State, the judicial commissioner must apply the same principles as would be applied by a court on an application for judicial review and consider the matter with a sufficient degree of care as to ensure compliance with the duties imposed by section 2 (general duties in relation to privacy): see Chapter 2, paragraphs 2.08–2.10.[145]

8.84 The Secretary of State or senior official, in deciding whether to give an approval, must have regard to the public interest in the confidentiality of items subject to legal privilege[146] and may only do so if two conditions are met. The first is that the arrangements made for storing the bulk dataset and protecting it from unauthorized disclosure of the material under section 205(6)(d) include specific arrangements in respect of items subject to legal privilege; and, secondly, where a purpose is to identify any items subject to legal privilege, the senior official considers that there are exceptional and compelling circumstances that make the use of the relevant criteria necessary.[147]

8.85 The threshold of 'exceptional and compelling' will not be met unless the public interest in obtaining the information outweighs the public interest in maintaining

---

[140] ibid s 221(3).
[141] Draft Code of Practice, paras 4.13–4.18 and Chapter 7.
[142] IPA, s 222(1).
[143] ibid s 222(2) and (4).
[144] ibid s 222(3).
[145] ibid s 222(8)(a)–(b).
[146] ibid s 222(6).
[147] ibid s 222(5)(a)–(b).

the confidentiality of the legal privilege, there are no other means by which the information could reasonably be obtained, and, obtaining the information is necessary in the interests of national security or for preventing death or significant injury.[148]

8.86 Where a selection of the protected data for examination retained under a specific BDP warrant is made and at least a purpose of using the criteria to be used for the selection of the data for examination is to identify data that, if it or any underlying material were not created or held with the intention of furthering a criminal purpose, would be an item subject to legal privilege and the person to whom the warrant is addressed considers that the data or any underlying material is likely to be created or held with the intention of furthering a criminal purpose, the data or underlying content may be selected for examination if the relevant criteria are referable to an individual known to be in the British Islands at the time of selection.[149] This again is referred to as 'the relevant criteria' for this purpose and the data are referred to as 'the targeted data' or underlying material. Its use in such circumstances is subject to the approval of the Secretary of State. In any other case, approval may be given by a senior official acting on behalf of the Secretary of State who has approved the use of those criteria.[150] Approval can only be given if the official considers that the targeted data or underlying material are likely to be communications created or held with the intention of furthering a criminal purpose.[151]

8.87 The term 'underlying material' for present purposes means any communications or other items of information from which the data was produced.[152]

3. Items Subject to Legal Privilege

(a) *Retention*

8.88 Where an item subject to legal privilege has been retained following its examination in reliance of a specific BPD warrant for purposes other than its destruction, the person to whom the warrant is addressed must inform the Investigatory Powers Commissioner of the retention of the item as soon as reasonably practicable.[153]

8.89 Other than in cases where the public interest in retention of the item outweighs the public interest in the confidentiality of items subject to items subject to legal privilege and retention is necessary in the interests of national security or for the purpose of preventing death or serious injury,[154] the Investigatory Powers Commissioner must either direct that the item is destroyed or impose conditions as to the retention and use of the item.[155] In determining which of these alternatives is appropriate, the

---

[148] ibid s 222(7)(a)–(c).
[149] ibid s 222(9)–(10).
[150] ibid s 222(11).
[151] ibid s 222(12).
[152] ibid s 222(13).
[153] ibid s 223(1).
[154] ibid s 223(4)(a)–(b).
[155] ibid s 223(2)(a)–(b).

D. Safeguards

Commissioner may require representations to be made by affected persons.[156] These are either the person to whom the warrant was or is addressed or the Secretary of State.[157] Where the Commissioner requires representations, these must be considered when determining whether the items should be destroyed or conditions imposed.[158]

4. Criminal Offence: Breaching Safeguards

Part 7 creates a new offence of breaching safeguards relating to examination of data. There are three ingredients: the person must select for examination any contained in a bulk personal dataset retained in reliance of either type of Part 7 warrant, know or believe that the selection of that data for examination does not comply with the statutory requirements provided for in the Act, and deliberately select that data for examination in breach of those requirements.[159] 8.90

The requirements are: first, that any selection for examination of the data is carried out only for the specified purposes at the time of the selection, that is, as far as is necessary for the operational purposes: see paragraphs 8.48–8.50 above;[160] secondly, that it is necessary and proportionate; and, thirdly, where the data is protected data, that it satisfies any conditions that have been imposed.[161] As to the when the offence is committed by a body corporate or Scottish partnership, see Chapter 10 paragraphs 10.125–10.127. 8.91

A person guilty of the offence is liable on summary conviction in England and Wales to imprisonment for a term not exceeding twelve months (or six months, if the offence was committed before the commencement of section 154(1) of the Criminal Justice Act 2003), or to a fine, or both.[162] On summary conviction in Scotland to imprisonment for a term not exceeding twelve months, or to a fine not exceeding the statutory maximum, or both.[163] In Northern Ireland, the maximum sentence on summary conviction is imprisonment for a term not exceeding six months, or to a fine not exceeding the statutory maximum, or both.[164] 8.92

On conviction on indictment, the maximum sentence is imprisonment for a term not exceeding two years or to a fine, or both.[165] 8.93

The consent of the relevant Director of Public Prosecutions is required before criminal proceedings for an offence under section 173 may be instituted against a person in England, Wales, or Northern Ireland.[166] 8.94

---

[156] ibid s 223(5)(a).
[157] ibid s 223(6)(a)–(b).
[158] ibid s 223(5)(b).
[159] ibid s 224(1)(a)–(c).
[160] ibid s 224(3).
[161] ibid s 224(2)(a)–(c).
[162] ibid s 224(4)(a).
[163] ibid s 224(4)(b).
[164] ibid s 224(4)(c).
[165] ibid s 224(4)(d).
[166] ibid s 224(5).

E. APPLICATION OF PART 7 TO OTHER PARTS OF THE IPA

1. Application for a 'Direction'

8.95 Where a bulk personal dataset has been obtained by an intelligence service under a warrant or other authorization issued or given under the IPA but not where it was obtained under a bulk acquisition warrant issued under Chapter 2 of Part 6, the head of the intelligence service may apply to the Secretary of State for what is referred to as a direction.[167]

8.96 There are three directions: that the intelligence service may retain and/or examine the bulk personal dataset by virtue of the direction; that section 201(1) also ceases to apply in relation to the bulk personal dataset; and that any other power of the intelligence service to retain or examine the bulk personal dataset, and any associated regulatory provision, ceases to apply in relation to the bulk personal dataset.[168] This latter direction may also provide for any associated regulatory provision specified in the direction to continue to apply in relation to the bulk personal dataset, with or without modifications specified in the direction.[169] However, the power to do so must only be exercised to ensure that where section 56 and Schedule 3 (exclusion from legal proceedings) and sections 57 to 59 (unauthorized and excepted disclosures) applied in relation to the bulk personal dataset immediately before the giving of the direction, and, in the case of the former, that they continue to apply in relation to it (without modification) and, in the latter, that they continue to apply in relation to it with the modification that the reference in section 58(7)(a) to the provisions of Part 2 is to be read as including a reference to the provisions of Part 7.[170] The term associated regulatory provision means that it is made by or for the purposes of the IPA and applied in relation to the retention, examination, disclosure, or other use of the bulk personal dataset immediately before the giving of the direction.[171]

8.97 Where a direction is given, the intelligence service may only exercise its power by virtue of the direction to retain, or to retain and examine, the bulk personal dataset if it applies for and is granted authority to do so by a class or specific BPD warrant, as the case may be.[172] An application for a warrant can be made concurrently with an application for a direction.[173]

8.98 Once given, a direction may not be revoked, although it may be varied. Variation is limited but only for the purpose of altering or removing the position in respect of associated regulatory provision.[174]

---

[167] ibid s 225(1)–(2).
[168] ibid s 225(3)(a)–(c).
[169] ibid s 225(5).
[170] ibid s 225(6)(a)–(b).
[171] ibid s 225(14).
[172] ibid s 225(4).
[173] ibid s 225(13).
[174] ibid s 225(11)(a)–(b).

E. Application of Part 7 to Other Parts of the IPA

2. Judicial Approval for Directions and Variations to Directions

8.99 The Secretary of State may only give a direction and a direction may only be varied with the approval of a judicial commissioner.[175]

8.100 When determining whether to approve a decision of the Secretary of State, the judicial commissioner must apply the same principles as would be applied by a court on an application for judicial review.[176]

8.101 The Secretary of State must be provided with reasons where approval is refused and, in cases where the refusal is by a judicial commissioner other than the Investigatory Powers Commissioner, there is a right to ask for the decision to modify to be reconsidered by the senior Commissioner.[177]

---

[175] ibid s 225(7) and (12).
[176] ibid s 225(8).
[177] ibid s 225(9)–(10).

9
OVERSIGHT ARRANGEMENTS

A.	Introduction	9.01
B.	Judicial Commissioners	9.10
	1. Abolition of Existing Oversight Bodies	9.10
	2. Appointment	9.12
	3. Terms and Conditions of Appointment	9.16
	4. Funding and Resources	9.18
	5. Main Functions of Commissioners	9.19
	6. Other Functions	9.32
	7. Investigation and Information-gathering Powers	9.46
C.	Reporting	9.49
	1. Annual and Other Reports	9.49
	2. Duties on Prime Minister in Respect of Reporting	9.54
D.	The Investigatory Powers Tribunal	9.57
	1. Jurisdictional Changes to the Investigatory Powers Tribunal	9.57
	2. Changes to the Exercise of the Investigatory Powers Tribunal's Jurisdiction	9.70
	3. The Right of Appeal from the Investigatory Powers Tribunal	9.78
E.	Advisory Bodies	9.85
	1. Technical Advisory Board	9.85
	2. Technology Advisory Panel	9.87
	3. Membership of the Panel	9.90

A. INTRODUCTION

There was rare unanimity in the reviews, opinions, submissions, and evidence published, expressed, and heard prior to the enactment of the Investigatory Powers Act 2016 (IPA) that some degree of consolidation and reformation of the oversight arrangements that were in place under the Intelligence Services Act 1994 (ISA), Police Act 1997, and Regulation of Investigatory Powers Act 2000 (RIPA) was necessary. The consensus, however, was, to quote Updike, but 'a thief, tiptoeing away with more than it brings'. What followed, the creation of the office of the Investigatory Powers Commissioner, divided opinion seemingly more than calls for reform had unified it. 9.01

9. Oversight Arrangements

9.02 The Royal United Services Institute's Independent Surveillance Review expressed the view that 'the system requires a radical overhaul which must include an enhanced role for the judiciary'.[1] David Anderson QC, the then Independent Reviewer of Terrorism Legislation, had recommended in his seminal report 'A Question of Trust' the establishment of an independent commission to replace the existing tripartite structure.[2] The Interception of Communications Commissioner's Office (IOCCO) echoed this in its evidence to the Joint Committee on the draft Investigatory Powers Bill[3] after Anderson's concept had failed to find its way into the draft Bill.[4] Deviating only in what to call it, IOCCO not only called for the creation of the Investigatory Powers Commission but also used as precedent, the establishment of the Independent Police Complaints Commission, under section 9 of the Police Reform Act 2002.[5] The Intelligence and Security Committee (ISC) was the lone voice arguing that 'it is therefore right that responsibility for authorising warrants for intrusive activity remains with Ministers'.[6]

9.03 The rationale underlying this thinking was, as far as Anderson was concerned, unification of purpose[7] and for IOCCO, the 'need [for] a clear legal mandate' of purpose.[8] The human rights organization, Liberty, conveyed its concerns about the consequences of, in effect continuing but consolidating, although not substantively reforming, the existing model:

> Liberty supports the consolidation of the byzantine model of surveillance oversight currently provided by several commissioners. However, we are deeply concerned the Bill hands over these functions to the new created body of [Judicial Commissioners], whose primary role is authorisation. [Judicial Commissioner's] independence and perceived independence will be wholly undermined the clear conflicts of interest that will likely arise on a regular basis. Therefore, we believe that oversight of intrusive powers should be invested and consolidated in a new commission independent from the [Investigatory Powers Commissioner, Investigatory Powers Tribunal] and Executive— proposed here, as per David Anderson's recommendation, as the Intelligence and Surveillance Commissioner.[9]

9.04 The use of the term 'authorization' by Liberty underscores an important mistake, perpetrated by a number of commentators, as to what the function of the judicial commissioners is or, more importantly, is not. The judicial commissioners do not 'authorize' but approve (although Anderson had recommended a scheme of judicial

---

[1] A Democratic Licence to Operate: report of the independent surveillance review, Royal United Services Institute (July 2015) xii (RUSI, 'A Democratic Licence to Operate').

[2] David Anderson QC, 'A Question of Trust: Report of the Investigatory Powers Review' (June 2015).

[3] HL paper 93. HC 651 (3 February 2016).

[4] Interception of Communications Commissioner's Office (IOCCO), Evidence for the Joint Committee for the Investigatory Powers Bill, 21 December 2015 (IOCCO, Evidence to Joint Committee).

[5] IOCCO, Evidence to the Joint Committee, 5.

[6] Intelligence and Security Committee, Privacy and Security: A Modern and Transparent Legal Framework, HC 1075 (12 March 2015) (ISC, Privacy and Security).

[7] See Anderson (n 2) 281, para 14.97.

[8] IOCCO, Evidence to the Joint Committee, 5.

[9] Liberty's briefing on Part 8 of the Investigatory Powers Bill for Committee Stage in the House of Commons, Liberty (April 2016).

A. Introduction

authority): see for an example of this in practice, *Chatwani and others v National Crime Agency* [2015] UKIPTrib 15_84_88–CH. This approval tests the original decision based on necessity and proportionality against the principles of judicial review and a requirement to consider applications 'with a sufficient degree of care as to ensure ... [compliance] with the duties imposed by section 2 (general duties in relation to privacy)'. This has limitations, as one respected practitioner, Matthew Ryder QC, noted in his evidence to the Joint Committee on the Draft Investigatory Powers Bill:

> In a judicial review situation, the judge is essentially bound by decisions and assessments of facts that have been made by the Secretary of State and is applying judicial review principles—which, as Martin [Chamberlain QC] rightly says, can be on a range of scrutiny—to that assessment that has already been made of the facts ...
>
> The final point to bear in mind is that, normally in judicial review, there is an element of an adversarial process. In other words, the judge is assessing it with somebody making representations in relation to the other side. There will be no adversarial process built into this, the way it stands at the moment. You will have a judicial review, but no one putting forward the argument to the judge in a different situation.[10]

9.05 An approval regime involving Commissioners existed under RIPA. The Protection of Freedoms Act 2012 amended RIPA so as to require local authorities to obtain approval from a sitting Justice of the Peace for those Part II activities they may engage in. In *Covert Policing Law and Practice*, these provisions were described as, 'a sea change', whether knowingly or not, to the United Kingdom's position on the notion that judges, not the state, should authorize covert surveillance activities.[11] From this can be traced the origins of the introduction of—for the first time in United Kingdom (UK) law—judicial approval of the decisions of the Secretary of State and others on behalf of the intelligence services of their most covert surveillance activities, or 'double-lock' as it became known. Anderson reflected that this was 'unnecessarily cumbersome' and he did not 'like it'.[12]

9.06 The review process gave rise to issues of constitutionality that were both of academic and practical significance, in particular in relation to the separation of powers and institutional capacity.[13] The House of Lords Select Committee on the

---

[10] HC 651 (16 December 2015) 190 http://data.parliament.uk/writtenevidence/committeeevidence.svc/evidencedocument/draft-investigatory-powers-bill-committee/draft-investigatory-powers-bill/oral/26441.html (last accessed 23 May 2017).

[11] S McKay, *Covert Policing Law and Practice* (OUP 2015) 170, para 5.97.

[12] David Anderson QC, 'The Investigatory Powers Act 2016: An Exercise in Democracy' (3 December 2016). https://terrorismlegislationreviewer.independent.gov.uk/the-investigatory-powers-act-2016-an-exercise-in-democracy/ (last accessed 22 April 2017).

[13] Byron Karemba, 'The Investigatory Powers Bill: Introducing Judicial Scrutiny of Surveillance Warrants and the Broader Constitutional Context (Part III)', UK Constitutional Law Blog (30 September 2016) (Karemba, IP Bill III) https://ukconstitutionallaw.org/2016/09/30/byron-karemba-the-investigatory-powers-bill-introducing-judicial-scrutiny-of-surveillance-warrants-and-the-broader-constitutional-context-part-iii/ (last accessed 2 June 2017).

9. Oversight Arrangements

Constitution recognizing that not just actually independence was at stake but 'the appearance of independence and hence public confidence' was clearly important.[14]

9.07 The confluence of oversight bodies did not include the role of the Information Commissioner, who retains oversight of aspects of the retention of communications data regime under Part 4 IPA.[15]

9.08 Part 8 IPA is structured over twenty-one provisions. Two elements are truly reformative: the introduction of the Investigatory Powers Commissioner and the right of appeal against a decision of the Investigatory Powers Tribunal (IPT). The remainder of Part 8 largely amends, supplements, or updates the existing framework under Part IV RIPA. Perhaps, incongruously, it also gives effect to Schedule 7, relating to the publication of the Codes of Practice.[16]

9.09 On 29 September 2017, the Home Office published the draft updated Tribunal Rules and a consultation paper.[17]

B. JUDICIAL COMMISSIONERS

1. Abolition of Existing Oversight Bodies

9.10 The IPA creates the Investigatory Powers Commissioner and judicial commissioners and abolishes the existing framework of oversight, so the offices of the Interception of Communications Commissioner, the Intelligence Services Commissioner, the Chief Surveillance Commissioner and the Scottish Chief Surveillance Commissioner, and the ordinary Surveillance Commissioners and Scottish Surveillance Commissioners.[18] There is repeal of the corresponding provisions of the Police Act 1997, RIPA, and the Regulation of Investigatory Powers Act (Scotland) 2000 (RIP(S)A) that conceived those entities.[19]

9.11 The Investigatory Powers Commissioner for Northern Ireland, an office never filled, remains on the statute book, although there is provision for its abolition and repeal of the relevant provision in RIPA subject to regulations made by the Secretary of State and the consent of the Northern Ireland Assembly.[20]

2. Appointment

9.12 Under Part 8 of the IPA, the prime minister must appoint the Investigatory Powers Commissioner and the necessary number of judicial commissioners required to carry out their functions.[21] They are to be known collectively as the 'judicial

---

[14] Select Committee on the Constitution, Report on the Investigatory Powers Bill, HL Paper 24 (11 July 2016).
[15] IPA, s 244.
[16] ibid s 241.
[17] https://www.gov.uk/government/consultations/investigatory-powers-tribunal-consultation-updated-rules and it was accessed on 29/9/17.
[18] ibid s 240(1)(a)–(f).
[19] ibid s 240(2)(a)–(d).
[20] ibid s 240(3)–(5).
[21] ibid s 227(1)(a)–(b).

commissioners'.[22] References to a judicial commissioner in any enactment are to be read as including the Investigatory Powers Commissioner and similarly, any references to the Investigatory Powers Commissioner are to be read as references to any other judicial commissioner where the former's functions have been delegated to the latter: see paragraphs 9.22–9.24 below.[23]

9.13 The first Investigatory Powers Commissioner, Lord Justice Fulford, was appointed on 3 March 2017.[24]

9.14 There are a number of determinative criteria common to the appointment of either role, as was also the case under RIPA 2000. The person must hold or have held a high judicial office[25] and may not be appointed unless recommended jointly by the Lord Chancellor, the Lord Chief Justice of England and Wales, the Lord President of the Court of Session, and the Lord Chief Justice of Northern Ireland.[26] The Investigatory Powers Commissioner must also recommend the appointment of judicial commissioners.[27]

9.15 In addition, certain requirements must be met. Before appointing any judicial commissioner, the prime minister must consult the Scottish Ministers and have regard to a memorandum of understanding agreed between the prime minister and the Scottish Ministers when exercising the functions of appointment.[28]

3. Terms and Conditions of Appointment

9.16 The terms and conditions of appointment of judicial commissioners include a minimum term of appointment of three years, although they may be reappointed unless they have been removed from office.[29]

9.17 Removal from office is by the prime minister and may arise in four circumstances: bankruptcy or arrangements with creditors; disqualification as a director; disqualification undertaking or subject to orders under section 429(2) of the Insolvency Act 1986; or conviction of an offence and a term of imprisonment.[30] Where any such circumstances arise, a judicial commissioner may be removed from office only after a resolution approving the removal has been passed by each House of Parliament.[31]

4. Funding and Resources

9.18 The funding for judicial commissioners and the allocation of staff, accommodation, and other resources necessary for the carrying out of their functions is to be

---

[22] ibid s 227(7).
[23] ibid s 227(13)(a)–(b).
[24] https://www.gov.uk/government/news/investigatory-powers-commissioner-appointed-lord-justice-fulford.
[25] Within the meaning of Part 3 of the Constitutional Reform Act 2005.
[26] IPA, s 227(2)–(4).
[27] ibid s 227(4)(e).
[28] ibid s 227(5)–(6).
[29] ibid s 228(1)–(3).
[30] ibid s 228(5)(a)–(d).
[31] ibid s 228(4).

provided by the Treasury following consultation between the Investigatory Powers Commissioner and the Secretary of State.[32] Where the functions are exercisable by reference to the exercise by Scottish public authorities of devolved functions (as those terms are defined in the Scotland Act 1998), Scottish Ministers may pay what they consider is appropriate by way of allowances to the judicial commissioners.[33]

5. Main Functions of Commissioners

(a) *Limitations on the Exercise of Functions*

9.19 A judicial commissioner must not, in discharging functions under Part 8, act in a way which the Investigatory Powers Commissioner considers is contrary to the public interest or prejudicial to national security, the prevention or detection of serious crime, or the economic well-being of the UK.[34] In addition, the Investigatory Powers Commissioner must ensure a judicial commissioner does not jeopardize the success of an intelligence or security operation or a law enforcement operation, compromise the safety or security of those involved, or unduly impede the operational effectiveness of an intelligence service, a police force, a government department, or Her Majesty's forces.[35]

9.20 The limitations on the exercise of judicial commissioners' functions do not apply to a number of areas of their decision-making: whether to serve, vary, or cancel a monetary penalty notice or its content; approving the issue, modification, or renewal of a warrant; directing the destruction or how otherwise to deal with circumstances where approval is not given in urgent cases of warrants having been issued or modified or where legal privilege has been retained and similarly destruction of records obtained and retained in intrusive surveillance cases where the authorization under RIPA, RIPSA, or the Police Act 1997.[36] In addition, the limitations do not apply to a range of other core statutory functions of judicial commissioners set out in section 229(8).

9.21 The Code of Practice issued under section 241 and which gives effect to Schedule 7 does not apply to the functions of the judicial commissioners.[37]

(b) *Delegable Functions*

9.22 The Investigatory Powers Commissioner may delegate powers, other than those relating to the appointment of judicial commissioners, to any other judicial commissioner.[38] This does not prevent the exercise of those powers by the Investigatory Powers Commissioner.[39] This broadly reflects the position under RIPA.[40]

---

[32] ibid s 238(1)–(2).
[33] ibid s 238(3).
[34] ibid s 229(6)(a)–(c).
[35] ibid s 229(7)(a)–(c).
[36] ibid s 229(8).
[37] ibid Schedule 7, para 1(2).
[38] ibid s 227(8)–(9).
[39] ibid s 227(10).
[40] RIPA 2000, s 64(1).

B. Judicial Commissioners

9.23 The functions of a judicial commissioner or judicial commissioners are exercisable by any of the judicial commissioners other than any function conferred on the Investigatory Powers Commissioner by name, unless otherwise delegated.[41]

9.24 Any judicial commissioner may, to such extent as it is open to them to do so, delegate the exercise of their functions to any member of staff of the judicial commissioners or any other person acting on behalf of the Commissioners including functions which have been delegated to a judicial commissioner by the Investigatory Powers Commissioner.[42] However, this does not extend to the Investigatory Powers Commissioner's function of authorizing a disclosure under section 58(4) or section 133(3) or making a recommendation in respect of the appointment of a judicial commissioner or appointments to the Technology Advisory Panel: see paragraphs 9.87–9.91 below.[43] Nor does it extend to the core functions of judicial commissioners under section 229(8): see paragraphs 9.19–9.21 above.[44]

(c) *Review Functions*

9.25 The review functions of the Investigatory Powers Commissioner extend beyond the IPA to other areas of covert policing. Those relating to the IPA include but are not limited to the audit, inspection, and investigation of the exercise of the statutory functions of public authorities relating to the interception of communications and any content of communications intercepted by an interception authorized or required by a warrant, the acquisition or retention of communications data, the acquisition of secondary data or related systems data under Chapter 1, Part 2 or Chapter 1, Part 6 of the IPA or equipment interference and communications, equipment data, or other information acquired by that means.[45] In keeping these matters under review, the Investigatory Powers Commissioner is under an overarching mandatory duty to keep under review the operation of safeguards to protect privacy.[46]

9.26 In addition, the main functions include the giving and operation of national security notices by the Secretary of State to telecommunications operators under section 252: see Chapter 10, paragraphs 10.03–10.12 and the acquisition, retention, use, or disclosure of bulk personal datasets by an intelligence service.[47] This is not limited to the use of the IPA to do so.

9.27 Schedule 7 of the IPA imposes additional review functions on the Investigatory Powers Commissioner in respect of the exercise by the Secretary of State in introducing subordinate legislation resulting in a provision being included in the Codes of Practice.[48] The Investigatory Powers Commissioner must also be consulted prior to

---

[41] IPA, s 227(11)–(12).
[42] ibid s 238(5) and (7).
[43] ibid s 238(6)(b)–(c).
[44] ibid s 238(6)(a).
[45] ibid s 229(1)–(2).
[46] ibid s 229(5).
[47] ibid s 229(3)(a)–(b).
[48] ibid Schedule 7, paras 1(2)(b) and 2(3).

any Code being issued or revised insofar as it relates to functions of the Information Commissioner.[49]

9.28 The review functions outside the scope of the IPA are exhaustive. These are the existing common functions under RIPA and (RIP(S)A) relating to oversight of surveillance activities (and the use and conduct of covert human intelligence sources) and the investigation of electronic data protected by encryption under RIPA only. This includes the adequacy of arrangements under section 55 RIPA and how they are discharged.[50] In addition, they extend to the use of property interference powers by police and police-related public authorities under Part 3 of the Police Act 1997 and the intelligence services under sections 5 to 7 of the ISA (as well as the exercise by the Scottish Ministers of functions under sections 5 and 6(3) and (4) of that Act).[51] Finally, there is a limited statutory extension to the oversight functions in respect of prisons. The exercise of functions by virtue of regulations provided for under section 80 of the Serious Crime Act 2015 in relation to the prevention or restriction of use of communication devices by prisoners and the exercise of functions by virtue of sections 1 to 4 of the Prisons (Interference with Wireless Telegraphy) Act 2012.[52] This reflects the consolidation of the previous oversight regime with that under the IPA.

9.29 There are a number of matters the Investigatory Powers Commissioner is expressly not required to keep under review, including the exercise of any function which is for the purpose of obtaining information or taking possession of any document or other property in connection with communications stored in or by a telecommunication system, or is carried out in accordance with an appropriate court order made for that purpose and not exercisable under any of the provisions set out in the preceding paragraph.[53] In addition, included is the exercise of any function by a judicial authority and the service of an encryption notice under section 49 RIPA or other function, exercisable with the permission of a judicial authority under Part 3 RIPA.[54] These are new provisions and some attempt to address jurisdictional issues that arose under RIPA.

9.30 The Investigatory Powers Commissioner's oversight functions to do include a review of the exercise of any function of a relevant minister to make subordinate legislation.[55]

9.31 Conduct authorized by sections 45 and 47 (interception for administrative or enforcement purposes), or 50 (interception in psychiatric hospitals) falls outside the Investigatory Powers Commissioner's jurisdiction.[56]

---

[49] ibid Schedule 7, paras 4(2) and 5(3).
[50] ibid s 229(3)(e)–(g).
[51] ibid s 229(3)(h)–(j).
[52] ibid s 229(3)(c)–(d).
[53] ibid s 229(4)(d)(i)–(ii).
[54] ibid s 229(4)(a) and (c).
[55] ibid s 229(4)(a).
[56] ibid s 229(4)(e).

6. Other Functions

(a) *Directed Oversight Functions*

In addition to the main oversight functions, the prime minister has the power to direct that the Investigatory Powers Commissioner keep under review the carrying out of any aspect of the functions of an intelligence service or its head or any part of the armed forces or Ministry of Defence that engage in intelligence activities. The term 'intelligence activities' is not defined but would almost certainly include those military personnel involved in allegations of mistreatment of detainees during armed conflict, for example.[57] This may provide an argument to government against holding a public inquiry in such circumstances.

9.32

A direction is likely to be at the request of the Investigatory Powers Commissioner or the ISC but it is not limited in any way to these organizations alone.[58] The ISC also has a free-standing power to refer a matter to the Investigatory Powers Commissioner whether or not a direction is made: see para 9.42 below.[59] Where a direction is given or for that matter revoked, it must be published unless it appears to the prime minister that such publication would be contrary to the public interest or prejudicial to national security, the prevention or detection of serious crime, the economic wellbeing of the UK, or the continued discharge of the functions of any public authority whose activities include activities that are subject to review by the Investigatory Powers Commissioner.[60] The use of the word 'appears' is unusual and incongruous with the consistent use of 'considers' throughout most of the text of the IPA. Either way, it is a highly subjective assessment.

9.33

(b) *Duty to Inform Public of Certain Acts of Non-compliance: 'Error Reporting'*

Appearing under the vague heading of 'error reporting' is a mandatory requirement on the Investigatory Powers Commissioner to inform a person of 'any relevant error relating to that person of which the Commissioner is aware'. This is subject to two qualifications: that the error is a serious error; and that it is in the public interest for the person to be informed of it.[61] Unless these criteria are met, no disclosure can be made.[62] Relevant error is defined as non-compliance by a public authority with any requirements imposed under the IPA or other statutory provision and which fall within the jurisdictional purview of the Investigatory Powers Commissioner.[63] The Investigatory Powers Commissioner must also keep this definition under review.[64]

9.34

A serious error is one the Investigatory Powers Commissioner considers has caused significant prejudice or harm to the person concerned.[65] Such guidance as is given

9.35

---

[57] ibid s 230(1)–(2).
[58] ibid s 230(3).
[59] ibid s 236.
[60] ibid s 230(4)(a)–(d).
[61] ibid s 231(1).
[62] ibid s 231(7).
[63] ibid s 231(9)(a)–(b).
[64] ibid s 231(9).
[65] ibid s 231(2).

9. Oversight Arrangements

in the IPA is that a breach of the person's rights under the European Convention on Human Rights for the purposes of the Human Rights Act 1998 is not sufficient by itself to constitute a serious error. A question arises as to how this aligns with the overarching requirement in section 2 IPA (general duties in relation to privacy): see Chapter 2, paragraphs 2.08–2.10.

9.36 In determining the public interest limb, the Investigatory Powers Commissioner must, in particular, consider a wide range of factors including the seriousness of the error and its effect on the person concerned, and the extent to which disclosing it would be contrary to the public interest or prejudicial to national security, the prevention or detection of serious crime, the economic well-being of the UK, or the continued discharge of the functions of any of the intelligence services.[66]

9.37 A public authority, telecommunications operator, or postal operator must report any relevant error of which it is aware to the Investigatory Powers Commissioner.[67]

9.38 The Investigatory Powers Commissioner must ask the public authority that has made the error to make submissions about the matters concerned prior to making a determination but there is no automatic right for the person to see such submission as may subsequently be made.[68] The procedural safeguards that exist for the person subject to the error are limited to the requirement to inform the person of any rights that the person may have to apply to the IPT, and provide such details of the error as the Commissioner considers to be necessary for the exercise of those rights, having regard to the factors curtailing a disclosure of the error in the public interest:[69] see para 9.36 above.

(c) Additional Functions under Part 8 IPA

9.39 There are two additional functions identified under section 232 IPA. The first is the duty on a judicial commissioner to give the IPT all such documents, information, and other assistance (including the Commissioner's opinion as to any issue falling to be determined by the tribunal) as the tribunal may require in connection with one of its investigations or otherwise for the purposes of its consideration or determination of any matter.[70]

9.40 The second is a discretionary function to provide advice or information to any public authority or other person in relation to matters for which a judicial commissioner is responsible (other than advice or information provided to the IPT).[71] This is a significant deviation from the role of at least the Chief Surveillance Commissioner under the RIPA oversight regime, who expressly indicated that its functions did not include the provision of advice.

9.41 The exercise of the discretion is not unfettered. Where it might be prejudicial to national security, the prevention or detection of serious crime, the economic

---

[66] ibid s 231(4)(a)–(b).
[67] ibid s 235(6).
[68] ibid s 231(6)(a).
[69] ibid s 231(6)(b).
[70] ibid s 232(1)(a)–(b).
[71] ibid s 232(6).

B. Judicial Commissioners

well-being of the UK, or the continued discharge of the functions of any public authority whose activities include activities that are subject to review by the Investigatory Powers Commissioner, the judicial commissioner must first consult the Secretary of State or, in appropriate cases, Scottish Ministers.[72]

(d) *ISC Referrals*
The ISC may refer a matter to the Investigatory Powers Commissioner with a view to the Commissioner carrying out an investigation, inspection, or audit into it.[73] Where it does so, the Investigatory Powers Commissioner must inform the ISC whether it accedes to the request.[74]   9.42

(e) *Reports by Public Authorities of Non-compliance by Telecommunication Operator*
A public authority may report to the Investigatory Powers Commissioner any refusal by a telecommunications or postal operator to comply with any requirements imposed on them under the IPA.[75]   9.43

(f) *Functions under Other Parts and Retained Functions under Other Enactments*
The Investigatory Powers Commissioner and the other judicial commissioners retain the functions that are exercisable by them by virtue of any other Part of the IPA or any other enactment.[76] The references to Chief Commissioner and Commissioner in Part 3 of the Police Act 1997, ss 96, 97, 103, 104, and 105 are amended to reflect the new statutory framework and are substituted with the Investigatory Powers Commissioner and the judicial commissioner, respectively.[77] Similarly, Part 2 RIPA, ss 35–39, Part 3 RIPA, ss 51, 54, and 55 and RIP(S)A, ss 13–17 are amended as appropriate to substitute Chief Surveillance Commissioner and ordinary Surveillance Commissioner for Investigatory Powers Commissioner and judicial commissioner, respectively.[78] The Regulation of Investigatory Powers (Covert Human Intelligence Sources: Relevant Sources) Order 2013 (introduced following the undercover policing controversy and requiring 'long term' undercover officers' authorizations to also be approved by a Surveillance Commissioner) is also amended, substituting the former designations to correlate with the new structure.[79]   9.44

(g) *Power to Modify Functions*
The Secretary of State may, by regulations, modify the functions of the Investigatory Powers or judicial commissioner but not in respect of any function relating to the approval, quashing, or cancellation of an authorization or warrant or its variation or   9.45

---

[72] ibid s 232(3)(a)–(d); the criteria to be met to consult Scottish Ministers is set out in ibid s (4)(a)–(b).
[73] ibid s 236(1).
[74] ibid s 236(2).
[75] ibid s 235(5).
[76] ibid s 233(1).
[77] ibid s 233(2)(a)–(h).
[78] ibid s 223(3)–(5).
[79] ibid s 223(6)(a)–(e).

renewal.[80] This power is extended by section 267(1)(c) and is exercisable by modifying any provision made by or under any enactment and not limited to the IPA: see Chapter 1, paragraphs 1.63–1.73.[81] This provision exercised the House of Lords Select Committee on the Constitution, which expressed the view that the use of a Henry VIII power to modify the functions of a judicial oversight body was not appropriate and recommended it be 'confined to the ability to extend and augment the oversight functions of the Commissioners, in order that those functions are able to keep up with the technological or other advances'.[82]

7. Investigation and Information-gathering Powers

9.46 A judicial commissioner may carry out such investigations, inspections, and audits as the Commissioner considers appropriate for the purposes of their functions.[83] Obligations are placed on 'relevant persons' in this connection. These are any person who holds, or has held, an office, rank, or position with a public authority, any telecommunications operator or postal operator who is, has been, or may become subject to a requirement imposed by the IPA, any person who is, has been, or may become subject to a requirement to provide assistance to implement warrants by virtue of sections 41 and 43 (interception of communications), 126 and 128 (equipment interference), 149 (bulk interception), 168 and 170 (bulk acquisition), or 190 (bulk equipment interference), or any person to whom a notice is given under section 49 of RIPA (encryption notice).

9.47 The obligations on relevant persons are must disclose or provide to a judicial commissioner all such documents and information as the Commissioner may and such assistance as the Commissioner may require in carrying out any investigation, inspection, or audit require for the purposes of the Commissioner's functions.[84] Assistance for these purposes include such access to apparatus, systems, or other facilities or services as the judicial commissioner concerned may require.[85]

9.48 Under section 237, 'information gateway', a disclosure of information to the Investigatory Powers Commissioner or another judicial commissioner for the purposes of any of their functions does not breach an obligation of confidence or restriction on disclosure owed by the person making the disclosure or imposed on him or her by any other statutory or common law provisions unless it would be a breach of the Data Protection Act 1998.[86]

(2) But sub-section (1) does not apply to a disclosure, in contravention of any provisions of the Data Protection Act 1998, of personal data which is not exempt from those provisions.

---

[80] ibid s 239(1)–(2).
[81] ibid s 239(3).
[82] Select Committee on the Constitution report on the IP Bill, para 22.
[83] IPA, s 235(1).
[84] ibid s 235(2)–(3).
[85] ibid s 235(4).
[86] ibid s 237(1)–(2).

C. REPORTING

1. Annual and Other Reports

(a) *Minimum Mandatory Reporting*

The Investigatory Powers Commissioner must, as soon as reasonably practicable after the end of each calendar year, make a report to the prime minister about the carrying out of the functions of the judicial commissioners.[87] This may include recommendations about the functions of the judicial commissioners.[88] Where the prime minister has at any time requested a report on any other matter, the Investigatory Powers Commissioner is required to make the report in accordance with the request.[89]

9.49

The annual report must cover a number of areas including statistics on the use of those investigatory powers the Investigatory Powers Commissioner is required to review. This is to include the number of warrants or authorizations issued, given, considered, or approved during the reporting year. In addition, it must include several classes of information about: the results of the use and impact of those investigatory powers; the operation of the safeguards provided for in the IPA relating to items subject to legal privilege, confidential journalistic material, and sources of journalistic information; the targeted interception, examination, equipment interference issued, considered, or approved during the reporting year; and the operational purposes specified during the year in warrants issued under Part 6 (see Chapter 7) or Part 7 (see Chapter 8) of the IPA.[90]

9.50

There is also a requirement to include data arising out of error reporting under section 231(8) consisting of the number of relevant errors, those of which were serious and the number of persons informed of those errors: see paras 9.34–9.38 above.[91]

9.51

In addition, the annual report must include information about the work of the Technology Advisory Panel: see paras 9.87–9.89 below and the information about the funding, staffing, and other resources of the judicial commissioners and details of any of their public engagements or those of its staff.[92]

9.52

(b) *Discretionary and Other Reporting*

The Investigatory Powers Commissioner may, at any time, make any such report to the prime minister, on any matter relating to the functions of the judicial commissioners, as the Investigatory Powers Commissioner considers appropriate.[93] This may include recommendations about any matter relating to the functions of the judicial

9.53

---

[87] ibid s 224(1).
[88] ibid s 224(5).
[89] ibid s 224(3).
[90] ibid s 224(2)(a)–(e).
[91] ibid s 224(2)(f).
[92] ibid s 2242)(g)–(i).
[93] ibid s 224(4).

commissioners.[94] The Investigatory Powers Commissioner may, at the request of the prime minister, publish either such report either in full or in part.[95]

2. Duties on Prime Minister in Respect of Reporting

(a) *Annual Reports*

9.54 Any part of an annual report from the Investigatory Powers Commissioner may be redacted if in the opinion of the prime minister publication would be contrary to the public interest or prejudicial to national security, the prevention or detection of serious crime, the economic well-being of the UK, or the continued discharge of the functions under the IPA of any public authority which is subject to oversight by the Investigatory Powers Commissioner. There is a duty to consult Scottish Ministers where any proposed redaction relates to functions under Part 3 of the Police Act 1997.[96]

9.55 Subject to any redactions, the prime minister must publish an annual report and, where parts have been excluded from publication, must provide a statement to this effect.[97] A copy of the report must be sent to the Scottish Ministers, who must lay the copy report and statement before the Scottish Parliament.[98]

(b) *Other Reports*

9.56 Where the prime minister receives an annual or other report from the Investigatory Powers Commissioner which relates to an investigation, inspection, or audit carried out following a referral by the ISC and a decision to accept the referral communicated to the ISC, the prime minister must send it to ISC so far as concerns the request and its functions under section 2 of the Justice and Security Act 2013.[99]

D. THE INVESTIGATORY POWERS TRIBUNAL

1. Jurisdictional Changes to the Investigatory Powers Tribunal

9.57 The existing IPT remains but is reformed in part and some provisions under RIPA are subject to amendment. The jurisdiction of the IPT, set out in section 65 of RIPA, the 'ouster' provision,[100] is widened to reflect the increased investigatory scope of the IPA and sub-section (2)(c), which relates to the tribunal's jurisdiction to hear claims of detriment where section 17 (the prohibition on, amongst other things, the use of intercept as evidence) is amended to reflect that this is now found in section 56 of the IPA.[101]

---

[94] ibid s 224(5).
[95] ibid s 224(9).
[96] ibid s 224(7).
[97] ibid s 224(6).
[98] ibid s 224(8).
[99] ibid s 234(10) and (11)(a)–(b).
[100] *R (on the application of A) v B* [2010] 1 WLR 1.
[101] IPA, s 243(1)(a).

D. The Investigatory Powers Tribunal

9.58 In terms of conduct in relation to which the tribunal has jurisdiction, section 65(5)(b) is amended to also include conduct for or in connection with the obtaining of secondary data from communications transmitted by means of such a postal service or telecommunications system; and the issue, modification, renewal, or service of an interception warrant issued under Part 2 or Chapter 1 of Part 6: see Chapter 7 generally.[102]

9.59 Since Chapter II of Part I RIPA is repealed, section 65(5)(c) is replaced with a new provision to reflect this and includes a raft of amendments set out in section 243(1)(c) IPA. It now relates to conduct of a kind that may be permitted or required by an authorization or notice under Part 3 of the IPA (obtaining communications data) or a warrant under Chapter 2 of Part 6 (bulk acquisition of communications data).

9.60 The further amendments to section 65(5)(c) fall into conduct, the giving of an authorization or notice, the issuing of a warrant, or ancillary matters relating to the authorization, notice or warrant, and failures.

(a) *Conduct: Additional Amendments*

9.61 The additional amendments beyond those to section 65(5)(c) relating to conduct are that relating to a kind that may be required by a national security or technical capability notice under sections 253 or 254, permitted by a retention notice under Part 4 (retention of communications data), or conduct falling within the other amendments.

(b) *The Giving of Notices or Authorizations: Amendments*

9.62 The amendments as to the giving of a notice or authorization or issue relate to those under Part 3 IPA, an authorization under section 152(5)(c) or 193(5)(c) (examination of intercepted content or protected material), and section 219(3)(b) (retention to consider whether to apply for a Lazarus warrant). In addition, they include the giving or varying of a retention notice under Part 4 IPA or a section 225 direction (relating to bulk personal datasets not subject to a warrant) and the giving or variation of a national security or technical capability notice under sections 252 or 253 IPA.

(c) *Issuing Warrants and Ancillary Matters: Amendments*

9.63 Those relating to the issue of a warrant or ancillary matters concern the issue, modification, or renewal or service of a bulk acquisition warrant, equipment interference or bulk equipment interference warrants, or bulk personal dataset warrants.

(d) *Failures: Amendments*

9.64 The failure to cancel a warrant or authorization under Part 3 IPA or revoke a national security or technical capability notice or a notice under Part 4 or a section 225 direction is now provided for in section 65(5) by the amendments under section 243(1) IPA.

---

[102] ibid s 243(1)(b).

9. Oversight Arrangements

(e) *Other Amendments*

9.65 The list of officials and bodies whose conduct may be subject to a complaint to the IPT is extended to include immigration officers and the Competition and Markets Authority.[103]

9.66 There is a new provision in section 65(6) RIPA. This new section 65(6A) provides that where the new provision relating to conduct of a kind that may be required or permitted by an equipment interference or bulk equipment interference warrant (now to be found in section 65(5)(czd)) sub-section 5(d) or (f) Part II RIPA conduct (including intrusive surveillance) and interference with property or wireless telegraphy does not apply.[104]

9.67 Section 65(7) RIPA is amended to qualify, first, that it is only conduct of a public authority that is caught by the provision. It is updated to reflect permission of a judicial authority under the IPA and the repeal of section 23A RIPA.[105] Conduct for the purposes of section 65(7) RIPA is now extended with the introduction of sub-section (7ZB) RIPA to include the widened investigatory scope under the IPA.[106]

9.68 Where section 65(7) RIPA correlated to something taking place with authority or purported authority under sub-section (8), which related to powers repealed under RIPA, these are now replaced to reflect those powers and the extended powers under the IPA, so includes the issue of any warrant, authorization or notice, retention, national security or technical capability notice, or a section 225 direction.[107]

9.69 There is a final amendment to section 65 to take account of the amendment to section 65(5). A new provision, sub-section (9A), does no more than ensure that this reconciles with section 16 IPA.[108]

2. Changes to the Exercise of the Investigatory Powers Tribunal's Jurisdiction

9.70 The power of the IPT to quash or cancel a warrant or authorization is amended and extended to reflect the new regime.[109]

(a) *Changes to the Investigatory Powers Tribunal's procedure*

9.71 The obligation on the IPT by virtue of section 68(5)(b) RIPA to report its findings to the prime minster where its determination relates to any act or omission or to conduct for which any warrant, authorization, or permission was issued, granted, or given by or behalf of the Secretary of State is extended to include a notice under Part 4 IPA, or a national security, technical capability notice under section 252 or 253 or a section 225 direction.[110]

---

[103] ibid s 243(1)(d).
[104] ibid s 243(1)(e).
[105] ibid s 243(1)(g).
[106] ibid s 243(1)(h).
[107] ibid s 243(1)(i).
[108] ibid s 243(1)(j).
[109] ibid s 243(2)(a)–(c).
[110] ibid s 243(3).

D. The Investigatory Powers Tribunal

Section 68(6)(b) is amended to include a reference to the IPA. 9.72

The list of persons subject to the duty to cooperate with the IPT and set out in section 68(7) RIPA is amended to take account of the new legislative scheme. This included those providing assistance with giving effect to an interception warrant for the purposes of section 11 RIPA. Since this provision is now repealed and the duty extended to other forms of warrant, sections 41, 126, 149, 168, or 190 IPA are substituted in its place and the generic term warrant replaces interception warrant.[111] 9.73

Similarly, the reference to section 12 in section 68(7)(f) is replaced with section 252 or 253 IPA.[112] 9.74

The persons by or to whom an authorization for the obtaining or disclosing communications data has been granted or a notice has been given under Part I, Chapter II RIPA is amended to provide for every person to whom a notice under Part 3 IPA has been given or to whom a retention notice under Part 4 or a national security, technical capability notice under section 252 or 253, or a section 225 direction has been given.[113] 9.75

The persons under a duty to disclose or provide information to the IPT, included under section 68(7)(k) RIPA, every person who has engaged in any conduct with the authority of an authorization under section 22 or Part II of this Act or under Part III of the Police Act 1997. The reference to section 22 RIPA is replaced with Part 3 IPA and now extends to a warrant under Chapter 2 of Part 6 IPA.[114] 9.76

The remaining amendments to section 68 RIPA are largely cosmetic and substitute references to warrants in place of authorization and Investigatory Powers Commissioner or judicial commissioner in place references to the former oversight regime.[115] 9.77

3. The Right of Appeal from the Investigatory Powers Tribunal

The most welcome reform to the legislative scheme under RIPA is the right of appeal from a decision of the IPT. This is the consequence of section 67A, introduced as a consequence of section 142 IPA. The right of appeal available to a 'relevant person'; the complainant or respondent or person complained against.[116] In the case of a reference made to the IPT, it includes a public authority.[117] 9.78

The right is exercisable in tightly prescribed circumstances, namely a point of law arising out of a determination by the IPT under section 86(4) RIPA (the determination by the IPT of any proceedings, complaint or reference) or the new section 86(4C) RIPA, also introduced by section 142.[118] 9.79

---

[111] ibid s 243(5)(a)(i)–(ii).
[112] ibid s 243(5)(b).
[113] ibid s 243(5)(c).
[114] ibid s 243(5)(d)(i)–(ii).
[115] ibid s 234(5)(e)–(f) and (6).
[116] RIPA, s 67A(8) (a)–(b).
[117] ibid s 67A(8)(c).
[118] ibid s 67A(1).

9.80   Prior to making a qualifying determination or decision, the IPT must specify the court where any appeal would be heard.[119] In England and Wales, this would normally be the Court of Appeal and, in Scotland, the Court of Session.[120] There is also scope, should the provisions enabling the appointment of the Investigatory Powers Commissioner of Northern Ireland be implemented, for the Court of Appeal Northern Ireland to also have jurisdiction to hear appeals.[121] The tribunal is not, under section 67A RIPA, required to allocate the case according to where it originated; this may be provided for in regulations subsequently.[122] RIPA is amended so as to provide for the making of these.[123]

9.81   Permission to appeal is required (although section 67A uses the out-of-vogue term 'leave to appeal') and may be granted by the IPT or the appropriate appellate court that must, if permission is given, hear the appeal.[124] The threshold for granting permission is high: an appeal must raise an important point of principle or practice or another compelling reason for granting permission must exist.[125]

9.82   The prohibition on appeal and ancillary provisions in section 67(8)–(12) RIPA are amended or removed by section 242 IPA to reflect the new route to appeal.[126]

9.83   There is a new procedural requirement introduced by section 242(3) IPA on the IPT to provide a notice where it makes a determination under section 68(4) RIPA also to give notice, as the case may be, to the respondent, the person complained against, or a local authority.[127] The content of such notice must be in the same terms as section 68(4) (a statement that the determination is, or is not, in the complainant's favour).[128]

9.84   Similarly, in cases where the IPT makes a final decision of a preliminary issue in relation to any proceedings, complaint, or reference but it is not a section 68(4) decision or a decision relating to a procedural matter a notice of that decision must be provided to the relevant parties as appropriate, unless the tribunal rules operate so as to prevent or are inconsistent with this.[129] A notice for this purpose must be confined to a statement as to what the decision is, although it too is subject to tribunal rules.[130] The provisions relating to the tribunal rules are amended to reflect the position in respect of the giving of notices and in respect of permission to appeal.[131]

---

[119] ibid s 67A(2).
[120] ibid s 67A(3)(a)–(b).
[121] ibid s 67A(4).
[122] ibid s 67A(5).
[123] IPA, s 242(4)(a)–(b).
[124] RIPA, s 67A(6)(a)–(b).
[125] ibid s 67A(7)(a)–(b).
[126] IPA, s 242(1).
[127] RIPA, s 68(4A).
[128] ibid s 68(4B).
[129] ibid s 68(4C) and (4E)(a)–(b).
[130] ibid s 68(4D) and (4E).
[131] IPA, s 242(4)(a)–(b).

E. ADVISORY BODIES

1. Technical Advisory Board

The Technical Advisory Board, a creature of RIPA, continues to exist under section 245 IPA. However, whereas membership was, under RIPA, by ministerial order, under section 245, this is now by way of regulations.

The regulations must also make provision about the constitution of the board. Its membership must include persons from two discrete interest groups: public authorities entitled to apply for warrants or authorizations under the IPA and those upon whom obligations are placed following service of retention, national security, or technical capability notices.[132] They must also provide for such other persons as appropriate to be appointed but subject to producing a balance between the two interest groups.[133] The regulations may also make provision about quorum and how vacancies on the board are filled.[134]

9.85

9.86

2. Technology Advisory Panel

The IPA conceives the Technology Advisory Panel, the purpose of which is to provide advice—whether directed or not—about the impact of changing technology on the exercise of those investigatory powers falling under the Investigatory Powers Commissioner's purview and the availability and development of techniques to use such powers while minimizing interference with privacy.[135] It is the Investigatory Powers Commissioner's responsibility to ensure it is established and maintained.

9.87

The panel must provide its advice to the Investigatory Powers Commissioner, the Secretary of State, and the Scottish Ministers, although, in respect of the latter, only in respect of matters for which they are responsible.[136]

9.88

The panel must report annually to the Investigatory Powers Commissioner about the carrying out of the functions of the panel and provide a copy of the report to the Secretary of State and, insofar as relevant to their responsibilities, the Scottish Ministers.[137]

9.89

3. Membership of the Panel

The Investigatory Powers Commissioner makes appointments to the panel and must appoint such number of persons considered necessary for the carrying out of its functions. Appointment is subject to the individual's terms and conditions.

9.90

---

[132] ibid s 245(2)(a)–(b).
[133] ibid s 245(2)(c)–(d).
[134] ibid s 245(3).
[135] ibid s 246(1)–(3).
[136] ibid s 246(5).
[137] ibid s 246(6).

9. Oversight Arrangements

However, a member must not act in a way that the member considers—so is based on a subjective, self-policing test—to be contrary to the public interest or prejudicial to national security, the prevention or detection of serious crime, or the economic well-being of the UK. In addition, and in particular, the member must ensure he or she does not jeopardize the success of an intelligence or security operation or a law enforcement operation, compromise the safety or security of those involved, or unduly impede the operational effectiveness of an intelligence service, a police force, a government department, or Her Majesty's forces.

9.91   A member of the panel has the same powers to require disclosure of documents and information from a relevant person as a judicial commissioner: see paragraph 9.39 above.

10
ADDITIONAL POWERS, COMBINING WARRANTS, AND MISCELLANEOUS PROVISIONS

A.	Introduction	10.01
B.	Additional Powers	10.03
	1. National Security Notices	10.03
	2. Technical Capability Notices	10.13
	3. Approval of Notices by judicial commissioners	10.26
	4. Other Matters Relating to National Security and Technical Capability Notices	10.30
	5. Variation and Revocation of Relevant Notices	10.39
	6. Review of Notices by the Secretary of State	10.45
	7. Approval of Relevant Notices Following a Reference and Review	10.49
C.	Amendments to Other Enactments Relating to Investigatory Powers	10.52
	1. Intelligence Services Act 1994	10.52
	2. Amendments to Warrants under Section 5 of the ISA	10.54
	3. Wireless Telegraphy Act 2006	10.55
D.	Combined Warrants or Authorizations	10.59
	1. Intelligence Services Act 1994	10.60
	2. Police Act 1997, Part III	10.64
	3. Regulation of Investigatory Powers Act 2000	10.71
	4. Schedule 8 IPA	10.93
E.	Miscellaneous	10.125
	1. Offences under the IPA Committed by a Body Corporate or Scottish Partnership	10.125
	2. Compliance with IPA	10.128

A. INTRODUCTION

Part 9 of the Investigatory Powers Act 2016 (IPA), described as 'miscellaneous **10.01** and general provisions', contains a number of important provisions, including the

10. Additional Powers, Combining Warrants, and Miscellaneous Provisions

additional power: the national security notice and expanding the reach of the technical capability notice previously found in section 12, RIPA and now repealed. It also includes provision to amend other covert surveillance legislation, albeit to a limited extent, the framework for combining warrants and authorizations as well as definitions.

10.02 Not all of the provisions can logically be left to the final chapter of this work. This chapter deals with those matters referred to above, except definitions. Definitions, particularly those relating to telecommunications and postal operators, have been dealt with in Chapter 1 since they are so pervasive throughout the IPA and an early consideration of them is essential. It is likely they will have to be constantly referred to when considering other aspects of the legislation: see Chapter 1, paragraphs 1.74–1.90.

B. ADDITIONAL POWERS

1. National Security Notices

10.03 A national security notice is a notice requiring a telecommunications operator to take such steps as the Secretary of State considers necessary in the interests of national security.[1] This provision replaces to an extent the provision in section 94 of the Telecommunications Act 1984, which the former Independent Reviewer of Terrorism Legislation, David Anderson QC, described as 'so baldly stated as to tell the citizen little about how [it is] liable to be used'.[2] This echoed one of the conclusions of the Intelligence and Security Committee, which reported that: 'the current arrangements in the Telecommunications Act 1984 lack clarity and transparency, and must be reformed. This capability must be clearly set out in law, including the safeguards governing its use and statutory oversight arrangements'.[3]

10.04 The Joint Committee on the draft Investigatory Powers Bill[4] recommended that national security should be defined for the purpose of this provision. This was rejected, the Home Office stating:

It has been the policy of successive governments not to define national security in statute. Threats to national security are constantly evolving and difficult to predict, and it is vital that legislation should not constrain the ability of the security and intelligence agencies to protect the UK from new and emerging threats.[5]

10.05 This reflects the long-established common law position that when considering decisions of the executive on the question of national security, the courts would not

---

[1] IPA, s 251(2).
[2] David Anderson QC, 'A Question of Trust' (June 2015) para 13.31(a).
[3] Intelligence and Security Committee, 'Privacy and Security: A Modern and Transparent Legal Framework' (12 March 2015) HC1075.
[4] HL Paper 93. HC 651 (3 February 2016).
[5] J Dawson, House of Commons Briefing Paper, No 75181 (11 March 2016) 72.

B. Additional Powers

usually interfere with the judgment of a decision-maker with special institutional competence: *Secretary of State for the Home Department v Rehman*.[6]

10.06 The steps that may be taken under a national security notice include, so are not limited to, requiring the telecommunications operator to carry out any conduct, including the provision of services or facilities, for the purpose of facilitating anything done by an intelligence service under any enactment other than the IPA or assist it to carry out its functions more securely or more effectively or dealing with an emergency for the purposes of Part 1 of the Civil Contingencies Act 2004 (an event or situation relating to a place in the United Kingdom (UK), which threatens serious damage to human welfare, to the environment, war, or terrorism).[7] The notice must specify such period as seems reasonable to the Secretary of State for the steps required to be taken.[8]

10.07 The draft Code of Practice on National Security Notices elaborates:

> It is not possible to give a list of the full range of the steps that telecommunications operators may be required to take in the interests of national security; not only would this affect the ability of the police and security and intelligence agencies to carry out their work, but as communications technology changes the Secretary of State will need to retain flexibility to respond. However, a notice may typically require a telecommunications operator to provide services to support secure communications by the agencies, for example by arranging for a communication to travel via a particular route in order to improve security, or asking a communications service provider to refrain from doing something they might otherwise do. They may additionally cover the confidential provision of services to the agencies within the telecommunications operator, such as by maintaining a pool of trusted staff for management and maintenance of sensitive communications services.[9]

10.08 A telecommunications operator may only be given a national security notice if the Secretary of State considers it is necessary in the interests of national security and the steps required as a consequence of giving the notice are proportionate to what is to be achieved through such conduct.[10] It requires approval by a judicial commissioner.[11]

10.09 In addition to judicial approval, there are rudimentary safeguards. Where a notice would require the taking of any steps that would otherwise require a warrant or authorization under a 'relevant enactment' to be lawful, the notice may require the taking of those steps only if such a warrant or authorization has been obtained.[12] However, the Secretary of State may not give a notice if its main purpose was to require the telecommunications operator to do something for which such a warrant or authorization was required.[13] The draft of Code of Practice puts it in the following terms: 'a national security notice cannot be used as an alternative to an

---

[6] [2001] UKHL 47, [2003] 1 AC 153.
[7] IPA, s 252(3)(a)–(b).
[8] ibid s 252(7).
[9] National Security Notices, Draft Code of Practice (draft Code of Practice) (February 2017) para 3.3.
[10] IPA, s 252(1)(a)–(b).
[11] ibid s 252(1)(c).
[12] ibid s 252(4)(a)–(b).
[13] ibid s 252(5).

10. Additional Powers, Combining Warrants, and Miscellaneous Provisions

interception warrant where the activity could be authorised by such a warrant'.[14] Relevant enactment means, in addition to the IPA, the Intelligence Services Act 1994 (ISA), the Regulation of Investigatory Powers Act 2000 (RIPA), and the Regulation of Investigatory Powers (Scotland) Act 2000 (RIP(S)A).

10.10 Although there is no express provision in Part 9 in respect of sensitive professions and journalists, the draft Code of Practice provides:

> Paragraph 2 of Schedule 7 of the Investigatory Powers Act provides that a code issued under the Act must contain particular provision designed to protect the public interest in the confidentiality of journalistic information and any data which relates to a member of a profession which routinely holds items subject to legal privilege or confidential information. Where a notice requires the taking of a step that involves an interference with privacy, and a warrant or other authorisation has been obtained to authorise that conduct, the Code of Practice relevant to that authorisation will contain provisions required by Paragraph 2 of Schedule 7 of the Act. Where a warrant or authorisation is not available to authorise an interference with privacy, it will never be appropriate to obtain journalistic information or any data which relates to a member of a profession which routinely holds items subject to legal privilege or confidential information via a national security notice. As such, it is not necessary to include more detailed safeguards in respect of such information in this code as they are not relevant.[15]

10.11 The draft Code of Practice provides guidance on the form and content of a notice.[16]

10.12 Conduct required by a national security notice is to be treated as lawful for all purposes.[17]

2. Technical Capability Notices

10.13 The technical capability notice is not new. The power to give a 'notice requiring the person who is to be subject to the obligations to take all such steps as may be specified or described in the notice' was provided for in section 12 RIPA. The provision for the giving of the technical capability notice is now found in section 253 IPA.

10.14 A technical capability notice is a notice imposing on the 'relevant operator' any applicable obligations specified in the notice, and requiring the person to take all the steps specified in the notice for the purpose of complying with those obligations.[18] Relevant operator means a postal or telecommunications operator or a person proposing to become one.[19] The term 'applicable obligation' means an obligation specified by the Secretary of State in regulations that may be imposed on relevant operators or on relevant operators of that description.[20] The order issued

---

[14] Draft Code of Practice, para 3.4.
[15] ibid para 3.8.
[16] ibid para 3.12.
[17] IPA, s 252(8).
[18] ibid s 253(2)(a)–(b).
[19] ibid s 253(3).
[20] ibid s 253(3).

B. Additional Powers

under section 12 RIPA was the Regulation of Investigatory Powers (Maintenance of Interception Capability) Order 2002.

10.15 A relevant operator may be given a technical capability notice if the Secretary of State considers it is necessary for securing that the operator has the capability to provide any assistance which the operator may be required to provide in relation to any relevant authorization and the conduct required as a consequence of giving the notice is proportionate to what is to be achieved through such conduct.[21] It requires approval by a judicial commissioner.[22]

10.16 There is no draft Code of Practice in respect of technical capability notices.

10.17 The notice must specify such period as seems reasonable to the Secretary of State to be reasonable for the steps required to be taken and may specify different time periods in relation to different steps.[23] It may be given to persons outside the UK whether or not it requires steps to be taken, or not to be taken, outside the UK.[24]

(a) *Regulations*

10.18 The regulations may specify an obligation that may be imposed on any relevant operators only if the Secretary of State considers it is reasonable to do so for the purpose of securing that it is and remains practicable: to impose requirements on those relevant operators to provide assistance in relation to relevant authorizations; and for those relevant operators to comply with those requirements.[25] The term 'relevant authorisation' means any warrant issued under IPA Parts 2, 5, or 6 or any authorization or notice given under Part 3.[26] This is a significant expansion on the scope of the previous regulations, which applied only to warrants for the interception of communications.[27]

10.19 The obligations that may be specified in any regulations include at least five obligations relating to: apparatus owned or operated by a relevant operator; the removal by a relevant operator of electronic protection applied by or on behalf of that operator to any communications or data; the security of any postal or telecommunications services provided by a relevant operator; and the handling or disclosure of any information. This is in addition to the provision of facilities or services of a specified description.[28]

10.20 There is a mandatory requirement on the Secretary of State to consult, before any regulations are made, the Technical Advisory Board, persons appearing to the Secretary of State to be likely to be subject to any obligations specified in the regulations or their representatives, or those with statutory functions in relation to such

---

[21] ibid s 253(1)(a)–(b).
[22] ibid s 253(1)(c).
[23] ibid s 253(7).
[24] ibid s 253(8).
[25] ibid s 253(4)(a)–(b).
[26] ibid s 253(3).
[27] RIPA, s 12(1).
[28] IPA, s 253(5)(a)–(e).

persons.[29] The first consultation on the unpublished Draft Investigatory Powers (Technical Capability) Regulations 2017 concluded on 19 May 2017.[30] The draft regulations, unlike the 2002 Order, are no longer limited to interception and their reach extends to private and public telecommunications providers.

10.21 The draft regulations contain some significant provisions that were not published during the Bill's evolution. This includes, in Schedule 1, paragraph 10:

> To install and maintain any apparatus provided to the operator by or on behalf of the Secretary of State for the purpose of enabling the operator to obtain or disclose communications data, including by providing and maintaining any apparatus, systems or other facilities or services necessary to install and maintain any apparatus so provided.

10.22 The respected commentator and solicitor, Graham Smith, has described this as a government 'black box' for the collection of communications data and 'a substantial departure in kind from previous RIPA obligations'.[31]

10.23 The draft regulations also provide in Schedule 1, paragraph 8:

> To provide and maintain the capability to disclose, where practicable, the content of communications or secondary data in an intelligible form and to remove electronic protection applied by or on behalf of the telecommunications operator to the communications or data, or to permit the person to whom the warrant is addressed to remove such electronic protection.

10.24 There is concern on the part of commentators that this is, on one view, capable of being interpreted as providing for a requirement to remove end-to-end encryption.[32] There are competing arguments for and against and it may be one of the early battlegrounds in the aftermath of the regulations coming into force. See also paragraph 10.36, below.

10.25 As to the making of regulations under the IPA generally, see Chapter 1, paragraphs 1.63–1.73.

3. Approval of Notices by judicial commissioners

10.26 For the purposes of judicial approval, a relevant notice means either a national security notice or a technical capability notice.[33]

10.27 In deciding whether to approve a decision to give a relevant notice, the judicial commissioner must review the conclusions reached by the Secretary of State as to two matters. The first is whether the notice is necessary for the reason it is proposed

---

[29] ibid s 253(6)(a)–(d).

[30] The draft regulations can be accessed via the Open Rights Group website: https://www.openrightsgroup.org/ourwork/reports/home-office-consultation:-investigatory-powers-%28technical-capability%29-regulations-2017 (last accessed 29 May 2017).

[31] Graham Smith, 'Back doors, black boxes and #IPAct technical capability regulations' *Cyberleagle* (8 May 2017) http://www.cyberleagle.com/2017/05/back-doors-black-boxes-and-ipact.html (last accessed 28 May 2017).

[32] See Privacy International, 'UK Investigatory Powers Bill will require tech companies to notify the Government of new products and services in advance of their launch' https://www.privacyinternational.org/node/829 (last accessed 28 May 2017); Smith (n 31).

[33] IPA, s 254(1).

B. Additional Powers

it should be given under either section 252(1) or 253(1), and the second is whether the conduct that would be authorized by the warrant is proportionate to the objective to be met through its use.[34]

In determining whether to approve the same principles as would be applied by a court on an application for judicial review are applicable, the judicial commissioner should 'consider the [necessity and proportionality of the application] with a sufficient degree of care' so as to ensure compliance with section 2 of the IPA (general duties in relation to privacy): see Chapter 2, paragraphs 2.08–2.10.[35]

10.28

A judicial commissioner who refuses to approve a decision to give a notice must give the Secretary of State written reasons for the refusal.[36] The Secretary of State in such circumstances may then ask the Investigatory Powers Commissioner for approval, unless the Investigatory Powers Commissioner was the judicial commissioner who refused it at first instance.[37]

10.29

4. Other Matters Relating to National Security and Technical Capability Notices

(a) *Relevant Notices*

The Secretary of State must consult the person to be given the relevant notice before he or she is given it.[38] In addition, the Secretary of State must take into account five matters: the likely benefits of the notice; the likely number of users (if known) of any postal or telecommunications service to which the notice relates; the technical feasibility of complying with the notice, the likely cost of complying with the notice; and any other effect of the notice on the person (or description of person) to whom it relates.[39]

10.30

The draft Code of Practice sets out how government envisages the process will work:

10.31

[I]n practice, consultation is likely to take place long before a notice is given. However, the time taken for the consultation will vary depending on the individual circumstances in each case, such as the complexity of the notice, the nature of the obligations to be imposed, and the resources available to the operator to consider the proposed obligations. The Government will engage with an operator who is likely to be subject to a notice in order to provide advice and guidance, and prepare them for the possibility of receiving a notice.

In the event that the Secretary of State considers it appropriate to give a notice, the Government will take steps to consult the telecommunications operator formally before the notice is given. Should the person to whom the notice is to be given have concerns about the reasonableness, cost or technical feasibility of requirements to be set out in the notice, these should be raised during

---

[34] ibid s 254(2)(a)–(b).
[35] ibid s 254(3)(a)–(b).
[36] ibid s 254(4).
[37] ibid s 254(5).
[38] ibid s 255(2).
[39] ibid s 255(3)(a)–(e).

10. Additional Powers, Combining Warrants, and Miscellaneous Provisions

the consultation process. Any concerns outstanding at the conclusion of these discussions will be presented to the Secretary of State and will form part of the decision making process.[40]

10.32 A relevant notice must be in writing and a person to whom it is given or any person employed or engaged for the purposes of that person's business must not disclose the existence or contents of the notice to any other person without the permission of the Secretary of State.[41]

(b) *Enforceability*

10.33 A person who is given a relevant notice must comply with it.[42] This requirement is enforceable in relation to a person in the UK by civil proceedings instituted by the Secretary of State for an injunction, or for specific performance of a statutory duty under section 45 of the Court of Session Act 1988, or for any other appropriate relief.[43]

10.34 A relevant notice that is a technical capability notice relating to a targeted interception or mutual assistance warrant under Chapter 1 of Part 2, a bulk interception warrant or an authorization or notice given under Part 3 (obtaining communications data) is also enforceable in relation to a person outside the UK,[44] although it is not clear how this will work in practice.

10.35 A relevant notice that is a national security notice is enforceable notwithstanding any other duty imposed on the person by or under Part 1, or Chapter 1 of Part 2, of the Communications Act 2003.[45]

(c) *Other Matters Relating to Technical Capability Notices*

10.36 In the case of a technical capability notice that would impose any obligations relating to the removal by a person of electronic protection applied by or on behalf of that person to any communications or data, in complying with the requirement to take various matters into account, the Secretary of State must in particular take into account the technical feasibility, and likely cost, of complying with those obligations.[46] See also paragraphs 10.23–10.24 above.

10.37 A technical capability notice may be given, electronically or by other means of giving a notice to a person, outside the UK by delivering it to the person's principal office within the UK or, if the person has no such office in the UK, to any place in the UK where the person carries on business or conducts activities; or if the person has specified an address in the UK as one at which the person, or someone on the person's behalf, will accept documents of the same description as a notice, by delivering it to that address.[47]

---

[40] Draft Code of Practice, paras 4.3–4.4.
[41] IPA, s 255(5) and (8).
[42] ibid s 255(9).
[43] ibid s 255(10) and (11).
[44] ibid s 255(10)(b).
[45] ibid s 255(12).
[46] ibid s 255(4).
[47] ibid s 255(6)(a)–(b).

B. Additional Powers

The Secretary of State may by regulations make further provision about the giving of relevant notices.[48] 10.38

5. Variation and Revocation of Relevant Notices

The Secretary of State must keep each relevant notice under review.[49] The draft Code of Practice provides limited guidance on the review process and states that 'a national security notice remains in force until cancelled' but must be cancelled if it is no longer necessary or proportionate for it to remain in place.[50] 10.39

The Secretary of State may vary, wholly or in part, or revoke a relevant notice.[51] In the case of a national security notice, the Secretary of State may only vary where the threshold for giving the notice is met (ie it is necessary in the interests of national security and it is proportionate).[52] The same position applies in the case of a technical capability notice (Secretary of State may only vary where it is considered that the variation is necessary for securing that the person has the capability to provide any assistance that the person may be required to provide in relation to any relevant authorization and is proportionate).[53] In both cases, judicial approval from a judicial commissioner is required.[54] The only exception to this requirement is where the Secretary of State is obligated to review a notice following a referral by the person who has been given it and the outcome of this has been approved by the Investigatory Powers Commissioner in accordance with section 257(1), (9), and (10): see paragraphs 10.45–10.48 below.[55] 10.40

The requirement to obtain the approval of notices by judicial commissioners applies in relation to a decision to vary a relevant notice as it applies in relation to a decision to give a relevant notice, but the references in section 254(2)(a)–(b) to the notice were to the variation and as varied respectively.[56] 10.41

The requirements in section 255(2)–(4) (the duty to consult) and (7) (the power to make further provision by way of regulations) apply to the variation or revocation of a relevant notice as they apply in relation to giving a relevant notice: see paragraphs 10.30–10.38 above.[57] The draft Code of Practice offers limited guidance on what this involves: 10.42

Before varying a notice, the Government is required to consult the communications service provider to understand the impact of the change, including cost and technical implications. Once this consultation process is complete, the Secretary of State will consider whether it is necessary to

---

[48] ibid s 255(7).
[49] ibid 256(2).
[50] Draft Code of Practice, paras 3.17–3.18.
[51] IPA, s 256(3)(a)–(b).
[52] ibid s 256(4)(a)–(b).
[53] ibid s 256(5)(a)–(b).
[54] ibid s 256(4)(c) and (5)(c).
[55] ibid s 256(6).
[56] ibid s 256(8)(a)–(b).
[57] ibid s 256(9)–(10).

10. Additional Powers, Combining Warrants, and Miscellaneous Provisions

vary the notice and whether the requirements imposed by the notice as varied are proportionate to what is sought to be achieved by that conduct.[58]

10.43   Similarly, any reference in section 256 or in section 255(8)–(12) to a notice given under section 252 or section 253 includes a reference to such a notice as varied.[59]

10.44   If the Secretary of State varies or revokes a relevant notice the person it was given to must also give that person notice of the variation or revocation.[60] Revocation in relation to a particular person or description of persons does not prevent the giving of another relevant notice of the same kind to that person or description of persons.[61]

6. Review of Notices by the Secretary of State

10.45   A person who is given a relevant notice may, within such period or circumstances as may be provided for by regulations made under Part 9, refer the notice, in whole or in part, back to the Secretary of State.[62] The Secretary of State must then review the notice insofar as it is referred. The draft Code of Practice is of limited assistance in this connection, in that 'the circumstances and timeframe within which a telecommunications operator may request a review are set out in regulations ... Details of how to submit a notice to the Secretary of State for review will be provided either before or at the time the notice is given'.[63]

10.46   Before determining the reference, the Secretary of State must consult the Technical Advisory Board (the Board) and a judicial commissioner.[64] They have separate and joint duties arising out of a referral. The Board must consider the technical requirements and the financial consequences, for the person who has made the reference, of the notice so far as referred and the judicial commissioner must consider whether the notice so far as referred is proportionate.[65] Jointly, they must give the person concerned and the Secretary of State the opportunity to provide evidence, or make representations, to them before reaching their conclusions, and report their conclusions to both parties.[66]

10.47   The Secretary of State may, after considering the conclusions of the Board and the Commissioner vary or revoke the notice under section 256, or give a notice under this section to the person confirming its effect.[67] Where it is the latter, prior approval by Investigatory Powers Commissioner is required.[68] The provisions of

---

[58] Draft Code of Practice, para 3.21.
[59] IPA, s 256(12).
[60] ibid s 256(7).
[61] ibid s 256(11).
[62] ibid s 257(1)–(2).
[63] Draft Code of Practice, para 4.17.
[64] IPA, s 257(5)(a)–(b).
[65] ibid s 257(6)–(7).
[66] ibid s 257(8)(a)–(b).
[67] ibid s 257(9).
[68] ibid s 257(10). This implies that the Judicial Commissioner must refer the matter to the Investigatory Powers Commissioner for this purpose.

section 255(5)–(8) apply as they would in respect of the original notice. References to a relevant notice for these purposes is, other than where judicial approval is given, to it as varied under section 256: see paragraphs 10.39–10.44 above.

10.48 There is no requirement for a person who has referred a notice to comply with the notice, insofar as referred, until the Secretary of State has reviewed the notice.[69]

7. Approval of Relevant Notices Following a Reference and Review

10.49 In deciding whether to approve a decision to vary a relevant notice the Investigatory Powers Commissioner (as opposed to a judicial commissioner) must review the conclusions reached by the Secretary of State as to two matters. The first is whether the notice as varied is necessary for the reason it is proposed it is given under either section 252(1)(a) or section 253(1)(a) and the second is whether the conduct that would be authorized by the warrant is proportionate to what the objective to be met through its use.[70]

10.50 In determining whether to approve the same principles as would be applied by a court on an application for judicial review are applicable and the Investigatory Powers Commissioner should 'consider the [necessity and proportionality of the application] with a sufficient degree of care' so as to ensure compliance with section 2 of the IPA (general duties in relation to privacy): see Chapter 2, paragraphs 2.08–2.10.[71]

10.51 If the Investigatory Powers Commissioner refuses to approve a decision to vary a notice or to give effect to it, written reasons for the refusal must be given to the Secretary of State.[72]

C. AMENDMENTS TO OTHER ENACTMENTS RELATING TO INVESTIGATORY POWERS

1. Intelligence Services Act 1994

(a) *Amendments to Functions of GCHQ*

10.52 Section 3 of the Intelligence Services Act 1994 (ISA) is amended by section 251 IPA. Whereas it was previously provided that GCHQ was empowered to 'monitor or interfere with electromagnetic, acoustic and other emissions and any equipment producing such emissions and to obtain and provide information derived from or related to such emissions or equipment and from encrypted material', this now expressly permits the exploitation of the fruits of this surveillance through the inclusion of the words 'make use of' after 'monitor'.[73]

---

[69] ibid 257(3).
[70] ibid s 258(2)(a)–(b).
[71] ibid s 258(3)(a)–(b).
[72] ibid s 258(4).
[73] ibid s 251(2)(a).

10. Additional Powers, Combining Warrants, and Miscellaneous Provisions

10.53 The organizations GCHQ was permitted to assist in section 3(1)(b)(ii) ISA was previously limited to government or those prescribed by the prime minister. This latter restriction has been repealed and replaced with 'or, in such cases as it considers appropriate, to other organizations or persons, or to the general public, in the United Kingdom or elsewhere'. GCHQ is now permitted to self-determine whom it assists.[74]

2. Amendments to Warrants under Section 5 of the ISA

10.54 The scheme under section 5 ISA is amended through the introduction of an amendment to sub-section (3A); sub-section (3) is now repealed. This extends the general prohibition on the exercise of the Security Service's functions in respect of property in the British Islands to 'the Intelligence Service or GCHQ' for the purposes of the exercise of their functions under section 1(2)(c) or 3(2)(c).[75] The reference to 'Intelligence Service' should, it is presumed, be a reference to the Secret Intelligence Service.

3. Wireless Telegraphy Act 2006

10.55 The offence of misuse or disclosure of wireless telegraphy in section 48 of the Wireless Telegraphy Act 2006 is amended as a result of section 259 IPA.

10.56 Whereas under section 48(1), the ingredients of the offence were prefaced with the words, '[a] person commits an offence if, otherwise than under the authority of a designated person', this is now substituted by 'without lawful authority'.[76]

10.57 A new sub-section (3A) is added to give primacy to the offence of unlawful interception in section 3(1) IPA.

10.58 Consequently, the entirety of section 49 of the Wireless Telegraphy Act 2006 (interception authorities) is repealed.[77]

D. COMBINED WARRANTS OR AUTHORIZATIONS

10.59 Section 248 IPA gives effect to Schedule 8, which provides for a single scheme for the combination of warrants and authorizations. This relates to warrants and authorizations under the IPA and other covert policing legislation: the ISA, Part III of the Police Act 1997, RIPA, and RIP(S)A. The relevant parts of these enactments are looked at in overview prior to examining the provisions of Schedule 8.

1. Intelligence Services Act 1994

10.60 Other than the amendments to the ISA dealt with in this chapter, section 5 (warrant for the interference with property of wireless telegraphy) remains unchanged: see paragraphs 10.52–10.54 above.

---

[74] ibid s 251(2)(b).
[75] ibid s 251(3)(a)–(c).
[76] ibid s 259(3).
[77] ibid s 259(6).

D. Combined Warrants or Authorizations

10.61 Section 5(1) ISA provides that no interference with property or wireless telegraphy will be unlawful providing it is authorized by a warrant issued by the Secretary of State. A warrant may be issued authorizing the taking of such action specified in the warrant in respect of any property or wireless telegraphy if the minister thinks it is necessary for the purposes of assisting the agencies in the discharge of their statutory functions.[78]

10.62 The functions of the Security Service are set out in section 1(2) to (4) of the Security Service Act 1989 and include the protection of national security[79] and the economic well-being of the UK, as well as supporting the activities of the National Crime Agency (NCA) and other law enforcement agencies in the prevention and detection of serious crime.[80]

10.63 The functions of the Secret Intelligence Service and GCHQ are identical. The former are set out in section 1(1) ISA and the latter in section 3(1). They are twofold: first, to obtain and provide information relating to the actions or intentions of persons outside the British Islands; and, secondly, to perform other tasks relating to the actions or intentions of such persons.[81] The functions are only exercisable in the interests of national security, the economic well-being of the UK, or the prevention and detection of serious crime.[82] The functions of GCHQ are exercisable on the same basis as those of SIS.[83] They are, as amended, to 'monitor, make use of, or interfere with electromagnetic, acoustic and other emissions and any equipment producing such emissions' and to provide information that derives from these resources and encrypted material and to provide advice and assistance about languages and cryptography.[84]

2. Police Act 1997, Part III

10.64 The amendments to the scheme under the Police Act 1997 relate to assimilating the changes under the IPA to the wording of the relevant provisions and transferring jurisdiction for approvals to the Investigatory Powers Commissioner. In every other respect, the provision remains unchanged.

10.65 The effect of an authorization is straightforward: 'no entry on or interference with property or with wireless telegraphy shall be unlawful if it is authorised by an authorisation' (Part III).[85]

10.66 Authorizing officers include a chief constable of a police force, the Provost Marshall of the Services' Police, the chairman of the Independent Police Complaints

---

[78] ISA 1994, s 5(2)(a)(i)–(iii).
[79] In particular, its protection against threats from espionage, terrorism, and sabotage, from the activities of agents of foreign powers, and from actions intended to overthrow or under parliamentary democracy by political, industrial, or violent means: ISA 1994, s 1(2).
[80] ISA 1994, s 1(4).
[81] ibid s 1(1)(a)–(b).
[82] ibid s 2(a)–(c).
[83] ibid s 3(2)(a)–(c).
[84] ibid s 3(1)(a)–(b)(ii).
[85] PA 1997, s 92.

10. Additional Powers, Combining Warrants, and Miscellaneous Provisions

Commission and the Director General of NCA, or any person holding the rank of assistant chief constable designated as an authorizing officer.[86]

10.67 Where an authorizing officer believes that it is necessary for the action specified in the authorization to be taken for the purpose of preventing or detecting serious crime, it is proportionate to what it seeks to achieve and cannot reasonably be achieved by other means.[87] Three forms of conduct may then be authorized. The first is the taking of action in respect of property in the relevant area as he or she may specify.[88] The second is such action in the relevant geographical area in respect of wireless telegraphy as he or she may specify.[89] The third is maintaining or extracting equipment that has been authorized under Part III of the Police Act 1997 or Part II of RIPA or the relevant Scottish enactment.[90]

10.68 The power to grant authorizations in respect of the chief constable or deputy chief constable of the Police Service of Northern Ireland extends so as to include the protection of the interests of national security.[91]

10.69 HM Revenue and Customs is limited to granting authorization to an assigned matter within the meaning of section 1(1) of the Customs and Excise Management Act 1979.[92]

10.70 As to the restrictions on the use of section 93 of the Police Act 1997, see Chapter 2, paragraph 2.73.

3. Regulation of Investigatory Powers Act 2000

10.71 The remaining substantive Parts of RIPA are Parts II (surveillance and use and conduct of covert human intelligence sources), III (encryption), and IV (oversight). The amendments to Part IV are dealt with in Chapter 9 of this work. Part II mirrors RIP(S)A. The following is an overview of the provisions that remain.

10.72 The amendments to Part II are set out in Schedule 10, Part 1, paragraphs, 3–6 IPA. There is none of significance for the purposes of this chapter.

10.73 The 2000 Act creates a regulatory regime for two types of surveillance: directed and intrusive.

(a) *Surveillance*

10.74 Surveillance includes (so is not limited to) monitoring, observing, or listening to persons, their movements, their conversations, or other activities or communications.[93] It extends to the recording of such activity and the use of a surveillance device (defined as 'any apparatus designed or adapted for use in surveillance') either

---

[86] ibid s 93(5).
[87] ibid s 93(2).
[88] ibid s 93(1)(a).
[89] ibid s 93(1)(b).
[90] ibid s 93(1)(ab) and s 93(1A).
[91] ibid s 93(2A).
[92] ibid s 93(4).
[93] RIPA, s 48(2)(a).

D. Combined Warrants or Authorizations

wholly or in part to carry out any of the surveillance activity.[94] Apparatus now has the meaning given to it in section 261(1) IPA and includes 'any equipment, machinery or device (whether physical or logical) and any wire or cable'.

10.75 It also extends to the interception of communications in the course of their transmission subject to the strict requirement that either the sender or recipient consents to the interception and there is no warrant issued in connection with the interception.[95]

10.76 It excludes any conduct of a covert human intelligence source whether he or she is wearing a surveillance device or not or information disclosed in the presence of a source and the use of a source for obtaining or recording information.[96] It also excludes trespass to and interference with property or wireless telegraphy.[97]

(b) Matters Common to Directed and Intrusive Surveillance

10.77 Section 26(9) RIPA sets out matters common to both forms of surveillance. The surveillance, whether directed or intrusive, must be carried out covertly and involve the acquisition of private information.

10.78 Surveillance is carried out covertly if, and only if, 'it is carried out in a manner that is calculated to ensure that persons that are subject to the surveillance are unaware that it is or may be taking place'.[98]

10.79 Private information is an express element of directed surveillance but it is axiomatic that it is also an element of intrusive surveillance. Private information in relation to a person includes any information relating to his or her private or family life.[99]

(c) Directed Surveillance

10.80 Section 26 RIPA provides for, amongst other things, directed and intrusive surveillance.[100] Directed surveillance is 'covert but not intrusive' and is carried out for the purposes of a specific investigation or a specific operation in such a manner as is likely to result in the obtaining of private information about a person (whether specifically identified as part of the specific investigation or operation, so in fact, *any* person) and is carried other than by way of an immediate response to events or circumstances that is such that it would be reasonably impracticable to obtain an authority to engage in the surveillance activity.[101]

(d) Intrusive Surveillance

10.81 Surveillance is intrusive if it is carried out in relation to anything taking place on any residential premises or in any private vehicle and involves the presence of an

---

[94] ibid s 48(2)(b)–(c).
[95] ibid s 48(4)(a)–(b).
[96] ibid s 48(3)(a)–(b).
[97] ibid s 48(3)(c)(i)–(ii).
[98] ibid s 26(9)(a).
[99] ibid s 26(2)(b) and (10).
[100] See generally Code of Practice, ch 2.
[101] RIPA, s 26(2)(a)–(c).

10. Additional Powers, Combining Warrants, and Miscellaneous Provisions

individual on the premises or in the vehicle or is carried out by means of a surveillance device.[102]

(e) *Covert Human Intelligence Sources, Other than Relevant Sources*

10.82 A person is a covert human intelligence source is he or she establishes or maintains a personal or other relationship with a person for the covert purpose of facilitating the covert use of such a relationship to obtain information or to provide access to any information to another person or the cover disclosure of information obtained by the use of such a relationship, or as a consequence of the existence of such a relationship.[103]

10.83 A purpose is covert, in relation to the establishment or maintenance of a personal or other relationship, if and only if, the relationship is conducted in a manner that is calculated to ensure that one of the parties to the relationship is unaware of the purpose; and a relationship is used covertly, and information obtained is disclosed covertly, if and only if, it is used, or as the case may be, disclosed in a manner that is calculated to ensure that one of the parties to the relationship is unaware of the use or disclosure in question.

(f) *Relevant Sources*

10.84 The Regulation of Investigatory Powers (Covert Human Intelligence Sources: Relevant Sources) Order 2013 (the Order) came into force on 1 January 2014. A relevant source for the purpose of the order is a source holding an office, rank, or position in a police force, national law enforcement organizations, or the military. It excludes the intelligence agencies.[104]

10.85 The order prescribes what should occur where the authorization of the relevant source in a 'long term authorisation'. This relates to two separate time periods taken together, the period of time it is proposed the relevant source will be authorized for (first time period) and the period or periods the relevant source has already been authorized as a source for in connection with the same investigation or operation (second time period).[105]

10.86 In respect of the first time period, where the period or periods of previous authorization is less than twelve months in total, any further authorization will cease to have effect, unless renewed, at the end of the period of twelve months, less the total period of time previously authorized (ie where the previous authorizations have totalled ten months, the new authorization would expire two months later, unless renewed).

10.87 The position in respect of the second time period is that if it ceased to have effect more than three years prior to the intended commencement date for the new authorization, the period in the first period of time should be disregarded.[106]

---

[102] ibid s 26(3)(a)–(b).
[103] ibid s 26(8)(a)–(c).
[104] SI 2013/2788, art 2.
[105] ibid art 3(2)(a)–(b).
[106] ibid art 3(5).

D. Combined Warrants or Authorizations

(g) *Grounds upon which Applications for Authority May Be Made*

10.88 The grounds upon which an authorization may be granted for directed surveillance and use and conduct of a covert human intelligence source are the same and must be necessary for one or more of the following: the interests of national security, for the purpose of preventing or detecting crime or of preventing disorder, the interests of the economic well-being of the UK, the interests of public safety, for the purpose of protecting public health, for the purpose of assessing or collecting any tax, duty, levy, or other imposition, contribution, or charge payable to a government department, or for any purpose other than the above which is specified for the purposes of this sub-section by any later order made by the Secretary of State, which must be laid before Parliament and approved by a resolution of each House.[107]

10.89 Authorization must also be proportionate to operational objective sought to be achieved through the conduct it is proposed is engaged in.[108] In the case of an authority for use and conduct, certain arrangements must also be in place.[109] There are different schemes in place for law enforcement, the intelligence services, and the Ministry of Defence. Local authorities are subject to a separate scheme under RIPA.[110] In connection with the latter, they may only obtain authorization were a minimum crime threshold is reached and are required to obtain judicial approval from a sitting magistrate.[111]

10.90 The public authorities entitled to apply for intrusive surveillance authorization is limited and excludes local authorities. The grounds are also narrower, limited to the interests of national security, the prevention and detection of serious crime, and the interests of the economic interests of the UK.[112]

10.91 In the case of the intelligence services, Ministry of Defence, and armed forces, authorization is by way of a warrant issued by the Secretary of State.[113] In every other case, judicial approval is required.[114]

10.92 Judicial approval is also required for long-term authorizations in respect of use and conduct of covert human intelligence sources that are relevant sources.[115]

4. Schedule 8 IPA

10.93 Schedule 8 is in four parts. Part 1 relates to combinations with targeted interception warrants; Part 2, other combinations involving targeted equipment interference

---

[107] RIPA, s 28(3)(a)–(g) and (5) and s 29(3)(a)–(g) and (6).
[108] ibid ss 28(2)(b) and 29(2)(b).
[109] ibid s 29(2)(c)(i)–(iii).
[110] ibid ss 33–40, 41–42, and 32A–32B.
[111] Regulation of Investigatory Powers (Directed Surveillance and Covert Human Intelligence Sources) Order 2010 as amended by the Regulation of Investigatory Powers (Directed Surveillance and Covert Human Intelligence Sources) (Amendment) Order 2012.
[112] RIPA, s 32(3)(a)–(c).
[113] ibid ss 41 and 42.
[114] ibid s 36.
[115] Regulation of Investigatory Powers (Covert Human Intelligence Sources: Relevant Sources) Order 2013.

10. Additional Powers, Combining Warrants, and Miscellaneous Provisions

warrants; Part 3, combinations involving targeted examination warrants only; and Part 4, supplementary provisions.

(a) *Combinations: Targeted Interception Warrants*

10.94 The Secretary of State may, on an application made by or on behalf of the head of an intelligence service, the Chief of Defence Intelligence or a relevant intercepting authority (the applicants) issue a warrant that combines a targeted interception warrant with one or more warrants or authorizations.

10.95 The following warrants or authorizations can be combined on an application from any of the applicants: a targeted equipment interference warrant, a directed surveillance authorization or an intrusive surveillance authorization.[116]

10.96 In addition to those matters common to each applicant, a head of an intelligence service may apply for any of the following to be combined with a targeted interception warrant: a targeted examination warrant in respect of the interception of communications or equipment interference or a property interference warrant under section 5 ISA.[117]

10.97 In addition, an intercepting authority may apply also for a property interference warrant under Part III of the Police Act 1997 to be combined with a targeted interception warrant.[118]

(i) *Scottish Ministers*

10.98 The Scottish Ministers may, on an application made by or on behalf of the head of an intelligence service, issue a warrant that combines a targeted interception warrant with: a targeted examination warrant in respect of the interception of communications or equipment interference, a targeted equipment interference warrant or a property interference warrant under section 5 ISA.[119]

10.99 The Scottish Ministers may, on an application made by or on behalf of the Police Service of Scotland issue a warrant that combines a targeted interception warrant with: a targeted equipment interference warrant, a property interference warrant under Part III of the Police Act 1997, a directed surveillance authorization or an intrusive surveillance authorization (under either RIPA or RIP(S)A).[120]

10.100 The Scottish Ministers may, on an application made by or on behalf of an intercepting authority issue a warrant that combines a targeted interception warrant with: a targeted equipment interference warrant or a property interference warrant under Part III of the Police Act 1997.[121]

---

[116] IPA, Schedule 8, paras 1(b), (e)–(f); 2(a)–(c); and 3(a), (c)–(d).
[117] ibid para 1(a), (c)–(d).
[118] ibid para 3(1)(b).
[119] ibid para 4(a)–(d).
[120] ibid paras 5(a)–(d) and 6(a)–(d).
[121] ibid para 7(a)–(b).

D. Combined Warrants or Authorizations

(b) *Combinations: Targeted Equipment Interference Warrants*

10.101 The Secretary of State may, on an application made by or on behalf of the head of an intelligence service or the Chief of Defence Intelligence (the applicants) issue a warrant that combines a targeted equipment interference warrant with one or more warrants or authorizations.

10.102 The following warrants or authorizations can be combined on an application from any of the applicants: a directed surveillance authorization or an intrusive surveillance authorization.[122]

10.103 In addition to those common to each applicant, a head of an intelligence service may apply for any of the following to be combined with a targeted interception warrant: a targeted examination warrant in respect of the interception of communications or equipment interference or a property interference warrant under section 5, ISA.[123]

(i) *Scottish Ministers*

10.104 The Scottish Ministers may, on an application made by or on behalf of the head of an intelligence service, issue a warrant that combines a targeted equipment interference warrant with: a targeted examination warrant in respect of the interception of communications or equipment interference or a property interference warrant under section 5, ISA.[124]

(c) *Law Enforcement Chiefs*

10.105 A law enforcement chief may, on an application made by an appropriate law enforcement officer in relation to the chief issue a warrant that combines a targeted equipment interference warrant with: a property interference warrant under Part III of the Police Act 1997, a directed surveillance authorization, or an intrusive surveillance authorization (under either RIPA or RIP(S)A).[125]

(d) *Combinations: Targeted Examination Warrants Only*

10.106 The Secretary of State may, on an application made by or on behalf of the head of an intelligence service, issue a warrant that combines targeted examination warrants in respect of the interception of communications or equipment interference.[126]

(i) *Scottish Ministers*

10.107 The Scottish Ministers may, on an application made by or on behalf of the head of an intelligence service issue a warrant that combines targeted examination warrants with in respect of the interception of communications or equipment interference.[127]

---

[122] ibid paras 8(d)–(e) and 9(a)–(b).
[123] ibid para 8(a)–(c).
[124] ibid para 10(a)–(c).
[125] ibid paras 11(1)(a)–(c) and 12(1)(a)–(c).
[126] ibid para 13(a)–(b).
[127] ibid para 14(a)–(b).

10. Additional Powers, Combining Warrants, and Miscellaneous Provisions

(g) Combined Warrants: Requirements and Rules

10.108 (i) *Requirements* A person to whom an application is made for a combined warrant is entitled to issue the warrant notwithstanding that person may not have the power to issue the warrant or authorization as a single instrument.[128] However the applicant for a combined warrant must be a person or a member of staff, an officer or someone acting on behalf of an organization entitled to apply for the warrant or authorization as a single instrument.[129]

10.109 A combined warrant must be addressed to the person by whom, or on whose behalf, the application for the combined warrant was made and must contain a provision stating which warrants or other authorizations are included in the combined warrant.[130]

10.110 Any reference in any enactment to a warrant or other authorization issued or given includes, in the case of a combined warrant containing a warrant or authorization of that description, a reference to so much of the combined warrant as consists of that warrant or authorization.[131]

10.111 (ii) *Rules: Application to each part of a combined warrant as a single instrument* The requirements of law insofar as they relate to a warrant or other authorization that may be included in a combined warrant, apply in relation to that part of a combined warrant as it would in respect of the warrant or authorization as if it was a single instrument. This means: any conditions or requirements that must be met, the grounds on which such a warrant or authorization may be issued or given and the conduct that may be authorized. It also extends to the law relating to renewal, modification, and the procedural rules relating to modification and cancellation. The duties imposed by section 2 (general duties in relation to privacy) also apply.[132]

10.112 The reference to procedural rules in connection with modification means the law governing the involvement of judicial commissioners in decisions, the delegation of decisions, the signing of instruments making a modification, and urgent cases.[133]

10.113 These rules are subject to those relating to combined warrants.[134]

10.114 (iii) *Rules: Application to combined warrants* A combined targeted interception, targeted equipment interference or targeted examination warrant addressed to any person may only be issued, renewed or cancelled in accordance with the procedural rules that would apply to the issue, renewal or cancellation of a warrant of that type addressed to that person as a single instrument.[135]

---

[128] ibid para 16(1).
[129] ibid para 16(2).
[130] ibid paras 17–18.
[131] ibid para 19.
[132] ibid para 20(1)(a)–(i).
[133] ibid para 20(2)(a)–(d).
[134] ibid para 20(3).
[135] ibid paras 21(1), 22(1), and 23(1).

D. Combined Warrants or Authorizations

10.115 The reference to procedural rules, in relation to a warrant, means the law governing the involvement of judicial commissioners in decisions, the delegation of decisions, the signing of warrants, and urgent cases.[136] The involvement of judicial commissioners does not apply where the warrant is combined with a property interference warrant under section 5, ISA in relation to that part of the combined warrant.[137]

10.116 Schedule 8, paragraph 24 provides that, as a consequence of the rules on combined warrants set out above, sections 96, 97, 103(1)–(2) and (4), and 104 of the Police Act 1997 and sections 25–38, RIPA, and 13–16 RIP(S)A do not apply in relation to an authorization under section 93 of the Police Act 1997, section 32 RIPA, and section 10 RIP(S)A, respectively, which is included in a combined warrant. This is because the procedural rules as to the issue of the warrant with which it is to be combined are to be followed.

10.117 Where a combined warrant containing an authorization under section 93 of the Police Act 1997 is cancelled the provisions in relation to retrieval of anything left on the property apply as they would if section 103(6) applied.[138]

10.118 Where a combined warrant includes warrants or authorizations which if treated as single instruments would cease to have effect at the end of different periods, the combined warrant is to cease to have effect, unless renewed, at the end of the shortest of the periods. However, this does not apply to a combined warrant that includes a directed surveillance authorization; it is a combined warrant addressed to the head of an intelligence service, and is issued with the approval of a judicial commissioner. In such circumstances, the combined warrant, unless renewed, cease to have effect at the end of the period of six months, beginning with the day on which it is issued.[139]

(h) *Application of Provisions of IPA to Combined Warrants: Special Rules*

10.119 Where, in the case of a targeted interception or examination warrant under section 24(3) IPA, a judicial commissioner refuses to approve a decision to issue on an urgent basis a combined warrant under Part 1 or 3 of Schedule 8, the provisions in section 25(3) IPA in relation to a judicial commissioner directing destruction of the material or imposing conditions on its retention apply and references in section 25 IPA to a warrant should be read as if it is a reference to a combined warrant.[140]

10.120 The same position applies where the combined warrant includes a targeted equipment interference or examination warrant issued under Part 5 or is a combined warrant under Part 2 of Schedule 8 and a judicial commissioner refuses to approve a decision to issue the warrant on an urgent basis. The provisions of section 110 IPA in relation to a judicial commissioner directing destruction of the material or imposing conditions on its retention and, if retained, examination apply, and references in

---

[136] ibid paras 21(2)(a)–(d), 22(2), and 23(2).
[137] ibid paras 21(3) and 22(3).
[138] ibid para 24(2).
[139] ibid para 27(1)–(3).
[140] ibid para 28(1)–(2).

the combined warrant to targeted equipment interference or targeted examination warrants should be read as a reference to the warrant as if it was a single instrument and all other reference to a warrant should be read as if it is a reference to a combined warrant.[141]

10.121 Where any provision in Part 2 or 5 IPA enables a person to whom the warrant is addressed to require assistance giving effect to the warrant, in the case of a combined warrant containing such a warrant, the provision is to be read as so as to give effect to so much of it as relates to the requirement to provide assistance. The power to serve a copy of a warrant for that purpose includes power, in the case of such a combined warrant, to serve the part of the combined warrant consisting of such a warrant.[142]

10.122 The prohibition in section 56 IPA relating to the exclusion of matters from legal proceedings applies to the making of an application for a combined warrant of an application as it does the application for a warrant under Chapter 1 of Part 2 of this Act where such a warrant is included in a combined warrant.[143]

10.123 The reference in section 58(7) to the provisions of Part 2 and section 133(4) to the provisions of Part 5 IPA is to be read, in the case of a combined warrant containing a targeted interception or equipment interference warrant or related examination warrants which the person who issued the combined warrant has power to issue under that Part, as including a reference to Schedule 8 IPA.[144]

(i) *Power to Make Consequential Amendments*

10.124 The Secretary of State may by regulations make such provision modifying any provision made by or under an enactment, including Schedule 8 IPA as the Secretary of State considers appropriate in consequence of any provision made by it. The term 'enactment' for this purpose does not include any primary legislation passed or made after the end of the parliament in which this Act is passed.[145]

E. MISCELLANEOUS

1. Offences under the IPA Committed by a Body Corporate or Scottish Partnership

10.125 Where any offence under the IPA is committed by a body corporate or a Scottish partnership the senior officer or person (as well as the body corporate or partnership) is guilty of the offence and liable to be proceeded against and punished accordingly.[146]

---

[141] ibid paras 28(3)(a)–(c) and 29(a)–(c).
[142] ibid para 30(1)–(3).
[143] ibid para 31(a)–(b).
[144] ibid para 32(1)–(2).
[145] ibid para 33(1)–(2).
[146] IPA, s 266(1).

10.126 The offence must be proved to have been committed with the consent or connivance of, or to be attributable to any neglect on the part of the senior officer of the body corporate or Scottish partnership, or a person purporting to act in such a capacity.[147]

10.127 The term 'director' means, in relation to a body corporate whose affairs are managed by its members, a member of the body corporate. The term 'senior officer' means, in relation to a body corporate, a director, manager, secretary or other similar officer of the body corporate, and in relation to a Scottish partnership, a partner in the partnership.[148]

2. Compliance with IPA

(a) *Payments towards Certain Compliance Costs*

10.128 Section 249 IPA replaces the former section 14 RIPA (grants for interception costs). The money for payments is provided by Parliament.[149]

10.129 The Secretary of State must ensure that arrangements are in force for securing that telecommunications and postal operators receive an appropriate contribution in respect of such of their relevant costs as the Secretary of State considers appropriate.[150] The term 'relevant costs' means 'costs incurred, or likely to be incurred, by telecommunications operators and postal operators in complying with [the IPA].[151]

10.130 The arrangements may provide for payment of a contribution to be subject to terms and conditions determined by the Secretary of State and for the scope and extent of the arrangements, and what the appropriate level of contribution which should be made in each case. The terms and conditions may, in particular, include a condition on the operator concerned to comply with any audit that may reasonably be required to monitor the claim for costs.[152] Different levels of contribution may apply for different cases or descriptions of case but it can never be the case that no contribution is made.[153]

10.131 In the case of either retention notice under Part 4 or a national security notice under section 252 given to a telecommunications or a postal operator, the level or levels of contribution which the Secretary of State has determined should be made in respect of the costs incurred, or likely to be incurred, by the operator as a result of the notice in complying with it must be specified in the notice.[154]

---

[147] ibid s 266(2)(a)–(b).
[148] ibid s 266(3)9a)–(b).
[149] ibid s 249(8).
[150] ibid s 249(1).
[151] ibid s 249(2).
[152] ibid s 249(3)–(5).
[153] ibid s 249(6).
[154] ibid s 249(7).

10. Additional Powers, Combining Warrants, and Miscellaneous Provisions

(b) *Power to Develop Compliance Systems*

10.132 The Secretary of State may develop, provide, maintain, or improve (or enter into financial or other arrangements with any person for such purposes) such apparatus, systems, or other facilities or services as the Secretary of State considers appropriate for enabling or otherwise facilitating compliance by the Secretary of State, another public authority, or any other person with the provisions of IPA.[155]

10.133 Where the Secretary of State has entered into financial or other arrangements these may, in particular, include giving financial assistance. This may be in the form of grant, loan, guarantee, or indemnity, investment, or incurring expenditure for the benefit of the person assisted. Any financial assistance may be subject to terms and conditions and these may include provision as to repayment with or without interest.[156]

---

[155] ibid s 250(1)(a)–(b).
[156] ibid s 250(2)–(4).

Appendix
Investigatory Powers Act 2016

CHAPTER 25

CONTENTS

PART 1
GENERAL PRIVACY PROTECTIONS

Overview and general privacy duties

1 Overview of Act
2 General duties in relation to privacy

Prohibitions against unlawful interception

3 Offence of unlawful interception
4 Definition of "interception" etc.
5 Conduct that is not interception
6 Definition of "lawful authority"
7 Monetary penalties for certain unlawful interceptions
8 Civil liability for certain unlawful interceptions
9 Restriction on requesting interception by overseas authorities
10 Restriction on requesting assistance under mutual assistance agreements etc.

Prohibition against unlawful obtaining of communications data

11 Offence of unlawfully obtaining communications data

Abolition or restriction of powers to obtain communications data

12 Abolition or restriction of certain powers to obtain communications data

Restrictions on interference with equipment

13 Mandatory use of equipment interference warrants
14 Restriction on use of section 93 of the Police Act 1997

PART 2
LAWFUL INTERCEPTION OF COMMUNICATIONS

CHAPTER 1 INTERCEPTION AND EXAMINATION WITH A WARRANT

Warrants under this Chapter

15 Warrants that may be issued under this Chapter

16 Obtaining secondary data
17 Subject-matter of warrants

Power to issue warrants

18 Persons who may apply for issue of a warrant
19 Power of Secretary of State to issue warrants
20 Grounds on which warrants may be issued by Secretary of State
21 Power of Scottish Ministers to issue warrants
22 "Relevant Scottish applications"

Approval of warrants by Judicial Commissioners

23 Approval of warrants by Judicial Commissioners
24 Approval of warrants issued in urgent cases
25 Failure to approve warrant issued in urgent case

Additional safeguards

26 Members of Parliament etc.
27 Items subject to legal privilege
28 Confidential journalistic material
29 Sources of journalistic information

Further provision about warrants

30 Decisions to issue warrants to be taken personally by Ministers
31 Requirements that must be met by warrants
32 Duration of warrants
33 Renewal of warrants
34 Modification of warrants
35 Persons who may make modifications
36 Further provision about modifications
37 Notification of major modifications
38 Approval of major modifications made in urgent cases
39 Cancellation of warrants
40 Special rules for certain mutual assistance warrants

Implementation of warrants

41 Implementation of warrants
42 Service of warrants
43 Duty of operators to assist with implementation

CHAPTER 2 OTHER FORMS OF LAWFUL INTERCEPTION

Interception with consent

44 Interception with the consent of the sender or recipient

Interception for administrative or enforcement purposes

45 Interception by providers of postal or telecommunications services

Appendix

46 Interception by businesses etc. for monitoring and record-keeping purposes
47 Postal services: interception for enforcement purposes
48 Interception by OFCOM in connection with wireless telegraphy

Interception taking place in certain institutions

49 Interception in prisons
50 Interception in psychiatric hospitals etc.
51 Interception in immigration detention facilities

Interception in accordance with overseas requests

52 Interception in accordance with overseas requests

CHAPTER 3 OTHER PROVISIONS ABOUT INTERCEPTION

Restrictions on use or disclosure of material obtained under warrants etc.

53 Safeguards relating to retention and disclosure of material
54 Safeguards relating to disclosure of material overseas
55 Additional safeguards for items subject to legal privilege
56 Exclusion of matters from legal proceedings etc.
57 Duty not to make unauthorised disclosures
58 Section 57: meaning of "excepted disclosure"
59 Offence of making unauthorised disclosures

Interpretation

60 Part 2: interpretation

PART 3
AUTHORISATIONS FOR OBTAINING COMMUNICATIONS DATA

Targeted authorisations for obtaining data

61 Power to grant authorisations
62 Restrictions in relation to internet connection records
63 Additional restrictions on grant of authorisations
64 Procedure for authorisations and authorised notices
65 Duration and cancellation of authorisations and notices
66 Duties of telecommunications operators in relation to authorisations

Filtering arrangements for obtaining data

67 Filtering arrangements for obtaining data
68 Use of filtering arrangements in pursuance of an authorisation
69 Duties in connection with operation of filtering arrangements

Relevant public authorities other than local authorities

70 Relevant public authorities and designated senior officers etc.

Appendix

71 Power to modify section 70 and Schedule 4
72 Certain regulations under section 71: supplementary

Local authorities

73 Local authorities as relevant public authorities
74 Requirement to be party to collaboration agreement
75 Judicial approval for local authority authorisations

Additional protections

76 Use of a single point of contact
77 Commissioner approval for authorisations to identify or confirm journalistic sources

Collaboration agreements

78 Collaboration agreements
79 Collaboration agreements: supplementary
80 Police collaboration agreements

Further and supplementary provision

81 Lawfulness of conduct authorised by this Part
82 Offence of making unauthorised disclosure
83 Certain transfer and agency arrangements with public authorities
84 Application of Part 3 to postal operators and postal services
85 Extra-territorial application of Part 3
86 Part 3: interpretation

PART 4
RETENTION OF COMMUNICATIONS DATA

General

87 Powers to require retention of certain data

Safeguards

88 Matters to be taken into account before giving retention notices
89 Approval of retention notices by Judicial Commissioners
90 Review by the Secretary of State
91 Approval of notices following review under section 90
92 Data integrity and security
93 Disclosure of retained data

Variation or revocation of notices

94 Variation or revocation of notices

Enforcement

95 Enforcement of notices and certain other requirements and restrictions

Appendix

Further and supplementary provision

96 Application of Part 4 to postal operators and postal services
97 Extra-territorial application of Part 4
98 Part 4: interpretation

PART 5
EQUIPMENT INTERFERENCE

Warrants under this Part

99 Warrants under this Part: general
100 Meaning of "equipment data"
101 Subject-matter of warrants

Power to issue warrants

102 Power to issue warrants to intelligence services: the Secretary of State
103 Power to issue warrants to intelligence services: the Scottish Ministers
104 Power to issue warrants to the Chief of Defence Intelligence
105 Decision to issue warrants under sections 102 to 104 to be taken personally by Ministers
106 Power to issue warrants to law enforcement officers
107 Restriction on issue of warrants to certain law enforcement officer

Approval of warrants by Judicial Commissioners

108 Approval of warrants by Judicial Commissioners
109 Approval of warrants issued in urgent cases
110 Failure to approve warrant issued in urgent case

Additional safeguards

111 Members of Parliament etc.
112 Items subject to legal privilege
113 Confidential journalistic material
114 Sources of journalistic information

Further provision about warrants

115 Requirements that must be met by warrants
116 Duration of warrants
117 Renewal of warrants
118 Modification of warrants issued by the Secretary of State or Scottish Ministers
119 Persons who may make modifications under section 118
120 Further provision about modifications under section 118
121 Notification of modifications
122 Approval of modifications under section 118 made in urgent cases
123 Modification of warrants issued by law enforcement chiefs
124 Approval of modifications under section 123 in urgent cases
125 Cancellation of warrants

Implementation of warrants

126 Implementation of warrants
127 Service of warrants
128 Duty of telecommunications operators to assist with implementation

Supplementary provision

129 Safeguards relating to retention and disclosure of material
130 Safeguards relating to disclosure of material overseas
131 Additional safeguards for items subject to legal privilege
132 Duty not to make unauthorised disclosures
133 Section 132: meaning of "excepted disclosure"
134 Offence of making unauthorised disclosure
135 Part 5: interpretation

PART 6
BULK WARRANTS

CHAPTER 1 BULK INTERCEPTION WARRANTS

Bulk interception warrants

136 Bulk interception warrants
137 Obtaining secondary data
138 Power to issue bulk interception warrants
139 Additional requirements in respect of warrants affecting overseas operators
140 Approval of warrants by Judicial Commissioners
141 Decisions to issue warrants to be taken personally by Secretary of State
142 Requirements that must be met by warrants

Duration, modification and cancellation of warrants

143 Duration of warrants
144 Renewal of warrants
145 Modification of warrants
146 Approval of major modifications by Judicial Commissioners
147 Approval of major modifications made in urgent cases
148 Cancellation of warrants

Implementation of warrants

149 Implementation of warrants

Restrictions on use or disclosure of material obtained under warrants etc.

150 Safeguards relating to retention and disclosure of material
151 Safeguards relating to disclosure of material overseas
152 Safeguards relating to examination of material
153 Additional safeguards for items subject to legal privilege
154 Additional safeguard for confidential journalistic material
155 Offence of breaching safeguards relating to examination of material
156 Application of other restrictions in relation to warrants

Appendix

Interpretation

157 Chapter 1: interpretation

CHAPTER 2 BULK ACQUISITION WARRANTS

Bulk acquisition warrants

158 Power to issue bulk acquisition warrants
159 Approval of warrants by Judicial Commissioners
160 Decisions to issue warrants to be taken personally by Secretary of State
161 Requirements that must be met by warrants

Duration, modification and cancellation of warrants

162 Duration of warrants
163 Renewal of warrants
164 Modification of warrants
165 Approval of major modifications by Judicial Commissioners
166 Approval of major modifications made in urgent cases
167 Cancellation of warrants

Implementation of warrants

168 Implementation of warrants
169 Service of warrants
170 Duty of operators to assist with implementation

Restrictions on use or disclosure of data obtained under warrants etc.

171 Safeguards relating to the retention and disclosure of data
172 Safeguards relating to examination of data
173 Offence of breaching safeguards relating to examination of data

Supplementary provision

174 Offence of making unauthorised disclosure
175 Chapter 2: interpretation

CHAPTER 3 BULK EQUIPMENT INTERFERENCE WARRANTS

Bulk equipment interference warrants

176 Bulk equipment interference warrants: general
177 Meaning of "equipment data"
178 Power to issue bulk equipment interference warrants
179 Approval of warrants by Judicial Commissioners
180 Approval of warrants issued in urgent cases
181 Failure to approve warrant issued in urgent case
182 Decisions to issue warrants to be taken personally by Secretary of State
183 Requirements that must be met by warrants

Duration, modification and cancellation of warrants

184 Duration of warrants
185 Renewal of warrants

Appendix

186 Modification of warrants
187 Approval of major modifications by Judicial Commissioners
188 Approval of major modifications made in urgent cases
189 Cancellation of warrants

Implementation of warrants

190 Implementation of warrants

Restrictions on use or disclosure of material obtained under warrants etc.

191 Safeguards relating to retention and disclosure of material
192 Safeguards relating to disclosure of material overseas
193 Safeguards relating to examination of material etc.
194 Additional safeguards for items subject to legal privilege
195 Additional safeguard for confidential journalistic material
196 Offence of breaching safeguards relating to examination of material
197 Application of other restrictions in relation to warrants

Interpretation

198 Chapter 3: interpretation

PART 7
BULK PERSONAL DATASET WARRANTS

Bulk personal datasets: interpretation

199 Bulk personal datasets: interpretation

Requirement for warrant

200 Requirement for authorisation by warrant: general
201 Exceptions to section 200(1) and (2)
202 Restriction on use of class BPD warrants
203 Meaning of "protected data"

Issue of warrants

204 Class BPD warrants
205 Specific BPD warrants
206 Additional safeguards for health records
207 Protected data: power to impose conditions
208 Approval of warrants by Judicial Commissioners
209 Approval of specific BPD warrants issued in urgent cases
210 Failure to approve specific BPD warrant issued in urgent case
211 Decisions to issue warrants to be taken personally by Secretary of State
212 Requirements that must be met by warrants

Duration, modification and cancellation

213 Duration of warrants

Appendix

214 Renewal of warrants
215 Modification of warrants
216 Approval of major modifications by Judicial Commissioners
217 Approval of major modifications made in urgent cases
218 Cancellation of warrants
219 Non-renewal or cancellation of BPD warrants

Further and supplementary provision

220 Initial examinations: time limits
221 Safeguards relating to examination of bulk personal datasets
222 Additional safeguards for items subject to legal privilege: examination
223 Additional safeguards for items subject to legal privilege: retention following examination
224 Offence of breaching safeguards relating to examination of material
225 Application of Part to bulk personal datasets obtained under this Act
226 Part 7: interpretation

PART 8
OVERSIGHT ARRANGEMENTS

CHAPTER 1 INVESTIGATORY POWERS COMMISSIONER AND OTHER JUDICIAL COMMISSIONERS

The Commissioners

227 Investigatory Powers Commissioner and other Judicial Commissioners
228 Terms and conditions of appointment

Main functions of Commissioners

229 Main oversight functions
230 Additional directed oversight functions
231 Error reporting
232 Additional functions under this Part
233 Functions under other Parts and other enactments

Reports and investigation and information powers

234 Annual and other reports
235 Investigation and information powers
236 Referrals by the Intelligence and Security Committee of Parliament
237 Information gateway

Supplementary provision

238 Funding, staff and facilities etc.
239 Power to modify functions
240 Abolition of existing oversight bodies

CHAPTER 2 OTHER ARRANGEMENTS

Codes of practice

241 Codes of practice

Investigatory Powers Tribunal

242 Right of appeal from Tribunal
243 Functions of Tribunal in relation to this Act etc.

Information Commissioner

244 Oversight by Information Commissioner in relation to Part 4

Advisory bodies

245 Technical Advisory Board
246 Technology Advisory Panel
247 Members of the Panel

PART 9
MISCELLANEOUS AND GENERAL PROVISIONS

CHAPTER 1 MISCELLANEOUS

Combined warrants and authorisations

248 Combination of warrants and authorisations

Compliance with Act

249 Payments towards certain compliance costs
250 Power to develop compliance systems etc.

Additional powers

251 Amendments of the Intelligence Services Act 1994
252 National security notices
253 Technical capability notices
254 Approval of notices by Judicial Commissioners
255 Further provision about notices under section 252 or 253
256 Variation and revocation of notices
257 Review of notices by the Secretary of State
258 Approval of notices following review under section 257

Wireless telegraphy

259 Amendments of the Wireless Telegraphy Act 2006

CHAPTER 2 GENERAL

Review of operation of Act

260 Review of operation of Act

Interpretation

261 Telecommunications definitions
262 Postal definitions

263 General definitions
264 General definitions: "journalistic material" etc.
265 Index of defined expressions

Supplementary provision

266 Offences by bodies corporate etc.
267 Regulations
268 Enhanced affirmative procedure
269 Financial provisions
270 Transitional, transitory or saving provision
271 Minor and consequential provision

Final provision

272 Commencement, extent and short title

Schedule 1—Monetary penalty notices
   Part 1—Monetary penalty notices
   Part 2—Information provisions
Schedule 2—Abolition of disclosure powers
Schedule 3—Exceptions to section 56
Schedule 4—Relevant public authorities and designated senior officers etc.
   Part 1—Table of authorities and officers etc.
   Part 2—Interpretation of table
Schedule 5—Transfer and agency arrangements with public authorities: further provisions
Schedule 6—Issue of warrants under section 106 etc.: table
   Part 1—Table: Part 1
   Part 2—Table: Part 2
   Part 3—Interpretation of the table
Schedule 7—Codes of practice
Schedule 8—Combination of warrants and authorisations
   Part 1—Combinations with targeted interception warrants
   Part 2—Other combinations involving targeted equipment interference warrants
   Part 3—Combinations involving targeted examination warrants only
   Part 4—Combined warrants: supplementary provision
Schedule 9—Transitional, transitory and saving provision
Schedule 10—Minor and consequential provision
Part 1—General amendments
Part 2—Lawful interception of communications
Part 3—Acquisition of communications data
Part 4—Retention of communications data
Part 5—Equipment interference
Part 6—Judicial Commissioners
Part 7—Other minor and consequential provision
Part 8—Repeals and revocations consequential on other repeals or amendments in this Act

Appendix

INVESTIGATORY POWERS ACT 2016
2016 CHAPTER 25

An Act to make provision about the interception of communications, equipment interference and the acquisition and retention of communications data, bulk personal datasets and other information; to make provision about the treatment of material held as a result of such interception, equipment interference or acquisition or retention; to establish the Investigatory Powers Commissioner and other Judicial Commissioners and make provision about them and other oversight arrangements; to make further provision about investigatory powers and national security; to amend sections 3 and 5 of the Intelligence Services Act 1994; and for connected purposes.

[29th November 2016]

BE IT ENACTED by the Queen's most Excellent Majesty, by and with the advice and consent of the Lords Spiritual and Temporal, and Commons, in this present Parliament assembled, and by the authority of the same, as follows:—

PART 1
GENERAL PRIVACY PROTECTIONS

Overview and general privacy duties

1 Overview of Act

(1) This Act sets out the extent to which certain investigatory powers may be used to interfere with privacy.
(2) This Part imposes certain duties in relation to privacy and contains other protections for privacy.
(3) These other protections include offences and penalties in relation to—
   (a) the unlawful interception of communications, and
   (b) the unlawful obtaining of communications data.
(4) This Part also abolishes and restricts various general powers to obtain communications data and restricts the circumstances in which equipment interference, and certain requests about the interception of communications, can take place.
(5) Further protections for privacy—
   (a) can be found, in particular, in the regimes provided for by Parts 2 to 7 and in the oversight arrangements in Part 8, and
   (b) also exist—
      (i) by virtue of the Human Rights Act 1998,
      (ii) in section 55 of the Data Protection Act 1998 (unlawful obtaining etc. of personal data),
      (iii) in section 48 of the Wireless Telegraphy Act 2006 (offence of interception or disclosure of messages),
      (iv) in sections 1 to 3A of the Computer Misuse Act 1990 (computer misuse offences),
      (v) in the common law offence of misconduct in public office, and
      (vi) elsewhere in the law.
(6) The regimes provided for by Parts 2 to 7 are as follows—

Appendix

(a) Part 2 and Chapter 1 of Part 6 set out circumstances (including under a warrant) in which the interception of communications is lawful and make further provision about the interception of communications and the treatment of material obtained in connection with it,

(b) Part 3 and Chapter 2 of Part 6 set out circumstances in which the obtaining of communications data is lawful in pursuance of an authorisation or under a warrant and make further provision about the obtaining and treatment of such data,

(c) Part 4 makes provision for the retention of certain communications data in pursuance of a notice,

(d) Part 5 and Chapter 3 of Part 6 deal with equipment interference warrants, and

(e) Part 7 deals with bulk personal dataset warrants.

(7) As to the rest of the Act—

(a) Part 8 deals with oversight arrangements for regimes in this Act and elsewhere, and

(b) Part 9 contains miscellaneous and general provisions including amendments to sections 3 and 5 of the Intelligence Services Act 1994 and provisions about national security and combined warrants and authorisations.

2 General duties in relation to privacy

(1) Subsection (2) applies where a public authority is deciding whether—

(a) to issue, renew or cancel a warrant under Part 2, 5, 6 or 7,

(b) to modify such a warrant,

(c) to approve a decision to issue, renew or modify such a warrant,

(d) to grant, approve or cancel an authorisation under Part 3,

(e) to give a notice in pursuance of such an authorisation or under Part 4 or section 252, 253 or 257,

(f) to vary or revoke such a notice,

(g) to approve a decision to give or vary a notice under Part 4 or section 252, 253 or 257,

(h) to approve the use of criteria under section 153, 194 or 222,

(i) to give an authorisation under section 219(3)(b),

(j) to approve a decision to give such an authorisation, or

(k) to apply for or otherwise seek any issue, grant, giving, modification, variation or renewal of a kind falling within paragraph (a), (b), (d), (e), (f) or (i).

(2) The public authority must have regard to—

(a) whether what is sought to be achieved by the warrant, authorisation or notice could reasonably be achieved by other less intrusive means,

(b) whether the level of protection to be applied in relation to any obtaining of information by virtue of the warrant, authorisation or notice is higher because of the particular sensitivity of that information,

(c) the public interest in the integrity and security of telecommunication systems and postal services, and

(d) any other aspects of the public interest in the protection of privacy.

(3) The duties under subsection (2)—

(a) apply so far as they are relevant in the particular context, and

(b) are subject to the need to have regard to other considerations that are also relevant in that context.

(4) The other considerations may, in particular, include—

(a) the interests of national security or of the economic well-being of the United Kingdom,

(b) the public interest in preventing or detecting serious crime,

(c) other considerations which are relevant to—
  (i) whether the conduct authorised or required by the warrant, authorisation or notice is proportionate, or
  (ii) whether it is necessary to act for a purpose provided for by this Act,
(d) the requirements of the Human Rights Act 1998, and
(e) other requirements of public law.
(5) For the purposes of subsection (2)(b), examples of sensitive information include—
  (a) items subject to legal privilege,
  (b) any information identifying or confirming a source of journalistic information, and
  (c) relevant confidential information within the meaning given by paragraph 2(4) of Schedule 7 (certain information held in confidence and consisting of personal records, journalistic material or communications between Members of Parliament and their constituents).
(6) In this section "public authority" includes the relevant judicial authority (within the meaning of section 75) where the relevant judicial authority is deciding whether to approve under that section an authorisation under Part 3.

Prohibitions against unlawful interception

3 Offence of unlawful interception

(1) A person commits an offence if—
  (a) the person intentionally intercepts a communication in the course of its transmission by means of—
    (i) a public telecommunication system,
    (ii) a private telecommunication system, or
    (iii) a public postal service,
  (b) the interception is carried out in the United Kingdom, and
  (c) the person does not have lawful authority to carry out the interception.
(2) But it is not an offence under subsection (1) for a person to intercept a communication in the course of its transmission by means of a private telecommunication system if the person—
  (a) is a person with a right to control the operation or use of the system, or
  (b) has the express or implied consent of such a person to carry out the interception.
(3) Sections 4 and 5 contain provision about—
  (a) the meaning of "interception", and
  (b) when interception is to be regarded as carried out in the United Kingdom.
(4) Section 6 contains provision about when a person has lawful authority to carry out an interception.
(5) For the meaning of the terms used in subsection (1)(a)(i) to (iii), see sections 261 and 262.
(6) A person who is guilty of an offence under subsection (1) is liable—
  (a) on summary conviction in England and Wales, to a fine;
  (b) on summary conviction in Scotland or Northern Ireland, to a fine not exceeding the statutory maximum;
  (c) on conviction on indictment, to imprisonment for a term not exceeding 2 years or to a fine, or to both.
(7) No proceedings for any offence which is an offence by virtue of this section may be instituted—
  (a) in England and Wales, except by or with the consent of the Director of Public Prosecutions;
  (b) in Northern Ireland, except by or with the consent of the Director of Public Prosecutions for Northern Ireland.

Appendix

4 Definition of "interception" etc.

Interception in relation to telecommunication systems

(1) For the purposes of this Act, a person intercepts a communication in the course of its transmission by means of a telecommunication system if, and only if—
   (a) the person does a relevant act in relation to the system, and
   (b) the effect of the relevant act is to make any content of the communication available, at a relevant time, to a person who is not the sender or intended recipient of the communication. For the meaning of "content" in relation to a communication, see section 261(6).

(2) In this section "relevant act", in relation to a telecommunication system, means—
   (a) modifying, or interfering with, the system or its operation;
   (b) monitoring transmissions made by means of the system;
   (c) monitoring transmissions made by wireless telegraphy to or from apparatus that is part of the system.

(3) For the purposes of this section references to modifying a telecommunication system include references to attaching any apparatus to, or otherwise modifying or interfering with—
   (a) any part of the system, or
   (b) any wireless telegraphy apparatus used for making transmissions to or from apparatus that is part of the system.

(4) In this section "relevant time", in relation to a communication transmitted by means of a telecommunication system, means—
   (a) any time while the communication is being transmitted, and
   (b) any time when the communication is stored in or by the system (whether before or after its transmission).

(5) For the purposes of this section, the cases in which any content of a communication is to be taken to be made available to a person at a relevant time include any case in which any of the communication is diverted or recorded at a relevant time so as to make any content of the communication available to a person after that time.

(6) In this section "wireless telegraphy" and "wireless telegraphy apparatus" have the same meaning as in the Wireless Telegraphy Act 2006 (see sections 116 and 117 of that Act).

Interception in relation to postal services

(7) Section 125(3) of the Postal Services Act 2000 applies for the purposes of determining for the purposes of this Act whether a postal item is in the course of its transmission by means of a postal service as it applies for the purposes of determining for the purposes of that Act whether a postal packet is in course of transmission by post.

Interception carried out in the United Kingdom

(8) For the purposes of this Act the interception of a communication is carried out in the United Kingdom if, and only if—
   (a) the relevant act or, in the case of a postal item, the interception is carried out by conduct within the United Kingdom, and
   (b) the communication is intercepted—
      (i) in the course of its transmission by means of a public telecommunication system or a public postal service, or
      (ii) in the course of its transmission by means of a private telecommunication system in a case where the sender or intended recipient of the communication is in the United Kingdom.

5 Conduct that is not interception

(1) References in this Act to the interception of a communication do not include references to the interception of any communication broadcast for general reception.
(2) References in this Act to the interception of a communication in the course of its transmission by means of a postal service do not include references to—
   (a) any conduct that takes place in relation only to so much of the communication as consists of any postal data comprised in, included as part of, attached to, or logically associated with a communication (whether by the sender or otherwise) for the purposes of any postal service by means of which it is being or may be transmitted, or
   (b) any conduct, in connection with conduct falling within paragraph (a), that gives a person who is neither the sender nor the intended recipient only so much access to a communication as is necessary for the purpose of identifying such postal data. For the meaning of "postal data", see section 262.

6 Definition of "lawful authority"

(1) For the purposes of this Act, a person has lawful authority to carry out an interception if, and only if—
   (a) the interception is carried out in accordance with—
      (i) a targeted interception warrant or mutual assistance warrant under Chapter 1 of Part 2, or
      (ii) a bulk interception warrant under Chapter 1 of Part 6,
   (b) the interception is authorised by any of sections 44 to 52, or
   (c) in the case of a communication stored in or by a telecommunication system, the interception—
      (i) is carried out in accordance with a targeted equipment interference warrant under Part 5 or a bulk equipment interference warrant under Chapter 3 of Part 6,
      (ii) is in the exercise of any statutory power that is exercised for the purpose of obtaining information or taking possession of any document or other property, or
      (iii) is carried out in accordance with a court order made for that purpose.
(2) Conduct which has lawful authority for the purposes of this Act by virtue of subsection (1)(a) or (b) is to be treated as lawful for all other purposes.
(3) Any other conduct which—
   (a) is carried out in accordance with a warrant under Chapter 1 of Part 2 or a bulk interception warrant, or
   (b) is authorised by any of sections 44 to 52, is to be treated as lawful for all purposes.

7 Monetary penalties for certain unlawful interceptions

(1) The Investigatory Powers Commissioner may serve a monetary penalty notice on a person if conditions A and B are met.
(2) A monetary penalty notice is a notice requiring the person on whom it is served to pay to the Investigatory Powers Commissioner ("the Commissioner") a monetary penalty of an amount determined by the Commissioner and specified in the notice.
(3) Condition A is that the Commissioner considers that—
   (a) the person has intercepted, in the United Kingdom, any communication in the course of its transmission by means of a public telecommunication system,
   (b) the person did not have lawful authority to carry out the interception, and

Appendix

(c) the person was not, at the time of the interception, making an attempt to act in accordance with an interception warrant which might, in the opinion of the Commissioner, explain the interception.

(4) Condition B is that the Commissioner does not consider that the person has committed an offence under section 3(1).

(5) The amount of a monetary penalty determined by the Commissioner under this section must not exceed £50,000.

(6) Schedule 1 (which makes further provision about monetary penalty notices) has effect.

(7) In this section "interception warrant" means—
   (a) a targeted interception warrant or mutual assistance warrant under Chapter 1 of Part 2, or
   (b) a bulk interception warrant under Chapter 1 of Part 6.

(8) For the meaning of "interception" and other key expressions used in this section, see sections 4 to 6.

8 Civil liability for certain unlawful interceptions

(1) An interception of a communication is actionable at the suit or instance of—
   (a) the sender of the communication, or
   (b) the recipient, or intended recipient, of the communication, if conditions A to D are met.

(2) Condition A is that the interception is carried out in the United Kingdom.

(3) Condition B is that the communication is intercepted—
   (a) in the course of its transmission by means of a private telecommunication system, or
   (b) in the course of its transmission, by means of a public telecommunication system, to or from apparatus that is part of a private telecommunication system.

(4) Condition C is that the interception is carried out by, or with the express or implied consent of, a person who has the right to control the operation or use of the private telecommunication system.

(5) Condition D is that the interception is carried out without lawful authority.

(6) For the meaning of "interception" and other key expressions used in this section, see sections 4 to 6.

9 Restriction on requesting interception by overseas authorities

(1) This section applies to a request for any authorities of a country or territory outside the United Kingdom to carry out the interception of communications sent by, or intended for, an individual who the person making the request believes will be in the British Islands at the time of the interception.

(2) A request to which this section applies may not be made by or on behalf of a person in the United Kingdom unless—
   (a) a targeted interception warrant has been issued under Chapter 1 of Part 2 authorising the person to whom it is addressed to secure the interception of communications sent by, or intended for, that individual, or
   (b) a targeted examination warrant has been issued under that Chapter authorising the person to whom it is addressed to carry out the selection of the content of such communications for examination.

10 Restriction on requesting assistance under mutual assistance agreements etc.

(1) This section applies to—
   (a) a request for assistance under an EU mutual assistance instrument, and
   (b) a request for assistance in accordance with an international mutual assistance agreement.

(2) A request to which this section applies may not be made by or on behalf of a person in the United Kingdom to the competent authorities of a country or territory outside the United Kingdom unless a mutual assistance warrant has been issued under Chapter 1 of Part 2 authorising the making of the request.

(3) In this section—

"EU mutual assistance instrument" means an EU instrument which—
- (a) relates to the provision of mutual assistance in connection with, or in the form of, the interception of communications,
- (b) requires the issue of a warrant, order or equivalent instrument in cases in which assistance is given, and
- (c) is designated as an EU mutual assistance instrument by regulations made by the Secretary of State;

"international mutual assistance agreement" means an international agreement which—
- (a) relates to the provision of mutual assistance in connection with, or in the form of, the interception of communications,
- (b) requires the issue of a warrant, order or equivalent instrument in cases in which assistance is given, and
- (c) is designated as an international mutual assistance agreement by regulations made by the Secretary of State.

Prohibition against unlawful obtaining of communications data

11 Offence of unlawfully obtaining communications data

(1) A relevant person who, without lawful authority, knowingly or recklessly obtains communications data from a telecommunications operator or a postal operator is guilty of an offence.

(2) In this section "relevant person" means a person who holds an office, rank or position with a relevant public authority (within the meaning of Part 3).

(3) Subsection (1) does not apply to a relevant person who shows that the person acted in the reasonable belief that the person had lawful authority to obtain the communications data.

(4) A person guilty of an offence under this section is liable—
- (a) on summary conviction in England and Wales—
  - (i) to imprisonment for a term not exceeding 12 months (or 6 months, if the offence was committed before the commencement of section 154(1) of the Criminal Justice Act 2003), or
  - (ii) to a fine, or to both;
- (b) on summary conviction in Scotland—
  - (i) to imprisonment for a term not exceeding 12 months, or
  - (ii) to a fine not exceeding the statutory maximum, or to both;
- (c) on summary conviction in Northern Ireland—
  - (i) to imprisonment for a term not exceeding 6 months, or
  - (ii) to a fine not exceeding the statutory maximum, or to both;
- (d) on conviction on indictment, to imprisonment for a term not exceeding 2 years or to a fine, or to both.

Appendix

Abolition or restriction of powers to obtain communications data

12 Abolition or restriction of certain powers to obtain communications data

(1) Schedule 2 (which repeals certain information powers so far as they enable public authorities to secure the disclosure by a telecommunications operator or postal operator of communications data without the consent of the operator) has effect.

(2) Any general information power which—
  (a) would (apart from this subsection) enable a public authority to secure the disclosure by a telecommunications operator or postal operator of communications data without the consent of the operator, and
  (b) does not involve a court order or other judicial authorisation or warrant and is not a regulatory power or a relevant postal power, is to be read as not enabling the public authority to secure such a disclosure.

(3) A regulatory power or relevant postal power which enables a public authority to secure the disclosure by a telecommunications operator or postal operator of communications data without the consent of the operator may only be exercised by the public authority for that purpose if it is not possible for the authority to use a power under this Act to secure the disclosure of the data.

(4) The Secretary of State may by regulations modify any enactment in consequence of subsection (2).

(5) In this section "general information power" means—
  (a) in relation to disclosure by a telecommunications operator, any power to obtain information or documents (however expressed) which—
    (i) is conferred by or under an enactment other than this Act or the Regulation of Investigatory Powers Act 2000, and
    (ii) does not deal (whether alone or with other matters) specifically with telecommunications operators or any class of telecommunications operators, and
  (b) in relation to disclosure by a postal operator, any power to obtain information or documents (however expressed) which—
    (i) is conferred by or under an enactment other than this Act or the Regulation of Investigatory Powers Act 2000, and
    (ii) does not deal (whether alone or with other matters) specifically with postal operators or any class of postal operators.

(6) In this section—
  "power" includes part of a power,
  "regulatory power" means any power to obtain information or documents (however expressed) which—
    (a) is conferred by or under an enactment other than this Act or the Regulation of Investigatory Powers Act 2000, and
    (b) is exercisable in connection with the regulation of—
      (i) telecommunications operators, telecommunications services or telecommunication systems, or
      (ii) postal operators or postal services, "relevant postal power" means any power to obtain information or documents (however expressed) which—
        (a) is conferred by or under an enactment other than this Act or the Regulation of Investigatory Powers Act 2000, and

(b) is exercisable in connection with the conveyance or expected conveyance of any postal item into or out of the United Kingdom, and references to powers include duties (and references to enabling and exercising are to be read as including references to requiring and performing).

Restrictions on interference with equipment

13 Mandatory use of equipment interference warrants

(1) An intelligence service may not, for the purpose of obtaining communications, private information or equipment data, engage in conduct which could be authorised by an equipment interference warrant except under the authority of such a warrant if—
   (a) the intelligence service considers that the conduct would (unless done under lawful authority) constitute one or more offences under sections 1 to 3A of the Computer Misuse Act 1990 (computer misuse offences), and
   (b) there is a British Islands connection.
(2) For the purpose of this section, there is a British Islands connection if—
   (a) any of the conduct would take place in the British Islands (regardless of the location of the equipment which would, or may, be interfered with),
   (b) the intelligence service believes that any of the equipment which would, or may, be interfered with would, or may, be in the British Islands at some time while the interference is taking place, or (c) a purpose of the interference is to obtain—
      (i) communications sent by, or to, a person who is, or whom the intelligence service believes to be, for the time being in the British Islands,
      (ii) private information relating to an individual who is, or whom the intelligence service believes to be, for the time being in the British Islands, or
      (iii) equipment data which forms part of, or is connected with, communications or private information falling within subparagraph (i) or (ii).
(3) This section does not restrict the ability of the head of an intelligence service to apply for an equipment interference warrant in cases where—
   (a) the intelligence service does not consider that the conduct for which it is seeking authorisation would (unless done under lawful authority) constitute one or more offences under sections 1 to 3A of the Computer Misuse Act 1990, or
   (b) there is no British Islands connection.
(4) In this section—
   "communications", "private information" and "equipment data" have the same meaning as in Part 5 (see section 135);
   "equipment interference warrant" means—
   (a) a targeted equipment interference warrant under Part 5;
   (b) a bulk equipment interference warrant under Chapter 3 of Part 6.

14 Restriction on use of section 93 of the Police Act 1997

(1) A person may not, for the purpose of obtaining communications, private information or equipment data, make an application under section 93 of the Police Act 1997 for authorisation to engage in conduct which could be authorised by a targeted equipment interference warrant under Part 5 if the applicant considers that the conduct would (unless done under lawful authority) constitute one or more offences under sections 1 to 3A of the Computer Misuse Act 1990 (computer misuse offences).
(2) In this section, "communications", "private information" and "equipment data" have the same meaning as in Part 5 (see section 135).

Appendix

PART 2

LAWFUL INTERCEPTION OF COMMUNICATIONS

CHAPTER 1

INTERCEPTION AND EXAMINATION WITH A WARRANT

Warrants under this Chapter
15 Warrants that may be issued under this Chapter

(1) There are three kinds of warrant that may be issued under this Chapter—
   (a) targeted interception warrants (see subsection (2)),
   (b) targeted examination warrants (see subsection (3)), and
   (c) mutual assistance warrants (see subsection (4)).
(2) A targeted interception warrant is a warrant which authorises or requires the person to whom it is addressed to secure, by any conduct described in the warrant, any one or more of the following—
   (a) the interception, in the course of their transmission by means of a postal service or telecommunication system, of communications described in the warrant;
   (b) the obtaining of secondary data from communications transmitted by means of a postal service or telecommunication system and described in the warrant (see section 16);
   (c) the disclosure, in any manner described in the warrant, of anything obtained under the warrant to the person to whom the warrant is addressed or to any person acting on that person's behalf.
(3) A targeted examination warrant is a warrant which authorises the person to whom it is addressed to carry out the selection of relevant content for examination, in breach of the prohibition in section 152(4) (prohibition on seeking to identify communications of individuals in the British Islands).

   In this Part "relevant content", in relation to a targeted examination warrant, means any content of communications intercepted by an interception authorised or required by a bulk interception warrant under Chapter 1 of Part 6.
(4) A mutual assistance warrant is a warrant which authorises or requires the person to whom it is addressed to secure, by any conduct described in the warrant, any one or more of the following—
   (a) the making of a request, in accordance with an EU mutual assistance instrument or an international mutual assistance agreement, for the provision of any assistance of a kind described in the warrant in connection with, or in the form of, an interception of communications;
   (b) the provision to the competent authorities of a country or territory outside the United Kingdom, in accordance with such an instrument or agreement, of any assistance of a kind described in the warrant in connection with, or in the form of, an interception of communications;
   (c) the disclosure, in any manner described in the warrant, of anything obtained under the warrant to the person to whom the warrant is addressed or to any person acting on that person's behalf.
(5) A targeted interception warrant or mutual assistance warrant also authorises the following conduct (in addition to the conduct described in the warrant)—
   (a) any conduct which it is necessary to undertake in order to do what is expressly authorised or required by the warrant, including—
      (i) the interception of communications not described in the warrant, and
      (ii) conduct for obtaining secondary data from such communications;

(b) any conduct by any person which is conduct in pursuance of a requirement imposed by or on behalf of the person to whom the warrant is addressed to be provided with assistance in giving effect to the warrant;

(c) any conduct for obtaining related systems data from any postal operator or telecommunications operator.

(6) For the purposes of subsection (5)(c)—

"related systems data", in relation to a warrant, means systems data relating to a relevant communication or to the sender or recipient, or intended recipient, of a relevant communication (whether or not a person), and "relevant communication", in relation to a warrant, means—

    (a) any communication intercepted in accordance with the warrant in the course of its transmission by means of a postal service or telecommunication system, or

    (b) any communication from which secondary data is obtained under the warrant.

(7) For provision enabling the combination of targeted interception warrants with certain other warrants or authorisations (including targeted examination warrants), see Schedule 8.

16 Obtaining secondary data

(1) This section has effect for the purposes of this Part.

(2) In relation to a communication transmitted by means of a postal service, references to obtaining secondary data from the communication are references to obtaining such data in the course of the transmission of the communication (as to which, see section 4(7)).

(3) In relation to a communication transmitted by means of a telecommunication system, references to obtaining secondary data from the communication are references to obtaining such data—

    (a) while the communication is being transmitted, or

    (b) at any time when the communication is stored in or by the system (whether before or after its transmission).

(4) "Secondary data"—

    (a) in relation to a communication transmitted by means of a postal service, means any data falling within subsection (5);

    (b) in relation to a communication transmitted by means of a telecommunication system, means any data falling within subsection (5) or (6).

(5) The data falling within this subsection is systems data which is comprised in, included as part of, attached to or logically associated with the communication (whether by the sender or otherwise).

(6) The data falling within this subsection is identifying data which—

    (a) is comprised in, included as part of, attached to or logically associated with the communication (whether by the sender or otherwise),

    (b) is capable of being logically separated from the remainder of the communication, and

    (c) if it were so separated, would not reveal anything of what might reasonably be considered to be the meaning (if any) of the communication, disregarding any meaning arising from the fact of the communication or from any data relating to the transmission of the communication.

(7) For the meaning of "systems data" and "identifying data", see section 263.

17 Subject-matter of warrants

(1) A warrant under this Chapter may relate to—

    (a) a particular person or organisation, or

    (b) a single set of premises.

(2) In addition, a targeted interception warrant or targeted examination warrant may relate to—
   (a) a group of persons who share a common purpose or who carry on, or may carry on, a particular activity;
   (b) more than one person or organisation, or more than one set of premises, where the conduct authorised or required by the warrant is for the purposes of a single investigation or operation;
   (c) testing or training activities.
(3) In subsection (2)(c) "testing or training activities" means—
   (a) in relation to a targeted interception warrant—
      (i) the testing, maintenance or development of apparatus, systems or other capabilities relating to the interception of communications in the course of their transmission by means of a telecommunication system or to the obtaining of secondary data from communications transmitted by means of such a system, or
      (ii) the training of persons who carry out, or are likely to carry out, such interception or the obtaining of such data;
   (b) in relation to a targeted examination warrant—
      (i) the testing, maintenance or development of apparatus, systems or other capabilities relating to the selection of relevant content for examination, or
      (ii) the training of persons who carry out, or are likely to carry out, the selection of relevant content for examination.

Power to issue warrants

18 Persons who may apply for issue of a warrant

(1) Each of the following is an "intercepting authority" for the purposes of this Part—
   (a) a person who is the head of an intelligence service;
   (b) the Director General of the National Crime Agency;
   (c) the Commissioner of Police of the Metropolis;
   (d) the Chief Constable of the Police Service of Northern Ireland;
   (e) the chief constable of the Police Service of Scotland;
   (f) the Commissioners for Her Majesty's Revenue and Customs;
   (g) the Chief of Defence Intelligence;
   (h) a person who is the competent authority of a country or territory outside the United Kingdom for the purposes of an EU mutual assistance instrument or an international mutual assistance agreement.
(2) For the meaning of "head of an intelligence service", see section 263.
(3) An application for the issue of a warrant under this Chapter may only be made on behalf of an intercepting authority by a person holding office under the Crown.

19 Power of Secretary of State to issue warrants

(1) The Secretary of State may, on an application made by or on behalf of an intercepting authority mentioned in section 18(1)(a) to (g), issue a targeted interception warrant if—
   (a) the Secretary of State considers that the warrant is necessary on grounds falling within section 20,
   (b) the Secretary of State considers that the conduct authorised by the warrant is proportionate to what is sought to be achieved by that conduct,
   (c) the Secretary of State considers that satisfactory arrangements made for the purposes of sections 53 and 54 (safeguards relating to disclosure etc.) are in force in relation to the warrant, and

(d) except where the Secretary of State considers that there is an urgent need to issue the warrant, the decision to issue the warrant has been approved by a Judicial Commissioner. This is subject to subsection (4).
(2) The Secretary of State may, on an application made by or on behalf of the head of an intelligence service, issue a targeted examination warrant if—
   (a) the Secretary of State considers that the warrant is necessary on grounds falling within section 20,
   (b) the Secretary of State considers that the conduct authorised by the warrant is proportionate to what is sought to be achieved by that conduct,
   (c) the Secretary of State considers that the warrant is or may be necessary to authorise the selection of relevant content for examination in breach of the prohibition in section 152(4) (prohibition on seeking to identify communications of individuals in the British Islands), and
   (d) except where the Secretary of State considers that there is an urgent need to issue the warrant, the decision to issue the warrant has been approved by a Judicial Commissioner. This is subject to subsection (4).
(3) The Secretary of State may, on an application made by or on behalf of an intercepting authority, issue a mutual assistance warrant if—
   (a) the Secretary of State considers that the warrant is necessary on grounds falling within section 20,
   (b) the Secretary of State considers that the conduct authorised by the warrant is proportionate to what is sought to be achieved by that conduct,
   (c) the Secretary of State considers that satisfactory arrangements made for the purposes of sections 53 and 54 (safeguards relating to disclosure etc.) are in force in relation to the warrant, and
   (d) except where the Secretary of State considers that there is an urgent need to issue the warrant, the decision to issue the warrant has been approved by a Judicial Commissioner. This is subject to subsection (4).
(4) The Secretary of State may not issue a warrant under this section if—
   (a) the application is a relevant Scottish application (see section 22), and
   (b) in the case of an application for a targeted interception warrant or a targeted examination warrant, the Secretary of State considers that the warrant is necessary only for the purpose of preventing or detecting serious crime.
   For the power of the Scottish Ministers to issue warrants under this Chapter, see section 21.
(5) But subsection (4) does not prevent the Secretary of State from doing anything under this section for the purposes specified in section 2(2) of the European Communities Act 1972.

20 Grounds on which warrants may be issued by Secretary of State

(1) This section has effect for the purposes of this Part.
(2) A targeted interception warrant or targeted examination warrant is necessary on grounds falling within this section if it is necessary—
   (a) in the interests of national security,
   (b) for the purpose of preventing or detecting serious crime, or
   (c) in the interests of the economic well-being of the United Kingdom so far as those interests are also relevant to the interests of national security (but see subsection (4)).
(3) A mutual assistance warrant is necessary on grounds falling within this section if—
   (a) it is necessary for the purpose of giving effect to the provisions of an EU mutual assistance instrument or an international mutual assistance agreement, and

(b) the circumstances appear to the Secretary of State to be equivalent to those in which the Secretary of State would issue a warrant by virtue of subsection (2)(b).

(4) A warrant may be considered necessary as mentioned in subsection (2)(c) only if the information which it is considered necessary to obtain is information relating to the acts or intentions of persons outside the British Islands.

(5) A warrant may not be considered necessary on grounds falling within this section if it is considered necessary only for the purpose of gathering evidence for use in any legal proceedings.

(6) The fact that the information which would be obtained under a warrant relates to the activities in the British Islands of a trade union is not, of itself, sufficient to establish that the warrant is necessary on grounds falling within this section.

21 Power of Scottish Ministers to issue warrants

(1) The Scottish Ministers may, on an application made by or on behalf of an intercepting authority mentioned in section 18(1)(a) to (g), issue a targeted interception warrant if—
   (a) the application is a relevant Scottish application (see section 22),
   (b) the Scottish Ministers consider that the warrant is necessary on grounds falling within subsection (4),
   (c) the Scottish Ministers consider that the conduct authorised by the warrant is proportionate to what is sought to be achieved by that conduct,
   (d) the Scottish Ministers consider that satisfactory arrangements made for the purposes of sections 53 and 54 (safeguards relating to disclosure etc.) are in force in relation to the warrant, and
   (e) except where the Scottish Ministers consider that there is an urgent need to issue the warrant, the decision to issue the warrant has been approved by a Judicial Commissioner.

(2) The Scottish Ministers may, on an application made by or on behalf of the head of an intelligence service, issue a targeted examination warrant if—
   (a) the application is a relevant Scottish application,
   (b) the Scottish Ministers consider that the warrant is necessary on grounds falling within subsection (4),
   (c) the Scottish Ministers consider that the conduct authorised by the warrant is proportionate to what is sought to be achieved by that conduct,
   (d) the Scottish Ministers consider that the warrant is or may be necessary to authorise the selection of relevant content for examination in breach of the prohibition in section 152(4) (prohibition on seeking to identify communications of individuals in the British Islands), and
   (e) except where the Scottish Ministers consider that there is an urgent need to issue the warrant, the decision to issue the warrant has been approved by a Judicial Commissioner.

(3) The Scottish Ministers may, on an application made by or on behalf of an intercepting authority, issue a mutual assistance warrant if—
   (a) the application is a relevant Scottish application,
   (b) the Scottish Ministers consider that the warrant is necessary on grounds falling within subsection (4),
   (c) the Scottish Ministers consider that the conduct authorised by the warrant is proportionate to what is sought to be achieved by that conduct,
   (d) the Scottish Ministers consider that satisfactory arrangements made for the purposes of sections 53 and 54 (safeguards relating to disclosure etc.) are in force in relation to the warrant, and
   (e) except where the Scottish Ministers consider that there is an urgent need to issue the warrant, the decision to issue the warrant has been approved by a Judicial Commissioner.

(4) A warrant is necessary on grounds falling within this subsection if—
  (a) in the case of a targeted interception warrant or targeted examination warrant, it is necessary for the purposes of preventing or detecting serious crime, and
  (b) in the case of a mutual assistance warrant—
    (i) it is necessary for the purpose of giving effect to the provisions of an EU mutual assistance instrument or an international mutual assistance agreement, and
    (ii) the circumstances appear to the Scottish Ministers to be equivalent to those in which the Scottish Ministers would issue a warrant by virtue of paragraph (a).
(5) A warrant may not be considered necessary on grounds falling within subsection (4) if it is considered necessary only for the purpose of gathering evidence for use in any legal proceedings.
(6) The fact that the information which would be obtained under a warrant relates to the activities in the British Islands of a trade union is not, of itself, sufficient to establish that the warrant is necessary on grounds falling within subsection (4).

22 "Relevant Scottish applications"

(1) An application for the issue of a warrant under this Chapter is a "relevant Scottish application" for the purposes of this Chapter if any of conditions A to C is met. In this section "the applicant" means the person by whom, or on whose behalf, the application is made.
(2) Condition A is that—
  (a) the application is for the issue of a targeted interception warrant or a targeted examination warrant, and
  (b) the warrant, if issued, would relate to—
    (i) a person who is in Scotland, or is reasonably believed by the applicant to be in Scotland, at the time of the issue of the warrant, or
    (ii) premises which are in Scotland, or are reasonably believed by the applicant to be in Scotland, at that time.
(3) Condition B is that—
  (a) the application is for the issue of a mutual assistance warrant which, if issued, would authorise or require—
    (i) the making of a request falling within section 15(4)(a), or (ii) the making of such a request and disclosure falling within section 15(4)(c), and
  (b) the application—
    (i) is made by, or on behalf of, the chief constable of the Police Service of Scotland, or
    (ii) is made by, or on behalf of, the Commissioners for Her Majesty's Revenue and Customs or the Director General of the National Crime Agency for the purpose of preventing or detecting serious crime in Scotland.
(4) Condition C is that—
  (a) the application is for the issue of a mutual assistance warrant which, if issued, would authorise or require—
    (i) the provision of assistance falling within section 15(4)(b), or
    (ii) the provision of such assistance and disclosure falling within section 15(4)(c), and
  (b) the warrant, if issued, would relate to—
    (i) a person who is in Scotland, or is reasonably believed by the applicant to be in Scotland, at the time of the issue of the warrant, or
    (ii) premises which are in Scotland, or are reasonably believed by the applicant to be in Scotland, at that time.

Approval of warrants by Judicial Commissioners

23 Approval of warrants by Judicial Commissioners

(1) In deciding whether to approve a person's decision to issue a warrant under this Chapter, a Judicial Commissioner must review the person's conclusions as to the following matters—
 (a) whether the warrant is necessary on relevant grounds (see subsection (3)), and
 (b) whether the conduct that would be authorised by the warrant is proportionate to what is sought to be achieved by that conduct.

(2) In doing so, the Judicial Commissioner must—
 (a) apply the same principles as would be applied by a court on an application for judicial review, and
 (b) consider the matters referred to in subsection (1) with a sufficient degree of care as to ensure that the Judicial Commissioner complies with the duties imposed by section 2 (general duties in relation to privacy).

(3) In subsection (1)(a) "relevant grounds" means—
 (a) in the case of a decision of the Secretary of State to issue a warrant, grounds falling within section 20;
 (b) in the case of a decision of the Scottish Ministers to issue a warrant, grounds falling within section 21(4).

(4) Where a Judicial Commissioner refuses to approve a person's decision to issue a warrant under this Chapter, the Judicial Commissioner must give the person written reasons for the refusal.

(5) Where a Judicial Commissioner, other than the Investigatory Powers Commissioner, refuses to approve a person's decision to issue a warrant under this Chapter, the person may ask the Investigatory Powers Commissioner to decide whether to approve the decision to issue the warrant.

24 Approval of warrants issued in urgent cases

(1) This section applies where—
 (a) a warrant under this Chapter is issued without the approval of a Judicial Commissioner, and
 (b) the person who decided to issue the warrant considered that there was an urgent need to issue it.

(2) The person who decided to issue the warrant must inform a Judicial Commissioner that it has been issued.

(3) The Judicial Commissioner must, before the end of the relevant period—
 (a) decide whether to approve the decision to issue the warrant, and (b) notify the person of the Judicial Commissioner's decision. "The relevant period" means the period ending with the third working day after the day on which the warrant was issued.

(4) If a Judicial Commissioner refuses to approve the decision to issue a warrant, the warrant—
 (a) ceases to have effect (unless already cancelled), and
 (b) may not be renewed, and section 23(5) does not apply in relation to the refusal to approve the decision.

(5) Section 25 contains further provision about what happens if a Judicial Commissioner refuses to approve the decision to issue a warrant.

25 Failure to approve warrant issued in urgent case

(1) This section applies where under section 24(3) a Judicial Commissioner refuses to approve the decision to issue a warrant.

(2) The person to whom the warrant was addressed must, so far as is reasonably practicable, secure that anything in the process of being done under the warrant stops as soon as possible.

(3) The Judicial Commissioner may—
  (a) direct that any of the material obtained under the warrant is destroyed;
  (b) impose conditions as to the use or retention of any of that material;
  (c) in the case of a targeted examination warrant, impose conditions as to the use of any relevant content selected for examination under the warrant.
(4) The Judicial Commissioner—
  (a) may require an affected party to make representations about how the Judicial Commissioner should exercise any function under subsection (3), and
  (b) must have regard to any such representations made by an affected party (whether or not as a result of a requirement imposed under paragraph (a)).
(5) Each of the following is an "affected party" for the purposes of subsection (4)—
  (a) the person who decided to issue the warrant;
  (b) the person to whom the warrant was addressed.
(6) The person who decided to issue the warrant may ask the Investigatory Powers Commissioner to review a decision made by any other Judicial Commissioner under subsection (3).
(7) On a review under subsection (6), the Investigatory Powers Commissioner may—
  (a) confirm the Judicial Commissioner's decision, or
  (b) make a fresh determination.
(8) Nothing in this section or section 24 affects the lawfulness of—
  (a) anything done under the warrant before it ceases to have effect;
  (b) if anything is in the process of being done under the warrant when it ceases to have effect—
    (i) anything done before that thing could be stopped, or
    (ii) anything done which it is not reasonably practicable to stop.

Additional safeguards

26 Members of Parliament etc.

(1) This section applies where—
  (a) an application is made to the Secretary of State for the issue of a targeted interception warrant or a targeted examination warrant, and (b) the purpose of the warrant is—
    (i) in the case of a targeted interception warrant, to authorise or require the interception of communications sent by, or intended for, a person who is a member of a relevant legislature, or
    (ii) in the case of a targeted examination warrant, to authorise the selection for examination of the content of such communications.
(2) The Secretary of State may not issue the warrant without the approval of the Prime Minister.
(3) In this section "member of a relevant legislature" means—
  (a) a member of either House of Parliament;
  (b) a member of the Scottish Parliament;
  (c) a member of the National Assembly for Wales;
  (d) a member of the Northern Ireland Assembly;
  (e) a member of the European Parliament elected for the United Kingdom.

27 Items subject to legal privilege

(1) Subsections (2) to (5) apply if—
  (a) an application is made by or on behalf of an intercepting authority for a warrant under this Chapter, and

(b) the purpose, or one of the purposes, of the warrant is—
  (i) in the case of a targeted interception warrant or mutual assistance warrant, to authorise or require the interception of items subject to legal privilege, or
  (ii) in the case of a targeted examination warrant, to authorise the selection of such items for examination.
(2) The application must contain a statement that the purpose, or one of the purposes, of the warrant is to authorise or require the interception, or (in the case of a targeted examination warrant) the selection for examination, of items subject to legal privilege.
(3) In deciding whether to issue the warrant, the person to whom the application is made must have regard to the public interest in the confidentiality of items subject to legal privilege.
(4) The person to whom the application is made may issue the warrant only if the person considers—
  (a) that there are exceptional and compelling circumstances that make it necessary to authorise or require the interception, or (in the case of a targeted examination warrant) the selection for examination, of items subject to legal privilege, and
  (b) that the arrangements made for the purposes of section 53 or (as the case may be) section 150 (safeguards relating to retention and disclosure of material) include specific arrangements for the handling, retention, use and destruction of such items.
(5) But the warrant may not be issued if it is considered necessary only as mentioned in section 20(2)(c).
(6) For the purposes of subsection (4)(a), there cannot be exceptional and compelling circumstances that make it necessary to authorise or require the interception, or the selection for examination, of items subject to legal privilege unless—
  (a) the public interest in obtaining the information that would be obtained by the warrant outweighs the public interest in the confidentiality of items subject to legal privilege,
  (b) there are no other means by which the information may reasonably be obtained, and
  (c) in the case of a warrant considered necessary as mentioned in section 20(2)(b) or (3) or (as the case may be) 21(4), obtaining the information is necessary for the purpose of preventing death or significant injury.
(7) Subsections (8) and (9) apply if—
  (a) an application is made by or on behalf of an intercepting authority for a warrant under this Chapter,
  (b) the intercepting authority considers that the relevant communications are likely to include items subject to legal privilege, and
  (c) subsections (2) to (5) do not apply.
(8) The application must contain—
  (a) a statement that the intercepting authority considers that the relevant communications are likely to include items subject to legal privilege, and
  (b) an assessment of how likely it is that the relevant communications will include such items.
(9) The person to whom the application is made may issue the warrant only if the person considers that the arrangements made for the purposes of section 53 or (as the case may be) section 150 include specific arrangements for the handling, retention, use and destruction of items subject to legal privilege.
(10) In this section "relevant communications" means—
  (a) in relation to a targeted interception warrant or mutual assistance warrant, any communications the interception of which is authorised or required by the warrant;
  (b) in relation to a targeted examination warrant, any communications the content of which the warrant authorises to be selected for examination.

(11) Subsections (12) and (13) apply if—
- (a) an application is made by or on behalf of an intercepting authority for a warrant under this Chapter,
- (b) the purpose, or one of the purposes, of the warrant is—
  - (i) in the case of a targeted interception warrant or mutual assistance warrant, to authorise or require the interception of communications that, if they were not made with the intention of furthering a criminal purpose, would be items subject to legal privilege, or
  - (ii) in the case of a targeted examination warrant, to authorise the selection of such communications for examination, and
- (c) the intercepting authority considers that the communications ("the targeted communications") are likely to be communications made with the intention of furthering a criminal purpose.

(12) The application must—
- (a) contain a statement that the purpose, or one of the purposes, of the warrant is to authorise or require the interception, or (in the case of a targeted examination warrant) the selection for examination, of communications that, if they were not made with the intention of furthering a criminal purpose, would be items subject to legal privilege, and
- (b) set out the reasons for believing that the targeted communications are likely to be communications made with the intention of furthering a criminal purpose.

(13) The person to whom the application is made may issue the warrant only if the person considers that the targeted communications are likely to be communications made with the intention of furthering a criminal purpose.

28 Confidential journalistic material

(1) This section applies if—
- (a) an application is made by or on behalf of an intercepting authority for a warrant under this Chapter, and
- (b) the purpose, or one of the purposes, of the warrant is—
  - (i) in the case of a targeted interception warrant or mutual assistance warrant, to authorise or require the interception of communications which the intercepting authority believes will be communications containing confidential journalistic material, or
  - (ii) in the case of a targeted examination warrant, to authorise the selection for examination of journalistic material which the intercepting authority believes is confidential journalistic material.

(2) The application must contain a statement that the purpose, or one of the purposes, of the warrant is—
- (a) in the case of a targeted interception warrant or mutual assistance warrant, to authorise or require the interception of communications which the intercepting authority believes will be communications containing confidential journalistic material, or
- (b) in the case of a targeted examination warrant, to authorise the selection for examination of journalistic material which the intercepting authority believes is confidential journalistic material.

(3) The person to whom the application is made may issue the warrant only if the person considers that the arrangements made for the purposes of section 53 or (as the case may be) section 150 (safeguards relating to retention and disclosure of material) include specific arrangements for the handling, retention, use and destruction of communications containing confidential journalistic material.

(4) For the meaning of "journalistic material" and "confidential journalistic material", see section 264.

Appendix

29 Sources of journalistic information

(1) This section applies if—
   (a) an application is made by or on behalf of an intercepting authority for a warrant under this Chapter, and
   (b) the purpose, or one of the purposes, of the warrant is to identify or confirm a source of journalistic information.
   (For the meaning of "source of journalistic information", see section 263(1).)
(2) The application must contain a statement that the purpose, or one of the purposes, of the warrant is to identify or confirm a source of journalistic information.
(3) The person to whom the application is made may issue the warrant only if the person considers that the arrangements made for the purposes of section 53 or (as the case may be) section 150 (safeguards relating to retention and disclosure of material) include specific arrangements for the handling, retention, use and destruction of communications that identify sources of journalistic information.

Further provision about warrants

30 Decisions to issue warrants to be taken personally by Ministers

(1) The decision to issue a warrant under this Chapter must be taken personally by—
   (a) the Secretary of State, or
   (b) in the case of a warrant to be issued by the Scottish Ministers, a member of the Scottish Government.
(2) Before a warrant under this Chapter is issued, it must be signed by the person who has taken the decision to issue it.
(3) Subsections (1) and (2) are subject to—
   (a) subsection (4), and
   (b) section 40 (special rules for certain mutual assistance warrants).
(4) If it is not reasonably practicable for a warrant to be signed by the person who has taken the decision to issue it, the warrant may be signed by a senior official designated by the Secretary of State or (as the case may be) the Scottish Ministers for that purpose.
(5) In such a case, the warrant must contain a statement that—
   (a) it is not reasonably practicable for the warrant to be signed by the person who took the decision to issue it, and
   (b) the Secretary of State or (as the case may be) a member of the Scottish Government has personally and expressly authorised the issue of the warrant.
(6) In this section "senior official" means—
   (a) in the case of a warrant to be issued by the Secretary of State, a member of the Senior Civil Service or a member of the Senior Management Structure of Her Majesty's Diplomatic Service;
   (b) in the case of a warrant to be issued by the Scottish Ministers, a member of the staff of the Scottish Administration who is a member of the Senior Civil Service.

31 Requirements that must be met by warrants

(1) A warrant under this Chapter must contain a provision stating whether it is a targeted interception warrant, a targeted examination warrant or a mutual assistance warrant.
(2) A warrant issued under this Chapter must be addressed to the person by whom, or on whose behalf, the application for the warrant was made.

(3) A warrant that relates to a particular person or organisation, or to a single set of premises, must name or describe that person or organisation or those premises.
(4) A warrant that relates to a group of persons who share a common purpose or who carry on (or may carry on) a particular activity must—
  (a) describe that purpose or activity, and
  (b) name or describe as many of those persons as it is reasonably practicable to name or describe.
(5) A warrant that relates to more than one person or organisation, or more than one set of premises, where the conduct authorised or required by the warrant is for the purposes of a single investigation or operation, must—
  (a) describe the investigation or operation, and
  (b) name or describe as many of those persons or organisations, or as many of those sets of premises, as it is reasonably practicable to name or describe.
(6) A warrant that relates to any testing or training activities must—
  (a) describe those activities, and
  (b) name or describe as many of the persons within subsection (7) as it is reasonably practicable to name or describe.
  "Testing or training activities" has the meaning given by section 17(3).
(7) A person is within this subsection if—
  (a) in the case of a targeted interception warrant—
    (i) communications from, or intended for, the person will or may be intercepted by an interception authorised or required by the warrant, or
    (ii) secondary data will or may be obtained under the warrant from communications from, or intended for, the person;
  (b) in the case of a targeted examination warrant, the content of communications from, or intended for, the person may be selected for examination under the warrant.
(8) Where—
  (a) a targeted interception warrant or mutual assistance warrant authorises or requires the interception of communications described in the warrant, or the obtaining of secondary data from such communications, or
  (b) a targeted examination warrant authorises the selection of the content of communications for examination, the warrant must specify the addresses, numbers, apparatus, or other factors, or combination of factors, that are to be used for identifying the communications.
(9) Any factor, or combination of factors, specified in accordance with subsection (8) must be one that identifies communications which are likely to be or to include—
  (a) communications from, or intended for, any person or organisation named or described in the warrant, or
  (b) communications originating on, or intended for transmission to, any premises named or described in the warrant.
(10) In this section any reference to communications from, or intended for, a person or organisation includes communications from, or intended for, anything owned, controlled or operated by that person or organisation.

32 Duration of warrants

(1) A warrant under this Chapter ceases to have effect at the end of the relevant period (see subsection (2)), unless—
  (a) it is renewed before the end of that period (see section 33), or

(b) it is cancelled or otherwise ceases to have effect before the end of that period (see sections 24 and 39).
(2) In this section "the relevant period"—
  (a) in the case of an urgent warrant which has not been renewed, means the period ending with the fifth working day after the day on which the warrant was issued;
  (b) in any other case, means the period of 6 months beginning with—
    (i) the day on which the warrant was issued, or
    (ii) in the case of a warrant that has been renewed, the day after the day at the end of which the warrant would have ceased to have effect if it had not been renewed.
(3) For the purposes of subsection (2)(a) a warrant is an "urgent warrant" if—
  (a) the warrant was issued without the approval of a Judicial Commissioner, and
  (b) the person who decided to issue the warrant considered that there was an urgent need to issue it.

33 Renewal of warrants

(1) If the renewal conditions are met, a warrant issued under this Chapter may be renewed, at any time during the renewal period, by an instrument issued by the appropriate person (see subsection (3)).
(2) The renewal conditions are—
  (a) that the appropriate person considers that the warrant continues to be necessary on any relevant grounds (see subsection (4)),
  (b) that the appropriate person considers that the conduct that would be authorised by the renewed warrant continues to be proportionate to what is sought to be achieved by that conduct,
  (c) that, in the case of a targeted examination warrant, the appropriate person considers that the warrant continues to be necessary to authorise the selection of relevant content for examination in breach of the prohibition in section 152(4), and
  (d) that the decision to renew the warrant has been approved by a Judicial Commissioner.
(3) The appropriate person is—
  (a) in the case of a warrant issued by the Secretary of State, the Secretary of State;
  (b) in the case of a warrant issued by the Scottish Ministers, a member of the Scottish Government.
(4) "Relevant grounds" means—
  (a) in the case of a warrant issued by the Secretary of State, grounds falling within section 20;
  (b) in the case of a warrant issued by the Scottish Ministers, grounds falling within section 21(4).
(5) "The renewal period" means—
  (a) in the case of an urgent warrant which has not been renewed, the relevant period;
  (b) in any other case, the period of 30 days ending with the day at the end of which the warrant would otherwise cease to have effect.
(6) The decision to renew a warrant must be taken personally by the appropriate person, and the instrument renewing the warrant must be signed by that person.
(7) Section 23 (approval of warrants by Judicial Commissioners) applies in relation to a decision to renew a warrant as it applies in relation to a decision to issue a warrant (and accordingly any reference in that section to the person who decided to issue the warrant is to be read as a reference to the person who decided to renew it).
(8) Sections 26 to 29 (additional safeguards) apply in relation to a decision to renew a warrant as they apply in relation to a decision to issue a warrant.

(9) In this section—
"the relevant period" has the same meaning as in section 32;
"urgent warrant" is to be read in accordance with subsection (3) of that section.
(10) This section is subject to section 40 (special rules for certain mutual assistance warrants).

34 Modification of warrants

(1) The provisions of a warrant issued under this Chapter may be modified at any time by an instrument issued by the person making the modification.
(2) The only modifications that may be made under this section are—
   (a) adding, varying or removing the name or description of a person, organisation or set of premises to which the warrant relates, and
   (b) adding, varying or removing any factor specified in the warrant in accordance with section 31(8).
(3) But a warrant may not be modified as mentioned in subsection (2)(a) if it relates only to a particular person or organisation, or to a single set of premises, as mentioned in section 17(1).
(4) The decision to modify the provisions of a warrant must be taken personally by the person making the modification, and the instrument making the modification must be signed by that person.
This is subject to section 36(8).
(5) In this Chapter—
   (a) a modification adding or varying a name or description as mentioned in paragraph (a) of subsection (2) is referred to as a "major modification", and
   (b) any other modification within that subsection is referred to as a "minor modification".
(6) Nothing in this section applies in relation to modifying the provisions of a warrant in a way which does not affect the conduct authorised or required by it.
(7) Sections 35 to 38 contain further provision about making modifications under this section.

35 Persons who may make modifications

(1) A major modification may be made by—
   (a) the Secretary of State, in the case of a warrant issued by the Secretary of State,
   (b) a member of the Scottish Government, in the case of a warrant issued by the Scottish Ministers, or
   (c) a senior official acting on behalf of the Secretary of State or (as the case may be) the Scottish Ministers.
(2) A minor modification may be made by—
   (a) the Secretary of State, in the case of a warrant issued by the Secretary of State,
   (b) a member of the Scottish Government, in the case of a warrant issued by the Scottish Ministers,
   (c) a senior official acting on behalf of the Secretary of State or (as the case may be) the Scottish Ministers,
   (d) the person to whom the warrant is addressed, or (e) a person who holds a senior position in the same public authority as the person mentioned in paragraph (d).
(3) But if a person within subsection (2)(d) or (e) considers that there is an urgent need to make a major modification, that person (as well as a person within subsection (1)) may do so.
Section 38 contains provision about the approval of major modifications made in urgent cases.
(4) Subsections (1) and (3) are subject to section 36(5) and (6) (special rules where any of sections 26 to 29 applies in relation to the making of a major modification).

(5) Subsections (2)(d) and (e) and (3) do not apply in the case of a mutual assistance warrant addressed to a person falling within section 18(1)(h) (competent authorities of overseas countries or territories).
(6) For the purposes of subsection (2)(e) a person holds a senior position in a public authority if—
   (a) in the case of any of the intelligence services—
      (i) the person is a member of the Senior Civil Service or a member of the Senior Management Structure of Her Majesty's Diplomatic Service, or
      (ii) the person holds a position in the intelligence service of equivalent seniority to such a person;
   (b) in the case of the National Crime Agency, the person is a National Crime Agency officer of grade 2 or above;
   (c) in the case of the metropolitan police force, the Police Service of Northern Ireland or the Police Service of Scotland, a person is of or above the rank of superintendent;
   (d) in the case of Her Majesty's Revenue and Customs, the person is a member of the Senior Civil Service;
   (e) in the case of the Ministry of Defence—
      (i) the person is a member of the Senior Civil Service, or
      (ii) the person is of or above the rank of brigadier, commodore or air commodore.
(7) In this section "senior official" means—
   (a) in the case of a warrant issued by the Secretary of State, a member of the Senior Civil Service or a member of the Senior Management Structure of Her Majesty's Diplomatic Service;
   (b) in the case of a warrant issued by the Scottish Ministers, a member of the staff of the Scottish Administration who is a member of the Senior Civil Service.

36 Further provision about modifications

(1) A person may make a modification within subsection (2) only if the person considers—
   (a) that the modification is necessary on any relevant grounds (see subsection (3)), and
   (b) that the conduct authorised by the modification is proportionate to what is sought to be achieved by that conduct.
(2) The modifications within this subsection are—
   (a) a major modification adding the name or description of a person, organisation or set of premises to which the warrant relates, and
   (b) a minor modification adding any factor specified in the warrant in accordance with section 31(8).
(3) In subsection (1)(a) "relevant grounds" means—
   (a) in the case of a warrant issued by the Secretary of State, grounds falling within section 20;
   (b) in the case of a warrant issued by the Scottish Ministers, grounds falling within section 21(4); and for the purposes of subsection (1) any reference to the Secretary of State in section 20(3)(b) or the Scottish Ministers in section 21(4)(b) is to be read as a reference to the person making the modification.
(4) Sections 26 to 29 (additional safeguards) apply in relation to the making of a major modification within subsection (2)(a) above as they apply in relation to the issuing of a warrant.
(5) Where section 26 applies in relation to the making of a major modification—
   (a) the modification must be made by the Secretary of State, and (b) the modification has effect only if the decision to make the modification has been approved by a Judicial Commissioner.

(6) Where section 27, 28 or 29 applies in relation to the making of a major modification—
   (a) the modification must be made by—
      (i) the Secretary of State or (in the case of a warrant issued by the Scottish Ministers) a member of the Scottish Government, or
      (ii) if a senior official acting on behalf of a person within subparagraph (i) considers that there is an urgent need to make the modification, that senior official, and
   (b) except where the person making the modification considers that there is an urgent need to make it, the modification has effect only if the decision to make the modification has been approved by a Judicial Commissioner.
(7) In a case where any of sections 26 to 29 applies in relation to the making of a major modification, section 23 (approval of warrants by Judicial Commissioners) applies in relation to the decision to make the modification as it applies in relation to a decision to issue a warrant, but as if—
   (a) the references in subsection (1)(a) and (b) of that section to the warrant were references to the modification,
   (b) any reference to the person who decided to issue the warrant were a reference to the person who decided to make the modification, and
   (c) subsection (3) of this section applied for the purposes of subsection (1) of that section as it applies for the purposes of subsection (1) of this section.
Section 38 contains provision about the approval of major modifications made in urgent cases.
(8) If, in a case where any of sections 26 to 29 applies in relation to the making of a major modification, it is not reasonably practicable for the instrument making the modification to be signed by the Secretary of State or (as the case may be) a member of the Scottish Government in accordance with section 34(4), the instrument may be signed by a senior official designated by the Secretary of State or (as the case may be) the Scottish Ministers for that purpose.
(9) In such a case, the instrument making the modification must contain a statement that—
   (a) it is not reasonably practicable for the instrument to be signed by the person who took the decision to make the modification, and
   (b) the Secretary of State or (as the case may be) a member of the Scottish Government has personally and expressly authorised the making of the modification.
(10) If at any time a person mentioned in section 35(2) considers that any factor specified in a warrant in accordance with section 31(8) is no longer relevant for identifying communications which, in the case of that warrant, are likely to be, or to include, communications falling within section 31(9)(a) or (b), the person must modify the warrant by removing that factor.
(11) In this section "senior official" has the same meaning as in section 35.

37 Notification of major modifications

(1) As soon as is reasonably practicable after a person makes a major modification of a warrant under this Chapter, a Judicial Commissioner must be notified of the modification and the reasons for making it.
(2) But subsection (1) does not apply where—
   (a) the modification is made by virtue of section 35(3), or
   (b) any of sections 26 to 29 applies in relation to the making of the modification.
(3) Where a major modification is made by a senior official in accordance with section 35(1) or section 36(6)(a)(ii), the Secretary of State or (in the case of a warrant issued by the Scottish Ministers) a member of the Scottish Government must be notified personally of the modification and the reasons for making it.
(4) In this section "senior official" has the same meaning as in section 35.

38 Approval of major modifications made in urgent cases

(1) This section applies where a person makes a major modification of a warrant under this Chapter by virtue of section 35(3).
(2) This section also applies where—
   (a) section 27, 28 or 29 applies in relation to the making of a major modification of a warrant under this Chapter,
   (b) the person making the modification does so without the approval of a Judicial Commissioner, and
   (c) the person considered that there was an urgent need to make the modification.
(3) The person who made the modification must inform the appropriate person that it has been made.
(4) In this section—
   "the appropriate person" is—
   (a) in a case falling within subsection (1), a designated senior official, and
   (b) in a case falling within subsection (2), a Judicial Commissioner, "designated senior official" means a senior official who has been designated by the Secretary of State or (in the case of warrants issued by the Scottish Ministers) the Scottish Ministers for the purposes of this section, and "senior official" has the same meaning as in section 35.
(5) The appropriate person must, before the end of the relevant period—
   (a) decide whether to approve the decision to make the modification, and
   (b) notify the person of the appropriate person's decision.
   "The relevant period" means the period ending with the third working day after the day on which the modification was made.
(6) As soon as is reasonably practicable after a designated senior official makes a decision under subsection (5)—
   (a) a Judicial Commissioner must be notified of—
      (i) the decision, and
      (ii) if the senior official has decided to approve the decision to make the modification, the modification in question, and
   (b) the Secretary of State or (in the case of a warrant issued by the Scottish Ministers) a member of the Scottish Government must be notified personally of the matters mentioned in paragraph (a)(i) and (ii).
(7) If the appropriate person refuses to approve the decision to make the modification—
   (a) the warrant (unless it no longer has effect) has effect as if the modification had not been made, and
   (b) the person to whom the warrant is addressed must, so far as is reasonably practicable, secure that anything in the process of being done under the warrant by virtue of that modification stops as soon as possible, and, in a case falling within subsection (2) above, section 23(5) does not apply in relation to the refusal to approve the decision.
(8) Nothing in this section affects the lawfulness of—
   (a) anything done under the warrant by virtue of the modification before the modification ceases to have effect;
   (b) if anything is in the process of being done under the warrant by virtue of the modification when the modification ceases to have effect—
      (i) anything done before that thing could be stopped, or
      (ii) anything done which it is not reasonably practicable to stop.

39 Cancellation of warrants

(1) Any of the appropriate persons may cancel a warrant issued under this Chapter at any time.
(2) If any of the appropriate persons considers that—
   (a) a warrant issued under this Chapter is no longer necessary on any relevant grounds, or
   (b) the conduct authorised by the warrant is no longer proportionate to what is sought to be achieved by that conduct, the person must cancel the warrant.
(3) In subsection (2)(a) "relevant grounds" means—
   (a) in the case of a warrant issued by the Secretary of State, grounds falling within section 20;
   (b) in the case of a warrant issued by the Scottish Ministers, grounds falling within section 21(4).
(4) For the purpose of this section "the appropriate persons" are—
   (a) in the case of a warrant issued by the Secretary of State, the Secretary of State or a senior official acting on behalf of the Secretary of State;
   (b) in the case of a warrant issued by the Scottish Ministers, a member of the Scottish Government or a senior official acting on behalf of the Scottish Ministers.
(5) Where a warrant is cancelled under this section, the person to whom the warrant was addressed must, so far as is reasonably practicable, secure that anything in the process of being done under the warrant stops as soon as possible.
(6) A warrant that has been cancelled under this section may not be renewed.
(7) In this section "senior official" means—
   (a) in the case of a warrant issued by the Secretary of State, a member of the Senior Civil Service or a member of the Senior Management Structure of Her Majesty's Diplomatic Service;
   (b) in the case of a warrant issued by the Scottish Ministers, a member of the staff of the Scottish Administration who is a member of the Senior Civil Service.
(8) See also section 40 (which imposes a duty to cancel mutual assistance warrants in certain circumstances).

40 Special rules for certain mutual assistance warrants

(1) For the purposes of this section a warrant is a "relevant mutual assistance warrant" if—
   (a) the warrant is for the purposes of a request for assistance made under an EU mutual assistance instrument or an international mutual assistance agreement by the competent authorities of a country or territory outside the United Kingdom, and
   (b) either—
      (i) it appears that the interception subject is outside the United Kingdom, or
      (ii) the interception authorised or required by the warrant is to take place in relation only to premises outside the United Kingdom.
(2) The decision to issue a relevant mutual assistance warrant may be taken by a senior official designated by the Secretary of State for that purpose.
(3) In such a case, the warrant must contain—
   (a) a statement that the warrant is issued for the purposes of a request for assistance made under an EU mutual assistance instrument or an international mutual assistance agreement (as the case may be) by the competent authorities of a country or territory outside the United Kingdom, and
   (b) whichever of the following statements is applicable—
      (i) a statement that the interception subject appears to be outside the United Kingdom;
      (ii) a statement that the interception authorised or required by the warrant is to take place in relation only to premises outside the United Kingdom.

(4) A relevant mutual assistance warrant may be renewed by a senior official designated by the Secretary of State for that purpose; and references in section 33 to the appropriate person include, in the case of such a warrant, references to that senior official.
(5) Where a senior official renews a relevant mutual assistance warrant in accordance with subsection (4), the instrument renewing the warrant must contain—
   (a) a statement that the renewal is for the purposes of a request for assistance made under an EU mutual assistance instrument or an international mutual assistance agreement (as the case may be) by the competent authorities of a country or territory outside the United Kingdom, and
   (b) whichever of the following statements is applicable—
      (i) a statement that the interception subject appears to be outside the United Kingdom;
      (ii) a statement that the interception authorised or required by the warrant is to take place in relation only to premises outside the United Kingdom.
(6) Subsection (7) applies in a case where—
   (a) a relevant mutual assistance warrant—
      (i) was issued containing the statement set out in subsection (3)(b)(i), or
      (ii) has been renewed by an instrument containing the statement set out in subsection (5)(b)(i), and
   (b) the last renewal (if any) of the warrant was a renewal by a senior official in accordance with subsection (4).
(7) If the Secretary of State, or a senior official acting on behalf of the Secretary of State, believes that the person, group or organisation named or described in the warrant as the interception subject is in the United Kingdom, that person must cancel the warrant under section 39.
(8) In this section—
"the interception subject", in relation to a warrant, means the person, group of persons or organisation to which the warrant relates;
"senior official" means a member of the Senior Civil Service or a member of the Senior Management Structure of Her Majesty's Diplomatic Service.

Implementation of warrants

41 Implementation of warrants

(1) This section applies to targeted interception warrants and mutual assistance warrants.
(2) In giving effect to a warrant to which this section applies, the person to whom it is addressed ("the intercepting authority") may (in addition to acting alone) act through, or together with, such other persons as the intercepting authority may require (whether under subsection (3) or otherwise) to provide the authority with assistance in giving effect to the warrant.
(3) For the purpose of requiring any person to provide assistance in relation to a warrant to which this section applies, the intercepting authority may—
   (a) serve a copy of the warrant on any person who the intercepting authority considers may be able to provide such assistance, or
   (b) make arrangements for the service of a copy of the warrant on any such person.
(4) A copy of a warrant may be served under subsection (3) on a person outside the United Kingdom for the purpose of requiring the person to provide such assistance in the form of conduct outside the United Kingdom.
(5) For the purposes of this Act, the provision of assistance in giving effect to a warrant to which this section applies includes any disclosure to the intercepting authority, or to persons acting on behalf of the intercepting authority, of anything obtained under the warrant.

(6) References in this section and sections 42 and 43 to the service of a copy of a warrant include—
   (a) the service of a copy of one or more schedules contained in the warrant with the omission of the remainder of the warrant, and
   (b) the service of a copy of the warrant with the omission of any schedule contained in the warrant.

42 Service of warrants

(1) This section applies to the service of warrants under section 41(3).
(2) A copy of the warrant must be served in such a way as to bring the contents of the warrant to the attention of the person who the intercepting authority considers may be able to provide assistance in relation to it.
(3) A copy of a warrant may be served on a person outside the United Kingdom in any of the following ways (as well as by electronic or other means of service)—
   (a) by serving it at the person's principal office within the United Kingdom or, if the person has no such office in the United Kingdom, at any place in the United Kingdom where the person carries on business or conducts activities;
   (b) if the person has specified an address in the United Kingdom as one at which the person, or someone on the person's behalf, will accept service of documents of the same description as a copy of a warrant, by serving it at that address;
   (c) by making it available for inspection (whether to the person or to someone acting on the person's behalf) at a place in the United Kingdom (but this is subject to subsection (4)).
(4) A copy of a warrant may be served on a person outside the United Kingdom in the way mentioned in subsection (3)(c) only if—
   (a) it is not reasonably practicable for a copy to be served by any other means (whether as mentioned in subsection (3)(a) or (b) or otherwise), and
   (b) the intercepting authority takes such steps as the authority considers appropriate for the purpose of bringing the contents of the warrant, and the availability of a copy for inspection, to the attention of the person.
(5) The steps mentioned in subsection (4)(b) must be taken as soon as reasonably practicable after the copy of the warrant is made available for inspection.
(6) In this section "the intercepting authority" has the same meaning as in section 41.

43 Duty of operators to assist with implementation

(1) A relevant operator that has been served with a copy of a warrant to which section 41 applies by (or on behalf of) the intercepting authority must take all steps for giving effect to the warrant that are notified to the relevant operator by (or on behalf of) the intercepting authority. This is subject to subsection (4).
(2) In this section—
   "relevant operator" means a postal operator or a telecommunications operator;
   "the intercepting authority" has the same meaning as in section 41.
(3) Subsection (1) applies whether or not the relevant operator is in the United Kingdom.
(4) The relevant operator is not required to take any steps which it is not reasonably practicable for the relevant operator to take.
(5) In determining for the purposes of subsection (4) whether it is reasonably practicable for a relevant operator outside the United Kingdom to take any steps in a country or territory outside the United Kingdom for giving effect to a warrant, the matters to be taken into account include the following—
   (a) any requirements or restrictions under the law of that country or territory that are relevant to the taking of those steps, and

(b) the extent to which it is reasonably practicable to give effect to the warrant in a way that does not breach any of those requirements or restrictions.

(6) Where obligations have been imposed on a relevant operator ("P") under section 253 (technical capability notices), for the purposes of subsection (4) the steps which it is reasonably practicable for P to take include every step which it would have been reasonably practicable for P to take if P had complied with all of those obligations.

(7) A person who knowingly fails to comply with subsection (1) is guilty of an offence and liable—
- (a) on summary conviction in England and Wales—
  - (i) to imprisonment for a term not exceeding 12 months (or 6 months, if the offence was committed before the commencement of section 154(1) of the Criminal Justice Act 2003), or
  - (ii) to a fine, or to both;
- (b) on summary conviction in Scotland—
  - (i) to imprisonment for a term not exceeding 12 months, or
  - (ii) to a fine not exceeding the statutory maximum, or to both;
- (c) on summary conviction in Northern Ireland—
  - (i) to imprisonment for a term not exceeding 6 months, or
  - (ii) to a fine not exceeding the statutory maximum, or to both;
- (d) on conviction on indictment, to imprisonment for a term not exceeding 2 years or to a fine, or to both.

(8) The duty imposed by subsection (1) is enforceable (whether or not the person is in the United Kingdom) by civil proceedings by the Secretary of State for an injunction, or for specific performance of a statutory duty under section 45 of the Court of Session Act 1988, or for any other appropriate relief.

CHAPTER 2

OTHER FORMS OF LAWFUL INTERCEPTION

Interception with consent

44 Interception with the consent of the sender or recipient

(1) The interception of a communication is authorised by this section if the sender and the intended recipient of the communication have each consented to its interception.

(2) The interception of a communication is authorised by this section if—
- (a) the communication is one sent by, or intended for, a person who has consented to the interception, and
- (b) surveillance by means of that interception has been authorised under—
  - (i) Part 2 of the Regulation of Investigatory Powers Act 2000, or
  - (ii) the Regulation of Investigatory Powers (Scotland) Act 2000 (2000 asp 11).

Interception for administrative or enforcement purposes

45 Interception by providers of postal or telecommunications services

(1) The interception of a communication is authorised by this section if the interception is carried out—
- (a) by, or on behalf of, a person who provides a postal service or a telecommunications service, and
- (b) for any of the purposes in subsection (2).

(2) The purposes referred to in subsection (1) are—
  (a) purposes relating to the provision or operation of the service;
  (b) purposes relating to the enforcement, in relation to the service, of any enactment relating to—
    (i) the use of postal or telecommunications services, or
    (ii) the content of communications transmitted by means of such services;
  (c) purposes relating to the provision of services or facilities aimed at preventing or restricting the viewing or publication of the content of communications transmitted by means of postal or telecommunications services.
(3) A reference in this section to anything carried out for purposes relating to the provision or operation of a telecommunications service includes, among other things, a reference to anything done for the purposes of identifying, combating or preventing anything which could affect—
  (a) any telecommunication system by means of which the service is provided, or
  (b) any apparatus attached to such a system.

46 Interception by businesses etc. for monitoring and record-keeping purposes

(1) Conduct is authorised by this section if it is authorised by regulations made under subsection (2).
(2) The Secretary of State may by regulations authorise conduct of a description specified in the regulations if that conduct appears to the Secretary of State to constitute a legitimate practice reasonably required for the purpose, in connection with the carrying on of any relevant activities (see subsection (4)), of monitoring or keeping a record of—
  (a) communications by means of which transactions are entered into in the course of the relevant activities, or
  (b) other communications relating to the relevant activities or taking place in the course of the carrying on of those activities.
(3) But nothing in any regulations under subsection (2) may authorise the interception of any communication except in the course of its transmission using apparatus or services provided by or to the person carrying on the relevant activities for use (whether wholly or partly) in connection with those activities.
(4) In this section "relevant activities" means—
  (a) any business,
  (b) any activities of a government department, the Welsh Government, a Northern Ireland department or any part of the Scottish Administration,
  (c) any activities of a public authority, and
  (d) any activities of any person or office holder on whom functions are conferred by or under any enactment.

47 Postal services: interception for enforcement purposes

(1) The interception of a communication in the course of its transmission by means of a public postal service is authorised by this section if it is carried out by an officer of Revenue and Customs under section 159 of the Customs and Excise Management Act 1979, as applied by virtue of—
  (a) section 105 of the Postal Services Act 2000 (power to open postal items etc.), or
  (b) that section and another enactment.
(2) The interception of a communication in the course of its transmission by means of a public postal service is authorised by this section if it is carried out under paragraph 9 of Schedule 7 to the Terrorism Act 2000 (port and border controls).

Appendix

48 Interception by OFCOM in connection with wireless telegraphy

(1) Conduct falling within subsection (2) is authorised by this section if it is carried out by OFCOM for purposes connected with a relevant matter (see subsection (3)).

(2) The conduct referred to in subsection (1) is—
   (a) the interception of a communication in the course of its transmission by means of a telecommunication system;
   (b) the obtaining, by or in connection with the interception, of information about the sender or recipient, or intended recipient, of the communication (whether or not a person);
   (c) the disclosure of anything obtained by conduct falling within paragraph (a) or (b).

(3) Each of the following is a relevant matter for the purposes of subsection (1)—
   (a) the grant of wireless telegraphy licences under the Wireless Telegraphy Act 2006 ("the 2006 Act");
   (b) the prevention or detection of anything which constitutes interference with wireless telegraphy;
   (c) the enforcement of—
      (i) any provision of Part 2 (other than Chapter 2 and sections 27 to 31) or Part 3 of the 2006 Act, or
      (ii) any enactment not falling within sub-paragraph (i) that relates to interference with wireless telegraphy.

(4) In this section—
"interference", in relation to wireless telegraphy, has the same meaning as in the Wireless Telegraphy Act 2006 (see section 115(3) of that Act);
"OFCOM" means the Office of Communications established by section 1 of the Office of Communications Act 2002;
"wireless telegraphy" has the same meaning as in the Wireless Telegraphy Act 2006 (see section 116 of that Act).

Interception taking place in certain institutions

49 Interception in prisons

(1) Conduct taking place in a prison is authorised by this section if it is conduct in exercise of any power conferred by or under prison rules.

(2) In this section "prison rules" means any rules made under—
   (a) section 47 of the Prison Act 1952,
   (b) section 39 of the Prisons (Scotland) Act 1989, or
   (c) section 13 of the Prison Act (Northern Ireland) 1953.

(3) In this section "prison" means—
   (a) any prison, young offender institution, young offenders centre, secure training centre, secure college or remand centre which—
      (i) is under the general superintendence of, or is provided by, the Secretary of State under the Prison Act 1952, or
      (ii) is under the general superintendence of, or is provided by, the Department of Justice in Northern Ireland under the Prison Act (Northern Ireland) 1953, or
   (b) any prison, young offenders institution or remand centre which is under the general superintendence of the Scottish Ministers under the Prisons (Scotland) Act 1989, and includes any contracted out prison, within the meaning of Part 4 of the Criminal Justice

Act 1991 or section 106(4) of the Criminal Justice and Public Order Act 1994, and any legalised police cells within the meaning of section 14 of the Prisons (Scotland) Act 1989.

50 Interception in psychiatric hospitals etc.

(1) Conduct is authorised by this section if—
   (a) it takes place in any hospital premises where high security psychiatric services are provided, and
   (b) it is conduct in pursuance of, and in accordance with, any relevant direction given to the body providing those services at those premises.
(2) "Relevant direction" means—
   (a) a direction under section 4(3A)(a) of the National Health Service Act 2006, or
   (b) a direction under section 19 or 23 of the National Health Service (Wales) Act 2006.
(3) Conduct is authorised by this section if—
   (a) it takes place in a state hospital, and
   (b) it is conduct in pursuance of, and in accordance with, any direction given to the State Hospitals Board for Scotland under section 2(5) of the National Health Service (Scotland) Act 1978 (regulations and directions as to the exercise of their functions by health boards).
   The reference to section 2(5) of that Act is to that provision as applied by Article 5(1) of, and the Schedule to, the State Hospitals Board for Scotland Order 1995 (which applies certain provisions of that Act to the State Hospitals Board).
(4) Conduct is authorised by this section if it is conduct in exercise of any power conferred by or under—
   (a) section 281 of the Mental Health (Care and Treatment) (Scotland) Act 2003 (2003 asp 13) (power to withhold correspondence of certain persons detained in hospital), or
   (b) section 284 of that Act (powers relating to the use of telephones by certain persons detained in hospital).
(5) In this section—
   "high security psychiatric services" has the same meaning as in section 4 of the National Health Service Act 2006;
   "hospital premises" has the same meaning as in section 4(3) of that Act;
   "state hospital" has the same meaning as in the National Health Service (Scotland) Act 1978.

51 Interception in immigration detention facilities

(1) Conduct taking place in immigration detention facilities is authorised by this section if it is conduct in exercise of any power conferred by or under relevant rules.
(2) In this section—
   "immigration detention facilities" means any removal centre, short-term holding facility or pre-departure accommodation;
   "removal centre", "short-term holding facility" and "pre-departure accommodation" have the meaning given by section 147 of the Immigration and Asylum Act 1999;
   "relevant rules" means—
      (a) in the case of a removal centre, rules made under section 153 of that Act;
      (b) in the case of a short-term holding facility, rules made under, or having effect by virtue of, section 157 of that Act;

(c) in the case of pre-departure accommodation, rules made under, or having effect by virtue of, section 157A of that Act.

Interception in accordance with overseas requests

52 Interception in accordance with overseas requests

(1) The interception of a communication in the course of its transmission by means of a telecommunication system is authorised by this section if conditions A to D are met.
(2) Condition A is that the interception—
    (a) is carried out by or on behalf of a telecommunications operator, and
    (b) relates to the use of a telecommunications service provided by the telecommunications operator.
(3) Condition B is that the interception is carried out in response to a request made in accordance with a relevant international agreement by the competent authorities of a country or territory outside the United Kingdom. In this subsection "relevant international agreement" means an international agreement to which the United Kingdom is a party and which is designated as a relevant international agreement by regulations made by the Secretary of State.
(4) Condition C is that the interception is carried out for the purpose of obtaining information about the communications of an individual—
    (a) who is outside the United Kingdom, or
    (b) who each of the following persons believes is outside the United Kingdom—
        (i) the person making the request;
        (ii) the person carrying out the interception.
(5) Condition D is that any further conditions specified in regulations made by the Secretary of State for the purposes of this section are met.

CHAPTER 3

OTHER PROVISIONS ABOUT INTERCEPTION

Restrictions on use or disclosure of material obtained under warrants etc.

53 Safeguards relating to retention and disclosure of material

(1) The issuing authority must ensure, in relation to every targeted interception warrant or mutual assistance warrant issued by that authority, that arrangements are in force for securing that the requirements of subsections (2) and (5) are met in relation to the material obtained under the warrant. This is subject to subsection (9).
(2) The requirements of this subsection are met in relation to the material obtained under a warrant if each of the following is limited to the minimum that is necessary for the authorised purposes (see subsection (3))—
    (a) the number of persons to whom any of the material is disclosed or otherwise made available;
    (b) the extent to which any of the material is disclosed or otherwise made available;
    (c) the extent to which any of the material is copied;
    (d) the number of copies that are made.

(3) For the purposes of this section something is necessary for the authorised purposes if, and only if—
    (a) it is, or is likely to become, necessary on any of the grounds falling within section 20 on which a warrant under Chapter 1 of this Part may be necessary,
    (b) it is necessary for facilitating the carrying out of any functions under this Act of the Secretary of State, the Scottish Ministers or the person to whom the warrant is or was addressed,
    (c) it is necessary for facilitating the carrying out of any functions of the Judicial Commissioners or the Investigatory Powers Tribunal under or in relation to this Act,
    (d) it is necessary to ensure that a person ("P") who is conducting a criminal prosecution has the information P needs to determine what is required of P by P's duty to secure the fairness of the prosecution, or (e) it is necessary for the performance of any duty imposed on any person by the Public Records Act 1958 or the Public Records Act (Northern Ireland) 1923.

(4) The arrangements for the time being in force under this section for securing that the requirements of subsection (2) are met in relation to the material obtained under the warrant must include arrangements for securing that every copy made of any of that material is stored, for so long as it is retained, in a secure manner.

(5) The requirements of this subsection are met in relation to the material obtained under a warrant if every copy made of any of that material (if not destroyed earlier) is destroyed as soon as there are no longer any relevant grounds for retaining it (see subsection (6)).

(6) For the purposes of subsection (5), there are no longer any relevant grounds for retaining a copy of any material if, and only if—
    (a) its retention is not necessary, or not likely to become necessary, on any of the grounds falling within section 20 on which a warrant under Chapter 1 of this Part may be necessary, and
    (b) its retention is not necessary for any of the purposes mentioned in paragraphs (b) to (e) of subsection (3) above.

(7) Where—
    (a) a communication which has been intercepted in accordance with a targeted interception warrant or mutual assistance warrant is retained, following its examination, for purposes other than the destruction of the communication, and
    (b) it is a communication that contains confidential journalistic material or identifies a source of journalistic information, the person to whom the warrant is addressed must inform the Investigatory Powers Commissioner as soon as is reasonably practicable.

(8) Subsection (9) applies if—
    (a) any material obtained under the warrant has been handed over to any overseas authorities, or
    (b) a copy of any such material has been given to any overseas authorities.

(9) To the extent that the requirements of subsections (2) and (5) relate to any of the material mentioned in subsection (8)(a), or to the copy mentioned in subsection (8)(b), the arrangements made for the purposes of this section are not required to secure that those requirements are met (see instead section 54).

(10) In this section—
"copy", in relation to material obtained under a warrant, means any of the following (whether or not in documentary form)—
    (a) any copy, extract or summary of the material which identifies the material as having been obtained under the warrant, and (b) any record which—

Appendix

      (i) refers to any interception or to the obtaining of any material, and
     (ii) is a record of the identities of the persons to or by whom the material was sent, or to whom the material relates, and "copied" is to be read accordingly;

"the issuing authority" means—
  (a) the Secretary of State, in the case of warrants issued by the Secretary of State;
  (b) the Scottish Ministers, in the case of warrants issued by the Scottish Ministers;

"overseas authorities" means authorities of a country or territory outside the United Kingdom.

54 Safeguards relating to disclosure of material overseas

(1) The issuing authority must ensure, in relation to every targeted interception warrant or mutual assistance warrant issued by that authority, that arrangements are in force for securing that—
  (a) any material obtained under the warrant is handed over to overseas authorities only if the requirements of subsection (2) are met, and
  (b) copies of any such material are given to overseas authorities only if those requirements are met.

(2) The requirements of this subsection are met in the case of a warrant if it appears to the issuing authority—
  (a) that requirements corresponding to the requirements of section 53(2) and (5) will apply, to such extent (if any) as the issuing authority considers appropriate, in relation to any of the material which is handed over, or any copy of which is given, to the authorities in question, and
  (b) that restrictions are in force which would prevent, to such extent (if any) as the issuing authority considers appropriate, the doing of anything in, for the purposes of or in connection with any proceedings outside the United Kingdom which would result in a prohibited disclosure.

(3) In subsection (2)(b) "prohibited disclosure" means a disclosure which, if made in the United Kingdom, would breach the prohibition in section 56(1).

(4) In this section—

"copy" has the same meaning as in section 53;

"the issuing authority" means—
  (a) the Secretary of State, in the case of warrants issued by the Secretary of State;
  (b) the Scottish Ministers, in the case of warrants issued by the Scottish Ministers;

"overseas authorities" means authorities of a country or territory outside the United Kingdom.

55 Additional safeguards for items subject to legal privilege

(1) This section applies where an item subject to legal privilege which has been intercepted in accordance with a targeted interception warrant or mutual assistance warrant is retained, following its examination, for purposes other than the destruction of the item.

(2) The person to whom the warrant is addressed must inform the Investigatory Powers Commissioner of the retention of the item as soon as is reasonably practicable.

(3) Unless the Investigatory Powers Commissioner considers that subsection (5) applies to the item, the Commissioner must—
  (a) direct that the item is destroyed, or
  (b) impose one or more conditions as to the use or retention of that item.

(4) If the Investigatory Powers Commissioner considers that subsection (5) applies to the item, the Commissioner may nevertheless impose such conditions under subsection (3)(b) as the Commissioner considers necessary for the purpose of protecting the public interest in the confidentiality of items subject to legal privilege.

(5) This subsection applies to an item subject to legal privilege if—
  (a) the public interest in retaining the item outweighs the public interest in the confidentiality of items subject to legal privilege, and
  (b) retaining the item is necessary in the interests of national security or for the purpose of preventing death or significant injury.
(6) The Investigatory Powers Commissioner—
  (a) may require an affected party to make representations about how the Commissioner should exercise any function under subsection (3), and
  (b) must have regard to any such representations made by an affected party (whether or not as a result of a requirement imposed under paragraph (a)).
(7) Each of the following is an "affected party" for the purposes of subsection (6)—
  (a) the person who decided to issue the warrant;
  (b) the person to whom the warrant is or was addressed.

56 Exclusion of matters from legal proceedings etc.

(1) No evidence may be adduced, question asked, assertion or disclosure made or other thing done in, for the purposes of or in connection with any legal proceedings or Inquiries Act proceedings which (in any manner)—
  (a) discloses, in circumstances from which its origin in interception-related conduct may be inferred—
    (i) any content of an intercepted communication, or
    (ii) any secondary data obtained from a communication, or
  (b) tends to suggest that any interception-related conduct has or may have occurred or may be going to occur.
  This is subject to Schedule 3 (exceptions).
(2) "Interception-related conduct" means—
  (a) conduct by a person within subsection (3) that is, or in the absence of any lawful authority would be, an offence under section 3(1) (offence of unlawful interception);
  (b) a breach of the prohibition imposed by section 9 (restriction on requesting interception by overseas authorities);
  (c) a breach of the prohibition imposed by section 10 (restriction on requesting assistance under mutual assistance agreements etc.);
  (d) the making of an application by any person for a warrant, or the issue of a warrant, under Chapter 1 of this Part;
  (e) the imposition of any requirement on any person to provide assistance in giving effect to a targeted interception warrant or mutual assistance warrant.
(3) The persons referred to in subsection (2)(a) are—
  (a) any person who is an intercepting authority (see section 18);
  (b) any person holding office under the Crown;
  (c) any person deemed to be the proper officer of Revenue and Customs by virtue of section 8(2) of the Customs and Excise Management Act 1979;
  (d) any person employed by, or for the purposes of, a police force;
  (e) any postal operator or telecommunications operator;
  (f) any person employed or engaged for the purposes of the business of a postal operator or telecommunications operator.
(4) Any reference in subsection (1) to interception-related conduct also includes any conduct taking place before the coming into force of this section and consisting of—
  (a) conduct by a person within subsection (3) that—

(i) was an offence under section 1(1) or (2) of the Regulation of Investigatory Powers Act 2000 ("RIPA"), or
(ii) would have been such an offence in the absence of any lawful authority (within the meaning of section 1(5) of RIPA);
(b) conduct by a person within subsection (3) that—
(i) was an offence under section 1 of the Interception of Communications Act 1985, or
(ii) would have been such an offence in the absence of subsections (2) and (3) of that section;
(c) a breach by the Secretary of State of the duty under section 1(4) of RIPA (restriction on requesting assistance under mutual assistance agreements);
(d) the making of an application by any person for a warrant, or the issue of a warrant, under—
(i) Chapter 1 of Part 1 of RIPA, or
(ii) the Interception of Communications Act 1985;
(e) the imposition of any requirement on any person to provide assistance in giving effect to a warrant under Chapter 1 of Part 1 of RIPA.
(5) In this section—
"Inquiries Act proceedings" means proceedings of an inquiry under the Inquiries Act 2005;
"intercepted communication" means any communication intercepted in the course of its transmission by means of a postal service or telecommunication system.

57 Duty not to make unauthorised disclosures

(1) A person to whom this section applies must not make an unauthorised disclosure to another person.
(2) A person makes an unauthorised disclosure for the purposes of this section if—
(a) the person discloses any of the matters within subsection (4) in relation to—
(i) a warrant under Chapter 1 of this Part, or
(ii) a warrant under Chapter 1 of Part 1 of the Regulation of Investigatory Powers Act 2000, and
(b) the disclosure is not an excepted disclosure (see section 58).
(3) This section applies to the following persons—
(a) any person who is an intercepting authority (see section 18);
(b) any person holding office under the Crown;
(c) any person employed by, or for the purposes of, a police force;
(d) any postal operator or telecommunications operator;
(e) any person employed or engaged for the purposes of the business of a postal operator or telecommunications operator;
(f) any person to whom any of the matters within subsection (4) have been disclosed in relation to a warrant mentioned in subsection (2)(a).
(4) The matters referred to in subsection (2)(a) are—
(a) the existence or contents of the warrant;
(b) the details of the issue of the warrant or of any renewal or modification of the warrant;
(c) the existence or contents of any requirement to provide assistance in giving effect to the warrant;
(d) the steps taken in pursuance of the warrant or of any such requirement;
(e) any of the material obtained under the warrant.

Appendix

58 Section 57: meaning of "excepted disclosure"

(1) For the purposes of section 57 a disclosure made in relation to a warrant is an "excepted disclosure" if it falls within any of the Heads set out in—
   (a) subsection (2) (disclosures authorised by warrant etc.);
   (b) subsection (4) (oversight bodies);
   (c) subsection (5) (legal advisers);
   (d) subsection (8) (disclosures of a general nature).

(2) Head 1 is—
   (a) a disclosure authorised by the warrant;
   (b) a disclosure authorised by the person to whom the warrant is or was addressed or under any arrangements made by that person for the purposes of this section;
   (c) a disclosure authorised by the terms of any requirement to provide assistance in giving effect to the warrant (including any requirement for disclosure imposed by virtue of section 41(5) or, in the case of a warrant under Chapter 1 of Part 1 of the Regulation of Investigatory Powers Act 2000 ("RIPA"), section 11(9) of RIPA).

(3) But subsection (2)(b) does not apply in the case of a mutual assistance warrant that is or was addressed to a person falling within section 18(1)(h) (competent authorities of overseas countries or territories).

(4) Head 2 is—
   (a) in the case of a warrant under Chapter 1 of this Part, a disclosure made to, or authorised by, a Judicial Commissioner;
   (b) in the case of a warrant under Chapter 1 of Part 1 of RIPA, a disclosure made to, or authorised by, the Interception of Communications Commissioner or a Judicial Commissioner;
   (c) a disclosure made to the Independent Police Complaints Commission for the purposes of facilitating the carrying out of any of its functions;
   (d) a disclosure made to the Intelligence and Security Committee of Parliament for the purposes of facilitating the carrying out of any of its functions.

(5) Head 3 is—
   (a) a disclosure made by a legal adviser—
      (i) in contemplation of, or in connection with, any legal proceedings, and
      (ii) for the purposes of those proceedings;
   (b) a disclosure made—
      (i) by a professional legal adviser ("L") to L's client or a representative of L's client, or
      (ii) by L's client, or by a representative of L's client, to L, in connection with the giving, by L to L's client, of advice about the effect of the relevant provisions (see subsection (7)).

(6) But a disclosure within Head 3 is not an excepted disclosure if it is made with the intention of furthering a criminal purpose.

(7) In subsection (5)(b) "the relevant provisions" means—
   (a) in the case of a warrant under Chapter 1 of this Part, the provisions of this Part;
   (b) in the case of a warrant under Chapter 1 of Part 1 of RIPA, the provisions of that Chapter.

(8) Head 4 is—
   (a) a disclosure that—
      (i) is made by a postal operator or a telecommunications operator in accordance with a requirement imposed by regulations made by the Secretary of State, and

(ii) consists of statistical information of a description specified in the regulations;
(b) a disclosure of information that does not relate to any particular warrant under Chapter 1 of this Part or under Chapter 1 of Part 1 of RIPA but relates to any such warrants in general.

(9) Nothing in this section affects the operation of section 56 (which, among other things, prohibits the making of certain disclosures in, for the purposes of or in connection with legal proceedings).

59 Offence of making unauthorised disclosures

(1) A person who fails to comply with section 57(1) commits an offence.
(2) A person who is guilty of an offence under this section is liable—
- (a) on summary conviction in England and Wales—
  - (i) to imprisonment for a term not exceeding 12 months (or 6 months, if the offence was committed before the commencement of section 154(1) of the Criminal Justice Act 2003), or
  - (ii) to a fine, or to both;
- (b) on summary conviction in Scotland—
  - (i) to imprisonment for a term not exceeding 12 months, or
  - (ii) to a fine not exceeding the statutory maximum, or to both;
- (c) on summary conviction in Northern Ireland—
  - (i) to imprisonment for a term not exceeding 6 months, or
  - (ii) to a fine not exceeding the statutory maximum, or to both;
- (d) on conviction on indictment, to imprisonment for a term not exceeding 5 years or to a fine, or to both.

(3) In proceedings against any person for an offence under this section in respect of any disclosure, it is a defence for the person to show that the person could not reasonably have been expected, after first becoming aware of the matter disclosed, to take steps to prevent the disclosure.

Interpretation

60 Part 2: interpretation

(1) In this Part—
"EU mutual assistance instrument" has the meaning given by section 10(3);
"intercepting authority" is to be read in accordance with section 18;
"international mutual assistance agreement" has the meaning given by section 10(3);
"mutual assistance warrant" has the meaning given by section 15(4);
"police force" means any of the following—
- (a) any police force maintained under section 2 of the Police Act 1996;
- (b) the metropolitan police force;
- (c) the City of London police force;
- (d) the Police Service of Scotland;
- (e) the Police Service of Northern Ireland;
- (f) the Ministry of Defence Police;
- (g) the Royal Navy Police;
- (h) the Royal Military Police;
- (i) the Royal Air Force Police;
- (j) the British Transport Police Force;

"relevant content", in relation to a targeted examination warrant, has the meaning given by section 15(3);
"relevant Scottish application" has the meaning given by section 22;
"secondary data" has the meaning given by section 16, and references to obtaining secondary data from a communication are to be read in accordance with that section;
"targeted examination warrant" has the meaning given by section 15(3).
(2) In this Part references to a member of a police force, in relation to the Royal Navy Police, the Royal Military Police or the Royal Air Force Police, do not include any member of that force who is not for the time being attached to, or serving with, that force or another of those police forces.
(3) See also—
section 261 (telecommunications definitions),
section 262 (postal definitions),
section 263 (general definitions),
section 264 (general definitions: "journalistic material" etc.),
section 265 (index of defined expressions).

PART 3

AUTHORISATIONS FOR OBTAINING COMMUNICATIONS DATA

Targeted authorisations for obtaining data

61 Power to grant authorisations

(1) Subsection (2) applies if a designated senior officer of a relevant public authority considers—
　(a) that it is necessary to obtain communications data for a purpose falling within subsection (7),
　(b) that it is necessary to obtain the data—
　　(i) for the purposes of a specific investigation or a specific operation, or
　　(ii) for the purposes of testing, maintaining or developing equipment, systems or other capabilities relating to the availability or obtaining of communications data, and
　(c) that the conduct authorised by the authorisation is proportionate to what is sought to be achieved.
(2) The designated senior officer may authorise any officer of the authority to engage in any conduct which—
　(a) is for the purpose of obtaining the data from any person, and
　(b) relates to—
　　(i) a telecommunication system, or
　　(ii) data derived from a telecommunication system.
(3) Subsections (1) and (2) are subject to—
　(a) section 62 (restrictions in relation to internet connection records),
　(b) section 63 (additional restrictions on grant of authorisations),
　(c) sections 70 and 73 to 75 and Schedule 4 (restrictions relating to certain relevant public authorities),
　(d) section 76 (requirement to consult a single point of contact), and
　(e) section 77 (Commissioner approval for authorisations to identify or confirm journalistic sources).

Appendix

(4) Authorised conduct may, in particular, consist of an authorised officer—
 (a) obtaining the communications data themselves from any person or telecommunication system,
 (b) asking any person whom the authorised officer believes is, or may be, in possession of the communications data or capable of obtaining it—
  (i) to obtain the data (if not already in possession of it), and
  (ii) to disclose the data (whether already in the person's possession or subsequently obtained by that person) to a person identified by, or in accordance with, the authorisation, or
 (c) requiring by notice a telecommunications operator whom the authorised officer believes is, or may be, in possession of the communications data or capable of obtaining it—
  (i) to obtain the data (if not already in possession of it), and
  (ii) to disclose the data (whether already in the operator's possession or subsequently obtained by the operator) to a person identified by, or in accordance with, the authorisation.

(5) An authorisation—
 (a) may relate to data whether or not in existence at the time of the authorisation,
 (b) may authorise the obtaining or disclosure of data by a person who is not an authorised officer, or any other conduct by such a person, which enables or facilitates the obtaining of the communications data concerned, and
 (c) may, in particular, require a telecommunications operator who controls or provides a telecommunication system to obtain or disclose data relating to the use of a telecommunications service provided by another telecommunications operator in relation to that system.

(6) An authorisation—
 (a) may not authorise any conduct consisting in the interception of communications in the course of their transmission by means of a telecommunication system, and
 (b) may not authorise an authorised officer to ask or require, in the circumstances mentioned in subsection (4)(b) or (c), a person to disclose the data to any person other than—
  (i) an authorised officer, or
  (ii) an officer of the same relevant public authority as an authorised officer.

(7) It is necessary to obtain communications data for a purpose falling within this subsection if it is necessary to obtain the data—
 (a) in the interests of national security,
 (b) for the purpose of preventing or detecting crime or of preventing disorder,
 (c) in the interests of the economic well-being of the United Kingdom so far as those interests are also relevant to the interests of national security,
 (d) in the interests of public safety,
 (e) for the purpose of protecting public health,
 (f) for the purpose of assessing or collecting any tax, duty, levy or other imposition, contribution or charge payable to a government department,
 (g) for the purpose of preventing death or injury or any damage to a person's physical or mental health, or of mitigating any injury or damage to a person's physical or mental health,
 (h) to assist investigations into alleged miscarriages of justice,
 (i) where a person ("P") has died or is unable to identify themselves because of a physical or mental condition—
  (i) to assist in identifying P, or

Appendix

(ii) to obtain information about P's next of kin or other persons connected with P or about the reason for P's death or condition, or

(j) for the purpose of exercising functions relating to—
  (i) the regulation of financial services and markets, or
  (ii) financial stability.

(8) The fact that the communications data which would be obtained in pursuance of an authorisation relates to the activities in the British Islands of a trade union is not, of itself, sufficient to establish that it is necessary to obtain the data for a purpose falling within subsection (7).

(9) See—
  (a) sections 70 and 73 for the meanings of "designated senior officer" and "relevant public authority";
  (b) section 84 for the way in which this Part applies to postal operators and postal services.

62 Restrictions in relation to internet connection records

(1) A designated senior officer of a local authority may not grant an authorisation for the purpose of obtaining data which is, or can only be obtained by processing, an internet connection record.

(2) A designated senior officer of a relevant public authority which is not a local authority may not grant an authorisation for the purpose of obtaining data which is, or can only be obtained by processing, an internet connection record unless condition A, B or C is met.

(3) Condition A is that the designated senior officer considers that it is necessary, for a purpose falling within section 61(7), to obtain the data to identify which person or apparatus is using an internet service where—
  (a) the service and time of use are already known, but
  (b) the identity of the person or apparatus using the service is not known.

(4) Condition B is that—
  (a) the purpose for which the data is to be obtained falls within section 61(7) but is not the purpose falling within section 61(7)(b) of preventing or detecting crime, and
  (b) the designated senior officer considers that it is necessary to obtain the data to identify—
    (i) which internet communications service is being used, and when and how it is being used, by a person or apparatus whose identity is already known,
    (ii) where or when a person or apparatus whose identity is already known is obtaining access to, or running, a computer file or computer program which wholly or mainly involves making available, or acquiring, material whose possession is a crime, or
    (iii) which internet service is being used, and when and how it is being used, by a person or apparatus whose identity is already known.

(5) Condition C is that—
  (a) the purpose for which the data is to be obtained is the purpose falling within section 61(7)(b) of preventing or detecting crime,
  (b) the crime to be prevented or detected is serious crime or other relevant crime, and
  (c) the designated senior officer considers that it is necessary to obtain the data to identify—
    (i) which internet communications service is being used, and when and how it is being used, by a person or apparatus whose identity is already known,
    (ii) where or when a person or apparatus whose identity is already known is obtaining access to, or running, a computer file or computer program which wholly or mainly involves making available, or acquiring, material whose possession is a crime, or
    (iii) which internet service is being used, and when and how it is being used, by a person or apparatus whose identity is already known.

Appendix

(6) In subsection (5) "other relevant crime" means crime which is not serious crime but where the offence, or one of the offences, which is or would be constituted by the conduct concerned is—
   (a) an offence for which an individual who has reached the age of 18 (or, in relation to Scotland or Northern Ireland, 21) is capable of being sentenced to imprisonment for a term of 12 months or more (disregarding any enactment prohibiting or restricting the imprisonment of individuals who have no previous convictions), or
   (b) an offence—
      (i) by a person who is not an individual, or
      (ii) which involves, as an integral part of it, the sending of a communication or a breach of a person's privacy.
(7) In this Act "internet connection record" means communications data which—
   (a) may be used to identify, or assist in identifying, a telecommunications service to which a communication is transmitted by means of a telecommunication system for the purpose of obtaining access to, or running, a computer file or computer program, and
   (b) comprises data generated or processed by a telecommunications operator in the process of supplying the telecommunications service to the sender of the communication (whether or not a person).

63 Additional restrictions on grant of authorisations

(1) A designated senior officer may not grant an authorisation for the purposes of a specific investigation or a specific operation if the officer is working on that investigation or operation.
(2) But, if the designated senior officer considers that there are exceptional circumstances which mean that subsection (1) should not apply in a particular case, that subsection does not apply in that case.
(3) Examples of exceptional circumstances include—
   (a) an imminent threat to life or another emergency,
   (b) the investigation or operation concerned is one where there is an exceptional need, in the interests of national security, to keep knowledge of it to a minimum,
   (c) there is an opportunity to obtain information where—
      (i) the opportunity is rare,
      (ii) the time to act is short, and
      (iii) the need to obtain the information is significant and in the interests of national security, or
   (d) the size of the relevant public authority concerned is such that it is not practicable to have a designated senior officer who is not working on the investigation or operation concerned.

64 Procedure for authorisations and authorised notices

(1) An authorisation must specify—
   (a) the office, rank or position held by the designated senior officer granting it,
   (b) the matters falling within section 61(7) by reference to which it is granted,
   (c) the conduct that is authorised,
   (d) the data or description of data to be obtained, and
   (e) the persons or descriptions of persons to whom the data is to be, or may be, disclosed or how to identify such persons.
(2) An authorisation which authorises a person to impose requirements by notice on a telecommunications operator must also specify—
   (a) the operator concerned, and

Appendix

  (b) the nature of the requirements that are to be imposed, but need not specify the other contents of the notice.
(3) The notice itself—
  (a) must specify—
    (i) the office, rank or position held by the person giving it,
    (ii) the requirements that are being imposed, and
    (iii) the telecommunications operator on whom the requirements are being imposed, and
  (b) must be given in writing or (if not in writing) in a manner that produces a record of its having been given.
(4) An authorisation must be applied for, and granted, in writing or (if not in writing) in a manner that produces a record of its having been applied for or granted.

65 Duration and cancellation of authorisations and notices

(1) An authorisation ceases to have effect at the end of the period of one month beginning with the date on which it is granted.
(2) An authorisation may be renewed at any time before the end of that period by the grant of a further authorisation.
(3) Subsection (1) has effect in relation to a renewed authorisation as if the period of one month mentioned in that subsection did not begin until the end of the period of one month applicable to the authorisation that is current at the time of the renewal.
(4) A designated senior officer who has granted an authorisation—
  (a) may cancel it at any time, and
  (b) must cancel it if the designated senior officer considers that the requirements of this Part would not be satisfied in relation to granting an equivalent new authorisation.
(5) The Secretary of State may by regulations provide for the person by whom any function under subsection (4) is to be exercised where the person who would otherwise have exercised it is no longer available to do so.
(6) Such regulations may, in particular, provide for the person by whom the function is to be exercised to be a person appointed in accordance with the regulations.
(7) A notice given in pursuance of an authorisation (and any requirement imposed by the notice)—
  (a) is not affected by the authorisation subsequently ceasing to have effect under subsection (1), but
  (b) is cancelled if the authorisation is cancelled under subsection (4).

66 Duties of telecommunications operators in relation to authorisations

(1) It is the duty of a telecommunications operator on whom a requirement is imposed by notice given in pursuance of an authorisation to comply with that requirement.
(2) It is the duty of a telecommunications operator who is obtaining or disclosing communications data, in response to a request or requirement for the data in pursuance of an authorisation, to obtain or disclose the data in a way that minimises the amount of data that needs to be processed for the purpose concerned.
(3) A person who is under a duty by virtue of subsection (1) or (2) is not required to take any steps in pursuance of that duty which it is not reasonably practicable for that person to take.
(4) For the purposes of subsection (3), where obligations have been imposed on a telecommunications operator ("P") under section 253 (maintenance of technical capability), the steps which it is reasonably practicable for P to take include every step which it would have been reasonably practicable for P to take if P had complied with all of those obligations.

(5) The duty imposed by subsection (1) or (2) is enforceable by civil proceedings by the Secretary of State for an injunction, or for specific performance of a statutory duty under section 45 of the Court of Session Act 1988, or for any other appropriate relief.

Filtering arrangements for obtaining data

67 Filtering arrangements for obtaining data

(1) The Secretary of State may establish, maintain and operate arrangements for the purposes of—
   (a) assisting a designated senior officer, who is considering whether to grant an authorisation, to determine whether the requirements of this Part in relation to granting the authorisation are satisfied, or
   (b) facilitating the lawful, efficient and effective obtaining of communications data from any person by relevant public authorities in pursuance of an authorisation.
(2) Arrangements under subsection (1) ("filtering arrangements") may, in particular, involve the obtaining of communications data in pursuance of an authorisation ("the target data") by means of—
   (a) a request to the Secretary of State to obtain the target data on behalf of an authorised officer, and
   (b) the Secretary of State—
      (i) obtaining the target data or data from which the target data may be derived,
      (ii) processing the target data or the data from which it may be derived (and retaining data temporarily for that purpose), and
      (iii) disclosing the target data to the person identified for this purpose by, or in accordance with, the authorisation.
(3) Filtering arrangements may, in particular, involve the generation or use by the Secretary of State of information—
   (a) for the purpose mentioned in subsection (1)(a), or
   (b) for the purposes of—
      (i) the support, maintenance, oversight, operation or administration of the arrangements, or
      (ii) the functions of the Investigatory Powers Commissioner mentioned in subsection (4) or (5).
(4) Filtering arrangements must involve the generation and retention of such information or documents as the Investigatory Powers Commissioner considers appropriate for the purposes of the functions of the Commissioner under section 229(1) of keeping under review the exercise by public authorities of functions under this Part.
(5) The Secretary of State must consult the Investigatory Powers Commissioner about the principles on the basis of which the Secretary of State intends to establish, maintain or operate any arrangements for the purpose mentioned in subsection (1)(a).

68 Use of filtering arrangements in pursuance of an authorisation

(1) This section applies in relation to the use of the filtering arrangements in pursuance of an authorisation.
(2) The filtering arrangements may be used—
   (a) to obtain and disclose communications data in pursuance of an authorisation, only if the authorisation specifically authorises the use of the arrangements to obtain and disclose the data,

(b) to process data in pursuance of an authorisation (and to retain the data temporarily for that purpose), only if the authorisation specifically authorises processing data of that description under the arrangements (and their temporary retention for that purpose).
(3) An authorisation must record the designated senior officer's decision as to—
   (a) whether the communications data to be obtained and disclosed in pursuance of the authorisation may be obtained and disclosed by use of the filtering arrangements,
   (b) whether the processing of data under the filtering arrangements (and its temporary retention for that purpose) is authorised, (c) if the processing of data under the filtering arrangements is authorised, the description of data that may be processed.
(4) A designated senior officer must not grant an authorisation which authorises—
   (a) use of the filtering arrangements, or
   (b) processing under the filtering arrangements, unless the condition in subsection (5) is met.
(5) The condition is that the designated senior officer (as well as considering that the other requirements of this Part in relation to granting the authorisation are satisfied) considers that what is authorised in relation to the filtering arrangements is proportionate to what is sought to be achieved.

69 Duties in connection with operation of filtering arrangements

(1) The Secretary of State must secure—
   (a) that no authorisation data is obtained or processed under the filtering arrangements except for the purposes of an authorisation,
   (b) that data which—
      (i) has been obtained or processed under the filtering arrangements, and
      (ii) is to be disclosed in pursuance of an authorisation or for the purpose mentioned in section 67(1)(a), is disclosed only to the person to whom the data is to be disclosed in pursuance of the authorisation or (as the case may be) to the designated senior officer concerned,
   (c) that any authorisation data which is obtained under the filtering arrangements in pursuance of an authorisation is immediately destroyed—
      (i) when the purposes of the authorisation have been met, or
      (ii) if at any time it ceases to be necessary to retain the data for the purposes or purpose concerned.
(2) The Secretary of State must secure that data (other than authorisation data) which is retained under the filtering arrangements is disclosed only—
   (a) for the purpose mentioned in section 67(1)(a),
   (b) for the purposes of support, maintenance, oversight, operation or administration of the arrangements,
   (c) to the Investigatory Powers Commissioner for the purposes of the functions of the Commissioner mentioned in section 67(4) or (5), or
   (d) otherwise as authorised by law.
(3) The Secretary of State must secure that—
   (a) only the Secretary of State and designated individuals are permitted to read, obtain or otherwise process data for the purposes of support, maintenance, oversight, operation or administration of the filtering arrangements, and
   (b) no other persons are permitted to access or use the filtering arrangements except in pursuance of an authorisation or for the purpose mentioned in section 67(1)(a).

(4) In subsection (3)(a) "designated" means designated by the Secretary of State; and the Secretary of State may designate an individual only if the Secretary of State thinks that it is necessary for the individual to be able to act as mentioned in subsection (3)(a).
(5) The Secretary of State must—
    (a) put in place and maintain an adequate security system to govern access to, and use of, the filtering arrangements and to protect against any abuse of the power of access, and
    (b) impose measures to protect against unauthorised or unlawful data retention, processing, access or disclosure.
(6) The Secretary of State must—
    (a) put in place and maintain procedures (including the regular testing of relevant software and hardware) to ensure that the filtering arrangements are functioning properly, and
    (b) report, as soon as possible after the end of each calendar year, to the Investigatory Powers Commissioner about the functioning of the filtering arrangements during that year.
(7) A report under subsection (6)(b) must, in particular, contain information about the destruction of authorisation data during the calendar year concerned.
(8) If the Secretary of State believes that significant processing errors have occurred giving rise to a contravention of any of the requirements of this Part which relate to the filtering arrangements, the Secretary of State must report that fact immediately to the Investigatory Powers Commissioner.
(9) In this section "authorisation data", in relation to an authorisation, means communications data that is, or is to be, obtained in pursuance of the authorisation or any data from which that data is, or may be, derived.

Relevant public authorities other than local authorities

70 Relevant public authorities and designated senior officers etc.

(1) Schedule 4 (relevant public authorities and designated senior officers etc.) has effect.
(2) A public authority listed in column 1 of the table in the Schedule is a relevant public authority for the purposes of this Part.
(3) In this Part "designated senior officer", in relation to a relevant public authority listed in column 1 of the table, means an individual who holds with the authority—
    (a) an office, rank or position specified in relation to the authority in column 2 of the table, or
    (b) an office, rank or position higher than that specified in relation to the authority in column 2 of the table (subject to subsections (4) and (5)).
(4) Subsection (5) applies where an office, rank or position specified in relation to a relevant public authority in column 2 of the table is specified by referenceto—
    (a) a particular branch, agency or other part of the authority, or
    (b) responsibility for functions of a particular description.
(5) A person is a designated senior officer by virtue of subsection (3)(b) only if the person—
    (a) holds an office, rank or position in that branch, agency or part, or
    (b) has responsibility for functions of that description.
(6) A person who is a designated senior officer of a relevant public authority by virtue of subsection (3) and an entry in column 2 of the table may grant an authorisation—
    (a) only for obtaining communications data of the kind specified in the corresponding entry in column 3 of the table, and
    (b) only if section 61(1)(a) is met in relation to a purpose within one of the paragraphs of section 61(7) specified in the corresponding entry in column 4 of the table.

(7) Where there is more than one entry in relation to a relevant public authority in column 2 of the table, and a person is a designated senior officer of the authority by virtue of subsection (3) as it applies to more than one of those entries, subsection (6) applies in relation to each entry.

71 Power to modify section 70 and Schedule 4

(1) The Secretary of State may by regulations modify section 70 or Schedule 4.
(2) Regulations under subsection (1) may in particular—
   (a) add a public authority to, or remove a public authority from, the list in column 1 of the table,
   (b) modify an entry in column 2 of the table,
   (c) impose or remove restrictions on the authorisations that may be granted by a designated senior officer with a specified public authority,
   (d) impose or remove restrictions on the circumstances in which or purposes for which such authorisations may be granted by a designated senior officer.
(3) The power to make regulations under subsection (1) includes power to make such modifications in any enactment (including this Act) as the Secretary of State considers appropriate in consequence of a person becoming, or ceasing to be, a relevant public authority because of regulations under that subsection.

72 Certain regulations under section 71: supplementary

(1) This section applies to regulations under section 71 other than regulations which do only one or both of the following—
   (a) remove a public authority from the list in column 1 of the table in Schedule 4 and make consequential modifications,
   (b) modify column 2 of the table in a way that does not involve replacing an office, rank or position specified in that column in relation to a particular public authority with a lower office, rank or position in relation to the same authority.
(2) Before making regulations to which this section applies, the Secretary of State must consult—
   (a) the Investigatory Powers Commissioner, and
   (b) the public authority to which the modifications relate.
(3) A statutory instrument containing regulations to which this section applies may not be made except in accordance with the enhanced affirmative procedure.

Local authorities

73 Local authorities as relevant public authorities

(1) A local authority is a relevant public authority for the purposes of this Part.
(2) In this Part "designated senior officer", in relation to a local authority, means an individual who holds with the authority—
   (a) the position of director, head of service or service manager (or equivalent), or
   (b) a higher position.
(3) A designated senior officer of a local authority may grant an authorisation for obtaining communications data only if section 61(1)(a) is met in relation to a purpose within section 61(7)(b).
(4) The Secretary of State may by regulations amend subsection (2).
(5) Before making regulations under subsection (4) which amend subsection (2) so as to replace an office, rank or position specified in that subsection with a lower office, rank or position, the Secretary of State must consult—

Appendix

    (a) the Investigatory Powers Commissioner, and
    (b) each local authority to which the amendment relates.
(6) A statutory instrument containing regulations under subsection (4) to which subsection (5) applies may not be made except in accordance with the enhanced affirmative procedure.
(7) Sections 74 and 75 impose further restrictions in relation to the grant of authorisations by local authorities.

74 Requirement to be party to collaboration agreement

(1) A designated senior officer of a local authority may not grant an authorisation unless—
    (a) the local authority is a party to a collaboration agreement (whether as a supplying authority or a subscribing authority or both), and
    (b) that collaboration agreement is certified by the Secretary of State (having regard to guidance given by virtue of section 79(6) and (7)) as being appropriate for the local authority.
(2) A designated senior officer of a local authority may only grant an authorisation to a person within subsection (3).
(3) A person is within this subsection if the person is an officer of a relevant public authority which is a supplying authority under a collaboration agreement to which the local authority is a party.
(4) If the local authority is itself a supplying authority under a collaboration agreement with the result that officers of the local authority are permitted to be granted authorisations by a designated senior officer of a subscribing authority, the persons within subsection (3) include officers of the local authority.
(5) In this section "collaboration agreement", "subscribing authority" and "supplying authority" have the same meaning as in section 78.

75 Judicial approval for local authority authorisations

(1) This section applies to an authorisation granted by a designated senior officer of a local authority other than an authorisation to which section 77 applies.
(2) The authorisation is not to take effect until such time (if any) as the relevant judicial authority has made an order under this section approving it.
(3) The local authority may apply to the relevant judicial authority for an order under this section approving the authorisation.
(4) The local authority is not required to give notice of the application to—
    (a) any person to whom the authorisation relates, or
    (b) that person's legal representatives.
(5) The relevant judicial authority may approve the authorisation if, and only if, the relevant judicial authority considers that—
    (a) at the time of the grant, there were reasonable grounds for considering that the requirements of this Part were satisfied in relation to the authorisation, and
    (b) at the time when the relevant judicial authority is considering the matter, there are reasonable grounds for considering that the requirements of this Part would be satisfied if an equivalent new authorisation were granted at that time.
(6) Where, on an application under this section, the relevant judicial authority refuses to approve the grant of the authorisation, the relevant judicial authority may make an order quashing the authorisation.
(7) In this section "the relevant judicial authority" means—
    (a) in relation to England and Wales, a justice of the peace,
    (b) in relation to Scotland, a sheriff, and
    (c) in relation to Northern Ireland, a district judge (magistrates' courts) in Northern Ireland.

(8) See also sections 77A and 77B of the Regulation of Investigatory Powers Act 2000 (procedure for orders under this section of a sheriff in Scotland or a district judge (magistrates' courts) in Northern Ireland).

Additional protections

76 Use of a single point of contact

(1) Before granting an authorisation, the designated senior officer must consult a person who is acting as a single point of contact in relation to the granting of authorisations.
(2) But, if the designated senior officer considers that there are exceptional circumstances which mean that subsection (1) should not apply in a particular case, that subsection does not apply in that case.
(3) Examples of exceptional circumstances include—
    (a) an imminent threat to life or another emergency, or
    (b) the interests of national security.
(4) A person is acting as a single point of contact if that person—
    (a) is an officer of a relevant public authority, and
    (b) is responsible for advising—
        (i) officers of the relevant public authority about applying for authorisations, or
        (ii) designated senior officers of the relevant public authority about granting authorisations.
(5) A person acting as a single point of contact may, in particular, advise an officer of a relevant public authority who is considering whether to apply for an authorisation about—
    (a) the most appropriate methods for obtaining data where the data concerned is processed by more than one telecommunications operator,
    (b) the cost, and resource implications, for—
        (i) the relevant public authority concerned of obtaining the data, and
        (ii) the telecommunications operator concerned of disclosing the data,
    (c) any unintended consequences of the proposed authorisation, and
    (d) any issues as to the lawfulness of the proposed authorisation.
(6) A person acting as a single point of contact may, in particular, advise a designated senior officer who is considering whether to grant an authorisation about—
    (a) whether it is reasonably practical to obtain the data sought in pursuance of the proposed authorisation,
    (b) the cost, and resource implications, for—
        (i) the relevant public authority concerned of obtaining the data, and
        (ii) the telecommunications operator concerned of disclosing the data,
    (c) any unintended consequences of the proposed authorisation, and
    (d) any issues as to the lawfulness of the proposed authorisation.
(7) A person acting as a single point of contact may also provide advice about—
    (a) whether requirements imposed by virtue of an authorisation have been met,
    (b) the use in support of operations or investigations of communications data obtained in pursuance of an authorisation, and
    (c) any other effects of an authorisation.
(8) Nothing in this section prevents a person acting as a single point of contact from also applying for, or being granted, an authorisation or, in the case of a designated senior officer, granting an authorisation.

Appendix

77 Commissioner approval for authorisations to identify or confirm journalistic sources

(1) Subsection (2) applies if—
   (a) a designated senior officer has granted an authorisation in relation to the obtaining by a relevant public authority of communications data for the purpose of identifying or confirming a source of journalistic information, and
   (b) the authorisation is not necessary because of an imminent threat to life.
(2) The authorisation is not to take effect until such time (if any) as a Judicial Commissioner has approved it.
(3) The relevant public authority for which the authorisation has been granted may apply to a Judicial Commissioner for approval of the authorisation.
(4) The applicant is not required to give notice of the application to—
   (a) any person to whom the authorisation relates, or
   (b) that person's legal representatives.
(5) A Judicial Commissioner may approve the authorisation if, and only if, the Judicial Commissioner considers that—
   (a) at the time of the grant, there were reasonable grounds for considering that the requirements of this Part were satisfied in relation to the authorisation, and
   (b) at the time when the Judicial Commissioner is considering the matter, there are reasonable grounds for considering that the requirements of this Part would be satisfied if an equivalent new authorisation were granted at that time.
(6) In considering whether the position is as mentioned in subsection (5)(a) and (b), the Judicial Commissioner must, in particular, have regard to—
   (a) the public interest in protecting a source of journalistic information, and
   (b) the need for there to be another overriding public interest before a relevant public authority seeks to identify or confirm a source of journalistic information.
(7) Where, on an application under this section, the Judicial Commissioner refuses to approve the grant of the authorisation, the Judicial Commissioner may quash the authorisation.

Collaboration agreements

78 Collaboration agreements

(1) A collaboration agreement is an agreement (other than a police collaboration agreement) under which—
   (a) a relevant public authority ("the supplying authority") puts the services of designated senior officers of that authority or other officers of that authority at the disposal of another relevant public authority ("the subscribing authority") for the purposes of the subscribing authority's functions under this Part, and
   (b) either—
      (i) a designated senior officer of the supplying authority is permitted to grant authorisations to officers of the subscribing authority,
      (ii) officers of the supplying authority are permitted to be granted authorisations by a designated senior officer of the subscribing authority, or
      (iii) officers of the supplying authority act as single points of contact for officers of the subscribing authority.
(2) The persons by whom, or to whom, authorisations may be granted (or who may act as single points of contact) under a collaboration agreement are additional to those persons by whom, or to whom, authorisations would otherwise be granted under this Part (or who could otherwise act as single points of contact).

(3) In a case falling within subsection (1)(b)(i)—
  (a) section 61 has effect as if—
    (i) in subsection (2) the reference to an officer of the authority were a reference to an officer of the subscribing authority, and
    (ii) in subsection (6)(b)(ii) the reference to an officer of the same relevant public authority as an authorised officer included a reference to an officer of the supplying authority,
  (b) section 63(3)(d) has effect as if the reference to the relevant public authority concerned were a reference to both authorities,
  (c) this Part has effect as if the designated senior officer of the supplying authority had the power to grant an authorisation to officers of the subscribing authority, and had other functions in relation to the authorisation, which were the same as (and subject to no greater or lesser restrictions than) the power and other functions which the designated senior officer of the subscribing authority who would otherwise have dealt with the authorisation would have had, and
  (d) section 75(1) applies to the authorisation as if it were granted by a designated senior officer of the subscribing authority.
(4) In a case falling within subsection (1)(b)(ii)—
  (a) section 61 has effect as if—
    (i) in subsection (2) the reference to an officer of the authority were a reference to an officer of the supplying authority, and
    (ii) in subsection (6)(b)(ii) the reference to an officer of the same relevant public authority as an authorised officer included a reference to an officer of the subscribing authority, and
  (b) section 63(3)(d) has effect as if the reference to the relevant public authority concerned were a reference to both authorities.
(5) In a case falling within subsection (1)(b)(iii), section 76(4)(b) has effect as if the references to the relevant public authority were references to the subscribing authority.
(6) In this section—
"force collaboration provision" has the meaning given by paragraph (a) of section 22A(2) of the Police Act 1996 but as if the reference in that paragraph to a police force included the National Crime Agency,
"police collaboration agreement" means a collaboration agreement under section 22A of the Police Act 1996 which contains force collaboration provision.

79 Collaboration agreements: supplementary

(1) A collaboration agreement may provide for payments to be made between parties to the agreement.
(2) A collaboration agreement—
  (a) must be in writing,
  (b) may be varied by a subsequent collaboration agreement, and
  (c) may be brought to an end by agreement between the parties to it.
(3) A person who makes a collaboration agreement must—
  (a) publish the agreement, or
  (b) publish the fact that the agreement has been made and such other details about it as the person considers appropriate.
(4) A relevant public authority may enter into a collaboration agreement as a supplying authority, a subscribing authority or both (whether or not it would have power to do so apart from this section).

(5) The Secretary of State may, after consulting a relevant public authority, direct it to enter into a collaboration agreement if the Secretary of State considers that entering into the agreement would assist the effective exercise by the authority, or another relevant public authority, of its functions under this Part.

(6) A code of practice under Schedule 7 must include guidance to relevant public authorities about collaboration agreements.

(7) The guidance must include guidance about the criteria the Secretary of State will use in considering whether a collaboration agreement is appropriate for a relevant public authority.

80 Police collaboration agreements

(1) This section applies if—
  (a) the chief officer of police of an England and Wales police force ("force 1") has entered into a police collaboration agreement for the purposes of a collaborating police force's functions under this Part, and
  (b) under the terms of the agreement—
    (i) a designated senior officer of force 1 is permitted to grant authorisations to officers of the collaborating police force, (ii) officers of force 1 are permitted to be granted authorisations by a designated senior officer of the collaborating police force, or
    (iii) officers of force 1 act as single points of contact for officers of the collaborating police force.

(2) The persons by whom, or to whom, authorisations may be granted (or who may act as single points of contact) under a police collaboration agreement are additional to those persons by whom, or to whom, authorisations would otherwise be granted under this Part (or who could otherwise act as single points of contact).

(3) In a case falling within subsection (1)(b)(i)—
  (a) section 61 has effect as if—
    (i) in subsection (2) the reference to an officer of the authority were a reference to an officer of the collaborating police force, and
    (ii) in subsection (6)(b)(ii) the reference to an officer of the same relevant public authority as an authorised officer included a reference to an officer of force 1,
  (b) section 63(3)(d) has effect as if the reference to the relevant public authority concerned were a reference to force 1 and the collaborating police force, and
  (c) this Part has effect as if the designated senior officer of force 1 had the power to grant an authorisation to officers of the collaborating police force, and had other functions in relation to the authorisation, which were the same as (and subject to no greater or lesser restrictions than) the power and other functions which the designated senior officer of the collaborating police force who would otherwise have dealt with the authorisation would have had.

(4) In a case falling within subsection (1)(b)(ii)—
  (a) section 61 has effect as if—
    (i) in subsection (2) the reference to an officer of the authority were a reference to an officer of force 1, and
    (ii) in subsection (6)(b)(ii) the reference to an officer of the same relevant public authority as an authorised officer included a reference to an officer of the collaborating police force, and
  (b) section 63(3)(d) has effect as if the reference to the relevant public authority concerned were a reference to force 1 and the collaborating police force.

(5) In a case falling within subsection (1)(b)(iii), section 76(4)(b) has effect as if the references to the relevant public authority were references to the collaborating police force.

Appendix

(6) In this section—
"collaborating police force", in relation to a police collaboration agreement, means a police force (other than force 1) whose chief officer of police is a party to the agreement,
"England and Wales police force" means—
   (a) any police force maintained under section 2 of the Police Act 1996 (police forces in England and Wales outside London),
   (b) the metropolitan police force, or
   (c) the City of London police force,
"police collaboration agreement" has the same meaning as in section 78 (see subsection (6) of that section), and references in this section to an England and Wales police force or a police force include the National Crime Agency (and references to the chief officer of police include the Director General of the National Crime Agency).

Further and supplementary provision

81 Lawfulness of conduct authorised by this Part

(1) Conduct is lawful for all purposes if—
   (a) it is conduct in which any person is authorised to engage by an authorisation or required to undertake by virtue of a notice given in pursuance of an authorisation, and
   (b) the conduct is in accordance with, or in pursuance of, the authorisation or notice.
(2) A person (whether or not the person so authorised or required) is not to be subject to any civil liability in respect of conduct that—
   (a) is incidental to, or is reasonably undertaken in connection with, conduct that is lawful by virtue of subsection (1), and
   (b) is not itself conduct for which an authorisation or warrant—
      (i) is capable of being granted under any of the enactments mentioned in subsection (3), and
      (ii) might reasonably have been expected to have been sought in the case in question.
(3) The enactments referred to in subsection (2)(b)(i) are—
   (a) an enactment contained in this Act,
   (b) an enactment contained in the Regulation of Investigatory Powers Act 2000,
   (c) an enactment contained in Part 3 of the Police Act 1997 (powers of the police and of customs officers), or
   (d) section 5 of the Intelligence Services Act 1994 (warrants for the intelligence services).

82 Offence of making unauthorised disclosure

(1) It is an offence for a telecommunications operator, or any person employed or engaged for the purposes of the business of a telecommunications operator, to disclose, without reasonable excuse, to any person the existence of—
   (a) any requirement imposed on the operator by virtue of this Part to disclose communications data relating to that person, or
   (b) any request made in pursuance of an authorisation for the operator to disclose such data.
(2) For the purposes of subsection (1), it is, in particular, a reasonable excuse if the disclosure is made with the permission of the relevant public authority which is seeking to obtain the data from the operator (whether the permission is contained in any notice requiring the operator to disclose the data or otherwise).
(3) A person guilty of an offence under this section is liable—
   (a) on summary conviction in England and Wales—

Appendix

   (i) to imprisonment for a term not exceeding 12 months (or 6 months, if the offence was committed before the commencement of section 154(1) of the Criminal Justice Act 2003), or
   (ii) to a fine, or to both;
 (b) on summary conviction in Scotland—
   (i) to imprisonment for a term not exceeding 12 months, or
   (ii) to a fine not exceeding the statutory maximum, or to both;
 (c) on summary conviction in Northern Ireland—
   (i) to imprisonment for a term not exceeding 6 months, or
   (ii) to a fine not exceeding the statutory maximum, or to both;
 (d) on conviction on indictment, to imprisonment for a term not exceeding 2 years or to a fine, or to both.

83 Certain transfer and agency arrangements with public authorities

(1) The Secretary of State may by regulations provide for—
 (a) any function under sections 67 to 69 which is exercisable by the Secretary of State to be exercisable instead by another public authority, or
 (b) any function under sections 67 to 69 which is exercisable by a public authority by virtue of paragraph (a) to be exercisable instead by the Secretary of State.
(2) The Secretary of State may by regulations modify any enactment about a public authority for the purpose of enabling or otherwise facilitating any function exercisable by the Secretary of State under this Part to be exercisable on behalf of the Secretary of State by the authority concerned.
(3) Regulations under subsection (2) do not affect the Secretary of State's responsibility for the exercise of the functions concerned.
(4) Subsection (2) does not apply in relation to any function of the Secretary of State of making regulations.
(5) Schedule 5 (which contains further safeguards and provisions supplementing this section) has effect.

84 Application of Part 3 to postal operators and postal services

(1) This Part applies to postal operators and postal services as it applies to telecommunications operators and telecommunications services.
(2) In its application by virtue of subsection (1), this Part has effect as if—
 (a) any reference to a telecommunications operator were a reference to a postal operator,
 (b) any reference to a telecommunications service were a reference to a postal service,
 (c) any reference to a telecommunication system were a reference to a postal service,
 (d) sections 61(3)(a) and 62 were omitted, and
 (e) in Part 2 of Schedule 4, for "which is entity data" there were substituted "within paragraph (c) of the definition of "communications data" in section 262(3)".

85 Extra-territorial application of Part 3

(1) An authorisation may relate to conduct outside the United Kingdom and persons outside the United Kingdom.
(2) A notice given in pursuance of an authorisation may relate to conduct outside the United Kingdom and persons outside the United Kingdom.
(3) Where such a notice is to be given to a person outside the United Kingdom, the notice may be given to the person in any of the following ways (as well as by electronic or other means of service)—

Appendix

(a) by delivering it to the person's principal office within the United Kingdom or, if the person has no such office in the United Kingdom, to any place in the United Kingdom where the person carries on business or conducts activities,

(b) if the person has specified an address in the United Kingdom as one at which the person, or someone on the person's behalf, will accept documents of the same description as a notice, by delivering it to that address,

(c) by notifying the person by such other means as the authorised officer considers appropriate (which may include notifying the person orally).

(4) In determining for the purposes of subsection (3) of section 66 whether it is reasonably practicable for a telecommunications operator outside the United Kingdom to take any steps in a country or territory outside the United Kingdom for the purpose of complying with a duty imposed by virtue of subsection (1) or (2) of that section, the matters to be taken into account include the following—

(a) any requirements or restrictions under the law of that country or territory that are relevant to the taking of those steps, and

(b) the extent to which it is reasonably practicable to comply with the duty in a way that does not breach any of those requirements or restrictions.

(5) Nothing in the definition of "telecommunications operator" limits the type of communications data in relation to which an authorisation, or a request or requirement of a kind which gives rise to a duty under section 66(1) or (2), may apply.

86 Part 3: interpretation

(1) In this Part—

"authorisation" means an authorisation under section 61 (including that section as modified by sections 78 and 80),

"designated senior officer"—

(a) in relation to a relevant public authority which is a local authority, has the meaning given by section 73(2), and

(b) in relation to any other relevant public authority, has the meaning given by section 70(3),

"filtering arrangements" means any arrangements under section 67(1),

"officer", in relation to a relevant public authority, means a person holding an office, rank or position with that authority,

"relevant public authority" means a public authority which is a relevant public authority for the purposes of this Part by virtue of section 70(2) or 73(1).

(2) In this Part "local authority" means—

(a) a district or county council in England,

(b) a London borough council,

(c) the Common Council of the City of London in its capacity as a local authority,

(d) the Council of the Isles of Scilly,

(e) a county council or county borough council in Wales,

(f) a council constituted under section 2 of the Local Government etc. (Scotland) Act 1994, and

(g) a district council in Northern Ireland.

(3) See also—

section 261 (telecommunications definitions),
section 262 (postal definitions),
section 263 (general definitions),
section 265 (index of defined expressions).

Appendix

PART 4
RETENTION OF COMMUNICATIONS DATA

General

87 Powers to require retention of certain data

(1) The Secretary of State may, by notice (a "retention notice") and subject as follows, require a telecommunications operator to retain relevant communications data if—
   (a) the Secretary of State considers that the requirement is necessary and proportionate for one or more of the purposes falling within paragraphs (a) to (j) of section 61(7) (purposes for which communications data may be obtained), and
   (b) the decision to give the notice has been approved by a Judicial Commissioner.
(2) A retention notice may—
   (a) relate to a particular operator or any description of operators,
   (b) require the retention of all data or any description of data,
   (c) identify the period or periods for which data is to be retained,
   (d) contain other requirements, or restrictions, in relation to the retention of data,
   (e) make different provision for different purposes,
   (f) relate to data whether or not in existence at the time of the giving, or coming into force, of the notice.
(3) A retention notice must not require any data to be retained for more than 12 months beginning with—
   (a) in the case of communications data relating to a specific communication, the day of the communication concerned,
   (b) in the case of entity data which does not fall within paragraph (a) above but does fall within paragraph (a)(i) of the definition of "communications data" in section 261(5), the day on which the entity concerned ceases to be associated with the telecommunications service concerned or (if earlier) the day on which the data is changed, and
   (c) in any other case, the day on which the data is first held by the operator concerned.
(4) A retention notice must not require an operator who controls or provides a telecommunication system ("the system operator") to retain data which—
   (a) relates to the use of a telecommunications service provided by another telecommunications operator in relation to that system,
   (b) is (or is capable of being) processed by the system operator as a result of being comprised in, included as part of, attached to or logically associated with a communication transmitted by means of the system as a result of the use mentioned in paragraph (a),
   (c) is not needed by the system operator for the functioning of the system in relation to that communication, and
   (d) is not retained or used by the system operator for any other lawful purpose, and which it is reasonably practicable to separate from other data which is subject to the notice.
(5) A retention notice which relates to data already in existence when the notice comes into force imposes a requirement to retain the data for only so much of a period of retention as occurs on or after the coming into force of the notice.
(6) A retention notice comes into force—
   (a) when the notice is given to the operator (or description of operators) concerned, or
   (b) (if later) at the time or times specified in the notice.
(7) A retention notice is given to an operator (or description of operators) by giving, or publishing, it in such manner as the Secretary of State considers appropriate for bringing it to the attention of the operator (or description of operators) to whom it relates.

Appendix

(8) A retention notice must specify—
   (a) the operator (or description of operators) to whom it relates,
   (b) the data which is to be retained,
   (c) the period or periods for which the data is to be retained,
   (d) any other requirements, or any restrictions, in relation to the retention of the data,
   (e) the information required by section 249(7) (the level or levels of contribution in respect of costs incurred as a result of the notice).
(9) The requirements or restrictions mentioned in subsection (8)(d) may, in particular, include—
   (a) a requirement to retain the data in such a way that it can be transmitted efficiently and effectively in response to requests,
   (b) requirements or restrictions in relation to the obtaining (whether by collection, generation or otherwise), generation or processing of—
      (i) data for retention, or
      (ii) retained data.
(10) The fact that the data which would be retained under a retention notice relates to the activities in the British Islands of a trade union is not, of itself, sufficient to establish that the requirement to retain the data is necessary for one or more of the purposes falling within paragraphs (a) to (j) of section 61(7).
(11) In this Part "relevant communications data" means communications data which may be used to identify, or assist in identifying, any of the following—
   (a) the sender or recipient of a communication (whether or not a person),
   (b) the time or duration of a communication,
   (c) the type, method or pattern, or fact, of communication,
   (d) the telecommunication system (or any part of it) from, to or through which, or by means of which, a communication is or may be transmitted, or
   (e) the location of any such system, and this expression therefore includes, in particular, internet connection records.

Safeguards

88 Matters to be taken into account before giving retention notices

(1) Before giving a retention notice, the Secretary of State must, among other matters, take into account—
   (a) the likely benefits of the notice,
   (b) the likely number of users (if known) of any telecommunications service to which the notice relates,
   (c) the technical feasibility of complying with the notice, (d) the likely cost of complying with the notice, and
   (e) any other effect of the notice on the telecommunications operator (or description of operators) to whom it relates.
(2) Before giving such a notice, the Secretary of State must take reasonable steps to consult any operator to whom it relates.

89 Approval of retention notices by Judicial Commissioners

(1) In deciding whether to approve a decision to give a retention notice, a Judicial Commissioner must review the Secretary of State's conclusions as to whether the requirement to be imposed by the notice to retain relevant communications data is necessary and proportionate for one or more of the purposes falling within paragraphs (a) to (j) of section 61(7).

(2) In doing so, the Judicial Commissioner must—
   (a) apply the same principles as would be applied by a court on an application for judicial review, and
   (b) consider the matters referred to in subsection (1) with a sufficient degree of care as to ensure that the Judicial Commissioner complies with the duties imposed by section 2 (general duties in relation to privacy).
(3) Where a Judicial Commissioner refuses to approve a decision to give a retention notice, the Judicial Commissioner must give the Secretary of State written reasons for the refusal.
(4) Where a Judicial Commissioner, other than the Investigatory Powers Commissioner, refuses to approve a decision to give a retention notice, the Secretary of State may ask the Investigatory Powers Commissioner to decide whether to approve the decision to give the notice.

90 Review by the Secretary of State

(1) A telecommunications operator to whom a retention notice is given may, within such period or circumstances as may be provided for by regulations made by the Secretary of State, refer the notice back to the Secretary of State.
(2) Such a reference may be in relation to the whole of a notice or any aspect of it.
(3) In the case of a notice given to a description of operators—
   (a) each operator falling within that description may make a reference under subsection (1), but
   (b) each such reference may only be in relation to the notice, or aspect of the notice, so far as it applies to that operator.
(4) There is no requirement for an operator who has referred a retention notice under subsection (1) to comply with the notice, so far as referred, until the Secretary of State has reviewed the notice in accordance with subsection (5).
(5) The Secretary of State must review any notice so far as referred to the Secretary of State under subsection (1).
(6) Before deciding the review, the Secretary of State must consult—
   (a) the Technical Advisory Board, and
   (b) a Judicial Commissioner.
(7) The Board must consider the technical requirements and the financial consequences, for the operator who has made the reference, of the notice so far as referred.
(8) The Commissioner must consider whether the notice so far as referred is proportionate.
(9) The Board and the Commissioner must—
   (a) give the operator concerned and the Secretary of State the opportunity to provide evidence, or make representations, to them before reaching their conclusions, and
   (b) report their conclusions to—
      (i) the operator, and
      (ii) the Secretary of State.
(10) The Secretary of State may, after considering the conclusions of the Board and the Commissioner—
   (a) vary or revoke the retention notice under section 94, or
   (b) give a notice under this section to the operator concerned confirming its effect.
(11) But the Secretary of State may vary the notice, or give a notice under subsection (10)(b) confirming its effect, only if the Secretary of State's decision to do so has been approved by the Investigatory Powers Commissioner.
(12) A report or notice under this section is given to an operator by giving or publishing it in such manner as the Secretary of State considers appropriate for bringing it to the attention of the operator.

(13) The Secretary of State must keep a retention notice under review (whether or not referred under subsection (1)).

91 Approval of notices following review under section 90

(1) In deciding whether to approve a decision to vary a retention notice as mentioned in section 90(10)(a), or to give a notice under section 90(10)(b) confirming the effect of a retention notice, the Investigatory Powers Commissioner must review the Secretary of State's conclusions as to whether the requirement to be imposed by the notice as varied or confirmed to retain relevant communications data is necessary and proportionate for one or more of the purposes falling within paragraphs (a) to (j) of section 61(7).
(2) In doing so, the Investigatory Powers Commissioner must—
   (a) apply the same principles as would be applied by a court on an application for judicial review, and
   (b) consider the matters referred to in subsection (1) with a sufficient degree of care as to ensure that the Investigatory Powers Commissioner complies with the duties imposed by section 2 (general duties in relation to privacy).
(3) Where the Investigatory Powers Commissioner refuses to approve a decision to vary a retention notice as mentioned in section 90(10)(a), or to give a notice under section 90(10)(b) confirming the effect of a retention notice, the Investigatory Powers Commissioner must give the Secretary of State written reasons for the refusal.

92 Data integrity and security

(1) A telecommunications operator who retains relevant communications data by virtue of this Part must—
   (a) secure that the data is of the same integrity, and subject to at least the same security and protection, as the data on any system from which it is derived,
   (b) secure, by appropriate technical and organisational measures, that the data can be accessed only by specially authorised personnel, and
   (c) protect, by appropriate technical and organisational measures, the data against accidental or unlawful destruction, accidental loss or alteration, or unauthorised or unlawful retention, processing, access or disclosure.
(2) A telecommunications operator who retains relevant communications data by virtue of this Part must destroy the data if the retention of the data ceases to be authorised by virtue of this Part and is not otherwise authorised by law.
(3) The destruction of the data may take place at such monthly or shorter intervals as appear to the operator to be practicable.

93 Disclosure of retained data

A telecommunications operator must put in place adequate security systems (including technical and organisational measures) governing access to relevant communications data retained by virtue of this Part in order to protect against any unlawful disclosure.

Variation or revocation of notices

94 Variation or revocation of notices

(1) The Secretary of State may vary a retention notice.
(2) The Secretary of State must give, or publish, notice of the variation in such manner as the Secretary of State considers appropriate for bringing the variation to the attention of the telecommunications operator (or description of operators) to whom it relates.

(3) A variation comes into force—
   (a) when notice of it is given or published in accordance with subsection (2), or
   (b) (if later) at the time or times specified in the notice of variation.
(4) A retention notice may not be varied so as to require the retention of additional relevant communications data unless—
   (a) the Secretary of State considers that the requirement is necessary and proportionate for one or more of the purposes falling within paragraphs (a) to (j) of section 61(7), and
   (b) subject to subsection (6), the decision to vary the notice has been approved by a Judicial Commissioner.
(5) The fact that additional relevant communications data which would be retained under a retention notice as varied relates to the activities in the British Islands of a trade union is not, of itself, sufficient to establish that the requirement to retain the data is necessary for one or more of the purposes falling within paragraphs (a) to (j) of section 61(7).
(6) Subsection (4)(b) does not apply to a variation to which section 90(11) applies.
(7) Section 87(2) and (5) apply in relation to a retention notice as varied as they apply in relation to a retention notice, but as if the references to the notice coming into force included references to the variation coming into force.
(8) Sections 87(3), (4) and (8), 95 and 97, and subsections (1), (4), (13) and (16) of this section, apply in relation to a retention notice as varied as they apply in relation to a retention notice.
(9) Section 88 applies in relation to the making of a variation as it applies in relation to the giving of a retention notice (and, accordingly, the references to the notice in section 88(1)(a) to (e) are to be read as references to the variation).
(10) Section 89 applies in relation to a decision to vary to which subsection (4)(b) above applies as it applies in relation to a decision to give a retention notice (and, accordingly, the reference in subsection (1) of that section to the requirement to be imposed by the notice is to be read as a reference to the requirement to be imposed by the variation).
(11) Section 90 applies (but only so far as the variation is concerned) in relation to a retention notice as varied (other than one varied as mentioned in subsection (10)(a) of that section) as it applies in relation to a retention notice.
(12) Section 91 applies in relation to a decision under section 90(10) to vary or confirm a variation as it applies in relation to a decision to vary or confirm a retention notice (and, accordingly, the reference in subsection (1) of that section to the requirement to be imposed by the notice as varied or confirmed is to be read as a reference to the requirement to be imposed by the variation as varied or confirmed).
(13) The Secretary of State may revoke (whether wholly or in part) a retention notice.
(14) The Secretary of State must give or publish notice of the revocation in such manner as the Secretary of State considers appropriate for bringing the revocation to the attention of the operator (or description of operators) to whom it relates.
(15) A revocation comes into force—
   (a) when notice of it is given or published in accordance with subsection (14), or
   (b) (if later) at the time or times specified in the notice of revocation.
(16) The fact that a retention notice has been revoked in relation to a particular description of communications data and a particular operator (or description of operators) does not prevent the giving of another retention notice in relation to the same description of data and the same operator (or description of operators).

Enforcement

95 Enforcement of notices and certain other requirements and restrictions

(1) It is the duty of a telecommunications operator on whom a requirement or restriction is imposed by—
    (a) a retention notice, or
    (b) section 92 or 93, to comply with the requirement or restriction.
(2) A telecommunications operator, or any person employed or engaged for the purposes of the business of a telecommunications operator, must not disclose the existence or contents of a retention notice to any other person.
(3) The Information Commissioner, or any member of staff of the Information Commissioner, must not disclose the existence or contents of a retention notice to any other person.
(4) Subsections (2) and (3) do not apply to a disclosure made with the permission of the Secretary of State.
(5) The duty under subsection (1) or (2) is enforceable by civil proceedings by the Secretary of State for an injunction, or for specific performance of a statutory duty under section 45 of the Court of Session Act 1988, or for any other appropriate relief.

Further and supplementary provision

96 Application of Part 4 to postal operators and postal services

(1) This Part applies to postal operators and postal services as it applies to telecommunications operators and telecommunications services.
(2) In its application by virtue of subsection (1), this Part has effect as if—
    (a) any reference to a telecommunications operator were a reference to a postal operator,
    (b) any reference to a telecommunications service were a reference to a postal service,
    (c) any reference to a telecommunication system were a reference to a postal service,
    (d) in section 87(3), for paragraph (b) there were substituted—
        "(b) in the case of communications data which does not fall within paragraph (a) above but does fall within paragraph (c) of the definition of "communications data" in section 262(3), the day on which the person concerned leaves the postal service concerned or (if earlier) the day on which the data is changed,",
    (e) for section 87(4) there were substituted—
        "(4) A retention notice must not require an operator who provides a postal service ("the network operator") to retain data which—
            (a) relates to the use of a postal service provided by another postal operator in relation to the postal service of the network operator,
            (b) is (or is capable of being) processed by the network operator as a result of being comprised in, included as part of, attached to or logically associated with a communication transmitted by means of the postal service of the network operator as a result of the use mentioned in paragraph (a),
            (c) is not needed by the network operator for the functioning of the network operator's postal service in relation to that communication, and
            (d) is not retained or used by the network operator for any other lawful purpose, and which it is reasonably practicable to separate from other data which is subject to the notice.", and
    (f) in section 87(11), the words from "and this expression" to the end were omitted.

Appendix

97 Extra-territorial application of Part 4

(1) A retention notice, and any requirement or restriction imposed by virtue of a retention notice or by section 92, 93 or 95(1) to (3), may relate to conduct outside the United Kingdom and persons outside the United Kingdom.

(2) But section 95(5), so far as relating to those requirements or restrictions, does not apply to a person outside the United Kingdom.

98 Part 4: interpretation

(1) In this Part—
"notice" means notice in writing,
"relevant communications data" has the meaning given by section 87(11),
"retention notice" has the meaning given by section 87(1).

(2) See also—
section 261 (telecommunications definitions),
section 262 (postal definitions),
section 263 (general definitions),
section 265 (index of defined expressions).

PART 5
EQUIPMENT INTERFERENCE

Warrants under this Part

99 Warrants under this Part: general

(1) There are two kinds of warrants which may be issued under this Part—
   (a) targeted equipment interference warrants (see subsection (2));
   (b) targeted examination warrants (see subsection (9)).

(2) A targeted equipment interference warrant is a warrant which authorises or requires the person to whom it is addressed to secure interference with any equipment for the purpose of obtaining—
   (a) communications (see section 135);
   (b) equipment data (see section 100);
   (c) any other information.

(3) A targeted equipment interference warrant—
   (a) must also authorise or require the person to whom it is addressed to secure the obtaining of the communications, equipment data or other information to which the warrant relates;
   (b) may also authorise that person to secure the disclosure, in any manner described in the warrant, of anything obtained under the warrant by virtue of paragraph (a).

(4) The reference in subsections (2) and (3) to the obtaining of communications or other information includes doing so by—
   (a) monitoring, observing or listening to a person's communications or other activities;
   (b) recording anything which is monitored, observed or listened to.

(5) A targeted equipment interference warrant also authorises the following conduct (in addition to the conduct described in the warrant)—
   (a) any conduct which it is necessary to undertake in order to do what is expressly authorised or required by the warrant, including conduct for securing the obtaining of communications, equipment data or other information;

Appendix

(b) any conduct by any person which is conduct in pursuance of a requirement imposed by or on behalf of the person to whom the warrant is addressed to be provided with assistance in giving effect to the warrant.

(6) A targeted equipment interference warrant may not, by virtue of subsection (3), authorise or require a person to engage in conduct, in relation to a communication other than a stored communication, which would (unless done with lawful authority) constitute an offence under section 3(1) (unlawful interception).

(7) Subsection (5)(a) does not authorise a person to engage in conduct which could not be expressly authorised under the warrant because of the restriction imposed by subsection (6).

(8) In subsection (6), "stored communication" means a communication stored in or by a telecommunication system (whether before or after its transmission).

(9) A targeted examination warrant is a warrant which authorises the person to whom it is addressed to carry out the selection of protected material obtained under a bulk equipment interference warrant for examination, in breach of the prohibition in section 193(4) (prohibition on seeking to identify communications of, or private information relating to, individuals in the British Islands). In this Part, "protected material", in relation to a targeted examination warrant, means any material obtained under a bulk equipment interference warrant under Chapter 3 of Part 6, other than material which is—
   (a) equipment data;
   (b) information (other than a communication or equipment data) which is not private information.

(10) For provision enabling the combination of targeted equipment interference warrants with certain other warrants or authorisations (including targeted examination warrants), see Schedule 8.

(11) Any conduct which is carried out in accordance with a warrant under this Part is lawful for all purposes.

100 Meaning of "equipment data"

(1) In this Part, "equipment data" means—
   (a) systems data;
   (b) data which falls within subsection (2).

(2) The data falling within this subsection is identifying data which—
   (a) is, for the purposes of a relevant system, comprised in, included as part of, attached to or logically associated with a communication (whether by the sender or otherwise) or any other item of information,
   (b) is capable of being logically separated from the remainder of the communication or the item of information, and
   (c) if it were so separated, would not reveal anything of what might reasonably be considered to be the meaning (if any) of the communication or the item of information, disregarding any meaning arising from the fact of the communication or the existence of the item of information or from any data relating to that fact.

(3) In subsection (2), "relevant system" means any system on or by means of which the data is held.

(4) For the meaning of "systems data" and "identifying data", see section 263.

101 Subject-matter of warrants

(1) A targeted equipment interference warrant may relate to any one or more of the following matters—
   (a) equipment belonging to, used by or in the possession of a particular person or organisation;

(b) equipment belonging to, used by or in the possession of a group of persons who share a common purpose or who carry on, or may carry on, a particular activity;
(c) equipment belonging to, used by or in the possession of more than one person or organisation, where the interference is for the purpose of a single investigation or operation;
(d) equipment in a particular location;
(e) equipment in more than one location, where the interference is for the purpose of a single investigation or operation;
(f) equipment which is being, or may be, used for the purposes of a particular activity or activities of a particular description;
(g) equipment which is being, or may be, used to test, maintain or develop capabilities relating to interference with equipment for the purpose of obtaining communications, equipment data or other information;
(h) equipment which is being, or may be, used for the training of persons who carry out, or are likely to carry out, such interference with equipment.
(2) A targeted examination warrant may relate to any one or more of the following matters—
 (a) a particular person or organisation;
 (b) a group of persons who share a common purpose or who carry on, or may carry on, a particular activity;
 (c) more than one person or organisation, where the conduct authorised by the warrant is for the purpose of a single investigation or operation;
 (d) the testing, maintenance or development of capabilities relating to the selection of protected material for examination;
 (e) the training of persons who carry out, or are likely to carry out, the selection of such material for examination.

Power to issue warrants

102 Power to issue warrants to intelligence services: the Secretary of State

(1) The Secretary of State may, on an application made by or on behalf of the head of an intelligence service, issue a targeted equipment interference warrant if—
 (a) the Secretary of State considers that the warrant is necessary on grounds falling within subsection (5),
 (b) the Secretary of State considers that the conduct authorised by the warrant is proportionate to what is sought to be achieved by that conduct,
 (c) the Secretary of State considers that satisfactory arrangements made for the purposes of sections 129 and 130 (safeguards relating to disclosure etc.) are in force in relation to the warrant, and
 (d) except where the Secretary of State considers that there is an urgent need to issue the warrant, the decision to issue the warrant has been approved by a Judicial Commissioner.
(2) But the Secretary of State may not issue a targeted equipment interference warrant under subsection (1) if—
 (a) the Secretary of State considers that the only ground for considering the warrant to be necessary is for the purpose of preventing or detecting serious crime, and
 (b) the warrant, if issued, would authorise interference only with equipment which would be in Scotland at the time of the issue of the warrant or which the Secretary of State believes would be in Scotland at that time.
 For the power of the Scottish Ministers to issue a targeted equipment interference warrant, see section 103.

(3) The Secretary of State may, on an application made by or on behalf of the head of an intelligence service, issue a targeted examination warrant if—
   (a) the Secretary of State considers that the warrant is necessary on grounds falling within subsection (5),
   (b) the Secretary of State considers that the conduct authorised by the warrant is proportionate to what is sought to be achieved by that conduct,
   (c) the Secretary of State considers that the warrant is or may be necessary to authorise the selection of protected material for examination in breach of the prohibition in section 193(4) (prohibition on seeking to identify communications of, or private information relating to, individuals in the British Islands), and
   (d) except where the Secretary of State considers that there is an urgent need to issue the warrant, the decision to issue the warrant has been approved by a Judicial Commissioner.
(4) But the Secretary of State may not issue a targeted examination warrant under subsection (3) if the warrant, if issued, would relate only to a person who would be in Scotland at the time of the issue of the warrant or whom the Secretary of State believes would be in Scotland at that time.
For the power of the Scottish Ministers to issue a targeted examination warrant, see section 103.
(5) A warrant is necessary on grounds falling within this subsection if it is necessary—
   (a) in the interests of national security,
   (b) for the purpose of preventing or detecting serious crime, or
   (c) in the interests of the economic well-being of the United Kingdom so far as those interests are also relevant to the interests of national security.
(6) A warrant may be considered necessary on the ground falling within subsection (5)(c) only if the interference with equipment which would be authorised by the warrant is considered necessary for the purpose of obtaining information relating to the acts or intentions of persons outside the British Islands.
(7) The fact that the information which would be obtained under a warrant relates to the activities in the British Islands of a trade union is not, of itself, sufficient to establish that the warrant is necessary on grounds falling within subsection (5).
(8) An application for the issue of a warrant under this section may only be made on behalf of the head of an intelligence service by a person holding office under the Crown.
(9) Nothing in subsection (2) or (4) prevents the Secretary of State from doing anything under this section for the purposes specified in section 2(2) of the European Communities Act 1972.

103 Power to issue warrants to intelligence services: the Scottish Ministers

(1) The Scottish Ministers may, on an application made by or on behalf of the head of an intelligence service, issue a targeted equipment interference warrant if—
   (a) the warrant authorises interference only with equipment which is in Scotland at the time the warrant is issued or which the Scottish Ministers believe to be in Scotland at that time,
   (b) the Scottish Ministers consider that the warrant is necessary for the purpose of preventing or detecting serious crime,
   (c) the Scottish Ministers consider that the conduct authorised by the warrant is proportionate to what is sought to be achieved by that conduct,
   (d) the Scottish Ministers consider that satisfactory arrangements made for the purposes of sections 129 and 130 (safeguards relating to disclosure etc.) are in force in relation to the warrant, and

(e) except where the Scottish Ministers consider that there is an urgent need to issue the warrant, the decision to issue the warrant has been approved by a Judicial Commissioner.
(2) The Scottish Ministers may, on an application made by or on behalf of the head of an intelligence service, issue a targeted examination warrant if—
  (a) the warrant relates only to a person who is in Scotland, or whom the Scottish Ministers believe to be in Scotland, at the time of the issue of the warrant,
  (b) the Scottish Ministers consider that the warrant is necessary for the purpose of preventing or detecting serious crime,
  (c) the Scottish Ministers consider that the conduct authorised by the warrant is proportionate to what is sought to be achieved by that conduct,
  (d) the Scottish Ministers consider that the warrant is or may be necessary to authorise the selection of protected material in breach of the prohibition in section 193(4) (prohibition on seeking to identify communications of, or private information relating to, individuals in the British Islands), and
  (e) except where the Scottish Ministers consider that there is an urgent need to issue the warrant, the decision to issue the warrant has been approved by a Judicial Commissioner.
(3) The fact that the information which would be obtained under a warrant relates to the activities in the British Islands of a trade union is not, of itself, sufficient to establish that the warrant is necessary as mentioned in subsection (1)(b) or (2)(b).
(4) An application for the issue of a warrant under this section may only be made on behalf of the head of an intelligence service by a person holding office under the Crown.

104 Power to issue warrants to the Chief of Defence Intelligence

(1) The Secretary of State may, on an application made by or on behalf of the Chief of Defence Intelligence, issue a targeted equipment interference warrant if—
  (a) the Secretary of State considers that the warrant is necessary in the interests of national security,
  (b) the Secretary of State considers that the conduct authorised by the warrant is proportionate to what is sought to be achieved by that conduct,
  (c) the Secretary of State considers that satisfactory arrangements made for the purposes of sections 129 and 130 (safeguards relating to disclosure etc.) are in force in relation to the warrant, and
  (d) except where the Secretary of State considers that there is an urgent need to issue the warrant, the decision to issue the warrant has been approved by a Judicial Commissioner.
(2) The fact that the information which would be obtained under a warrant relates to the activities in the British Islands of a trade union is not, of itself, sufficient to establish that the warrant is necessary as mentioned in subsection (1)(a).
(3) An application for the issue of a warrant under this section may only be made on behalf of the Chief of Defence Intelligence by a person holding office under the Crown.

105 Decision to issue warrants under sections 102 to 104 to be taken personally by Ministers

(1) The decision to issue a warrant under section 102 or 104 must be taken personally by the Secretary of State.
(2) The decision to issue a warrant under section 103 must be taken personally by a member of the Scottish Government.
(3) Before a warrant under section 102, 103 or 104 is issued, it must be signed by the person who has taken the decision to issue it (subject to subsection (4)).

(4) If it is not reasonably practicable for a warrant to be signed by the person who has taken the decision to issue it, the warrant may be signed by a senior official designated by the Secretary of State or (as the case may be) the Scottish Ministers for that purpose.

(5) In such a case, the warrant must contain a statement that—
  (a) it is not reasonably practicable for the warrant to be signed by the person who took the decision to issue it, and
  (b) the Secretary of State or (as the case may be) a member of the Scottish Government has personally and expressly authorised the issue of the warrant.

106 Power to issue warrants to law enforcement officers

(1) A law enforcement chief described in Part 1 or 2 of the table in Schedule 6 may, on an application made by a person who is an appropriate law enforcement officer in relation to the chief, issue a targeted equipment interference warrant if—
  (a) the law enforcement chief considers that the warrant is necessary for the purpose of preventing or detecting serious crime,
  (b) the law enforcement chief considers that the conduct authorised by the warrant is proportionate to what is sought to be achieved by that conduct,
  (c) the law enforcement chief considers that satisfactory arrangements made for the purposes of sections 129 and 130 (safeguards relating to disclosure etc.) are in force in relation to the warrant, and
  (d) except where the law enforcement chief considers that there is an urgent need to issue the warrant, the decision to issue the warrant has been approved by a Judicial Commissioner.

(2) The fact that the information which would be obtained under a warrant relates to the activities in the British Islands of a trade union is not, of itself, sufficient to establish that the warrant is necessary as mentioned in subsection (1)(a).

(3) A law enforcement chief described in Part 1 of the table in Schedule 6 may, on an application made by a person who is an appropriate law enforcement officer in relation to the chief, issue a targeted equipment interference warrant if—
  (a) the law enforcement chief considers that the warrant is necessary for the purpose of preventing death or any injury or damage to a person's physical or mental health or of mitigating any injury or damage to a person's physical or mental health,
  (b) the law enforcement chief considers that the conduct authorised by the warrant is proportionate to what is sought to be achieved by that conduct,
  (c) the law enforcement chief considers that satisfactory arrangements made for the purposes of sections 129 and 130 (safeguards relating to disclosure etc.) are in force in relation to the warrant, and
  (d) except where the law enforcement chief considers that there is an urgent need to issue the warrant, the decision to issue the warrant has been approved by a Judicial Commissioner.

(4) If it is not reasonably practicable for a law enforcement chief to consider an application under this section, an appropriate delegate may, in an urgent case, exercise the power to issue a targeted equipment interference warrant.

(5) For the purposes of this section—
  (a) a person is a law enforcement chief if the person is listed in the first column of the table in Schedule 6;
  (b) a person is an appropriate delegate in relation to a law enforcement chief listed in the first column if the person is listed in the corresponding entry in the second column of that table;

Appendix

  (c) a person is an appropriate law enforcement officer in relation to a law enforcement chief listed in the first column if the person is listed in the corresponding entry in the third column of that table.

(6) Where the law enforcement chief is the Chief Constable or the Deputy Chief Constable of the Police Service of Northern Ireland, the reference in subsection (1)(a) to the purpose of preventing or detecting serious crime includes a reference to the interests of national security.

(7) A law enforcement chief who is an immigration officer may consider that the condition in subsection (1)(a) is satisfied only if the serious crime relates to an offence which is an immigration or nationality offence (whether or not it also relates to other offences).

(8) A law enforcement chief who is an officer of Revenue and Customs may consider that the condition in subsection (1)(a) is satisfied only if the serious crime relates to an assigned matter within the meaning of section 1(1) of the Customs and Excise Management Act 1979.

(9) A law enforcement chief who is a designated customs official may consider that the condition in subsection (1)(a) is satisfied only if the serious crime relates to a matter in respect of which a designated customs official has functions.

(10) A law enforcement chief who is the chair of the Competition and Markets Authority may consider that the condition in subsection (1)(a) is satisfied only if the offence, or all of the offences, to which the serious crime relates are offences under section 188 of the Enterprise Act 2002.

(11) A law enforcement chief who is the chairman, or a deputy chairman, of the Independent Police Complaints Commission may consider that the condition in subsection (1)(a) is satisfied only if the offence, or all of the offences, to which the serious crime relates are offences that are being investigated as part of an investigation by the Commission under Schedule 3 to the Police Reform Act 2002.

(12) A law enforcement chief who is the Police Investigations and Review Commissioner may consider that the condition in subsection (1)(a) is satisfied only if the offence, or all of the offences, to which the serious crime relates are offences that are being investigated under section 33A(b)(i) of the Police, Public Order and Criminal Justice (Scotland) Act 2006.

(13) For the purpose of subsection (7), an offence is an immigration or nationality offence if conduct constituting the offence—
  (a) relates to the entitlement of one or more persons who are not nationals of the United Kingdom to enter, transit across, or be in, the United Kingdom (including conduct which relates to conditions or other controls on any such entitlement), or
  (b) is undertaken for the purposes of or otherwise in relation to—
    (i) the British Nationality Act 1981;
    (ii) the Hong Kong Act 1985;
    (iii) the Hong Kong (War Wives and Widows) Act 1996;
    (iv) the British Nationality (Hong Kong) Act 1997;
    (v) the British Overseas Territories Act 2002;
    (vi) an instrument made under any of those Acts.

(14) In this section—
"designated customs official" has the same meaning as in Part 1 of the Borders, Citizenship and Immigration Act 2009 (see section 14(6) of that Act);
"immigration officer" means a person appointed as an immigration officer under paragraph 1 of Schedule 2 to the Immigration Act 1971.

Appendix

107 Restriction on issue of warrants to certain law enforcement officers

(1) A law enforcement chief specified in subsection (2) may not issue a targeted equipment interference warrant under section 106 unless the law enforcement chief considers that there is a British Islands connection.

(2) The law enforcement chiefs specified in this subsection are—
   (a) the Chief Constable of a police force maintained under section 2 of the Police Act 1996;
   (b) the Commissioner, or an Assistant Commissioner, of the metropolitan police force;
   (c) the Commissioner of Police for the City of London;
   (d) the chief constable of the Police Service of Scotland;
   (e) the Chief Constable or a Deputy Chief Constable of the Police Service of Northern Ireland;
   (f) the Chief Constable of the British Transport Police Force;
   (g) the Chief Constable of the Ministry for Defence Police;
   (h) the chairman, or a deputy chairman, of the Independent Police Complaints Commission;
   (i) the Police Investigations and Review Commissioner.

(3) The Director General of the National Crime Agency may not issue a targeted equipment interference warrant on the application of a member of a collaborative police force unless the Director General considers that there is a British Islands connection.
   "Collaborative police force" has the meaning given by paragraph 2 of Part 3 of Schedule 6.

(4) For the purpose of this section, there is a British Islands connection if—
   (a) any of the conduct authorised by the warrant would take place in the British Islands (regardless of the location of the equipment that would, or may, be interfered with),
   (b) any of the equipment which would, or may, be interfered with would, or may, be in the British Islands at some time while the interference is taking place, or
   (c) a purpose of the interference is to obtain—
      (i) communications sent by, or to, a person who is, or whom the law enforcement officer believes to be, for the time being in the British Islands,
      (ii) information relating to an individual who is, or whom the law enforcement officer believes to be, for the time being in the British Islands, or
      (iii) equipment data which forms part of, or is connected with, communications or information falling within sub-paragraph (i) or (ii).

(5) Except as provided by subsections (1) to (3), a targeted equipment interference warrant may be issued under section 106 whether or not the person who has power to issue the warrant considers that there is a British Islands connection.

Approval of warrants by Judicial Commissioners

108 Approval of warrants by Judicial Commissioners

(1) In deciding whether to approve a person's decision to issue a warrant under this Part, a Judicial Commissioner must review the person's conclusions as to the following matters—
   (a) whether the warrant is necessary on any relevant grounds (see subsection (3)), and
   (b) whether the conduct which would be authorised by the warrant is proportionate to what is sought to be achieved by that conduct.

(2) In doing so, the Judicial Commissioner must—
   (a) apply the same principles as would be applied by a court on an application for judicial review, and
   (b) consider the matters referred to in subsection (1) with a sufficient degree of care as to ensure that the Judicial Commissioner complies with the duties imposed by section 2 (general duties in relation to privacy).

(3) In subsection (1)(a), "relevant grounds" means—
   (a) in the case of a decision to issue a warrant under section 102, grounds falling within section 102(5);
   (b) in the case of a decision to issue a warrant under section 103, the purpose of preventing or detecting serious crime;
   (c) in the case of a decision to issue a warrant under section 104, the interests of national security;
   (d) in the case of a decision to issue a warrant under section 106(1), the purpose mentioned in section 106(1)(a);
   (e) in the case of a decision to issue a warrant under section 106(3), the purpose mentioned in section 106(3)(a).
(4) Where a Judicial Commissioner refuses to approve a person's decision to issue a warrant under this Part, the Judicial Commissioner must give the person written reasons for the refusal.
(5) Where a Judicial Commissioner, other than the Investigatory Powers Commissioner, refuses to approve a person's decision to issue a warrant under this Part, the person may ask the Investigatory Powers Commissioner to decide whether to approve the decision to issue the warrant.

109 Approval of warrants issued in urgent cases

(1) This section applies where—
   (a) a warrant under this Part is issued without the approval of a Judicial Commissioner, and
   (b) the person who issued the warrant considered that there was an urgent need to issue it.
(2) The person who issued the warrant must inform a Judicial Commissioner that it has been issued.
(3) The Judicial Commissioner must, before the end of the relevant period—
   (a) decide whether to approve the decision to issue the warrant, and
   (b) notify the person of the Judicial Commissioner's decision.
   "The relevant period" means the period ending with the third working day after the day on which the warrant was issued.
(4) If a Judicial Commissioner refuses to approve the decision to issue a warrant, the warrant—
   (a) ceases to have effect (unless already cancelled), and
   (b) may not be renewed, and section 108(5) does not apply in relation to the refusal to approve the decision.
(5) Section 110 contains further provision about what happens if a Judicial Commissioner refuses to approve the decision to issue a warrant.

110 Failure to approve warrant issued in urgent case

(1) This section applies where under section 109(3) a Judicial Commissioner refuses to approve the decision to issue a warrant.
(2) The person to whom the warrant was addressed must, so far as is reasonably practicable, secure that anything in the process of being done under the warrant stops as soon as possible.
(3) Where the refusal relates to a targeted equipment interference warrant, the Judicial Commissioner may—
   (a) authorise further interference with equipment for the purpose of enabling the person to whom the warrant was addressed to secure that anything in the process of being done under the warrant stops as soon as possible;
   (b) direct that any of the material obtained under the warrant is destroyed;
   (c) impose conditions as to the use or retention of any of that material.

(4) Where the refusal relates to a targeted examination warrant, the Judicial Commissioner may impose conditions as to the use of any protected material selected for examination under the warrant.
(5) The Judicial Commissioner—
 (a) may require an affected party to make representations about how the Judicial Commissioner should exercise any function under subsection (3) or (4), and
 (b) must have regard to any such representations made by an affected party (whether or not as a result of a requirement imposed under paragraph (a)).
(6) Each of the following is an "affected party" for the purposes of subsection (5)—
 (a) the person who decided to issue the warrant;
 (b) the person to whom the warrant was addressed.
(7) The person who decided to issue the warrant may ask the Investigatory Powers Commissioner to review a decision made by any other Judicial Commissioner under subsection (3) or (4).
(8) On a review under subsection (7), the Investigatory Powers Commissioner may—
 (a) confirm the Judicial Commissioner's decision, or
 (b) make a fresh determination.
(9) Nothing in this section or section 109 affects the lawfulness of—
 (a) anything done under the warrant before it ceases to have effect;
 (b) if anything is in the process of being done under the warrant when it ceases to have effect—
  (i) anything done before that thing could be stopped, or
  (ii) anything done that it is not reasonably practicable to stop.

Additional safeguards

111 Members of Parliament etc.

(1) Subsection (3) applies where—
 (a) an application is made to the Secretary of State for a targeted equipment interference warrant, and
 (b) the purpose of the warrant is to obtain—
  (i) communications sent by, or intended for, a person who is a member of a relevant legislature, or
  (ii) a member of a relevant legislature's private information.
(2) Subsection (3) also applies where—
 (a) an application is made to the Secretary of State for a targeted examination warrant, and
 (b) the purpose of the warrant is to authorise the selection for examination of protected material which consists of—
  (i) communications sent by, or intended for, a person who is a member of a relevant legislature, or
  (ii) a member of a relevant legislature's private information.
(3) The Secretary of State may not issue the warrant without the approval of the Prime Minister.
(4) Subsection (5) applies where—
 (a) an application is made under section 106 to a law enforcement chief for a targeted equipment interference warrant, and
 (b) the purpose of the warrant is to obtain—
  (i) communications sent by, or intended for, a person who is a member of a relevant legislature, or
  (ii) a member of a relevant legislature's private information.

Appendix

(5) The law enforcement chief may not issue the warrant without the approval of the Secretary of State unless the law enforcement chief believes that the warrant (if issued) would authorise interference only with equipment which would be in Scotland at the time of the issue of the warrant or which the law enforcement chief believes would be in Scotland at that time.

(6) The Secretary of State may give approval for the purposes of subsection (5) only with the approval of the Prime Minister.

(7) In a case where the decision whether to issue a targeted equipment interference warrant is to be taken by an appropriate delegate in relation to a law enforcement chief under section 106(4), the reference in subsection (5) to the law enforcement chief is to be read as a reference to the appropriate delegate.

(8) In this section "member of a relevant legislature" means—
   (a) a member of either House of Parliament;
   (b) a member of the Scottish Parliament;
   (c) a member of the National Assembly for Wales;
   (d) a member of the Northern Ireland Assembly;
   (e) a member of the European Parliament elected for the United Kingdom.

112 Items subject to legal privilege

(1) Subsections (2) to (5) apply if—
   (a) an application is made for a warrant under this Part, and
   (b) the purpose, or one of the purposes, of the warrant is—
      (i) in the case of a targeted equipment interference warrant, to authorise or require interference with equipment for the purpose of obtaining items subject to legal privilege, or
      (ii) in the case of a targeted examination warrant, to authorise the selection of such items for examination.

(2) The application must contain a statement that the purpose, or one of the purposes, of the warrant is to authorise or require interference with equipment for the purpose of obtaining items subject to legal privilege or (in the case of a targeted examination warrant) the selection for examination of items subject to legal privilege.

(3) In deciding whether to issue the warrant, the person to whom the application is made must have regard to the public interest in the confidentiality of items subject to legal privilege.

(4) The person to whom the application is made may issue the warrant only if the person considers—
   (a) that there are exceptional and compelling circumstances which make it necessary to authorise or require interference with equipment for the purpose of obtaining items subject to legal privilege or (in the case of a targeted examination warrant) the selection for examination of items subject to legal privilege, and
   (b) that the arrangements made for the purposes of section 129 or (as the case may be) section 191 (safeguards relating to retention and disclosure of material) include specific arrangements for the handling, retention, use and destruction of such items.

(5) But the warrant may not be issued if it is considered necessary only as mentioned in section 102(5)(c).

(6) For the purposes of subsection (4)(a), there cannot be exceptional and compelling circumstances that make it necessary to authorise or require interference with equipment for the purpose of obtaining, or the selection for examination of, items subject to legal privilege unless—
   (a) the public interest in obtaining the information that would be obtained by the warrant outweighs the public interest in the confidentiality of items subject to legal privilege,

(b) there are no other means by which the information may reasonably be obtained, and

(c) in the case of a warrant considered necessary for the purposes of preventing or detecting serious crime or as mentioned in section 106(3)(a), obtaining the information is necessary for the purpose of preventing death or significant injury.

(7) Subsections (8) and (9) apply if—

(a) an application is made for a warrant under this Part,

(b) the applicant considers that the relevant material is likely to include items subject to legal privilege, and

(c) subsections (2) to (5) do not apply.

(8) The application must contain—

(a) a statement that the applicant considers that the relevant material is likely to include items subject to legal privilege, and

(b) an assessment of how likely it is that the relevant material will include such items.

(9) The person to whom the application is made may issue the warrant only if the person considers that the arrangements made for the purposes of section 129 or (as the case may be) section 191 include specific arrangements for the handling, retention, use and destruction of items subject to legal privilege.

(10) In this section, "relevant material" means—

(a) in relation to a targeted equipment interference warrant, any material the obtaining of which is authorised or required under the warrant;

(b) in relation to a targeted examination warrant, any protected material which the warrant authorises to be selected for examination.

(11) Subsections (12) and (13) apply if—

(a) an application is made for a warrant under this Part,

(b) the purpose, or one of the purposes, of the warrant is—

(i) in the case of a targeted equipment interference warrant, to authorise or require interference with equipment for the purpose of obtaining communications or other items of information that, if they were not communications made or (as the case may be) other items of information created or held with the intention of furthering a criminal purpose, would be items subject to legal privilege, or

(ii) in the case of a targeted examination warrant, to authorise the selection of such communications or other items of information for examination, and

(c) the applicant considers that the communications or the other items of information ("the targeted communications or other items of information") are likely to be communications made or (as the case may be) other items of information created or held with the intention of furthering a criminal purpose.

(12) The application must—

(a) contain a statement that the purpose, or one of the purposes, of the warrant is—

(i) to authorise or require interference with equipment for the purpose of obtaining communications or other items of information that, if they were not communications made or (as the case may be) other items of information created or held with the intention of furthering a criminal purpose, would be items subject to legal privilege, or

(ii) (in the case of a targeted examination warrant) to authorise the selection of such communications or other items of information for examination, and

(b) set out the reasons for believing that the targeted communications or other items of information are likely to be communications made or (as the case may be) other items of information created or held with the intention of furthering a criminal purpose.

(13) The person to whom the application is made may issue the warrant only if the person considers that the targeted communications or other items of information are likely to be communications made or (as the case may be) other items of information created or held with the intention of furthering a criminal purpose.

113 Confidential journalistic material

(1) This section applies if an application is made for a warrant under this Part and the purpose, or one of the purposes, of the warrant—
   (a) in the case of a targeted equipment interference warrant, to authorise or require interference with equipment for the purpose of obtaining communications or other items of information which the applicant for the warrant believes will be communications or other items of information containing confidential journalistic material, or
   (b) in the case of a targeted examination warrant, to authorise the selection for examination of journalistic material which the applicant for the warrant believes is confidential journalistic material.
(2) The application must contain a statement that the purpose, or one of the purposes, of the warrant is—
   (a) in the case of a targeted equipment interference warrant, to authorise or require interference with equipment for the purpose of obtaining communications or other items of information which the applicant for the warrant believes will be communications or other items of information containing confidential journalistic material, or
   (b) in the case of a targeted examination warrant, to authorise the selection for examination of journalistic material which the applicant for the warrant believes is confidential journalistic material.
(3) The person to whom the application is made may issue the warrant only if the person considers that the arrangements made for the purposes of section 129 or (as the case may be) section 191 (safeguards relating to retention and disclosure of material) include specific arrangements for the handling, retention, use and destruction of communications or other items of information containing confidential journalistic material.
(4) For the meaning of "journalistic material" and "confidential journalistic material", see section 264.

114 Sources of journalistic information

(1) This section applies if an application is made for a warrant under this Part and the purpose, or one of the purposes, of the warrant is to identify or confirm a source of journalistic information. (For the meaning of "source of journalistic information", see section 263(1).)
(2) The application must contain a statement that the purpose, or one of the purposes, of the warrant is to identify or confirm a source of journalistic information.
(3) The person to whom the application is made may issue the warrant only if the person considers that the arrangements made for the purposes of section 129 or (as the case may be) section 191 (safeguards relating to retention and disclosure of material) include specific arrangements for the handling, retention, use and destruction of communications or other items of information that identify sources of journalistic information.

Further provision about warrants
115 Requirements that must be met by warrants

(1) A warrant under this Part must contain a provision stating whether it is a targeted equipment interference warrant or a targeted examination warrant.

Appendix

(2) A warrant under this Part must be addressed—
   (a) in the case of a warrant issued under section 102 or 103, to the head of the intelligence service by whom or on whose behalf the application for the warrant was made;
   (b) in the case of a warrant issued under section 104, to the Chief of Defence Intelligence;
   (c) in the case of a warrant issued under section 106 by a law enforcement chief (or by an appropriate delegate in relation to a law enforcement chief), to a person who—
      (i) is an appropriate law enforcement officer in relation to the law enforcement chief, and
      (ii) is named or described in the warrant.

(3) In the case of a targeted equipment interference warrant which relates to a matter described in the first column of the Table below, the warrant must include the details specified in the second column.

Matter	Details to be included in the warrant
Equipment belonging to, used by or in the possession of a particular person or organisation	The name of the person or organisation or a description of the person or organisation
Equipment belonging to, used by or in the possession of persons who form a group which shares a common purpose or who carry on, or may carry on, a particular activity	A description of the purpose or activity and the name of, or a description of, as many of the persons as it is reasonably practicable to name or describe
Equipment used by or in the possession of more than one person or organisation, where the interference is for the purpose of a single investigation or operation	A description of the nature of the investigation or operation and the name of, or a description of, as many of the persons or organisations as it is reasonably practicable to name or describe
Equipment in a particular location	A description of the location
Equipment in more than one location, where the interference is for the purpose of a single investigation or operation	A description of the nature of the investigation or operation and a description of as many of the locations as it is reasonably practicable to describe
Equipment which is being, or may be, used for the purposes of a particular activity or activities of a particular description	A description of the particular activity or activities
Equipment which is being, or may be, used to test, maintain or develop capabilities relating to interference with equipment	A description of the nature of the testing, maintenance or development of capabilities
Equipment which is being, or may be, used for the training of persons who carry out, or are likely to carry out, interference with equipment	A description of the nature of the training

(4) A targeted equipment interference warrant must also describe—
   (a) the type of equipment which is to be interfered with, and
   (b) the conduct which the person to whom the warrant is addressed is authorised to take.
(5) In the case of a targeted examination warrant which relates to a matter described in the first column of the Table below, the warrant must include the details specified in the second column.

Matter	Details to be included in the warrant
A particular person or organisation	The name of the person or organisation or a description of the person or organisation
A group of persons who share a common purpose or who carry on or may carry on a particular activity	A description of the purpose or activity and the name of, or a description of, as many of the persons as it is reasonably practicable to name or describe
More than one person or organisation, where the interference is for the purpose of a single investigation or operation	A description of the nature of the investigation or operation and the name of, or a description of, as many of the persons or organisations as it is reasonably practicable to name or describe
The testing, maintenance or development of capabilities relating to the selection of protected material for examination	A description of the nature of the testing, maintenance or development of capabilities
The training of persons who carry out, or are likely to carry out, the selection of protected material for examination	A description of the nature of the training

116 Duration of warrants

(1) A warrant issued under this Part ceases to have effect at the end of the relevant period (see subsection (2)), unless—
 (a) it is renewed before the end of that period (see section 117), or
 (b) it is cancelled or otherwise ceases to have effect before the end of that period (see sections 109 and 125).
(2) In this section, "the relevant period"—
 (a) in the case of an urgent warrant which has not been renewed, means the period ending with the fifth working day after the day on which the warrant was issued;
 (b) in any other case, means the period of 6 months beginning with—
  (i) the day on which the warrant was issued, or
  (ii) in the case of a warrant which has been renewed, the day after the day at the end of which the warrant would have ceased to have effect if it had not been renewed.
(3) For the purposes of subsection (2)(a), a warrant is an "urgent warrant" if—
 (a) the warrant was issued without the approval of a Judicial Commissioner, and
 (b) the person who decided to issue the warrant considered that there was an urgent need to issue it.

117 Renewal of warrants

(1) If the renewal conditions are met, a warrant issued under this Part may be renewed, at any time during the renewal period, by an instrument issued by the appropriate person (see subsection (3)).
(2) The renewal conditions are—
 (a) that the appropriate person considers that the warrant continues to be necessary on any relevant grounds,
 (b) that the appropriate person considers that the conduct that would be authorised by the renewed warrant continues to be proportionate to what is sought to be achieved by that conduct,

(c) that, in the case of a targeted examination warrant, the appropriate person considers that the warrant continues to be necessary to authorise the selection of protected material for examination in breach of the prohibition in section 193(4), and
(d) that the decision to renew the warrant has been approved by a Judicial Commissioner.
(3) The appropriate person is—
  (a) in the case of a warrant issued under section 102 or 104, the Secretary of State;
  (b) in the case of a warrant issued under section 103, a member of the Scottish Government;
  (c) in the case of a warrant issued under section 106 by a law enforcement chief or by an appropriate delegate in relation to the law enforcement chief, either—
    (i) the law enforcement chief, or
    (ii) if the warrant was issued by an appropriate delegate, that person.
(4) In subsection (2)(a), "relevant grounds" means—
  (a) in the case of a warrant issued under section 102, grounds falling within section 102(5),
  (b) in the case of a warrant issued under section 103, the purpose of preventing or detecting serious crime,
  (c) in the case of a warrant issued under section 104, the interests of national security,
  (d) in the case of a warrant issued under section 106(1), the purpose mentioned in section 106(1)(a), or
  (e) in the case of a warrant issued under section 106(3), the purpose mentioned in section 106(3)(a).
(5) "The renewal period" means—
  (a) in the case of an urgent warrant which has not been renewed, the relevant period;
  (b) in any other case, the period of 30 days ending with the day at the end of which the warrant would otherwise cease to have effect.
(6) The decision to renew a warrant issued under section 102 or 104 must be taken personally by the Secretary of State, and the instrument renewing the warrant must be signed by the Secretary of State.
(7) The decision to renew a warrant issued under section 103 must be taken personally by a member of the Scottish Government, and the instrument renewing the warrant must be signed by the person who took that decision.
(8) The instrument renewing a warrant issued under section 106 must be signed by the person who renews it.
(9) Section 108 (approval of warrants by Judicial Commissioners) applies in relation to a decision to renew a warrant under this Part as it applies in relation to a decision to issue such a warrant (and accordingly any reference in that section to the person who decided to issue the warrant is to be read as a reference to the person who decided to renew it).
(10) Sections 111 to 114 (additional safeguards) apply in relation to a decision to renew a warrant under this Part as they apply in relation to a decision to issue such a warrant.
(11) In this section—
"relevant period" has the same meaning as in section 116;
"urgent warrant" is to be read in accordance with subsection (3) of that section.

118 Modification of warrants issued by the Secretary of State or Scottish Ministers

(1) The provisions of a warrant issued under section 102, 103 or 104 may be modified at any time by an instrument issued by the person making the modification.
(2) The only modifications which may be made under this section are—
  (a) adding to the matters to which the warrant relates (see section 101(1) and (2)), by including the details required in relation to that matter by section 115(3) or (5);

(b) removing a matter to which the warrant relates;
(c) adding (in relation to a matter to which the warrant relates) a name or description to the names or descriptions included in the warrant in accordance with section 115(3) or (5);
(d) varying or removing (in relation to a matter to which the warrant relates) a name or description included in the warrant in accordance with section 115(3) or (5);
(e) adding to the descriptions of types of equipment included in the warrant in accordance with section 115(4)(a);
(f) varying or removing a description of a type of equipment included in the warrant in accordance with section 115(4)(a).
(3) But—
(a) where a targeted equipment interference warrant relates only to a matter specified in section 101(1)(a), only to a matter specified in section 101(1)(d), or only to both such matters, the details included in the warrant in accordance with section 115(3) may not be modified;
(b) where a targeted examination warrant relates only to a matter specified in section 101(2)(a), the details included in the warrant in accordance with section 115(5) may not be modified.
(4) The decision to modify the provisions of a warrant must be taken personally by the person making the modification, and the instrument making the modification must be signed by that person.
This is subject to section 120(7).
(5) Nothing in this section applies in relation to modifying the provisions of a warrant in a way which does not affect the conduct authorised or required by it.
(6) Sections 119 to 122 contain further provision about making modifications under this section.

119 Persons who may make modifications under section 118

(1) The persons who may make modifications under section 118 of a warrant are (subject to subsection (2))—
(a) in the case of a warrant issued by the Secretary of State under section 102 or 104—
(i) the Secretary of State, or
(ii) a senior official acting on behalf of the Secretary of State;
(b) in the case of a warrant issued by the Scottish Ministers under section 103—
(i) a member of the Scottish Government, or
(ii) a senior official acting on behalf of the Scottish Ministers.
(2) Any of the following persons may also make modifications under section 118 of a warrant, but only where the person considers that there is an urgent need to make the modification—
(a) the person to whom the warrant is addressed;
(b) a person who holds a senior position in the same public authority as the person mentioned in paragraph (a).
Section 122 contains provision about the approval of modifications made in urgent cases.
(3) Subsection (2) is subject to section 120(4) and (5) (special rules where any of sections 111 to 114 applies in relation to the making of a modification under section 118).
(4) For the purposes of subsection (2)(b), a person holds a senior position in a public authority if—
(a) in the case of any of the intelligence services—
(i) the person is a member of the Senior Civil Service or a member of the Senior Management Structure of Her Majesty's Diplomatic Service, or
(ii) the person holds a position in the intelligence service of equivalent seniority to such a person;

Appendix

(b) in the case of the Ministry of Defence—
  (i) the person is a member of the Senior Civil Service, or
  (ii) the person is of or above the rank of brigadier, commodore or air commodore.

120 Further provision about modifications under section 118

(1) A modification, other than a modification removing any matter, name or description, may be made under section 118 only if the person making the modification considers—
  (a) that the modification is necessary on any relevant grounds (see subsection (2)), and
  (b) that the conduct authorised by the modification is proportionate to what is sought to be achieved by that conduct.
(2) In subsection (1)(a), "relevant grounds" means—
  (a) in the case of a warrant issued under section 102, grounds falling within section 102(5);
  (b) in the case of a warrant issued under section 103, the purpose of preventing or detecting serious crime;
  (c) in the case of a warrant issued under section 104, the interests of national security.
(3) Sections 111 to 114 (additional safeguards) apply in relation to the making of a modification to a warrant under section 118, other than a modification removing any matter, name or description, as they apply in relation to the issuing of a warrant.
(4) Where section 111 applies in relation to the making of a modification—
  (a) the modification must be made by the Secretary of State, and
  (b) the modification has effect only if the decision to make the modification has been approved by a Judicial Commissioner.
(5) Where section 112, 113 or 114 applies in relation to the making of a modification—
  (a) the modification must be made by —
    (i) the Secretary of State or (in the case of a warrant issued by the Scottish Ministers) a member of the Scottish Government, or
    (ii) if a senior official acting on behalf of a person within subparagraph (i) considers that there is an urgent need to make the modification, that senior official, and
  (b) except where the person making the modification considers that there is an urgent need to make it, the modification has effect only if the decision to make the modification has been approved by a Judicial Commissioner.
(6) In a case where any of sections 111 to 114 applies in relation to the making of a modification, section 108 (approval of warrants by Judicial Commissioners) applies in relation to the decision to make the modification as it applies in relation to a decision to issue a warrant, but as if—
  (a) the references in subsection (1)(a) and (b) of that section to the warrant were references to the modification, and
  (b) any reference to the person who decided to issue the warrant were a reference to the person who decided to make the modification. Section 122 contains provision about the approval of modifications made in urgent cases.
(7) If, in a case where any of sections 111 to 114 applies in relation to the making of a modification, it is not reasonably practicable for the instrument making the modification to be signed by the Secretary of State or (as the case may be) a member of the Scottish Government in accordance with section 118(4), the instrument may be signed by a senior official designated by the Secretary of State or (as the case may be) the Scottish Ministers for that purpose.
(8) In such a case, the instrument making the modification must contain a statement that—

(a) it is not reasonably practicable for the instrument to be signed by the person who took the decision to make the modification, and
(b) the Secretary of State or (as the case may be) a member of the Scottish Government has personally and expressly authorised the making of the modification.

121 Notification of modifications

(1) As soon as is reasonably practicable after a person makes a modification of a warrant under section 118, a Judicial Commissioner must be notified of the modification and the reasons for making it.
(2) But subsection (1) does not apply where—
    (a) the modification is to remove any matter, name or description included in the warrant in accordance with section 115(3) to (5),
    (b) the modification is made by virtue of section 119(2), or
    (c) any of sections 111 to 114 applies in relation to the making of the modification.
(3) Where a modification is made by a senior official in accordance with section 119(1) or section 120(5)(a)(ii), the Secretary of State or (in the case of a warrant issued by the Scottish Ministers) a member of the Scottish Government must be notified personally of the modification and the reasons for making it.

122 Approval of modifications under section 118 made in urgent cases

(1) This section applies where a person makes a modification of a warrant by virtue of section 119(2).
(2) This section also applies where—
    (a) section 112, 113 or 114 applies in relation to the making of a modification under section 118,
    (b) the person making the modification does so without the approval of a Judicial Commissioner, and
    (c) the person considered that there was an urgent need to make the modification.
(3) The person who made the modification must inform the appropriate person that it has been made.
(4) In this section—
    "the appropriate person" is—
        (a) in a case falling within subsection (1), a designated senior official, and
        (b) in a case falling within subsection (2), a Judicial Commissioner;
    "designated senior official" means a senior official who has been designated by the Secretary of State or (in the case of warrants issued by the Scottish Ministers) the Scottish Ministers for the purposes of this section.
(5) The appropriate person must, before the end of the relevant period—
    (a) decide whether to approve the decision to make the modification, and
    (b) notify the person of the appropriate person's decision.
    "The relevant period" means the period ending with the third working day after the day on which the modification was made.
(6) As soon as is reasonably practicable after a designated senior official makes a decision under subsection (5)—
    (a) a Judicial Commissioner must be notified of—
        (i) the decision, and
        (ii) if the senior official has decided to approve the decision to make the modification, the modification in question, and

(b) the Secretary of State or (in the case of a warrant issued by the Scottish Ministers) a member of the Scottish Government must be notified personally of the matters mentioned in paragraph (a)(i) and (ii).

(7) If the appropriate person refuses to approve the decision to make the modification—
    (a) the warrant (unless it no longer has effect) has effect as if the modification had not been made, and
    (b) the person to whom the warrant is addressed must, so far as is reasonably practicable, secure that anything in the process of being done under the warrant by virtue of that modification stops as soon as possible; and, in a case falling within subsection (2) above, section 108(5) does not apply in relation to the refusal to approve the decision.

(8) In a case where the appropriate person refuses to approve a decision to make a modification of a targeted equipment interference warrant, the appropriate person may authorise further interference with equipment for the purpose of enabling the person to whom the warrant is addressed to secure that anything in the process of being done under the warrant by virtue of the modification stops as soon as possible.

(9) If the appropriate person authorises further interference with equipment under subsection (8), the Secretary of State or (in the case of a warrant issued by the Scottish Ministers) a member of the Scottish Government must be notified personally of the authorisation.

(10) Nothing in this section affects the lawfulness of—
    (a) anything done under the warrant by virtue of the modification before the modification ceases to have effect;
    (b) if anything is in the process of being done under the warrant by virtue of the modification when the modification ceases to have effect—
        (i) anything done before that thing could be stopped, or
        (ii) anything done which it is not reasonably practicable to stop.

123 Modification of warrants issued by law enforcement chiefs

(1) The provisions of a warrant issued under section 106 by a law enforcement chief, or by an appropriate delegate in relation to that chief, may be modified at any time—
    (a) by the law enforcement chief, or
    (b) if the warrant was issued by an appropriate delegate, by that person.

(2) The only modifications which may be made under this section are—
    (a) adding to the matters to which the warrant relates (see section 101(1) and (2)), by including the details required in relation to that matter by section 115(3) or (5);
    (b) removing a matter to which the warrant relates;
    (c) adding (in relation to a matter to which the warrant relates) a name or description to the names or descriptions included in the warrant in accordance with section 115(3) or (5);
    (d) varying or removing (in relation to a matter to which the warrant relates) a name or description included in the warrant in accordance with section 115(3) or (5);
    (e) adding to the descriptions of types of equipment included in the warrant in accordance with section 115(4)(a);
    (f) varying or removing a description of a type of equipment included in the warrant in accordance with section 115(4)(a).

(3) But where a warrant relates only to a matter specified in section 101(1)(a), only to a matter specified in section 101(1)(d), or only to both such matters, the details included in the warrant in accordance with section 115(3) may not be modified.

(4) A modification may be made only if—

Appendix

    (a) except in the case of a modification removing any matter, name or description, the person making the modification considers that—
        (i) the modification is necessary on any relevant grounds (see subsection (5)), and
        (ii) the conduct authorised by the modification is proportionate to what is sought to be achieved by that conduct, and
    (b) except where the person making the modification considers that there is an urgent need to make it, the decision to make the modification has been approved by a Judicial Commissioner.

(5) In subsection (4)(a), "relevant grounds" means—
    (a) in the case of a warrant issued under section 106(1), the purpose mentioned in section 106(1)(a);
    (b) in the case of a warrant issued under section 106(3), the purpose mentioned in section 106(3)(a).

(6) The decision to make any modification must be taken personally by the person making the modification, and the instrument making the modification must be signed by that person.

(7) Section 108 (approval of warrants by Judicial Commissioners) applies in relation to a decision to make a modification of a warrant issued under section 106 as it applies in relation to a decision to issue such a warrant, but as if—
    (a) the references in subsection (1)(a) and (b) of that section to the warrant were references to the modification, and
    (b) any reference to the person who decided to issue the warrant were a reference to the person who decided to make the modification.

(8) Sections 111 to 114 (additional safeguards) apply in relation to the making of a modification to a warrant under this section, other than a modification removing any matter, name or description, as they apply in relation to the issuing of a warrant.

(9) In the application of section 111 in accordance with subsection (8), subsection (5) is to be read as if for the words from "unless" to the end of the subsection there were substituted "unless the law enforcement chief believes that the warrant (as modified) would authorise interference only with equipment which would be in Scotland at the time of the making of the modification or which the law enforcement chief believes would be in Scotland at that time".

(10) Where section 111 applies in relation to the making of a modification to a warrant under this section, subsection (4)(b) of this section has effect in relation to the making of the modification as if the words "except where the person making the modification considers that there is an urgent need to make it" were omitted.

(11) Nothing in this section applies in relation to modifying the provisions of a warrant in a way which does not affect the conduct authorised or required by it.

124 Approval of modifications under section 123 in urgent cases

(1) This section applies where—
    (a) a modification is made under section 123 without the approval of a Judicial Commissioner, and
    (b) the person who made the modification considered that there was an urgent need to make it.

(2) The person who made the modification must inform a Judicial Commissioner that it has been made.

(3) The Judicial Commissioner must, before the end of the relevant period—
    (a) decide whether to approve the decision to make the modification, and

Appendix

    (b) notify the person of the Judicial Commissioner's decision.

"The relevant period" means the period ending with the third working day after the day on which the modification was made.

(4) If the Judicial Commissioner refuses to approve the decision to make the modification—
- (a) the person who issued the warrant must be notified of the refusal,
- (b) the warrant (unless it no longer has effect) has effect as if the modification had not been made, and
- (c) the person to whom the warrant is addressed must, so far as is reasonably practicable, secure that anything in the process of being done under the warrant by virtue of that modification stops as soon as possible; and section 108(5) does not apply in relation to the refusal to approve the decision.

(5) In a case where a Judicial Commissioner refuses to approve a decision to make a modification of a targeted equipment interference warrant, the Judicial Commissioner may authorise further interference with equipment for the purpose of enabling the person to whom the warrant is addressed to secure that anything in the process of being done under the warrant by virtue of the modification stops as soon as possible.

(6) If the Judicial Commissioner authorises further interference with equipment under subsection (5), the person who issued the warrant must be informed of the authorisation.

(7) Nothing in this section affects the lawfulness of—
- (a) anything done under the warrant by virtue of the modification before the modification ceases to have effect;
- (b) if anything is in the process of being done under the warrant by virtue of the modification when the modification ceases to have effect—
  - (i) anything done before that thing could be stopped, or
  - (ii) anything done which it is not reasonably practicable to stop.

125 Cancellation of warrants

(1) Any of the appropriate persons may cancel a warrant issued under this Part at any time.

(2) If any of the appropriate persons considers that—
- (a) a warrant issued under this Part is no longer necessary on any relevant grounds, or
- (b) the conduct authorised by a warrant issued under this Part is no longer proportionate to what is sought to be achieved by the conduct, the person must cancel the warrant.

(3) In subsection (2)(a), "relevant grounds" means—
- (a) in the case of a warrant issued under section 102, grounds falling within section 102(5);
- (b) in the case of a warrant issued under section 103, the purpose of preventing or detecting serious crime;
- (c) in the case of a warrant issued under section 104, the interests of national security;
- (d) in the case of a warrant issued under section 106(1), the purpose mentioned in section 106(1)(a);
- (e) in the case of a warrant issued under section 106(3), the purpose mentioned in section 106(3)(a).

(4) For the purposes of this section, "the appropriate persons" are—
- (a) in the case of a warrant issued by the Secretary of State under section 102 or 104, the Secretary of State or a senior official acting on behalf of the Secretary of State;
- (b) in the case of a warrant issued by the Scottish Ministers under section 103, a member of the Scottish Government or a senior official acting on behalf of the Scottish Ministers;
- (c) in the case of a warrant issued under section 106 by a law enforcement chief or by an appropriate delegate in relation to the law enforcement chief, either—

(i) the law enforcement chief, or
(ii) if the warrant was issued by an appropriate delegate, that person.
(5) Where a warrant is cancelled under this section, the person to whom the warrant was addressed must, so far as is reasonably practicable, secure that anything in the process of being done under the warrant stops as soon as possible.
(6) A warrant that has been cancelled under this section may not be renewed.

Implementation of warrants

126 Implementation of warrants

(1) In giving effect to a targeted equipment interference warrant, the person to whom it is addressed ("the implementing authority") may (in addition to acting alone) act through, or together with, such other persons as the implementing authority may require (whether under subsection (2) or otherwise) to provide the authority with assistance in giving effect to the warrant.
(2) For the purpose of requiring any person to provide assistance in relation to a targeted equipment interference warrant, the implementing authority may—
  (a) serve a copy of the warrant on any person whom the implementing authority considers may be able to provide such assistance, or
  (b) make arrangements for the service of a copy of the warrant on any such person.
(3) A copy of a warrant may be served under subsection (2) on a person outside the United Kingdom for the purpose of requiring the person to provide such assistance in the form of conduct outside the United Kingdom.
(4) For the purposes of this Act, the provision of assistance in giving effect to a targeted equipment interference warrant includes any disclosure to the implementing authority, or to persons acting on that person's behalf, of material obtained under the warrant.
(5) The references in subsections (2) and (3) and sections 127 and 128 to the service of a copy of a warrant include—
  (a) the service of a copy of one or more schedules contained in the warrant with the omission of the remainder of the warrant, and
  (b) the service of a copy of the warrant with the omission of any schedule contained in it.

127 Service of warrants

(1) This section applies to the service of warrants under section 126(2).
(2) A copy of the warrant must be served in such a way as to bring the contents of the warrant to the attention of the person who the implementing authority considers may be able to provide assistance in relation to it.
(3) A copy of a warrant may be served on a person outside the United Kingdom in any of the following ways (as well as by electronic or other means of service)—
  (a) by serving it at the person's principal office within the United Kingdom or, if the person has no such office in the United Kingdom, at any place in the United Kingdom where the person carries on business or conducts activities;
  (b) if the person has specified an address in the United Kingdom as one at which the person, or someone on the person's behalf, will accept service of documents of the same description as a copy of a warrant, by serving it at that address;
  (c) by making it available for inspection (whether to the person or to someone acting on the person's behalf) at a place in the United Kingdom (but this is subject to subsection (4)).

(4) A copy of a warrant may be served on a person outside the United Kingdom in the way mentioned in subsection (3)(c) only if—
   (a) it is not reasonably practicable for a copy to be served by any other means (whether as mentioned in subsection (3)(a) or (b) or otherwise), and
   (b) the implementing authority takes such steps as it considers appropriate for the purpose of bringing the contents of the warrant, and the availability of a copy for inspection, to the attention of the person.
(5) The steps mentioned in subsection (4)(b) must be taken as soon as reasonably practicable after the copy of the warrant is made available for inspection.
(6) In this section, "the implementing authority" has the same meaning as in section 126.

128 Duty of telecommunications operators to assist with implementation

(1) A telecommunications operator that has been served with a copy of a targeted equipment interference warrant issued by the Secretary of State under section 102 or 104, or by the Scottish Ministers under section 103, must take all steps for giving effect to the warrant which are notified to the telecommunications operator by or on behalf of the person to whom the warrant is addressed.
(2) A telecommunications operator that has been served with a copy of a targeted equipment interference warrant issued under section 106 and addressed to a law enforcement officer mentioned in subsection (3) must take all steps for giving effect to the warrant which—
   (a) were approved by the Secretary of State or, in the case of a warrant addressed to a constable of the Police Service of Scotland, by the Scottish Ministers, before the warrant was served, and
   (b) are notified to the telecommunications operator by or on behalf of the law enforcement officer.
(3) The law enforcement officers mentioned in this subsection are—
   (a) a National Crime Agency officer;
   (b) an officer of Revenue and Customs;
   (c) a constable of the Police Service of Scotland;
   (d) a member of the Police Service of Northern Ireland;
   (e) a member of the metropolitan police force.
(4) The Secretary of State or the Scottish Ministers may give approval for the purposes of subsection (2)(a) if the Secretary of State or (as the case may be) the Scottish Ministers consider that—
   (a) it is necessary for the telecommunications operator to be required to take the steps, and
   (b) the steps are proportionate to what is sought to be achieved by them.
(5) A telecommunications operator is not required to take any steps which it is not reasonably practicable for the telecommunications operator to take.
(6) Where obligations have been imposed on a telecommunications operator ("P") under section 253 (technical capability notices), for the purposes of subsection (5) the steps which it is reasonably practicable for P to take include every step which it would have been reasonably practicable for P to take if P had complied with all of those obligations.
(7) The duty imposed by subsection (1) or (2) is enforceable against a person in the United Kingdom by civil proceedings by the Secretary of State for an injunction, or for specific performance of a statutory duty under section 45 of the Court of Session Act 1988, or for any other appropriate relief.

Supplementary provision

129 Safeguards relating to retention and disclosure of material

(1) The issuing authority must ensure, in relation to every targeted equipment interference warrant issued by that authority, that arrangements are in force for securing that the requirements of subsections (2) and (5) are met in relation to the material obtained under the warrant.
This is subject to subsection (10).

(2) The requirements of this subsection are met in relation to the material obtained under a warrant if each of the following is limited to the minimum that is necessary for the authorised purposes (see subsection (3))—
   (a) the number of persons to whom any of the material is disclosed or otherwise made available;
   (b) the extent to which any of the material is disclosed or otherwise made available;
   (c) the extent to which any of the material is copied;
   (d) the number of copies that are made.

(3) For the purposes of subsection (2), something is necessary for the authorised purposes if, and only if—
   (a) it is, or is likely to become, necessary on any relevant grounds (see subsection (7)),
   (b) it is necessary for facilitating the carrying out of any functions under this Act of the Secretary of State, the Scottish Ministers or the person to whom the warrant is or was addressed,
   (c) it is necessary for facilitating the carrying out of any functions of the Judicial Commissioners or of the Investigatory Powers Tribunal under or in relation to this Act,
   (d) it is necessary for the purpose of legal proceedings, or
   (e) it is necessary for the performance of the functions of any person under any enactment.

(4) The arrangements for the time being in force under this section for securing that the requirements of subsection (2) are met in relation to the material obtained under the warrant must include arrangements for securing that every copy made of any of that material is stored, for so long as it is retained, in a secure manner.

(5) The requirements of this subsection are met in relation to the material obtained under a warrant if every copy made of any of that material (if not destroyed earlier) is destroyed as soon as there are no longer any grounds for retaining it (see subsection (6)).

(6) For the purposes of subsection (5), there are no longer any grounds for retaining a copy of any material if, and only if—
   (a) its retention is not necessary, or not likely to become necessary, on any relevant grounds (see subsection (7)), and
   (b) its retention is not necessary for any of the purposes mentioned in paragraphs (b) to (e) of subsection (3) above.

(7) In subsections (3) and (6), "relevant grounds" means—
   (a) in relation to a warrant issued under section 102, grounds falling within section 102(5);
   (b) in relation to a warrant issued under section 103, the purpose of preventing or detecting serious crime;
   (c) in relation to a warrant issued under section 104, the interests of national security;
   (d) in the case of a warrant issued under section 106(1), the purpose mentioned in section 106(1)(a);
   (e) in the case of a warrant issued under section 106(3), the purpose mentioned in section 106(3)(a).

(8) Where—
  (a) material obtained under a targeted equipment interference warrant is retained, following its examination, for purposes other than the destruction of the material, and
  (b) it is material that contains confidential journalistic material or identifies a source of journalistic material, the person to whom the warrant is addressed must inform the Investigatory Powers Commissioner as soon as is reasonably practicable.
(9) Subsection (10) applies if—
  (a) any material obtained under the warrant has been handed over to any overseas authorities, or
  (b) a copy of any such material has been given to any overseas authorities.
(10) To the extent that the requirements of subsections (2) and (5) relate to any of the material mentioned in subsection (9)(a), or to the copy mentioned in subsection (9)(b), the arrangements made for the purpose of this section are not required to secure that those requirements are met (see instead section 130).
(11) In this section—
  "copy", in relation to material obtained under a warrant, means any of the following (whether or not in documentary form)—
  (a) any copy, extract or summary of the material which identifies the material as having been obtained under the warrant, and
  (b) any record which is a record of the identities of persons who owned, used or were in possession of the equipment which was interfered with to obtain that material, and "copied" is to be read accordingly;
  "the issuing authority" means—
  (a) in the case of a warrant issued under section 102 or 104, the Secretary of State;
  (b) in the case of a warrant issued under section 103, the Scottish Ministers;
  (c) in the case of a warrant issued under section 106, the law enforcement chief who issued the warrant (or on whose behalf it was issued);
  "overseas authorities" means authorities of a country or territory outside the United Kingdom.

130 Safeguards relating to disclosure of material overseas

(1) The issuing authority must ensure, in relation to every targeted equipment interference warrant, that arrangements are in force for securing that—
  (a) any material obtained under the warrant is handed over to overseas authorities only if the requirements of subsection (2) are met, and
  (b) copies of any such material are given to overseas authorities only if those requirements are met.
(2) The requirements of this subsection are met in the case of a warrant if it appears to the issuing authority that requirements corresponding to the requirements of section 129(2) and (5) will apply, to such extent (if any) as the issuing authority considers appropriate, in relation to any of the material which is handed over, or any copy of which is given, to the authorities in question.
(3) In this section—
  "copy" has the same meaning as in section 129;
  "issuing authority" also has the same meaning as in that section;
  "overseas authorities" means authorities of a country or territory outside the United Kingdom.

131 Additional safeguards for items subject to legal privilege

(1) This section applies where an item subject to legal privilege which has been obtained under a targeted equipment interference warrant is retained, following its examination, for purposes other than the destruction of the item.

(2) The person to whom the warrant is addressed must inform the Investigatory Powers Commissioner of the retention of the item as soon as is reasonably practicable.
(3) Unless the Investigatory Powers Commissioner considers that subsection (5) applies to the item, the Commissioner must—
  (a) direct that the item is destroyed, or
  (b) impose one or more conditions as to the use or retention of that item.
(4) If the Investigatory Powers Commissioner considers that subsection (5) applies to the item, the Commissioner may nevertheless impose such conditions under subsection (3)(b) as the Commissioner considers necessary for the purpose of protecting the public interest in the confidentiality of items subject to legal privilege.
(5) This subsection applies to an item subject to legal privilege if—
  (a) the public interest in retaining the item outweighs the public interest in the confidentiality of items subject to legal privilege, and
  (b) retaining the item is necessary in the interests of national security or for the purpose of preventing death or significant injury.
(6) The Investigatory Powers Commissioner—
  (a) may require an affected party to make representations about how the Commissioner should exercise any function under subsection (3), and
  (b) must have regard to any such representations made by an affected party (whether or not as a result of a requirement imposed under paragraph (a)).
(7) Each of the following is an "affected party" for the purposes of subsection (6)—
  (a) the issuing authority (within the meaning given by section 129(11));
  (b) the person to whom the warrant is or was addressed.

132 Duty not to make unauthorised disclosures

(1) A person to whom this section applies must not make an unauthorised disclosure to another person.
(2) A person makes an unauthorised disclosure for the purposes of this section if—
  (a) the person discloses any of the matters within subsection (4) in relation to a warrant under this Part, and
  (b) the disclosure is not an excepted disclosure (see section 133).
(3) This section applies to the following persons—
  (a) any person who may apply for a warrant under this Part;
  (b) any person holding office under the Crown;
  (c) any person employed by, or for the purposes of, a police force;
  (d) any telecommunications operator;
  (e) any person employed or engaged for the purposes of any business of a telecommunications operator;
  (f) any person to whom any of the matters within subsection (4) have been disclosed in relation to a warrant under this Part.
(4) The matters referred to in subsection (2)(a) are—
  (a) the existence or contents of the warrant;
  (b) the details of the issue of the warrant or of any renewal or modification of the warrant;
  (c) the existence or contents of any requirement to provide assistance in giving effect to the warrant;
  (d) the steps taken in pursuance of the warrant or of any such requirement;
  (e) any of the material obtained under the warrant in a form which identifies it as having been obtained under a warrant under this Part .

133 Section 132: meaning of "excepted disclosure"

(1) For the purposes of section 132, a disclosure made in relation to a warrant is an excepted disclosure if it falls within any of the Heads set out in—
   (a) subsection (2) (disclosures authorised by warrant etc.);
   (b) subsection (3) (oversight bodies);
   (c) subsection (4) (legal proceedings);
   (d) subsection (6) (disclosures of a general nature).
(2) Head 1 is—
   (a) a disclosure authorised by the warrant;
   (b) a disclosure authorised by the person to whom the warrant is or was addressed or under any arrangements made by that person for the purposes of this section;
   (c) a disclosure authorised by the terms of any requirement to provide assistance in giving effect to the warrant (including any requirement for disclosure imposed by virtue of section 126(4)).#
(3) Head 2 is—
   (a) a disclosure made to, or authorised by, a Judicial Commissioner;
   (b) a disclosure made to the Independent Police Complaints Commission for the purposes of facilitating the carrying out of any of its functions;
   (c) a disclosure made to the Intelligence and Security Committee of Parliament for the purposes of facilitating the carrying out of any of its functions.
(4) Head 3 is—
   (a) a disclosure made—
      (i) in contemplation of, or in connection with, any legal proceedings, and
      (ii) for the purposes of those proceedings;
   (b) a disclosure made—
      (i) by a professional legal adviser ("L") to L's client or a representative of L's client, or
      (ii) by L's client, or by a representative of L's client, to L, in connection with the giving, by L to L's client, of advice about the effect of the provisions of this Part.
(5) But a disclosure within Head 3 is not an excepted disclosure if it is made with the intention of furthering a criminal purpose.
(6) Head 4 is—
   (a) a disclosure which—
      (i) is made by a telecommunications operator in accordance with a requirement imposed by regulations made by the Secretary of State, and
      (ii) consists of statistical information of a description specified in the regulations;
   (b) a disclosure of information that does not relate to any particular warrant under this Part but relates to such warrants in general.

134 Offence of making unauthorised disclosure

(1) A person commits an offence if—
   (a) the person discloses any matter in breach of section 132(1), and
   (b) the person knew that the disclosure was in breach of that section.
(2) A person who is guilty of an offence under this section is liable—
   (a) on summary conviction in England and Wales—

        (i) to imprisonment for a term not exceeding 12 months (or 6 months, if the offence was committed before the commencement of section 154(1) of the Criminal Justice Act 2003), or
        (ii) to a fine, or to both;
    (b) on summary conviction in Scotland—
        (i) to imprisonment for a term not exceeding 12 months, or
        (ii) to a fine not exceeding the statutory maximum, or to both;
    (c) on summary conviction in Northern Ireland—
        (i) to imprisonment for a term not exceeding 6 months, or
        (ii) to a fine not exceeding the statutory maximum, or to both;
    (d) on conviction on indictment, to imprisonment for a term not exceeding 5 years or to a fine, or to both.
(3) In proceedings against any person for an offence under this section in respect of any disclosure, it is a defence for the person to show that the person could not reasonably have been expected, after first becoming aware of the matter disclosed, to take steps to prevent the disclosure.

135 Part 5: interpretation

(1) In this Part—
    "communication" includes—
    (a) anything comprising speech, music, sounds, visual images or data of any description, and
    (b) signals serving either for the impartation of anything between persons, between a person and a thing or between things or for the actuation or control of any apparatus;
    "equipment" means equipment producing electromagnetic, acoustic or other emissions or any device capable of being used in connection with such equipment;
    "equipment data" has the meaning given by section 100;
    "private information" includes information relating to a person's private or family life;
    "protected material", in relation to a targeted examination warrant, has the meaning given by section 99(9);
    "senior official" means—
    (a) in the case of a targeted equipment interference warrant which is or may be issued by the Secretary of State or a law enforcement chief, or in the case of a targeted examination warrant which is or may be issued by the Secretary of State, a member of the Senior Civil Service or a member of the Senior Management Structure of Her Majesty's Diplomatic Service;
    (b) in the case of a targeted equipment interference warrant or a targeted examination warrant which is or may be issued by the Scottish Ministers, a member of the staff of the Scottish Administration who is a member of the Senior Civil Service;
    "targeted examination warrant" has the meaning given by section 99(9).
(2) See also—
    section 261 (telecommunications definitions),
    section 263 (general definitions),
    section 264 (general definitions: "journalistic material" etc.),
    section 265 (index of defined expressions).

Appendix

PART 6
BULK WARRANTS

CHAPTER 1

BULK INTERCEPTION WARRANTS

Bulk interception warrants

136 Bulk interception warrants

(1) For the purposes of this Act a "bulk interception warrant" is a warrant issued under this Chapter which meets conditions A and B.
(2) Condition A is that the main purpose of the warrant is one or more of the following—
   (a) the interception of overseas-related communications (see subsection (3));
   (b) the obtaining of secondary data from such communications (see section 137).
(3) In this Chapter "overseas-related communications" means—
   (a) communications sent by individuals who are outside the British Islands, or
   (b) communications received by individuals who are outside the British Islands.
(4) Condition B is that the warrant authorises or requires the person to whom it is addressed to secure, by any conduct described in the warrant, any one or more of the following activities—
   (a) the interception, in the course of their transmission by means of a telecommunication system, of communications described in the warrant;
   (b) the obtaining of secondary data from communications transmitted by means of such a system and described in the warrant;
   (c) the selection for examination, in any manner described in the warrant, of intercepted content or secondary data obtained under the warrant;
   (d) the disclosure, in any manner described in the warrant, of anything obtained under the warrant to the person to whom the warrant is addressed or to any person acting on that person's behalf.
(5) A bulk interception warrant also authorises the following conduct (in addition to the conduct described in the warrant)—
   (a) any conduct which it is necessary to undertake in order to do what is expressly authorised or required by the warrant, including—
      (i) the interception of communications not described in the warrant, and
      (ii) conduct for obtaining secondary data from such communications;
   (b) conduct by any person which is conduct in pursuance of a requirement imposed by or on behalf of the person to whom the warrant is addressed to be provided with assistance in giving effect to the warrant;
   (c) any conduct for obtaining related systems data from any telecommunications operator.
(6) For the purposes of subsection (5)(c)—
"related systems data", in relation to a warrant, means systems data relating to a relevant communication or to the sender or recipient, or intended recipient, of a relevant communication (whether or not a person), and
"relevant communication", in relation to a warrant, means—
   (a) any communication intercepted in accordance with the warrant in the course of its transmission by means of a telecommunication system, or
   (b) any communication from which secondary data is obtained under the warrant.

Appendix

137 Obtaining secondary data

(1) This section has effect for the purposes of this Chapter.
(2) References to obtaining secondary data from a communication transmitted by means of a telecommunication system are references to obtaining such data—
   (a) while the communication is being transmitted, or
   (b) at any time when the communication is stored in or by the system (whether before or after its transmission), and references to secondary data obtained under a bulk interception warrant are to be read accordingly.
(3) "Secondary data", in relation to a communication transmitted by means of a telecommunication system, means any data falling within subsection (4) or (5).
(4) The data falling within this subsection is systems data which is comprised in, included as part of, attached to or logically associated with the communication (whether by the sender or otherwise).
(5) The data falling within this subsection is identifying data which—
   (a) is comprised in, included as part of, attached to or logically associated with the communication (whether by the sender or otherwise),
   (b) is capable of being logically separated from the remainder of the communication, and
   (c) if it were so separated, would not reveal anything of what might reasonably be considered to be the meaning (if any) of the communication, disregarding any meaning arising from the fact of the communication or from any data relating to the transmission of the communication.
(6) For the meaning of "systems data" and "identifying data", see section 263.

138 Power to issue bulk interception warrants

(1) The Secretary of State may, on an application made by or on behalf of the head of an intelligence service, issue a bulk interception warrant if—
   (a) the Secretary of State considers that the main purpose of the warrant is one or more of the following—
      (i) the interception of overseas-related communications, and
      (ii) the obtaining of secondary data from such communications, (b) the Secretary of State considers that the warrant is necessary—
         (i) in the interests of national security, or
         (ii) on that ground and on any other grounds falling within subsection (2),
   (c) the Secretary of State considers that the conduct authorised by the warrant is proportionate to what is sought to be achieved by that conduct,
   (d) the Secretary of State considers that—
      (i) each of the specified operational purposes (see section 142) is a purpose for which the examination of intercepted content or secondary data obtained under the warrant is or may be necessary, and
      (ii) the examination of intercepted content or secondary data for each such purpose is necessary on any of the grounds on which the Secretary of State considers the warrant to be necessary,
   (e) the Secretary of State considers that satisfactory arrangements made for the purposes of sections 150 and 151 (safeguards relating to disclosure etc.) are in force in relation to the warrant,
   (f) in a case where the Secretary of State considers that a telecommunications operator outside the United Kingdom is likely to be required to provide assistance in giving effect to the warrant if it is issued, the Secretary of State has complied with section 139, and

(g) the decision to issue the warrant has been approved by a Judicial Commissioner.
For the meaning of "head of an intelligence service", see section 263.
(2) A warrant is necessary on grounds falling within this subsection if it is necessary—
   (a) for the purpose of preventing or detecting serious crime, or
   (b) in the interests of the economic well-being of the United Kingdom so far as those interests are also relevant to the interests of national security (but see subsection (3)).
(3) A warrant may be considered necessary on the ground falling within subsection (2)(b) only if the information which it is considered necessary to obtain is information relating to the acts or intentions of persons outside the British Islands.
(4) A warrant may not be considered necessary in the interests of national security or on any other grounds falling within subsection (2) if it is considered necessary only for the purpose of gathering evidence for use in any legal proceedings.
(5) An application for the issue of a bulk interception warrant may only be made on behalf of the head of an intelligence service by a person holding office under the Crown.

139 Additional requirements in respect of warrants affecting overseas operators

(1) This section applies where—
   (a) an application for a bulk interception warrant has been made, and
   (b) the Secretary of State considers that a telecommunications operator outside the United Kingdom is likely to be required to provide assistance in giving effect to the warrant if it is issued.
(2) Before issuing the warrant, the Secretary of State must consult the operator.
(3) Before issuing the warrant, the Secretary of State must, among other matters, take into account—
   (a) the likely benefits of the warrant,
   (b) the likely number of users (if known) of any telecommunications service which is provided by the operator and to which the warrant relates,
   (c) the technical feasibility of complying with any requirement that may be imposed on the operator to provide assistance in giving effect to the warrant,
   (d) the likely cost of complying with any such requirement, and
   (e) any other effect of the warrant on the operator.

140 Approval of warrants by Judicial Commissioners

(1) In deciding whether to approve a decision to issue a warrant under section 138, a Judicial Commissioner must review the Secretary of State's conclusions as to the following matters—
   (a) whether the warrant is necessary as mentioned in subsection (1)(b) of that section,
   (b) whether the conduct that would be authorised by the warrant is proportionate to what is sought to be achieved by that conduct,
   (c) whether—
      (i) each of the specified operational purposes (see section 142) is a purpose for which the examination of intercepted content or secondary data obtained under the warrant is or may be necessary, and
      (ii) the examination of intercepted content or secondary data for each such purpose is necessary as mentioned in section 138(1)(d)(ii), and
   (d) any matters taken into account in accordance with section 139.
(2) In doing so, the Judicial Commissioner must—

(a) apply the same principles as would be applied by a court on an application for judicial review, and
(b) consider the matters referred to in subsection (1) with a sufficient degree of care as to ensure that the Judicial Commissioner complies with the duties imposed by section 2 (general duties in relation to privacy).

(3) Where a Judicial Commissioner refuses to approve a decision to issue a warrant under section 138, the Judicial Commissioner must give the Secretary of State written reasons for the refusal.

(4) Where a Judicial Commissioner, other than the Investigatory Powers Commissioner, refuses to approve a decision to issue a warrant under section 138, the Secretary of State may ask the Investigatory Powers Commissioner to decide whether to approve the decision to issue the warrant.

141 Decisions to issue warrants to be taken personally by Secretary of State

(1) The decision to issue a bulk interception warrant must be taken personally by the Secretary of State.

(2) Before a bulk interception warrant is issued, it must be signed by the Secretary of State.

142 Requirements that must be met by warrants

(1) A bulk interception warrant must contain a provision stating that it is a bulk interception warrant.

(2) A bulk interception warrant must be addressed to the head of the intelligence service by whom, or on whose behalf, the application for the warrant was made.

(3) A bulk interception warrant must specify the operational purposes for which any intercepted content or secondary data obtained under the warrant may be selected for examination.

(4) The operational purposes specified in the warrant must be ones specified, in a list maintained by the heads of the intelligence services ("the list of operational purposes"), as purposes which they consider are operational purposes for which intercepted content or secondary data obtained under bulk interception warrants may be selected for examination.

(5) The warrant may, in particular, specify all of the operational purposes which, at the time the warrant is issued, are specified in the list of operational purposes.

(6) An operational purpose may be specified in the list of operational purposes only with the approval of the Secretary of State.

(7) The Secretary of State may give such approval only if satisfied that the operational purpose is specified in a greater level of detail than the descriptions contained in section 138(1)(b) or (2).

(8) At the end of each relevant three-month period the Secretary of State must give a copy of the list of operational purposes to the Intelligence and Security Committee of Parliament.

(9) In subsection (8) "relevant three-month period" means—
(a) the period of three months beginning with the day on which this section comes into force, and
(b) each successive period of three months.

(10) The Prime Minister must review the list of operational purposes at least once a year.

(11) In this Chapter "the specified operational purposes", in relation to a bulk interception warrant, means the operational purposes specified in the warrant in accordance with this section.

Duration, modification and cancellation of warrants

143 Duration of warrants

(1) A bulk interception warrant (unless already cancelled) ceases to have effect at the end of the period of 6 months beginning with—
   (a) the day on which the warrant was issued, or
   (b) in the case of a warrant that has been renewed, the day after the day at the end of which the warrant would have ceased to have effect if it had not been renewed.
(2) For provision about the renewal of warrants, see section 144.

144 Renewal of warrants

(1) If the renewal conditions are met, a bulk interception warrant may be renewed, at any time during the renewal period, by an instrument issued by the Secretary of State.
This is subject to subsection (6).
(2) The renewal conditions are—
   (a) that the Secretary of State considers that the warrant continues to be necessary—
      (i) in the interests of national security, or
      (ii) on that ground and on any other grounds falling within section 138(2),
   (b) that the Secretary of State considers that the conduct that would be authorised by the renewed warrant continues to be proportionate to what is sought to be achieved by that conduct,
   (c) that the Secretary of State considers that—
      (i) each of the specified operational purposes (see section 142) is a purpose for which the examination of intercepted content or secondary data obtained under the warrant continues to be, or may be, necessary, and
      (ii) the examination of intercepted content or secondary data for each such purpose continues to be necessary on any of the grounds on which the Secretary of State considers that the warrant continues to be necessary, and
   (d) that the decision to renew the warrant has been approved by a Judicial Commissioner.
(3) "The renewal period" means the period of 30 days ending with the day at the end of which the warrant would otherwise cease to have effect.
(4) The decision to renew a bulk interception warrant must be taken personally by the Secretary of State, and the instrument renewing the warrant must be signed by the Secretary of State.
(5) Section 140 (approval of warrants by Judicial Commissioners) applies in relation to a decision to renew a bulk interception warrant as it applies in relation to a decision to issue a bulk interception warrant, but with the omission of paragraph (d) of subsection (1).
This is subject to subsection (6).
(6) In the case of the renewal of a bulk interception warrant that has been modified so that it no longer authorises or requires the interception of communications or the obtaining of secondary data—
   (a) the renewal condition in subsection (2)(a) is to be disregarded,
   (b) the reference in subsection (2)(c)(ii) to the grounds on which the Secretary of State considers the warrant to be necessary is to be read as a reference to any grounds falling within section 138(1)(b) or (2), and
   (c) section 140 has effect as if—
      (i) paragraph (a) of subsection (1) were omitted, and
      (ii) the reference in subsection (1)(c)(ii) to the grounds on which the Secretary of State considers the warrant to be necessary were a reference to any grounds falling within section 138(1)(b) or (2).

145 Modification of warrants

(1) The provisions of a bulk interception warrant may be modified at any time by an instrument issued by the person making the modification.

(2) The only modifications that may be made under this section are—
   (a) adding, varying or removing any operational purpose specified in the warrant as a purpose for which any intercepted content or secondary data obtained under the warrant may be selected for examination, and (b) providing that the warrant no longer authorises or requires (to the extent that it did so previously)—
      (i) the interception of any communications in the course of their transmission by means of a telecommunication system, or
      (ii) the obtaining of any secondary data from communications transmitted by means of such a system.

(3) In this section—
   (a) a modification adding or varying any operational purpose as mentioned in paragraph (a) of subsection (2) is referred to as a "major modification", and
   (b) any other modification within that subsection is referred to as a "minor modification".

(4) A major modification—
   (a) must be made by the Secretary of State, and
   (b) may be made only if the Secretary of State considers that it is necessary on any of the grounds on which the Secretary of State considers the warrant to be necessary (see section 138(1)(b)).

(5) Except where the Secretary of State considers that there is an urgent need to make the modification, a major modification has effect only if the decision to make the modification is approved by a Judicial Commissioner.

(6) A minor modification may be made by—
   (a) the Secretary of State, or
   (b) a senior official acting on behalf of the Secretary of State.

(7) Where a minor modification is made by a senior official, the Secretary of State must be notified personally of the modification and the reasons for making it.

(8) If at any time a person mentioned in subsection (6) considers that any operational purpose specified in a warrant is no longer a purpose for which the examination of intercepted content or secondary data obtained under the warrant is or may be necessary, the person must modify the warrant by removing that operational purpose.

(9) The decision to modify the provisions of a warrant must be taken personally by the person making the modification, and the instrument making the modification must be signed by that person.

This is subject to subsection (10).

(10) If it is not reasonably practicable for an instrument making a major modification to be signed by the Secretary of State, the instrument may be signed by a senior official designated by the Secretary of State for that purpose.

(11) In such a case, the instrument making the modification must contain a statement that—
   (a) it is not reasonably practicable for the instrument to be signed by the Secretary of State, and
   (b) the Secretary of State has personally and expressly authorised the making of the modification.

(12) Despite section 136(2), the modification of a bulk interception warrant as mentioned in subsection (2)(b) above does not prevent the warrant from being a bulk interception warrant.

(13) Nothing in this section applies in relation to modifying the provisions of a warrant in a way which does not affect the conduct authorised or required by it.

146 Approval of major modifications by Judicial Commissioners

(1) In deciding whether to approve a decision to make a major modification of a bulk interception warrant, a Judicial Commissioner must review the Secretary of State's conclusions as to whether the modification is necessary on any of the grounds on which the Secretary of State considers the warrant to be necessary.
(2) In doing so, the Judicial Commissioner must—
  (a) apply the same principles as would be applied by a court on an application for judicial review, and
  (b) consider the matter referred to in subsection (1) with a sufficient degree of care as to ensure that the Judicial Commissioner complies with the duties imposed by section 2 (general duties in relation to privacy).
(3) Where a Judicial Commissioner refuses to approve a decision to make a major modification under section 145, the Judicial Commissioner must give the Secretary of State written reasons for the refusal.
(4) Where a Judicial Commissioner, other than the Investigatory Powers Commissioner, refuses to approve a decision to make a major modification under section 145, the Secretary of State may ask the Investigatory Powers Commissioner to decide whether to approve the decision to make the modification.

147 Approval of major modifications made in urgent cases

(1) This section applies where—
  (a) the Secretary of State makes a major modification of a bulk interception warrant without the approval of a Judicial Commissioner, and
  (b) the Secretary of State considered that there was an urgent need to make the modification.
(2) The Secretary of State must inform a Judicial Commissioner that the modification has been made.
(3) The Judicial Commissioner must, before the end of the relevant period—
  (a) decide whether to approve the decision to make the modification, and (b) notify the Secretary of State of the Judicial Commissioner's decision.
  "The relevant period" means the period ending with the third working day after the day on which the modification was made.
(4) If the Judicial Commissioner refuses to approve the decision to make the modification—
  (a) the warrant (unless it no longer has effect) has effect as if the modification had not been made, and
  (b) the person to whom the warrant is addressed must, so far as is reasonably practicable, secure that anything in the process of being done under the warrant by virtue of that modification stops as soon as possible, and section 146(4) does not apply in relation to the refusal to approve the decision.
(5) Nothing in this section affects the lawfulness of—
  (a) anything done under the warrant by virtue of the modification before the modification ceases to have effect;
  (b) if anything is in the process of being done under the warrant by virtue of the modification when the modification ceases to have effect—
    (i) anything done before that thing could be stopped, or
    (ii) anything done which it is not reasonably practicable to stop.

Appendix

148 Cancellation of warrants

(1) The Secretary of State, or a senior official acting on behalf of the Secretary of State, may cancel a bulk interception warrant at any time.
(2) If the Secretary of State, or a senior official acting on behalf of the Secretary of State, considers that any of the cancellation conditions are met in relation to a bulk interception warrant, the person must cancel the warrant.
(3) The cancellation conditions are—
   (a) that the warrant is no longer necessary in the interests of national security;
   (b) that the conduct authorised by the warrant is no longer proportionate to what is sought to be achieved by that conduct;
   (c) that the examination of intercepted content or secondary data obtained under the warrant is no longer necessary for any of the specified operational purposes (see section 142).
(4) But the condition in subsection (3)(a) does not apply where the warrant has been modified so that it no longer authorises or requires the interception of communications or the obtaining of secondary data.
(5) Where a warrant is cancelled under this section, the person to whom the warrant was addressed must, so far as is reasonably practicable, secure that anything in the process of being done under the warrant stops as soon as possible.
(6) A warrant that has been cancelled under this section may not be renewed.

Implementation of warrants

149 Implementation of warrants

(1) In giving effect to a bulk interception warrant, the person to whom it is addressed ("the implementing authority") may (in addition to acting alone) act through, or together with, such other persons as the implementing authority may require (whether under subsection (2) or otherwise) to provide the authority with assistance in giving effect to the warrant.
(2) For the purpose of requiring any person to provide assistance in relation to a bulk interception warrant, the implementing authority may—
   (a) serve a copy of the warrant on any person who the implementing authority considers may be able to provide such assistance, or
   (b) make arrangements for the service of a copy of the warrant on any such person.
(3) A copy of a warrant may be served under subsection (2) on a person outside the United Kingdom for the purpose of requiring the person to provide such assistance in the form of conduct outside the United Kingdom.
(4) For the purposes of this Act, the provision of assistance in giving effect to a bulk interception warrant includes any disclosure to the implementing authority, or to persons acting on behalf of the implementing authority, of anything obtained under the warrant.
(5) Sections 42 (service of warrants) and 43 (duty of operators to assist with implementation) apply in relation to a bulk interception warrant as they apply in relation to a targeted interception warrant.
(6) References in this section (and in sections 42 and 43 as they apply in relation to bulk interception warrants) to the service of a copy of a warrant include—
   (a) the service of a copy of one or more schedules contained in the warrant with the omission of the remainder of the warrant, and
   (b) the service of a copy of the warrant with the omission of any schedule contained in the warrant.

Restrictions on use or disclosure of material obtained under warrants etc.

150 Safeguards relating to retention and disclosure of material

(1) The Secretary of State must ensure, in relation to every bulk interception warrant, that arrangements are in force for securing—
   (a) that the requirements of subsections (2) and (5) are met in relation to the material obtained under the warrant, and
   (b) that the requirements of section 152 are met in relation to the intercepted content or secondary data obtained under the warrant.
   This is subject to subsection (8).

(2) The requirements of this subsection are met in relation to the material obtained under a warrant if each of the following is limited to the minimum that is necessary for the authorised purposes (see subsection (3))—
   (a) the number of persons to whom any of the material is disclosed or otherwise made available;
   (b) the extent to which any of the material is disclosed or otherwise made available;
   (c) the extent to which any of the material is copied;
   (d) the number of copies that are made.

(3) For the purposes of subsection (2) something is necessary for the authorised purposes if, and only if—
   (a) it is, or is likely to become, necessary in the interests of national security or on any other grounds falling within section 138(2),
   (b) it is necessary for facilitating the carrying out of any functions under this Act of the Secretary of State, the Scottish Ministers or the head of the intelligence service to whom the warrant is or was addressed,
   (c) it is necessary for facilitating the carrying out of any functions of the Judicial Commissioners or the Investigatory Powers Tribunal under or in relation to this Act,
   (d) it is necessary to ensure that a person ("P") who is conducting a criminal prosecution has the information P needs to determine what is required of P by P's duty to secure the fairness of the prosecution, or
   (e) it is necessary for the performance of any duty imposed on any person by the Public Records Act 1958 or the Public Records Act (Northern Ireland) 1923.

(4) The arrangements for the time being in force under this section for securing that the requirements of subsection (2) are met in relation to the material obtained under the warrant must include arrangements for securing that every copy made of any of that material is stored, for so long as it is retained, in a secure manner.

(5) The requirements of this subsection are met in relation to the material obtained under a warrant if every copy made of any of that material (if not destroyed earlier) is destroyed as soon as there are no longer any relevant grounds for retaining it (see subsection (6)).

(6) For the purposes of subsection (5), there are no longer any relevant grounds for retaining a copy of any material if, and only if—
   (a) its retention is not necessary, or not likely to become necessary, in the interests of national security or on any other grounds falling within section 138(2), and
   (b) its retention is not necessary for any of the purposes mentioned in paragraphs (b) to (e) of subsection (3) above.

(7) Subsection (8) applies if—
   (a) any material obtained under the warrant has been handed over to any overseas authorities, or
   (b) a copy of any such material has been given to any overseas authorities.

Appendix

(8) To the extent that the requirements of subsections (2) and (5) and section 152 relate to any of the material mentioned in subsection (7)(a), or to the copy mentioned in subsection (7)(b), the arrangements made for the purposes of this section are not required to secure that those requirements are met (see instead section 151).

(9) In this section—

"copy", in relation to material obtained under a warrant, means any of the following (whether or not in documentary form)—
   (a) any copy, extract or summary of the material which identifies the material as having been obtained under the warrant, and
   (b) any record which—
      (i) refers to any interception or to the obtaining of any material, and
      (ii) is a record of the identities of the persons to or by whom the material was sent, or to whom the material relates, and "copied" is to be read accordingly;

"overseas authorities" means authorities of a country or territory outside the United Kingdom.

151 Safeguards relating to disclosure of material overseas

(1) The Secretary of State must ensure, in relation to every bulk interception warrant, that arrangements are in force for securing that—
   (a) any material obtained under the warrant is handed over to overseas authorities only if the requirements of subsection (2) are met, and
   (b) copies of any such material are given to overseas authorities only if those requirements are met.

(2) The requirements of this subsection are met in the case of a warrant if it appears to the Secretary of State—
   (a) that requirements corresponding to the requirements of section 150(2) and (5) and section 152 will apply, to such extent (if any) as the Secretary of State considers appropriate, in relation to any of the material which is handed over, or any copy of which is given, to the authorities in question, and
   (b) that restrictions are in force which would prevent, to such extent (if any) as the Secretary of State considers appropriate, the doing of anything in, for the purposes of or in connection with any proceedings outside the United Kingdom which would result in a prohibited disclosure.

(3) In subsection (2)(b) "prohibited disclosure" means a disclosure which, if made in the United Kingdom, would breach the prohibition in section 56(1) (see section 156).

(4) In this section—

"copy" has the same meaning as in section 150;

"overseas authorities" means authorities of a country or territory outside the United Kingdom.

152 Safeguards relating to examination of material

(1) For the purposes of section 150 the requirements of this section are met in relation to the intercepted content and secondary data obtained under a warrant if—
   (a) the selection of any of the intercepted content or secondary data for examination is carried out only for the specified purposes (see subsection (2)),
   (b) the selection of any of the intercepted content or secondary data for examination is necessary and proportionate in all the circumstances, and
   (c) the selection of any of the intercepted content for examination meets any of the selection conditions (see subsection (3)).

(2) The selection of intercepted content or secondary data for examination is carried out only for the specified purposes if the intercepted content or secondary data is selected for examination only so far as is necessary for the operational purposes specified in the warrant in accordance with section 142.

In this subsection "specified in the warrant" means specified in the warrant at the time of the selection of the intercepted content or secondary data for examination.

(3) The selection conditions referred to in subsection (1)(c) are—
   (a) that the selection of the intercepted content for examination does not breach the prohibition in subsection (4);
   (b) that the person to whom the warrant is addressed considers that the selection of the intercepted content for examination would not breach that prohibition;
   (c) that the selection of the intercepted content for examination in breach of that prohibition is authorised by subsection (5);
   (d) that the selection of the intercepted content for examination in breach of that prohibition is authorised by a targeted examination warrant issued under Chapter 1 of Part 2.

(4) The prohibition referred to in subsection (3)(a) is that intercepted content may not at any time be selected for examination if—
   (a) any criteria used for the selection of the intercepted content for examination are referable to an individual known to be in the British Islands at that time, and
   (b) the purpose of using those criteria is to identify the content of communications sent by, or intended for, that individual.

It does not matter for the purposes of this subsection whether the identity of the individual is known.

(5) The selection of intercepted content ("the relevant content") for examination is authorised by this subsection if—
   (a) criteria referable to an individual have been, or are being, used for the selection of intercepted content for examination in circumstances falling within subsection (3)(a) or (b),
   (b) at any time it appears to the person to whom the warrant is addressed that there has been a relevant change of circumstances in relation to the individual (see subsection (6)) which would mean that the selection of the relevant content for examination would breach the prohibition in subsection (4),
   (c) since that time, a written authorisation to examine the relevant content using those criteria has been given by a senior officer, and
   (d) the selection of the relevant content for examination is made before the end of the permitted period (see subsection (7)).

(6) For the purposes of subsection (5)(b) there is a relevant change of circumstances in relation to an individual if—
   (a) the individual has entered the British Islands, or
   (b) a belief by the person to whom the warrant is addressed that the individual was outside the British Islands was in fact mistaken.

(7) In subsection (5)—
"senior officer", in relation to a warrant addressed to the head of an intelligence service, means a member of the intelligence service who—
   (a) is a member of the Senior Civil Service or a member of the Senior Management Structure of Her Majesty's Diplomatic Service, or
   (b) holds a position in the intelligence service of equivalent seniority to such a member;
"the permitted period" means the period ending with the fifth working day after the time mentioned in subsection (5)(b).

(8) In a case where the selection of intercepted content for examination is authorised by subsection (5), the person to whom the warrant is addressed must notify the Secretary of State that the selection is being carried out.

153 Additional safeguards for items subject to legal privilege

(1) Subsection (2) applies if, in a case where intercepted content obtained under a bulk interception warrant is to be selected for examination—
  (a) the selection of the intercepted content for examination meets any of the selection conditions in section 152(3)(a) to (c), and
  (b) either—
    (i) the purpose, or one of the purposes, of using the criteria to be used for the selection of the intercepted content for examination ("the relevant criteria") is to identify any items subject to legal privilege, or
    (ii) the use of the relevant criteria is likely to identify such items.
(2) The intercepted content may be selected for examination using the relevant criteria only if a senior official acting on behalf of the Secretary of State has approved the use of those criteria.
(3) In deciding whether to give an approval under subsection (2) in a case where subsection (1)(b)(i) applies, a senior official must have regard to the public interest in the confidentiality of items subject to legal privilege.
(4) A senior official may give an approval under subsection (2) only if—
  (a) the official considers that the arrangements made for the purposes of section 150 (safeguards relating to retention and disclosure of material) include specific arrangements for the handling, retention, use and destruction of items subject to legal privilege, and
  (b) where subsection (1)(b)(i) applies, the official considers that there are exceptional and compelling circumstances that make it necessary to authorise the use of the relevant criteria.
(5) For the purposes of subsection (4)(b), there cannot be exceptional and compelling circumstances that make it necessary to authorise the use of the relevant criteria unless—
  (a) the public interest in obtaining the information that would be obtained by the selection of the intercepted content for examination outweighs the public interest in the confidentiality of items subject to legal privilege,
  (b) there are no other means by which the information may reasonably be obtained, and
  (c) obtaining the information is necessary in the interests of national security or for the purpose of preventing death or significant injury.
(6) Subsection (7) applies if, in a case where intercepted content obtained under a bulk interception warrant is to be selected for examination—
  (a) the selection of the intercepted content for examination meets any of the selection conditions in section 152(3)(a) to (c),
  (b) the purpose, or one of the purposes, of using the criteria to be used for the selection of the intercepted content for examination ("the relevant criteria") is to identify communications that, if they were not made with the intention of furthering a criminal purpose, would be items subject to legal privilege, and
  (c) the person to whom the warrant is addressed considers that the communications ("the targeted communications") are likely to be communications made with the intention of furthering a criminal purpose.
(7) The intercepted content may be selected for examination using the relevant criteria only if a senior official acting on behalf of the Secretary of State has approved the use of those criteria.

(8) A senior official may give an approval under subsection (7) only if the official considers that the targeted communications are likely to be communications made with the intention of furthering a criminal purpose.

(9) Where an item subject to legal privilege which has been intercepted in accordance with a bulk interception warrant is retained following its examination, for purposes other than the destruction of the item, the person to whom the warrant is addressed must inform the Investigatory Powers Commissioner as soon as is reasonably practicable.
(For provision about the grounds for retaining material obtained under a warrant, see section 150.)

(10) Unless the Investigatory Powers Commissioner considers that subsection (12) applies to the item, the Commissioner must—
   (a) direct that the item is destroyed, or
   (b) impose one or more conditions as to the use or retention of that item.

(11) If the Investigatory Powers Commissioner considers that subsection (12) applies to the item, the Commissioner may nevertheless impose such conditions under subsection (10)(b) as the Commissioner considers necessary for the purpose of protecting the public interest in the confidentiality of items subject to legal privilege.

(12) This subsection applies to an item subject to legal privilege if—
   (a) the public interest in retaining the item outweighs the public interest in the confidentiality of items subject to legal privilege, and
   (b) retaining the item is necessary in the interests of national security or for the purpose of preventing death or significant injury.

(13) The Investigatory Powers Commissioner—
   (a) may require an affected party to make representations about how the Commissioner should exercise any function under subsection (10), and (b) must have regard to any such representations made by an affected party (whether or not as a result of a requirement imposed under paragraph (a)).

(14) Each of the following is an "affected party" for the purposes of subsection (13)—
   (a) the Secretary of State;
   (b) the person to whom the warrant is or was addressed.

154 Additional safeguard for confidential journalistic material

Where—
   (a) a communication which has been intercepted in accordance with a bulk interception warrant is retained, following its examination, for purposes other than the destruction of the communication, and
   (b) it is a communication containing confidential journalistic material, the person to whom the warrant is addressed must inform the Investigatory Powers Commissioner as soon as is reasonably practicable.

(For provision about the grounds for retaining material obtained under a warrant, see section 150.)

155 Offence of breaching safeguards relating to examination of material

(1) A person commits an offence if—
   (a) the person selects for examination any intercepted content or secondary data obtained under a bulk interception warrant,
   (b) the person knows or believes that the selection of that intercepted content or secondary data for examination does not comply with a requirement imposed by section 152 or 153, and

(c) the person deliberately selects that intercepted content or secondary data for examination in breach of that requirement.
(2) A person guilty of an offence under this section is liable—
  (a) on summary conviction in England and Wales—
    (i) to imprisonment for a term not exceeding 12 months (or 6 months, if the offence was committed before the commencement of section 154(1) of the Criminal Justice Act 2003), or
    (ii) to a fine, or to both;
  (b) on summary conviction in Scotland—
    (i) to imprisonment for a term not exceeding 12 months, or
    (ii) to a fine not exceeding the statutory maximum, or to both;
  (c) on summary conviction in Northern Ireland—
    (i) to imprisonment for a term not exceeding 6 months, or
    (ii) to a fine not exceeding the statutory maximum, or to both;
  (d) on conviction on indictment, to imprisonment for a term not exceeding 2 years or to a fine, or to both.
(3) No proceedings for any offence which is an offence by virtue of this section may be instituted—
  (a) in England and Wales, except by or with the consent of the Director of Public Prosecutions;
  (b) in Northern Ireland, except by or with the consent of the Director of Public Prosecutions for Northern Ireland.

156 Application of other restrictions in relation to warrants

(1) Section 56 and Schedule 3 (exclusion of matters from legal proceedings etc.) apply in relation to bulk interception warrants as they apply in relation to targeted interception warrants.
(2) Sections 57 to 59 (duty not to make unauthorised disclosures) apply in relation to bulk interception warrants as they apply in relation to targeted interception warrants, but as if the reference in section 58(2)(c) to a requirement for disclosure imposed by virtue of section 41(5) were a reference to such a requirement imposed by virtue of section 149(4).

Interpretation

157 Chapter 1: interpretation

(1) In this Chapter—
  "intercepted content", in relation to a bulk interception warrant, means any content of communications intercepted by an interception authorised or required by the warrant;
  "overseas-related communications" has the meaning given by section 136;
  "secondary data" has the meaning given by section 137, and references to obtaining secondary data from a communication are to be read in accordance with that section;
  "senior official" means a member of the Senior Civil Service or a member of the Senior Management Structure of Her Majesty's Diplomatic Service;
  "the specified operational purposes" has the meaning given by section 142(11).
(2) See also—
  section 261 (telecommunications definitions),
  section 263 (general definitions),
  section 264 (general definitions: "journalistic material" etc.),
  section 265 (index of defined expressions).

CHAPTER 2

BULK ACQUISITION WARRANTS

Bulk acquisition warrants

158 Power to issue bulk acquisition warrants

(1) The Secretary of State may, on an application made by or on behalf of the head of an intelligence service, issue a bulk acquisition warrant if—
   (a) the Secretary of State considers that the warrant is necessary—
       (i) in the interests of national security, or
       (ii) on that ground and on any other grounds falling within subsection (2),
   (b) the Secretary of State considers that the conduct authorised by the warrant is proportionate to what is sought to be achieved by that conduct,
   (c) the Secretary of State considers that—
       (i) each of the specified operational purposes (see section 161) is a purpose for which the examination of communications data obtained under the warrant is or may be necessary, and
       (ii) the examination of such data for each such purpose is necessary on any of the grounds on which the Secretary of State considers the warrant to be necessary,
   (d) the Secretary of State considers that satisfactory arrangements made for the purposes of section 171 (safeguards relating to the retention and disclosure of data) are in force in relation to the warrant, and
   (e) the decision to issue the warrant has been approved by a Judicial Commissioner.
   For the meaning of "head of an intelligence service", see section 263.

(2) A warrant is necessary on grounds falling within this subsection if it is necessary—
   (a) for the purpose of preventing or detecting serious crime, or
   (b) in the interests of the economic well-being of the United Kingdom so far as those interests are also relevant to the interests of national security (but see subsection (3)).

(3) A warrant may be considered necessary on the ground falling within subsection (2)(b) only if the communications data which it is considered necessary to obtain is communications data relating to the acts or intentions of persons outside the British Islands.

(4) The fact that the communications data which would be obtained under a warrant relates to the activities in the British Islands of a trade union is not, of itself, sufficient to establish that the warrant is necessary in the interests of national security or on that ground and a ground falling within subsection (2).

(5) A bulk acquisition warrant is a warrant which authorises or requires the person to whom it is addressed to secure, by any conduct described in the warrant, any one or more of the activities in subsection (6).

(6) The activities are—
   (a) requiring a telecommunications operator specified in the warrant—
       (i) to disclose to a person specified in the warrant any communications data which is specified in the warrant and is in the possession of the operator,
       (ii) to obtain any communications data specified in the warrant which is not in the possession of the operator but which the operator is capable of obtaining, or
       (iii) to disclose to a person specified in the warrant any data obtained as mentioned in sub-paragraph (ii),

(b) the selection for examination, in any manner described in the warrant, of communications data obtained under the warrant,
(c) the disclosure, in any manner described in the warrant, of communications data obtained under the warrant to the person to whom the warrant is addressed or to any person acting on that person's behalf.
(7) A bulk acquisition warrant also authorises the following conduct (in addition to the conduct described in the warrant)—
  (a) any conduct which it is necessary to undertake in order to do what is expressly authorised or required by the warrant, and
  (b) conduct by any person which is conduct in pursuance of a requirement imposed by or on behalf of the person to whom the warrant is addressed to be provided with assistance in giving effect to the warrant.
(8) A bulk acquisition warrant may relate to data whether or not in existence at the time of the issuing of the warrant.
(9) An application for the issue of a bulk acquisition warrant may only be made on behalf of the head of an intelligence service by a person holding office under the Crown.

159 Approval of warrants by Judicial Commissioners

(1) In deciding whether to approve a decision to issue a warrant under section 158, a Judicial Commissioner must review the Secretary of State's conclusions as to the following matters—
  (a) whether the warrant is necessary as mentioned in subsection (1)(a) of that section,
  (b) whether the conduct that would be authorised by the warrant is proportionate to what is sought to be achieved by that conduct, and
  (c) whether—
    (i) each of the specified operational purposes (see section 161) is a purpose for which the examination of communications data obtained under the warrant is or may be necessary, and
    (ii) the examination of such data for each such purpose is necessary as mentioned in section 158(1)(c)(ii).
(2) In doing so, the Judicial Commissioner must—
  (a) apply the same principles as would be applied by a court on an application for judicial review, and
  (b) consider the matters referred to in subsection (1) with a sufficient degree of care as to ensure that the Judicial Commissioner complies with the duties imposed by section 2 (general duties in relation to privacy).
(3) Where a Judicial Commissioner refuses to approve a decision to issue a warrant under section 158, the Judicial Commissioner must give the Secretary of State written reasons for the refusal.
(4) Where a Judicial Commissioner, other than the Investigatory Powers Commissioner, refuses to approve a decision to issue a warrant under section 158, the Secretary of State may ask the Investigatory Powers Commissioner to decide whether to approve the decision to issue the warrant.

160 Decisions to issue warrants to be taken personally by Secretary of State

(1) The decision to issue a bulk acquisition warrant must be taken personally by the Secretary of State.
(2) Before a bulk acquisition warrant is issued, it must be signed by the Secretary of State.

161 Requirements that must be met by warrants

(1) A bulk acquisition warrant must contain a provision stating that it is a bulk acquisition warrant.
(2) A bulk acquisition warrant must be addressed to the head of the intelligence service by whom, or on whose behalf, the application for the warrant was made.
(3) A bulk acquisition warrant must specify the operational purposes for which any communications data obtained under the warrant may be selected for examination.
(4) The operational purposes specified in the warrant must be ones specified, in a list maintained by the heads of the intelligence services ("the list of operational purposes"), as purposes which they consider are operational purposes for which communications data obtained under bulk acquisition warrants may be selected for examination.
(5) The warrant may, in particular, specify all of the operational purposes which, at the time the warrant is issued, are specified in the list of operational purposes.
(6) An operational purpose may be specified in the list of operational purposes only with the approval of the Secretary of State.
(7) The Secretary of State may give such approval only if satisfied that the operational purpose is specified in a greater level of detail than the descriptions contained in section 158(1)(a) or (2).
(8) At the end of each relevant three-month period the Secretary of State must give a copy of the list of operational purposes to the Intelligence and Security Committee of Parliament.
(9) In subsection (8) "relevant three-month period" means—
 (a) the period of three months beginning with the day on which this section comes into force, and
 (b) each successive period of three months.
(10) The Prime Minister must review the list of operational purposes at least once a year.
(11) In this Chapter "the specified operational purposes", in relation to a bulk acquisition warrant, means the operational purposes specified in the warrant in accordance with this section.

Duration, modification and cancellation of warrants

162 Duration of warrants

(1) A bulk acquisition warrant (unless already cancelled) ceases to have effect at the end of the period of 6 months beginning with—
 (a) the day on which the warrant was issued, or
 (b) in the case of a warrant that has been renewed, the day after the day at the end of which the warrant would have ceased to have effect if it had not been renewed.
(2) For provision about the renewal of warrants, see section 163.

163 Renewal of warrants

(1) If the renewal conditions are met, a bulk acquisition warrant may be renewed, at any time during the renewal period, by an instrument issued by the Secretary of State. This is subject to subsection (6).
(2) The renewal conditions are—
 (a) that the Secretary of State considers that the warrant continues to be necessary—
  (i) in the interests of national security, or
  (ii) on that ground and on any other grounds falling within section 158(2),

(b) that the Secretary of State considers that the conduct that would be authorised by the renewed warrant continues to be proportionate to what is sought to be achieved by that conduct,
(c) that the Secretary of State considers that—
  (i) each of the specified operational purposes (see section 161) is a purpose for which the examination of communications data obtained under the warrant continues to be, or may be, necessary, and
  (ii) the examination of such data for each such purpose continues to be necessary on any of the grounds on which the Secretary of State considers that the warrant continues to be necessary, and
(d) that the decision to renew the warrant has been approved by a Judicial Commissioner.
(3) "The renewal period" means the period of 30 days ending with the day at the end of which the warrant would otherwise cease to have effect.
(4) The decision to renew a bulk acquisition warrant must be taken personally by the Secretary of State, and the instrument renewing the warrant must be signed by the Secretary of State.
(5) Section 159 (approval of warrants by Judicial Commissioners) applies in relation to a decision to renew a bulk acquisition warrant as it applies in relation to a decision to issue a bulk acquisition warrant. This is subject to subsection (6).
(6) In the case of the renewal of a bulk acquisition warrant that has been modified so that it no longer authorises or requires the carrying out of activities falling within section 158(6)(a)—
  (a) the renewal condition in subsection (2)(a) is to be disregarded,
  (b) the reference in subsection (2)(c)(ii) to the grounds on which the Secretary of State considers the warrant to be necessary is to be read as a reference to any grounds falling within section 158(1)(a) or (2), and
  (c) section 159 has effect as if—
    (i) paragraph (a) of subsection (1) were omitted, and
    (ii) the reference in subsection (1)(c)(ii) to the grounds on which the Secretary of State considers the warrant to be necessary were a reference to any grounds falling within section 158(1)(a) or (2).

164 Modification of warrants

(1) The provisions of a bulk acquisition warrant may be modified at any time by an instrument issued by the person making the modification.
(2) The only modifications that may be made under this section are—
  (a) adding, varying or removing any operational purpose specified in the warrant as a purpose for which any communications data obtained under the warrant may be selected for examination, and
  (b) providing that the warrant no longer authorises or requires the carrying out of activities falling within section 158(6)(a).
(3) In this section—
  (a) a modification adding or varying any operational purpose as mentioned in paragraph (a) of subsection (2) is referred to as a "major modification", and
  (b) any other modification within that subsection is referred to as a "minor modification".
(4) A major modification—
  (a) must be made by the Secretary of State, and
  (b) may be made only if the Secretary of State considers that it is necessary on any of the grounds on which the Secretary of State considers the warrant to be necessary (see section 158(1)(a)).

(5) Except where the Secretary of State considers that there is an urgent need to make the modification, a major modification has effect only if the decision to make the modification is approved by a Judicial Commissioner.
(6) A minor modification may be made by—
  (a) the Secretary of State, or
  (b) a senior official acting on behalf of the Secretary of State.
(7) Where a minor modification is made by a senior official, the Secretary of State must be notified personally of the modification and the reasons for making it.
(8) If at any time a person mentioned in subsection (6) considers that any operational purpose specified in a warrant is no longer a purpose for which the examination of communications data obtained under the warrant is or may be necessary, the person must modify the warrant by removing that operational purpose.
(9) The decision to modify the provisions of a warrant must be taken personally by the person making the modification, and the instrument making the modification must be signed by that person. This is subject to subsection (10).
(10) If it is not reasonably practicable for an instrument making a major modification to be signed by the Secretary of State, the instrument may be signed by a senior official designated by the Secretary of State for that purpose.
(11) In such a case, the instrument making the modification must contain a statement that—
  (a) it is not reasonably practicable for the instrument to be signed by the Secretary of State, and
  (b) the Secretary of State has personally and expressly authorised the making of the modification.
(12) Nothing in this section applies in relation to modifying the provisions of a warrant in a way which does not affect the conduct authorised or required by it.

165 Approval of major modifications by Judicial Commissioners

(1) In deciding whether to approve a decision to make a major modification of a bulk acquisition warrant, a Judicial Commissioner must review the Secretary of State's conclusions as to whether the modification is necessary on any of the grounds on which the Secretary of State considers the warrant to be necessary.
(2) In doing so, the Judicial Commissioner must—
  (a) apply the same principles as would be applied by a court on an application for judicial review, and
  (b) consider the matter referred to in subsection (1) with a sufficient degree of care as to ensure that the Judicial Commissioner complies with the duties imposed by section 2 (general duties in relation to privacy).
(3) Where a Judicial Commissioner refuses to approve a decision to make a major modification under section 164, the Judicial Commissioner must give the Secretary of State written reasons for the refusal.
(4) Where a Judicial Commissioner, other than the Investigatory Powers Commissioner, refuses to approve a decision to make a major modification under section 164, the Secretary of State may ask the Investigatory Powers Commissioner to decide whether to approve the decision to make the modification.

166 Approval of major modifications made in urgent cases

(1) This section applies where—
  (a) the Secretary of State makes a major modification of a bulk acquisition warrant without the approval of a Judicial Commissioner, and

Appendix

    (b) the Secretary of State considered that there was an urgent need to make the modification.
(2) The Secretary of State must inform a Judicial Commissioner that the modification has been made.
(3) The Judicial Commissioner must, before the end of the relevant period—
    (a) decide whether to approve the decision to make the modification, and
    (b) notify the Secretary of State of the Judicial Commissioner's decision.
"The relevant period" means the period ending with the third working day after the day on which the modification was made.
(4) If the Judicial Commissioner refuses to approve the decision to make the modification—
    (a) the warrant (unless it no longer has effect) has effect as if the modification had not been made, and
    (b) the person to whom the warrant is addressed must, so far as is reasonably practicable, secure that anything in the process of being done under the warrant by virtue of that modification stops as soon as possible, and section 165(4) does not apply in relation to the refusal to approve the decision.
(5) Nothing in this section affects the lawfulness of—
    (a) anything done under the warrant by virtue of the modification before the modification ceases to have effect,
    (b) if anything is in the process of being done under the warrant by virtue of the modification when the modification ceases to have effect—
        (i) anything done before that thing could be stopped, or
        (ii) anything done which it is not reasonably practicable to stop.

167 Cancellation of warrants

(1) The Secretary of State, or a senior official acting on behalf of the Secretary of State, may cancel a bulk acquisition warrant at any time.
(2) If the Secretary of State, or a senior official acting on behalf of the Secretary of State, considers that any of the cancellation conditions are met in relation to a bulk acquisition warrant, the person must cancel the warrant.
(3) The cancellation conditions are—
    (a) that the warrant is no longer necessary in the interests of national security,
    (b) that the conduct authorised by the warrant is no longer proportionate to what is sought to be achieved by that conduct,
    (c) that the examination of communications data obtained under the warrant is no longer necessary for any of the specified operational purposes (see section 161).
(4) But the condition in subsection (3)(a) does not apply where the warrant has been modified so that it no longer authorises or requires the carrying out of activities falling within section 158(6)(a).
(5) Where a warrant is cancelled under this section, the person to whom the warrant was addressed must, so far as is reasonably practicable, secure that anything in the process of being done under the warrant stops as soon as possible.
(6) A warrant that has been cancelled under this section may not be renewed.

Implementation of warrants

168 Implementation of warrants

(1) In giving effect to a bulk acquisition warrant, the person to whom it is addressed ("the implementing authority") may (in addition to acting alone) act through, or together with, such

other persons as the implementing authority may require (whether under subsection (2) or otherwise) to provide the authority with assistance in giving effect to the warrant.
(2) For the purpose of requiring any person to provide assistance in relation to a bulk acquisition warrant, the implementing authority may—
   (a) serve a copy of the warrant on any person whom the implementing authority considers may be able to provide such assistance, or
   (b) make arrangements for the service of a copy of the warrant on any such person.
(3) A copy of a warrant may be served under subsection (2) on a person outside the United Kingdom for the purpose of requiring the person to provide such assistance in the form of conduct outside the United Kingdom.
(4) For the purposes of this Act, the provision of assistance in giving effect to a bulk acquisition warrant includes any disclosure to the implementing authority, or to persons acting on behalf of the implementing authority, of communications data as authorised or required under the warrant.
(5) References in this section and in sections 169 and 170 to the service of a copy of a warrant include—
   (a) the service of a copy of one or more schedules contained in the warrant with the omission of the remainder of the warrant, and
   (b) the service of a copy of the warrant with the omission of any schedule contained in the warrant.

169 Service of warrants

(1) This section applies to the service of bulk acquisition warrants under section 168(2).
(2) A copy of the warrant must be served in such a way as to bring the contents of the warrant to the attention of the person whom the implementing authority considers may be able to provide assistance in relation to it.
(3) A copy of a warrant may be served on a person outside the United Kingdom in any of the following ways (as well as by electronic or other means of service)—
   (a) by serving it at the person's principal office within the United Kingdom or, if the person has no such office in the United Kingdom, at any place in the United Kingdom where the person carries on business or conducts activities;
   (b) if the person has specified an address in the United Kingdom as one at which the person, or someone on the person's behalf, will accept service of documents of the same description as a copy of a warrant, by serving it at that address;
   (c) by making it available for inspection (whether to the person or to someone acting on the person's behalf) at a place in the United Kingdom (but this is subject to subsection (4)).
(4) A copy of a warrant may be served on a person outside the United Kingdom in the way mentioned in subsection (3)(c) only if—
   (a) it is not reasonably practicable for a copy to be served by any other means (whether as mentioned in subsection (3)(a) or (b) or otherwise), and
   (b) the implementing authority takes such steps as the authority considers appropriate for the purpose of bringing the contents of the warrant, and the availability of a copy for inspection, to the attention of the person.
(5) The steps mentioned in subsection (4)(b) must be taken as soon as reasonably practicable after the copy of the warrant is made available for inspection.
(6) In this section "the implementing authority" has the same meaning as in section 168.

Appendix

170 Duty of operators to assist with implementation

(1) A telecommunications operator that has been served with a copy of a bulk acquisition warrant by (or on behalf of) the implementing authority must take all steps for giving effect to the warrant that are notified to the operator by (or on behalf of) the implementing authority.
This is subject to subsection (3).
(2) Subsection (1) applies whether or not the operator is in the United Kingdom.
(3) The operator is not required to take any steps which it is not reasonably practicable for the operator to take.
(4) Where obligations have been imposed on a telecommunications operator ("P") under section 253 (technical capability notices), for the purposes of subsection (3) the steps which it is reasonably practicable for P to take include every step which it would have been reasonably practicable for P to take if P had complied with all of those obligations.
(5) The duty imposed by subsection (1) is enforceable against a person in the United Kingdom by civil proceedings by the Secretary of State for an injunction, or for specific performance of a statutory duty under section 45 of the Court of Session Act 1988, or for any other appropriate relief.
(6) In this section "the implementing authority" has the same meaning as in section 168.

Restrictions on use or disclosure of data obtained under warrants etc.

171 Safeguards relating to the retention and disclosure of data

(1) The Secretary of State must ensure, in relation to every bulk acquisition warrant, that arrangements are in force for securing—
   (a) that the requirements of subsections (2) and (5) are met in relation to the communications data obtained under the warrant, and
   (b) that the requirements of section 172 are met in relation to that data.

This is subject to subsection (8).
(2) The requirements of this subsection are met in relation to the communications data obtained under a warrant if each of the following is limited to the minimum that is necessary for the authorised purposes (see subsection (3))—
   (a) the number of persons to whom any of the data is disclosed or otherwise made available,
   (b) the extent to which any of the data is disclosed or otherwise made available,
   (c) the extent to which any of the data is copied,
   (d) the number of copies that are made.
(3) For the purposes of subsection (2) something is necessary for the authorised purposes if, and only if—
   (a) it is, or is likely to become, necessary in the interests of national security or on any other grounds falling within section 158(2),
   (b) it is necessary for facilitating the carrying out of any functions under this Act of the Secretary of State, the Scottish Ministers or the head of the intelligence service to whom the warrant is or was addressed,
   (c) it is necessary for facilitating the carrying out of any functions of the Judicial Commissioners or the Investigatory Powers Tribunal under or in relation to this Act,
   (d) it is necessary to ensure that a person ("P") who is conducting a criminal prosecution has the information P needs to determine what is required of P by P's duty to secure the fairness of the prosecution,
   (e) it is necessary for use as evidence in legal proceedings, or

Appendix

    (f) it is necessary for the performance of any duty imposed on any person by the Public Records Act 1958 or the Public Records Act (Northern Ireland) 1923.

(4) The arrangements for the time being in force under subsection (1) for securing that the requirements of subsection (2) are met in relation to the communications data obtained under the warrant must include arrangements for securing that every copy made of any of that data is stored, for so long as it is retained, in a secure manner.

(5) The requirements of this subsection are met in relation to the communications data obtained under a warrant if every copy made of any of that data (if not destroyed earlier) is destroyed as soon as there are no longer any relevant grounds for retaining it (see subsection (6)).

(6) For the purposes of subsection (5), there are no longer any relevant grounds for retaining a copy of any data if, and only if—
    (a) its retention is not necessary, or not likely to become necessary, in the interests of national security or on any other grounds falling within section 158(2), and
    (b) its retention is not necessary for any of the purposes mentioned in paragraphs (b) to (f) of subsection (3) above.

(7) Subsection (8) applies if—
    (a) any communications data obtained under the warrant has been handed over to any overseas authorities, or
    (b) a copy of any such data has been given to any overseas authorities.

(8) To the extent that the requirements of subsections (2) and (5) and section 172 relate to any of the data mentioned in subsection (7)(a), or to the copy mentioned in subsection (7)(b), the arrangements made for the purposes of subsection (1) are not required to secure that those requirements are met.

(9) But the Secretary of State must instead ensure that arrangements are in force for securing that communications data obtained under a bulk acquisition warrant, or any copy of such data, is handed over or given to an overseas authority only if the Secretary of State considers that requirements corresponding to the requirements of subsections (2) and (5) and section 172 will apply, to such extent (if any) as the Secretary of State considers appropriate, in relation to such data or copy.

(10) In this section—
"copy", in relation to communications data obtained under a warrant, means any of the following (whether or not in documentary form)—
    (a) any copy, extract or summary of the data which identifies the data as having been obtained under the warrant, and
    (b) any record referring to the obtaining of the data which is a record of the identities of the persons to whom the data relates, and "copied" is to be read accordingly,
"overseas authorities" means authorities of a country or territory outside the United Kingdom.

172 Safeguards relating to examination of data

(1) For the purposes of section 171 the requirements of this section are met in relation to the communications data obtained under a warrant if—
    (a) any selection of the data for examination is carried out only for the specified purposes (see subsection (2)), and
    (b) the selection of any of the data for examination is necessary and proportionate in all the circumstances.

(2) The selection of communications data for examination is carried out only for the specified purposes if the data is selected for examination only so far as is necessary for the operational purposes specified in the warrant in accordance with section 161.

Appendix

(3) In subsection (2) "specified in the warrant" means specified in the warrant at the time of the selection of the data for examination.

173 Offence of breaching safeguards relating to examination of data

(1) A person commits an offence if—
   (a) the person selects for examination any communications data obtained under a bulk acquisition warrant,
   (b) the person knows or believes that the selection of that data for examination does not comply with a requirement imposed by section 172, and
   (c) the person deliberately selects that data for examination in breach of that requirement.
(2) A person guilty of an offence under this section is liable—
   (a) on summary conviction in England and Wales—
      (i) to imprisonment for a term not exceeding 12 months (or 6 months, if the offence was committed before the commencement of section 154(1) of the Criminal Justice Act 2003), or
      (ii) to a fine, or to both;
   (b) on summary conviction in Scotland—
      (i) to imprisonment for a term not exceeding 12 months, or
      (ii) to a fine not exceeding the statutory maximum, or to both;
   (c) on summary conviction in Northern Ireland—
      (i) to imprisonment for a term not exceeding 6 months, or
      (ii) to a fine not exceeding the statutory maximum, or to both;
   (d) on conviction on indictment, to imprisonment for a term not exceeding 2 years or to a fine, or to both.
(3) No proceedings for any offence which is an offence by virtue of this section may be instituted—
   (a) in England and Wales, except by or with the consent of the Director of Public Prosecutions;
   (b) in Northern Ireland, except by or with the consent of the Director of Public Prosecutions for Northern Ireland.

Supplementary provision

174 Offence of making unauthorised disclosure

(1) It is an offence for—
   (a) a telecommunications operator who is under a duty by virtue of section 170 to assist in giving effect to a bulk acquisition warrant, or
   (b) any person employed or engaged for the purposes of the business of such an operator,
to disclose to any person, without reasonable excuse, the existence or contents of the warrant.
(2) For the purposes of subsection (1), it is, in particular, a reasonable excuse if the disclosure is made with the permission of the Secretary of State.
(3) A person guilty of an offence under this section is liable—
   (a) on summary conviction in England and Wales—
      (i) to imprisonment for a term not exceeding 12 months (or 6 months, if the offence was committed before the commencement of section 154(1) of the Criminal Justice Act 2003), or
      (ii) to a fine, or to both;

Appendix

  (b) on summary conviction in Scotland—
    (i) to imprisonment for a term not exceeding 12 months, or
    (ii) to a fine not exceeding the statutory maximum, or to both;
  (c) on summary conviction in Northern Ireland—
    (i) to imprisonment for a term not exceeding 6 months, or
    (ii) to a fine not exceeding the statutory maximum, or to both;
  (d) on conviction on indictment, to imprisonment for a term not exceeding 2 years or to a fine, or to both.

175 Chapter 2: interpretation

(1) In this Chapter—
  "communications data" does not include communications data within the meaning given by section 262(3),
  "senior official" means—
    (a) a member of the Senior Civil Service, or
    (b) a member of the Senior Management Structure of Her Majesty's Diplomatic Service,
  "the specified operational purposes" has the meaning given by section 161(11).
(2) See also—
  section 261 (telecommunications definitions),
  section 263 (general definitions),
  section 265 (index of defined expressions).

CHAPTER 3

BULK EQUIPMENT INTERFERENCE WARRANTS

Bulk equipment interference warrants

176 Bulk equipment interference warrants: general

(1) For the purposes of this Act, a warrant is a "bulk equipment interference warrant" if—
  (a) it is issued under this Chapter;
  (b) it authorises or requires the person to whom it is addressed to secure interference with any equipment for the purpose of obtaining—
    (i) communications (see section 198);
    (ii) equipment data (see section 177);
    (iii) any other information; and
  (c) the main purpose of the warrant is to obtain one or more of the following—
    (i) overseas-related communications;
    (ii) overseas-related information;
    (iii) overseas-related equipment data.
(2) In this Chapter—
  "overseas-related communications" means—
    (a) communications sent by individuals who are outside the British Islands, or
    (b) communications received by individuals who are outside the British Islands;
  "overseas-related information" means information of individuals who are outside the British Islands.
(3) For the purpose of this Chapter, equipment data is "overseas-related equipment data" if—

Appendix

(a) it forms part of, or is connected with, overseas-related communications or overseas-related information;
(b) it would or may assist in establishing the existence of overseas-related communications or overseas-related information or in obtaining such communications or information;
(c) it would or may assist in developing capabilities in relation to obtaining overseas-related communications or overseas-related information.

(4) A bulk equipment interference warrant—
  (a) must authorise or require the person to whom it is addressed to secure the obtaining of the communications, equipment data or other information to which the warrant relates;
  (b) may also authorise or require the person to whom it is addressed to secure—
    (i) the selection for examination, in any manner described in the warrant, of any material obtained under the warrant by virtue of paragraph (a);
    (ii) the disclosure, in any manner described in the warrant, of any such material to the person to whom the warrant is addressed or to any person acting on that person's behalf.

(5) A bulk equipment interference warrant also authorises the following conduct (in addition to the conduct described in the warrant)—
  (a) any conduct which it is necessary to undertake in order to do what is expressly authorised or required by the warrant, including conduct for securing the obtaining of communications, equipment data or other information;
  (b) any conduct by any person which is conduct in pursuance of a requirement imposed by or on behalf of the person to whom the warrant is addressed to be provided with assistance in giving effect to the warrant.

(6) A bulk equipment interference warrant may not, by virtue of subsection (4)(a), authorise a person to engage in conduct, in relation to a communication other than a stored communication, which would (unless done with lawful authority) constitute an offence under section 3(1) (unlawful interception).

(7) Subsection (5)(a) does not authorise a person to engage in conduct which could not be expressly authorised under the warrant because of the restriction imposed by subsection (6).

(8) In subsection (6), "stored communication" means a communication stored in or by a telecommunication system (whether before or after its transmission).

(9) Any conduct which is carried out in accordance with a bulk equipment interference warrant is lawful for all purposes.

177 Meaning of "equipment data"

(1) In this Chapter, "equipment data" means—
  (a) systems data;
  (b) data which falls within subsection (2).

(2) The data falling within this subsection is identifying data which—
  (a) is, for the purposes of a relevant system, comprised in, included as part of, attached to or logically associated with a communication (whether by the sender or otherwise) or any other item of information,
  (b) is capable of being logically separated from the remainder of the communication or the item of information, and
  (c) if it were so separated, would not reveal anything of what might reasonably be considered to be the meaning (if any) of the communication or the item of information, disregarding any meaning arising from the fact of the communication or the existence of the item of information or from any data relating to that fact.

(3) In subsection (2), "relevant system" means any system on or by means of which the data is held.
(4) For the meaning of "systems data" and "identifying data", see section 263.

178 Power to issue bulk equipment interference warrants

(1) The Secretary of State may, on an application made by or on behalf of the head of an intelligence service, issue a bulk equipment interference warrant if—
   (a) the Secretary of State considers that the main purpose of the warrant is to obtain overseas-related communications, overseas-related information or overseas-related equipment data,
   (b) the Secretary of State considers that the warrant is necessary—
      (i) in the interests of national security, or
      (ii) on that ground and on any other grounds falling within subsection (2),
   (c) the Secretary of State considers that the conduct authorised by the warrant is proportionate to what is sought to be achieved by that conduct,
   (d) the Secretary of State considers that—
      (i) each of the specified operational purposes (see section 183) is a purpose for which the examination of material obtained under the warrant is or may be necessary, and
      (ii) the examination of such material for each such purpose is necessary on any of the grounds on which the Secretary of State considers the warrant to be necessary,
   (e) the Secretary of State considers that satisfactory arrangements made for the purposes of sections 191 and 192 (safeguards relating to disclosure etc.) are in force in relation to the warrant, and
   (f) except where the Secretary of State considers that there is an urgent need to issue the warrant, the decision to issue the warrant has been approved by a Judicial Commissioner.
For the meaning of "head of an intelligence service", see section 263.
(2) A warrant is necessary on grounds falling within this subsection if it is necessary—
   (a) for the purpose of preventing or detecting serious crime, or
   (b) in the interests of the economic well-being of the United Kingdom so far as those interests are also relevant to the interests of national security (but see subsection (3)).
(3) A warrant may be considered necessary on the ground falling within subsection (2)(b) only if the interference with equipment which would be authorised by the warrant is considered necessary for the purpose of obtaining information relating to the acts or intentions of persons outside the British Islands.
(4) An application for the issue of a bulk equipment interference warrant may only be made on behalf of the head of an intelligence service by a person holding office under the Crown.

179 Approval of warrants by Judicial Commissioners

(1) In deciding whether to approve a decision to issue a warrant under section 178, a Judicial Commissioner must review the Secretary of State's conclusions as to the following matters—
   (a) whether the warrant is necessary as mentioned in subsection (1)(b) of that section,
   (b) whether the conduct that would be authorised by the warrant is proportionate to what is sought to be achieved by that conduct, and
   (c) whether—
      (i) each of the specified operational purposes (see section 183) is a purpose for which the examination of material obtained under the warrant is or may be necessary, and
      (ii) the examination of such material for each such purpose is necessary as mentioned in section 178(1)(d)(ii).

(2) In doing so, the Judicial Commissioner must—
    (a) apply the same principles as would be applied by a court on an application for judicial review, and
    (b) consider the matters referred to in subsection (1) with a sufficient degree of care as to ensure that the Judicial Commissioner complies with the duties imposed by section 2 (general duties in relation to privacy).
(3) Where a Judicial Commissioner refuses to approve a decision to issue a warrant under section 178, the Judicial Commissioner must give the Secretary of State written reasons for the refusal.
(4) Where a Judicial Commissioner, other than the Investigatory Powers Commissioner, refuses to approve a decision to issue a warrant under section 178, the Secretary of State may ask the Investigatory Powers Commissioner to decide whether to approve the decision to issue the warrant.

180 Approval of warrants issued in urgent cases

(1) This section applies where—
    (a) a warrant under section 178 is issued without the approval of a Judicial Commissioner, and
    (b) the Secretary of State considered that there was an urgent need to issue it.
(2) The Secretary of State must inform a Judicial Commissioner that it has been issued.
(3) The Judicial Commissioner must, before the end of the relevant period—
    (a) decide whether to approve the decision to issue the warrant, and
    (b) notify the Secretary of State of the Judicial Commissioner's decision. "The relevant period" means the period ending with the third working day after the day on which the warrant was issued.
(4) If a Judicial Commissioner refuses to approve the decision to issue a warrant, the warrant—
    (a) ceases to have effect (unless already cancelled), and
    (b) may not be renewed, and section 179(4) does not apply in relation to the refusal to approve the decision.
(5) Section 181 contains further provision about what happens if a Judicial Commissioner refuses to approve a decision to issue a warrant.

181 Failure to approve warrant issued in urgent case

(1) This section applies where under section 180(3) a Judicial Commissioner refuses to approve a decision to issue a warrant.
(2) The person to whom the warrant was addressed must, so far as is reasonably practicable, secure that anything in the process of being done under the warrant stops as soon as possible.
(3) The Judicial Commissioner may—
    (a) authorise further interference with equipment for the purpose of enabling the person to whom the warrant was addressed to secure that anything in the process of being done under the warrant stops as soon as possible;
    (b) direct that any material obtained under the warrant is destroyed;
    (c) impose conditions as to the use or retention of any of that material.
(4) The Judicial Commissioner—
    (a) may require an affected party to make representations about how the Judicial Commissioner should exercise any function under subsection (3), and
    (b) must have regard to any such representations made by an affected party (whether or not as a result of a requirement imposed under paragraph (a)).

(5) Each of the following is an "affected party" for the purposes of subsection (4)—
   (a) the Secretary of State;
   (b) the person to whom the warrant was addressed.
(6) The Secretary of State may ask the Investigatory Powers Commissioner to review a decision made by any other Judicial Commissioner under subsection (3).
(7) On a review under subsection (6), the Investigatory Powers Commissioner may—
   (a) confirm the Judicial Commissioner's decision, or
   (b) make a fresh determination.
(8) Nothing in this section or section 180 affects the lawfulness of—
   (a) anything done under the warrant before it ceases to have effect;
   (b) if anything is in the process of being done under the warrant when it ceases to have effect—
      (i) anything done before that thing could be stopped, or
      (ii) anything done that it is not reasonably practicable to stop.

182 Decisions to issue warrants to be taken personally by Secretary of State

(1) The decision to issue a bulk equipment interference warrant must be taken personally by the Secretary of State.
(2) Before a bulk equipment interference warrant is issued, it must be signed by the Secretary of State.
(3) If it is not reasonably practicable for a warrant to be signed by the Secretary of State, the warrant may be signed by a senior official designated by the Secretary of State for that purpose.
(4) In such a case, the warrant must contain a statement that—
   (a) it is not reasonably practicable for the warrant to be signed by the Secretary of State, and
   (b) the Secretary of State has personally and expressly authorised the issue of the warrant.

183 Requirements that must be met by warrants

(1) A bulk equipment interference warrant must contain a provision stating that it is a bulk equipment interference warrant.
(2) A bulk equipment interference warrant must be addressed to the head of the intelligence service by whom, or on whose behalf, the application for the warrant was made.
(3) A bulk equipment interference warrant must describe the conduct that is authorised by the warrant.
(4) A bulk equipment interference warrant must specify the operational purposes for which any material obtained under the warrant may be selected for examination.
(5) The operational purposes specified in the warrant must be ones specified, in a list maintained by the heads of the intelligence services ("the list of operational purposes"), as purposes which they consider are operational purposes for which material obtained under bulk equipment interference warrants may be selected for examination.
(6) The warrant may, in particular, specify all of the operational purposes which, at the time the warrant is issued, are specified in the list of operational purposes.
(7) An operational purpose may be specified in the list of operational purposes only with the approval of the Secretary of State.
(8) The Secretary of State may give such approval only if satisfied that the operational purpose is specified in a greater level of detail than the descriptions contained in section 178(1)(b) or (2).
(9) At the end of each relevant three-month period, the Secretary of State must give a copy of the list of operational purposes to the Intelligence and Security Committee of Parliament.

(10) In subsection (9), "relevant three-month period" means—
  (a) the period of three months beginning with the day on which this section comes into force, and
  (b) each successive period of three months.
(11) The Prime Minister must review the list of operational purposes at least once a year.
(12) In this Chapter, "the specified operational purposes", in relation to a bulk equipment interference warrant, means the operational purposes specified in the warrant in accordance with this section.

Duration, modification and cancellation of warrants
184 Duration of warrants

(1) A bulk equipment interference warrant ceases to have effect at the end of the relevant period (see subsection (2)), unless—
  (a) it is renewed before the end of that period (see section 185), or
  (b) it is cancelled or otherwise ceases to have effect before the end of that period (see sections 180 and 189).
(2) In this section, "the relevant period"—
  (a) in the case of an urgent warrant (see subsection (3)), means the period ending with the fifth working day after the day on which the warrant was issued;
  (b) in any other case, means the period of 6 months beginning with—
    (i) the day on which the warrant was issued, or
    (ii) in the case of a warrant which has been renewed, the day after the day at the end of which the warrant would have ceased to have effect if it had not been renewed.
(3) For the purposes of subsection (2)(a), a warrant is an "urgent warrant" if—
  (a) the warrant was issued without the approval of a Judicial Commissioner, and
  (b) the person who decided to issue the warrant considered that there was an urgent need to issue it.

185 Renewal of warrants

(1) If the renewal conditions are met, a bulk equipment interference warrant may be renewed, at any time during the renewal period, by an instrument issued by the Secretary of State.
This is subject to subsection (6).
(2) The renewal conditions are—
  (a) that the Secretary of State considers that the warrant continues to be necessary—
    (i) in the interests of national security, or
    (ii) on that ground and on any other grounds falling within section 178(2),
  (b) that the Secretary of State considers that the conduct that would be authorised by the renewed warrant continues to be proportionate to what is sought to be achieved by that conduct,
  (c) that the Secretary of State considers that—
    (i) each of the specified operational purposes (see section 183) is a purpose for which the examination of material obtained under the warrant continues to be, or may be, necessary, and
    (ii) the examination of such material for each such purpose continues to be necessary on any of the grounds on which the Secretary of State considers that the warrant continues to be necessary, and
  (d) that the decision to renew the warrant has been approved by a Judicial Commissioner.

(3) "The renewal period" means—
   (a) in the case of an urgent warrant which has not been renewed, the relevant period;
   (b) in any other case, the period of 30 days ending with the day at the end of which the warrant would otherwise cease to have effect.
(4) The decision to renew a bulk equipment interference warrant must be taken personally by the Secretary of State, and the instrument renewing the warrant must be signed by the Secretary of State.
(5) Section 179 (approval of warrants by Judicial Commissioners) applies in relation to a decision to renew a bulk equipment interference warrant as it applies in relation to a decision to issue a bulk equipment interference warrant.
This is subject to subsection (6).
(6) In the case of a bulk equipment interference warrant which has been modified so that it no longer authorises or requires the securing of interference with any equipment or the obtaining of any communications, equipment data or other information—
   (a) the renewal condition in subsection (2)(a) is to be disregarded,
   (b) the reference in subsection (2)(c)(ii) to the grounds on which the Secretary of State considers the warrant to be necessary is to be read as a reference to any grounds falling within section 178(1)(b) or (2), and
   (c) section 179 has effect as if—
      (i) paragraph (a) of subsection (1) were omitted, and
      (ii) the reference in subsection (1)(c)(ii) to the grounds on which the Secretary of State considers the warrant to be necessary were a reference to any grounds falling within section 178(1)(b) or (2).
(7) In this section—
"the relevant period" has the same meaning as in section 184;
"urgent warrant" is to be read in accordance with subsection (3) of that section.

186 Modification of warrants

(1) The provisions of a bulk equipment interference warrant may be modified at any time by an instrument issued by the person making the modification.
(2) The modifications which may be made under this section are—
   (a) adding, varying or removing any operational purpose specified in the warrant as a purpose for which any material obtained under the warrant may be selected for examination, and
   (b) adding, varying or removing any description of conduct authorised by the warrant.
(3) In this section—
   (a) a modification adding or varying any operational purpose, or any description of conduct, as mentioned in subsection (2) is referred to as a "major modification", and
   (b) any other modification within that subsection is referred to as a "minor modification".
(4) A major modification adding or varying any operational purpose—
   (a) must be made by the Secretary of State, and
   (b) may be made only if the Secretary of State considers that it is necessary on any of the grounds on which the Secretary of State considers the warrant to be necessary (see section 178(1)(b)).
(5) A major modification adding or varying any description of conduct—
   (a) must be made by the Secretary of State, and
   (b) may be made only if the Secretary of State considers—
      (i) that the modification is necessary on any of the grounds on which the Secretary of State considers the warrant to be necessary (see section 178(1)(b)), and

Appendix

    (ii) that the conduct authorised by the modification is proportionate to what is sought to be achieved by that conduct.

(6) Except where the Secretary of State considers that there is an urgent need to make the modification, a major modification has effect only if the decision to make the modification is approved by a Judicial Commissioner.

(7) A minor modification may be made by—
  (a) the Secretary of State, or
  (b) a senior official acting on behalf of the Secretary of State.

(8) Where a minor modification is made by a senior official, the Secretary of State must be notified personally of the modification and the reasons for making it.

(9) If at any time a person mentioned in subsection (7) considers that any operational purpose specified in a warrant is no longer a purpose for which the examination of material obtained under the warrant is or may be necessary, the person must modify the warrant by removing that operational purpose.

(10) The decision to modify the provisions of a warrant must be taken personally by the person making the modification, and the instrument making the modification must be signed by that person. This is subject to subsection (11).

(11) If it is not reasonably practicable for an instrument making a major modification to be signed by the Secretary of State, the instrument may be signed by a senior official designated by the Secretary of State for that purpose.

(12) In such a case, the instrument making the modification must contain a statement that—
  (a) it is not reasonably practicable for the instrument to be signed by the Secretary of State, and
  (b) the Secretary of State has personally and expressly authorised the making of the modification.

(13) Despite section 176(1)(b) and (4)(a), the modification of a bulk equipment interference warrant so that it no longer authorises or requires the securing of interference with any equipment or the obtaining of any communications, equipment data or other information does not prevent the warrant from being a bulk equipment interference warrant.

(14) Nothing in this section applies in relation to modifying the provisions of a warrant in a way which does not affect the conduct authorised by it.

187 Approval of major modifications by Judicial Commissioners

(1) In deciding whether to approve a decision to make a major modification of a bulk equipment interference warrant, a Judicial Commissioner must review the Secretary of State's conclusions as to the following matters—
  (a) whether the modification is necessary on any of the grounds on which the Secretary of State considers the warrant to be necessary, and
  (b) in the case of a major modification adding or varying any description of conduct authorised by the warrant, whether the conduct authorised by the modification is proportionate to what is sought to be achieved by that conduct.

(2) In doing so, the Judicial Commissioner must—
  (a) apply the same principles as would be applied by a court on an application for judicial review, and
  (b) consider the matters referred to in subsection (1) with a sufficient degree of care as to ensure that the Judicial Commissioner complies with the duties imposed by section 2 (general duties in relation to privacy).

(3) Where a Judicial Commissioner refuses to approve a decision to make a major modification under section 186, the Judicial Commissioner must give the Secretary of State written reasons for the refusal.
(4) Where a Judicial Commissioner, other than the Investigatory Powers Commissioner, refuses to approve a decision to make a major modification under section 186, the Secretary of State may ask the Investigatory Powers Commissioner to decide whether to approve the decision to make the modification.

188 Approval of major modifications made in urgent cases

(1) This section applies where—
   (a) the Secretary of State makes a major modification of a bulk equipment interference warrant without the approval of a Judicial Commissioner, and
   (b) the Secretary of State considered that there was an urgent need to make the modification.
(2) The Secretary of State must inform a Judicial Commissioner that the modification has been made.
(3) The Judicial Commissioner must, before the end of the relevant period—
   (a) decide whether to approve the decision to make the modification, and
   (b) notify the Secretary of State of the Judicial Commissioner's decision.
   "The relevant period" means the period ending with the third working day after the day on which the modification was made.
(4) If the Judicial Commissioner refuses to approve the decision to make the modification—
   (a) the warrant (unless it no longer has effect) has effect as if the modification had not been made, and
   (b) the person to whom the warrant is addressed must, so far as is reasonably practicable, secure that anything in the process of being done under the warrant by virtue of that modification stops as soon as possible, and section 187(4) does not apply in relation to the refusal to approve the decision.
(5) The Judicial Commissioner may authorise further interference with equipment for the purpose of enabling the person to whom the warrant is addressed to secure that anything in the process of being done under the warrant by virtue of the modification stops as soon as possible.
(6) Nothing in this section affects the lawfulness of—
   (a) anything done under the warrant by virtue of the modification before the modification ceases to have effect;
   (b) if anything is in the process of being done under the warrant by virtue of the modification when the modification ceases to have effect—
      (i) anything done before that thing could be stopped, or
      (ii) anything done which it is not reasonably practicable to stop.

189 Cancellation of warrants

(1) The Secretary of State, or a senior official acting on behalf of the Secretary of State, may cancel a bulk equipment interference warrant at any time.
(2) If the Secretary of State, or a senior official acting on behalf of the Secretary of State, considers that any of the cancellation conditions are met in relation to a bulk equipment interference warrant, the person must cancel the warrant.
(3) The cancellation conditions are—
   (a) that the warrant is no longer necessary in the interests of national security;

(b) that the conduct authorised by the warrant is no longer proportionate to what is sought to be achieved by that conduct;
(c) that the examination of material obtained under the warrant is no longer necessary for any of the specified operational purposes (see section 183).
(4) But the condition in subsection (3)(a) does not apply where the warrant has been modified so that it no longer authorises or requires the securing of interference with any equipment or the obtaining of any communications, equipment data or other information.
(5) Where a warrant is cancelled under this section, the person to whom the warrant was addressed must, so far as is reasonably practicable, secure that anything in the process of being done under the warrant stops as soon as possible.
(6) A warrant that has been cancelled under this section may not be renewed.

Implementation of warrants

190 Implementation of warrants

(1) In giving effect to a bulk equipment interference warrant, the person to whom it is addressed ("the implementing authority") may (in addition to acting alone) act through, or together with, such other persons as the implementing authority may require (whether under subsection (2) or otherwise) to provide the authority with assistance in giving effect to the warrant.
(2) For the purpose of requiring any person to provide assistance in relation to a bulk equipment interference warrant, the implementing authority may—
   (a) serve a copy of the warrant on any person who the implementing authority considers may be able to provide such assistance, or
   (b) make arrangements for the service of a copy of the warrant on any such person.
(3) A copy of a warrant may be served under subsection (2) on a person outside the United Kingdom for the purpose of requiring the person to provide such assistance in the form of conduct outside the United Kingdom.
(4) For the purposes of this Act, the provision of assistance in giving effect to a bulk equipment interference warrant includes any disclosure to the implementing authority, or to persons acting on behalf of the implementing authority, of material obtained under the warrant.
(5) Sections 127 (service of warrants) and 128 (duty of telecommunications operators to assist with implementation) apply in relation to a bulk equipment interference warrant as they apply in relation to a targeted equipment interference warrant issued under section 102 by the Secretary of State.
(6) References in this section (and in sections 127 and 128 as they apply in relation to bulk equipment interference warrants) to the service of a copy of a warrant include—
   (a) the service of a copy of one or more schedules contained in the warrant with the omission of the remainder of the warrant, and
   (b) the service of a copy of the warrant with the omission of any schedule contained in the warrant.

Restrictions on use or disclosure of material obtained under warrants etc.

191 Safeguards relating to retention and disclosure of material

(1) The Secretary of State must ensure, in relation to every bulk equipment interference warrant, that arrangements are in force for securing—
   (a) that the requirements of subsections (2) and (5) are met in relation to the material obtained under the warrant, and

(b) that the requirements of section 193 are met in relation to that material. This is subject to subsection (8).
(2) The requirements of this subsection are met in relation to the material obtained under the warrant if each of the following is limited to the minimum that is necessary for the authorised purposes (see subsection (3))—
  (a) the number of persons to whom any of the material is disclosed or otherwise made available;
  (b) the extent to which any of the material is disclosed or otherwise made available;
  (c) the extent to which any of the material is copied;
  (d) the number of copies that are made.
(3) For the purposes of subsection (2) something is necessary for the authorised purposes if, and only if—
  (a) it is, or is likely to become, necessary in the interests of national security or on any other grounds falling within section 178(2),
  (b) it is necessary for facilitating the carrying out of any functions under this Act of the Secretary of State, the Scottish Ministers or the head of the intelligence service to whom the warrant is or was addressed,
  (c) it is necessary for facilitating the carrying out of any functions of the Judicial Commissioners or of the Investigatory Powers Tribunal under or in relation to this Act,
  (d) it is necessary for the purpose of legal proceedings, or
  (e) it is necessary for the performance of the functions of any person under any enactment.
(4) The arrangements for the time being in force under this section for securing that the requirements of subsection (2) are met in relation to the material obtained under the warrant must include arrangements for securing that every copy made of any of that material is stored, for so long as it is retained, in a secure manner.
(5) The requirements of this subsection are met in relation to the material obtained under the warrant if every copy made of any of that material (if not destroyed earlier) is destroyed as soon as there are no longer any relevant grounds for retaining it (see subsection (6)).
(6) For the purposes of subsection (5), there are no longer any relevant grounds for retaining a copy of any material if, and only if—
  (a) its retention is not necessary, or not likely to become necessary, in the interests of national security or on any other grounds falling within section 178(2), and
  (b) its retention is not necessary for any of the purposes mentioned in paragraphs (b) to (e) of subsection (3) above.
(7) Subsection (8) applies if—
  (a) any material obtained under the warrant has been handed over to any overseas authorities, or
  (b) a copy of any such material has been given to any overseas authorities.
(8) To the extent that the requirements of subsections (2) and (5) and section 193 relate to any of the material mentioned in subsection (7)(a), or to the copy mentioned in subsection (7)(b), the arrangements made for the purpose of this section are not required to secure that those requirements are met (see instead section 192).
(9) In this section—
  "copy", in relation to any material obtained under a warrant, means any of the following (whether or not in documentary form)—
    (a) any copy, extract or summary of the material which identifies the material as having been obtained under the warrant, and

(b) any record which is a record of the identities of persons who owned, used or were in possession of the equipment which was interfered with to obtain that material, and "copied" is to be read accordingly;

"overseas authorities" means authorities of a country or territory outside the United Kingdom.

192 Safeguards relating to disclosure of material overseas

(1) The Secretary of State must ensure, in relation to every bulk equipment interference warrant, that arrangements are in force for securing that—
  (a) any material obtained under the warrant is handed over to overseas authorities only if the requirements of subsection (2) are met, and
  (b) copies of any such material are given to overseas authorities only if those requirements are met.
(2) The requirements of this subsection are met in the case of a warrant if it appears to the Secretary of State that requirements corresponding to the requirements of section 191(2) and (5) and section 193 will apply, to such extent (if any) as the Secretary of State considers appropriate, in relation to any of the material which is handed over, or any copy of which is given, to the authorities in question.
(3) In this section—
"copy" has the same meaning as in section 191;
"overseas authorities" means authorities of a country or territory outside the United Kingdom.

193 Safeguards relating to examination of material etc.

(1) For the purposes of section 191, the requirements of this section are met in relation to the material obtained under a warrant if—
  (a) the selection of any of the material obtained under the warrant for examination is carried out only for the specified purposes (see subsection (2)),
  (b) the selection of any of the material for examination is necessary and proportionate in all the circumstances, and
  (c) where any such material is protected material, the selection of the material for examination meets any of the selection conditions (see subsection (3)).
(2) The selection of material obtained under the warrant for examination is carried out only for the specified purposes if the material is selected for examination only so far as is necessary for the operational purposes specified in the warrant in accordance with section 183.
In this subsection "specified in the warrant" means specified in the warrant at the time of the selection of the material for examination.
(3) The selection conditions referred to in subsection (1)(c) are—
  (a) that the selection of the protected material for examination does not breach the prohibition in subsection (4);
  (b) that the person to whom the warrant is addressed reasonably considers that the selection of the protected material for examination would not breach that prohibition;
  (c) that the selection of the protected material for examination in breach of that prohibition is authorised by subsection (5);
  (d) that the selection of the protected material for examination in breach of that prohibition is authorised by a targeted examination warrant issued under Part 5.
(4) The prohibition referred to in subsection (3)(a) is that the protected material may not at any time be selected for examination if—
  (a) any criteria used for the selection of the material for examination are referable to an individual known to be in the British Islands at that time, and

Appendix

    (b) the purpose of using those criteria is to identify protected material consisting of communications sent by, or intended for, that individual or private information relating to that individual.

It does not matter for the purposes of this subsection whether the identity of the individual is known.

(5) The selection of protected material ("the relevant material") for examination is authorised by this subsection if—
  (a) criteria referable to an individual have been, or are being, used for the selection of material for examination in circumstances falling within subsection (3)(a) or (b),
  (b) at any time it appears to the person to whom the warrant is addressed that there has been a relevant change of circumstances in relation to the individual (see subsection (6)) which would mean that the selection of the relevant material for examination would breach the prohibition in subsection (4),
  (c) since that time, a written authorisation to examine the relevant material using those criteria has been given by a senior officer, and
  (d) the selection of the relevant material for examination is made before the end of the permitted period (see subsection (7)).

(6) For the purposes of subsection (5)(b) there is a relevant change of circumstances in relation to an individual if—
  (a) the individual has entered the British Islands, or
  (b) a belief by the person to whom the warrant is addressed that the individual was outside the British Islands was in fact mistaken.

(7) In subsection (5)—
"senior officer", in relation to a warrant addressed to the head of an intelligence service, means a member of the intelligence service who—
  (a) is a member of the Senior Civil Service or a member of the Senior Management Structure of Her Majesty's Diplomatic Service, or
  (b) holds a position in the intelligence service of equivalent seniority to such a member;
"the permitted period" means the period ending with the fifth working day after the time mentioned in subsection (5)(b).

(8) In a case where the selection of protected material for examination is authorised by subsection (5), the person to whom the warrant is addressed must notify the Secretary of State that the selection is being carried out.

(9) In this Part, "protected material" means any material obtained under the warrant other than material which is—
  (a) equipment data;
  (b) information (other than a communication or equipment data) which is not private information.

194 Additional safeguards for items subject to legal privilege

(1) Subsection (2) applies if, in a case where protected material obtained under a bulk equipment interference warrant is to be selected for examination—
  (a) the selection of the material for examination meets any of the selection conditions in section 193(3)(a) to (c), and
  (b) either—
    (i) the purpose, or one of the purposes, of using the criteria to be used for the selection of the material for examination ("the relevant criteria") is to identify any items subject to legal privilege, or
    (ii) the use of the relevant criteria is likely to identify such items.

Appendix

(2) The material may be selected for examination using the relevant criteria only if a senior official acting on behalf of the Secretary of State has approved the use of those criteria.

(3) In deciding whether to give an approval under subsection (2) in a case where subsection (1)(b)(i) applies, a senior official must have regard to the public interest in the confidentiality of items subject to legal privilege.

(4) A senior official may give an approval under subsection (2) only if—
  (a) the official considers that the arrangements made for the purposes of section 191 (safeguards relating to retention and disclosure of material) include specific arrangements for the handling, retention, use and destruction of items subject to legal privilege, and
  (b) where subsection (1)(b)(i) applies, the official considers that there are exceptional and compelling circumstances that make it necessary to authorise the use of the relevant criteria.

(5) For the purposes of subsection (4)(b), there cannot be exceptional and compelling circumstances that make it necessary to authorise the use of the relevant criteria unless—
  (a) the public interest in obtaining the information that would be obtained by the selection of the material for examination outweighs the public interest in the confidentiality of items subject to legal privilege,
  (b) there are no other means by which the information may reasonably be obtained, and
  (c) obtaining the information is necessary in the interests of national security or for the purpose of preventing death or significant injury.

(6) Subsection (7) applies if, in a case where protected material obtained under a bulk equipment interference warrant is to be selected for examination—
  (a) the selection of the material for examination meets any of the selection conditions in section 193(3)(a) to (c),
  (b) the purpose, or one of the purposes, of using the criteria to be used for the selection of the material for examination ("the relevant criteria") is to identify communications or other items of information that, if they were not communications made or (as the case may be) other items of information created or held with the intention of furthering a criminal purpose, would be items subject to legal privilege, and
  (c) the person to whom the warrant is addressed considers that the communications or other items of information ("the targeted communications or other items of information") are likely to be communications made or (as the case may be) other items of information created or held with the intention of furthering a criminal purpose.

(7) The material may be selected for examination using the relevant criteria only if a senior official acting on behalf of the Secretary of State has approved the use of those criteria.

(8) A senior official may give an approval under subsection (7) only if the official considers that the targeted communications or other items of information are likely to be communications made or (as the case may be) other items of information created or held with the intention of furthering a criminal purpose.

(9) Where an item subject to legal privilege which has been obtained under a bulk equipment interference warrant is retained following its examination, for purposes other than the destruction of the item, the person to whom the warrant is addressed must inform the Investigatory Powers Commissioner as soon as is reasonably practicable.

(For provision about the grounds for retaining material obtained under a bulk equipment interference warrant, see section 191.)

(10) Unless the Investigatory Powers Commissioner considers that subsection (12) applies to the item, the Commissioner must—
  (a) direct that the item is destroyed, or
  (b) impose one or more conditions as to the use or retention of that item.

(11) If the Investigatory Powers Commissioner considers that subsection (12) applies to the item, the Commissioner may nevertheless impose such conditions under subsection (10)(b) as the Commissioner considers necessary for the purpose of protecting the public interest in the confidentiality of items subject to legal privilege.
(12) This subsection applies to an item subject to legal privilege if—
(a) the public interest in retaining the item outweighs the public interest in the confidentiality of items subject to legal privilege, and
(b) retaining the item is necessary in the interests of national security or for the purpose of preventing death or significant injury.
(13) The Investigatory Powers Commissioner—
(a) may require an affected party to make representations about how the Commissioner should exercise any function under subsection (10), and (b) must have regard to any such representations made by an affected party (whether or not as a result of a requirement imposed under paragraph (a)).
(14) Each of the following is an "affected party" for the purposes of subsection (13)—
(a) the Secretary of State;
(b) the person to whom the warrant is or was addressed.

195 Additional safeguard for confidential journalistic material

Where—
(a) material obtained under a bulk equipment interference warrant is retained, following its examination, for purposes other than the destruction of the material, and
(b) it is material containing confidential journalistic material, the person to whom the warrant is addressed must inform the Investigatory Powers Commissioner as soon as is reasonably practicable.
(For provision about the grounds for retaining material obtained under a bulk equipment interference warrant, see section 191.)

196 Offence of breaching safeguards relating to examination of material

(1) A person commits an offence if—
(a) the person selects for examination any material obtained under a bulk equipment interference warrant,
(b) the person knows or believes that the selection of that material does not comply with a requirement imposed by section 193 or 194, and
(c) the person deliberately selects that material in breach of that requirement.
(2) A person guilty of an offence under this section is liable—
(a) on summary conviction in England and Wales—
(i) to imprisonment for a term not exceeding 12 months (or 6 months, if the offence was committed before the commencement of section 154(1) of the Criminal Justice Act 2003), or
(ii) to a fine, or to both;
(b) on summary conviction in Scotland—
(i) to imprisonment for a term not exceeding 12 months, or
(ii) to a fine not exceeding the statutory maximum, or to both;
(c) on summary conviction in Northern Ireland—
(i) to imprisonment for a term not exceeding 6 months, or
(ii) to a fine not exceeding the statutory maximum, or to both;
(d) on conviction on indictment, to imprisonment for a term not exceeding 2 years or to a fine, or to both.

(3) No proceedings for any offence which is an offence by virtue of this section may be instituted—
   (a) in England and Wales, except by or with the consent of the Director of Public Prosecutions;
   (b) in Northern Ireland, except by or with the consent of the Director of Public Prosecutions for Northern Ireland.

197 Application of other restrictions in relation to warrants

Sections 132 to 134 (duty not to make unauthorised disclosures) apply in relation to bulk equipment interference warrants as they apply in relation to targeted equipment interference warrants, but as if the reference in section 133(2)(c) to a requirement for disclosure imposed by virtue of section 126(4) were a reference to such a requirement imposed by virtue of section 190(4).

Interpretation

198 Chapter 3: interpretation

(1) In this Chapter—
"communication" includes—
   (a) anything comprising speech, music, sounds, visual images or data of any description, and
   (b) signals serving either for the impartation of anything between persons, between a person and a thing or between things or for the actuation or control of any apparatus;

"equipment" means equipment producing electromagnetic, acoustic or other emissions or any device capable of being used in connection with such equipment;

"equipment data" has the meaning given by section 177;

"private information" includes information relating to a person's private or family life;

"protected material", in relation to a bulk equipment interference warrant, has the meaning given by section 193(9);

"senior official" means a member of the Senior Civil Service or a member of the Senior Management Structure of Her Majesty's Diplomatic Service;

"the specified operational purposes" has the meaning given by section 183(12).

(2) See also—
section 261 (telecommunications definitions);
section 263 (general definitions);
section 264 (general definitions: "journalistic material" etc.);
section 265 (index of defined expressions).

PART 7
BULK PERSONAL DATASET WARRANTS

Bulk personal datasets: interpretation

199 Bulk personal datasets: interpretation

(1) For the purposes of this Part, an intelligence service retains a bulk personal dataset if—
   (a) the intelligence service obtains a set of information that includes personal data relating to a number of individuals,

Appendix

    (b) the nature of the set is such that the majority of the individuals are not, and are unlikely to become, of interest to the intelligence service in the exercise of its functions,
    (c) after any initial examination of the contents, the intelligence service retains the set for the purpose of the exercise of its functions, and
    (d) the set is held, or is to be held, electronically for analysis in the exercise of those functions.
(2) In this Part, "personal data" has the same meaning as in the Data Protection Act 1998 except that it also includes data relating to a deceased individual where the data would be personal data within the meaning of that Act if it related to a living individual.

Requirement for warrant

200 Requirement for authorisation by warrant: general

(1) An intelligence service may not exercise a power to retain a bulk personal dataset unless the retention of the dataset is authorised by a warrant under this Part.
(2) An intelligence service may not exercise a power to examine a bulk personal dataset retained by it unless the examination is authorised by a warrant under this Part.
(3) For the purposes of this Part, there are two kinds of warrant—
    (a) a warrant, referred to in this Part as "a class BPD warrant", authorising an intelligence service to retain, or to retain and examine, any bulk personal dataset of a class described in the warrant;
    (b) a warrant, referred to in this Part as "a specific BPD warrant", authorising an intelligence service to retain, or to retain and examine, any bulk personal dataset described in the warrant.
(4) Section 201 sets out exceptions to the restrictions imposed by subsections (1) and (2) of this section.

201 Exceptions to section 200(1) and (2)

(1) Section 200(1) or (2) does not apply to the exercise of a power of an intelligence service to retain or (as the case may be) examine a bulk personal dataset if the intelligence service obtained the bulk personal dataset under a warrant or other authorisation issued or given under this Act.
(2) Section 200(1) or (2) does not apply at any time when a bulk personal dataset is being retained or (as the case may be) examined for the purpose of enabling any of the information contained in it to be destroyed.
(3) Sections 210(8), 219(8) and 220(5) provide for other exceptions to section 200(1) or (2) (in connection with cases where a Judicial Commissioner refuses to approve a specific BPD warrant, the non-renewal or cancellation of BPD warrants and initial examinations).

202 Restriction on use of class BPD warrants

(1) An intelligence service may not retain, or retain and examine, a bulk personal dataset in reliance on a class BPD warrant if the head of the intelligence service considers that the bulk personal dataset consists of, or includes, protected data. For the meaning of "protected data", see section 203.
(2) An intelligence service may not retain, or retain and examine, a bulk personal dataset in reliance on a class BPD warrant if the head of the intelligence service considers—
    (a) that the bulk personal dataset consists of, or includes, health records, or
    (b) that a substantial proportion of the bulk personal dataset consists of sensitive personal data.

Appendix

(3) An intelligence service may not retain, or retain and examine, a bulk personal dataset in reliance on a class BPD warrant if the head of the intelligence service considers that the nature of the bulk personal dataset, or the circumstances in which it was created, is or are such that its retention, or retention and examination, by the intelligence service raises novel or contentious issues which ought to be considered by the Secretary of State and a Judicial Commissioner on an application by the head of the intelligence service for a specific BPD warrant.

(4) In subsection (2)—
"health records" has the same meaning as in section 206;
"sensitive personal data" means personal data consisting of information about an individual (whether living or deceased) which is of a kind mentioned in section 2(a) to (f) of the Data Protection Act 1998.

203 Meaning of "protected data"

(1) In this Part, "protected data" means any data contained in a bulk personal dataset other than data which is one or more of the following—
  (a) systems data;
  (b) data which falls within subsection (2);
  (c) data which is not private information.
(2) The data falling within this subsection is identifying data which—
  (a) is contained in the bulk personal dataset,
  (b) is capable of being logically separated from the bulk personal dataset, and
  (c) if it were so separated, would not reveal anything of what might reasonably be considered to be the meaning (if any) of any of the data which would remain in the bulk personal dataset or of the bulk personal dataset itself, disregarding any meaning arising from the existence of that data or (as the case may be) the existence of the bulk personal dataset or from any data relating to that fact.
(3) For the meaning of "systems data" see section 263(4).
(4) In this section, "private information" includes information relating to a person's private or family life.

Issue of warrants

204 Class BPD warrants

(1) The head of an intelligence service, or a person acting on his or her behalf, may apply to the Secretary of State for a class BPD warrant.
(2) The application must include—
  (a) a description of the class of bulk personal datasets to which the application relates, and
  (b) in a case where the intelligence service is seeking authorisation for the examination of bulk personal datasets of that class, the operational purposes which it is proposing should be specified in the warrant (see section 212).
(3) The Secretary of State may issue the warrant if—
  (a) the Secretary of State considers that the warrant is necessary—
    (i) in the interests of national security,
    (ii) for the purposes of preventing or detecting serious crime, or
    (iii) in the interests of the economic well-being of the United Kingdom so far as those interests are also relevant to the interests of national security,
  (b) the Secretary of State considers that the conduct authorised by the warrant is proportionate to what is sought to be achieved by the conduct,

(c) where the warrant authorises the examination of bulk personal datasets of the class described in the warrant, the Secretary of State considers that—
   (i) each of the specified operational purposes (see section 212) is a purpose for which the examination of bulk personal datasets of that class is or may be necessary, and
   (ii) the examination of bulk personal datasets of that class for each such purpose is necessary on any of the grounds on which the Secretary of State considers the warrant to be necessary,
(d) the Secretary of State considers that the arrangements made by the intelligence service for storing bulk personal datasets of the class to which the application relates and for protecting them from unauthorised disclosure are satisfactory, and
(e) the decision to issue the warrant has been approved by a Judicial Commissioner.

(4) The fact that a class BPD warrant would authorise the retention, or the retention and examination, of bulk personal datasets relating to activities in the British Islands of a trade union is not, of itself, sufficient to establish that the warrant is necessary on grounds falling within subsection (3)(a).

(5) An application for a class BPD warrant may only be made on behalf of the head of an intelligence service by a person holding office under the Crown.

205 Specific BPD warrants

(1) The head of an intelligence service, or a person acting on his or her behalf, may apply to the Secretary of State for a specific BPD warrant in the following cases.

(2) Case 1 is where—
   (a) the intelligence service is seeking authorisation to retain, or to retain and examine, a bulk personal dataset, and
   (b) the bulk personal dataset does not fall within a class described in a class BPD warrant.

(3) Case 2 is where—
   (a) the intelligence service is seeking authorisation to retain, or to retain and examine, a bulk personal dataset, and
   (b) the bulk personal dataset falls within a class described in a class BPD warrant but either—
      (i) the intelligence service is prevented by section 202(1), (2) or (3) from retaining, or retaining and examining, the bulk personal dataset in reliance on the class BPD warrant, or
      (ii) the intelligence service at any time considers that it would be appropriate to seek a specific BPD warrant.

(4) The application must include—
   (a) a description of the bulk personal dataset to which the application relates, and
   (b) in a case where the intelligence service is seeking authorisation for the examination of the bulk personal dataset, the operational purposes which it is proposing should be specified in the warrant (see section 212).

(5) Where subsection (3)(b)(i) applies, the application must include an explanation of why the intelligence service is prevented by section 202(1), (2) or (3) from retaining, or retaining and examining, the bulk personal dataset in reliance on a class BPD warrant.

(6) The Secretary of State may issue the warrant if—
   (a) the Secretary of State considers that the warrant is necessary—
      (i) in the interests of national security,
      (ii) for the purposes of preventing or detecting serious crime, or
      (iii) in the interests of the economic well-being of the United Kingdom so far as those interests are also relevant to the interests of national security,

Appendix

    (b) the Secretary of State considers that the conduct authorised by the warrant is proportionate to what is sought to be achieved by the conduct,

    (c) where the warrant authorises the examination of a bulk personal dataset, the Secretary of State considers that—
        (i) each of the specified operational purposes (see section 212) is a purpose for which the examination of the bulk personal dataset is or may be necessary, and
        (ii) the examination of the bulk personal dataset for each such purpose is necessary on any of the grounds on which the Secretary of State considers the warrant to be necessary,

    (d) the Secretary of State considers that the arrangements made by the intelligence service for storing the bulk personal dataset and for protecting it from unauthorised disclosure are satisfactory, and

    (e) except where the Secretary of State considers that there is an urgent need to issue the warrant, the decision to issue it has been approved by a Judicial Commissioner.

(7) The fact that a specific BPD warrant would authorise the retention, or the retention and examination, of bulk personal datasets relating to activities in the British Islands of a trade union is not, of itself, sufficient to establish that the warrant is necessary on grounds falling within subsection (6)(a).

(8) A specific BPD warrant relating to a bulk personal dataset ("dataset A") may also authorise the retention or examination of other bulk personal datasets ("replacement datasets") that do not exist at the time of the issue of the warrant but may reasonably be regarded as replacements for dataset A.

(9) An application for a specific BPD warrant may only be made on behalf of the head of an intelligence service by a person holding office under the Crown.

206 Additional safeguards for health records

(1) Subsections (2) and (3) apply if—
    (a) an application is made by or on behalf of the head of an intelligence service for the issue of a specific BPD warrant, and
    (b) the purpose, or one of the purposes, of the warrant is to authorise the retention, or the retention and examination, of health records.

(2) The application must contain a statement that the purpose, or one of the purposes, of the warrant is to authorise the retention, or the retention and examination, of health records.

(3) The Secretary of State may issue the warrant only if the Secretary of State considers that there are exceptional and compelling circumstances that make it necessary to authorise the retention, or the retention and examination, of health records.

(4) Subsection (5) applies if—
    (a) an application is made by or on behalf of the head of an intelligence service for a specific BPD warrant,
    (b) the head of the intelligence service considers that the bulk personal dataset includes, or is likely to include, health records, and
    (c) subsections (2) and (3) do not apply.

(5) The application must contain either—
    (a) a statement that the head of the intelligence service considers that the bulk personal dataset includes health records, or
    (b) a statement that the head of the intelligence service considers that it is likely that the bulk personal dataset includes health records and an assessment of how likely this is.

Appendix

(6) In this section, "health record" means a record, or a copy of a record, which—
  (a) consists of information relating to the physical or mental health or condition of an individual,
  (b) was made by or on behalf of a health professional in connection with the care of that individual, and
  (c) was obtained by the intelligence service from a health professional or a health service body or from a person acting on behalf of a health professional or a health service body in relation to the record or the copy.
(7) In subsection (6)—
  "health professional" has the same meaning as in the Data Protection Act 1998 (see section 69 of that Act);
  "health service body" has the meaning given by section 69(3) of that Act.

207 Protected data: power to impose conditions

Where the Secretary of State decides to issue a specific BPD warrant, the Secretary of State may impose conditions which must be satisfied before protected data retained in reliance on the warrant may be selected for examination on the basis of criteria which are referable to an individual known to be in the British Islands at the time of the selection.

208 Approval of warrants by Judicial Commissioners

(1) In deciding whether to approve a decision to issue a class BPD warrant or a specific BPD warrant, a Judicial Commissioner must review the Secretary of State's conclusions as to the following matters—
  (a) whether the warrant is necessary on grounds falling within section 204(3)(a) or (as the case may be) section 205(6)(a),
  (b) whether the conduct that would be authorised by the warrant is proportionate to what is sought to be achieved by that conduct, and
  (c) where the warrant authorises examination of bulk personal datasets of a class described in the warrant or (as the case may be) of a bulk personal dataset described in the warrant, whether—
    (i) each of the specified operational purposes (see section 212) is a purpose for which the examination of bulk personal datasets of that class or (as the case may be) the bulk personal dataset is or may be necessary, and
    (ii) the examination of bulk personal datasets of that class or (as the case may be) the bulk personal dataset is necessary as mentioned in section 204(3)(c)(ii) or (as the case may be) section 205(6)(c)(ii).
(2) In doing so, the Judicial Commissioner must—
  (a) apply the same principles as would be applied by a court on an application for judicial review, and
  (b) consider the matters referred to in subsection (1) with a sufficient degree of care as to ensure that the Judicial Commissioner complies with the duties imposed by section 2 (general duties in relation to privacy).
(3) Where a Judicial Commissioner refuses to approve a decision to issue a class BPD warrant or a specific BPD warrant, the Judicial Commissioner must give the Secretary of State written reasons for the refusal.
(4) Where a Judicial Commissioner, other than the Investigatory Powers Commissioner, refuses to approve a decision to issue a class BPD warrant or a specific BPD warrant, the Secretary of State may ask the Investigatory Powers Commissioner to decide whether to approve the decision to issue the warrant.

209 Approval of specific BPD warrants issued in urgent cases

(1) This section applies where—
   (a) a specific BPD warrant is issued without the approval of a Judicial Commissioner, and
   (b) the Secretary of State considered that there was an urgent need to issue it.
(2) The Secretary of State must inform a Judicial Commissioner that it has been issued.
(3) The Judicial Commissioner must, before the end of the relevant period—
   (a) decide whether to approve the decision to issue the warrant, and
   (b) notify the Secretary of State of the Judicial Commissioner's decision.
   "The relevant period" means the period ending with the third working day after the day on which the warrant was issued.
(4) If a Judicial Commissioner refuses to approve the decision to issue a specific BPD warrant, the warrant—
   (a) ceases to have effect (unless already cancelled), and
   (b) may not be renewed, and section 208(4) does not apply in relation to the refusal to approve the decision.
(5) Section 210 contains further provision about what happens if a Judicial Commissioner refuses to approve a decision to issue a warrant.

210 Failure to approve specific BPD warrant issued in urgent case

(1) This section applies where under section 209(3) a Judicial Commissioner refuses to approve the decision to issue a warrant.
(2) The head of the intelligence service to whom the warrant was addressed must, so far as is reasonably practicable, secure that anything in the process of being done in reliance on the warrant stops as soon as possible.
(3) The Judicial Commissioner may—
   (a) direct that the whole or part of a bulk personal dataset retained in reliance on the warrant is destroyed;
   (b) impose conditions as to the use or retention of the whole or part of any such bulk personal dataset.
(4) The Judicial Commissioner—
   (a) may require an affected party to make representations about how the Judicial Commissioner should exercise any function under subsection (3), and
   (b) must have regard to any such representations made by an affected party (whether or not as a result of a requirement imposed under paragraph (a)).
(5) Each of the following is an "affected party" for the purposes of subsection (4)—
   (a) the Secretary of State;
   (b) the head of the intelligence service to whom the warrant was addressed.
(6) The Secretary of State may ask the Investigatory Powers Commissioner to review a decision made by any other Judicial Commissioner under subsection (3).
(7) On a review under subsection (6), the Investigatory Powers Commissioner may—
   (a) confirm the Judicial Commissioner's decision, or
   (b) make a fresh determination.
(8) An intelligence service is not to be regarded as in breach of section 200(1) or (2) where it retains or (as the case may be) examines a bulk personal dataset in accordance with conditions imposed under subsection (3)(b).
(9) Nothing in this section or section 209 affects the lawfulness of—
   (a) anything done in reliance on the warrant before it ceases to have effect;

(b) if anything is in the process of being done in reliance on the warrant when it ceases to have effect—
- (i) anything done before that thing could be stopped, or
- (ii) anything done that it is not reasonably practicable to stop.

211 Decisions to issue warrants to be taken personally by Secretary of State

(1) The decision to issue a class BPD warrant or a specific BPD warrant must be taken personally by the Secretary of State.
(2) Before a class BPD warrant is issued, it must be signed by the Secretary of State.
(3) Before a specific BPD warrant is issued, it must be signed by the Secretary of State (subject to subsection (4)).
(4) If it is not reasonably practicable for a specific BPD warrant to be signed by the Secretary of State, it may be signed by a senior official designated by the Secretary of State for that purpose.
(5) In such a case, the warrant must contain a statement that—
- (a) it is not reasonably practicable for the warrant to be signed by the Secretary of State, and
- (b) the Secretary of State has personally and expressly authorised the issue of the warrant.

212 Requirements that must be met by warrants

(1) A class BPD warrant or a specific BPD warrant must contain a provision stating whether it is a class BPD warrant or (as the case may be) a specific BPD warrant.
(2) A class BPD warrant or a specific BPD warrant must be addressed to the head of the intelligence service by whom, or on whose behalf, the application for the warrant was made.
(3) A class BPD warrant must—
- (a) include a description of the class of bulk personal datasets to which the warrant relates, and
- (b) where the warrant authorises examination of bulk personal datasets of that class, specify the operational purposes for which data contained in bulk personal datasets of that class may be selected for examination.
(4) A specific BPD warrant must—
- (a) describe the bulk personal dataset to which the warrant relates,
- (b) where the warrant authorises the retention or examination of replacement datasets, include a description that will enable those datasets to be identified,
- (c) where the warrant authorises the examination of the bulk personal dataset or replacement datasets, specify the operational purposes for which data contained in the bulk personal dataset and any replacement datasets may be selected for examination, and
- (d) where the Secretary of State has imposed conditions under section 207, specify those conditions.
(5) The operational purposes specified in a class BPD warrant or a specific BPD warrant must be ones specified, in a list maintained by the heads of the intelligence services ("the list of operational purposes"), as purposes which they consider are operational purposes for which data contained in bulk personal datasets retained in reliance on class BPD warrants or specific BPD warrants may be selected for examination.
(6) A class BPD warrant or a specific BPD warrant may, in particular, specify all of the operational purposes which, at the time the warrant is issued, are specified in the list of operational purposes.
(7) An operational purpose may be specified in the list of operational purposes only with the approval of the Secretary of State.

Appendix

(8) The Secretary of State may give such approval only if satisfied that the operational purpose is specified in a greater level of detail than the descriptions contained in section 204(3)(a) or (as the case may be) section 205(6)(a).

(9) At the end of each relevant three-month period, the Secretary of State must give a copy of the list of operational purposes to the Intelligence and Security Committee of Parliament.

(10) In subsection (9), "relevant three-month period" means—
  (a) the period of three months beginning with the day on which this section comes into force, and
  (b) each successive period of three months.

(11) The Prime Minister must review the list of operational purposes at least once a year.

(12) In this Part, "the specified operational purposes", in relation to a class BPD warrant or a specific BPD warrant, means the operational purposes specified in the warrant in accordance with this section.

Duration, modification and cancellation

213 Duration of warrants

(1) A class BPD warrant or a specific BPD warrant ceases to have effect at the end of the relevant period (see subsection (2)) unless—
  (a) it is renewed before the end of that period (see section 214), or
  (b) it is cancelled or (in the case of a specific BPD warrant) otherwise ceases to have effect before the end of that period (see sections 209 and 218).

(2) In this section, "the relevant period"—
  (a) in the case of an urgent specific BPD warrant (see subsection (3)), means the period ending with the fifth working day after the day on which the warrant was issued;
  (b) in any other case, means the period of 6 months beginning with—
    (i) the day on which the warrant was issued, or
    (ii) in the case of a warrant that has been renewed, the day after the day at the end of which the warrant would have ceased to have effect if it had not been renewed.

(3) For the purposes of subsection (2)(a), a specific BPD warrant is an "urgent specific BPD warrant" if—
  (a) the warrant was issued without the approval of a Judicial Commissioner, and
  (b) the Secretary of State considered that there was an urgent need to issue it.

(4) For provision about the renewal of warrants, see section 214.

214 Renewal of warrants

(1) If the renewal conditions are met, a class BPD warrant or a specific BPD warrant may be renewed, at any time during the renewal period, by an instrument issued by the Secretary of State.

(2) The renewal conditions are—
  (a) that the Secretary of State considers that the warrant continues to be necessary on grounds falling within section 204(3)(a) or (as the case may be) section 205(6)(a),
  (b) that the Secretary of State considers that the conduct that would be authorised by the renewed warrant continues to be proportionate to what is sought to be achieved by the conduct,
  (c) where the warrant authorises examination of bulk personal datasets of a class described in the warrant or (as the case may be) of a bulk personal dataset described in the warrant, that the Secretary of State considers that—

(i) each of the specified operational purposes (see section 212) is a purpose for which the examination of bulk personal datasets of that class or (as the case may be) the bulk personal dataset continues to be, or may be, necessary, and

(ii) the examination of bulk personal datasets of that class or (as the case may be) the bulk personal dataset continues to be necessary on any of the grounds on which the Secretary of State considers that the warrant continues to be necessary, and

(d) that the decision to renew the warrant has been approved by a Judicial Commissioner.

(3) "The renewal period" means—
(a) in the case of an urgent specific BPD warrant which has not been renewed, the relevant period;
(b) in any other case, the period of 30 days ending with the day at the end of which the warrant would otherwise cease to have effect.

(4) The decision to renew a class BPD warrant or a specific BPD warrant must be taken personally by the Secretary of State, and the instrument renewing the warrant must be signed by the Secretary of State.

(5) Section 207 (protected data: power to impose conditions) applies in relation to the renewal of a specific BPD warrant as it applies in relation to the issue of such a warrant (whether or not any conditions have previously been imposed in relation to the warrant under that section).

(6) Section 208 (approval of warrants by Judicial Commissioner) applies in relation to a decision to renew a warrant as it applies in relation to a decision to issue a warrant.

(7) In this section—
"the relevant period" has the same meaning as in section 213;
"urgent specific BPD warrant" is to be read in accordance with subsection (3) of that section.

215 Modification of warrants

(1) The provisions of a class BPD warrant or a specific BPD warrant may be modified at any time by an instrument issued by the person making the modification.

(2) The only modifications which may be made under this section are—
(a) in the case of a class BPD warrant, adding, varying or removing any operational purpose specified in the warrant as a purpose for which bulk personal datasets of a class described in the warrant may be examined;
(b) in the case of a specific BPD warrant, adding, varying or removing any operational purpose specified in the warrant as a purpose for which the bulk personal dataset described in the warrant may be examined.

(3) In this section—
(a) a modification adding or varying any operational purpose is referred to as a "major modification", and
(b) a modification removing any operational purpose is referred to as a "minor modification".

(4) A major modification—
(a) must be made by the Secretary of State, and
(b) may be made only if the Secretary of State considers that it is necessary on any of the grounds on which the Secretary of State considers the warrant to be necessary (see section 204(3)(a) or (as the case may be) section 205(6)(a)).

(5) Except where the Secretary of State considers that there is an urgent need to make the modification, a major modification has effect only if the decision to make the modification is approved by a Judicial Commissioner.

(6) A minor modification may be made by—
(a) the Secretary of State, or
(b) a senior official acting on behalf of the Secretary of State.

(7) Where a minor modification is made by a senior official, the Secretary of State must be notified personally of the modification and the reasons for making it.
(8) If at any time a person mentioned in subsection (6) considers that any operational purpose specified in a warrant is no longer a purpose for which the examination of any bulk personal datasets to which the warrant relates is or may be necessary, the person must modify the warrant by removing that operational purpose.
(9) The decision to modify the provisions of a class BPD warrant or a specific BPD warrant must be taken personally by the person making the modification, and the instrument making the modification must be signed by that person.

This is subject to subsection (10).

(10) If it is not reasonably practicable for an instrument making a major modification to be signed by the Secretary of State, the instrument may be signed by a senior official designated by the Secretary of State for that purpose.
(11) In such a case, the instrument making the modification must contain a statement that—
   (a) it is not reasonably practicable for the instrument to be signed by the Secretary of State, and
   (b) the Secretary of State has personally and expressly authorised the making of the modification.

216 Approval of major modifications by Judicial Commissioners

(1) In deciding whether to approve a decision to make a major modification of a class BPD warrant or a specific BPD warrant, a Judicial Commissioner must review the Secretary of State's conclusions as to whether the modification is necessary on any of the grounds on which the Secretary of State considers the warrant to be necessary.
(2) In doing so, the Judicial Commissioner must—
   (a) apply the same principles as would be applied by a court on an application for judicial review, and
   (b) consider the matter referred to in subsection (1) with a sufficient degree of care as to ensure that the Judicial Commissioner complies with the duties imposed by section 2 (general duties in relation to privacy).
(3) Where a Judicial Commissioner refuses to approve a decision to make a major modification under section 215, the Judicial Commissioner must give the Secretary of State written reasons for the refusal.
(4) Where a Judicial Commissioner, other than the Investigatory Powers Commissioner, refuses to approve a decision to make a major modification under section 215, the Secretary of State may ask the Investigatory Powers Commissioner to decide whether to approve the decision to make the modification.

217 Approval of major modifications made in urgent cases

(1) This section applies where—
   (a) the Secretary of State makes a major modification of a class BPD warrant or a specific BPD warrant without the approval of a Judicial Commissioner, and
   (b) the Secretary of State considered that there was an urgent need to make the modification.
(2) The Secretary of State must inform a Judicial Commissioner that the modification has been made.
(3) The Judicial Commissioner must, before the end of the relevant period—
   (a) decide whether to approve the decision to make the modification, and
   (b) notify the Secretary of State of the Judicial Commissioner's decision.

Appendix

"The relevant period" means the period ending with the third working day after the day on which the modification was made.

(4) If the Judicial Commissioner refuses to approve the decision to make the modification—
   (a) the warrant (unless it no longer has effect) has effect as if the modification had not been made, and
   (b) the person to whom the warrant is addressed must, so far as is reasonably practicable, secure that anything in the process of being done in reliance on the warrant by virtue of that modification stops as soon as possible, and section 216(4) does not apply in relation to the refusal to approve the decision.

(5) Nothing in this section affects the lawfulness of—
   (a) anything done in reliance on the warrant by virtue of the modification before the modification ceases to have effect;
   (b) if anything is in the process of being done in reliance on the warrant by virtue of the modification when the modification ceases to have effect—
      (i) anything done before that thing could be stopped, or
      (ii) anything done which it is not reasonably practicable to stop.

218 Cancellation of warrants

(1) The Secretary of State, or a senior official acting on behalf of the Secretary of State, may cancel a class BPD warrant or a specific BPD warrant at any time.

(2) If the Secretary of State, or a senior official acting on behalf of the Secretary of State, considers that any of the cancellation conditions are met in relation to a class BPD warrant or a specific BPD warrant, the person must cancel the warrant.

(3) The cancellation conditions are—
   (a) that the warrant is no longer necessary on any grounds falling within section 204(3)(a) or (as the case may be) section 205(6)(a);
   (b) that the conduct authorised by the warrant is no longer proportionate to what is sought to be achieved by that conduct;
   (c) where the warrant authorises examination of bulk personal datasets of a class described in the warrant or (as the case may be) of a bulk personal dataset described in the warrant, that the examination of bulk personal datasets of that class or (as the case may be) of the bulk personal dataset is no longer necessary for any of the specified operational purposes (see section 212).

219 Non-renewal or cancellation of BPD warrants

(1) This section applies where a class BPD warrant or a specific BPD warrant ceases to have effect because it expires without having been renewed or because it is cancelled.

(2) The head of the intelligence service to whom the warrant was addressed may, before the end of the period of 5 working days beginning with the day on which the warrant ceases to have effect—
   (a) apply for—
      (i) a specific BPD warrant authorising the retention, or the retention and examination, of the whole or any part of the material retained by the intelligence service in reliance on the warrant which has ceased to have effect;
      (ii) a class BPD warrant authorising the retention or (as the case may be) the retention and examination of bulk personal datasets of a class that is described in a way that would authorise the retention or (as the case may be) the retention and examination of the whole or any part of such material, or

Appendix

    (b) where the head of the intelligence service wishes to give further consideration to whether to apply for a warrant of a kind mentioned in paragraph (a)(i) or (ii), apply to the Secretary of State for authorisation to retain, or to retain and examine, the whole or any part of the material retained by the intelligence service in reliance on the warrant.

(3) On an application under subsection (2)(b), the Secretary of State may—
    (a) direct that any of the material to which the application relates be destroyed;
    (b) with the approval of a Judicial Commissioner, authorise the retention or (as the case may be) the retention and examination of any of that material, subject to such conditions as the Secretary of State considers appropriate, for a period specified by the Secretary of State which may not exceed 3 months.

(4) In deciding whether to give approval for the purposes of subsection (3)(b), the Judicial Commissioner must—
    (a) apply the same principles as would be applied by a court on an application for judicial review, and
    (b) consider the matter with a sufficient degree of care as to ensure that the Judicial Commissioner complies with the duties imposed by section 2 (general duties in relation to privacy).

(5) Where a Judicial Commissioner refuses to approve a decision by the Secretary of State to authorise the retention or (as the case may be) the retention and examination of any material under subsection (3)(b), the Judicial Commissioner must give the Secretary of State written reasons for the decision.

(6) Where a Judicial Commissioner, other than the Investigatory Powers Commissioner, refuses to approve such a decision, the Secretary of State may ask the Investigatory Powers Commissioner to decide whether to approve the decision.

(7) If, during the period specified by the Secretary of State under subsection (3)(b), the head of the intelligence service decides to apply for a warrant of a kind mentioned in subsection (2)(a)(i) or (ii), the head of the intelligence service must make the application as soon as reasonably practicable and before the end of the period specified by the Secretary of State.

(8) Where a class BPD warrant or a specific BPD warrant ceases to have effect because it expires without having been renewed or it is cancelled, an intelligence service is not to be regarded as in breach of section 200(1) or (2) by virtue of its retention or examination of any material to which the warrant related during any of the following periods.

First period
The period of 5 working days beginning with the day on which the warrant ceases to have effect.

Second period
The period beginning with the day on which the head of the intelligence service makes an application under subsection (2)(a) or (b) in relation to the material and ending with the determination of the application.

Third period
The period during which the retention or examination of the material is authorised under subsection (3)(b).

Fourth period
Where authorisation under subsection (3)(b) is given and the head of the intelligence service subsequently makes, in accordance with subsection (7), an application for a specific BPD warrant or a class BPD warrant in relation to the material, the period (if any) beginning with the expiry of the authorisation under subsection (3)(b) and ending with the determination of the application for the warrant.

Further and supplementary provision

220 Initial examinations: time limits

(1) This section applies where—
   (a) an intelligence service obtains a set of information otherwise than in the exercise of a power conferred by a warrant or other authorisation issued or given under this Act, and
   (b) the head of the intelligence service believes that—
      (i) the set includes, or may include, personal data relating to a number of individuals, and
      (ii) the nature of the set is, or may be, such that the majority of the individuals are not, and are unlikely to become, of interest to the intelligence service in the exercise of its functions.

(2) The head of the intelligence service must take the following steps before the end of the permitted period.

   Step 1 Carry out an initial examination of the set for the purpose of deciding whether, if the intelligence service were to retain it after that initial examination and hold it electronically for analysis for the purposes of the exercise of its functions, the intelligence service would be retaining a bulk personal dataset (see section 199).

   Step 2 If the intelligence service would be retaining a bulk personal dataset as mentioned in step 1, decide whether to retain the set and hold it electronically for analysis for the purposes of the exercise of the functions of the intelligence service.

   Step 3 If the head of the intelligence service decides to retain the set and hold it electronically for analysis as mentioned in step 2, apply for a specific BPD warrant as soon as reasonably practicable after making that decision (unless the retention of the dataset is authorised by a class BPD warrant).

(3) The permitted period begins when the head of the intelligence service first forms the beliefs mentioned in subsection (1)(b).

(4) The permitted period ends—
   (a) where the set of information was created in the United Kingdom, 3 months after the day on which it begins;
   (b) where the set of information was created outside the United Kingdom, 6 months after the day on which it begins.

(5) If the head of the intelligence service applies for a specific BPD warrant in accordance with step 3 (set out in subsection (2))—
   (a) the intelligence service is not to be regarded as in breach of section 200(1) by virtue of retaining the bulk personal dataset during the period between the taking of the decision mentioned in step 2 and the determination of the application for the specific BPD warrant, and
   (b) the intelligence service is not to be regarded as in breach of section 200(2) by virtue of examining the bulk personal dataset during that period if the examination is necessary for the purposes of the making of the application for the warrant.

221 Safeguards relating to examination of bulk personal datasets

(1) The Secretary of State must ensure, in relation to every class BPD warrant or specific BPD warrant which authorises examination of bulk personal datasets of a class described in the warrant or (as the case may be) of a bulk personal dataset described in the warrant, that arrangements are in force for securing that—

Appendix

(a) any selection of data contained in the datasets (or dataset) for examination is carried out only for the specified purposes (see subsection (2)), and
(b) the selection of any such data for examination is necessary and proportionate in all the circumstances.

(2) The selection of data contained in bulk personal datasets for examination is carried out only for the specified purposes if the data is selected for examination only so far as is necessary for the operational purposes specified in the warrant in accordance with section 212.

(3) The Secretary of State must also ensure, in relation to every specific BPD warrant which specifies conditions imposed under section 207, that arrangements are in force for securing that any selection for examination of protected data on the basis of criteria which are referable to an individual known to be in the British Islands at the time of the selection is in accordance with the conditions specified in the warrant.

(4) In this section "specified in the warrant" means specified in the warrant at the time of the selection of the data for examination.

222 Additional safeguards for items subject to legal privilege: examination

(1) Subsections (2) and (3) apply if, in a case where protected data retained in reliance on a specific BPD warrant is to be selected for examination—
   (a) the purpose, or one of the purposes, of using the criteria to be used for the selection of the data for examination ("the relevant criteria") is to identify any items subject to legal privilege, or
   (b) the use of the relevant criteria is likely to identify such items.

(2) If the relevant criteria are referable to an individual known to be in the British Islands at the time of the selection, the data may be selected for examination using the relevant criteria only if the Secretary of State has approved the use of those criteria.

(3) In any other case, the data may be selected for examination using the relevant criteria only if a senior official acting on behalf of the Secretary of State has approved the use of those criteria.

(4) The Secretary of State may give approval for the purposes of subsection (2) only with the approval of a Judicial Commissioner.

(5) Approval may be given under subsection (2) or (3) only if—
   (a) the Secretary of State or (as the case may be) the senior official considers that the arrangements mentioned in section 205(6)(d) include specific arrangements in respect of items subject to legal privilege, and (b) where subsection (1)(a) applies, the Secretary of State or (as the case may be) the senior official considers that there are exceptional and compelling circumstances that make it necessary to authorise the use of the relevant criteria.

(6) In deciding whether to give an approval under subsection (2) or (3) in a case where subsection (1)(a) applies, the Secretary of State or (as the case may be) the senior official must have regard to the public interest in the confidentiality of items subject to legal privilege.

(7) For the purposes of subsection (5)(b), there cannot be exceptional and compelling circumstances that make it necessary to authorise the use of the relevant criteria unless—
   (a) the public interest in obtaining the information that would be obtained by the selection of the data for examination outweighs the public interest in the confidentiality of items subject to legal privilege,
   (b) there are no other means by which the information may reasonably be obtained, and
   (c) obtaining the information is necessary in the interests of national security or for the purpose of preventing death or significant injury.

(8) In deciding whether to give approval for the purposes of subsection (4), the Judicial Commissioner must—

(a) apply the same principles as would be applied by a court on an application for judicial review, and
(b) consider the matter with a sufficient degree of care as to ensure that the Judicial Commissioner complies with the duties imposed by section 2 (general duties in relation to privacy).

(9) Subsections (10) and (11) apply if, in a case where protected data retained in reliance on a specific BPD warrant is to be selected for examination—
(a) the purpose, or one of the purposes, of using the criteria to be used for the selection of the data for examination ("the relevant criteria") is to identify data that, if the data or any underlying material were not created or held with the intention of furthering a criminal purpose, would be an item subject to legal privilege, and
(b) the person to whom the warrant is addressed considers that the data ("the targeted data") or any underlying material is likely to be data or underlying material created or held with the intention of furthering a criminal purpose.

(10) If the relevant criteria are referable to an individual known to be in the British Islands at the time of the selection, the data may be selected for examination using the relevant criteria only if the Secretary of State has approved the use of those criteria.

(11) In any other case, the data may be selected for examination using the relevant criteria only if a senior official acting on behalf of the Secretary of State has approved the use of those criteria.

(12) Approval may be given under subsection (10) or (11) only if the Secretary of State or (as the case may be) the senior official considers that the targeted data or the underlying material is likely to be data or underlying material created or held with the intention of furthering a criminal purpose.

(13) In this section, "underlying material", in relation to data retained in reliance on a specific BPD warrant, means any communications or other items of information from which the data was produced.

223 Additional safeguards for items subject to legal privilege: retention following examination

(1) Where an item subject to legal privilege is retained following its examination in reliance on a specific BPD warrant, for purposes other than the destruction of the item, the person to whom the warrant is addressed must inform the Investigatory Powers Commissioner as soon as is reasonably practicable.

(2) Unless the Investigatory Powers Commissioner considers that subsection (4) applies to the item, the Commissioner must—
(a) direct that the item is destroyed, or
(b) impose one or more conditions as to the use or retention of that item.

(3) If the Investigatory Powers Commissioner considers that subsection (4) applies to the item, the Commissioner may nevertheless impose such conditions under subsection (2)(b) as the Commissioner considers necessary for the purpose of protecting the public interest in the confidentiality of items subject to legal privilege.

(4) This subsection applies to an item subject to legal privilege if—
(a) the public interest in retaining the item outweighs the public interest in the confidentiality of items subject to legal privilege, and
(b) retaining the item is necessary in the interests of national security or for the purpose of preventing death or significant injury.

(5) The Investigatory Powers Commissioner—
(a) may require an affected party to make representations about how the Commissioner should exercise any function under subsection (2), and

Appendix

    (b) must have regard to any such representations made by an affected party (whether or not as a result of a requirement imposed under paragraph (a)).

(6) Each of the following is an "affected party" for the purposes of subsection (5)—
    (a) the Secretary of State;
    (b) the person to whom the warrant is or was addressed.

224 Offence of breaching safeguards relating to examination of material

(1) A person commits an offence if—
    (a) the person selects for examination any data contained in a bulk personal dataset retained in reliance on a class BPD warrant or a specific BPD warrant,
    (b) the person knows or believes that the selection of that data is in breach of a requirement specified in subsection (2), and
    (c) the person deliberately selects that data in breach of that requirement.

(2) The requirements specified in this subsection are that any selection for examination of the data—
    (a) is carried out only for the specified purposes (see subsection (3)),
    (b) is necessary and proportionate, and
    (c) if the data is protected data, satisfies any conditions imposed under section 207.

(3) The selection for examination of the data is carried out only for the specified purposes if the data is selected for examination only so far as is necessary for the operational purposes specified in the warrant in accordance with section 212.

In this subsection, "specified in the warrant" means specified in the warrant at the time of the selection of the data for examination.

(4) A person guilty of an offence under this section is liable—
    (a) on summary conviction in England and Wales—
        (i) to imprisonment for a term not exceeding 12 months (or 6 months, if the offence was committed before the commencement of section 154(1) of the Criminal Justice Act 2003), or
        (ii) to a fine, or to both;
    (b) on summary conviction in Scotland—
        (i) to imprisonment for a term not exceeding 12 months, or
        (ii) to a fine not exceeding the statutory maximum, or to both;
    (c) on summary conviction in Northern Ireland—
        (i) to imprisonment for a term not exceeding 6 months, or
        (ii) to a fine not exceeding the statutory maximum, or to both;
    (d) on conviction on indictment, to imprisonment for a term not exceeding 2 years or to a fine, or to both.

(5) No proceedings for any offence which is an offence by virtue of this section may be instituted—
    (a) in England and Wales, except by or with the consent of the Director of Public Prosecutions;
    (b) in Northern Ireland, except by or with the consent of the Director of Public Prosecutions for Northern Ireland.

225 Application of Part to bulk personal datasets obtained under this Act

(1) Subject to subsection (2), this section applies where a bulk personal dataset has been obtained by an intelligence service under a warrant or other authorisation issued or given under this Act (and, accordingly, section 200(1) and (2) do not apply by virtue of section 201(1)).

(2) This section does not apply where the bulk personal dataset was obtained by the intelligence service under a bulk acquisition warrant issued under Chapter 2 of Part 6.

Appendix

(3) Where this section applies, the Secretary of State may, on the application of the head of the intelligence service, give a direction that—
  (a) the intelligence service may retain, or retain and examine, the bulk personal dataset by virtue of the direction,
  (b) any other power of the intelligence service to retain or examine the bulk personal dataset, and any associated regulatory provision, ceases to apply in relation to the bulk personal dataset (subject to subsection (5)), and
  (c) section 201(1) also ceases to apply in relation to the bulk personal dataset.
(4) Accordingly, where a direction is given under subsection (3), the intelligence service may exercise its power by virtue of the direction to retain, or to retain and examine, the bulk personal dataset only if authorised to do so by a class BPD warrant or a specific BPD warrant under this Part.
(5) A direction under subsection (3) may provide for any associated regulatory provision specified in the direction to continue to apply in relation to the bulk personal dataset, with or without modifications specified in the direction.
(6) The power conferred by subsection (5) must be exercised to ensure that—
  (a) where section 56 and Schedule 3 applied in relation to the bulk personal dataset immediately before the giving of the direction, they continue to apply in relation to it (without modification);
  (b) where sections 57 to 59 applied in relation to the bulk personal dataset immediately before the giving of the direction, they continue to apply in relation to it with the modification that the reference in section 58(7)(a) to the provisions of Part 2 is to be read as including a reference to the provisions of this Part.
(7) The Secretary of State may only give a direction under subsection (3) with the approval of a Judicial Commissioner.
(8) In deciding whether to give approval for the purposes of subsection (7), the Judicial Commissioner must apply the same principles as would be applied by a court on an application for judicial review.
(9) Where a Judicial Commissioner refuses to approve a decision by the Secretary of State to give a direction under subsection (3), the Judicial Commissioner must give the Secretary of State written reasons for the decision.
(10) Where a Judicial Commissioner, other than the Investigatory Powers Commissioner, refuses to approve such a decision, the Secretary of State may ask the Investigatory Powers Commissioner to decide whether to approve the decision.
(11) A direction under subsection (3)—
  (a) may not be revoked;
  (b) may be varied but only for the purpose of altering or removing any provision included in the direction under subsection (5).
(12) Subsections (7) to (10) apply in relation to the variation of a direction under subsection (3) as they apply in relation to the giving of a direction under that subsection.
(13) The head of an intelligence service may, at the same time as applying for a direction under subsection (3), apply for a specific BPD warrant under section 205 (and the Secretary of State may issue such a warrant at the same time as giving the direction).
(14) In this section, "associated regulatory provision", in relation to a power of an intelligence service to retain or examine a bulk personal dataset, means any provision which—
  (a) is made by or for the purposes of this Act (other than this Part), and
  (b) applied in relation to the retention, examination, disclosure or other use of the bulk personal dataset immediately before the giving of a direction under subsection (3).

Appendix

226 Part 7: interpretation

(1) In this Part—
"class BPD warrant" has the meaning given by section 200(3)(a);
"personal data" has the meaning given by section 199(2);
"senior official" means a member of the Senior Civil Service or a member of the Senior Management Structure of Her Majesty's Diplomatic Service;
"specific BPD warrant" has the meaning given by section 200(3)(b);
"the specified operational purposes" has the meaning given by section 212(12).

(2) See also—
section 263 (general definitions),
section 265 (index of defined expressions).

PART 8

OVERSIGHT ARRANGEMENTS

CHAPTER 1

INVESTIGATORY POWERS COMMISSIONER AND OTHER JUDICIAL COMMISSIONERS

The Commissioners

227 Investigatory Powers Commissioner and other Judicial Commissioners

(1) The Prime Minister must appoint—
   (a) the Investigatory Powers Commissioner, and
   (b) such number of other Judicial Commissioners as the Prime Minister considers necessary for the carrying out of the functions of the Judicial Commissioners.

(2) A person is not to be appointed as the Investigatory Powers Commissioner or another Judicial Commissioner unless the person holds or has held a high judicial office (within the meaning of Part 3 of the Constitutional Reform Act 2005).

(3) A person is not to be appointed as the Investigatory Powers Commissioner unless recommended jointly by—
   (a) the Lord Chancellor,
   (b) the Lord Chief Justice of England and Wales,
   (c) the Lord President of the Court of Session, and
   (d) the Lord Chief Justice of Northern Ireland.

(4) A person is not to be appointed as a Judicial Commissioner under subsection (1)(b) unless recommended jointly by—
   (a) the Lord Chancellor,
   (b) the Lord Chief Justice of England and Wales,
   (c) the Lord President of the Court of Session,
   (d) the Lord Chief Justice of Northern Ireland, and
   (e) the Investigatory Powers Commissioner.

(5) Before appointing any person under subsection (1), the Prime Minister must consult the Scottish Ministers.

Appendix

(6) The Prime Minister must have regard to a memorandum of understanding agreed between the Prime Minister and the Scottish Ministers when exercising functions under subsection (1) or (5).

(7) The Investigatory Powers Commissioner is a Judicial Commissioner and the Investigatory Powers Commissioner and the other Judicial Commissioners are to be known, collectively, as the Judicial Commissioners.

(8) The Investigatory Powers Commissioner may, to such extent as the Investigatory Powers Commissioner may decide, delegate the exercise of functions of the Investigatory Powers Commissioner to any other Judicial Commissioner.

(9) Subsection (8) does not apply to the function of the Investigatory Powers Commissioner of making a recommendation under subsection (4)(e) or making an appointment under section 247(1).

(10) The delegation under subsection (8) to any extent of functions by the Investigatory Powers Commissioner does not prevent the exercise of the functions to that extent by that Commissioner.

(11) Any function exercisable by a Judicial Commissioner or any description of Judicial Commissioners is exercisable by any of the Judicial Commissioners or (as the case may be) any of the Judicial Commissioners of that description.

(12) Subsection (11) does not apply to—
   (a) any function conferred on the Investigatory Powers Commissioner by name (except so far as its exercise by any of the Judicial Commissioners or any description of Judicial Commissioners is permitted by a delegation under subsection (8)), or
   (b) any function conferred on, or delegated under subsection (8) to, any other particular named Judicial Commissioner.

(13) References in any enactment—
   (a) to a Judicial Commissioner are to be read as including the Investigatory Powers Commissioner, and
   (b) to the Investigatory Powers Commissioner are to be read, so far as necessary for the purposes of subsection (8), as references to the Investigatory Powers Commissioner or any other Judicial Commissioner.

228 Terms and conditions of appointment

(1) Subject as follows, each Judicial Commissioner holds and vacates office in accordance with the Commissioner's terms and conditions of appointment.

(2) Each Judicial Commissioner is to be appointed for a term of three years.

(3) A person who ceases to be a Judicial Commissioner (otherwise than under subsection (5)) may be re-appointed under section 227(1).

(4) A Judicial Commissioner may not, subject to subsection (5), be removed from office before the end of the term for which the Commissioner is appointed unless a resolution approving the removal has been passed by each House of Parliament.

(5) A Judicial Commissioner may be removed from office by the Prime Minister if, after the appointment of the Commissioner—
   (a) a bankruptcy order is made against the Commissioner or the Commissioner's estate is sequestrated or the Commissioner makes a composition or arrangement with, or grants a trust deed for, the Commissioner's creditors,
   (b) any of the following orders is made against the Commissioner—

Appendix

      (i)   a disqualification order under the Company Directors Disqualification Act 1986 or the Company Directors Disqualification (Northern Ireland) Order 2002,
     (ii)   an order under section 429(2)(b) of the Insolvency Act 1986 (failure to pay under county court administration order),
    (iii)   an order under section 429(2) of the Insolvency Act 1986 (disabilities on revocation of county court administration order),
  (c) the Commissioner's disqualification undertaking is accepted under section 7 or 8 of the Company Directors Disqualification Act 1986 or under the Company Directors Disqualification (Northern Ireland) Order 2002, or
  (d) the Commissioner is convicted in the United Kingdom, the Channel Islands or the Isle of Man of an offence and receives a sentence of imprisonment (whether suspended or not).

Main functions of Commissioners

229 Main oversight functions

(1) The Investigatory Powers Commissioner must keep under review (including by way of audit, inspection and investigation) the exercise by public authorities of statutory functions relating to—
  (a) the interception of communications,
  (b) the acquisition or retention of communications data,
  (c) the acquisition of secondary data or related systems data under Chapter 1 of Part 2 or Chapter 1 of Part 6, or
  (d) equipment interference.

(2) Such statutory functions include, in particular, functions relating to the disclosure, retention or other use of—
  (a) any content of communications intercepted by an interception authorised or required by a warrant under Chapter 1 of Part 2 or Chapter 1 of Part 6,
  (b) acquired or retained communications data,
  (c) data acquired as mentioned in subsection (1)(c), or
  (d) communications, equipment data or other information acquired by means of equipment interference.

(3) The Investigatory Powers Commissioner must keep under review (including by way of audit, inspection and investigation)—
  (a) the acquisition, retention, use or disclosure of bulk personal datasets by an intelligence service,
  (b) the giving and operation of notices under section 252 (national security notices),
  (c) the exercise of functions by virtue of section 80 of the Serious Crime Act 2015 (prevention or restriction of use of communication devices by prisoners etc.),
  (d) the exercise of functions by virtue of sections 1 to 4 of the Prisons (Interference with Wireless Telegraphy) Act 2012,
  (e) the exercise of functions by virtue of Part 2 or 3 of the Regulation of Investigatory Powers Act 2000 (surveillance, covert human intelligence sources and investigation of electronic data protected by encryption etc.),
  (f) the adequacy of the arrangements by virtue of which the duties imposed by section 55 of that Act are sought to be discharged,
  (g) the exercise of functions by virtue of the Regulation of Investigatory Powers (Scotland) Act 2000 (2000 asp 11) (surveillance and covert human intelligence sources),

(h) the exercise of functions under Part 3 of the Police Act 1997 (authorisation of action in respect of property),

(i) the exercise by the Secretary of State of functions under sections 5 to 7 of the Intelligence Services Act 1994 (warrants for interference with wireless telegraphy, entry and interference with property etc.), and

(j) the exercise by the Scottish Ministers (by virtue of provision made under section 63 of the Scotland Act 1998) of functions under sections 5 and 6(3) and (4) of the Act of 1994.

(4) But the Investigatory Powers Commissioner is not to keep under review—

(a) the exercise of any function of a relevant Minister to make subordinate legislation,

(b) the exercise of any function by a judicial authority,

(c) the exercise of any function by virtue of Part 3 of the Regulation of Investigatory Powers Act 2000 which is exercisable with the permission of a judicial authority,

(d) the exercise of any function which—

  (i) is for the purpose of obtaining information or taking possession of any document or other property in connection with communications stored in or by a telecommunication system, or

  (ii) is carried out in accordance with an order made by a judicial authority for that purpose, and is not exercisable by virtue of this Act, the Regulation of Investigatory Powers Act 2000, the Regulation of Investigatory Powers (Scotland) Act 2000 or an enactment mentioned in subsection (3)(c), (h), (i) or (j) above,

(e) the exercise of any function where the conduct concerned is—

  (i) conduct authorised by section 45, 47 or 50, or

  (ii) conduct authorised by section 46 which is not conduct by or on behalf of an intercepting authority (within the meaning given by section 18(1)), or

(f) the exercise of any function which is subject to review by the Information Commissioner or the Investigatory Powers Commissioner for Northern Ireland.

(5) In keeping matters under review in accordance with this section, the Investigatory Powers Commissioner must, in particular, keep under review the operation of safeguards to protect privacy.

(6) In exercising functions under this Act, a Judicial Commissioner must not act in a way which the Commissioner considers to be contrary to the public interest or prejudicial to—

(a) national security,

(b) the prevention or detection of serious crime, or

(c) the economic well-being of the United Kingdom.

(7) A Judicial Commissioner must, in particular, ensure that the Commissioner does not—

(a) jeopardise the success of an intelligence or security operation or a law enforcement operation,

(b) compromise the safety or security of those involved, or

(c) unduly impede the operational effectiveness of an intelligence service, a police force, a government department or Her Majesty's forces.

(8) Subsections (6) and (7) do not apply in relation to any of the following functions of a Judicial Commissioner—

(a) deciding—

  (i) whether to serve, vary or cancel a monetary penalty notice under section 7 or paragraph 16 of Schedule 1, a notice of intent under paragraph 4 of that Schedule or an information notice under Part 2 of that Schedule, or

  (ii) the contents of any such notice,

Appendix

- (b) deciding whether to approve the issue, modification or renewal of a warrant,
- (c) deciding whether to direct the destruction of material or how otherwise to deal with the situation where—
  - (i) a warrant issued, or modification made, for what was considered to be an urgent need is not approved, or
  - (ii) an item subject to legal privilege is retained, following its examination, for purposes other than the destruction of the item,
- (d) deciding whether to—
  - (i) approve the grant, modification or renewal of an authorisation, or
  - (ii) quash or cancel an authorisation or renewal,
- (e) deciding whether to approve—
  - (i) the giving or varying of a retention notice under Part 4 or a notice under section 252 or 253, or
  - (ii) the giving of a notice under section 90(10)(b) or 257(9)(b),
- (f) participating in a review under section 90 or 257,
- (g) deciding whether to approve an authorisation under section 219(3)(b),
- (h) deciding whether to give approval under section 222(4),
- (i) deciding whether to approve the giving or varying of a direction under section 225(3),
- (j) making a decision under section 231(1),
- (k) deciding whether to order the destruction of records under section 103 of the Police Act 1997, section 37 of the Regulation of Investigatory Powers Act 2000 or section 15 of the Regulation of Investigatory Powers (Scotland) Act 2000,
- (l) deciding whether to make an order under section 103(6) of the Police Act 1997 (order enabling the taking of action to retrieve anything left on property in pursuance of an authorisation),
- (m) deciding—
  - (i) an appeal against, or a review of, a decision by another Judicial Commissioner, and
  - (ii) any action to take as a result.

(9) In this section—
"bulk personal dataset" is to be read in accordance with section 199,
"equipment data" has the same meaning as in Part 5 (see section 100),
"judicial authority" means a judge, court or tribunal or any person exercising the functions of a judge, court or tribunal (but does not include a Judicial Commissioner),
"police force" has the same meaning as in Part 2 (see section 60(1)),
"related systems data" has the meaning given by section 15(6),
"relevant Minister" means a Minister of the Crown or government department, the Scottish Ministers, the Welsh Ministers or a Northern Ireland department,
"secondary data" has the same meaning as in Part 2 (see section 16).

230 Additional directed oversight functions

(1) So far as directed to do so by the Prime Minister and subject to subsection (2), the Investigatory Powers Commissioner must keep under review the carrying out of any aspect of the functions of—
- (a) an intelligence service,
- (b) a head of an intelligence service, or
- (c) any part of Her Majesty's forces, or of the Ministry of Defence, so far as engaging in intelligence activities.

(2) Subsection (1) does not apply in relation to anything which is required to be kept under review by the Investigatory Powers Commissioner under section 229.
(3) The Prime Minister may give a direction under this section at the request of the Investigatory Powers Commissioner or the Intelligence and Security Committee of Parliament or otherwise.
(4) The Prime Minister must publish, in a manner which the Prime Minister considers appropriate, any direction under this section (and any revocation of such a direction) except so far as it appears to the Prime Minister that such publication would be contrary to the public interest or prejudicial to—
    (a) national security,
    (b) the prevention or detection of serious crime,
    (c) the economic well-being of the United Kingdom, or
    (d) the continued discharge of the functions of any public authority whose activities include activities that are subject to review by the Investigatory Powers Commissioner.

231 Error reporting

(1) The Investigatory Powers Commissioner must inform a person of any relevant error relating to that person of which the Commissioner is aware if the Commissioner considers that—
    (a) the error is a serious error, and
    (b) it is in the public interest for the person to be informed of the error.
(2) In making a decision under subsection (1)(a), the Investigatory Powers Commissioner may not decide that an error is a serious error unless the Commissioner considers that the error has caused significant prejudice or harm to the person concerned.
(3) Accordingly, the fact that there has been a breach of a person's Convention rights (within the meaning of the Human Rights Act 1998) is not sufficient by itself for an error to be a serious error.
(4) In making a decision under subsection (1)(b), the Investigatory Powers Commissioner must, in particular, consider—
    (a) the seriousness of the error and its effect on the person concerned, and
    (b) the extent to which disclosing the error would be contrary to the public interest or prejudicial to—
        (i) national security,
        (ii) the prevention or detection of serious crime,
        (iii) the economic well-being of the United Kingdom, or
        (iv) the continued discharge of the functions of any of the intelligence services.
(5) Before making a decision under subsection (1)(a) or (b), the Investigatory Powers Commissioner must ask the public authority which has made the error to make submissions to the Commissioner about the matters concerned.
(6) When informing a person under subsection (1) of an error, the Investigatory Powers Commissioner must—
    (a) inform the person of any rights that the person may have to apply to the Investigatory Powers Tribunal, and
    (b) provide such details of the error as the Commissioner considers to be necessary for the exercise of those rights, having regard in particular to the extent to which disclosing the details would be contrary to the public interest or prejudicial to anything falling within subsection (4)(b)(i) to (iv).
(7) The Investigatory Powers Commissioner may not inform the person to whom it relates of a relevant error except as provided by this section.
(8) A report under section 234(1) must include information about—

(a) the number of relevant errors of which the Investigatory Powers Commissioner has become aware during the year to which the report relates,
(b) the number of relevant errors which the Commissioner has decided during that year were serious errors, and
(c) the number of persons informed under subsection (1) during that year.
(9) In this section "relevant error" means an error—
(a) by a public authority in complying with any requirements which are imposed on it by virtue of this Act or any other enactment and which are subject to review by a Judicial Commissioner, and
(b) of a description identified for this purpose in a code of practice under Schedule 7, and the Investigatory Powers Commissioner must keep under review the definition of "relevant error".

232 Additional functions under this Part

(1) A Judicial Commissioner must give the Investigatory Powers Tribunal all such documents, information and other assistance (including the Commissioner's opinion as to any issue falling to be determined by the Tribunal) as the Tribunal may require—
(a) in connection with the investigation of any matter by the Tribunal, or
(b) otherwise for the purposes of the Tribunal's consideration or determination of any matter.
(2) A Judicial Commissioner may provide advice or information to any public authority or other person in relation to matters for which a Judicial Commissioner is responsible.
(3) But a Judicial Commissioner must consult the Secretary of State before providing any advice or information under subsection (2) if it appears to the Commissioner that providing the advice or information might be contrary to the public interest or prejudicial to—
(a) national security,
(b) the prevention or detection of serious crime,
(c) the economic well-being of the United Kingdom, or
(d) the continued discharge of the functions of any public authority whose activities include activities that are subject to review by the Investigatory Powers Commissioner.
(4) In addition to consulting the Secretary of State under subsection (3), the Judicial Commissioner must also consult the Scottish Ministers if it appears to the Commissioner that providing the advice or information might be prejudicial to—
(a) the prevention or detection of serious crime by a Scottish public authority, or
(b) the continued discharge of any devolved functions of a Scottish public authority whose activities include activities that are subject to review by the Investigatory Powers Commissioner.
(5) In subsection (4)—
"devolved function" means a function that does not relate to reserved matters (within the meaning of the Scotland Act 1998), and
"Scottish public authority" has the same meaning as in the Scotland Act 1998.
(6) Subsections (3) and (4) do not apply to any advice or information provided under subsection (2) to the Investigatory Powers Tribunal.

233 Functions under other Parts and other enactments

(1) The Investigatory Powers Commissioner and the other Judicial Commissioners have the functions that are exercisable by them by virtue of any other Part of this Act or by virtue of any other enactment.

Appendix

(2) In Part 3 of the Police Act 1997 (authorisations of action in respect of property: approval by Commissioners)—
   (a) in sections 96(1), 103(7)(b) and (8), 104(3) to (8) and 105(1) and (2) for "Chief Commissioner" substitute "Investigatory Powers Commissioner",
   (b) in sections 96(1), 97(1)(a) and 103(1), (2), (4) and (5)(b) for "a Commissioner appointed under section 91(1)(b)" substitute "a Judicial Commissioner",
   (c) in sections 96(4), 97(4) and (6) and 103(3) and (6) for "a Commissioner" substitute "a Judicial Commissioner",
   (d) in section 103(7) for "a Commissioner" substitute "a Judicial Commissioner (other than the Investigatory Powers Commissioner)",
   (e) in section 104(1) for "Chief Commissioner" substitute "Investigatory Powers Commissioner (except where the original decision was made by that Commissioner)",
   (f) in section 104(3) and (8)(a) for "the Commissioner" substitute "the Judicial Commissioner concerned",
   (g) in section 105(1)(a)(ii) and (b)(ii) for "the Commissioner" substitute "the Judicial Commissioner", and
   (h) in sections 97(5) and 103(9) for "A Commissioner" substitute "A Judicial Commissioner".
(3) In Part 2 of the Regulation of Investigatory Powers Act 2000 (surveillance and covert human intelligence sources: approval by Commissioners)—
   (a) in sections 35(1) and (4), 36(2)(a) and (5) and 37(2) to (6) and (8) for "an ordinary Surveillance Commissioner", wherever it appears, substitute "a Judicial Commissioner",
   (b) in sections 35(2)(b), 36(6)(g), 37(9)(b), 38(1) and (4) to (6) and 39(1), (2) and (4) and in the heading of section 39 for "Chief Surveillance Commissioner", wherever it appears, substitute "Investigatory Powers Commissioner",
   (c) in sections 35(3)(a) and 36(4)(a) and (b) for "Surveillance Commissioner" substitute "Judicial Commissioner",
   (d) in section 37(8)(b) for "Chief Surveillance Commissioner" substitute "Investigatory Powers Commissioner (if he is not that Commissioner)",
   (e) in section 38(1)(a) for "an ordinary Surveillance Commissioner" substitute "a Judicial Commissioner (other than the Investigatory Powers Commissioner)",
   (f) in sections 38(5)(b) and 39(1)(b) for "ordinary Surveillance Commissioner" substitute "Judicial Commissioner", and
   (g) in the heading of section 38 for "Surveillance Commissioners" substitute "Judicial Commissioners".
(4) In Part 3 of the Act of 2000 (investigation of electronic data protected by encryption etc.)—
   (a) in section 51(6) (notification to Intelligence Services Commissioner or Chief Surveillance Commissioner of certain directions relating to the disclosure of a key to protected information) for the words from "done so" to the end substitute "done so to the Investigatory Powers Commissioner",
   (b) in section 54(9) (tipping-off: protected disclosures to a relevant Commissioner) for "relevant Commissioner" substitute "Judicial Commissioner",
   (c) in section 55(7) (court to have regard to opinion of a relevant Commissioner in certain circumstances relating to a disclosed key) for "relevant Commissioner" substitute "Judicial Commissioner or the Investigatory Powers Commissioner for Northern Ireland", and
   (d) omit sections 54(11) and 55(8) (definitions of "relevant Commissioner").

Appendix

(5) In the Regulation of Investigatory Powers (Scotland) Act 2000 (2000 asp 11) (surveillance and covert human intelligence sources: approval by Commissioners and review by the Chief Commissioner)—
  (a) in sections 13(1) and (4), 14(1)(a) and (4) and 15(1) to (5) and (7) for "an ordinary Surveillance Commissioner", wherever it appears, substitute "a Judicial Commissioner",
  (b) in sections 13(2)(b), 15(8)(b), 16(1) and (4) to (6) and 17 and in the heading of section 17 for "Chief Surveillance Commissioner", wherever it appears, substitute "Investigatory Powers Commissioner",
  (c) in sections 13(3)(a) and 14(3)(a) and (b) for "Surveillance Commissioner" substitute "Judicial Commissioner",
  (d) in section 15(7)(b) for "Chief Surveillance Commissioner" substitute "Investigatory Powers Commissioner (if the Commissioner is not that Commissioner)",
  (e) in section 16(1)(a) for "an ordinary Surveillance Commissioner" substitute "a Judicial Commissioner (other than the Investigatory Powers Commissioner)",
  (f) in sections 16(5)(b) and 17(1)(b) for "ordinary Surveillance Commissioner" substitute "Judicial Commissioner", and
  (g) in section 16(5) for "ordinary Surveillance Commissioner's" substitute "Judicial Commissioner's".

(6) In Part 2 of the Regulation of Investigatory Powers (Covert Human Intelligence Sources: Relevant Sources) Order 2013 (S.I. 2013/2788) (notification of certain authorisations to, and approval of certain authorisations by, ordinary Surveillance Commissioner)—
  (a) in article 4(1), for "an ordinary Surveillance Commissioner" substitute "a Judicial Commissioner",
  (b) in article 5(8) and the heading of Part 2, for "ordinary Surveillance Commissioner" substitute "Judicial Commissioner",
  (c) in article 6(1) and (3) for "Chief Surveillance Commissioner" substitute "Investigatory Powers Commissioner",
  (d) in article 6(1) for "an ordinary Surveillance Commissioner" substitute "a Judicial Commissioner (other than the Investigatory Powers Commissioner)", and
  (e) in the heading of article 6 for "Surveillance Commissioners" substitute "Judicial Commissioners".

Reports and investigation and information powers

234 Annual and other reports

(1) The Investigatory Powers Commissioner must, as soon as reasonably practicable after the end of each calendar year, make a report to the Prime Minister about the carrying out of the functions of the Judicial Commissioners.
(2) A report under subsection (1) must, in particular, include—
  (a) statistics on the use of the investigatory powers which are subject to review by the Investigatory Powers Commissioner (including the number of warrants or authorisations issued, given, considered or approved during the year),
  (b) information about the results of such use (including its impact),
  (c) information about the operation of the safeguards conferred by this Act in relation to items subject to legal privilege, confidential journalistic material and sources of journalistic information,
  (d) information about the following kinds of warrants issued, considered or approved during the year—

(i) targeted interception warrants or targeted examination warrants of the kind referred to in section 17(2),
(ii) targeted equipment interference warrants relating to matters within paragraph (b), (c), (e), (f), (g) or (h) of section 101(1), and
(iii) targeted examination warrants under Part 5 relating to matters within any of paragraphs (b) to (e) of section 101(2),

(e) information about the operational purposes specified during the year in warrants issued under Part 6 or 7,
(f) the information on errors required by virtue of section 231(8), (g) information about the work of the Technology Advisory Panel,
(h) information about the funding, staffing and other resources of the Judicial Commissioners, and
(i) details of public engagements undertaken by the Judicial Commissioners or their staff.

(3) The Investigatory Powers Commissioner must, at any time, make any report to the Prime Minister which has been requested by the Prime Minister.

(4) The Investigatory Powers Commissioner may, at any time, make any such report to the Prime Minister, on any matter relating to the functions of the Judicial Commissioners, as the Investigatory Powers Commissioner considers appropriate.

(5) A report under subsection (1) or (4) may, in particular, include such recommendations as the Investigatory Powers Commissioner considers appropriate about any matter relating to the functions of the Judicial Commissioners.

(6) On receiving a report from the Investigatory Powers Commissioner under subsection (1), the Prime Minister must—
(a) publish the report, and
(b) lay a copy of the published report before Parliament together with a statement as to whether any part of the report has been excluded from publication under subsection (7).

(7) The Prime Minister may, after consultation with the Investigatory Powers Commissioner and (so far as the report relates to functions under Part 3 of the Police Act 1997) the Scottish Ministers, exclude from publication any part of a report under subsection (1) if, in the opinion of the Prime Minister, the publication of that part would be contrary to the public interest or prejudicial to—
(a) national security,
(b) the prevention or detection of serious crime,
(c) the economic well-being of the United Kingdom, or
(d) the continued discharge of the functions of any public authority whose activities include activities that are subject to review by the Investigatory Powers Commissioner.

(8) The Prime Minister must send a copy of every report and statement as laid before Parliament under subsection (6)(b) to the Scottish Ministers and the Scottish Ministers must lay the copy report and statement before the Scottish Parliament.

(9) The Investigatory Powers Commissioner may publish any report under subsection (3) or (4), or any part of such a report, if requested to do so by the Prime Minister.

(10) Subsection (11) applies if the Prime Minister receives a report from the Investigatory Powers Commissioner under subsection (1) or (4) which relates to an investigation, inspection or audit carried out by the Commissioner following a decision to do so of which the Intelligence and Security Committee of Parliament was informed under section 236(2).

(11) The Prime Minister must send to the Intelligence and Security Committee of Parliament a copy of the report so far as it relates to—
   (a) the investigation, inspection or audit concerned, and
   (b) the functions of the Committee falling within section 2 of the Justice and Security Act 2013.

235 Investigation and information powers

(1) A Judicial Commissioner may carry out such investigations, inspections and audits as the Commissioner considers appropriate for the purposes of the Commissioner's functions.
(2) Every relevant person must disclose or provide to a Judicial Commissioner all such documents and information as the Commissioner may require for the purposes of the Commissioner's functions.
(3) Every relevant person must provide a Judicial Commissioner with such assistance as the Commissioner may require in carrying out any investigation, inspection or audit for the purposes of the Commissioner's functions.
(4) Assistance under subsection (3) may, in particular, include such access to apparatus, systems or other facilities or services as the Judicial Commissioner concerned may require in carrying out any investigation, inspection or audit for the purposes of the Commissioner's functions.
(5) A public authority may report to the Investigatory Powers Commissioner any refusal by a telecommunications operator or postal operator to comply with any requirements imposed by virtue of this Act.
(6) A public authority, telecommunications operator or postal operator must report to the Investigatory Powers Commissioner any relevant error (within the meaning given by section 231(9)) of which it is aware.
(7) In this section "relevant person" means—
   (a) any person who holds, or has held, an office, rank or position with a public authority,
   (b) any telecommunications operator or postal operator who is, has been or may become subject to a requirement imposed by virtue of this Act,
   (c) any person who is, has been or may become subject to a requirement to provide assistance by virtue of section 41, 43, 126, 128, 149, 168, 170 or 190, or
   (d) any person to whom a notice is given under section 49 of the Regulation of Investigatory Powers Act 2000.

236 Referrals by the Intelligence and Security Committee of Parliament

(1) Subsection (2) applies if the Intelligence and Security Committee of Parliament refers a matter to the Investigatory Powers Commissioner with a view to the Commissioner carrying out an investigation, inspection or audit into it.
(2) The Investigatory Powers Commissioner must inform the Intelligence and Security Committee of Parliament of the Commissioner's decision as to whether to carry out the investigation, inspection or audit.

237 Information gateway

(1) A disclosure of information to the Investigatory Powers Commissioner or another Judicial Commissioner for the purposes of any function of the Commissioner does not breach—
   (a) an obligation of confidence owed by the person making the disclosure, or

Appendix

 (b) any other restriction on the disclosure of information (whether imposed by virtue of this Act or otherwise).

(2) But subsection (1) does not apply to a disclosure, in contravention of any provisions of the Data Protection Act 1998, of personal data which is not exempt from those provisions.

Supplementary provision

238 Funding, staff and facilities etc.

(1) There is to be paid to the Judicial Commissioners out of money provided by Parliament such remuneration and allowances as the Treasury may determine.

(2) The Secretary of State must, after consultation with the Investigatory Powers Commissioner and subject to the approval of the Treasury as to numbers of staff, provide the Judicial Commissioners with—
 (a) such staff, and
 (b) such accommodation, equipment and other facilities and services, as the Secretary of State considers necessary for the carrying out of the Commissioners' functions.

(3) The Scottish Ministers may pay to the Judicial Commissioners such allowances as the Scottish Ministers consider appropriate in respect of the exercise by the Commissioners of functions which relate to the exercise by Scottish public authorities of devolved functions.

(4) In subsection (3)—
"devolved function" means a function that does not relate to reserved matters (within the meaning of the Scotland Act 1998), and
"Scottish public authority" has the same meaning as in the Scotland Act 1998.

(5) The Investigatory Powers Commissioner or any other Judicial Commissioner may, to such extent as the Commissioner concerned may decide, delegate the exercise of functions of that Commissioner to any member of staff of the Judicial Commissioners or any other person acting on behalf of the Commissioners.

(6) Subsection (5) does not apply to—
 (a) the function of the Investigatory Powers Commissioner of making a recommendation under section 227(4)(e) or making an appointment under section 247(1),
 (b) any function which falls within section 229(8), or
 (c) any function under section 58(4) or 133(3) of authorising a disclosure, but, subject to this and the terms of the delegation, does include functions which have been delegated to a Judicial Commissioner by the Investigatory Powers Commissioner.

(7) The delegation under subsection (5) to any extent of functions by the Investigatory Powers Commissioner or any other Judicial Commissioner does not prevent the exercise of the functions to that extent by the Commissioner concerned.

239 Power to modify functions

(1) The Secretary of State may by regulations modify the functions of the Investigatory Powers Commissioner or any other Judicial Commissioner.

(2) But such regulations may not modify any function conferred by virtue of this Act on a Judicial Commissioner to approve, quash or cancel—
 (a) an authorisation or warrant, or
 (b) the variation or renewal of an authorisation or warrant.

(3) The power to make regulations under this section (including that power as extended by section 267(1)(c)) may, in particular, be exercised by modifying any provision made by or under an enactment (including this Act).

240 Abolition of existing oversight bodies

(1) The offices of the following are abolished—
   (a) the Interception of Communications Commissioner,
   (b) the Intelligence Services Commissioner,
   (c) the Chief Surveillance Commissioner,
   (d) the other Surveillance Commissioners,
   (e) the Scottish Chief Surveillance Commissioner, and
   (f) the other Scottish Surveillance Commissioners.
(2) Accordingly, the following enactments are repealed—
   (a) sections 57 and 58 of the Regulation of Investigatory Powers Act 2000 (the Interception of Communications Commissioner),
   (b) sections 59, 59A and 60 of that Act (the Intelligence Services Commissioner),
   (c) sections 62 and 63 of that Act and sections 91 and 107 of the Police Act 1997 (the Surveillance Commissioners), and
   (d) sections 2(1) to (9), 3 and 4 of the Regulation of Investigatory Powers (Scotland) Act 2000 (2000 asp 11) (the Scottish Surveillance Commissioners).
(3) The Secretary of State may by regulations, with the consent of the Northern Ireland Assembly, provide for the abolition of the office of the Investigatory Powers Commissioner for Northern Ireland.
(4) The power to make regulations under subsection (3) (including that power as extended by section 267(1)(c)) may, in particular, be exercised by modifying any provision made by or under an enactment (including this Act).
(5) Regulations made by virtue of subsection (4) may, in particular, repeal—
   (a) section 61 of the Regulation of Investigatory Powers Act 2000 (the Investigatory Powers Commissioner for Northern Ireland), and
   (b) the words "or the Investigatory Powers Commissioner for Northern Ireland" in section 229(4)(f) of this Act.
(6) In this section—
"the Chief Surveillance Commissioner" means the Chief Commissioner appointed under section 91(1)(a) of the Police Act 1997,
"the other Scottish Surveillance Commissioners" means—
   (a) the Surveillance Commissioners appointed under section 2(1)(b) of the Regulation of Investigatory Powers (Scotland) Act 2000, and
   (b) the Assistant Surveillance Commissioners appointed under section 3 of that Act,
"the other Surveillance Commissioners" means—
   (a) the Commissioners appointed under section 91(1)(b) of the Police Act 1997, and
   (b) the Assistant Surveillance Commissioners appointed under section 63(1) of the Regulation of Investigatory Powers Act 2000,
"the Scottish Chief Surveillance Commissioner" means the Chief Surveillance Commissioner appointed under section 2(1)(a) of the Regulation of Investigatory Powers (Scotland) Act 2000.

Appendix

CHAPTER 2

OTHER ARRANGEMENTS

Codes of practice

241 Codes of practice

Schedule 7 (codes of practice) has effect.

Investigatory Powers Tribunal

242 Right of appeal from Tribunal

(1) After section 67 of the Regulation of Investigatory Powers Act 2000 insert—

"**67A Appeals from the Tribunal**

  (1) A relevant person may appeal on a point of law against any determination of the Tribunal of a kind mentioned in section 68(4) or any decision of the Tribunal of a kind mentioned in section 68(4C).

  (2) Before making a determination or decision which might be the subject of an appeal under this section, the Tribunal must specify the court which is to have jurisdiction to hear the appeal (the "relevant appellate court").

  (3) This court is whichever of the following courts appears to the Tribunal to be the most appropriate—
   (a) the Court of Appeal in England and Wales,
   (b) the Court of Session.

  (4) The Secretary of State may by regulations, with the consent of the Northern Ireland Assembly, amend subsection (3) so as to add the Court of Appeal in Northern Ireland to the list of courts mentioned there.

  (5) The Secretary of State may by regulations specify criteria to be applied by the Tribunal in making decisions under subsection (2) as to the identity of the relevant appellate court.

  (6) An appeal under this section—
   (a) is to be heard by the relevant appellate court, but
   (b) may not be made without the leave of the Tribunal or, if that is refused, of the relevant appellate court.

  (7) The Tribunal or relevant appellate court must not grant leave to appeal unless it considers that—
   (a) the appeal would raise an important point of principle or practice, or
   (b) there is another compelling reason for granting leave.

  (8) In this section—
   "relevant appellate court" has the meaning given by subsection (2),
   "relevant person", in relation to any proceedings, complaint or reference, means the complainant or—
   (a) in the case of proceedings, the respondent,
   (b) in the case of a complaint, the person complained against, and
   (c) in the case of a reference, any public authority to whom the reference relates."

(2) In section 67 of that Act (no appeal from the Investigatory Powers Tribunal except as provided by order of the Secretary of State)—
  (a) in subsection (8) for "Except to such extent as the Secretary of State may by order otherwise provide," substitute "Except as provided by virtue of section 67A,", and
  (b) omit subsections (9) to (12).

(3) After section 68(4) of that Act (requirement to give notice of determinations to complainant) insert—

"(4A) Where the Tribunal make any determination of a kind mentioned in subsection (4), they must also give notice to—
  (a) in the case of proceedings, the respondent,
  (b) in the case of a complaint, the person complained against, and
  (c) in the case of a reference, any public authority to whom the reference relates.

(4B) A notice under subsection (4A) is (subject to any rules made by virtue of section 69(2)(j)) to be confined, as the case may be, to either—
  (a) a statement that they have made a determination in the complainant's favour, or
  (b) a statement that no determination has been made in the complainant's favour.

(4C) Where the Tribunal make any decision which—
  (a) is a final decision of a preliminary issue in relation to any proceedings, complaint or reference brought before or made to them, and
  (b) is neither a determination of a kind mentioned in subsection (4) nor a decision relating to a procedural matter, they must give notice of that decision to every person who would be entitled to receive notice of the determination under subsection (4) or (4A).

(4D) A notice under subsection (4C) is (subject to any rules made by virtue of section 69(2)(i) or (j)) to be confined to a statement as to what the decision is.

(4E) Subsections (4C) and (4D) do not apply so far as—
  (a) the Tribunal are prevented from giving notice of a decision to a person by rules made by virtue of section 69(4) or decide under such rules not to give such a notice, or
  (b) the giving of such a notice is inconsistent with such rules."

(4) In section 69(2) of that Act (Tribunal rules)—
  (a) in paragraph (i), after "section 68(4)" insert "or notice under section 68(4C)", and
  (b) after paragraph (i), insert ";
  (j) require information about any determination, award, order or other decision made by the Tribunal in relation to any proceedings, complaint or reference to be provided (in addition to any statement under section 68(4A) or notice under section 68(4C)) to—
    (i) in the case of proceedings, the respondent,
    (ii) in the case of a complaint, the person complained against, and
    (iii) in the case of a reference, any public authority to whom the reference relates, or to the person representing their interests;
  (k) make provision about the making and determination of applications to the Tribunal for permission to appeal".

(5) In section 78 of that Act (orders, regulations and rules)—
  (a) in subsection (4), after "applies" insert "(other than regulations under section 67A(5))", and
  (b) after subsection (4) insert—

  "(4A) A statutory instrument containing regulations under section 67A(5) may not be made unless a draft of the instrument has been laid before, and approved by a resolution of, each House of Parliament."

243 Functions of Tribunal in relation to this Act etc.

(1) In section 65 of the Regulation of Investigatory Powers Act 2000 (the Investigatory Powers Tribunal)—
  (a) in subsection (2)(c) (jurisdiction of the Investigatory Powers Tribunal where possible detriment due to evidential bar) for "section 17" substitute "section 56 of the Investigatory Powers Act 2016",

(b) in subsection (5) (conduct in relation to which the Tribunal has jurisdiction) after paragraph (b) insert—

"(ba) conduct for or in connection with the obtaining of secondary data from communications transmitted by means of such a service or system;

(bb) the issue, modification, renewal or service of a warrant under Part 2 or Chapter 1 of Part 6 of the Investigatory Powers Act 2016 (interception of communications);",

(c) in subsection (5) for paragraph (c) substitute—

"(c) conduct of a kind which may be permitted or required by an authorisation or notice under Part 3 of that Act or a warrant under Chapter 2 of Part 6 of that Act (acquisition of communications data);

(cza) the giving of an authorisation or notice under Part 3 of that Act or the issue, modification, renewal or service of a warrant under Chapter 2 of Part 6 of that Act;

(czb) conduct of a kind which may be required or permitted by a retention notice under Part 4 of that Act (retention of communications data) but excluding any conduct which is subject to review by the Information Commissioner;

(czc) the giving or varying of a retention notice under that Part of that Act;

(czd) conduct of a kind which may be required or permitted by a warrant under Part 5 or Chapter 3 of Part 6 of that Act (equipment interference);

(cze) the issue, modification, renewal or service of a warrant under Part 5 or Chapter 3 of Part 6 of that Act;

(czf) the issue, modification, renewal or service of a warrant under Part 7 of that Act (bulk personal dataset warrants);

(czg) the giving of an authorisation under section 219(3)(b) (authorisation for the retention, or retention and examination, of material following expiry of bulk personal dataset warrant);

(czh) the giving or varying of a direction under section 225 of that Act (directions where no bulk personal dataset warrant required);

(czi) conduct of a kind which may be required by a notice under section 252 or 253 of that Act (national security or technical capability notices);

(czj) the giving or varying of such a notice;

(czk) the giving of an authorisation under section 152(5)(c) or 193(5)(c) of that Act (certain authorisations to examine intercepted content or protected material);

(czl) any failure to—
  (i) cancel a warrant under Part 2, 5, 6 or 7 of that Act or an authorisation under Part 3 of that Act;
  (ii) cancel a notice under Part 3 of that Act;
  (iii) revoke a notice under Part 4, or section 252 or 253, of that Act; or
  (iv) revoke a direction under section 225 of that Act;

(czm) any conduct in connection with any conduct falling within paragraph (c), (czb), (czd) or (czi);",

(d) in subsection (6) (limitation for certain purposes of what is conduct falling within subsection (5))—
  (i) after "on behalf of" insert "an immigration officer or", and
  (ii) after paragraph (d) insert—
    "(dza) the Competition and Markets Authority;",

(e) after subsection (6) insert—

"(6A) Subsection (6) does not apply to anything mentioned in paragraph (d) or (f) of subsection (5) which also falls within paragraph (czd) of that subsection.",

Appendix

(f) in subsection (7) after "if" insert "it is conduct of a public authority and",
(g) in subsection (7ZA) (role for Tribunal where judicial authority involved) for "under section 23A or 32A" substitute "by a Judicial Commissioner or under section 32A of this Act or section 75 of the Investigatory Powers Act 2016",
(h) after subsection (7ZA) insert—
"(7ZB) For the purposes of this section conduct also takes place in challengeable circumstances if it is, or purports to be, conduct falling within subsection (5)(bb), (cza), (czc), (cze), (czf), (czg), (czh), (czj), (czk) or (czl) or (so far as the conduct is, or purports to be, the giving of a notice under section 49) subsection (5)(e).",
(i) in subsection (8) (matters that may be challenged before the Tribunal) for paragraphs (a) and (b) substitute—
"(a) a warrant under Part 2, 5, 6 or 7 of the Investigatory Powers Act 2016;
(b) an authorisation or notice under Part 3 of that Act;
(ba) a retention notice under Part 4 of that Act;
(bb) a direction under section 225 of that Act;
(bc) a notice under section 252 or 253 of that Act;", and
(j) after subsection (9) insert—
"(9A) In subsection (5)(ba) the reference to obtaining secondary data from communications transmitted by means of a postal service or telecommunication system is to be read in accordance with section 16 of the Investigatory Powers Act 2016."
(2) In section 67(7) of the Act of 2000 (powers of the Tribunal)—
(a) after paragraph (a) insert—
"(aza) an order quashing or cancelling a notice under Part 3 of the Investigatory Powers Act 2016 or a retention notice under Part 4 of that Act;
(azb) an order quashing or revoking a direction under section 225 of that Act;
(azc) an order quashing or revoking a notice under section 252 or 253 of that Act;",
(b) in paragraph (aa) for "section 23A or 32A" substitute "section 75 of the Investigatory Powers Act 2016 or section 32A of this Act", and
(c) in paragraph (b)(i) after "authorisation" insert "or by a notice under Part 3 of the Investigatory Powers Act 2016".
(3) In section 68(5)(b) of the Act of 2000 (report of certain findings to the Prime Minister) after "permission" insert ", or notice under Part 4 of the Investigatory Powers Act 2016 or under section 252 or 253 of that Act or direction under section 225 of that Act,".
(4) In section 68(6)(b) of the Act of 2000 (disclosures etc. to the Tribunal to enable the exercise of functions conferred by or under that Act) after "this Act" insert "or the Investigatory Powers Act 2016".
(5) In section 68(7) of the Act of 2000 (persons subject to duty to co-operate with the Tribunal)—
(a) in paragraph (e)—
(i) for "section 11" substitute "section 41, 126, 149, 168 or 190 of the Investigatory Powers Act 2016", and
(ii) for "an interception warrant" substitute "a warrant", (b) in paragraph (f) for "section 12" substitute "section 252 or 253 of that Act",
(c) for paragraphs (g) and (h) substitute—
"(g) every person by or to whom an authorisation under Part 3 of that Act has been granted;
(h) every person to whom a notice under Part 3 of that Act has been given;
(ha) every person to whom a retention notice under Part 4 of that Act or a notice under section 252 or 253 of that Act has been given;",

(d) in paragraph (k), for the words from "an authorisation" to the end substitute "—
   (i) an authorisation under Part 3 of the Investigatory Powers Act 2016, Part 2 of this Act or Part 3 of the Police Act 1997, or
   (ii) a warrant under Chapter 2 of Part 6 of the Investigatory Powers Act 2016;",
(e) in paragraph (l) after "authorisation" insert "or warrant", and
(f) in paragraph (n) after "(h)" insert ", (ha)".
(6) In section 68(8) of the Act of 2000 (meaning of "relevant Commissioner") for the words from "Interception" to the end substitute "Investigatory Powers Commissioner or any other Judicial Commissioner or the Investigatory Powers Commissioner for Northern Ireland".

Information Commissioner

244 Oversight by Information Commissioner in relation to Part 4

The Information Commissioner must audit compliance with requirements or restrictions imposed by virtue of Part 4 in relation to the integrity, security or destruction of data retained by virtue of that Part.

Advisory bodies

245 Technical Advisory Board

(1) There is to continue to be a Technical Advisory Board consisting of such number of persons appointed by the Secretary of State as the Secretary of State may by regulations provide.
(2) The regulations providing for the membership of the Technical Advisory Board must also make provision which is calculated to ensure—
   (a) that the membership of the Board includes persons likely effectively to represent the interests of persons on whom obligations may be imposed by virtue of retention notices under Part 4, national security notices under section 252 or technical capability notices under section 253,
   (b) that the membership of the Board includes persons likely effectively to represent the interests of persons entitled to apply for warrants under Part 2, 5, 6 or 7 or authorisations under Part 3,
   (c) that such other persons (if any) as the Secretary of State considers appropriate may be appointed to be members of the Board, and (d) that the Board is so constituted as to produce a balance between the representation of the interests mentioned in paragraph (a) and the representation of those mentioned in paragraph (b).
(3) Regulations under this section may also make provision about quorum and the filling of vacancies.

246 Technology Advisory Panel

(1) The Investigatory Powers Commissioner must ensure that there is a Technology Advisory Panel to provide advice to the Investigatory Powers Commissioner, the Secretary of State and the Scottish Ministers about—
   (a) the impact of changing technology on the exercise of investigatory powers whose exercise is subject to review by the Commissioner, and
   (b) the availability and development of techniques to use such powers while minimising interference with privacy.
(2) The Technology Advisory Panel must provide advice to the Investigatory Powers Commissioner about such matters falling within subsection (1)(a) or (b) as the Commissioner may direct.
(3) Subject to this, the Panel may provide advice to the Investigatory Powers Commissioner about such matters falling within subsection (1)(a) or (b) as it considers appropriate (whether or not requested to do so).

(4) The Panel may provide advice to the Secretary of State or the Scottish Ministers about such matters falling within subsection (1)(a) or (b) as it considers appropriate (whether or not requested to do so) but such advice to the Scottish Ministers may only relate to matters for which the Scottish Ministers are responsible.

(5) The Panel must, as soon as reasonably practicable after the end of each calendar year, make a report to the Investigatory Powers Commissioner about the carrying out of the functions of the Panel.

(6) The Panel must, at the same time, send a copy of the report to the Secretary of State and (so far as relating to matters for which the Scottish Ministers are responsible) the Scottish Ministers.

247 Members of the Panel

(1) The Investigatory Powers Commissioner must appoint such number of persons as members of the Technology Advisory Panel as the Commissioner considers necessary for the carrying out of the functions of the Panel.

(2) Subject as follows, each member of the Panel holds and vacates office in accordance with the member's terms and conditions of appointment.

(3) A member of the Panel must not act in a way which the member considers to be contrary to the public interest or prejudicial to—
   (a) national security,
   (b) the prevention or detection of serious crime, or
   (c) the economic well-being of the United Kingdom.

(4) A member of the Panel must, in particular, ensure that the member does not—
   (a) jeopardise the success of an intelligence or security operation or a law enforcement operation,
   (b) compromise the safety or security of those involved, or
   (c) unduly impede the operational effectiveness of an intelligence service, a police force, a government department or Her Majesty's forces.

(5) Section 235(2) and (7) (information powers) apply to a member of the Panel as they apply to a Judicial Commissioner.

PART 9

MISCELLANEOUS AND GENERAL PROVISIONS

CHAPTER 1

MISCELLANEOUS

Combined warrants and authorisations

248 Combination of warrants and authorisations

Schedule 8 (which makes provision for the combination of certain warrants and authorisations in a single instrument) has effect.

Compliance with Act

249 Payments towards certain compliance costs

(1) The Secretary of State must ensure that arrangements are in force for securing that telecommunications operators and postal operators receive an appropriate contribution in respect of such of their relevant costs as the Secretary of State considers appropriate.

(2) In subsection (1) "relevant costs" means costs incurred, or likely to be incurred, by telecommunications operators and postal operators in complying with this Act.
(3) The arrangements may provide for payment of a contribution to be subject to terms and conditions determined by the Secretary of State.
(4) Such terms and conditions may, in particular, include a condition on the operator concerned to comply with any audit that may reasonably be required to monitor the claim for costs.
(5) The arrangements may provide for the Secretary of State to determine—
    (a) the scope and extent of the arrangements, and
    (b) the appropriate level of contribution which should be made in each case.
(6) Different levels of contribution may apply for different cases or descriptions of case but the appropriate contribution must never be nil.
(7) A retention notice under Part 4 given to a telecommunications operator or a postal operator, or a national security notice under section 252 given to a telecommunications operator, must specify the level or levels of contribution which the Secretary of State has determined should be made in respect of the costs incurred, or likely to be incurred, by the operator as a result of the notice in complying with that Part or (as the case may be) with the national security notice.
(8) For the purpose of complying with this section the Secretary of State may make, or arrange for the making of, payments out of money provided by Parliament.

250 Power to develop compliance systems etc.

(1) The Secretary of State may—
    (a) develop, provide, maintain or improve, or
    (b) enter into financial or other arrangements with any person for the development, provision, maintenance or improvement of, such apparatus, systems or other facilities or services as the Secretary of State considers appropriate for enabling or otherwise facilitating compliance by the Secretary of State, another public authority or any other person with this Act.
(2) Arrangements falling within subsection (1)(b) may, in particular, include arrangements consisting of the giving of financial assistance by the Secretary of State.
(3) Such financial assistance—
    (a) may, in particular, be given by way of—
        (i) grant,
        (ii) loan,
        (iii) guarantee or indemnity,
        (iv) investment, or
        (v) incurring expenditure for the benefit of the person assisted, and
    (b) may be given subject to terms and conditions determined by the Secretary of State.
(4) Terms and conditions imposed by virtue of subsection (3)(b) may include terms and conditions as to repayment with or without interest.

Additional powers

251 Amendments of the Intelligence Services Act 1994

(1) The Intelligence Services Act 1994 is amended as follows.
(2) In section 3 (the Government Communications Headquarters)—
    (a) in subsection (1)(a), after "monitor" insert ", make use of", and
    (b) in the words following subsection (1)(b)(ii), for the words from "or to any other organisation" to the end substitute "or, in such cases as it considers appropriate, to other organisations or persons, or to the general public, in the United Kingdom or elsewhere."

(3) In section 5 (warrants: general)—
- (a) in subsection (2), omit ", subject to subsection (3) below,",
- (b) omit subsection (3), and
- (c) in subsection (3A), after "1989" insert ", or on the application of the Intelligence Service or GCHQ for the purposes of the exercise of their functions by virtue of section 1(2)(c) or 3(2)(c),".

252 National security notices

(1) The Secretary of State may give any telecommunications operator in the United Kingdom a national security notice under this section if—
- (a) the Secretary of State considers that the notice is necessary in the interests of national security,
- (b) the Secretary of State considers that the conduct required by the notice is proportionate to what is sought to be achieved by that conduct, and
- (c) the decision to give the notice has been approved by a Judicial Commissioner.

(2) A "national security notice" is a notice requiring the operator to take such specified steps as the Secretary of State considers necessary in the interests of national security.

(3) A national security notice may, in particular, require the operator to whom it is given—
- (a) to carry out any conduct, including the provision of services or facilities, for the purpose of—
  - (i) facilitating anything done by an intelligence service under any enactment other than this Act, or
  - (ii) dealing with an emergency (within the meaning of Part 1 of the Civil Contingencies Act 2004);
- (b) to provide services or facilities for the purpose of assisting an intelligence service to carry out its functions more securely or more effectively.

(4) In a case where—
- (a) a national security notice would require the taking of any steps, and
- (b) in the absence of such a notice requiring the taking of those steps, the taking of those steps would be lawful only if a warrant or authorisation under a relevant enactment had been obtained, the notice may require the taking of those steps only if such a warrant or authorisation has been obtained.

(5) But the Secretary of State may not give any telecommunications operator a national security notice the main purpose of which is to require the operator to do something for which a warrant or authorisation under a relevant enactment is required.

(6) In this section "relevant enactment" means—
- (a) this Act;
- (b) the Intelligence Services Act 1994;
- (c) the Regulation of Investigatory Powers Act 2000;
- (d) the Regulation of Investigatory Powers (Scotland) Act 2000 (2000 asp 11).

(7) A national security notice must specify such period as appears to the Secretary of State to be reasonable as the period within which the steps specified in the notice are to be taken.

(8) Conduct required by a national security notice is to be treated as lawful for all purposes (to the extent that it would not otherwise be so treated).

(9) Sections 254 to 258 contain further provision about national security notices.

253 Technical capability notices

(1) The Secretary of State may give a relevant operator a technical capability notice under this section if—
  (a) the Secretary of State considers that the notice is necessary for securing that the operator has the capability to provide any assistance which the operator may be required to provide in relation to any relevant authorisation,
  (b) the Secretary of State considers that the conduct required by the notice is proportionate to what is sought to be achieved by that conduct, and
  (c) the decision to give the notice has been approved by a Judicial Commissioner.
(2) A "technical capability notice" is a notice—
  (a) imposing on the relevant operator any applicable obligations specified in the notice, and
  (b) requiring the person to take all the steps specified in the notice for the purpose of complying with those obligations.
(3) In this section—
  "applicable obligation", in relation to a relevant operator of a particular description, means an obligation specified by the Secretary of State in regulations as an obligation that may be imposed on relevant operators, or on relevant operators of that description;
  "relevant authorisation" means—
    (a) any warrant issued under Part 2, 5 or 6, or
    (b) any authorisation or notice given under Part 3;
  "relevant operator" means—
    (a) a postal operator,
    (b) a telecommunications operator, or
    (c) a person who is proposing to become a postal operator or a telecommunications operator.
(4) Regulations under this section may specify an obligation that may be imposed on any relevant operators only if the Secretary of State considers it is reasonable to do so for the purpose of securing—
  (a) that it is (and remains) practicable to impose requirements on those relevant operators to provide assistance in relation to relevant authorisations, and
  (b) that it is (and remains) practicable for those relevant operators to comply with those requirements.
(5) The obligations that may be specified in regulations under this section include, among other things—
  (a) obligations to provide facilities or services of a specified description;
  (b) obligations relating to apparatus owned or operated by a relevant operator;
  (c) obligations relating to the removal by a relevant operator of electronic protection applied by or on behalf of that operator to any communications or data;
  (d) obligations relating to the security of any postal or telecommunications services provided by a relevant operator;
  (e) obligations relating to the handling or disclosure of any information.
(6) Before making any regulations under this section, the Secretary of State must consult the following persons—
  (a) the Technical Advisory Board,
  (b) persons appearing to the Secretary of State to be likely to be subject to any obligations specified in the regulations,
  (c) persons representing persons falling within paragraph (b), and

Appendix

    (d) persons with statutory functions in relation to persons falling within that paragraph.
(7) A technical capability notice—
    (a) must specify such period as appears to the Secretary of State to be reasonable as the period within which the steps specified in the notice are to be taken, and
    (b) may specify different periods in relation to different steps.
(8) A technical capability notice may be given to persons outside the United Kingdom (and may require things to be done, or not to be done, outside the United Kingdom).
(9) Sections 254 to 258 contain further provision about technical capability notices.

254 Approval of notices by Judicial Commissioners

(1) In this section "relevant notice" means—
    (a) a national security notice under section 252, or
    (b) a technical capability notice under section 253.
(2) In deciding whether to approve a decision to give a relevant notice, a Judicial Commissioner must review the Secretary of State's conclusions as to the following matters—
    (a) whether the notice is necessary as mentioned in section 252(1)(a) or (as the case may be) section 253(1)(a), and
    (b) whether the conduct that would be required by the notice is proportionate to what is sought to be achieved by that conduct.
(3) In doing so, the Judicial Commissioner must—
    (a) apply the same principles as would be applied by a court on an application for judicial review, and
    (b) consider the matters referred to in subsection (2) with a sufficient degree of care as to ensure that the Judicial Commissioner complies with the duties imposed by section 2 (general duties in relation to privacy).
(4) Where a Judicial Commissioner refuses to approve a decision to give a relevant notice, the Judicial Commissioner must give the Secretary of State written reasons for the refusal.
(5) Where a Judicial Commissioner, other than the Investigatory Powers Commissioner, refuses to approve a decision to give a relevant notice, the Secretary of State may ask the Investigatory Powers Commissioner to decide whether to approve the decision to give the notice.

255 Further provision about notices under section 252 or 253

(1) In this section "relevant notice" means—
    (a) a national security notice under section 252, or
    (b) a technical capability notice under section 253.
(2) Before giving a relevant notice to a person, the Secretary of State must consult that person.
(3) Before giving a relevant notice, the Secretary of State must, among other matters, take into account—
    (a) the likely benefits of the notice,
    (b) the likely number of users (if known) of any postal or telecommunications service to which the notice relates,
    (c) the technical feasibility of complying with the notice,
    (d) the likely cost of complying with the notice, and
    (e) any other effect of the notice on the person (or description of person) to whom it relates.
(4) In the case of a technical capability notice that would impose any obligations relating to the removal by a person of electronic protection applied by or on behalf of that person to any communications or data, in complying with subsection (3) the Secretary of State must in particular take into account the technical feasibility, and likely cost, of complying with those obligations.

(5) A relevant notice must be in writing.
(6) A technical capability notice may be given to a person outside the United Kingdom in any of the following ways (as well as by electronic or other means of giving a notice)—
    (a) by delivering it to the person's principal office within the United Kingdom or, if the person has no such office in the United Kingdom, to any place in the United Kingdom where the person carries on business or conducts activities;
    (b) if the person has specified an address in the United Kingdom as one at which the person, or someone on the person's behalf, will accept documents of the same description as a notice, by delivering it to that address.
(7) The Secretary of State may by regulations make further provision about the giving of relevant notices.
(8) A person to whom a relevant notice is given, or any person employed or engaged for the purposes of that person's business, must not disclose the existence or contents of the notice to any other person without the permission of the Secretary of State.
(9) A person to whom a relevant notice is given must comply with the notice.
(10) The duty imposed by subsection (9) is enforceable—
    (a) in relation to a person in the United Kingdom, and
    (b) so far as relating to a technical capability notice within subsection (11), in relation to a person outside the United Kingdom, by civil proceedings by the Secretary of State for an injunction, or for specific performance of a statutory duty under section 45 of the Court of Session Act 1988, or for any other appropriate relief.
(11) A technical capability notice is within this subsection if it relates to any of the following—
    (a) a targeted interception warrant or mutual assistance warrant under Chapter 1 of Part 2;
    (b) a bulk interception warrant;
    (c) an authorisation or notice given under Part 3.
(12) Subsection (9) applies to a person to whom a national security notice is given despite any other duty imposed on the person by or under Part 1, or Chapter 1 of Part 2, of the Communications Act 2003.

256 Variation and revocation of notices

(1) In this section "relevant notice" means—
    (a) a national security notice under section 252, or
    (b) a technical capability notice under section 253.
(2) The Secretary of State must keep each relevant notice under review.
(3) The Secretary of State may—
    (a) vary a relevant notice;
    (b) revoke a relevant notice (whether wholly or in part).
(4) The Secretary of State may vary a national security notice given to a person only if—
    (a) the Secretary of State considers that the variation is necessary in the interests of national security,
    (b) the Secretary of State considers that the conduct required by the notice as varied is proportionate to what is sought to be achieved by that conduct, and
    (c) if the variation would impose further requirements on the person, the decision to vary the notice has been approved by a Judicial Commissioner (but see subsection (6)).
(5) The Secretary of State may vary a technical capability notice given to a person only if—
    (a) the Secretary of State considers that the variation is necessary for securing that the person has the capability to provide any assistance which the person may be required to provide in relation to any relevant authorisation (within the meaning of section 253),

(b) the Secretary of State considers that the conduct required by the notice as varied is proportionate to what is sought to be achieved by that conduct, and
(c) if the variation would impose further requirements on the person, the decision to vary the notice has been approved by a Judicial Commissioner (but see subsection (6)).
(6) The condition in subsection (4)(c) or (as the case may be) subsection (5)(c) does not apply in the case of a variation to which section 257(10) applies.
(7) If the Secretary of State varies or revokes a relevant notice given to any person, the Secretary of State must give that person notice of the variation or revocation.
(8) Section 254 (approval of notices by Judicial Commissioners) applies in relation to a decision to vary a relevant notice (other than a decision to which section 257(10) applies) as it applies in relation to a decision to give a relevant notice, but as if—
(a) the reference in section 254(2)(a) to the notice were to the variation, and
(b) the reference in section 254(2)(b) to the notice were to the notice as varied.
(9) Subsections (2) to (4) and (7) of section 255 apply in relation to varying or revoking a relevant notice as they apply in relation to giving a relevant notice (and in the application of section 255(3) and (4) in relation to varying a relevant notice, references to the notice are to be read as references to the notice as varied).
(10) Subsections (5) and (6) of section 255 apply to any notice of the variation or revocation of a relevant notice as they apply to a relevant notice.
(11) The fact that a relevant notice has been revoked in relation to a particular person (or description of persons) does not prevent the giving of another relevant notice of the same kind in relation to the same person (or description of persons).
(12) Any reference in this section or section 255(8) to (12) to a notice given under section 252 or 253 includes a reference to such a notice as varied under this section.

257 Review of notices by the Secretary of State

(1) A person who is given a notice under section 252 or 253 may, within such period or circumstances as may be provided for by regulations made by the Secretary of State, refer the notice back to the Secretary of State.
(2) Such a reference may be in relation to the whole of a notice or any aspect of it.
(3) There is no requirement for a person who has referred a notice under subsection (1) to comply with the notice, so far as referred, until the Secretary of State has reviewed the notice in accordance with subsection (4).
(4) The Secretary of State must review any notice so far as referred to the Secretary of State under subsection (1).
(5) Before deciding the review, the Secretary of State must consult—
(a) the Technical Advisory Board, and
(b) a Judicial Commissioner.
(6) The Board must consider the technical requirements and the financial consequences, for the person who has made the reference, of the notice so far as referred.
(7) The Commissioner must consider whether the notice so far as referred is proportionate.
(8) The Board and the Commissioner must—
(a) give the person concerned and the Secretary of State the opportunity to provide evidence, or make representations, to them before reaching their conclusions, and
(b) report their conclusions to—
(i) the person, and
(ii) the Secretary of State.

(9) The Secretary of State may, after considering the conclusions of the Board and the Commissioner—
   (a) vary or revoke the notice under section 256, or
   (b) give a notice under this section to the person confirming its effect.
(10) But the Secretary of State may vary the notice, or give a notice under subsection (9)(b) confirming its effect, only if the Secretary of State's decision to do so has been approved by the Investigatory Powers Commissioner.
(11) Subsections (5) to (8) of section 255 apply in relation to a notice under subsection (9)(b) above as they apply in relation to a notice under section 252 or 253.
(12) Any reference in this section or section 258 to a notice under section 252 or 253 includes such a notice as varied under section 256, but only so far as the variation is concerned.
But it does not include a notice varied as mentioned in subsection (9)(a) above.

258 Approval of notices following review under section 257

(1) In this section "relevant notice" means—
   (a) a national security notice under section 252, or
   (b) a technical capability notice under section 253.
(2) In deciding whether to approve a decision to vary a relevant notice as mentioned in section 257(9)(a), or to give a notice under section 257(9)(b) confirming the effect of a relevant notice, the Investigatory Powers Commissioner must review the Secretary of State's conclusions as to the following matters—
   (a) whether the relevant notice as varied or confirmed is necessary as mentioned in section 252(1)(a) or (as the case may be) section 253(1)(a), and
   (b) whether the conduct required by the relevant notice, as varied or confirmed, is proportionate to what is sought to be achieved by that conduct.
(3) In doing so, the Investigatory Powers Commissioner must—
   (a) apply the same principles as would be applied by a court on an application for judicial review, and
   (b) consider the matters referred to in subsection (2) with a sufficient degree of care as to ensure that the Investigatory Powers Commissioner complies with the duties imposed by section 2 (general duties in relation to privacy).
(4) Where the Investigatory Powers Commissioner refuses to approve a decision to vary a relevant notice as mentioned in section 257(9)(a), or to give a notice under section 257(9)(b) confirming the effect of a relevant notice, the Investigatory Powers Commissioner must give the Secretary of State written reasons for the refusal.

Wireless telegraphy

259 Amendments of the Wireless Telegraphy Act 2006

(1) The Wireless Telegraphy Act 2006 is amended as follows.
(2) Section 48 (interception and disclosure of messages) is amended as follows.
(3) In subsection (1), for "otherwise than under the authority of a designated person" substitute "without lawful authority".
(4) After subsection (3) insert—

"(3A) A person does not commit an offence under this section consisting in any conduct if the conduct—
   (a) constitutes an offence under section 3(1) of the Investigatory Powers Act 2016 (offence of unlawful interception), or

(b) would do so in the absence of any lawful authority (within the meaning of section 6 of that Act).".

(5) Omit subsection (5).
(6) Omit section 49 (interception authorities).
(7) In consequence of the repeal made by subsection (6)—
- (a) in sections 50(5) and 119(2)(a), for "49" substitute "48";
- (b) in section 121(2), omit paragraph (b).

CHAPTER 2
GENERAL

Review of operation of Act

260 Review of operation of Act

(1) The Secretary of State must, within the period of 6 months beginning with the end of the initial period, prepare a report on the operation of this Act.
(2) In subsection (1) "the initial period" is the period of 5 years and 6 months beginning with the day on which this Act is passed.
(3) In preparing the report under subsection (1), the Secretary of State must, in particular, take account of any report on the operation of this Act made by a Select Committee of either House of Parliament (whether acting alone or jointly).
(4) The Secretary of State must—
- (a) publish the report prepared under subsection (1), and
- (b) lay a copy of it before Parliament.

Interpretation

261 Telecommunications definitions

(1) The definitions in this section have effect for the purposes of this Act.

Communication

(2) "Communication", in relation to a telecommunications operator, telecommunications service or telecommunication system, includes—
- (a) anything comprising speech, music, sounds, visual images or data of any description, and
- (b) signals serving either for the impartation of anything between persons, between a person and a thing or between things or for the actuation or control of any apparatus.

Entity data

(3) "Entity data" means any data which—
- (a) is about—
  - (i) an entity,
  - (ii) an association between a telecommunications service and an entity, or
  - (iii) an association between any part of a telecommunication system and an entity,
- (b) consists of, or includes, data which identifies or describes the entity (whether or not by reference to the entity's location), and
- (c) is not events data.

Events data

(4) "Events data" means any data which identifies or describes an event (whether or not by reference to its location) on, in or by means of a telecommunication system where the event consists of one or more entities engaging in a specific activity at a specific time.

Communications data

(5) "Communications data", in relation to a telecommunications operator, telecommunications service or telecommunication system, means entity data or events data—
- (a) which is (or is to be or is capable of being) held or obtained by, or on behalf of, a telecommunications operator and—
  - (i) is about an entity to which a telecommunications service is provided and relates to the provision of the service,
  - (ii) is comprised in, included as part of, attached to or logically associated with a communication (whether by the sender or otherwise) for the purposes of a telecommunication system by means of which the communication is being or may be transmitted, or
  - (iii) does not fall within sub-paragraph (i) or (ii) but does relate to the use of a telecommunications service or a telecommunication system,
- (b) which is available directly from a telecommunication system and falls within sub-paragraph (ii) of paragraph (a), or
- (c) which—
  - (i) is (or is to be or is capable of being) held or obtained by, or on behalf of, a telecommunications operator,
  - (ii) is about the architecture of a telecommunication system, and
  - (iii) is not about a specific person, but does not include any content of a communication or anything which, in the absence of subsection (6)(b), would be content of a communication.

Content of a communication

(6) "Content", in relation to a communication and a telecommunications operator, telecommunications service or telecommunication system, means any element of the communication, or any data attached to or logically associated with the communication, which reveals anything of what might reasonably be considered to be the meaning (if any) of the communication, but—
- (a) any meaning arising from the fact of the communication or from any data relating to the transmission of the communication is to be disregarded, and
- (b) anything which is systems data is not content.

Other definitions

(7) "Entity" means a person or thing.

(8) "Public telecommunications service" means any telecommunications service which is offered or provided to the public, or a substantial section of the public, in any one or more parts of the United Kingdom.

(9) "Public telecommunication system" means a telecommunication system located in the United Kingdom—
- (a) by means of which any public telecommunications service is provided, or
- (b) which consists of parts of any other telecommunication system by means of which any such service is provided.

(10) "Telecommunications operator" means a person who—

(a) offers or provides a telecommunications service to persons in the United Kingdom, or
(b) controls or provides a telecommunication system which is (wholly or partly)—
    (i) in the United Kingdom, or
    (ii) controlled from the United Kingdom.
(11) "Telecommunications service" means any service that consists in the provision of access to, and of facilities for making use of, any telecommunication system (whether or not one provided by the person providing the service).
(12) For the purposes of subsection (11), the cases in which a service is to be taken to consist in the provision of access to, and of facilities for making use of, a telecommunication system include any case where a service consists in or includes facilitating the creation, management or storage of communications transmitted, or that may be transmitted, by means of such a system.
(13) "Telecommunication system" means a system (including the apparatus comprised in it) that exists (whether wholly or partly in the United Kingdom or elsewhere) for the purpose of facilitating the transmission of communications by any means involving the use of electrical or electromagnetic energy.
(14) "Private telecommunication system" means any telecommunication system which—
    (a) is not a public telecommunication system,
    (b) is attached, directly or indirectly, to a public telecommunication system (whether or not for the purposes of the communication in question), and
    (c) includes apparatus which is both located in the United Kingdom and used (with or without other apparatus) for making the attachment to that public telecommunication system.

262 Postal definitions

(1) The definitions in this section have effect for the purposes of this Act.

Communication

(2) "Communication", in relation to a postal operator or postal service (but not in the definition of "postal service" in this section), includes anything transmitted by a postal service.

Communications data

(3) "Communications data", in relation to a postal operator or postal service, means—
    (a) postal data comprised in, included as part of, attached to or logically associated with a communication (whether by the sender or otherwise) for the purposes of a postal service by means of which it is being or may be transmitted,
    (b) information about the use made by any person of a postal service (but excluding any content of a communication (apart from information within paragraph (a)), or
    (c) information not within paragraph (a) or (b) that is (or is to be or is capable of being) held or obtained by or on behalf of a person providing a postal service, is about those to whom the service is provided by that person and relates to the service so provided.

Postal data

(4) "Postal data" means data which—
    (a) identifies, or purports to identify, any person, apparatus or location to or from which a communication is or may be transmitted,
    (b) identifies or selects, or purports to identify or select, apparatus through which, or by means of which, a communication is or may be transmitted,

(c) identifies, or purports to identify, the time at which an event relating to a communication occurs, or
(d) identifies the data or other data as data comprised in, included as part of, attached to or logically associated with a particular communication.
For the purposes of this definition "data", in relation to a postal item, includes anything written on the outside of the item.

Other definitions

(5) "Postal item" means—
(a) any letter, postcard or other such thing in writing as may be used by the sender for imparting information to the recipient, or
(b) any packet or parcel.
(6) "Postal operator" means a person providing a postal service to persons in the United Kingdom.
(7) "Postal service" means a service that—
(a) consists in the following, or in any one or more of them, namely, the collection, sorting, conveyance, distribution and delivery (whether in the United Kingdom or elsewhere) of postal items, and
(b) has as its main purpose, or one of its main purposes, to make available, or to facilitate, a means of transmission from place to place of postal items containing communications.
(8) "Public postal service" means a postal service that is offered or provided to the public, or a substantial section of the public, in any one or more parts of the United Kingdom.

263 General definitions

(1) In this Act—
"apparatus" includes any equipment, machinery or device (whether physical or logical) and any wire or cable,
"civil proceedings" means any proceedings in or before any court or tribunal that are not criminal proceedings,
"crime" means conduct which—
(a) constitutes one or more criminal offences, or
(b) is, or corresponds to, any conduct which, if it all took place in any one part of the United Kingdom, would constitute one or more criminal offences,
"criminal proceedings" includes proceedings before a court in respect of a service offence within the meaning of the Armed Forces Act 2006 (and references to criminal prosecutions are to be read accordingly),
"data" includes data which is not electronic data and any information (whether or not electronic),
"destroy", in relation to electronic data, means delete the data in such a way as to make access to the data impossible (and related expressions are to be read accordingly),
"enactment" means an enactment whenever passed or made; and includes—
(a) an enactment contained in subordinate legislation within the meaning of the Interpretation Act 1978,
(b) an enactment contained in, or in an instrument made under, an Act of the Scottish Parliament,
(c) an enactment contained in, or in an instrument made under, a Measure or Act of the National Assembly for Wales, and

(d) an enactment contained in, or in an instrument made under, Northern Ireland legislation,

"enhanced affirmative procedure" is to be read in accordance with section 268,

"functions" includes powers and duties,

"GCHQ" has the same meaning as in the Intelligence Services Act 1994,

"head", in relation to an intelligence service, means—
(a) in relation to the Security Service, the Director-General,
(b) in relation to the Secret Intelligence Service, the Chief, and
(c) in relation to GCHQ, the Director,

"Her Majesty's forces" has the same meaning as in the Armed Forces Act 2006,

"identifying data" has the meaning given by subsection (2),

"intelligence service" means the Security Service, the Secret Intelligence Service or GCHQ,

"the Investigatory Powers Commissioner" means the person appointed under section 227(1)(a) (and the expression is also to be read in accordance with section 227(13)(b)),

"the Investigatory Powers Tribunal" means the tribunal established under section 65 of the Regulation of Investigatory Powers Act 2000,

"items subject to legal privilege"—
(a) in relation to England and Wales, has the same meaning as in the Police and Criminal Evidence Act 1984 (see section 10 of that Act),
(b) in relation to Scotland, means—
    (i) communications between a professional legal adviser and the adviser's client, or
    (ii) communications made in connection with, or in contemplation of, legal proceedings and for the purposes of those proceedings, which would, by virtue of any rule of law relating to the confidentiality of communications, be protected in legal proceedings from disclosure, and
(c) in relation to Northern Ireland, has the same meaning as in the Police and Criminal Evidence (Northern Ireland) Order 1989 (S.I. 1989/1341 (N.I. 12)) (see Article 12 of that Order),

"Judicial Commissioner" means a person appointed under section 227(1)(a) or (b) (and the expression is therefore to be read in accordance with section 227(13)(a)),

"legal proceedings" means—
(a) civil or criminal proceedings in or before a court or tribunal, or
(b) proceedings before an officer in respect of a service offence within the meaning of the Armed Forces Act 2006,

"modify" includes amend, repeal or revoke (and related expressions are to be read accordingly),

"person holding office under the Crown" includes any servant of the Crown and any member of Her Majesty's forces,

"premises" includes any land, movable structure, vehicle, vessel, aircraft or hovercraft (and "set of premises" is to be read accordingly),

"primary legislation" means—
(a) an Act of Parliament,
(b) an Act of the Scottish Parliament,
(c) a Measure or Act of the National Assembly for Wales, or
(d) Northern Ireland legislation,

"public authority" means a public authority within the meaning of section 6 of the Human Rights Act 1998, other than a court or tribunal,

"serious crime" means crime where—
- (a) the offence, or one of the offences, which is or would be constituted by the conduct concerned is an offence for which a person who has reached the age of 18 (or, in relation to Scotland or Northern Ireland, 21) and has no previous convictions could reasonably be expected to be sentenced to imprisonment for a term of 3 years or more, or
- (b) the conduct involves the use of violence, results in substantial financial gain or is conduct by a large number of persons in pursuit of a common purpose,

"source of journalistic information" means an individual who provides material intending the recipient to use it for the purposes of journalism or knowing that it is likely to be so used,

"specified", in relation to an authorisation, warrant, notice or regulations, means specified or described in the authorisation, warrant, notice or (as the case may be) regulations (and "specify" is to be read accordingly),

"statutory", in relation to any function, means conferred by virtue of this Act or any other enactment,

"subordinate legislation" means—
- (a) subordinate legislation within the meaning of the Interpretation Act 1978, or
- (b) an instrument made under an Act of the Scottish Parliament, Northern Ireland legislation or a Measure or Act of the National Assembly for Wales,

"systems data" has the meaning given by subsection (4),

"the Technical Advisory Board" means the Board provided for by section 245,

"the Technology Advisory Panel" means the panel established in accordance with section 246(1),

"working day" means a day other than a Saturday, a Sunday, Christmas Day, Good Friday or a bank holiday under the Banking and Financial Dealings Act 1971 in any part of the United Kingdom.

(2) In this Act "identifying data" means—
- (a) data which may be used to identify, or assist in identifying, any person, apparatus, system or service,
- (b) data which may be used to identify, or assist in identifying, any event, or
- (c) data which may be used to identify, or assist in identifying, the location of any person, event or thing.

(3) For the purposes of subsection (2), the reference to data which may be used to identify, or assist in identifying, any event includes—
- (a) data relating to the fact of the event;
- (b) data relating to the type, method or pattern of event;
- (c) data relating to the time or duration of the event.

(4) In this Act "systems data" means any data that enables or facilitates, or identifies or describes anything connected with enabling or facilitating, the functioning of any of the following—
- (a) a postal service;
- (b) a telecommunication system (including any apparatus forming part of the system);
- (c) any telecommunications service provided by means of a telecommunication system;
- (d) a relevant system (including any apparatus forming part of the system);
- (e) any service provided by means of a relevant system.

(5) For the purposes of subsection (4), a system is a "relevant system" if any communications or other information are held on or by means of the system.

(6) For the purposes of this Act detecting crime or serious crime is to be taken to include—
   (a) establishing by whom, for what purpose, by what means and generally in what circumstances any crime or (as the case may be) serious crime was committed, and
   (b) the apprehension of the person by whom any crime or (as the case may be) serious crime was committed.
(7) References in this Act to the examination of material obtained under a warrant are references to the material being read, looked at or listened to by the persons to whom it becomes available as a result of the warrant.

264 General definitions: "journalistic material" etc.

(1) The definitions in this section have effect for the purposes of this Act.

Journalistic material

(2) "Journalistic material" means material created or acquired for the purposes of journalism.
(3) For the purposes of this section, where—
   (a) a person ("R") receives material from another person ("S"), and
   (b) S intends R to use the material for the purposes of journalism, R is to be taken to have acquired it for those purposes. Accordingly, a communication sent by S to R containing such material is to be regarded as a communication containing journalistic material.
(4) For the purposes of determining whether a communication contains material acquired for the purposes of journalism, it does not matter whether the material has been acquired for those purposes by the sender or recipient of the communication or by some other person.
(5) For the purposes of this section—
   (a) material is not to be regarded as created or acquired for the purposes of journalism if it is created or acquired with the intention of furthering a criminal purpose, and
   (b) material which a person intends to be used to further such a purpose is not to be regarded as intended to be used for the purposes of journalism.

Confidential journalistic material

(6) "Confidential journalistic material" means—
   (a) in the case of material contained in a communication, journalistic material which the sender of the communication—
      (i) holds in confidence, or
      (ii) intends the recipient, or intended recipient, of the communication to hold in confidence;
   (b) in any other case, journalistic material which a person holds in confidence.
(7) A person holds material in confidence for the purposes of this section if—
   (a) the person holds it subject to an express or implied undertaking to hold it in confidence, or
   (b) the person holds it subject to a restriction on disclosure or an obligation of secrecy contained in an enactment.

265 Index of defined expressions

In this Act, the expressions listed in the left-hand column have the meaning given by, or are to be interpreted in accordance with, the provisions listed in the right-hand column.

Appendix

Expression	Provision
Apparatus Section	263(1)
Bulk equipment interference warrant	Section 176(1)
Bulk interception warrant	Section 136(1)
Civil proceedings	Section 263(1)
Communication	Sections 261(2) and 262(2)
Communications data	Sections 261(5) and 262(3)
Confidential journalistic material	Section 264(6) and (7)
Content of a communication (in relation to a telecommunications operator, telecommunications service or telecommunication system)	Section 261(6)
Crime	Section 263(1)
Criminal proceedings	Section 263(1)
Criminal prosecution	Section 263(1)
Data	Section 263(1)
Destroy (in relation to electronic data) and related expressions	Section 263(1)
Detecting crime or serious crime	Section 263(6)
Enactment	Section 263(1)
Enhanced affirmative procedure	Section 263(1)
Entity	Section 261(7)
Entity data	Section 261(3)
Events data	Section 261(4)
Examination (in relation to material obtained under a warrant)	Section 263(7)
Functions	Section 263(1)
GCHQ	Section 263(1)
Head (in relation to an intelligence service)	Section 263(1)
Her Majesty's forces	Section 263(1)
Identifying data	Section 263(2) and (3)
Intelligence service	Section 263(1)
Interception of communication (postal service)	Sections 4(7) and 5
Interception of communication (telecommunication system)	Sections 4(1) to (6) and 5(1)
Interception of communication in the United Kingdom	Section 4(8)
Internet connection record	Section 62(7)
Investigatory Powers Commissioner	Section 263(1)
Investigatory Powers Tribunal	Section 263(1)
Items subject to legal privilege	Section 263(1)
Journalistic material	Section 264(2) to (5)
Judicial Commissioner	Section 263(1)
Judicial Commissioners	Section 227(7)
Lawful authority (in relation to interception of communication)	Section 6
Legal proceedings	Section 263(1)

Appendix

Expression	Provision
Modify (and related expressions)	Section 263(1)
Person holding office under the Crown	Section 263(1)
Postal data	Section 262(4)
Postal item	Section 262(5)
Postal item in course of transmission by postal service	Section 4(7)
Postal operator	Section 262(6)
Postal service	Section 262(7)
Premises	Section 263(1)
Primary legislation	Section 263(1)
Private telecommunication system	Section 261(14)
Public authority	Section 263(1)
Public postal service	Section 262(8)
Public telecommunications service	Section 261(8)
Public telecommunication system	Section 261(9)
Serious crime	Section 263(1) (and paragraph 6 of Schedule 9)
Source of journalistic information	Section 263(1)
Specified and specify (in relation to an authorisation, warrant, notice or regulations)	Section 263(1)
Statutory (in relation to any function)	Section 263(1)
Subordinate legislation	Section 263(1)
Systems data	Section 263(4) and (5)
Technical Advisory Board	Section 263(1)
Technology Advisory Panel	Section 263(1)
Telecommunications operator	Section 261(10)
Telecommunications service	Section 261(11) and (12)
Telecommunication system	Section 261(13)
Working day	Section 263(1)

Supplementary provision

266 Offences by bodies corporate etc.

(1) This section applies if an offence under this Act is committed by a body corporate or a Scottish partnership.
(2) If the offence is proved to have been committed with the consent or connivance of, or to be attributable to any neglect on the part of—
   (a) a senior officer of the body corporate or Scottish partnership, or
   (b) a person purporting to act in such a capacity, the senior officer or person (as well as the body corporate or partnership) is guilty of the offence and liable to be proceeded against and punished accordingly.

(3) In this section—
"director", in relation to a body corporate whose affairs are managed by its members, means a member of the body corporate,
"senior officer" means—
  (a) in relation to a body corporate, a director, manager, secretary or other similar officer of the body corporate, and
  (b) in relation to a Scottish partnership, a partner in the partnership.

267 Regulations

(1) Any power of the Secretary of State or the Treasury to make regulations under this Act—
  (a) is exercisable by statutory instrument,
  (b) may be exercised so as to make different provision for different purposes or different areas, and
  (c) includes power to make supplementary, incidental, consequential, transitional, transitory or saving provision.
(2) See sections 72(3) and 73(6) for the procedure for a statutory instrument containing regulations under section 71 to which section 72 applies or (as the case may be) regulations under section 73(4) to which section 73(5) applies (enhanced affirmative procedure).
(3) A statutory instrument containing regulations under—
  (a) section 12(4) or 271(2) which amend or repeal any provision of primary legislation,
  (b) section 46(2),
  (c) section 52(5),
  (d) section 83,
  (e) section 90(1),
  (f) section 239,
  (g) section 240(3),
  (h) section 245,
  (i) section 253,
  (j) section 257(1), or
  (k) paragraph 33 of Schedule 8, may not be made unless a draft of the instrument has been laid before, and approved by a resolution of, each House of Parliament.
(4) A statutory instrument containing—
  (a) regulations under section 12(4) or 271(2) to which subsection (3) does not apply,
  (b) regulations under section 65(5), or
  (c) regulations under paragraph 2(1)(b) of Schedule 5, is (if a draft of the instrument has not been laid before, and approved by a resolution of, each House of Parliament) subject to annulment in pursuance of a resolution of either House of Parliament.
(5) A statutory instrument containing—
  (a) regulations under section 10(3),
  (b) regulations under section 52(3),
  (c) regulations under section 58(8)(a),
  (d) regulations under section 71 to which section 72 does not apply,
  (e) regulations under section 73(4) to which section 73(5) does not apply,
  (f) regulations under section 133(6)(a), or
  (g) regulations under section 255(7), is subject to annulment in pursuance of a resolution of either House of Parliament.
(6) A statutory instrument containing regulations under paragraph 4 of Schedule 5 is subject to annulment in pursuance of a resolution of the House of Commons.

(7) See paragraphs 4(4) and 5(5) of Schedule 7 for the procedure for a statutory instrument containing regulations about the coming into force of a code of practice under that Schedule or of any revisions to such a code of practice (affirmative procedure or, in the case of the coming into force of revisions, a choice between that procedure and laying before Parliament after being made).
(8) A statutory instrument containing regulations which are subject to a particular parliamentary procedure under this Act may also include regulations which are subject to a different or no parliamentary procedure under this Act (but this subsection does not apply to regulations mentioned in subsection (2), (4), (6) or (7)).
(9) A statutory instrument which, by virtue of subsection (8), contains regulations which are subject to different parliamentary procedures, or one or more parliamentary procedure and no parliamentary procedure, is subject to whichever procedure is the higher procedure; and the order is as follows (the highest first)—
   (a) the procedure set out in subsection (3) (the affirmative procedure),
   (b) the procedure set out in subsection (5) above (the negative procedure),
   (c) no procedure.
(10) Provision is not prevented from being included in regulations made under this Act merely because the provision could have been included in other regulations made under this Act which would have been subject to a different or no parliamentary procedure.

268 Enhanced affirmative procedure

(1) For the purposes of regulations under section 71 to which section 72 applies and regulations under section 73(4) to which section 73(5) applies, the enhanced affirmative procedure is as follows.
(2) Subsection (3) applies if—
   (a) the Secretary of State has consulted under section 72(2) or (as the case may be) 73(5) in relation to making such regulations,
   (b) a period of at least 12 weeks, beginning with the day on which any such consultation first began, has elapsed, and
   (c) the Secretary of State considers it appropriate to proceed with making such regulations.
(3) The Secretary of State must lay before Parliament—
   (a) draft regulations, and
   (b) a document which explains the regulations.
(4) The Secretary of State may make regulations in the terms of the draft regulations laid under subsection (3) if, after the end of the 40-day period, the draft regulations are approved by a resolution of each House of Parliament.
(5) But subsections (6) to (9) apply instead of subsection (4) if—
   (a) either House of Parliament so resolves within the 30-day period, or
   (b) a committee of either House charged with reporting on the draft regulations so recommends within the 30-day period and the House to which the recommendation is made does not by resolution reject the recommendation within that period.
(6) The Secretary of State must have regard to—
   (a) any representations,
   (b) any resolution of either House of Parliament, and
   (c) any recommendations of a committee of either House of Parliament charged with reporting on the draft regulations, made during the 60-day period with regard to the draft regulations.

(7) If after the end of the 60-day period the draft regulations are approved by a resolution of each House of Parliament, the Secretary of State may make regulations in the terms of the draft regulations.

(8) If after the end of the 60-day period the Secretary of State wishes to proceed with the draft regulations but with material changes, the Secretary of State may lay before Parliament—
   (a) revised draft regulations, and
   (b) a statement giving a summary of the changes proposed.

(9) If the revised draft regulations are approved by a resolution of each House of Parliament, the Secretary of State may make regulations in the terms of the revised draft regulations.

(10) For the purposes of this section regulations are made in the terms of draft regulations or revised draft regulations if they contain no material changes to the provisions of the draft, or revised draft, regulations.

(11) References in this section to the "30-day", "40-day" and "60-day" periods in relation to any draft regulations are to the periods of 30, 40 and 60 days beginning with the day on which the draft regulations were laid before Parliament; and, for this purpose, no account is to be taken of any time during which Parliament is dissolved or prorogued or during which either House is adjourned for more than four days.

269 Financial provisions

There is to be paid out of money provided by Parliament—

(a) any expenditure incurred by a Minister of the Crown or government department by virtue of this Act, and
(b) any increase attributable to this Act in the sums payable by virtue of any other Act out of money so provided.

270 Transitional, transitory or saving provision

(1) Schedule 9 (which contains transitional, transitory and saving provision including a general saving for lawful conduct) has effect.
(2) The Secretary of State may by regulations make such transitional, transitory or saving provision as the Secretary of State considers appropriate in connection with the coming into force of any provision of this Act.

271 Minor and consequential provision

(1) Schedule 10 (which contains minor and consequential provision) has effect.
(2) The Secretary of State may by regulations make such provision as the Secretary of State considers appropriate in consequence of this Act.
(3) The power to make regulations under subsection (2) may, in particular, be exercised by modifying any provision made by or under an enactment.
(4) In subsection (3) "enactment" does not include any primary legislation passed or made after the end of the Session in which this Act is passed.

Final provision

272 Commencement, extent and short title

(1) Subject to subsections (2) and (3), this Act comes into force on such day as the Secretary of State may by regulations appoint; and different days may be appointed for different purposes.
(2) Sections 260 to 269, 270(2), 271(2) to (4) and this section come into force on the day on which this Act is passed.

Appendix

(3) Sections 227 and 228 come into force at the end of the period of two months beginning with the day on which this Act is passed.

(4) Subject to subsections (5) to (7), this Act extends to England and Wales, Scotland and Northern Ireland.

(5) An amendment, repeal or revocation made by this Act of an enactment has the same extent within the United Kingdom as the enactment amended, repealed or revoked.

(6) Her Majesty may by Order in Council provide for any of the provisions of this Act to extend, with or without modifications, to the Isle of Man or any of the British overseas territories.

(7) Any power under an Act to extend any provision of that Act by Order in Council to any of the Channel Islands may be exercised so as to extend there (with or without modifications) any amendment or repeal of that provision which is made by or under this Act.

(8) This Act may be cited as the Investigatory Powers Act 2016.

SCHEDULES
SCHEDULE 1 SECTION 7
MONETARY PENALTY NOTICES

PART 1

MONETARY PENALTY NOTICES

Payment of monetary penalties

1   (1) A monetary penalty imposed by a monetary penalty notice must be paid to the Commissioner within the period specified in the notice.

(2) The period specified under sub-paragraph (1) must not be less than 28 days beginning with the day after the day on which the notice is served.

(3) Any sum received by the Commissioner by virtue of a monetary penalty notice must be paid into the Consolidated Fund.

Contents of monetary penalty notices

2   A monetary penalty notice must, in particular—

   (a) state the name and address of the person on whom it is to be served,
   (b) provide details of the notice of intent served on that person (see paragraph 4),
   (c) state whether the Commissioner has received written representations in accordance with that notice of intent,
   (d) state the grounds on which the Commissioner serves the monetary penalty notice,
   (e) state the grounds on which the Commissioner decided the amount of the monetary penalty imposed by the monetary penalty notice,
   (f) state the details of how the monetary penalty is to be paid,
   (g) provide details of the person's rights of appeal under paragraph 8 in respect of the monetary penalty notice,
   (h) provide details of the Commissioner's rights of enforcement under paragraph 9 in respect of the monetary penalty notice.

Appendix

Enforcement obligations

3 (1) The Commissioner may include an enforcement obligation, or enforcement obligations, in a monetary penalty notice if the Commissioner considers that the interception to which the notice relates is continuing.
 (2) Each of the following is an enforcement obligation—
   (a) a requirement on the person on whom the notice is served to cease the interception on a specified day or within a specified period;
   (b) (where appropriate for achieving such a cessation) a requirement on the person to take specified steps within a specified period, or to refrain from taking specified steps after the end of a specified period.
 (3) An enforcement obligation may not have effect before the end of the period of 7 days beginning with the day after the day on which the notice is served.
 (4) Where an enforcement obligation is included in a monetary penalty notice under this paragraph, the notice must state what the obligation is and the grounds for including it.

Consultation requirements before service of monetary penalty notices

4 (1) The Commissioner must proceed in accordance with sub-paragraphs (2) to (7) before serving a monetary penalty notice on a person.
 (2) The Commissioner must serve a notice of intent on the person.
 (3) A notice of intent is a notice that the Commissioner proposes to serve a monetary penalty notice on the person.
 (4) A notice of intent served on a person must, in particular—
   (a) state the name and address of the person,
   (b) state the grounds on which the Commissioner proposes to serve the monetary penalty notice,
   (c) provide an indication of the amount of the monetary penalty that the Commissioner proposes to impose and the Commissioner's grounds for deciding that amount,
   (d) state whether the monetary penalty notice is to include any enforcement obligation and, if so, what the obligation is and the grounds for including it,
   (e) state the date on which the Commissioner proposes to serve the monetary penalty notice, (f) inform the person that the person may make written representations in relation to the Commissioner's proposal within a period specified in the notice, and
   (g) inform the person that the person may, within a period specified in the notice, request an oral hearing before the Commissioner in order to make representations of the kind mentioned in sub-paragraph (6)(b).
 (5) No period specified as mentioned in sub-paragraph (4)(f) or (g) may be less than 21 days beginning with the day after the day on which the notice is served.
 (6) Where the person has requested an oral hearing within the period specified for the purpose in the notice—
   (a) the Commissioner must arrange such a hearing, and
   (b) the person may make representations at the hearing about—
     (i) any matter falling within section 7(3)(c), or
     (ii) any other matter relating to the Commissioner's proposal which, by virtue of section 56, the person would be unable to raise on an appeal under paragraph 8.

Appendix

- (7) The Commissioner must consider any representations which have been made by the person in accordance with the notice or sub-paragraph (6).
- (8) If the Commissioner decides not to serve a monetary penalty notice on a person as a result of any representations which have been made by the person in accordance with a notice of intent or sub-paragraph (6), the Commissioner must inform the person of that fact.

5 (1) The Commissioner may not vary a notice of intent except as set out in subparagraph (2).
- (2) The Commissioner may vary a notice of intent by extending the period mentioned in paragraph 4(4)(f) or (g).
- (3) Sub-paragraph (1) does not prevent the Commissioner from serving a new notice of intent instead of varying such a notice.
- (4) The Commissioner may cancel a notice of intent.
- (5) A variation or cancellation of a notice of intent is effected by serving on the person on whom the notice was served a notice setting out the variation or cancellation.

6 (1) The Commissioner must not serve a monetary penalty notice on a person in respect of an interception if any notice of intent in respect of that interception was served on the person more than 3 months earlier.
- (2) But the Commissioner may serve a monetary penalty notice on a person where the service of the notice would otherwise be prevented by subparagraph (1) if the Commissioner—
  - (a) considers it reasonable to do so, and
  - (b) includes the reasons for doing so in the monetary penalty notice.

Variation or cancellation of monetary penalty notices

7 (1) The Commissioner may vary or cancel a monetary penalty notice.
- (2) But the Commissioner may not vary a monetary penalty notice in a way that is detrimental to the person on whom it was served (whether by increasing the amount of the monetary penalty, by reducing the period specified in the notice as the period within which the penalty must be paid, by imposing a new enforcement obligation or making an existing enforcement obligation effective earlier or otherwise more onerous, or otherwise).
- (3) The Commissioner must—
  - (a) in the case of a variation which reduces the amount of a monetary penalty, repay any excess already paid in accordance with the notice, and
  - (b) in the case of a cancellation, repay any amount already paid in accordance with the notice.
- (4) A variation or cancellation of a monetary penalty notice is effected by serving on the person on whom the monetary penalty notice was served a notice setting out the variation or cancellation.
- (5) The Commissioner may not serve another monetary penalty notice on a person in respect of an interception if the Commissioner has cancelled a previous notice served on the person in respect of the same interception.
- (6) If the Commissioner refuses a request by a person to vary or cancel a monetary penalty notice which has been served on the person, the Commissioner must inform the person of that fact.

Appeals in relation to monetary penalty notices

8 (1) A person on whom a monetary penalty notice is served may appeal to the First-tier Tribunal against—
   (a) the monetary penalty notice or any provision of it, or
   (b) any refusal of a request by the person to serve a notice of variation or cancellation in relation to the monetary penalty notice.
   (2) Where there is an appeal under sub-paragraph (1)(a) in relation to a monetary penalty notice or any provision of it, any requirement in the notice or (as the case may be) provision which does not relate to the imposition of an enforcement obligation need not be complied with until the appeal is withdrawn or finally determined.
   (3) Sub-paragraphs (4) to (6) apply in relation to an appeal under sub-paragraph (1)(a).
   (4) The First-tier Tribunal must allow the appeal or substitute such other monetary penalty notice as could have been served by the Commissioner if the Tribunal considers—
   (a) that the notice to which the appeal relates is not in accordance with the law, or
   (b) to the extent that the notice involved an exercise of discretion by the Commissioner, that the Commissioner ought to have exercised the discretion differently.
   (5) In any other case, the First-tier Tribunal must dismiss the appeal.
   (6) The First-tier Tribunal may review any determination of fact on which the notice was based.
   (7) Sub-paragraphs (8) to (10) apply in relation to an appeal under subparagraph (1)(b).
   (8) The First-tier Tribunal must direct the Commissioner to serve, on such terms as the Tribunal considers appropriate, a notice of variation or cancellation in relation to the monetary penalty notice if the Tribunal considers that the monetary penalty notice ought to be varied or cancelled on those terms.
   (9) In any other case, the First-tier Tribunal must dismiss the appeal.
   (10) The First-tier Tribunal may review any determination of fact on which the refusal to serve the notice of variation or cancellation was based.

Enforcement of monetary penalty notices

9 (1) This paragraph applies in relation to any penalty payable to the Commissioner by virtue of a monetary penalty notice.
   (2) In England and Wales or Northern Ireland, the penalty is recoverable—
   (a) if the county court in England and Wales or a county court in Northern Ireland so orders, as if it were payable under an order of that court, and
   (b) if the High Court so orders, as if it were payable under an order of that court.
   (3) In Scotland, the penalty is recoverable as if it were payable under an extract registered decree arbitral bearing a warrant for execution issued by the sheriff for any sheriffdom in Scotland.

10 (1) A person on whom a monetary penalty notice containing an enforcement obligation is served must comply with the obligation.
   (2) The duty imposed by sub-paragraph (1) is enforceable by civil proceedings by the Commissioner for an injunction, or for specific performance of a statutory duty under section 45 of the Court of Session Act 1988, or for any other appropriate relief.

Guidance

11 (1) The Commissioner must prepare and issue guidance on how the Commissioner proposes to exercise the Commissioner's functions under section 7 and this Schedule.
   (2) The guidance must, in particular, deal with—

Appendix

    (a) the manner in which the Commissioner is to deal with claims of a description specified in the guidance which may give rise to grounds for serving a monetary penalty notice,
    (b) the circumstances in which the Commissioner would consider it appropriate to serve a monetary penalty notice,
    (c) how the Commissioner will determine the amount of the penalty, and
    (d) the circumstances in which the Commissioner would consider it appropriate to impose an enforcement obligation.
(3) The Commissioner may alter or replace the guidance.
(4) If the guidance is altered or replaced, the Commissioner must issue the altered or replacement guidance.
(5) The Commissioner must arrange for the publication, in such form and manner as the Commissioner considers appropriate, of any guidance issued under this paragraph.

Interpretation of Part 1

12 In this Part of this Schedule—
"address" means—
(a) in the case of a registered company, the address of its registered office,
(b) in the case of a person (other than a registered company) carrying on a business, the address of the person's principal place of business in the United Kingdom, and
(c) in any other case, the person's last known address;
"the Commissioner" means the Investigatory Powers Commissioner;
"enforcement obligation" has the meaning given by paragraph 3(2);
"monetary penalty notice" means a monetary penalty notice under section 7;
"notice" means notice in writing;
"notice of intent" has the meaning given by paragraph 4(3);
"registered company" means a company registered under the enactments relating to companies for the time being in force in the United Kingdom.

PART 2

INFORMATION PROVISIONS

Information notices

13 (1) The Commissioner may by notice (an "information notice") request any person on whom the Commissioner is considering whether to serve a Part 1 notice of intent or a Part 1 monetary penalty notice to provide such information as the Commissioner reasonably requires for the purpose of deciding whether to serve it.
(2) Where the Commissioner requests that documents be produced, the Commissioner may take copies of, or extracts from, any document so produced.
(3) An information notice must—
    (a) specify or describe the information to be provided,
    (b) specify the manner in which, and the period within which, the information is to be provided,
    (c) state that the Commissioner considers that the information is information which the Commissioner reasonably requires for the purpose of deciding whether to serve a Part 1 notice of intent or (as the case may be) a Part 1 monetary penalty notice,
    (d) state the Commissioner's grounds for this view, and

Appendix

   (e) provide details of the rights of appeal under paragraph 15 in respect of the information notice.
(4) For the purposes of sub-paragraph (3)(b)—
   (a) specifying the manner in which the information is to be provided may include specifying the form in which it is to be provided, and
   (b) the specified period within which the information is to be provided must not be less than 28 days beginning with the day after the day on which the information notice is served.
14 (1) The Commissioner may not vary an information notice except as set out in sub-paragraph (2).
   (2) The Commissioner may vary an information notice by extending the period within which the information is to be provided if the person on whom the notice is served appeals under paragraph 15 in relation to the notice.
   (3) Sub-paragraph (1) does not prevent the Commissioner from serving a new information notice instead of varying such a notice.
   (4) The Commissioner may cancel an information notice.
   (5) A variation or cancellation of an information notice is effected by serving on the person on whom the notice was served a notice setting out the variation or cancellation.

Appeals in relation to information notices

15 (1) A person on whom an information notice is served may appeal to the Firsttier Tribunal against—
   (a) the information notice or any provision of it, or
   (b) any refusal of a request by the person to serve a notice of variation or cancellation in relation to the information notice.
   (2) Subject to paragraph 14(2), an appeal under this paragraph does not affect the need to comply with the information notice while the appeal has not been withdrawn or finally determined.
   (3) Sub-paragraphs (4) to (6) apply in relation to an appeal under sub-paragraph (1)(a).
   (4) The First-tier Tribunal must allow the appeal or substitute such other information notice as could have been served by the Commissioner if the Tribunal considers—
      (a) that the notice to which the appeal relates is not in accordance with the law, or
      (b) to the extent that the notice involved an exercise of discretion by the Commissioner, that the Commissioner ought to have exercised the discretion differently.
   (5) In any other case, the First-tier Tribunal must dismiss the appeal.
   (6) The First-tier Tribunal may review any determination of fact on which the notice was based.
   (7) Sub-paragraphs (8) to (10) apply in relation to an appeal under subparagraph (1)(b).
   (8) The First-tier Tribunal must direct the Commissioner to issue, on such terms as the Tribunal considers appropriate, a notice of variation or cancellation in relation to the information notice if the Tribunal considers that the information notice ought to be varied or cancelled on those terms.
   (9) In any other case, the First-tier Tribunal must dismiss the appeal.
   (10) The First-tier Tribunal may review any determination of fact on which the refusal to serve the notice of variation or cancellation was based.

Enforcement of information notices

16 (1) The Commissioner may serve a Part 2 monetary penalty notice on a person if the person—

Appendix

    (a) without reasonable excuse fails to comply with an information notice, or

    (b) knowingly or recklessly gives any information which is false in a material particular in response to an information notice.

(2) A Part 2 monetary penalty notice is a notice requiring the person on whom it is served to pay to the Commissioner a monetary penalty of an amount determined by the Commissioner and specified in the notice.

(3) The amount of a monetary penalty determined by the Commissioner under this paragraph may be—

    (a) a fixed amount,

    (b) an amount calculated by reference to a daily rate, or

    (c) a fixed amount and an amount calculated by reference to a daily rate.

(4) But the total amount payable must not exceed £10,000.

(5) In the case of an amount calculated by reference to a daily rate—

    (a) no account is to be taken of the day on which the Part 2 monetary penalty notice is served or any day before that day, and

    (b) the Part 2 monetary penalty notice must specify—

        (i) the day on which the amount first starts to accumulate and the circumstances in which it is to cease to accumulate, and

        (ii) the period or periods within which the amount, or any part or parts so far accumulated, must be paid to the Commissioner.

Any period falling within paragraph (b)(ii) must not be less than 28 days beginning with the day after the day on which the notice is served.

17 (1) Part 1 of this Schedule applies in relation to a Part 2 monetary penalty notice and the penalty that relates to that notice as it applies in relation to a Part 1 monetary penalty notice and the penalty that relates to that notice.

This is subject to the following modifications.

(2) The provisions in Part 1 of this Schedule so far as relating to enforcement obligations do not apply in relation to a Part 2 monetary penalty notice.

(3) Paragraph 4 has effect in relation to a Part 2 monetary penalty notice as if in sub-paragraph (6)(b) the reference to making representations about matters falling within sub-paragraph (6)(b)(i) or (ii) were a reference to making representations about matters falling within sub-paragraph (6)(b)(ii) only.

(4) Paragraph 6 has effect in relation to a Part 2 monetary penalty notice as if the references in sub-paragraph (1) to an interception were references to conduct falling within paragraph 16(1)(a) or (b).

(5) Paragraph 7(5) has effect in relation to a Part 2 monetary penalty notice as if the references to an interception were references to conduct falling within paragraph 16(1)(a) or (b).

Technical assistance for the Commissioner

18 (1) OFCOM must comply with any reasonable request made by the Commissioner, in connection with the Commissioner's functions under section 7 and this Schedule, for advice on technical and similar matters relating to electronic communications.

(2) For this purpose, the Commissioner may disclose to OFCOM any information obtained by the Commissioner under this Schedule.

(3) In this paragraph "OFCOM" means the Office of Communications established by section 1 of the Office of Communications Act 2002.

Interpretation of Part 2

19 In this Part of this Schedule—
"the Commissioner" means the Investigatory Powers Commissioner;
"enforcement obligation" has the meaning given by paragraph 3(2);
"information" includes documents; and any reference to providing or giving information includes a reference to producing a document;
"information notice" has the meaning given by paragraph 13(1);
"notice" means notice in writing;
"Part 1 monetary penalty notice" means a monetary penalty notice under section 7;
"Part 1 notice of intent" means a notice of intent (within the meaning of paragraph 4(3)) relating to a Part 1 monetary penalty notice;
"Part 2 monetary penalty notice" means a monetary penalty notice under paragraph 16.

SCHEDULE 2 SECTION 12(1)
ABOLITION OF DISCLOSURE POWERS

Health and Safety at Work etc. Act 1974

1 In section 20 of the Health and Safety at Work etc. Act 1974 (powers of inspectors), at end, insert—

"(9) Nothing in this section is to be read as enabling an inspector to secure the disclosure by a telecommunications operator or postal operator of communications data without the consent of the operator.

(10) In subsection (9) "communications data", "postal operator" and "telecommunications operator" have the same meanings as in the Investigatory Powers Act 2016 (see sections 261 and 262 of that Act)."

Criminal Justice Act 1987

2 In section 2 of the Criminal Justice Act 1987 (investigation powers of Director of Serious Fraud Office), after subsection (10), insert—

"(10A) Nothing in this section is to be read as enabling a person to secure the disclosure by a telecommunications operator or postal operator of communications data without the consent of the operator.

(10B) In subsection (10A) "communications data", "postal operator" and "telecommunications operator" have the same meanings as in the Investigatory Powers Act 2016 (see sections 261 and 262 of that Act)."

Consumer Protection Act 1987

3 In section 29 of the Consumer Protection Act 1987 (powers of search etc.), at end, insert—

"(8) The officer may not exercise a power under this section to secure the disclosure by a telecommunications operator or postal operator of communications data without the consent of the operator.

(9) In subsection (8) "communications data", "postal operator" and "telecommunications operator" have the same meanings as in the Investigatory Powers Act 2016 (see sections 261 and 262 of that Act)."

Appendix

Environmental Protection Act 1990

4 In section 71 of the Environmental Protection Act 1990 (obtaining of information from persons and authorities), at end, insert—

"(5) Nothing in this section is to be read as enabling a person to secure the disclosure by a telecommunications operator or postal operator of communications data without the consent of the operator.

(6) In subsection (5) "communications data", "postal operator" and "telecommunications operator" have the same meanings as in the Investigatory Powers Act 2016 (see sections 261 and 262 of that Act)."

Social Security Administration Act 1992

5 In section 109B of the Social Security Administration Act 1992 (power to require information)—
   (a) in subsection (2A) omit paragraph (j),
   (b) in subsection (2E) for the words from "for" to the end of the subsection substitute "so as to secure the disclosure by a telecommunications operator or postal operator of communications data without the consent of the operator.",
   (c) omit subsection (2F), and
   (d) in subsection (7)—
       (i) after the definition of "bank" insert—
           ""communications data" has the same meaning as in the Investigatory Powers Act 2016 (see sections 261 and 262 of that Act);",
       (ii) after the definition of "insurer" insert—
           ""postal operator" has the same meaning as in the Investigatory Powers Act 2016 (see section 262 of that Act);", and
       (iii) for the definition of "telecommunications service" substitute—
           ""telecommunications operator" has the same meaning as in the Investigatory Powers Act 2016 (see section 261 of that Act)."

6 In section 109C of the Social Security Administration Act 1992 (powers of entry) for subsection (6) substitute—

"(6) Subsections (2E) and (5) of section 109B apply for the purposes of this section as they apply for the purposes of that section."

Social Security Administration (Northern Ireland) Act 1992

7 In section 103B of the Social Security Administration (Northern Ireland) Act 1992 (power to require information)—
   (a) in subsection (2A) omit paragraph (i),
   (b) in subsection (2E) for the words from "for" to the end of the subsection substitute "so as to secure the disclosure by a telecommunications operator or postal operator of communications data without the consent of the operator.",
   (c) omit subsection (2F), and
   (d) in subsection (7)—
       (i) after the definition of "bank" insert—
           ""communications data" has the same meaning as in the Investigatory Powers Act 2016 (see sections 261 and 262 of that Act);",
       (ii) after the definition of "insurer" insert—
           ""postal operator" has the same meaning as in the Investigatory Powers Act 2016 (see section 262 of that Act);", and

(iii) for the definition of "telecommunications service" substitute—
""telecommunications operator" has the same meaning as in the Investigatory Powers Act 2016 (see section 261 of that Act)."

8   In section 103C of the Social Security Administration (Northern Ireland) Act 1992 (powers of entry) for subsection (6) substitute—
"(6) Subsections (2E) and (5) of section 103B apply for the purposes of this section as they apply for the purposes of that section."

Financial Services and Markets Act 2000

9   In section 175 of the Financial Services and Markets Act 2000 (information gathering and investigations: supplemental provision), after subsection (5), insert—
"(5A) Nothing in this Part is to be read as enabling a person to secure the disclosure by a telecommunications operator or postal operator of communications data without the consent of the operator.
(5B) In subsection (5A) "communications data", "postal operator" and "telecommunications operator" have the same meanings as in the Investigatory Powers Act 2016 (see sections 261 and 262 of that Act)."

Finance Act 2008

10 In Schedule 36 to the Finance Act 2008 (information and inspection powers), in paragraph 19 (restrictions on powers: types of information), at end, insert—
"(4) An information notice does not require a telecommunications operator or postal operator to provide or produce communications data.
(5) In sub-paragraph (4) "communications data", "postal operator" and "telecommunications operator" have the same meanings as in the Investigatory Powers Act 2016 (see sections 261 and 262 of that Act)."

Prevention of Social Housing Fraud (Power to Require Information) (England) Regulations 2014 (S.I. 2014/899)

11 In regulation 4 of the Prevention of Social Housing Fraud (Power to Require Information) (England) Regulations 2014 (power to require information from persons who provide telecommunications services etc.)—
(a) omit sub-paragraph (f) of paragraph (3),
(b) in sub-paragraph (g) of that paragraph for "(f)" substitute "(e)",
(c) omit paragraphs (6) and (7),
(d) after paragraph (10) insert—
"(10A) Nothing in this regulation is to be read as enabling a person to secure the disclosure by a telecommunications operator or postal operator of communications data without the consent of the operator.", and
(e) in paragraph (11)—
(i) after the definition of "bank" insert—
""communications data" has the same meaning as in the Investigatory Powers Act 2016 (see sections 261 and 262 of that Act);",
(ii) after the definition of "family" insert—
""postal operator" has the same meaning as in the Investigatory Powers Act 2016 (see section 262 of that Act);", and
(iii) for the definition of "telecommunications service" substitute—
""telecommunications operator" has the same meaning as in the Investigatory Powers Act 2016 (see section 261 of that Act)."

Appendix

SCHEDULE 3 SECTION 56

EXCEPTIONS TO SECTION 56

Introductory

1 This Schedule contains—
  (a) exceptions to the exclusion by section 56(1) of certain matters from legal proceedings, and
  (b) limitations on those exceptions where that exclusion will still apply.

Disclosures of lawfully intercepted communications

2 (1) Section 56(1)(a) does not prohibit the disclosure of any content of a communication, or any secondary data obtained from a communication, if the interception of that communication was lawful by virtue of any of the following provisions—
  (a) sections 6(1)(c) and 44 to 52;
  (b) sections 1(5)(c), 3 and 4 of the Regulation of Investigatory Powers Act 2000;
  (c) section 1(2)(b) and (3) of the Interception of Communications Act 1985.
 (2) Where any disclosure is proposed to be, or has been, made on the grounds that it is authorised by sub-paragraph (1), section 56(1) does not prohibit the doing of anything in, or for the purposes of, so much of any proceedings as relates to the question whether that disclosure is or was so authorised.

Disclosures of convictions for certain offences

3 Section 56(1)(b) does not prohibit the doing of anything that discloses any conduct of a person for which that person has been convicted of—
  (a) an offence under section 3(1), 43(7), 59 or 155,
  (b) an offence under section 1(1) or (2), 11(7) or 19 of the Regulation of Investigatory Powers Act 2000, or
  (c) an offence under section 1 of the Interception of Communications Act 1985.

Proceedings before the Investigatory Powers Tribunal etc.

4 Section 56(1) does not apply in relation to—
  (a) any proceedings before the Investigatory Powers Tribunal,
  (b) any proceedings on an appeal under section 67A of the Regulation of Investigatory Powers Act 2000 (appeal against decisions of the Tribunal etc.), or
  (c) any proceedings arising out of such an appeal.

Proceedings before Special Immigration Appeals Commission

5 (1) Section 56(1) does not apply in relation to—
  (a) any proceedings before the Special Immigration Appeals Commission, or
  (b) any proceedings arising out of proceedings before that Commission.
 (2) But sub-paragraph (1) does not permit the disclosure of anything to—
  (a) the appellant or (as the case may be) applicant to the Special Immigration Appeals Commission, or
  (b) any person who—
    (i) represents that appellant or applicant for the purposes of the proceedings, and
    (ii) does so otherwise than by virtue of appointment under section 6 of the Special Immigration Appeals Commission Act 1997.

Appendix

Proceedings before Proscribed Organisations Appeal Commission

6 (1) Section 56(1) does not apply in relation to—
  (a) any proceedings before the Proscribed Organisations Appeal Commission, or
  (b) any proceedings arising out of proceedings before that Commission.
 (2) But sub-paragraph (1) does not permit the disclosure of anything to any of the following—
  (a) the applicant to the Commission;
  (b) the organisation concerned (if different);
  (c) any person designated under paragraph 6 of Schedule 3 to the Terrorism Act 2000 to conduct the proceedings on behalf of that organisation;
  (d) any person who—
    (i) represents that appellant or that organisation for the purposes of the proceedings, and
    (ii) does so otherwise than by virtue of an appointment under paragraph 7 of that Schedule.

Closed material proceedings

7 (1) Section 56(1) does not apply in relation to any section 6 proceedings within the meaning given by section 14(1) of the Justice and Security Act 2013 (certain civil proceedings in which closed material applications may be made).
 (2) But sub-paragraph (1) does not permit a prohibited section 6 disclosure.
 (3) In the case of section 6 proceedings where the only relevant person is the Secretary of State, a "prohibited section 6 disclosure" means a disclosure of anything to—
  (a) any person, other than the Secretary of State, who is or was a party to the proceedings, or
  (b) any person who—
    (i) represents such a person for the purposes of the proceedings, and
    (ii) does so otherwise than by virtue of appointment as a special advocate.
 (4) In the case of section 6 proceedings where the Secretary of State is not the only relevant person, or is not a relevant person but is a party to the proceedings, a "prohibited section 6 disclosure" means a disclosure of anything to—
  (a) any person, other than the relevant person concerned or the Secretary of State, who is or was a party to the proceedings, or
  (b) any person who—
    (i) represents a person within paragraph (a) for the purposes of the proceedings, and
    (ii) does so otherwise than by virtue of appointment as a special advocate.
 (5) In this paragraph "relevant person", in relation to section 6 proceedings, has the meaning given by section 14(1) of the Justice and Security Act 2013.

TPIM proceedings

8 (1) Section 56(1) does not apply in relation to—
  (a) any TPIM proceedings, or
  (b) any proceedings arising out of any TPIM proceedings.
 (2) But sub-paragraph (1) does not permit the disclosure of anything to—
  (a) any person, other than the Secretary of State, who is or was a party to the proceedings, or
  (b) any person who—
    (i) represents such a person for the purposes of the proceedings, and
    (ii) does so otherwise than by virtue of appointment as a special advocate under Schedule 4 to the Terrorism Prevention and Investigation Measures Act 2011.

(3) In this paragraph "TPIM proceedings" has the same meaning as in the Terrorism Prevention and Investigation Measures Act 2011.

TEO proceedings

9   (1) Section 56(1) does not apply in relation to—
    (a) any TEO proceedings, or
    (b) any proceedings arising out of any TEO proceedings.
   (2) But sub-paragraph (1) does not permit the disclosure of anything to—
    (a) any person, other than the Secretary of State, who is or was a party to the proceedings, or
    (b) any person who—
        (i) represents such a person for the purposes of the proceedings, and
        (ii) does so otherwise than by virtue of appointment as a special advocate under Schedule 3 to the Counter-Terrorism and Security Act 2015.
   (3) In this paragraph "TEO proceedings" has the meaning given by paragraph 1 of Schedule 3 to the Counter-Terrorism and Security Act 2015 (temporary exclusion orders: proceedings).

Proceedings relating to freezing of terrorist assets etc.

10 (1) Section 56(1) does not apply in relation to—
    (a) any financial restrictions proceedings, or
    (b) any proceedings arising out of such proceedings.
   (2) In this paragraph "financial restrictions proceedings" has the meaning given by section 65 of the Counter-Terrorism Act 2008.
11 Section 56(1) does not apply in relation to any proceedings—
    (a) on an appeal under section 26, or an application under section 27, of the Terrorist Asset-Freezing etc. Act 2010 (appeals and reviews by the court), or
    (b) on a claim arising from any matter to which such an appeal or application relates, or any proceedings arising out of such proceedings.
12 But neither paragraph 10 nor paragraph 11 permits the disclosure of anything to—
    (a) any person, other than the Treasury, who is or was a party to the proceedings, or
    (b) any person who—
        (i) represents such a person for the purposes of the proceedings, and
        (ii) does so otherwise than by virtue of appointment as a special advocate.

Proceedings relating to release of prisoners etc. in Northern Ireland

13 (1) Section 56(1) does not apply in relation to—
    (a) any proceedings before—
        (i) the Parole Commissioners for Northern Ireland, or
        (ii) any Sentence Review Commissioners appointed under section 1 of the Northern Ireland (Sentences) Act 1998, or
    (b) any proceedings arising out of such proceedings.
   (2) But sub-paragraph (1) does not permit the disclosure of anything to—
    (a) any person, other than the Secretary of State, who is or was a party to the proceedings, or
    (b) any person who—
        (i) represents such a person for the purposes of the proceedings, and
        (ii) does so otherwise than by virtue of appointment as a special advocate.

Employment or industrial tribunal proceedings

14 (1) Section 56(1) does not apply in relation to any proceedings before an employment tribunal where the applicant, or the applicant's representatives, are excluded for all or part of the proceedings pursuant to—
   (a) a direction to the tribunal by virtue of section 10(5)(b) or (c) of the Employment Tribunals Act 1996 (exclusion from Crown employment proceedings by direction of Minister in interests of national security), or
   (b) a determination of the tribunal by virtue of section 10(6) of that Act (determination by tribunal in interests of national security).
(2) Section 56(1) does not apply in relation to any proceedings before an industrial tribunal in Northern Ireland where the applicant, or the applicant's representatives, are excluded for all or part of the proceedings pursuant to—
   (a) a direction to the tribunal by virtue of Article 12(5)(b) or (c) of the Industrial Tribunals (Northern Ireland) Order 1996 (S.I. 1996/1921 (N.I. 18)) (exclusion from Crown employment proceedings by direction of Minister in interests of national security), or
   (b) a determination of the tribunal by virtue of Article 12(6) of that Order (determination by tribunal in interests of national security).
(3) Section 56(1) does not apply in relation to any proceedings arising out of proceedings within sub-paragraph (1) or (2).

15 But paragraph 14 does not permit the disclosure of anything to—
   (a) the person who is or was the applicant in the proceedings before the employment or industrial tribunal, or
   (b) any person who—
      (i) represents that person for the purposes of any proceedings within paragraph 14, and
      (ii) does so otherwise than by virtue of appointment as a special advocate.

Proceedings relating to dismissal for certain offences

16 Section 56(1) does not prohibit anything done in, for the purposes of, or in connection with, so much of any legal proceedings as relates to the fairness or unfairness of a dismissal on the following grounds—
   (a) any conduct constituting an offence under section 3(1), 43(7), 59 or 155;
   (b) any conduct taking place before the coming into force of this paragraph and constituting—
      (i) an offence under section 1(1) or (2), 11(7) or 19 of the Regulation of Investigatory Powers Act 2000, or
      (ii) an offence under section 1 of the Interception of Communications Act 1985.

Proceedings on appeals relating to claims of discrimination in Northern Ireland

17 (1) Section 56(1) does not apply in relation to any proceedings on an appeal under Article 80(2) of the Fair Employment and Treatment (Northern Ireland) Order 1998 (S.I. 1998/3162 (N.I. 21)) where—
   (a) the appeal relates to a claim of discrimination in contravention of Part 3 of that Order (employment cases) and to a certificate of the Secretary of State that the act concerned was justified for the purpose of safeguarding national security, and
   (b) a party to the appeal, or the party's representatives, are excluded for all or part of the proceedings by virtue of section 91(4)(b) of the Northern Ireland Act 1998.
(2) Section 56(1) does not apply in relation to any proceedings arising out of proceedings within sub-paragraph (1).

18 But paragraph 17 does not permit the disclosure of anything to—
  (a) any person who is or was excluded from all or part of the proceedings mentioned in paragraph 17(1), or
  (b) any person who—
    (i) represents such a person for the purposes of any proceedings within paragraph 17, and
    (ii) does so otherwise than by virtue of appointment as a special advocate.

Civil proceedings for enforcement of duty to assist with implementation of warrants

19 Section 56(1) does not apply in relation to any civil proceedings under section 43(8) of this Act or section 11(8) of the Regulation of Investigatory Powers Act 2000 (enforcement of duty of operators to assist with implementation of warrants).

Proceedings for certain offences

20 (1) Section 56(1) does not apply in relation to any proceedings for a relevant offence.
  (2) "Relevant offence" means—
    (a) an offence under any provision of this Act;
    (b) an offence under section 1 of the Interception of Communications Act 1985;
    (c) an offence under any provision of the Regulation of Investigatory Powers Act 2000;
    (d) an offence under section 47 or 48 of the Wireless Telegraphy Act 2006;
    (e) an offence under section 83 or 84 of the Postal Services Act 2000;
    (f) an offence under section 4 of the Official Secrets Act 1989 relating to any such information, document or article as is mentioned in subsection (3)(a) or (c) of that section;
    (g) an offence under section 1 or 2 of the Official Secrets Act 1911 relating to any sketch, plan, model, article, note, document or information which—
      (i) incorporates, or relates to, the content of any intercepted communication or any secondary data obtained from a communication, or
      (ii) tends to suggest that any interception-related conduct has or may have occurred or may be going to occur;
    (h) an offence of perjury committed in the course of any relevant proceedings;
    (i) an offence of attempting or conspiring to commit an offence falling within any of paragraphs (a) to (h);
    (j) an offence under Part 2 of the Serious Crime Act 2007 in relation to an offence falling within any of those paragraphs;
    (k) an offence of aiding, abetting, counselling or procuring the commission of an offence falling within any of those paragraphs;
    (l) contempt of court committed in the course of, or in relation to, any relevant proceedings.
  (3) In this paragraph—
    "intercepted communication" and "interception-related conduct" have the same meaning as in section 56;
    "relevant proceedings" means any proceedings mentioned in paragraphs 4 to 19.

Disclosures to prosecutors and judges

21 (1) Nothing in section 56(1) prohibits—
  (a) a disclosure to a person ("P") conducting a criminal prosecution that is made for the purpose only of enabling P to determine what is required of P by P's duty to secure the fairness of the prosecution, or

(b) a disclosure to a relevant judge in a case in which the judge has ordered the disclosure to be made to the judge alone.

(2) A relevant judge may order a disclosure under sub-paragraph (1)(b) only if the judge considers that the exceptional circumstances of the case make the disclosure essential in the interests of justice.

(3) Where in any criminal proceedings—
   (a) a relevant judge orders a disclosure under sub-paragraph (1)(b), and
   (b) in consequence of that disclosure, the judge considers that there are exceptional circumstances requiring the judge to make a direction under this sub-paragraph, the judge may direct the person conducting the prosecution to make for the purposes of the proceedings any admission of fact which the judge considers essential in the interests of justice.

(4) But nothing in any direction under sub-paragraph (3) may authorise or require anything to be done in contravention of section 56(1).

(5) In this paragraph "relevant judge" means—
   (a) any judge of the High Court or of the Crown Court or any Circuit judge,
   (b) any judge of the High Court of Justiciary or any sheriff,
   (c) in relation to proceedings before the Court Martial, the judge advocate for those proceedings, or
   (d) any person holding a judicial office that entitles the person to exercise the jurisdiction of a judge falling within paragraph (a) or (b).

Disclosures to inquiries and inquests

22 (1) Nothing in section 56(1) prohibits—
   (a) a disclosure to the panel of an inquiry held under the Inquiries Act 2005, or
   (b) a disclosure to a person appointed as legal adviser to such an inquiry, where, in the course of the inquiry, the panel has ordered the disclosure to be made to the panel alone or (as the case may be) to the panel and any person appointed as legal adviser to the inquiry.

(2) The panel of an inquiry may order a disclosure under sub-paragraph (1) only if it considers that the exceptional circumstances of the case make the disclosure essential to enable the inquiry to fulfil its terms of reference.

(3) Any reference in this paragraph to a person appointed as legal adviser to an inquiry is a reference to a person appointed as solicitor or counsel to the inquiry.

23 (1) Section 56(1) does not apply in relation to any restricted proceedings of an inquiry held under the Inquiries Act 2005.

(2) Proceedings of an inquiry held under that Act are "restricted proceedings" for the purposes of this paragraph if restrictions imposed under section 19 of that Act are in force prohibiting attendance at the proceedings by any person who is not—
   (a) a member of the panel of the inquiry,
   (b) a person appointed as legal adviser to the inquiry,
   (c) a person who is a relevant party to the proceedings,
   (d) a person representing such a person for the purposes of the proceedings, or
   (e) a person performing functions necessary for the proper functioning of the proceedings.

(3) But sub-paragraph (1) does not permit any disclosure which has not been made in accordance with paragraph 22(1).

(4) In this paragraph "relevant party", in relation to any proceedings of an inquiry, means—
   (a) any person making a disclosure to the panel of the inquiry, or to a person appointed as legal adviser to the inquiry, in accordance with paragraph 22(1);
   (b) any person giving evidence to the inquiry in circumstances where, in the absence of sub-paragraph (1), the prohibition imposed by section 56(1) would be breached;
   (c) any person whose conduct is the interception-related conduct (within the meaning of section 56) to which the disclosure or evidence relates (whether or not that conduct has in fact occurred);
   (d) any other person to whom the subject-matter of the disclosure or evidence has been lawfully disclosed in accordance with section 58.

(5) Any reference in this paragraph to a person appointed as legal adviser to an inquiry is to be read in accordance with paragraph 22(3).

24 (1) Nothing in section 56(1) prohibits—
   (a) a disclosure to a person (the "nominated person") nominated under paragraph 3(1) of Schedule 10 to the Coroners and Justice Act 2009 (investigation by judge or former judge) to conduct an investigation into a person's death, or
   (b) a disclosure to a person appointed as legal adviser to an inquest forming part of an investigation conducted by the nominated person, where, in the course of the investigation, the nominated person has ordered the disclosure to be made to the nominated person alone or (as the case may be) to the nominated person and any person appointed as legal adviser to the inquest.

(2) The nominated person may order a disclosure under sub-paragraph (1) only if the person considers that the exceptional circumstances of the case make the disclosure essential in the interests of justice.

(3) In a case where a person who is not a nominated person is or has been conducting an investigation under Part 1 of the Coroners and Justice Act 2009 into a person's death, nothing in section 56(1) prohibits—
   (a) a disclosure to the person that there is intercepted material in existence which is, or may be, relevant to the investigation;
   (b) a disclosure to a person appointed as legal adviser to an inquest forming part of the investigation which is made for the purposes of determining—
      (i) whether any intercepted material is, or may be, relevant to the investigation, and
      (ii) if so, whether it is necessary for the material to be disclosed to the person conducting the investigation.

(4) In sub-paragraph (3) "intercepted material" means—
   (a) any content of an intercepted communication (within the meaning of section 56), or
   (b) any secondary data obtained from a communication.

(5) Any reference in this paragraph to a person appointed as legal adviser to an inquest is a reference to a person appointed as solicitor or counsel to the inquest.

Appendix

SCHEDULE 4 SECTION 70(1)
RELEVANT PUBLIC AUTHORITIES AND DESIGNATED SENIOR OFFICERS ETC.

PART 1
TABLE OF AUTHORITIES AND OFFICERS ETC.

Table

(1) *Relevant public authority*	(2) *DSO: minimum office, rank or position*	(3) *Type of communications data that may be obtained by DSO*	(4) *Paragraphs of section 61(7) specified for DSO*
Police force maintained under section 2 of the Police Act 1996	Inspector	Entity data	(a), (b), (c), (d), (e), (g) and (i)
	Superintendent	All	(a), (b), (c), (d), (e), (g) and (i)
Metropolitan police force	Inspector	Entity data	(a), (b), (c), (d), (e), (g) and (i)
	Superintendent	All	(a), (b), (c), (d), (e), (g) and (i)
City of London police force	Inspector	Entity data	(a), (b), (c), (d), (e), (g) and (i)
	Superintendent	All	(a), (b), (c), (d), (e), (g) and (i)
Police Service of Scotland	Inspector	Entity data	(a), (b), (c), (d), (e), (g) and (i)
	Superintendent	All	(a), (b), (c), (d), (e), (g) and (i)
Police Service of Northern Ireland	Inspector	Entity data	(a), (b), (c), (d), (e), (g) and (i)
	Superintendent	All	(a), (b), (c), (d), (e), (g) and (i)
British Transport Police Force	Inspector	Entity data	(a), (b), (c), (d), (e), (g) and (i)
	Superintendent	All	(a), (b), (c), (d), (e), (g) and (i)
Ministry of Defence Police	Inspector	Entity data	(a), (b), (c) and (g)
	Superintendent	All	(a), (b), (c) and (g)
Royal Navy Police	Lieutenant Commander	Entity data	(a), (b), (c) and (g)
	Commander	All	(a), (b), (c) and (g)
Royal Military Police	Major	Entity data	(a), (b), (c) and (g)
	Lieutenant Colonel	All	(a), (b), (c) and (g)

Appendix

(1) Relevant public authority	(2) DSO: minimum office, rank or position	(3) Type of communications data that may be obtained by DSO	(4) Paragraphs of section 61(7) specified for DSO
Royal Air Force Police	Squadron Leader	Entity data	(a), (b), (c) and (g)
	Wing Commander Security Service	All	(a), (b), (c) and (g)
Security Service	General Duties 4 or any other level 4 officer	Entity data	(a), (b) and (c)
		All	(a), (b) and (c)
	General Duties 3 or any other level 3 officer		
Secret Intelligence Service	Grade 6	All	(a), (b) and (c)
GCHQ	GC8	All	(a), (b) and (c)
Ministry of Defence	Member of the Senior Civil Service or equivalent	All	(a)
		All	(b)
	Grade 7 in the Fraud Defence Unit		
Department of Health	Grade 7 in the Medicines and Healthcare Products Regulatory Agency	All	(b), (d) and (e)
		All	(b)
	Grade 7 in the Anti-Fraud Unit		
Home Office	Immigration inspector or equivalent with responsibility for investigations or other functions relating to immigration and border security	All	(b)
		All	(b)
		All	(b)
		All	(b), (d) and (i)
	Immigration inspector or equivalent with responsibility for anti-corruption in relation to investigations or other functions relating to immigration and border security Immigration inspector or equivalent with responsibility for asylum fraud investigations Immigration inspector or equivalent with responsibility for security and intelligence in the immigration detention estate		
Ministry of Justice	Manager in the security group of the National Offender Management Service responsible for Intelligence	Entity data	(b) and (d)
		All	(b) and (d)
	Senior manager in the security group of the National Offender Management Service responsible for intelligence		

(continued)

465

Appendix

(1) Relevant public authority	(2) DSO: minimum office, rank or position	(3) Type of communications data that may be obtained by DSO	(4) Paragraphs of section 61(7) specified for DSO
National Crime Agency	Grade 3 Grade 2	Entity data Entity data (b), (g) and (i) Grade 2 All	(b), (g) and (i) (b), (g) and (i)
Her Majesty's Revenue and Customs	Higher officer Senior officer	Entity data All	(b) and (f) (b) and (f)
Department for Transport	Enforcement Officer in Maritime and Coastguard Agency Head of Enforcement in Maritime and Coastguard Agency Maritime Operations Commander (grade 7) in the Maritime and Coastguard Agency Principal Inspector in the Air Accident Investigation Branch, the Marine Accident Investigation Branch or the Rail Accident Investigation Branch	Entity data All All All	(b) and (d) (b) and (d) (g) (d)
Department for Work and Pensions	Senior Executive Officer in Fraud and Error Services Senior Executive Officer in the Child Maintenance Group Central Legal Services	All All	(b) (b)
An ambulance trust in England	Duty Manager of Ambulance Trust Control Rooms	All	(g)
Common Services Agency for the Scottish Health Service	Head of Counter Fraud Services	All	(b)
Competition and Markets Authority	Member of the Senior Civil Service with responsibility for cartels or criminal enforcement	All	(b)

Appendix

(1) Relevant public authority	(2) DSO: minimum office, rank or position	(3) Type of communications data that may be obtained by DSO	(4) Paragraphs of section 61(7) specified for DSO
Criminal Cases Review Commission	Investigations Adviser	All	(h)
Department for Communities in Northern Ireland	Deputy Principal	All	(b)
Department for the Economy in Northern Ireland	Deputy chief inspector in trading standards services	All	(b)
Department of Justice in Northern Ireland	Governor 4 in the Northern Ireland Prison Service	All	(b), (d) and (i)
Financial Conduct Authority	Head of department in the Enforcement and Market Oversight Division	All	(b) and (j)
A fire and rescue authority under the Fire and Rescue Services Act 2004	Watch Manager (Control)	All	(g)
Food Standards Agency	Grade 6	All	(b)
Food Standards Scotland	Head of the Scottish Food Crime and Incidents Unit	All	(b)
Gambling Commission	Senior manager	All	(b)
Gangmasters and Labour Abuse Authority	Head of operations	All	(b)
Health and Safety Executive	Band 1 inspector	All	(b), (d) and (e)
Independent Police Complaints Commission	Deputy Chair or Director	All	(b) and (i)
Information Commissioner	Group Manager	Entity data	(b)
	Head of enforcement or an equivalent grade	All	(b)
National Health Service Business Services Authority	Senior manager (of pay b and 8b) in the Counter Fraud and Security Management Services Division	All	(b)

(continued)

Appendix

(1) Relevant public authority	(2) DSO: minimum office, rank or position	(3) Type of communications data that may be obtained by DSO	(4) Paragraphs of section 61(7) specified for DSO
Northern Ireland Ambulance Service Health and Social Care Trust	Watch Manager (Control)	All	(g)
Northern Ireland Fire and Rescue Service Board	Watch Manager (Control)	All	(g)
Northern Ireland Health and Social Care Regional Business Services Organisation	Assistant Director Counter Fraud and Probity Services	All	(b)
Office of Communications	Senior associate	All	(b)
Office of the Police Ombudsman for Northern Ireland	Senior investigating officer	All	(b)
Police Investigations and Review Commissioner	Commissioner or Director of Operations	All	(b) and (i)
Scottish Ambulance Service Board	Watch Manager (Control)	All	(g)
Scottish Criminal Cases Review Commission	Investigations Adviser	All	(h)
Serious Fraud Office	Grade 6	All	(b)
Welsh Ambulance Services National Health Service Trust	Watch Manager (Control)	All	(g)

Appendix

PART 2

INTERPRETATION OF TABLE

1 In the table in Part 1 of this Schedule—
"ambulance trust in England" means—
   (a) an NHS trust all or most of whose hospitals, establishments and facilities are in England and which provides ambulance services, or
   (b) an NHS foundation trust which provides such services, "entity data" means any communications data which is entity data.

SCHEDULE 5 SECTION 83(5)

TRANSFER AND AGENCY ARRANGEMENTS WITH PUBLIC AUTHORITIES: FURTHER PROVISIONS

Particular safeguards in connection with operation of section 69

1 (1) The following provisions apply where the functions of the Secretary of State under section 67 are exercisable by a public authority by virtue of regulations under section 83(1).

(2) The measures adopted or arrangements made by the public authority for the purpose of complying with the requirements of section 69 must be such as are approved by the Secretary of State.

(3) Any report required by section 69(6)(b) or (8) must be made to the Secretary of State as well as to the Investigatory Powers Commissioner.

Requirement for public authority to provide reports to Secretary of State

2 (1) A public authority, when exercising functions by virtue of regulations under section 83(1), must at least once in each calendar year make a report to the Secretary of State on—
   (a) the discharge of the functions, and
   (b) such other matters as the Secretary of State may by regulations require.

(2) Regulations under section 83(1) may, in particular, modify sub-paragraph (1) as it has effect in relation to the calendar year in which the regulations come into force or are revoked.

(3) The Secretary of State may agree to a report under this paragraph being combined with any other report which the public authority concerned is required to, or may, make to the Secretary of State.

Transfer schemes in connection with transfer of functions

3 (1) The Secretary of State may, in connection with regulations under section 83(1), make a scheme for the transfer of property, rights or liabilities.

(2) The things that may be transferred under a transfer scheme include—
   (a) property, rights and liabilities which could not otherwise be transferred,
   (b) property acquired, and rights and liabilities arising, after the making of the scheme.

(3) A transfer scheme may make consequential, supplementary, incidental, transitional, transitory or saving provision and may, in particular—

Appendix

(a) create rights, or impose liabilities, in relation to property or rights transferred,
(b) make provision about the continuing effect of things done by, on behalf of or in relation to the transferor in respect of anything transferred,
(c) make provision about the continuation of things (including legal proceedings) in the process of being done by, on behalf of or in relation to the transferor in respect of anything transferred,
(d) make provision for references to the transferor in an instrument or other document in respect of anything transferred to be treated as references to the transferee,
(e) make provision for the shared ownership or use of property, (f) if the TUPE regulations do not apply in relation to the transfer, make provision which is the same or similar.

(4) A transfer scheme may provide—
  (a) for modification by agreement,
  (b) for modifications to have effect from the date when the original scheme came into effect.

(5) A transfer scheme may confer a discretion on the Secretary of State to pay compensation to any person whose interests are adversely affected by the scheme.

(6) A transfer scheme may be included in regulations under section 83(1) but, if not so included, must be laid before Parliament after being made.

(7) For the purposes of this paragraph references to rights and liabilities include references to—
  (a) rights and liabilities relating to a contract of employment, and
  (b) rights and liabilities of the Crown relating to the terms of employment of individuals in the civil service.

(8) Accordingly, a transfer scheme may, in particular, provide—
  (a) for—
    (i) an individual employed in the civil service to become an employee of the transferee, or
    (ii) an employee of the transferor to become an employee of the transferee or an individual employed in the civil service,
  (b) for—
    (i) the individual's terms of employment in the civil service to have effect (subject to any necessary modifications) as the terms of the individual's contract of employment with the transferee, or
    (ii) (as the case may be) the individual's contract of employment to have effect (subject to any necessary modifications) as the terms of the individual's contract of employment with the transferee or, where the transferee is the Secretary of State, the individual's terms of employment with the civil service, (c) for the transfer of rights and liabilities of the Crown or another public authority under or in connection with the individual's terms of employment.

(9) In this paragraph—
"civil service" means the civil service of the State,
"TUPE regulations" means the Transfer of Undertakings (Protection of Employment) Regulations 2006 (S.I. 2006/246), and references to the transfer of property include the grant of a lease.

Appendix

Tax in connection with transfer schemes

4 (1) The Treasury may by regulations make provision varying the way in which a relevant tax has effect in relation to—
   (a) anything transferred under a transfer scheme, or
   (b) anything done for the purposes of, or in relation to, a transfer under a transfer scheme.
   (2) The provision which may be made under sub-paragraph (1)(a) includes, in particular, provision for—
   (a) a tax provision not to apply, or to apply with modifications, in relation to anything transferred,
   (b) anything transferred to be treated in a specified way for the purposes of a tax provision,
   (c) the Secretary of State to be required or permitted to determine, or specify the method for determining, anything which needs to be determined for the purposes of any tax provision so far as relating to anything transferred.
   (3) The provision which may be made under sub-paragraph (1)(b) includes, in particular, provision for—
   (a) a tax provision not to apply, or to apply with modifications, in relation to anything done for the purposes of, or in relation to, the transfer,
   (b) anything done for the purposes of, or in relation to, the transfer to have or not have a specified consequence or be treated in a specified way,
   (c) the Secretary of State to be required or permitted to determine, or specify the method for determining, anything which needs to be determined for the purposes of any tax provision so far as relating to anything done for the purposes of, or in relation to, the transfer.
   (4) In this paragraph—
   "relevant tax" means income tax, corporation tax, capital gains tax, stamp duty, stamp duty reserve tax or stamp duty land tax,
   "tax provision" means any provision—
   (a) about a relevant tax, and
   (b) made by an enactment,
   "transfer scheme" means a transfer scheme under paragraph 3, and references to the transfer of property include the grant of a lease.

Supplementary and other general provision

5 The power to make regulations under section 83(1) includes, in particular, power to—
   (a) modify any enactment about a public authority for the purpose of enabling or otherwise facilitating any function under sections 67 to 69 to be exercisable by the public authority,
   (b) impose requirements or confer other functions on a public authority in connection with functions transferred by the regulations.

6 The power to make regulations under—
   (a) section 83, or
   (b) paragraph 4 above, including that power as extended (whether by section 267(1) or otherwise) may, in particular, be exercised by modifying any enactment (including this Act).

Appendix

SCHEDULE 6 SECTION 106
ISSUE OF WARRANTS UNDER SECTION 106 ETC: TABLE

Part 1
TABLE: PART 1

Law enforcement chiefs	*Appropriate delegates*	*Appropriate law enforcement officers*
The Chief Constable of a police force maintained under section 2 of the Police Act 1996.	The person who is the appropriate deputy chief constable for the purposes of section 12A(1) of the Police Act 1996. The person holding the rank of assistant chief constable designated to act under section 12A(2) of that Act. If it is not reasonably practicable for either of those persons to act, any other person holding the rank of assistant chief constable in the force.	A member of the police force, a member of a collaborative force or a National Crime Agency officer who is included in a collaboration agreement with the police force.
The Commissioner, or an Assistant Commissioner, of the metropolitan police force.	A person holding the rank of commander in the metropolitan police force.	A member of the metropolitan police force, a member of a collaborative force or a National Crime Agency officer who is included in a collaboration agreement with the metropolitan police force.
The Commissioner of Police for the City of London.	The person authorised to act under section 25 of the City of London Police Act 1839 or, if it is not reasonably practicable for that person to act, a person holding the rank of commander in the City of London police force.	A member of the City of London police force, a member of a collaborative force or a National Crime Agency officer who is included in a collaboration agreement with the City of London police force.
The chief constable of the Police Service of Scotland.	Any deputy chief constable or assistant chief constable of the Police Service of Scotland who is designated for the purpose by the chief constable.	A constable of the Police Service of Scotland.
The Chief Constable or a Deputy Chief Constable of the Police Service of Northern Ireland.	A person holding the rank of assistant chief constable in the Police Service of Northern Ireland.	A member of the Police Service of Northern Ireland.
The Director General of the National Crime Agency.	A senior National Crime Agency Officer designated for the purpose by the Director General of the National Crime Agency.	A National Crime Agency officer or a member of a collaborative police force.
The Chief Constable of the British Transport Police Force.	A person holding the rank of deputy or assistant chief constable in the British Transport Police Force.	A member of the British Transport Police Force.

Appendix

Law enforcement chiefs	Appropriate delegates	Appropriate law enforcement officers
The Chief Constable of the Ministry of Defence Police.	A person holding the rank of deputy chief constable or assistant chief constable in the Ministry of Defence Police.	A member of the Ministry of Defence Police.
The Provost Marshal of the Royal Navy Police.	A person holding the position of deputy Provost Marshal in the Royal Navy Police.	A member of the Royal Navy Police.
The Provost Marshal of the Royal Military Police.	A person holding the position of deputy Provost Marshal in the Royal Military Police.	A member of the Royal Military Police.
The Provost Marshal of the Royal Air Force Police.	A person holding the position of deputy Provost Marshal in the Royal Air Force Police.	A member of the Royal Air Force Police.

Part 2
TABLE: PART 2

Law enforcement chiefs	Appropriate delegates	Appropriate law enforcement officers
An immigration officer who is a senior official and who is designated for the purpose by the Secretary of State.	A senior official in the department of the Secretary of State by whom functions relating to immigration are exercisable who is designated for the purpose by the Secretary of State.	An immigration officer.
An officer of Revenue and Customs who is a senior official and who is designated for the purpose by the Commissioners for Her Majesty's Revenue and Customs.	An officer of Revenue and Customs who is a senior official and who is designated for the purpose by the Commissioners for Her Majesty's Revenue and Customs.	An officer of Revenue and Customs.
A designated customs official who is a senior official and who is designated for the purpose by the Secretary of State.	A designated customs official who is a senior official and who is designated for the purpose by the Secretary of State.	A designated customs official.
The Chair of the Competition and Markets Authority.	An officer of the Competition and Markets Authority designated by it for the purpose.	An officer of the Competition and Markets Authority.
The chairman, or a deputy chairman, of the Independent Police Complaints Commission.	A member (other than the chair or a deputy chairman) of the Independent Police Complaints Commission who is designated by the chairman for the purpose.	A person designated under paragraph 19(2) of Schedule 3 to the Police Reform Act 2002 to take charge of, or to assist with, the investigation to which the warrant under section 106(1) relates (or would relate if issued).
The Police Investigations and Review Commissioner.	A staff officer of the Police Investigations and Review Commissioner who is designated by the Commissioner for the purpose.	A staff officer of the Police Investigations and Review Commissioner.

Part 3
INTERPRETATION OF THE TABLE

1 (1) This paragraph applies for the purposes of the first three entries in Part 1 of the table.
   (2) A police force (police force 1) is a collaborative force in relation to another police force (police force 2) if—
      (a) the chief officers of both police forces are parties to the same agreement under section 22A of the Police Act 1996, and
      (b) the members of police force 1 are permitted by the terms of the agreement to make applications under section 106 to the chief officer of police force 2.
   (3) A National Crime Agency officer is included in a collaboration agreement with a police force if—
      (a) the Director General of the National Crime Agency and the chief officer of the police force are parties to the same agreement under section 22A of the Police Act 1996, and
      (b) the National Crime Agency officer is permitted by the terms of the agreement to make applications under section 106 to the chief officer of the police force.
2 (1) This paragraph applies for the purposes of the sixth entry in Part 1 of the table (which relates to the National Crime Agency).
   (2) A police force is a collaborative police force in relation to the National Crime Agency if—
      (a) the chief officer of the police force and the Director General of the National Crime Agency are parties to the same agreement under section 22A of the Police Act 1996, and
      (b) the members of the police force are permitted by the terms of the agreement to make applications under section 106 to the Director General of the National Crime Agency.
3 For the purpose of the sixth entry in Part 2 of the table, the reference to a staff officer of the Police Investigations and Review Commissioner is a reference to any person who—
      (a) is a member of the Commissioner's staff appointed under paragraph 7A of schedule 4 to the Police, Public Order and Criminal Justice (Scotland) Act 2006 (asp 10), or
      (b) is a member of the Commissioner's staff appointed under paragraph 7 of that schedule to whom paragraph 7B(2) of that schedule applies.
4 In this Schedule, "police force" means—
      (a) any police force maintained under section 2 of the Police Act 1996;
      (b) the metropolitan police force;
      (c) the City of London police force.

SCHEDULE 7 SECTION 241

CODES OF PRACTICE

Scope of codes

1 (1) The Secretary of State must issue one or more codes of practice about the exercise of functions conferred by virtue of this Act.
   (2) Sub-paragraph (1) does not apply in relation to—
      (a) any functions conferred by virtue of this Act on—
         (i) the Investigatory Powers Commissioner or any other Judicial Commissioner,

(ii) the Information Commissioner,
(iii) the Investigatory Powers Tribunal,
(iv) any other court or tribunal,
(v) the Technical Advisory Board, or
(vi) the Technology Advisory Panel,
- (b) any function to make subordinate legislation which is conferred by virtue of this Act on the Secretary of State or the Treasury.

(3) A code may, in particular, contain provision about the training of people who may exercise functions in relation to which sub-paragraph (1) applies.

2 (1) Each code must include—
- (a) provision designed to protect the public interest in the confidentiality of sources of journalistic information, and
- (b) provision about particular considerations applicable to any data which relates to a member of a profession which routinely holds items subject to legal privilege or relevant confidential information.

(2) A code about the exercise of functions conferred by virtue of Part 2, Part 5 or Chapter 1 or 3 of Part 6 must also contain provision about when circumstances are to be regarded as "exceptional and compelling circumstances" for the purposes of any provision of that Part or Chapter that restricts the exercise of functions in relation to items subject to legal privilege by reference to the existence of such circumstances.

(3) The Investigatory Powers Commissioner must keep under review any provision included in a code by virtue of sub-paragraph (2).

(4) In this paragraph—
"relevant confidential information" means information which is held in confidence by a member of a profession and consists of—
- (a) personal records or journalistic material which are (or would be if held in England and Wales) excluded material as defined by section 11 of the Police and Criminal Evidence Act 1984, or
- (b) communications between Members of Parliament and their constituents, and the references in this paragraph to a member of a profession include references to any person acting in the course of any trade, business, profession or other occupation or for the purposes of any paid or unpaid office.

3 (1) A code about the exercise of functions conferred by virtue of Part 3 must contain provision about communications data held by public authorities by virtue of that Part.

(2) Such provision must, in particular, include provision about—
- (a) why, how and where the data is held,
- (b) who may access the data on behalf of the authority,
- (c) to whom, and under what conditions, the data may be disclosed,
- (d) the processing of the data for purposes otherwise than in connection with the purposes for which it was obtained or retained,
- (e) the processing of the data together with other data,
- (f) the processes for determining how long the data should be held and for the destruction of the data.

Procedural requirements

4 (1) Before issuing a code the Secretary of State must—
- (a) prepare and publish a draft of the code, and
- (b) consider any representations made about it, and may modify the draft.

(2) The Secretary of State must, in particular, consult the Investigatory Powers Commissioner and, in the case of a code relating to the exercise of functions conferred by virtue of Part 4, the Information Commissioner.
(3) A code comes into force in accordance with regulations made by the Secretary of State.
(4) A statutory instrument containing such regulations may not be made unless a draft of the instrument has been laid before, and approved by a resolution of, each House of Parliament.
(5) When a draft instrument is laid, the code to which it relates must also be laid.
(6) No draft instrument may be laid until the consultation required by subparagraphs (1) and (2) has taken place.

Revision of codes

5 (1) The Secretary of State may from time to time revise the whole or part of a code.
 (2) Before issuing any revision of a code the Secretary of State must—
   (a) prepare and publish a draft, and
   (b) consider any representations made about it, and may modify the draft.
 (3) The Secretary of State must, in particular, consult the Investigatory Powers Commissioner and, in the case of a code relating to the exercise of functions conferred by virtue of Part 4, the Information Commissioner.
 (4) A revision of a code comes into force in accordance with regulations made by the Secretary of State.
 (5) A statutory instrument containing such regulations must be laid before Parliament if the regulations have been made without a draft having been laid before, and approved by a resolution of, each House of Parliament.
 (6) When an instrument or draft instrument is laid, the revision of a code to which it relates must also be laid.
 (7) No instrument or draft instrument may be laid until the consultation required by sub-paragraphs (2) and (3) has taken place.

Effect of codes

6 (1) A person must have regard to a code when exercising any functions to which the code relates.
 (2) A failure on the part of a person to comply with any provision of a code does not of itself make that person liable to criminal or civil proceedings.
 (3) A code is admissible in evidence in any such proceedings.
 (4) A court or tribunal may, in particular, take into account a failure by a person to have regard to a code in determining a question in any such proceedings.
 (5) A supervisory authority exercising functions by virtue of this Act may take into account a failure by a person to have regard to a code in determining a question which arises in connection with the exercise of those functions.
 (6) In this paragraph "supervisory authority" means—
   (a) the Investigatory Powers Commissioner or any other Judicial Commissioner,
   (b) the Information Commissioner, or
   (c) the Investigatory Powers Tribunal.

Appendix

SCHEDULE 8 SECTION 248

COMBINATION OF WARRANTS AND AUTHORISATIONS

PART 1

COMBINATIONS WITH TARGETED INTERCEPTION WARRANTS

Warrants that may be issued by Secretary of State

1   The Secretary of State may, on an application made by or on behalf of the head of an intelligence service, issue a warrant that combines a targeted interception warrant which the Secretary of State has power to issue under section 19(1) with one or more of the following—
   (a) a targeted examination warrant which the Secretary of State has power to issue under section 19(2);
   (b) a targeted equipment interference warrant which the Secretary of State has power to issue under section 102(1);
   (c) a targeted examination warrant which the Secretary of State has power to issue under section 102(3);
   (d) a warrant which the Secretary of State has power to issue under section 5 of the Intelligence Services Act 1994 (warrants for entry or interference with property or wireless telegraphy);
   (e) an authorisation under section 28 of the Regulation of Investigatory Powers Act 2000 (authorisation of directed surveillance);
   (f) an authorisation under section 32 of that Act (authorisation of intrusive surveillance).

2   The Secretary of State may, on an application made by or on behalf of the Chief of Defence Intelligence, issue a warrant that combines a targeted interception warrant which the Secretary of State has power to issue under section 19(1) with one or more of the following—
   (a) a targeted equipment interference warrant which the Secretary of State has power to issue under section 104;
   (b) an authorisation under section 28 of the Regulation of Investigatory Powers Act 2000 (authorisation of directed surveillance);
   (c) an authorisation under section 32 of that Act (authorisation of intrusive surveillance).

3   (1) The Secretary of State may, on an application made by or on behalf of a relevant intercepting authority, issue a warrant that combines a targeted interception warrant which the Secretary of State has power to issue under section 19(1) with one or more of the following—
   (a) a targeted equipment interference warrant which a law enforcement chief has power to issue under section 106;
   (b) an authorisation under section 93 of the Police Act 1997 (authorisations to interfere with property);
   (c) an authorisation under section 28 of the Regulation of Investigatory Powers Act 2000 (authorisation of directed surveillance);
   (d) an authorisation under section 32 of that Act (authorisation of intrusive surveillance).
   (2) For the purposes of sub-paragraph (1), each of the following is a "relevant intercepting authority"—
   (a) the Director General of the National Crime Agency;
   (b) the Commissioner of Police of the Metropolis;
   (c) the Chief Constable of the Police Service of Northern Ireland;
   (d) the chief constable of the Police Service of Scotland;

(e) the Commissioners for Her Majesty's Revenue and Customs.

Warrants that may be issued by Scottish Ministers

4 The Scottish Ministers may, on an application made by or on behalf of the head of an intelligence service, issue a warrant that combines a targeted interception warrant which the Scottish Ministers have power to issue under section 21(1) with one or more of the following—
   (a) a targeted examination warrant which the Scottish Ministers have power to issue under section 21(2);
   (b) a targeted equipment interference warrant which the Scottish Ministers have power to issue under section 103(1);
   (c) a targeted examination warrant which the Scottish Ministers have power to issue under section 103(2);
   (d) a warrant which the Scottish Ministers have power to issue under section 5 of the Intelligence Services Act 1994 (warrants for entry or interference with property or wireless telegraphy).

5 The Scottish Ministers may, on an application made by or on behalf of the chief constable of the Police Service of Scotland, issue a warrant that combines a targeted interception warrant which the Scottish Ministers have power to issue under section 21(1) with one or more of the following—
   (a) a targeted equipment interference warrant which a law enforcement chief has power to issue under section 106;
   (b) an authorisation under section 93 of the Police Act 1997 (authorisations to interfere with property);
   (c) an authorisation under section 28 of the Regulation of Investigatory Powers Act 2000 (authorisation of directed surveillance);
   (d) an authorisation under section 32 of that Act (authorisation of intrusive surveillance).

6 The Scottish Ministers may, on an application made by or on behalf of the chief constable of the Police Service of Scotland, issue a warrant that combines a targeted interception warrant which the Scottish Ministers have power to issue under section 21(1) with one or more of the following—
   (a) a targeted equipment interference warrant which a law enforcement chief has power to issue under section 106;
   s(b) an authorisation under section 93 of the Police Act 1997 (authorisations to interfere with property);
   (c) an authorisation under section 6 of the Regulation of Investigatory Powers (Scotland) Act 2000 (2000 asp 11) (authorisation of directed surveillance);
   (d) an authorisation under section 10 of that Act (authorisation of intrusive surveillance).

7 (1) The Scottish Ministers may, on an application made by or on behalf of a relevant intercepting authority, issue a warrant that combines a targeted interception warrant which the Scottish Ministers have power to issue under section 21(1) with one or more of the following—
   (a) a targeted equipment interference warrant which a law enforcement chief has power to issue under section 106;
   (b) an authorisation under section 93 of the Police Act 1997 (authorisations to interfere with property).

Appendix

(2) For the purposes of sub-paragraph (1), each of the following is a "relevant intercepting authority"—
- (a) the Director General of the National Crime Agency;
- (b) the Commissioner of Police of the Metropolis;
- (c) the Chief Constable of the Police Service of Northern Ireland;
- (d) the Commissioners for Her Majesty's Revenue and Customs.

PART 2
OTHER COMBINATIONS INVOLVING TARGETED EQUIPMENT INTERFERENCE WARRANTS

Warrants that may be issued by Secretary of State

8. The Secretary of State may, on an application made by or on behalf of the head of an intelligence service, issue a warrant that combines a targeted equipment interference warrant which the Secretary of State has power to issue under section 102(1) with one or more of the following—
   - (a) a targeted examination warrant which the Secretary of State has power to issue under section 102(3);
   - (b) a targeted examination warrant which the Secretary of State has power to issue under section 19(2);
   - (c) a warrant which the Secretary of State has power to issue under section 5 of the Intelligence Services Act 1994 (warrants for entry or interference with property or wireless telegraphy);
   - (d) an authorisation under section 28 of the Regulation of Investigatory Powers Act 2000 (authorisation of directed surveillance);
   - (e) an authorisation under section 32 of that Act (authorisation of intrusive surveillance).

9. The Secretary of State may, on an application made by or on behalf of the Chief of Defence Intelligence, issue a warrant that combines a targeted equipment interference warrant which the Secretary of State has power to issue under section 104 with one or more of the following—
   - (a) an authorisation under section 28 of the Regulation of Investigatory Powers Act 2000 (authorisation of directed surveillance);
   - (b) an authorisation under section 32 of that Act (authorisation of intrusive surveillance).

Warrants that may be issued by Scottish Ministers

10. The Scottish Ministers may, on an application made by or on behalf of the head of an intelligence service, issue a warrant that combines a targeted equipment interference warrant which the Scottish Ministers have power to issue under section 103(1) with one or more of the following—
    - (a) a targeted examination warrant which the Scottish Ministers have power to issue under section 103(2);
    - (b) a targeted examination warrant which the Scottish Ministers have power to issue under section 21(2);
    - (c) a warrant which the Scottish Ministers have power to issue under section 5 of the Intelligence Services Act 1994 (warrants for entry or interference with property or wireless telegraphy).

Appendix

Warrants that may be issued by other persons

11 (1) A law enforcement chief may, on an application made by a person who is an appropriate law enforcement officer in relation to the chief, issue a warrant that combines a targeted equipment interference warrant which the law enforcement chief has power to issue under section 106 with one or more of the following—
   (a) an authorisation under section 93 of the Police Act 1997 (authorisations to interfere with property);
   (b) an authorisation under section 28 of the Regulation of Investigatory Powers Act 2000 (authorisation of directed surveillance);
   (c) an authorisation under section 32 of that Act (authorisation of intrusive surveillance).
   (2) For the purposes of this paragraph, references to a "law enforcement chief" and an "appropriate law enforcement officer" are to be read in accordance with section 106(5).

12 (1) A law enforcement chief within sub-paragraph (2) may, on an application made by a person who is an appropriate law enforcement officer in relation to the chief, issue a warrant that combines a targeted equipment interference warrant which the law enforcement chief has power to issue under section 106 with one or more of the following—
   (a) an authorisation under section 93 of the Police Act 1997 (authorisations to interfere with property);
   (b) an authorisation under section 6 of the Regulation of Investigatory Powers (Scotland) Act 2000 (2000 asp 11) (authorisation of directed surveillance);
   (c) an authorisation under section 10 of that Act (authorisation of intrusive surveillance).
   (2) The law enforcement chiefs mentioned in sub-paragraph (1) are—
   (a) the chief constable of the Police Service of Scotland, and
   (b) the Police Investigations and Review Commissioner.
   (3) For the purposes of this paragraph, references to a "law enforcement chief" and an "appropriate law enforcement officer" are to be read in accordance with section 106(5).

PART 3

COMBINATIONS INVOLVING TARGETED EXAMINATION WARRANTS ONLY

13 The Secretary of State may, on an application made by or on behalf of the head of an intelligence service, issue a warrant that combines—
   (a) a targeted examination warrant which the Secretary of State has power to issue under section 19(2), with
   (b) a targeted examination warrant which the Secretary of State has power to issue under section 102(3).

14 The Scottish Ministers may, on an application made by or on behalf of the head of an intelligence service, issue a warrant that combines—
   (a) a targeted examination warrant which the Scottish Ministers have power to issue under section 21(2), with
   (b) a targeted examination warrant which the Scottish Ministers have power to issue under section 103(2).

Appendix

PART 4

COMBINED WARRANTS: SUPPLEMENTARY PROVISION

Introductory

15 In this Part of this Schedule "combined warrant" means a warrant issued under any of Parts 1 to 3 of this Schedule.

General

16 (1) Where Part 1, 2 or 3 of this Schedule provides for a person to have power, on an application made by or on behalf of any person ("the applicant"), to issue a combined warrant that includes any warrant or other authorisation, the person may issue a combined warrant containing that warrant or authorisation, whether or not that person would have power, on an application made by or on behalf of the applicant, to issue that warrant, or to give that authorisation, as a single instrument.

(2) Where Part 1, 2 or 3 of this Schedule provides for a person to have power to apply for a combined warrant, the person may apply for a combined warrant containing any warrant or other authorisation that may be included in it, provided that—
   (a) the person could apply for that warrant or authorisation as a single instrument, or
   (b) the organisation on whose behalf the person is acting, or another person who is a member of staff or an officer of the organisation or who is otherwise acting on its behalf, could apply for that warrant or authorisation as a single instrument.

17 (1) A combined warrant must be addressed to the person by whom, or on whose behalf, the application for the combined warrant was made.

(2) Any reference in this Act to the person to whom a warrant is or was addressed is to be read, in the case of a combined warrant containing such a warrant, as a reference to the person to whom the combined warrant is or was addressed.

18 A combined warrant must contain a provision stating which warrants or other authorisations are included in the combined warrant.

19 Any reference in any enactment to a warrant or other authorisation of a particular description issued or given under any enactment includes, in the case of a combined warrant containing a warrant or authorisation of that description, a reference to so much of the combined warrant as consists of such a warrant or authorisation.

This is subject to any provision made by or under the following provisions of this Schedule.

Rules about issue etc. applying separately in relation to each part of a combined warrant

20 (1) The law about the following matters, so far as relating to a warrant or other authorisation that may be included in a combined warrant, applies in relation to so much of a combined warrant as consists of such a warrant or authorisation—
   (a) the duties imposed by section 2 (general duties in relation to privacy);
   (b) any conditions that must be met before such a warrant or authorisation may be issued or given;
   (c) the grounds on which such a warrant or authorisation may be issued or given;
   (d) the conduct that may be authorised by such a warrant or authorisation;
   (e) any requirements as to what must be included in such a warrant or authorisation;
   (f) any conditions that must be met before such a warrant or authorisation may be renewed and the grounds on which it may be renewed;

Appendix

  (g) any conditions that must be met before such a warrant or authorisation may be modified;
  (h) the grounds on which such a warrant or authorisation may be modified and the procedural rules that apply to such a modification;
  (i) the circumstances in which such a warrant or authorisation may or must be cancelled.
 (2) In sub-paragraph (1)(h) "procedural rules", in relation to the modification of a warrant or other authorisation, means the law about any of the following matters—
  (a) the involvement of Judicial Commissioners in decisions;
  (b) the delegation of decisions;
  (c) the signing of instruments making a modification;
  (d) urgent cases.
 (3) Sub-paragraph (1) is subject to paragraphs 21 to 26.

Rules about issue etc. applying in relation to combined warrants

21 (1) A combined warrant under Part 1 of this Schedule addressed to any person may only be issued, renewed or cancelled in accordance with the procedural rules that would apply to the issue, renewal or cancellation of a targeted interception warrant addressed to that person (see Chapter 1 of Part 2 of this Act).
 (2) In sub-paragraph (1) "procedural rules", in relation to a warrant, means the law about any of the following matters—
  (a) the involvement of Judicial Commissioners in decisions;
  (b) the delegation of decisions;
  (c) the signing of warrants;
  (d) urgent cases.
 (3) But if a combined warrant under paragraph 1 or 4 includes a warrant which the person issuing the combined warrant has power to issue under section 5 of the Intelligence Services Act 1994 (a "section 5 warrant"), any requirement (arising from sub-paragraph (1) above) for the involvement of Judicial Commissioners in the decision whether to issue or renew the combined warrant does not apply in relation to the part of the combined warrant consisting of the section 5 warrant.

22 (1) A combined warrant under Part 2 of this Schedule addressed to any person may only be issued, renewed or cancelled in accordance with the procedural rules that would apply to the issue, renewal or cancellation of a targeted equipment interference warrant addressed to that person (see Part 5 of this Act).
 (2) In sub-paragraph (1) "procedural rules" has the same meaning as in paragraph 21(1).
 (3) But if a combined warrant under paragraph 8 or 10 includes a warrant which the person issuing the combined warrant has power to issue under section 5 of the Intelligence Services Act 1994 (a "section 5 warrant"), any requirement (arising from sub-paragraph (1) above) for the involvement of Judicial Commissioners in the decision whether to issue or renew the combined warrant does not apply in relation to the part of the combined warrant consisting of the section 5 warrant.

23 (1) A combined warrant under Part 3 of this Schedule addressed to any person may only be issued, renewed or cancelled in accordance with the procedural rules that would apply to the issue, renewal or cancellation of a targeted examination warrant under section 19(2) addressed to that person (see Chapter 1 of Part 2 of this Act).
 (2) In sub-paragraph (1) "procedural rules" has the same meaning as in paragraph 21(1).

24 (1) In consequence of paragraphs 21 and 22, the following provisions of the Police Act 1997 do not apply in relation to an authorisation under section 93 of that Act which is included in a combined warrant—
   (a) section 96 (notification of authorisations to Judicial Commissioner);
   (b) section 97 (authorisations requiring approval);
   (c) section 103(1), (2) and (4) (power to quash or cancel authorisations);
   (d) section 104 (appeals to Investigatory Powers Commissioner).
(2) Section 103(6) of that Act applies where a combined warrant containing an authorisation under section 93 of that Act is cancelled as it applies where such an authorisation is cancelled under section 103(4) of that Act.

25 In consequence of paragraphs 21 and 22, the following provisions of the Regulation of Investigatory Powers Act 2000 do not apply in relation to an authorisation under section 32 of that Act which is included in a combined warrant—
   (a) section 35 (notification of authorisations to Judicial Commissioner);
   (b) section 36 (approval required for authorisations to take effect);
   (c) section 37(2) to (4) (power to quash or cancel authorisations);
   (d) section 38 (appeals to Investigatory Powers Commissioner).

26 In consequence of paragraphs 21 and 22, the following provisions of the Regulation of Investigatory Powers (Scotland) Act 2000 do not apply in relation to an authorisation under section 10 of that Act which is included in a combined warrant—
   (a) section 13 (notification of authorisations to Judicial Commissioner);
   (b) section 14 (approval required for authorisations to take effect);
   (c) section 15(1) to (3) (power to quash or cancel authorisations);
   (d) section 16 (appeals to Investigatory Powers Commissioner).

Modification of rules as to duration

27 (1) Where a combined warrant includes warrants or authorisations which (as single instruments) would cease to have effect at the end of different periods, the combined warrant is to cease to have effect at the end of the shortest of the periods (unless renewed).
(2) But sub-paragraph (1) does not apply to a combined warrant which—
   (a) includes an authorisation under section 28 of the Regulation of Investigatory Powers Act 2000 (authorisation of directed surveillance),
   (b) is addressed to the head of an intelligence service, and
   (c) is issued with the approval of a Judicial Commissioner.
(3) In such a case, the combined warrant (unless it is renewed) is to cease to have effect at the end of the period of 6 months beginning with the day on which it is issued.

Special rules about the application of this Act to combined warrants

28 (1) This paragraph applies where under section 24(3) a Judicial Commissioner refuses to approve a decision to issue a combined warrant under Part 1 or 3 of this Schedule.
(2) Section 25 has effect in relation to the combined warrant as if—
   (a) any reference in subsection (3) of that section to a targeted interception warrant or targeted examination warrant were a reference to so much of the combined warrant as consisted of such a warrant, and
   (b) any other reference in that section to a warrant were a reference to the combined warrant.

Appendix

(3) Where the combined warrant included a targeted equipment interference warrant or targeted examination warrant which the person who issued the combined warrant has power to issue under Part 5 of this Act, section 110 has effect in relation to the combined warrant as if—

  (a) any reference in subsection (3)(b) or (c) of that section to a targeted equipment interference warrant were a reference to so much of the combined warrant as consisted of such a warrant,

  (b) any reference in subsection (4) of that section to a targeted examination warrant were a reference to so much of the combined warrant as consisted of such a warrant, and

  (c) any other reference in that section to a warrant were a reference to the combined warrant.

29 Where under section 109(3) a Judicial Commissioner refuses to approve the decision to issue a combined warrant under Part 2 of this Schedule, section 110 has effect in relation to the combined warrant as if—

  (a) any reference in subsection (3)(b) or (c) of that section to a targeted equipment interference warrant were a reference to so much of the combined warrant as consisted of such a warrant,

  (b) any reference in subsection (4) of that section to a targeted examination warrant were a reference to so much of the combined warrant as consisted of such a warrant, and

  (c) any other reference in that section to a warrant were a reference to the combined warrant.

30 (1) This paragraph applies to any provision in Part 2 or 5 of this Act that enables a person to whom a warrant is addressed to require the provision of assistance in giving effect to the warrant.

  (2) In the case of a combined warrant containing such a warrant, the provision is to be read as enabling the person to whom the combined warrant is addressed to require the provision of assistance in giving effect to so much of the combined warrant as consists of such a warrant.

  (3) Accordingly, any power to serve a copy of a warrant for that purpose includes power, in the case of such a combined warrant, to serve the part of the combined warrant consisting of such a warrant.

31 Any reference in section 56 (exclusion of matters from legal proceedings etc.) to the making of an application for a warrant, or the issue of a warrant, under Chapter 1 of Part 2 of this Act includes a reference to—

  (a) the making of an application for a combined warrant that includes a warrant under that Chapter, so far as relating to disclosing or suggesting the inclusion of such a warrant, or

  (b) the inclusion of a warrant under that Chapter in a combined warrant.

32 (1) The reference in section 58(7) to the provisions of Part 2 of this Act is to be read, in the case of a combined warrant containing a targeted interception warrant or targeted examination warrant which the person who issued the combined warrant has power to issue under that Part, as including a reference to this Schedule.

  (2) The reference in section 133(4) to the provisions of Part 5 of this Act is to be read, in the case of a combined warrant containing a targeted equipment interference warrant or targeted examination warrant which the person who issued the combined warrant has power to issue under that Part, as including a reference to this Schedule.

Appendix

Power to make consequential amendments

33 (1) The Secretary of State may by regulations make such provision modifying any provision made by or under an enactment (including this Schedule) as the Secretary of State considers appropriate in consequence of any provision made by this Schedule.

(2) In sub-paragraph (1) "enactment" does not include any primary legislation passed or made after the end of the Session in which this Act is passed.

SCHEDULE 9 SECTION 270(1)

TRANSITIONAL, TRANSITORY AND SAVING PROVISION

Lawful interception of communications

1 Any agreement which, immediately before the day on which section 10 comes into force, is designated for the purposes of section 1(4) of the Regulation of Investigatory Powers Act 2000 is to be treated, on and after that day, as designated as an international mutual assistance agreement by regulations under section 10(3) of this Act.

Authorisations for obtaining communications data

2 The reference to the Gangmasters and Labour Abuse Authority in the table in Part 1 of Schedule 4 is to be read, in relation to any time before the day on which section 10(1) of the Immigration Act 2016 (renaming of Gangmasters Licensing Authority) comes into force, as a reference to the Gangmasters Licensing Authority.

Retention of communications data

3 (1) A retention notice under section 1 of the Data Retention and Investigatory Powers Act 2014 which is in force immediately before the commencement day is to be treated, on or after that day, as a retention notice under section 87 of this Act; and Part 4 of this Act is to be read accordingly but as if sections 87(1)(b), (4) and (8)(e), 89, 90(1) to (12), 91, 94(4)(b), (6), (10) and (12) and 96(2)(e) were omitted.

(2) In particular—
  (a) anything which, immediately before the commencement day, is in the process of being done by virtue of, or in relation to, a retention notice under section 1 of the Act of 2014 may be continued as if being done by virtue of, or in relation to, a retention notice under section 87 of this Act, and
  (b) anything done by virtue of, or in relation to, a retention notice under section 1 of the Act of 2014 is, if in force or effective immediately before the commencement day, to have effect as if done by virtue of, or in relation to, a retention notice under section 87 of this Act so far as that is required for continuing its effect on or after the commencement day.

(3) Sub-paragraphs (1) and (2) cease to apply, in relation to any retention notice under section 1 of the Act of 2014—
  (a) at the end of the period of six months beginning with the commencement day, or
  (b) if earlier, on the revocation in full of the notice; but this is without prejudice to the continued operation of section 95(2) to (5) in relation to the notice.

(4) Section 249 applies in relation to costs incurred in complying with a retention notice under section 1 of the Act of 2014 which has continued in force on or after the

Appendix

commencement day as it applies in relation to costs incurred in complying with retention notices under section 87 of this Act but as if section 249(7) were omitted.

(5) The Secretary of State may revoke (whether wholly or in part) a retention notice under section 1 of the Act of 2014.

(6) The fact that a retention notice under section 1 of the Act of 2014 has, in relation to a particular description of data and a particular operator (or description of operators), ceased to have effect or been revoked does not prevent the giving of a retention notice under section 87 of this Act in relation to the same description of data and the same operator (or description of operators).

(7) In this paragraph "the commencement day" is the day on which section 1(1) of the Act of 2014 is repealed.

4 (1) Sub-paragraph (2) applies if any power to give, vary or confirm a retention notice under section 87 of this Act (excluding any power to vary a notice which has effect as such a notice by virtue of paragraph 3(1)) is brought into force without any requirement for approval by a Judicial Commissioner of the decision to give, vary or (as the case may be) confirm the notice.

(2) The notice as given, varied or confirmed ceases to have effect (so far as not previously revoked) at the end of the period of three months beginning with the day on which the requirement for approval comes into force.

5 (1) The repeal of section 1(7) of the Data Retention and Investigatory Powers Act 2014 does not affect the continued operation, during the transitional period mentioned in sub-paragraph (2), of regulations made under section 1(7) of that Act.

(2) The transitional period mentioned in this sub-paragraph is the period of six months beginning with the day on which section 1(7) of the Act of 2014 is repealed.

(3) In their continued operation by virtue of sub-paragraph (1), the regulations made under section 1(7) of the Act of 2014 have effect subject to such modifications (if any) as may be specified in regulations under section 270(2).

Definitions of "other relevant crime" and "serious crime"

6 (1) The definitions of—
 (a) "other relevant crime" in section 62(6), and
 (b) "serious crime" in section 263(1), are to be read, until the appointed day, as if for the words "the age of 18 (or, in relation to Scotland or Northern Ireland, 21)" there were substituted "the age of 21".

(2) In sub-paragraph (1), "the appointed day" means the day on which the amendment made to section 81(3)(a) of the Regulation of Investigatory Powers Act 2000 by paragraph 211 of Schedule 7 to the Criminal Justice and Court Services Act 2000 comes into force.

Savings for particular purposes

7 Nothing in this Act affects any power conferred on a postal operator (within the meaning given by section 27(3) of the Postal Services Act 2011) by or under any enactment to open, detain or delay any postal packet (within the meaning given by section 125(1) of the Postal Services Act 2000) or to deliver any such packet to a person other than the person to whom it is addressed.

8 Nothing in Part 4 of this Act prevents the retention of data for the purposes of, or in connection with, legal proceedings (including proceedings which might arise in the future).

9 The amendments made to the Regulation of Investigatory Powers Act 2000 by sections 3 to 6 of the Data Retention and Investigatory Powers Act 2014 (and those sections) continue to

Appendix

have effect despite section 8(3) of the Act of 2014 (sunset provision for that Act) until the provisions they amend (and those sections) are repealed by this Act in connection with the coming into force of provisions of this Act.

General saving for lawful conduct

10   Nothing in any of the provisions of this Act by virtue of which conduct of any description is or may be authorised by any warrant, authorisation or notice, or by virtue of which information may be obtained in any manner, is to be read—
   (a)   as making it unlawful to engage in any conduct of that description which is not otherwise unlawful under this Act and would not be unlawful apart from this Act,
   (b)   as otherwise requiring—
      (i)   the issue, grant or giving of such a warrant, authorisation or notice, or
      (ii)   the taking of any step for or towards obtaining the authority of such a warrant, authorisation or notice, before any such conduct of that description is engaged in, or
   (c)   as prejudicing any power to obtain information by any means not involving conduct that may be authorised under this Act.

SCHEDULE 10 SECTION 271(1)

MINOR AND CONSEQUENTIAL PROVISION

PART 1

GENERAL AMENDMENTS

Police Act 1997

1   In section 93(1A) of the Police Act 1997 (authorisations to interfere with property etc.) after "this Part" insert "or the Investigatory Powers Act 2016".

Northern Ireland Act 1998

2   In paragraph 9(1) of Schedule 3 to the Northern Ireland Act 1998 (reserved matters) for paragraph (a) substitute—

   "(a)   the subject-matter of Parts 2 and 3 of the Regulation of Investigatory Powers Act 2000, so far as relating to the prevention or detection of crime (within the meaning of that Act) or the prevention of disorder;
   (aa)   the subject-matter of the following provisions of the Investigatory Powers Act 2016, so far as relating to the prevention or detection of serious crime (within the meaning of that Act)—
      (i)   sections 3 to 10 and Schedule 1,
      (ii)   Part 2, and
      (iii) Chapter 1 of Part 6;
   (ab)   the subject-matter of section 11, Parts 3 and 4 and Chapter 2 of Part 6 of the Investigatory Powers Act 2016, so far as relating to the prevention or detection of crime (within the meaning of that Act) or the prevention of disorder;
   (ac)   the subject-matter of section 12 of, and Schedule 2 to, the Investigatory Powers Act 2016, so far as relating to the prevention or detection of crime (within the meaning of that Act);".

Regulation of Investigatory Powers Act 2000

3   The Regulation of Investigatory Powers Act 2000 is amended as follows.
4   In section 27(4)(a) (lawful surveillance etc.: conduct to be dealt with under other enactments) after "Act" insert "or the Investigatory Powers Act 2016".
5   (1) Section 71 (issue and revision of codes of practice) is amended as follows.
    (2) In subsection (2)(a), for "Parts I to III" substitute "Parts 2 and 3".
    (3) Omit subsection (2A).
    (4) In subsection (8) for "(2A)" substitute "(3)".
6   (1) Section 81(1) (general definitions) is amended as follows.
    (2) For the definition of "apparatus" substitute—
    ""apparatus" has the same meaning as in the Investigatory Powers Act 2016 (see section 263(1) of that Act);".
    (3) In paragraph (a) of the definition of "communication" omit "(except in the definition of "postal service" in section 2(1))".
    (4) In the definition of "interception" and cognate expressions, for "section 2" substitute "sections 4 and 5 of the Investigatory Powers Act 2016".
    (5) For the definitions of "postal service" and "public postal service" substitute—
    ""postal service" has the same meaning as in the Investigatory Powers Act 2016 (see section 262(7) of that Act);".
    (6) Omit the definitions of "private telecommunication system", "public telecommunications service" and "public telecommunication system".
    (7) In the definitions of "telecommunication system" and "telecommunications service", for "the meanings given by section 2(1)" substitute "the same meanings as in the Investigatory Powers Act 2016 (see section 261(11) to (13) of that Act)".

Political Parties, Elections and Referendums Act 2000

7   In paragraph 28(4) of Schedule 19C to the Political Parties, Elections and Referendums Act 2000 (civil sanctions: disclosure of information) for paragraph (b) substitute—
    "(b) any of Parts 1 to 7 or Chapter 1 of Part 9 of the Investigatory Powers Act 2016."

Public Finance and Accountability (Scotland) Act 2000 (2000 asp 1)

8   (1) The Public Finance and Accountability (Scotland) Act 2000 is amended as follows.
    (2) In section 26B(3) (voluntary disclosure of data to Audit Scotland) for paragraph (b) substitute—
    "(b) which is prohibited by any of Parts 1 to 7 or Chapter 1 of Part 9 of the Investigatory Powers Act 2016,".
    (3) In section 26C(3) (power to require disclosure of data) for paragraph (b) substitute—
    "(b) the disclosure is prohibited by any of Parts 1 to 7 or Chapter 1 of Part 9 of the Investigatory Powers Act 2016."

Social Security Fraud Act 2001

9   In section 4(1)(b) of the Social Security Fraud Act 2001 (arrangements for payments in relation to persons providing a telecommunications service etc.) for "the Regulation of Investigatory Powers Act 2000 (c. 23)" substitute "the Investigatory Powers Act 2016".

Appendix

Social Security Fraud Act (Northern Ireland) 2001

10 In section 4(1)(b) of the Social Security Fraud Act (Northern Ireland) 2001 (arrangements for payments in relation to persons providing a telecommunications service etc.) for "the Regulation of Investigatory Powers Act 2000 (c. 23)" substitute "the Investigatory Powers Act 2016".

Justice (Northern Ireland) Act 2002

11 In section 5A(3)(b) of the Justice (Northern Ireland) Act 2002 (disclosure of information to the Northern Ireland Judicial Appointments Commission) for "Part 1 of the Regulation of Investigatory Powers Act 2000" substitute "any of Parts 1 to 7 or Chapter 1 of Part 9 of the Investigatory Powers Act 2016".

Proceeds of Crime Act 2002

12 (1) The Proceeds of Crime Act 2002 is amended as follows.
 (2) In section 436(3)(b) (disclosure of information to certain Directors) for "Part 1 of the Regulation of Investigatory Powers Act 2000 (c. 23)" substitute "any of Parts 1 to 7 or Chapter 1 of Part 9 of the Investigatory Powers Act 2016".
 (3) In section 438(8)(b) (disclosure of information by certain Directors) for "Part 1 of the Regulation of Investigatory Powers Act 2000 (c. 23)" substitute "any of Parts 1 to 7 or Chapter 1 of Part 9 of the Investigatory Powers Act 2016".
 (4) In section 439(3)(b) (disclosure of information to Lord Advocate and to Scottish Ministers) for "Part 1 of the Regulation of Investigatory Powers Act 2000" substitute "any of Parts 1 to 7 or Chapter 1 of Part 9 of the Investigatory Powers Act 2016".
 (5) In section 441(7)(b) (disclosure of information by Lord Advocate and by Scottish Ministers) for "Part 1 of the Regulation of Investigatory Powers Act 2000 (c. 23)" substitute "any of Parts 1 to 7 or Chapter 1 of Part 9 of the Investigatory Powers Act 2016".

Police Reform Act 2002

13 In paragraph 19ZA(2)(c) of Schedule 3 to the Police Reform Act 2002 (handling of complaints and conduct matters etc.: power to serve information notice) for "Part 1 of the Regulation of Investigatory Powers Act 2000" substitute "any of Parts 1 to 7 or Chapter 1 of Part 9 of the Investigatory Powers Act 2016".

Privacy and Electronic Communications (EC Directive) Regulations 2003 (S.I. 2003/2426)

14 After regulation 5A(8) of the Privacy and Electronic Communications (EC Directive) Regulations 2003 (personal data breach) insert—
"(9) This regulation does not apply in relation to any personal data breach which is to be notified to the Investigatory Powers Commissioner in accordance with a code of practice made under the Investigatory Powers Act 2016."

Audit and Accountability (Northern Ireland) Order 2003 (S.I. 2003/418 (N.I. 5))

15 In Article 4C(3)(b) of the Audit and Accountability (Northern Ireland) Order 2003 (voluntary provision of data) for "Part 1 of the Regulation of Investigatory Powers Act 2000 (c. 23)" substitute "any of Parts 1 to 7 or Chapter 1 of Part 9 of the Investigatory Powers Act 2016".

Public Audit (Wales) Act 2004

16   In section 64C(3)(b) of the Public Audit (Wales) Act 2004 (voluntary provision of data) for "Part 1 of the Regulation of Investigatory Powers Act 2000 (c. 23)" substitute "any of Parts 1 to 7 or Chapter 1 of Part 9 of the Investigatory Powers Act 2016".

Constitutional Reform Act 2005

17   In section 107(3)(b) of the Constitutional Reform Act 2005 (disclosure of information to the Judicial Appointments Commission) for "Part 1 of the Regulation of Investigatory Powers Act 2000 (c. 23)" substitute "any of Parts 1 to 7 or Chapter 1 of Part 9 of the Investigatory Powers Act 2016".

Commissioners for Revenue and Customs Act 2005

18   In section 22(b) of the Commissioners for Revenue and Customs Act 2005 (data protection, etc.) for "Part 1 of the Regulation of Investigatory Powers Act 2000 (c. 23)" substitute "any of Parts 1 to 7 or Chapter 1 of Part 9 of the Investigatory Powers Act 2016".

Serious Crime Act 2007

19   (1) The Serious Crime Act 2007 is amended as follows.
   (2) In section 68(4)(b) (disclosure of information to prevent fraud) for "Part 1 of the Regulation of Investigatory Powers Act 2000 (c. 23)" substitute "any of Parts 1 to 7 or Chapter 1 of Part 9 of the Investigatory Powers Act 2016".
   (3) In section 85(8)(b) (disclosure of information by Revenue and Customs) for "Part 1 of the Regulation of Investigatory Powers Act 2000 (c. 23)" substitute "any of Parts 1 to 7 or Chapter 1 of Part 9 of the Investigatory Powers Act 2016".

Legal Services Act 2007

20   In section 169(3)(b) of the Legal Services Act 2007 (disclosure of information to the Legal Services Board) for "Part 1 of the Regulation of Investigatory Powers Act 2000 (c. 23)" substitute "any of Parts 1 to 7 or Chapter 1 of Part 9 of the Investigatory Powers Act 2016".

Regulatory Enforcement and Sanctions Act 2008

21   In section 70(4) of the Regulatory Enforcement and Sanctions Act 2008 (disclosure of information) for paragraph (b) substitute—
   "(b) any of Parts 1 to 7 or Chapter 1 of Part 9 of the Investigatory Powers Act 2016."

Counter-Terrorism Act 2008

22   In section 20(2)(b) of the Counter-Terrorism Act 2008 (disclosure and the intelligence services: supplementary provisions) for "Part 1 of the Regulation of Investigatory Powers Act 2000 (c. 23)" substitute "any of Parts 1 to 7 or Chapter 1 of Part 9 of the Investigatory Powers Act 2016".

Borders, Citizenship and Immigration Act 2009

23   In section 19(1)(b) of the Borders, Citizenship and Immigration Act 2009 (application of statutory provisions) for "Part 1 of the Regulation of Investigatory Powers Act 2000 (c. 23)" substitute "any of Parts 1 to 7 or Chapter 1 of Part 9 of the Investigatory Powers Act 2016".

Marine and Coastal Access Act 2009

24 (1) The Marine and Coastal Access Act 2009 is amended as follows.
   (2) In paragraph 13(5) of Schedule 7 (further provision about civil sanctions under Part 4: disclosure of information) for paragraph (b) substitute—
   "(b) any of Parts 1 to 7 or Chapter 1 of Part 9 of the Investigatory Powers Act 2016."
   (3) In paragraph 9(5) of Schedule 10 (further provision about fixed monetary penalties under section 142: disclosure of information) for paragraph (b) substitute—
   "(b) any of Parts 1 to 7 or Chapter 1 of Part 9 of the Investigatory Powers Act 2016."

Terrorist Asset-Freezing etc. Act 2010

25 In section 25(2)(b) of the Terrorist Asset-Freezing etc. Act 2010 (application of provisions) for "Part 1 of the Regulation of Investigatory Powers Act 2000" substitute "any of Parts 1 to 7 or Chapter 1 of Part 9 of the Investigatory Powers Act 2016".

Marine (Scotland) Act 2010 (2010 asp 5)

26 In paragraph 12(5) of Schedule 2 to the Marine (Scotland) Act 2010 (further provision about civil sanctions under Part 4: disclosure of information) for paragraph (b) substitute—
   "(b) any of Parts 1 to 7 or Chapter 1 of Part 9 of the Investigatory Powers Act 2016."

Charities Act 2011

27 In section 59(b) of the Charities Act 2011 (disclosure: supplementary) for "Part 1 of the Regulation of Investigatory Powers Act 2000" substitute "any of Parts 1 to 7 or Chapter 1 of Part 9 of the Investigatory Powers Act 2016".

Prisons (Interference with Wireless Telegraphy) Act 2012

28 In section 4(6) of the Prisons (Interference with Wireless Telegraphy) Act 2012 (meaning of "telecommunication system") for "Regulation of Investigatory Powers Act 2000" substitute "Investigatory Powers Act 2016 (see section 261(13) of that Act)".

Crime and Courts Act 2013

29 In paragraph 1(b) of Schedule 7 to the Crime and Courts Act 2013 (information: restrictions on disclosure) for "Part 1 of the Regulation of Investigatory Powers Act 2000" substitute "any of Parts 1 to 7 or Chapter 1 of Part 9 of the Investigatory Powers Act 2016".

Marine Act (Northern Ireland) 2013 (c. 10 (N.I.))

30 In paragraph 8(5) of Schedule 2 to the Marine Act (Northern Ireland) 2013 (further provision about fixed monetary penalties under section 35: disclosure of information) for paragraph (b) substitute—
   "(b) any of Parts 1 to 7 or Chapter 1 of Part 9 of the Investigatory Powers Act 2016."

Local Audit and Accountability Act 2014

31 In paragraph 3(3)(b) of Schedule 9 to the Local Audit and Accountability Act 2014 (data matching: voluntary provision of data) for "Part 1 of the Regulation of Investigatory Powers Act 2000" substitute "any of Parts 1 to 7 or Chapter 1 of Part 9 of the Investigatory Powers Act 2016".

Appendix

Anti-social Behaviour, Crime and Policing Act 2014

32 In paragraph 7(4)(b) of Schedule 4 to the Anti-social Behaviour, Crime and Policing Act 2014 (ASB case reviews: information) for "Part 1 of the Regulation of Investigatory Powers Act 2000" substitute "any of Parts 1 to 7 or Chapter 1 of Part 9 of the Investigatory Powers Act 2016".

Immigration Act 2014

33 In paragraph 6(b) of Schedule 6 to the Immigration Act 2014 (information) for "Part 1 of the Regulation of Investigatory Powers Act 2000" substitute "any of Parts 1 to 7 or Chapter 1 of Part 9 of the Investigatory Powers Act 2016".

Data Retention and Investigatory Powers Act 2014

34 Omit sections 4(1), 7 and 8 of the Data Retention and Investigatory Powers Act 2014 (introductory, review and final provisions).

Immigration Act 2016

35 In section 7(2)(b) of the Immigration Act 2016 (information gateways: supplementary) for "Part 1 of the Regulation of Investigatory Powers Act 2000" substitute "any of Parts 1 to 7 or Chapter 1 of Part 9 of the Investigatory Powers Act 2016".

PART 2

LAWFUL INTERCEPTION OF COMMUNICATIONS

Security Service Act 1989

36 In section 1(5) of the Security Service Act 1989 (meaning of "prevention" and "detection") for the words from "the provisions" to the end substitute "that Act".

Official Secrets Act 1989

37 In section 4(3) of the Official Secrets Act 1989 (crime and special investigation powers) omit the "and" after paragraph (a) and after paragraph (b) insert "and(c) any information obtained under a warrant under Chapter 1 of Part 2 or Chapter 1 of Part 6 of the Investigatory Powers Act 2016, any information relating to the obtaining of information under such a warrant and any document or other article which is or has been used or held for use in, or has been obtained by reason of, the obtaining of information under such a warrant."

Intelligence Services Act 1994

38 In section 11(1A) of the Intelligence Services Act 1994 (meaning of "prevention" and "detection") for the words from "apply" to the end substitute "apply for the purposes of this Act as it applies for the purposes of that Act, except that for the purposes of section 3 above it shall not include a reference to gathering evidence for use in any legal proceedings (within the meaning of that Act)."

Criminal Procedure and Investigations Act 1996

39 (1) The Criminal Procedure and Investigations Act 1996 is amended as follows.

(2) In section 3(7) (initial duty of prosecutor to disclose) for "section 17 of the Regulation of Investigatory Powers Act 2000" substitute "section 56 of the Investigatory Powers Act 2016".

(3) In section 7A(9) (continuing duty of prosecutor to disclose) for "section 17 of the Regulation of Investigatory Powers Act 2000 (c. 23)" substitute "section 56 of the Investigatory Powers Act 2016".

(4) In section 8(6) (application by accused for disclosure) for "section 17 of the Regulation of Investigatory Powers Act 2000" substitute "section 56 of the Investigatory Powers Act 2016".

(5) In section 23 (code of practice) for subsection (6) substitute—

"(6) The code must be so framed that it does not apply to any of the following—
  (a) material intercepted in obedience to a warrant issued under section 2 of the Interception of Communications Act 1985;
  (b) material intercepted under the authority of an interception warrant under section 5 of the Regulation of Investigatory Powers Act 2000;
  (c) material obtained under the authority of a warrant issued under Chapter 1 of Part 2 of the Investigatory Powers Act 2016;
  (d) material obtained under the authority of a warrant issued under Chapter 1 of Part 6 of that Act."

Police Act 1997

40 In section 133A of the Police Act 1997 (meaning of "prevention" and "detection") for the words from "the provisions" to the end substitute "that Act".

Scotland Act 1998

41 In Section B8 of Part 2 of Schedule 5 to the Scotland Act 1998 (reserved matters: national security, interception of communications etc.), in the definition of "private telecommunication system", for "section 2(1) of the Regulation of Investigatory Powers Act 2000" substitute "section 261(14) of the Investigatory Powers Act 2016".

Northern Ireland Act 1998

42 In paragraph 17 of Schedule 2 to the Northern Ireland Act 1998 (excepted matters) for paragraph (b) substitute—
"(b) the subject-matter of sections 3 to 10, Schedule 1, Part 2 and Chapter 1 of Part 6 of the Investigatory Powers Act 2016, except so far as relating to the prevention or detection of serious crime (within the meaning of that Act);".

Financial Services and Markets Act 2000

43 In section 394(7)(a) of the Financial Services and Markets Act 2000 (access to FCA or PRA material) for "section 17 of the Regulation of Investigatory Powers Act 2000" substitute "section 56 of the Investigatory Powers Act 2016".

Regulation of Investigatory Powers Act 2000

44 The Regulation of Investigatory Powers Act 2000 is amended as follows.

45 Omit Chapter 1 of Part 1 (interception of communications).

46 (1) Section 49 (investigation of electronic data protected by encryption etc.: powers under which data obtained) is amended as follows.
   (2) In subsection (1)(b) after "communications" insert "or obtain secondary data from communications".
   (3) After subsection (9) insert—
   "(9A) In subsection (1)(b) the reference to obtaining secondary data from communications is to be read in accordance with section 16 of the Investigatory Powers Act 2016."
47 In section 71 (issue and revision of codes of practice) omit subsection (10).
48 In section 78(3)(a) (affirmative orders) omit "12(10), 13(3),".
49 (1) Section 81 (general interpretation) is amended as follows.
   (2) In subsection (1)—
      (a) in the definition of "criminal", omit "or prosecution", and
      (b) in the definition of "interception warrant", for "a warrant under section 5" substitute —
         "(a) a targeted interception warrant or mutual assistance warrant under Chapter 1 of Part 2 of the Investigatory Powers Act 2016, or
         (b) a bulk interception warrant under Chapter 1 of Part 6 of that Act".
   (3) In subsection (4) omit the words from "; and references" to the end.
   (4) In subsection (5) omit the words from ", except that" to the end.
50 In section 82 (amendments, repeals and savings etc.) omit subsections (4) to (6).

Criminal Justice and Licensing (Scotland) Act 2010 (2010 asp 13)

51 In section 159 of the Criminal Justice and Licensing (Scotland) Act 2010, for "section 17 of the Regulation of Investigatory Powers Act 2000 (c. 23)" substitute "section 56 of the Investigatory Powers Act 2016".

Justice and Security Act 2013

52 In section 6(4)(b) of the Justice and Security Act 2013 (declaration permitting closed material applications in proceedings) for sub-paragraph (iii) substitute—
   "(iii) section 56(1) of the Investigatory Powers Act 2016 (exclusion for intercept material),".

PART 3

ACQUISITION OF COMMUNICATIONS DATA

Regulation of Investigatory Powers Act 2000

53 The Regulation of Investigatory Powers Act 2000 is amended as follows.
54 Omit Chapter 2 of Part 1 (acquisition and disclosure of communications data).
55 In section 49(1)(c) (investigation of electronic data protected by encryption etc.: powers under which data obtained)—
   (a) for the words from "section 22(3)" to "Part II" substitute "Part 3 of the Investigatory Powers Act 2016 or Part 2 of this Act", and
   (b) for "under section 22(4)" substitute "in pursuance of an authorisation under Part 3 of the Act of 2016 or as the result of the issue of a warrant under Chapter 2 of Part 6 of the Act of 2016".
56 In section 71(2) (issue and revision of codes of practice) omit "23A or".

Appendix

57 (1) Section 77A (procedure for order of sheriff under section 23A or 32A: Scotland) is amended as follows.
   (2) In the heading and in subsection (1)—
      (a) for "23A" substitute "75 of the Investigatory Powers Act 2016", and
      (b) for "or 32A" substitute "or section 32A of this Act".
   (3) In subsection (3) for "sections 23B and 32B and this section" substitute "this section, section 32B of this Act and section 75 of the Investigatory Powers Act 2016".
58 (1) Section 77B (procedure for order of district judge under section 23A or 32A: Northern Ireland) is amended as follows.
   (2) In the heading and in subsections (1) and (4) for "section 23A or 32A" substitute "section 32A of this Act or section 75 of the Investigatory Powers Act 2016".
   (3) In subsection (4) for "sections 23B and 32B" substitute "section 32B of this Act and section 75 of that Act".
59 In section 78(3)(a) (affirmative orders) omit "22(9), 23A(6), 25(5),".
60 In section 81(9) (general interpretation: certain references relating to Northern Ireland) omit "23A(7)(b),".

Police Reform Act 2002

61 (1) Paragraph 19ZA of Schedule 3 to the Police Reform Act 2002 (investigations by the IPCC: information notices) is amended as follows.
   (2) In sub-paragraph (3) omit—
      (a) the words from "(within the meaning of Chapter 2" to "2000)", and
      (b) the words "(within the meaning of that Chapter)".
   (3) After sub-paragraph (3) insert—
      "(3A) In sub-paragraph (3) "communications data", "postal operator" and "telecommunications operator" have the same meanings as in the Investigatory Powers Act 2016 (see sections 261 and 262 of that Act)."

PART 4

RETENTION OF COMMUNICATIONS DATA

Anti-terrorism, Crime and Security Act 2001

62 Omit Part 11 of the Anti-terrorism, Crime and Security Act 2001 (retention of communications data).

Data Retention and Investigatory Powers Act 2014

63 Omit sections 1 and 2 of the Data Retention and Investigatory Powers Act 2014 (retention of relevant communications data).

PART 5

EQUIPMENT INTERFERENCE

Regulation of Investigatory Powers Act 2000

64 The Regulation of Investigatory Powers Act 2000 is amended as follows.

Appendix

65 In section 48 (interpretation of Part 2), in subsection (3)(c)—
  (a) omit the "or" at the end of sub-paragraph (i);
  (b) after sub-paragraph (ii) insert "; or (iii) Part 5, or Chapter 3 of Part 6, of the Investigatory Powers Act 2016 (equipment interference)."

66 (1) Paragraph 2 of Schedule 2 (persons having the appropriate permission where data obtained under warrant etc.) is amended as follows.
  (2) In sub-paragraph (1)—
    (a) omit the "or" at the end of paragraph (a);
    (b) after paragraph (b) insert "; or
    (c) a targeted equipment interference warrant issued under section 106 of the Investigatory Powers Act 2016 (powers of law enforcement chiefs to issue warrants to law enforcement officers)."
  (3) In sub-paragraph (5), at the end insert "or under a targeted equipment interference warrant issued under section 106 of the Investigatory Powers Act 2016."
  (4) In sub-paragraph (6)—
    (a) omit the "and" at the end of paragraph (b);
    (b) after paragraph (c) insert "; and
    (d) in relation to protected information obtained under a warrant issued under section 106 of the Investigatory Powers Act 2016, means the person who issued the warrant or, if that person was an appropriate delegate in relation to a law enforcement chief, either that person or the law enforcement chief."
  (5) After sub-paragraph (6) insert—
    "(6A) In sub-paragraph (6)(d), the references to a law enforcement chief and to an appropriate delegate in relation to a law enforcement chief are to be read in accordance with section 106(5) of the Investigatory Powers Act 2016."

Regulation of Investigatory Powers (Scotland) Act 2000 (2000 asp 11)

67 The Regulation of Investigatory Powers (Scotland) Act 2000 is amended as follows.

68 In section 5(3) (lawful surveillance etc.), after paragraph (a) (and before the "or" at the end of the paragraph), insert—
"(aa) an enactment contained in Part 5 of the Investigatory Powers Act 2016 (equipment interference) so far as relating to the Police Service;".

69 In section 24(2) (issue and revision of codes of practice), after paragraph (a) (and before the "and" at the end of the paragraph), insert—
"(aa) Part 5 of the Investigatory Powers Act 2016 (equipment interference) so far as relating to the Police Service or the Police Investigations and Review Commissioner;".

Crime and Courts Act 2013

70 (1) In Schedule 1 to the Crime and Courts Act 2013 (the NCA and NCA officers), paragraph 6A (investigatory activity in Northern Ireland) is amended as follows.
  (2) In sub-paragraph (3)—
    (a) in the opening words, omit "an authorisation granted under any of the following provisions";
    (b) before paragraph (a) insert—
      "(za) a targeted equipment interference warrant under Part 5 of the Investigatory Powers Act 2016;";
    (c) in paragraph (a), for "in the" substitute "an authorisation granted under any of the following provisions of the";

Appendix

  (d) in paragraph (b), at the beginning insert "an authorisation granted under".
(3) After sub-paragraph (3) insert—
"(4) For the purpose of sub-paragraph (1), a relevant investigatory activity falling within sub-paragraph (3)(za) is to be regarded as carried out in Northern Ireland if (and to the extent that)—
  (a) the equipment that is being interfered with under the warrant is in Northern Ireland, and
  (b) at the time of the carrying out of the activity, the NCA officer knows that the equipment is in Northern Ireland.
(5) Sub-paragraph (6) applies where—
  (a) in the carrying out by an NCA officer of a relevant investigatory activity falling within sub-paragraph (3)(za), equipment in Northern Ireland is interfered with under the warrant,
  (b) at the time the interference begins, the NCA officer does not know that the equipment is in Northern Ireland, and
  (c) at any time while the interference is continuing, the NCA officer becomes aware that the equipment is in Northern Ireland.
(6) The NCA officer is not to be regarded as in breach of subparagraph (1) if the interference continues after the NCA officer becomes aware that the equipment is in Northern Ireland, provided that the officer informs the Chief Constable of the Police Service of Northern Ireland about the interference as soon as reasonably practicable."

PART 6

JUDICIAL COMMISSIONERS

Police Act 1997

71 The Police Act 1997 is amended as follows.
72 In section 103(8) (appeals) for "the period" substitute "any period".
73 In section 105(1)(b)(iii) (reports of appeals dismissed) omit "under section 107(2),".
74 In section 108(1) (interpretation of Part 3) after the definition of "designated deputy" insert—
""the Investigatory Powers Commissioner" and "Judicial Commissioner" have the same meanings as in the Investigatory Powers Act 2016 (see section 263(1) of that Act);".

Regulation of Investigatory Powers Act 2000

75 The Regulation of Investigatory Powers Act 2000 is amended as follows.
76 In section 37(9)(a) (appeals against decisions of ordinary Surveillance Commissioners) for "the period" substitute "any period".
77 In section 39(3) (appeals: reports of Chief Surveillance Commissioner)—
  (a) for "Subsections (3) and (4) of section 107 of the Police Act 1997" substitute "Subsections (6) to (8) of section 234 of the Investigatory Powers Act 2016", and
  (b) for "subsection (2) of that section" substitute "subsection (1) of that section".
78 Omit section 40 (information to be provided to Surveillance Commissioners).
79 In section 51(7)(b) (notification to Intelligence Services Commissioner or Chief Surveillance Commissioner of certain directions relating to the disclosure of a key to protected information) for "the Commissioner in question" substitute "the Investigatory Powers Commissioner".

80 (1) Section 64 (delegation of Commissioners' functions) is amended as follows.
  (2) In the heading for "Commissioners' functions" substitute "functions of the Investigatory Powers Commissioner for Northern Ireland".
  (3) In subsection (1)—
    (a) omit "or any provision of an Act of the Scottish Parliament", and
    (b) for "a relevant Commissioner" substitute "the Investigatory Powers Commissioner for Northern Ireland".
  (4) Omit subsection (2).
81 In section 71(2) (issue and revision of codes of practice) for "the Surveillance Commissioners" substitute "a Judicial Commissioner".
82 (1) Section 72 (effect of codes of practice) is amended as follows.
  (2) In subsection (4) for paragraphs (c) to (e) (and the word "or" between paragraphs (d) and (e)) substitute—
    "(ba) the Investigatory Powers Commissioner for Northern Ireland carrying out functions under this Act, or
    (bb) the Investigatory Powers Commissioner or any other Judicial Commissioner carrying out functions under this Act, the Investigatory Powers Act 2016 or the Police Act 1997,".
  (3) Omit subsection (5).
83 (1) Section 81(1) (general definitions) is amended as follows.
  (2) Omit the definitions of "Assistant Surveillance Commissioner", "ordinary Surveillance Commissioner", "Surveillance Commissioner" and "Chief Surveillance Commissioner".
  (3) After the definition of "interception warrant" insert—
    ""the Investigatory Powers Commissioner" and "Judicial Commissioner" have the same meanings as in the Investigatory Powers Act 2016 (see section 263(1) of that Act);".

Regulation of Investigatory Powers (Scotland) Act 2000 (2000 asp 11)

84 The Regulation of Investigatory Powers (Scotland) Act 2000 is amended as follows.
85 In the cross-heading before section 2 (Surveillance Commissioners) for "Surveillance" substitute "Judicial".
86 In section 2(10) (restrictions on appeals against Commissioners)—
  (a) for "Chief Surveillance Commissioner" substitute "Investigatory Powers Commissioner", and
  (b) for "other Surveillance Commissioner" substitute "other Judicial Commissioner".
87 In the heading of section 16 for "Surveillance Commissioners" substitute "Judicial Commissioners".
88 Omit section 18 (information to be provided to Surveillance Commissioners).
89 In the cross-heading before section 21 (Chief Surveillance Commissioner) for "Chief Surveillance" substitute "Investigatory Powers".
90 Omit section 21 (functions of Chief Surveillance Commissioner).
91 (1) Section 22 (co-operation with, and reports by, Chief Surveillance Commissioner) is amended as follows.
  (2) Omit subsection (1).
  (3) In subsection (2) for "Chief Surveillance Commissioner" substitute "Investigatory Powers Commissioner".
  (4) In subsection (3)—
    (a) for "Chief Surveillance Commissioner" substitute "Investigatory Powers Commissioner", and
    (b) after "under" insert ", and in relation to,".

Appendix

92 In section 24(2) (issue and revision of codes of practice) for "the Surveillance Commissioners appointed under this Act or the Commissioners holding office under section 91 of that Act" substitute "the Judicial Commissioners".

93 In section 26(4) (effect of codes of practice)—
   (a) in paragraph (b) for "Chief Surveillance Commissioner" substitute "Investigatory Powers Commissioner", and
   (b) in paragraph (c) for "a Surveillance Commissioner" substitute "a Judicial Commissioner (other than the Investigatory Powers Commissioner)".

94 (1) Section 31(1) (interpretation) is amended as follows.
   (2) After the definitions of "directed" and "intrusive" insert—
   ""the Investigatory Powers Commissioner" and "Judicial Commissioner" have the same meanings as in the Investigatory Powers Act 2016 (see section 263(1) of that Act);".
   (3) Omit the definitions of "ordinary Surveillance Commissioner", "Surveillance Commissioner" and "Chief Surveillance Commissioner".

Terrorism Prevention and Investigation Measures Act 2011

95 In section 21(3)(b) of the Terrorism Prevention and Investigation Measures Act 2011 (duty to consult certain persons before making an order for the continuation, repeal etc. of TPIM powers) for "the Intelligence Services Commissioner" substitute "the Investigatory Powers Commissioner".

Protection of Freedoms Act 2012

96 The Protection of Freedoms Act 2012 is amended as follows.

97 (1) Section 29 (code of practice for surveillance camera systems) is amended as follows.
   (2) In subsection (5)(d) (duty to consult certain persons in preparing code) for "the Chief Surveillance Commissioner" substitute "the Investigatory Powers Commissioner".
   (3) In subsection (7) omit the definition of "the Chief Surveillance Commissioner".

98 In section 33(8)(d) (duty to consult before making an order identifying who must have regard to the code) for "the Chief Surveillance Commissioner" substitute "the Investigatory Powers Commissioner".

PART 7

OTHER MINOR AND CONSEQUENTIAL PROVISION

Telecommunications Act 1984

99 Omit section 94 of the Telecommunications Act 1984 (directions in the interests of national security etc.).

Northern Ireland Act 1998

100 In paragraph 17 of Schedule 2 to the Northern Ireland Act 1998 (excepted matters) after "subversion;" insert "the Technical Advisory Board provided for by section 245 of the Investigatory Powers Act 2016;".

Communications Act 2003

101 (1) The Communications Act 2003 is amended as follows.
   (2) In section 401(5)(g), for "sections 47 to 49" substitute "section 47 or 48".
   (3) In Schedule 18 (transitional provisions), omit paragraph

Appendix

PART 8
REPEALS AND REVOCATIONS CONSEQUENTIAL ON OTHER REPEALS OR AMENDMENTS IN THIS ACT

General amendments

Title	Extent of repeal or revocation
Serious Crime Act 2015	Section 83.
	Section 86(12).
	In Schedule 4, paragraph 18.

Lawful interception of communications

Title	Extent of repeal or revocation
Regulation of Investigatory Powers Act 2000	In Schedule 4, paragraphs 7(2) and 9.
Anti-terrorism, Crime and Security Act 2001	Section 116(3).
Inquiries Act 2005	In Schedule 2, paragraphs 20 and 21.
Terrorism Act 2006	Section 32.
Wireless Telegraphy Act 2006	In Schedule 7, paragraphs 22 and 23.
National Health Service (Consequential Provisions) Act 2006	In Schedule 1, paragraph 208.
Armed Forces Act 2006	In Schedule 16, paragraph 169.
Serious Crime Act 2007	In Schedule 12, paragraph 6.
Counter-Terrorism Act 2008	Sections 69 and 74.
Policing and Crime Act 2009	Section 100.
Terrorist Asset-Freezing etc. Act 2010	Section 28(2) and (3).
Terrorism Prevention and Investigation Measures Act 2011	In Schedule 7, paragraph 4.
Regulation of Investigatory Powers (Monetary Penalty Notices and Consents for Interceptions) Regulations 2011 (S.I. 2011/1340)	The whole Regulations.
Health and Social Care Act 2012	In Schedule 5, paragraph 98.
Justice and Security Act 2013	Section 16.
	In Schedule 2, paragraph 11.
Crime and Courts Act 2013	In Schedule 8, paragraph 78.
	In Schedule 9, paragraph 125.
Data Retention and Investigatory Powers Act 2014	Section 3(1) and (2).
	Section 4(2) to (7).
	Section 5.
Counter-Terrorism and Security Act 2015	Section 15(3).
	In Schedule 8, paragraph 2.

Appendix

Acquisition and retention of communications data

Title	Extent of repeal or revocation
Serious Organised Crime and Police Act 2005	In Schedule 4, paragraph 135.
Serious Crime Act 2007	In Schedule 12, paragraphs 7 and 8.
Police, Public Order and Criminal Justice (Scotland) Act 2006 (Consequential Provisions and Modifications) Order 2007 (S.I. 2007/1098)	In the Schedule, paragraph 4(5).
Policing and Crime Act 2009	Section 7. In Schedule 7, paragraphs 13 and 14.
Protection of Freedoms Act 2012	Section 37. In Schedule 9, paragraphs 7 and 8 and, in paragraph 16(b), sub-paragraph (i) (and the word "and" at the end of sub-paragraph (i)).
Crime and Courts Act 2013	In Schedule 8, paragraph 81.
Police and Fire Reform (Scotland) Act 2012 (Consequential Provisions and Modifications) Order 2013 (S.I. 2013/602)	In Schedule 2, paragraph 33(5) to (8) and (15)(a).
Data Retention and Investigatory Powers Act 2014	Section 3(3) and (4). Section 4(8) to (10).
Counter-Terrorism and Security Act 2015	Section 21. Section 52(3)(a).

Judicial Commissioners

Title	Extent of repeal or revocation
Scotland Act 1998 (Cross-Border Public Authorities) (Adaptation of Functions etc.) Order 1999 (S.I. 1999/1747)	In Schedule 6, paragraph 2(2) and (5).
Regulation of Investigatory Powers Act 2000	In Schedule 4, paragraph 8(1), (10) and (11).
Insolvency Act 2000	In Schedule 4, paragraph 22(2).
Scotland Act 1998 (Transfer of Functions to the Scottish Ministers etc.) (No. 2) Order 2000 (S.I. 2000/3253)	In Schedule 3, paragraphs 9 to 12.
Insolvency Act 2000 (Company Directors Disqualification Undertakings) Order 2004 (S.I. 2004/1941)	In the Schedule, paragraph 10.
Constitutional Reform Act 2005	In Schedule 17, paragraphs 27 and 30(2)(a) and (b).
Tribunals, Courts and Enforcement Act 2007	In Schedule 16, paragraph 11(2).
Serious Crime Act 2007	In Schedule 12, paragraph 3.

(continued)

Appendix

Title	Extent of repeal or revocation
Companies Act 2006 (Consequential Amendments, Transitional Provisions and Savings) Order 2009 (S.I. 2009/1941)	In Schedule 1, paragraph 169.
Police Reform and Social Responsibility Act 2011	In Schedule 16, paragraph 222.
Protection of Freedoms Act 2012	In Schedule 9, paragraphs 10 and 11.
Justice and Security Act 2013	Section 5. In Schedule 2, paragraph 4.
Crime and Courts Act 2013	In Schedule 8, paragraph 59. In Schedule 21, paragraph 4.
Police and Fire Reform (Scotland) Act 2012 (Consequential Provisions and Modifications) Order 2013 (S.I. 2013/602)	In Schedule 1, paragraph 6(6). In Schedule 2, paragraph 33(20) and (22)(c).
Anti-social Behaviour, Crime and Policing Act 2014	Section 150.
Data Retention and Investigatory Powers Act 2014	Section 6.

Other minor and consequential provision

Title	Extent of repeal or revocation
Communications Act 2003	In Schedule 17, paragraph 70.

Index

additional powers 10.03–10.44
  approval of notices
    following a reference and review 10.49–10.51
    by judicial commissioners 10.26–10.29
  national security notices 10.03–10.12
  other matters relating to national security and technical capability notices 10.30–10.38
  enforceability 10.33–10.35
  other matters relating to technical capability notices 10.36–10.38
  relevant notices 10.30–10.32
  review of notices by the Secretary of State 10.45–10.48
  technical capability notices 10.13–10.25
    regulations 10.18–10.25
  variation and revocation of relevant notices 10.39–10.44
  see also **amendments**; **combined warrants**; **miscellaneous provisions**
additional protections 4.77–4.97
  authorizations to identify or confirm journalistic sources 4.83–4.86
  collaboration agreements 4.87–4.95
  lawfulness of conduct authorized by this Part 4.96–4.97
  Single Point of Contact (SPOC), use of 4.77–4.82
  see also **authorization**
advisory bodies 9.85–9.91
  membership of the panel 9.90–9.91
  Technical Advisory Board 9.85–9.86
  Technology Advisory Panel 9.87–9.89
  see also **oversight arrangements**
agency arrangements *see* **transfer and agency arrangements**
amendments
  to other enactments relating to investigatory powers 10.52–10.58
  to warrants under Section 5 of the ISA 10.54
  Intelligence Services Act (1994) 10.52–10.53
    amendments to functions of GCHQ 10.52–10.53
  Wireless Telegraphy Act (2006) 10.55–10.58
  see also **additional powers**; **combined warrants**; **miscellaneous provisions**
annual reports 9.49–9.53
  see also **reporting**
apparatus, definition 1.76, 10.74
applicable obligation, definition 10.14
approval of notices
  by judicial commissioners 10.26–10.29
  following a reference and review 10.49–10.51
authorization 4.06–4.37, 10.59–10.124
  additional protections 4.77–4.97
  authorization 4.06–4.37
  authorization data, definition 4.46
  authorized notices and 4.29–4.32
    duration and cancellation of 4.33–4.34
  context 4.01–4.05
  definition 9.04
  Designated Senior Officer (DSO) 4.07–4.11
  duties of telecommunications operators 4.35–4.37
  filtering 4.38–4.52
  internet connection records (ICR) 4.21–4.28
  local authorities 4.63–4.76
  for obtaining communications data 4.01–4.111
  power to authorize 4.12–4.20
    limits on authorization 4.18–4.20
    permissible conduct 4.15–4.17
    requirements under Section 61 4.13–4.14
  public authorities 4.53–4.62
  see also **additional protections**; **authorization**; **combined warrants**; **filtering**; **local authorities**; **public authorities**
authorized disclosures, definition 6.115
authorized purposes, definition 7.42, 7.109, 7.170

British Islands connection, definition 2.71, 6.41
bulk acquisition warrants 7.65–7.119
  approval of warrants by judicial commissioners 7.74–7.76
  bulk acquisition warrants: provisions 7.65–7.73
  cancellation of warrants 7.98–7.99
  duration of warrants 7.84
  duty of operators to assist with implementation 7.106–7.108
  implementation of warrants 7.100–7.101
  modification of warrants 7.89–7.97
    approval by judicial commissioners 7.93–7.94
    approval made in urgent cases 7.95–7.97
  offence of breaching safeguards relating to examination of data 7.113–7.116
  offence of making unauthorized disclosure 7.117–7.119
  renewal 7.85–7.88
    exceptions 7.88
  requirements that must be met by warrants 7.77–7.83
    non-operational purpose requirements 7.78
    operational purposes: procedural matters 7.79–7.81

Index

bulk acquisition warrants (*cont.*)
　operational purposes: requirements 7.82–7.83
　safeguards 7.109–7.112
　　examination of data 7.112
　　retention and disclosure of data 7.109–7.111
　service of warrants 7.102–7.105
bulk equipment interference warrants 7.120–7.191
　additional safeguards 7.180–7.186
　　confidential journalistic material 7.186
　　items subject to legal privilege 7.180–7.185
　application of other restrictions in relations to warrants 7.191
　approval of warrants 7.132–7.137
　　non-urgent cases 7.132–7.134
　　urgent cases 7.135–7.137
　bulk equipment interference warrants 7.120–7.127
　　meaning of 'equipment data' 7.127
　cancellation of warrants 7.165–7.166
　duration of warrants 7.149
　failure to approve warrant issued in urgent case 7.138–7.141
　implementation of warrants 7.167–7.169
　modification of warrants 7.154–7.164
　　approval in non-urgent cases 7.159–7.160
　　approval in urgent cases 7.161–7.164
　offence of breaching safeguards relating to examination of material 7.187–7.190
　power to issue bulk equipment interference warrants 7.128–7.131
　renewal of warrants 7.150–7.153
　　exceptions 7.153
　requirements that must be met by warrants 7.142–7.148
　　non-operational purpose requirements 7.143
　　operational purposes: procedural matters 7.144–7.146
　　operational purposes: requirements 7.147–7.148
　safeguards 7.170–7.179
　　disclosure of material overseas 7.173–7.174
　　examination of material 7.175–7.179
　　retention and disclosure of material 7.170–7.172
bulk personal dataset (BPD) warrants 8.01–8.101
　application of Part 7 to other parts of the IPA 8.95–8.101
　　application for a 'Direction' 8.95–8.98
　　judicial approval for Directions and variations to Directions 8.99–8.101
　approval of specific 8.39–8.41
　class BPD warrants 8.23–8.26
　　conditions to be met prior to issue 8.24–8.26
　　restrictions on use 8.16
　context 8.01–8.09
　non-renewal or cancellation of 8.69–8.75
　　applications 8.69–8.72

　　approval of warrants 8.73–8.75
　safeguards 8.79–8.94
　　criminal offence: breaching safeguards 8.90–8.94
　　general 8.79–8.81
　　items subject to legal privilege 8.82–8.89
　specific BPD warrants 8.27–8.32
　　additional requirements 8.33–8.35
　　conditions to be met prior to issue 8.29–8.32
　　health records 8.33–8.34
　　protected data 8.35
　urgent cases 8.39–8.41
　warrants 8.10–8.53
　　approval of warrants by judicial commissioners 8.36–8.41
　　class BPD warrants 8.23–8.26
　　consequences where judicial commissioner refuses to approve in urgent cases 8.42–8.45
　　requirements that must be met by 8.46–8.53
　　specific BPD: additional requirements 8.33–8.35
　　specific BPD warrants 8.27–8.32
　　types of warrants 8.12–8.22
　　when Part 7 is engaged 8.10–8.11
　warrants: post-issue matters 8.54–8.78
　　acquisition of bulk personal datasets outside statutory scheme 8.76–8.78
　　cancellation of warrants 8.68
　　duration of warrants 8.54
　　judicial approval 8.63–8.67
　　Lazarus/ non-renewal or cancellation of BPD warrants 8.69–8.75
　　modification of warrants 8.59–8.62
　　renewal of warrants 8.55–8.58
bulk warrants 7.01–7.191
　see also **bulk acquisition warrants**; **bulk equipment interference warrants**; **bulk personal dataset warrants**

change of circumstances, definition 7.50, 7.178
Chief of Defence Intelligence 6.31
civil liability
　for unlawful interceptions 2.54
collaborating police force, definition 4.90
collaboration agreements 4.87–4.95
collaborative agreements, definition 6.34
collaborative police force, definition 6.34, 6.40
combination of factors, definition 3.74
combined warrants
　application to 10.114–10.118
　　each part as a single instrument 10.111–10.113
　authorizations 10.59–10.124
　Intelligence Services Act (1994) 10.60–10.63
　Police Act (1997), Part III 10.64–10.70
　Regulation of Investigatory Powers Act (2000) 10.71–10.92
　requirements and rules 10.108–10.118

504

Index

requirements 10.108–10.110
Schedule 8 IPA 10.93–10.124
special rules 10.119–10.123
targeted equipment interference warrants 10.101–10.103
targeted interception warrants 10.94–10.97
targeted examination warrants only 10.106–10.107
see also additional powers; amendments; miscellaneous provisions; Regulation of Investigatory Powers Act (2000); Schedule 8 IPA
communication, definition 1.75, 1.84
communications, definition 2.69
communications data
 abolition of powers to obtain 2.62–2.72
 definition 1.53, 1.79, 1.85–1.86, 5.10
 interception and 1.47
 see also retention of communications data
compliance cuts
 payment towards 10.128–10.131
compliance systems
 power to develop 10.132–10.133
confidentiality, principle of 2.11
consequential amendments
 power to make 10.124
content, definition 1.53, 1.80, 2.32
copy, definition 6.107, 7.44, 7.111, 7.172
corporate bodies
 offences under the IPA 10.125–10.127
covert human intelligence sources 1.16
 other than relevant sources 10.82–10.83

data 1.88–1.90
 definition of 1.77
 identifying 1.88–1.89
 systems data 1.90
Data Retention and Investigatory Powers Act (DRIPA) (2014) 1.39
designated, definition 4.50
designated customs official, definition 6.33
Designated Senior Officer (DSO)
 authorization 4.07–4.11
 definition 4.09, 4.55, 4.64
 relevant public authorities 4.53–4.57
designated senior official, definition 3.95, 3.104
Directions
 applications for 8.95–8.98
 judicial approval for 8.99–8.101
 variations to 8.99–8.101
director, definition 10.127
disclosure, definition 3.158, 3.161, 6.115–6.118
disclosure in connection with oversight bodies, definition 6.116
disclosures of a general nature, definition 6.118
discretionary reporting 9.52
 see also reporting

enactment, definition 10.124
enforceability 10.33–10.35
enforcement 5.40–5.44
entity data, definition 1.77
equipment data
 definition 2.69, 7.127
 types of warrants 6.08
equipment interference 6.01–6.121
 context 6.01–6.04
 disclosure 6.104–6.121
  duty not to make unauthorized disclosures 6.111–6.113
  excepted disclosures 6.114–6.118
  offence of making unauthorized disclosure 6.119–6.121
  safeguards 6.104–6.111
 safeguards 6.52–6.65
  confidential journalistic material and journalistic sources 6.60–6.62
  items subject to legal privilege 6.55–6.59
  Members of Parliament 6.52–6.54
  requirements that must be met by warrants 6.63–6.65
 warrants 6.05–6.51
  approval by judicial commissioners 6.42–6.51
  definition 2.69
  issuing 6.17–6.41
  scope of 6.10–6.11
  subject matter of 6.12–6.16
  types of 6.05–6.09
 warrants: post-issue matters 6.66–6.103
  cancellation 6.93–6.95
  duration 6.66
  duty of telecommunications operators to assist with implementation 6.101–6.103
  implementation 6.96–6.97
  modification 6.71–6.92
  renewal of warrants 6.67–6.70
  service of warrants 6.98–6.100
events data, definition 1.78
examination, concept of 1.45
external communications, definition 1.25, 1.35, 3.06
extra-territoriality
 application of Part 3 4.110–4.111
 retention of communications data 5.44

factor, definition 3.74
filtering 4.38–4.52
 arrangements 4.40–4.42
 access 4.50
 acquisition 4.46–4.48
 functioning 4.52
 retention 4.49
 Secretary of State's duties 4.45–4.52
 security 4.51
 use of following authorization 4.43–4.44
 provision 4.38–4.39
future-proofing, definition 1.03

505

Index

GCHQ
  amendments to functions of 10.52–10.53
general information power, definition 2.63, 2.66
general privacy protections 2.01–2.73
  abolition of powers to obtain communications data 2.62–2.72
  civil liability for unlawful interceptions 2.54
  context 2.01–2.05
  interception of communications 2.19–2.38
    conduct amounting to 2.19–2.36
    conduct that is not interception 2.37–2.38
    in the course of transmission 2.24–2.36
    relevant act 2.22
    relevant time 2.23
  lawful authority 2.39–2.42
  monetary penalties for unlawful interceptions 2.43–2.53
    Schedule 1 IPA 2.46–2.53
  offence of unlawfully obtaining communications data 2.59–2.61
  restriction on requesting interception by overseas authorities 2.55–2.58
  restriction on use of Section 93 of the Police Act (1997) 2.73
  Section 1 IPA and 'overview' provisions 2.06–2.10
  unlawful interception 2.11–2.18

health professional, definition 8.19
health records 8.33–8.34
  definition 8.19
health service body, definition 8.19
Henry VIII clauses 1.64–1.65

identifying data, definition 1.88, 3.22, 7.05
immigration detention facilities 3.140–3.141
  definition 3.141
immigration or nationality offence, definition 6.38
immigration officer, definition 6.33
'in the course of transmission' 2.24–2.36
  definition 2.24
  see also interception of communications
Independent Surveillance Review (ISR) 1.54–1.58
initial period, definition 1.61
instrument, definition 3.77
intelligence activities, definition 9.32
intelligence services 6.24–6.28
  in Scotland 6.29–6.30
Intelligence Services Act (1994) 10.52–10.53
  amendments to functions of GCHQ 10.52–10.53
  combined warrants or authorizations 10.60–10.63
intercept material, handling of 3.143–3.147
interception, definition 1.45, 2.15, 2.44, 2.37
interception of communications 2.19–2.38
  conduct amounting to 2.19–2.36
    in the course of transmission 2.24–2.36

    relevant act 2.22
    relevant time 2.23
  conduct that is not interception 2.37–2.38
  legislative overview 1.05–1.19
    general saving for lawful conduct 1.14–1.19
    Interception of Communications Act (1985) 1.06–1.07
    Regulation of Investigatory Powers Act (2000) 1.08–1.13
Interception of Communications Act (1985)
  interception of communications 1.06–1.07
interception-related conduct, definition 3.154–3.155
internal, definition 3.06
internet connection records (ICR) 4.21–4.28
investigatory powers, definition 1.47
Investigatory Powers Act (2016) 1.01–1.99
  background 1.01–1.04
  commencement 1.91–1.93
  developments 1.38–1.39
    Data Retention and Investigatory Powers Act (DRIPA) (2014) 1.39
  events leading to reform 1.20–1.26
    early legal challenges 1.23–1.26
  evolution 1.05–1.58
  interception of communications, legislative overview 1.05–1.19
    general saving for lawful conduct 1.14–1.19
    Interception of Communications Act (1985) 1.06–1.07
    Regulation of Investigatory Powers Act (2000) 1.08–1.13
  making of regulations 1.63–1.73
  overview 1.59–1.60
  postal definitions 1.83–1.87
  preliminary assessment of 1.94–1.99
  provisions of general application 1.59–1.90
    data 1.88–1.90
    identifying data 1.88–1.89
    systems data 1.90
  review of operation of act 1.61–1.62
  reviews 1.40–1.58
    Independent Surveillance Review (ISR) 1.54–1.58
    overview 1.40–1.43
    privacy and security 1.44–1.46
    Question of Trust 1.47–1.53
  Section 8 RIPA 1.27–1.37
    competing interpretations of 1.30–1.37
    external communications 1.29
    internal communications 1.28
  telecommunications definitions 1.74–1.82
    communications data 1.79–1.80
    definitions 1.81–1.82
Investigatory Powers Tribunal (IPT) 9.57–9.84
  changes to the exercise of jurisdiction 9.70–9.77
    procedural change 9.71–9.77
  jurisdictional changes to 9.57–9.69
    amendments 9.61–9.69

Index

conduct 9.61
failures 9.64
giving of notices or authorizations 9.62
issuing warrants and ancillary matters 9.63
right of appeal from 9.78–9.84
issuing authority, definition 6.107

journalistic material
confidential 6.60–6.62, 7.58, 7.186
definition 3.64, 6.60
journalistic sources
authorizations to identify or confirm 4.83–4.86
judicial commissioners
approval of notices by 10.26–10.29
approval of warrants by:
bulk acquisition warrants 7.74–7.76
bulk personal dataset warrants 8.36–8.41
bulk warrants 7.13–7.15
equipment interference 6.42–6.51
lawful interception of communications 3.45–3.56
major modifications 7.93–7.94
non-urgent cases 3.46–3.47, 6.42–6.44, 8.36–8.38
refusal to approve 3.51–3.56, 6.48–6.51, 8.42–8.45
urgent cases 3.48–3.56, 6.48–6.51, 8.39–8.45
functions 9.19–9.45
additional functions under Part 8 IPA 9.39–9.41
delegable functions 9.22–9.24
directed oversight functions 9.32–9.33
duty to inform public of certain acts of non-compliance/error reporting 9.34–9.38
ISC referrals 9.42
limitations on the exercise of 9.19–9.21
other 9.32–9.45
power to modify 9.45
reports by public authorities of non-compliance by telecommunication operator 9.43
review 9.25–9.31
under Other Parts/Enactments 9.44
oversight arrangements 9.10–9.48
abolition of existing oversight bodies 9.10–9.11
appointment 9.12–9.15
functions of commissioners 9.19–9.45
funding and resources 9.18
investigation and information-gathering powers 9.46–9.48
terms and conditions of appointment 9.16–9.17
judicial review principles 1.97, 9.04

law enforcement chiefs 10.105
modification of warrants issued by 6.84–6.92
non-urgent cases 6.84–6.87
urgent cases 6.88–6.92
law enforcement officers
definition 6.102
restriction on issue of warrants 6.39–6.41
Schedule 6 IPA 6.32–6.34
law enforcement officials 6.38
police 6.35–6.37
lawful authority 2.39–2.42
definition 2.18, 2.39
lawful conduct
general saving for 1.14–1.19
lawful interception of communications 3.01–3.166
additional safeguards 3.57–3.66
items subject to legal privilege 3.59–3.66
Members of Parliament 3.57–3.58
approval of warrants by judicial commissioners 3.45–3.56
background 3.45
failure to approve 3.51–3.56
non-urgent cases 3.46–3.47
urgent cases 3.48–3.56
context 3.01–3.05
disclosure of intercept material 3.150–3.162
disclosure overseas 3.150–3.151
duty not to make unauthorized disclosures 3.156–3.162
exclusion of matters from legal proceedings 3.152–3.155
forms of lawful interception 3.121–3.142
consent 3.121–3.122
interception for administrative, enforcement or regulatory purposes 3.123–3.133
handling intercept material 3.143–3.147
interception in prisons and other institutions 3.134–3.142
immigration detention facilities 3.140–3.141
interception in accordance with overseas requests 3.142
prisons 3.134–3.136
psychiatric hospitals 3.137–3.139
issuing warrants 3.26–3.44
grounds on which warrants may be issued 3.33–3.44
Secretary of State's power 3.29–3.32
offence of making unauthorized disclosures 3.163–3.166
privileged items 3.148–3.149
restrictions on handling and disclosure of intercept material obtained under warrants 3.143–3.162
warrants 3.05–3.25
formalities 3.67–3.82
types of 3.06–3.25
see also **warrants**
lawfulness of conduct 4.96–4.97
leave to appeal 9.81

507

Index

legal privilege, items subject to 8.82–8.89
  bulk equipment interference
    warrants 7.180–7.185
  definition 6.117
  examination 8.82–8.87
  lawful interception of
    communications 3.59–3.66
  retention 8.88–8.89
  safeguards 3.59–3.66, 6.55–6.59
  warrants 7.52–7.57
  see also **safeguards**
legal proceedings
  definition 7.11
  exclusion of matters from 3.152–3.155
local authorities 4.63–4.76
  authorizations:
    judicial approval 4.72–4.76
    procedure 4.73–4.76
  definition 4.07
  see also **public authorities**
long term authorisation,
  definition 10.85, 10.92

Members of Parliament (MPs)
  equipment interference 6.52–6.54
  lawful interception of
    communications 3.57–3.58
  member of a relevant legislature,
    definition 3.58
minimum mandatory reporting 9.49–9.52
  see also **reporting**
miscellaneous provisions 10.125–10.133
  authorizations 4.102–4.111
  compliance with IPA 10.128–10.133
    payments towards cuts 10.128–10.131
    power to develop systems 10.132–10.133
  extra-territorial application of Part 3
    4.110–4.111
  offences under the IPA committed
    by a body corporate or Scottish
    partnership 10.125–10.127
  transfer and agency arrangements/
    regulations 4.102–4.109
  see also **additional powers; amendments; combined warrants; miscellaneous provisions**
modification of warrants 6.71–6.92
  issued by law enforcement chiefs 6.84–6.92
  issued by the Secretary of State of Scottish
    Ministers 6.71–6.73
  judicial approval in urgent and safeguarded
    cases 6.79–6.83
  non-urgent cases 6.84–6.87
  persons entitled to make
    modifications 6.74–6.76
  requirement to notify 6.77–6.78
  urgent cases 6.88–6.92
mutual assistance warrants 3.15–3.17,
  3.102–3.106

national security
  definition in statute 10.04
  matters relating to 10.30–10.38
  notices 10.03–10.12
necessary for the authorised purposes,
  definition 3.145
notices
  national security 10.03–10.12
  relevant 10.30–10.32
    variation and revocation of 10.39–10.44
  review by the Secretary of State 10.45–10.48
  technical capability 10.13–10.25, 10.36–10.38
  regulations 10.18–10.25
  see also **approval of notices**

obtaining communications, definition 6.06
obtaining secondary data 3.21–3.22
only for the specified purposes, definition 7.112
other relevant crime, definition 4.27
overseas
  authorities
    restriction on requesting
      interception 2.55–2.58
  disclosure of material or
    data 3.150–3.151, 6.108
  overseas-related communications,
    definition 7.05, 7.121
  overseas-related equipment data,
    definition 7.121–7.122
  overseas-related information, definition 7.121
  requests, interception in accordance with 3.142
oversight arrangements 9.01–9.91
  advisory bodies 9.85–9.91
    membership of the panel 9.90–9.91
    Technical Advisory Board 9.85–9.86
    Technology Advisory Panel 9.87–9.89
  context 9.01–9.09
  Investigatory Powers Tribunal 9.57–9.84
    amendments 9.61–9.69
    changes to the exercise of the IPT's
      jurisdiction 9.70–9.77
    changes to procedure 9.71–9.77
    conduct 9.61
    failures 9.64
    giving of notices or authorizations 9.62
    issuing warrants and ancillary matters 9.63
    jurisdictional changes to 9.57–9.69
    right of appeal from 9.78–9.84
  judicial commissioners 9.10–9.48
    abolition of existing oversight
      bodies 9.10–9.11
    appointment 9.12–9.15
    functions of 9.19–9.45
    funding and resources 9.18
    investigation and information-gathering
      powers 9.46–9.48
    terms and conditions of
      appointment 9.16–9.17

Index

reporting 9.49–9.56
  annual and other reports 9.49–9.55
  discretionary and other reporting 9.53
  minimum mandatory reporting 9.49–9.52
  other reports 9.56
  Prime Ministerial duties 9.54–9.56
'overview' provisions 2.06–2.10

part of a power, definition 2.66
permissible conduct 4.15–4.17
see also authorization
person, definition 2.21
personal data, definition 8.10
phone hacking inquiry 1.20
Police Act (1997)
  Part III 10.64–10.70
  restriction on use of Section 93 2.73
post-issue 5.17–5.23
see also retention of communications data
postal definitions 1.83–1.87
  postal data, definition 1.85–1.86, 2.38
  postal item, definition 1.83
  postal operator, definition 1.83
  postal service, definition 1.83–1.84, 1.86–1.87
  public postal service, definition 1.87, 2.15
postal operators
  duties of 3.115–3.120
  failure to comply with duties 3.118–3.120
power, definition 2.66
pre-issue 5.12–5.16
see also retention of communications data
Prime Ministerial duties
  reporting 9.54–9.56
  annual reports 9.54–9.55
  other reports 9.56
prison 3.134–3.136
  definition 3.135
see also lawful interception of communications
privacy and security 1.44–1.46
  concept of 1.48
  private information, definition 2.69
see also general privacy protections
private telecommunication system,
  definition 1.82, 2.15
privileged items 3.148–3.149
protected data 8.17–8.22, 8.35
  definition 8.17
protected material 6.09
  concept of 8.17
psychiatric hospitals 3.137–3.139
public authorities
  addition or removal from the table 4.58–4.62
  Designated Senior Officers and 4.53–4.57
  enhanced affirmative procedure 4.60–4.62
  other than local authorities 4.53–4.62
  transfer and agency arrangements 4.102–4.109
see also local authorities
public postal service, definition 1.87, 2.15

public telecommunication system, definition 1.81
public telecommunications service, definition 1.81
public telecommunications systems,
  definition 2.15

Question of Trust 1.47–1.53

reasonable excuse, definition 4.99
Regulation of Investigatory Powers Act
  (2000) 10.71–10.92
  covert human intelligence sources, other than
    relevant sources 10.82–10.83
  directed surveillance 10.80
  grounds upon which applications for authority
    may be made 10.88–10.92
  interception of communications 1.08–1.13
  intrusive surveillance 10.81
  matters common to directed and intrusive
    surveillance 10.77–10.79
  relevant sources 10.84–10.87
  surveillance 10.74–10.76
regulatory functions, definition 2.66
regulatory power, definition 2.66
related systems data, definition 3.17, 7.07
relevant act, definition 2.22
relevant activities, definition 3.129
relevant authorisation, definition 10.18
relevant communication, definition 3.17, 7.07
relevant communications data, definition 1.39
relevant content, definition 3.19
relevant costs, definition 10.129
relevant enactment, definition 10.09
relevant error, definition 9.34
relevant grounds, definition 6.42, 6.104, 7.42,
  7.109, 7.170
relevant international agreement,
  definition 3.142
relevant material, definition 7.178
relevant matter, definition 3.131
relevant mutual assistance warrant,
  definition 3.102–3106
relevant notice, definition 10.26
relevant operator, definition 3.116, 10.14
relevant person, definition 2.59
relevant postal power, definition 2.67
relevant public authority, definition 2.59
relevant rules, definition 3.141
relevant Scottish application, definition 3.37
relevant time, definition 2.22–2.23
reporting 9.49–9.56
  annual and other reports 9.49–9.53
    discretionary reporting 9.53
    minimum mandatory reporting 9.49–9.52
  duties of Prime Minister in respect of 9.54–9.56
    annual reports 9.54–9.55
    other reports 9.56
requirements, definition 5.16
restrictions, definition 5.16

Index

retention of communications data 5.01–5.44
  context 5.01–5.04
  enforcement 5.40–5.44
    extra-territoriality 5.44
  post-issue 5.17–5.23
  pre-issue 5.12–5.16
  safeguards 5.24–5.33
    judicial approval 5.24–5.29
    notices 5.24–5.26
    other 5.30–5.33
    variations 5.27–5.29
  scope of retention powers 5.05–5.11
  variation or revocation of notices 5.34–5.39
    matters common to variation and revocation 5.35–5.39
    variation 5.37–5.39
  see also communications data
revocation of notices 5.34–5.39
  variation and revocation 5.35–5.39
  see also **retention of communications data**

safeguards 6.52–6.65, 8.79–8.94
  breaching 8.90–8.94
    examination of data 7.113–7.116
    examination of material 7.187–7.190
  bulk acquisition warrants 7.109–7.112
    examination of data 7.112
    retention and disclosure of data 7.109–7.111
  bulk equipment interference warrants 7.170–7.179
    disclosure of material overseas 7.173–7.174
    examination of material 7.175–7.179
    retention and disclosure of material 7.170–7.172
  confidential journalistic material 6.60–6.62, 7.58, 7.186
  general 8.79–8.81
  legal privilege, items subject to 6.55–6.59, 8.82–8.89
    bulk equipment interference warrants 7.180–7.185
    examination 8.82–8.87
    lawful interception of communications 3.59–3.66
    Members of Parliament 6.52–6.54
    retention 8.88–8.89
  retention of communications data 5.24–5.33
    judicial approval 5.24–5.26
    notices 5.24–5.26
    other safeguards 5.30–5.33
    variations 5.27–5.29
  warrant requirements 6.63–6.65
Schedule 8 IPA 10.93–10.124
  applications of provisions of IPA to combined warrants: special rules 10.119–10.123
  combinations
    targeted interception warrants 10.94–10.97

  targeted equipment interference warrants 10.101–10.103
  targeted examination warrants only 10.106–10.107
  combined warrants: requirements and rules 10.108–10.118
    application to 10.114–10.118
    application to each part as a single instrument 10.111–10.113
    requirements 10.108–10.110
  law enforcement chiefs 10.105
  power to make consequential amendments 10.124
  Scottish Ministers 10.98–10.100, 10.104
Scotland (other grounds) 3.41–3.44
Scotland (Prevention or Detection of Crime) 3.36
Scottish application 3.37–3.40
Scottish Ministers
  modification of warrants by 3.83–3.85, 6.71–6.73
  Schedule 8 IPA 10.98–10.100, 10.104
  Secretary of State of 3.29–3.32, 3.83–3.85, 6.71–6.73
  requirements 3.29–3.32
Scottish partnership
  offences under the IPA 10.125–10.127
senior officer, definition 10.127
senior official, definition 3.68, 6.74, 7.51, 7.179
sensitive personal data, definition 8.20
signals, definition 7.120
Single Point of Contact (SPOC) 4.77–4.82
source of journalistic information, definition 4.86
specified in the warrant, definition 8.79
specified operational purposes, definition 7.18, 7.79, 7.144, 8.48
specified purposes, definition 7.47–7.48, 7.175, 8.79
stored communication, definition 6.10, 7.125
subscribing authority, concept of 4.66
supplying authority, concept of 4.66
surveillance 10.74–10.76
  directed 10.77–10.80
  intrusive 10.77–10.79, 10.81
  surveillance device, definition 10.74
  see also **Regulation of Investigatory Powers Act (2000)**
systems data 1.90
  definition 1.90, 2.33, 3.22, 7.05
  see also **data**

targeted equipment interference warrants 6.12–6.15
targeted examination warrants 3.18–3.20, 6.16
targeted interception 3.16–3.17
  concept of 3.04
targeted warrants 3.12–3.14
targets of warrants 3.23–3.25
  definition 3.23

Index

Technical Advisory Board 9.85–9.86
technical capability notices 10.13–10.25, 10.36–10.38
    regulations 10.18–10.25
    see also notices
Technology Advisory Panel 9.87–9.89
telecommunication system, definition 1.76
telecommunications definitions 1.74–1.82
    communications data 1.79–1.80
    definitions 1.81–1.82
telecommunications operator
    definition 1.76, 2.32, 4.35
    duties in relation to authorizations 4.35–4.37
    duties of 3.115–3.120
    offence of failure to comply 3.118–3.120
    duty to assist with implementation 6.101–6.103
telecommunications service, definition 1.76, 2.32
telecommunications system, definition 2.32
testing or training activities, definition 3.25
'the other contents of the notice', definition 4.31
transfer and agency arrangements
    public authorities and regulations 4.102–4.109

unauthorized disclosure
    definition 3.160
    duty not to make 3.156–3.162
    offence of making 3.163–3.166, 7.117–7.119
underlying material, definition 8.87
unlawful disclosure 4.98–4.101
unlawful interceptions
    civil liability for 2.54
    general privacy protections 2.11–2.18
    monetary penalties for 2.43–2.53
    Schedule 1 IPA 2.46–2.53
    unlawfully obtaining communications data 2.59–2.61

warrants
    acquisition of bulk personal datasets outside statutory scheme 8.76–8.78
        initial examinations: time limits 8.76–8.78
    additional safeguards 7.52–7.58
        confidential journalistic material 7.58
        items subject to legal privilege 7.52–7.57
    affecting overseas operators 7.12
    application of other restrictions in relation to 7.63–7.64
    approval by judicial commissioners 7.13–7.15, 8.36–8.41
        BPD warrants: urgent cases 8.39–8.41
        equipment interference 6.42–6.51
        non-urgent cases 6.42–6.44, 8.36–8.38
        refusal to approve 6.48–6.51
        urgent cases 6.45–6.47
    bulk 7.04–7.64
    bulk interception 7.04–7.07
        power to issue 7.08–7.12
    bulk personal dataset warrants 8.10–8.53
    class BPD warrants 8.23–8.26
        conditions to be met prior to issue 8.24–8.26
        consequences where judicial commissioner refuses to approve in urgent cases 8.42–8.45
    equipment interference 6.05–6.51
    formalities 3.67–3.82
        cancellation 3.99–3.101, 6.93–6.95, 7.37–7.38, 8.68
        duration 3.75–3.76, 6.66, 7.23, 8.54
        duty of postal and telecommunications operators 3.115–3.120, 6.101–6.103
        implementation 3.107–3.110, 6.96–6.97, 7.39–7.41
        modification of 3.83–3.98, 6.71–6.92, 7.28–7.31, 8.59–8.62
        renewal 3.77–3.82, 6.67–6.70, 7.24–7.27, 8.55–8.58
        requirements that must be met 3.69–3.74
        service of warrants 3.111–3.114, 6.98–6.100
        special rules for mutual assistance warrants 3.102–3.106
    issuing 3.26–3.44, 6.17–6.41
        Chief of Defence Intelligence 6.31
        grounds on which warrants may be issued 3.33–3.44
        intelligence services 6.24–6.28
        intelligence services in Scotland 6.29–6.30
        Law Enforcement Officers: Schedule 6 IPA 6.32–6.34
        matters common to all applications for warrants under Part 5 6.19–6.23
        other law enforcement officials 6.38
        police law enforcement officials 6.35–6.37
        restriction on issue of warrants to certain law enforcement officers 6.39–6.41
        Secretary of State's power 3.29–3.32
    judicial approval of 8.63–8.67
        non-urgent cases 8.63–8.64
        urgent cases 8.65–8.67
    lawful interception of communications 3.05–3.25
    Lazarus/ non-renewal or cancellation of BPD warrants 8.69–8.75
        applications 8.69–8.72
        approval of warrants 8.73–8.75
    offence of breaching safeguards relating to examination of material 7.59–7.62
    post-issue matters 6.66–6.103, 8.54–8.78
    requirements that must be met by 3.69–3.74, 7.16–7.22, 8.46–8.53
        non-operational purpose requirements 7.17, 8.47
        operational purposes: procedural matters 7.18–7.20, 8.48–8.50
        operational purposes: requirements 7.21–7.22, 8.51–8.53
    safeguards 7.42–7.46
        disclosure of material overseas 7.45–7.46

Index

warrants (*cont.*)
    examination of material 7.47–7.51
    retention and disclosure of material 7.42–7.44
  scope of 6.10–6.11
  specific BPD: additional requirements 8.33–8.35
    health records 8.33–8.34
    protected data 8.35
  specific BPD warrants 8.27–8.32
    conditions to be met prior
      to issue 8.29–8.32
  subject matter of 6.12–6.16
    targeted equipment interference
      warrants 6.12–6.15
    targeted examination warrants 6.16
  types of 3.06–3.25, 6.05–6.09, 8.12–8.22
    background 3.06–3.11
    class BPD warrants: restrictions on use 8.16
    equipment data 6.08
    matters common to targeted interception and
      mutual assistance warrants 3.16–3.17
    mutual assistance warrants 3.15
    obtaining secondary data 3.21–3.22
    protected data 8.17–8.22
    protected material 6.09
    scope 8.13–8.15
    targeted examination warrants 3.18–3.20
    targeted warrants 3.12–3.14
    targets of warrants 3.23–3.25
  when Part 7 is engaged 8.10–8.11
  see also **bulk acquisition warrants; bulk equipment interference warrants; bulk personal dataset warrants; modification of warrants**
wireless telegraphy, definition 2.34
Wireless Telegraphy Act (2006) 10.55–10.58
wireless telegraphy apparatus, definition 2.34